Social Problems

Seventh Edition

James William Coleman
California Polytechnic State University

Donald R. Cressey
Late, University of California, Santa Barbara

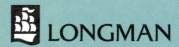

LONGMAN

An Imprint of Addison Wesley Longman, Inc.

New York • Reading, Massachusetts • Menlo Park, California • Harlow, England
Don Mills, Ontario • Sydney • Mexico City • Madrid • Amsterdam

Editor-in-Chief: Priscilla McGeehon
Acquisitions Editor: Alan McClare
Development Manager: Lisa Pinto
Development Editor: Nancy Crochiere
Supplements Editor: Lisa Ziccardi
Marketing Manager: Megan Galvin
Project Manager: Ellen MacElree
Design Manager/Text and Cover Design: Rubina Yeh
Cover: *Liberation* by Ben Shahn, 1945. Tempura on cardboard mounted on composition board,
    39¾ × 40″ (75.6 × 101.4 cm.). The Museum of Modern Art, New York. James Thrall Soby
    Bequest. Photograph © 1999 by The Museum of Modern Art, New York.
Art Studio: ElectraGraphics, Inc.
Photo Researcher: Mira Schachne
Prepress Services Supervisor: Valerie A. Vargas
Electronic Production Specialist: Sarah Johnson
Print Buyer: Denise Sandler
Electronic Page Makeup: Ruttle, Shaw & Wetherill, Inc.
Printer and Binder: World Color—Taunton
Cover Printer: Phoenix Color Corp.

For permission to use copyrighted material, grateful acknowledgment is made to the copyright
holders on p. 626, which are hereby made part of this copyright page.

Library of Congress Cataloging-in-Publication Data

Coleman, James William, 1947–
    Social problems / James William Coleman, Donald R. Cressey. — 7th
ed.
        p.   cm.
    Includes bibliographical references (p.   ) and index.
    ISBN 0-321-01848-6
    1. Sociology.   2. Social problems.   3. Social institutions.
    4. United States—Social conditions—1980–   5. United States—Social
policy—1980–1993.   I. Cressey, Donald Ray, 1919–   .   II. Title
    HM51.C593   1999
    361.1—dc21   98-38657
                                                                                        CIP

Please visit our website at http://www.longman.awl.com

ISBN 0-321-01848-6

2345678910—WCT—010099

Contents

Contents

Chapter 9   The Old and the Young   285

Chapter 10   Women and Men   312

Part III   Conformity and Deviance   343

Chapter 11   Sexual Behavior   345

Chapter 12   Drug Use   380

Preface

From the first rough draft to this seventh edition, we wrote this book for students. Our objective has been not only to familiarize undergraduates with the most trying problems of their times, but also to stimulate them to think in a critical scientific way. We encourage them to challenge the half-truths and pat answers that many people accept simply because they have heard them repeated so often. We ask students to participate in the dialogue about these issues rather than merely stand back and observe.

Features of the Seventh Edition

In preparing the seventh edition, I have tried to enhance the strengths that have made this book so successful over the years. Users of the previous editions have praised the broad coverage, the strongly worded debates on controversial issues, the informative graphics, and, most significantly, the consistent theoretical organization, including a section on the major theoretical perspectives in each chapter. These features have been retained or strengthened in this edition. Moreover, I have strived to maintain the same clear, straightforward style of writing—one that does not talk down to the reader or oversimplify complex issues—for which this book has become known.

Boxed Features

I have also continued three special boxed features that were exceedingly well received in previous editions. First, to counterbalance the "gloom and doom" that inevitably creeps into social problems classes, each chapter contains a special "Signs of Hope" box that highlights some positive trend or development. Every chapter also has a "Personal Perspectives" box that seeks to get students more personally involved in the issues by providing a vivid commentary from someone directly affected by a major social problem. Finally, "Debate" boxes present two sides of a controversial issue to show students the complexity of various problems and encourage them to consider both sides.

Student Aids

In addition to these special features, this new edition incorporates a much more comprehensive set of pedagogical aids than any previous edition. They include the following:

- *New "Quick Review"* questions at the end of each major section to aid students in reviewing the material they have just read
- *New "Questions for Critical Thinking"* at the end of each chapter to encourage students to think critically about the issues discussed and apply them to their own lives
- *Chapter-opening questions* that preview the major issues addressed in each chapter
- *Marginal definitions* that provide easy access to the definition of new or important terms
- *Chapter summaries* giving a brief overview of the important issues covered
- *Lists of key terms* at the end of the chapters to help students review the terms they have learned
- *"Further Readings,"* a list of related books that students might consult for additional information

Feminist Theory

Another major change is theoretical. In past editions, feminist theory was usually covered under the heading of conflict theory. But given its ever growing importance in sociology, the feminist perspective is now given independent treatment in each chapter.

Solutions to Social Problems

I also made an effort to put more emphasis on what we can do to deal with our social problems, and each chapter now has an expanded section on solving social problems. The section appears toward the end of each chapter, just before the summary.

Chapter-Opening Vignettes

Each chapter was also given a new introduction that uses some real event to introduce the problem being discussed. These personal vignettes will engage student interest and help draw readers into the chapter.

Organizational Changes

Those familiar with the sixth edition will notice that there has been some change in the overall organization of the book and the order of the chapters. Part I, "Troubled Institutions," now starts with the problems of the family and then works up to larger institutions. In response to reviewer comments, the chapter on health and illness was also moved into Part I, since much of that chapter's focus is on health care institutions. A new introduction at the beginning of each part shows the student the common features shared by the problems each chapter discusses.

New Coverage

Even more than most books, a social problems text needs to be updated constantly to reflect the ever changing array of issues, problems, and attempted solutions that concern and involve us. Below is a summary of some of the major changes and additions to this edition.

Chapter 1: Sociology and Social Problems This opening chapter has a new introduction and an expanded treatment of the basic sociological perspectives that includes a new section on feminist theory.

Chapter 2: Problems of the Family This chapter opens with a comparison of two typical families and their

problems. It also has two new sections: one on the blended family and a second on changing social expectations as a means of solving family problems. There is also a reexamination of statistical trends in family formation and dissolution.

Chapter 3: Problems of Education This chapter sets the stage for a discussion of the difficult problems of education with a new opener that deals with the efforts of a group of New York parents to keep a popular teacher from being laid off by paying her salary themselves. The chapter presents new comparative data on education both internationally and among different ethnic groups. There is also a new discussion of home schooling and a new subsection on valuing education in the section on solving the problems of education.

Chapter 4: Problems of the Economy This chapter has been heavily rewritten to reflect the changing economic realities of our current era. It now begins with the story of an English professor who is laid off and becomes a construction worker. The third section has been retitled "The New Economic Realities" and completely revised. The following section on the solutions to our economic problems has a new discussion of some ideas for building a sustainable economy.

Chapter 5: Problems of Government The introduction to this chapter focuses on people who claim to have been harassed by the Internal Revenue Service. There is new attention to the critical problem of campaign finance, and a new section examines growing public cynicism about our government. The examination of the ways to solve the problems of government now has new sections on reforming campaign finance and restructuring government.

Chapter 6: Health and Illness The story of a family that lost its health insurance now opens the chapter. The latest information on the AIDS epidemic is included, and the discussion of the causes of mental disorders is significantly expanded to include separate sections on developmental theories, traumas and social stress, and labeling theory. There is also considerable new data on the costs of health care and who pays them.

Chapter 7: The Poor This chapter begins with the story of some of the problems faced by a typical welfare mother. New data are presented on the amount and distribution of poverty, and the whole section on welfare was extensively reworked to reflect the sweeping changes recently enacted by the federal government. There is a new section titled "The Current Welfare

System," and the discussion on solving the problems of poverty has a new section titled "Distributing the Wealth More Fairly."

Chapter 8: The Ethnic Minorities We now begin with a powerful story of ethnic conflict in Rwanda. New data compare the social circumstances of the different ethnic groups in North America, and a new section treats those of mixed backgrounds as a distinct ethnic group. There is also new information on immigration and its impact on society.

Chapter 9: The Old and the Young We begin with an interesting account of a California day-care center that also accepts elderly clients. There is a great deal of new data on current status of children, adolescents, and the elderly, and a new section, "The Graying of America," analyzes our current demographic trends.

Chapter 10: Women and Men This chapter opens with a disturbing look at the repressive policies pursued by the victorious Taliban rebels in Afghanistan. There is new data on gender inequality, and the discussion of the ways to solve the problems it creates was expanded to include two new sections, "Fighting Gender Discrimination" and "Changing Gender Roles."

Chapter 11: Sexual Behavior The introduction to this chapter tells the story of a boy who was beaten up and abused by his schoolmates because he is gay. There is also new information about discrimination against gays and lesbians and about the latest court rulings. The discussion of prostitution was greatly expanded, and it now includes separate sections on the social world of prostitution, becoming a prostitute, and prostitution and the law. The discussion of pornography was also expanded to include more on "cyberporn."

Chapter 12: Drug Use We begin with the story of an MIT student who died from an alcohol overdose at a fraternity party. All the latest data on the trends in drug use are included, and the section on tobacco includes most recent new issues. A new section titled "Where Do We Stand?" was added to provide a fresh appraisal of the drug problem.

Chapter 13: Crime and Violence This chapter starts with the story of a 14-year-old boy whose best friend was gunned down in front of him. The discussion of the various types of crime was completely reorganized, and a new section on victimless crimes was added. A great deal of new information was added on the distribution and trends in crime, and a new section, "Combating White-

Collar Crime," was added to the discussion of ways to solve the crime problem.

Chapter 14: Urbanization The introduction to this chapter tells the story of a gang fight in Austin, Texas. There are new data on the patterns of growth and decline in cities, suburbs, and rural areas, and there is a new section on creating community as a way to help solve our urban problems.

Chapter 15: Population We begin with a sketch of a typical Guatemalan woman's attitudes toward family and birth control. Extensive new data were added on population trends, and two new sections, "Social Change" and "Birth Control," were added to the discussion of ways to control the population problem.

Chapter 16: The Environment The chapter begins with the story of the air pollution crisis caused by massive forest fires in Southeast Asia. All the latest information on air, land, and water pollution, and resource depletion is included, and a new section, "Changing Our Lives," discusses ways to solve the environmental problem.

Chapter 17: The Global Divide: Problems of International Inequality The chapter begins with the story of a poor Ethiopian woman's daily struggle for survival. Current data showing the comparative status of the people of the rich and poor nations were added throughout the chapter, and a new section, "Being Good Neighbors," deals with the global responsibilities of the wealthy nations.

Chapter 18: Warfare: Revolutionary, Ethnic, and International Conflict We begin with the story of Jody Williams, who won the Nobel Peace Prize for her efforts to restrict the use of military land mines. Because of recent changes in the geopolitical environment, more emphasis was given the ethnic conflicts, and there is a new section on ethnic and regional conflicts.

Supplements

This edition is accompanied by the usual array of excellent supplements. For the instructor, there is the *Instructor's Manual/Test Bank,* which I authored. The instructor's manual features detailed chapter outlines, additional resources for lecture material, class projects, recommended films, and discussion questions. The test bank offers multiple-choice, true/false, and essay questions. A computerized version of the test bank is available for both IBM and Macintosh computers.

For the student, there is a *Study Guide* prepared by Laurence Basirico of Elon College. The study guide provides a series of exercises directed toward reinforcing each chapter's learning objectives. Each chapter is designed to improve study habits and promote better comprehension of key themes and concepts. Practice tests for every chapter, including multiple-choice, short-answer, and essay questions, are also featured.

Acknowledgments

Space permits the mention of only a few of the many people who contributed to this book. First and foremost are the hundreds of students who have given countless invaluable suggestions over the years. I would also like to thank the following instructors who served as academic reviewers for this edition:

Barbara Atchinson, *Colorado State University*

Debbie Baiano Berman, *Framingham State College*

Melissa Brown, *Blinn College*

Arlen D. Carey, *University of Central Florida*

Michael Collins, *University of Wisconsin, Fox Valley*

Kathy Dietrich, *Blinn College*

Rita Duncan, *Tulsa Community College*

Kurt Finsterbush, *University of Maryland*

Pam Flaherty, *Sacramento City College*

Brenda Forster, *Elmhurst College*

Aleta Geib, *University of Akron*

Billy Gunter, *University of South Florida, Tampa*

John Hall, *Tulane University*

Julia Glover Hall, *Drexel University*

Mary Holley, *Montclair State University*

Leslie B. Inniss, *Florida State University*

Kenneth Land, *Duke University*

Lori Maida, *Concordia College*

Thomas McDonald, *North Dakota State University*

Judith S. McIlwee, *Mira Costa College*

John McKeon, *Walsh University*

Barbara Mueller, *Casper College*

Charles Mulford, *Iowa State University*

Joseph Obi, *University of Richmond*

Raymond O'Connor, *Holyoke Community College*

Ronald Penton, *Gulf Coast Community College*

Nelson Pichardo, *SUNY Albany*

Earl R. Schaeffer, *Columbus State University*

Jon Schlenker, *University of Maine, Augusta*

Raghu Singh, *Texas A & M University, Commerce*

David R. Spady, *Northern Michigan University*

Jerry Tyler, *Stephen F. Austin State University*

The insightful suggestions of these reviewers were a great help, as were those made by professors who used earlier editions of *Social Problems* and kindly volunteered their comments. The work of Alan McClare, Nancy Crochiere, and other members of the Longman team who have labored on this project over the years is also greatly appreciated.

James William Coleman

CHAPTER 1

Sociology and Social Problems

What is a social problem?

What part do social movements play in creating social problems?

What are the sociological perspectives used to analyze social problems?

How do sociologists study social problems?

How can we evaluate the claims made about social problems?

It was the best of times, it was the worst of times, it was the age of wisdom, it was the age of foolishness, . . . it was the season of Light, it was the season of Darkness, it was the spring of hope, it was the winter of despair. . . .

Thesе are opening words in Charles Dickens's famous novel *A Tale of Two Cities,* and they apply as well as we head into the twenty-first century as they did when he wrote them in the nineteenth. On the one hand, we are healthier, longer lived, and better educated, and we enjoy more technological conveniences than in any other period in human history. Yet such perennial problems as war, poverty, discrimination, and violence show no sign of fading away, and the specter of overpopulation and environmental catastrophe looms menacingly on the horizon. Indeed, the list of our social problems is so depressingly long that many people just throw their hands up and decide there is nothing they can do to help. But is that really true? The sociological study of social problems is founded on the belief that something can indeed be done if we first make the effort to study our problems systematically and then act on our understanding.

Politicians and community officials spend much of their careers trying to solve social problems that include everything from double parking to the threat of nuclear war. Voters select the candidates who claim to have the best solutions, but the public's ideas about many social problems are distorted or confused. While the serious study of social problems can clear up much of this confusion and misunderstanding, beginning students often have the uncomfortable feeling that the more they read, the less they understand. There are many conflicting viewpoints, and even the results of objective, scientific research may appear to be contradictory.

sociology
The scientific study of societies and social behavior.

Sociology—the scientific study of society and social behavior—provides a framework for sorting out all these facts, ideas, and beliefs. It provides the perspective and the tools we need to make sense of our social problems. Using this perspective, we can develop programs to deal with our problems and evaluate their results once they have been put into effect. This is not to say, of course, that all sociologists agree on the exact causes of our social problems or how we should solve them, but fortunately, such disagreements can result in a richer understanding for the student who is willing to examine all sides of the issues involved.

What Is a Social Problem?

social problem
(1) A condition that a significant number of people believe to be a problem. (2) A condition in which there is a sizable difference between the ideals of a society and its actual achievements.

Most people think of a **social problem** as any condition that is harmful to society; but the matter is not so simple, for the meanings of such everyday terms as *harm* and *society* are far from clear. Conditions that some people see as social problems harm some segments of society but are beneficial to others. Consider air pollution. On the one hand, an automobile manufacturer might argue that government regulation of free enterprise is a social problem because laws requiring antipollution devices on cars raise costs, decrease gasoline mileage, and stimulate inflation. On the other hand, residents of a polluted city might argue that the government's failure to outlaw noxious automobile emissions is a social problem because the smog created by such emissions harms their health and well-being. One person's social problem is another person's solution. Clearly, most people define a social problem as something that harms—or seems to harm—their own interests.

A more precise sociological definition holds that *a social problem exists when there is a sizable difference between the ideals of a society and its actual achievements.*[1] From this perspective, social problems are created by the failure to close the gap between the way people want things to be and the way things really are. Thus, racial discrimination is a social problem because although we believe that everyone should receive fair and equal treatment, some groups are still denied equal access to education, employment, and housing. Before this definition can be applied, someone must first examine the ideals and values of society and then decide whether these goals are being achieved. Sociologists and other experts thus decide what is or is not a problem because they are the ones with the skills necessary for measuring the desires and achievements of society.

Critics of this approach point out that no contemporary society has a single, unified set of values and ideals. When using this definition, sociologists must therefore decide which standards they will use for judging whether or not a certain condition is a social problem. Critics charge that those ideals and values used as standards are selected on the basis of the researcher's personal opinions and prejudices, not objective analysis.

Another widely accepted sociological definition holds that *a social problem exists when a significant number of people believe that a certain condition is in fact a problem.*[2] Here "the public"—not a sociologist—decides what is or is not a social problem. The sociologist's job is to determine which problems concern a substantial number of people. Thus, in this view, pollution did not become a social problem until environmental activists and news reports attracted the public's attention to conditions that had actually existed for some time.

The advantage of this definition is that it does not require a value judgment by sociologists who try to decide what is and is not a social problem; such decisions are made by "the public." However, a serious shortcoming of this approach is that the public is often uninformed or misguided and does not clearly understand its problems. If thousands of people were being poisoned by radiation leaking from a nuclear power plant but didn't know it, wouldn't that still be a social problem?

All the topics discussed in the chapters that follow qualify as social problems according to both sociological definitions. Each involves conditions that conflict with strongly held ideals and values, and all are considered social problems by significant groups of people. The goal of every chapter is to discuss these problems fairly and objectively. It is important to understand, however, that even selecting the problems requires a value judgment, whether by social scientists or by concerned citizens, and honest disagreements about the nature and importance of the various issues competing for public attention cannot be avoided.

Quick Review

What are the two common definitions of social problems?

What are the advantages and disadvantages of each?

Social Problems and Social Movements

The social issues that concern the public change from time to time, and a comparison of the numerous surveys of public opinion that have been done over the years reveals some interesting trends. War and peace and various economic issues have consistently ranked high on the public's list of social concerns. Interest in other problems seems to move in cycles. Thus, concern about taxes, foreign policy, illegal drug use, and lack of religious belief and morality is high in some years and low in others. Still other social problems are like fads, attracting a great deal of interest for a few years before dropping from public attention.[3]

These changes have many different causes: shifts in ideals and values, the solution of an old problem, the creation of new ones. One of the most important forces affecting changes in public opinion is **social movements**—groups of people that have banded together to promote a particular cause. For example, none of the polls in the 1930s and 1940s showed civil rights or race relations to be significant problems, even though racial discrimination was widespread and openly practiced. It was not until the civil rights movement began in the late 1950s that polls began to reflect an interest in this problem. The problem of racial discrimination would probably have remained buried if a powerful social movement had not developed to demand that society change its ways.

Such movements tend to follow a typical pattern of development. They begin when a large number of people start complaining about some problem they share. Such a group may be composed of people who believe they have been victimized, such as African American victims of racial discrimination or female victims of sexual discrimination; or it may be made up of concerned outsiders, such as opponents of alcohol use or those favoring the death penalty. As people with a common interest in an issue begin to talk with one another and express their feelings about the problem, individuals step forward to lead the developing movement.[4] Martin Luther King, Jr., was such a leader for the civil rights movement in the United States, as Nelson Mandela was for the movement to liberate South Africa from its racial oppression.

The leader's first job is to mold separate groups of dissatisfied people into an organized political movement. The success of the movement depends on publicity, for it is only through publicity that the general public can be made aware of the problem and encouraged to do something about it. In other words, it is through publicity that the problem of a particular group becomes a social problem.

Three factors help a social movement gain public support and favorable action by government. The most important is the political power of the movement and its supporters. If the movement's supporters are numerous, highly organized, wealthy, or in key positions of power, it is more likely to be successful.

A second factor is the strength of the movement's appeal to the people's values and prejudices. For example, a movement to protect children from sexual abuse is much more likely to gain widespread support than an effort to protect the civil liberties of child molesters.

The strength of the opposition to a movement is a third element determining its success or failure. Money is always limited, and the advocates of various social programs must compete with one another for funds. For example, few people object to the proposition that our children deserve a better education; however, a variety of opponents quickly emerge when someone suggests raising taxes to pay for improving

social movements
Groups of people who have banded together to promote a particular cause.

Social movements create public awareness about social problems and push the government to take action to resolve them. The Native American leaders depicted here are protesting the celebration of Christopher Columbus as a national hero.

the schools. Opposition to social movements also comes from people whose special interests are threatened by the goals of the movement. Thus, a proposal to raise the minimum wage for farmworkers is bound to be opposed by agricultural businesses.

A principal goal of many social movements is to create awareness of a social problem and then mobilize government action to resolve it; but even when a movement achieves these objectives, government action may be ineffective. Governments all over the world have created huge bureaucracies to deal with poverty (departments of welfare), health care (national health services), pollution (environmental protection agencies), and crime (police, courts, and prisons), but like all bureaucracies, these agencies are clumsy and slow-moving, and they are often more concerned with their own survival than with the problems they are supposed to solve. After all, if narcotics enforcement agencies stopped all drug abuse, if police departments prevented all crime, or if mental hospitals quickly cured all disturbed people, most of the employees of these agencies would soon be out of work. Occasionally, it appears that the agencies set up to deal with a particular social problem are not actually expected to solve it. Politicians have been known to approve funds for a social program just to silence troublesome protesters, creating new agencies with impressive titles but no real power.

Quick Review

How do social movements affect our social problems?

Foundations of the Sociological Approach

Over the years sociologists have built up a body of basic knowledge about society and how it operates that can help us get perspective on conflicting claims and counterclaims about our social problems. A great deal of this book is devoted to helping students develop this kind of sociological understanding of the world. Before we can proceed, however, we must look at some basic concepts that provide the foundation on which the sociological approach is built. (A wide variety of sociological concepts, including all the key terms defined [in the margins], are included in the glossary at the end of the book, so if you run across an unfamiliar concept while you are reading, be sure to check the glossary.)

As we go though our daily lives dealing with our friends, relatives, and acquaintances, most of us see a group of unique individual people, but the sociologist also sees a set of social roles. In the theater or the movies, a role is the part a particular person plays in the show. Sociologists use the term in much the same way, except that the role is played in real-life social situations. A **role** is usually defined as the set of behaviors and expectations associated with a particular social position (often known as a *status*). All roles—daughter, son, student, automobile driver, and countless others—offer certain rights and duties to the player. A student, for example, has the right to attend classes, to use the school's facilities, and to be graded fairly. The student also has the duty to read the texts, complete assigned work, and behave in an orderly manner. However, the way actual people carry out their roles often differs enormously from such idealized expectations.

Roles are one of the basic building blocks of our social world, and every society has countless positions with roles attached. Roles are interwoven in complex ways, so it is often impossible to understand a particular role apart from the social network in which it is embedded. How, for example, can the role of wife be defined without reference to the roles of husband, daughter, son, mother, and father? This interdependence stems from the fact that the rights of one position—wife, for example—are interlaced with the duties of other positions—husband, daughter, son. Each of us is judged by our performance as we carry out our roles. The negligent mother, the abusive father, the incompetent professor, and the disruptive student are judged harshly because they fail to meet our role expectations.

The standards we use to make such judgments are known as **norms.** A norm is simply a social rule that tells us what behavior is acceptable in a certain situation and what is not. Every human group, be it a small circle of friends or an entire society, generates norms that govern its members' conduct. An individual who violates a group's norms is often labeled a **deviant** and given some kind of formal or informal punishment. A person who violates the norm against taking the lives of others may be tried and formally punished with a prison term, whereas a person who violates the trust of his or her friends is informally punished by ridicule or exclusion from the group. Just as the various roles we play may place conflicting demands upon us, so the norms of various groups may conflict. Thus, we are sometimes placed in the uncomfortable position of being forced to violate the norms of one group in order to meet the norms of another.

Although some of the roles we play involve nothing more than a small group or a single individual, social roles tend to be woven together into larger units.

role

A set of expectations and behaviors associated with a social position.

norm

A social rule that tells us what behavior is acceptable in a certain situation and what is not.

deviant

(1) An individual who violates a social norm. (2) An individual who is labeled as a deviant by others.

Social institutions are relatively stable patterns of roles and behavior centered around some particular social tasks. The family, for example, is a basic institution in all known societies. It usually handles many of the duties of child rearing and provides emotional and sometimes economic support for its older members.

Social class is one of the most useful of all these basic sociological ideas. Although everyone has some idea of what it means, few of us use the concept in a very clear or consistent way. Sociologists define **social class** as a category of people with similar shares of the things that are valued in a society. People of the same social class have a similar chance in life: a similar opportunity to get an education, to receive health care, to acquire material possessions, and so on. Thus, the people you see sleeping on the heating grates outside an office building are from one social class, and the executives who speed past them on their way to the parking lot are from another.

Many nineteenth-century thinkers, including Karl Marx and his followers, defined social class solely in economic terms.[5] Today, most sociologists use a broader definition taken from the work of the German sociologist Max Weber.[6] According to Weber, the valuables a society distributes include social status and power as well as money, so to accurately assess the class positions of individuals or groups, we must know where they stand on all three. *Status* rests on a claim to social prestige, inherited from one's family or derived from occupation and life-style. *Power* is the ability to force others to do something whether they want to or not, and it is another key to understanding not just the class system but social life in general. Power is often associated with politics in the public mind, and high political position certainly brings a large measure of power with it; but power has many other sources as well, such as wealth or control of the means of violent force.

Sociologists use several different schemes to describe the class system in contemporary societies, but the most common divides these societies into four different classes (see Figure 1.1). The *upper class* is composed of individuals with great wealth, who often hold key positions of corporate power. Next comes the *middle class,* made up of an upper segment of highly paid professionals, successful executives and entrepreneurs, and a much larger group of middle-level managers and white-collar (nonmanual) workers. The *working class* is about the same size as the middle class, but its members are mainly blue-collar (manual) workers and lower-level service workers who would traditionally have been defined as white-collar workers but actually have the low pay and low prestige associated with working-class jobs. Although the best-paid blue-collar workers earn more money than many white-collar employees, the average members of the working class make far less than their middle-class counterparts. At the bottom of the social hierarchy is the *lower class,* whose members live in conditions of poverty or very close to them. There is a popular belief that most Americans are middle class, perhaps because the majority of the people we see on television and in the movies are from that class, but the truth of the matter is much different. Of every 100 people in the United States, only 1 is from the upper class, 15 to 20 are from the lower class, and the remainder are more or less evenly divided between the working class and the middle class (see Figure 1.1).[7]

The most all-encompassing concepts in sociology are those of society and culture. In everyday speech, culture refers to the refinements of civilization, such as art, music, and literature; but to sociologists, **culture** is the way of life of the people in a certain geographic area, and particularly the ideas, beliefs, values, patterns of

social institutions
Relatively stable patterns of roles and behavior centered on the performance of important social tasks.

social class
A category of people with similar shares of the things that are valued in a society.

culture
The way of life of the people in a certain geographic area, particularly their ideas, beliefs, values, patterns of thought, and symbols.

Figure 1.1
The Class System

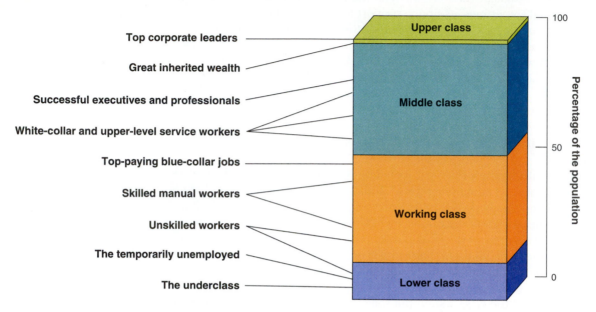

Source: Harold R. Kerbo, *Social Stratification and Inequality* (New York: McGraw-Hill, 1996) and current reports of the U.S. Bureau of the Census.

subculture
A culture that exists within and is influenced by a larger culture but has its own unique ideas and beliefs.

society
A group of people in a geographic area who share common institutions and traditions.

social structure
The organized patterns of human behavior and social relationships in a society.

thought, and symbols that make it possible. A culture provides individuals with a way of understanding the world and making it meaningful. A **subculture** is a culture that exists within a larger culture that influences it, but has its own distinctive ideas and beliefs; for example, the gang members who cover our cities with their graffiti are part of a subculture that places its own special meaning on such symbols.

Although culture and society cannot be separated in real life, sociologists sometimes distinguish between the two so that each can be studied more easily. **Society** refers to a group of people in a particular geographic area who share common institutions and traditions, while culture refers to the physical and mental products of those people. All societies have an overall **social structure,** which is simply an organized pattern of behavior and social relationships. They also have many more focused social structures, such as a particular pattern of family life, social class, and government.

Quick Review

Look at the list of key terms at the end of this chapter and make sure you can define each one.

Sociological Perspectives on Social Problems

All sociologists use the concepts discussed in the preceding section, but there are significant differences in their perspectives and approaches. Although the profusion of different theories and opinions can be confusing, there are a few broad theoretical perspectives that underlie many of these differences. Aside from helping us make sense of the theories themselves, a knowledge of these basic perspectives leads to a better understanding of our social problems by drawing our attention to important social forces that are often neglected by the media and politicians when they discuss these issues. These general sociological perspectives (and other more narrow theories as well) tend to focus on one of two different levels. Theories of society (*macro theories*) try to make sense of the behavior of large groups of people and the workings of entire societies, while **social psychological theories** (*micro theories*) are concerned primarily with the behavior of individuals and small groups. Of course, society depends on its individual members, and those individuals depend on society; in the last two decades, sociologists have increasingly come to recognize that a complete understanding depends on the integration of these two different levels of analysis.

> **social psychological theories**
> A large group of theories that attempts to explain the effects of individuals and social groups on each other.

Supporters of one theory often have harsh criticisms of other theories. But even though some theories are clearly more effective than others in analyzing a particular problem, none of the broad perspectives can be said to be "right" or "wrong." Not only can many different theories be applied to the same problem, but in most cases the deepest understanding comes from combining the insights gained from different theoretical perspectives. In this book, for example, some chapters draw more heavily from one theoretical perspective and some from another, depending on the nature of the problem under discussion, but all the problems are examined from many different standpoints. The objective is always to keep an open mind and draw insight wherever it can be found.

Most sociologists divide the macro-level theories of society into two broad perspectives—*functionalism* and *conflict theory*—and we will begin with those two approaches. Next we will look at *feminist theory*, which combines both macro and micro levels of analysis, and then at *interactionist theory*, which is by far the most influential of the social psychological (micro) theories in sociology. When reading the following explanations of these approaches, remember that they are only broad summaries. There are many theoretical differences among functionalists, conflict theorists, feminists, and interactionists, yet many sociologists combine elements from all these theories into a more integrated approach.

The Functionalist Perspective

Many early theorists who held a **functionalist perspective** saw society as something like a living organism. Just as people have a heart and circulatory system, muscles, blood, and a brain, a society has a set of economic, political, religious, family, and educational institutions. Just as all the parts of a living organism work together to keep it alive, so all the parts of society must work together to keep it going. Each

> **functionalist perspective**
> A broad sociological approach that sees society as a delicate balance of parts, each with its own functions and dysfunctions, and holds that most social problems result from the disorganization of society.

function

The contribution of each part of society to the maintenance of a balanced order.

institution has a set of **functions** it must perform in order to keep society healthy; for instance, the function of the economic institution is to provide the food, shelter, and clothing that people need in order to survive, while the functions of the government include coordinating the activities of other institutions, dealing with unmet social needs, and protecting society from foreign aggressors. These various institutions make up a balanced whole, so changes in one institution are likely to require changes in another. Thus, from the functionalist perspective, we all have a common stake in helping to maintain society, and all of a society's institutions work together for the common good.

Societies, like machines and biological organisms, do not always work the way they are supposed to work, however. Things get out of whack. Even when things are going well, changes introduced to correct one imbalance may produce other problems. An action that interferes with the effort to carry out essential social tasks is said to be **dysfunctional.** For example, educators may train too many people for certain jobs. Those who cannot find positions in their area of expertise may become resentful, rebelling against the system that they feel has treated them unfairly. Thus, "overeducation" may be said to be a dysfunction of our educational institutions.

dysfunction

The way a social phenomenon interferes with the maintenance of a balanced social order.

Functionalists see a common set of norms and values as the glue that holds groups, institutions, and whole societies together. Small tribal societies in which everyone is in constant close contact usually have little difficulty in maintaining these common ideals, but as the great French sociologist Emile Durkheim pointed out, as societies have become ever larger and more complex, it has become increasingly difficult to maintain a social consensus about basic norms and values.[8] Thus, one of the major sources of contemporary social problems is the weakening of the social consensus. Functionalists can cite considerable evidence to show that when the social rules lose their power to control our behavior, people become lost and confused and are more susceptible to suicide, mental disorders, and drug problems.

social disorganization

The condition that exists when an institution or an entire society is poorly organized and fails to carry out essential social functions satisfactorily.

Functionalists also feel that social problems arise when society, or some part of it, becomes disorganized. This **social disorganization** involves a breakdown of social structure, so that its various parts no longer work together as smoothly as they should. Functionalists see many causes of social disorganization: young people may be inadequately socialized because of problems in the institution of the family, or society may fail to provide enough social and economic opportunities to some of its members, thus encouraging them to become involved in crime or other antisocial activities. Sometimes a society's relationship to its environment may be disrupted, so that it no longer has sufficient food, energy, building materials, or other resources. However, in modern industrial societies, one cause of social disorganization—rapid social change—promotes all the others.

Social disorganization is particularly severe in the modern era because more change has occurred in less time than during any other period of human history. Basic institutions have undergone drastic changes with technology advancing so rapidly that other parts of the culture have failed to keep pace. This *cultural lag* is one of the major sources of social disorganization. For instance, when knowledge about nutrition, public health, and medical technology began spreading through the world in the nineteenth century, many lives, especially those of infants, were saved. Yet traditional attitudes toward the family have not changed fast enough to adjust to the fact that more children survive to adulthood. The result has been a worldwide population explosion.[9]

Although functionalism has been a standard theoretical approach to social problems for many years, it has numerous critics. Despite its claims of objectivity, many sociologists see functionalism as a politically conservative philosophy that too quickly assumes that society is good as it is and should be preserved without major changes. Functionalism sometimes blames social problems on individual deviance or temporary social disorganization while seeming to ignore what some see as more basic deficiencies in the structure of society. The critics of functionalism claim that it is often impossible to say whether or not a particular social phenomenon is functional for society as a whole because such phenomena usually have different impacts on different groups. For example, a law that forbids sleeping in the lobbies of public buildings would benefit wealthy people who may be disturbed by such behavior but hurt the homeless, who have nowhere else to go. The critics charge that what the functionalists often really mean when they say something is functional is that it works to the benefit of the status quo.

The Conflict Perspective

When theorists with a **conflict perspective** look out at contemporary society, they see a very different world. Where the functionalists see a more or less integrated whole working to maintain itself and promote the common good, the conflict theorists see a diverse collection of social groups all struggling for wealth, power, and prestige. While functionalists emphasize the importance of shared values, attitudes, and norms in holding society together, conflict theorists insist that social order is maintained more by authority backed by the use of force. For example, functionalists hold that most people obey the law because they believe that is the right thing to do. Conflict theorists, on the other hand, say that most people obey the law because they are afraid of being arrested, jailed, or even killed if they don't. Another important difference between the functionalist and conflict perspectives is seen in their assumptions about social change. Functionalists tend to view a healthy society as being relatively stable; they assert that too much change is disruptive and that society has a natural tendency to regain its balance whenever it is disturbed. Conflict theorists see society in more dynamic terms: because people are constantly struggling with one another to gain power, change is inevitable. One individual or group is bound to gain the upper hand, only to be defeated in later struggles.

Neither the conflict nor the functionalist perspective can be said to be a single unified theory. Rather, each consists of a number of related theories that share many common elements. One of the most important differences among conflict theorists concerns the type of conflicts they see as most central to modern society. Karl Marx, the famous nineteenth-century scholar and revolutionary who had so much to do with the origins of conflict theory, placed primary emphasis on **class conflict.** For Marx, the position a person holds in the system of production determines his or her class position. In a capitalist society (see Chapter 4 for a discussion of the nature of capitalism), a person may be in one of two different positions. Some people own capital and capital-producing property (for example, factory owners, landlords, and merchants) and are therefore members of the *bourgeoisie.* Other people work for wages as producers of capital (for example, factory workers, miners, and laborers of all kinds). Marx called this class the *proletariat.* He asserted that these two classes have directly opposing economic interests because the wealth of

conflict perspective
A broad sociological approach that sees the conflict between different groups as a basic sociological process and holds that the principal source of social problems is the exploitation and oppression of one group by another.

class conflict
The struggle for wealth, power, and prestige among the social classes.

the bourgeoisie is based on exploitation of the proletariat. He thought that workers would develop an increasing awareness of their exploitation by the bourgeoisie and that this awareness, combined with growing political organization, would eventually result in violent class conflict. Marx believed that the workers would overthrow their masters in this great revolution and establish a classless society. Private property and inheritance would be abolished; steeply graduated income taxes would be introduced; education and training would be free; and production would be organized for use, not profit.[10]

Modern conflict theorists continue to see class conflict as a central fact of life in contemporary society. Even though Marx's ideas have had an enormous impact on the twentieth-century world, many conflict theorists look at the class structure in very different terms than Marx did, instead preferring the approach of another famous German sociologist, Max Weber, which we have already discussed. And even many contemporary Marxists have come to see the vision of a popular revolution that will establish a just society without class distinctions as something that will occur in the distant future, if at all.

Although virtually no conflict theorists would deny the importance of class conflict in modern society, some place greater emphasis on other types of conflict. In the wake of the civil rights and ethnic power movements in the United States and the worldwide epidemic of ethnic conflict in the 1990s, some have come to place more importance on *ethnic conflict*—he struggle for power, wealth, and status be-

Contemporary society has huge inequalities in the distribution of wealth, power, and prestige, and conflict theorists hold that fact to be one of the most basic causes of our social problems.

tween the members of different ethnic groups. Conflict theorists influenced by feminism place greater emphasis on gender and the inequalities based on it. But whether they emphasize class, ethnicity, or gender, conflict theorists generally agree on some basic criticisms of the functionalists. Conflict theorists deny that our most serious problems arise from a weakening of social values or the unintentional problems created when an important social institution becomes disorganized. Rather, most social problems are the result of the intentional exploitation of weak groups by powerful ones. For example, conflict theorists argue that the serious problems faced by Latinos and African Americans in the United States are not caused by the disorganization of the social system that makes it difficult to fully integrate these minorities into the mainstream of society, but rather by exploitation by whites who profit from the economic and political subordination of minority groups.

Just as functionalism has been criticized for being too conservative, the conflict perspective has been criticized for being too radical. Critics say that conflict theorists overemphasize the role of conflict, arguing that if there were as much of it as these theorists claim, society would have collapsed long ago. Moreover, they charge that conflict theorists are too one-sided in their approach. The critics say that while conflict theorists see nothing but the bad side of capitalism, capitalist nations actually do a much better job of dealing with their social problems than other kinds of societies do.

The Feminist Perspective

Like the other approaches examined here, **feminist theory** is not really a single theory but a group of theories that share a concern with the same basic questions. In their analysis of contemporary feminist theory, Patricia Madoo Lengermann and Jill Niebrugge-Brantley hold that the two most important of those questions are "And what about the women?" and "Why is woman's situation as it is?"[11] Throughout most of its history, sociology, like the rest of the humanities and social sciences, saw human experience from a male perspective. While there was certainly much in this approach that applied to both genders, women's experience was often ignored or given a decidedly secondary importance. So when feminist theory was first beginning to emerge as an influential force in sociology in the 1960s, the first question it posed was "What about the women?" In other words, these thinkers set out to describe the world and women's place in it from a female perspective to counterbalance the male-oriented view of the traditional sociological theories. Feminist theory emphasizes the idea that women's lives are markedly different from men's because women are given the primary responsibility for child rearing and for the care of the emotional and physical needs of others. But the position of women is not just different from that of men, it is *unequal* as well. On the average, women have less wealth, less power, and lower status than men. Thus, feminists often describe contemporary society as a **patriarchy**—that is, a society dominated by men and run in their interests.

In their attempts to explain why woman's situation is the way it is, feminists tend to split into different theoretical camps. The largest group is probably the *liberal feminists*. Liberal feminists see social activity in our society divided into two separate spheres—the public sphere, which is man's central concern, and the private sphere, which is woman's realm. Liberal feminists view the private sphere as an endless round of demanding, undervalued tasks such as housework and child care, while the real rewards of life—power, money, and prestige—are to be found in the

feminist theory
An approach to understanding society and social behavior that focuses on the importance of gender and the inequalities based on it.

patriarchy
A society dominated by men and run in their interests.

public sphere. They generally accept the American values of freedom and individualism, but they argue that women have been confined to the private sphere and denied a fair opportunity to compete. The fundamental cause of this exclusion is **sexism**—stereotypes, prejudice, and discrimination based on gender. The solution to this injustice is therefore to attack the sexist traditions that have been handed down from previous generations and to allow everyone to develop their own unique abilities and pursue their interests regardless of their gender.

To the *socialist feminists*, the liberals take a far too rosy view of contemporary society. In their view, the roots of the exploitation of women are to be found in the capitalist economic system and the feudal system from which it evolved. Capitalism is based on the exploitation of labor, and women are the most exploited group of all. They are exploited by their husbands, providing unpaid labor for child care and housework, and they are exploited by the larger economy, providing a reserve pool of low-wage industrial labor to be used when necessary and then cast out. To the socialist feminists, a mere attack on sexist stereotypes will have little real impact on women's oppression unless the capitalist system itself is fundamentally transformed to free both women and men.

The *radical feminists* go a step beyond the others, arguing not just that the women's world is different than the men's world but that it is *better*. Men created and sustain our current social order, which is an oppressive patriarchal system that exploits and represses women, and their primary tool has been violence against women—rape, spouse abuse, incest, and murder. The radical feminists call for a "woman-centered" society that separates women from the repression of men.

The critics of feminist theory fall into two different camps. One group argues that the feminists are completely wrong when they charge that society, and especially the family, oppresses women. In this view, the family fulfills and enriches women, and the feminists are leading a misguided effort to make women become more like men. The other group of critics accepts the idea that women are indeed oppressed, but argues that most men are oppressed too. These critics assert that feminists foster the same kinds of stereotypes of men that our culture has created of women and that feminists try to blame men for injustices that are actually caused by impersonal historical forces.

The Interactionist Perspective

The sociological approach to social psychology is dominated by a single broad perspective known as **interactionism.** In fact, many of the ideas of the interactionists have become so widely accepted that oftentimes they are not even seen as part of a separate theory, but simply as a standard part of basic sociology. Interactionism explains our behavior in terms of the patterns of thoughts and beliefs we have and in terms of the meaning we give to our lives. To understand individual behavior, the interactionist tries to look at the world through the eyes of the actors involved, to see how they define themselves and their environment. This understanding of the conditions in which we find ourselves, known as the **definition of the situation,** is learned through interaction with other people and is the foundation we base all our behavior on. For example, a gang member who sees the police as the storm troopers of a racist society will respond differently to an officer's calls for help than a banker who sees the police as the defenders of law and order. Our interactions with others, however, teach us far more than how to define a particular social situation or even how to define the world in general. They are also the basis for the ideas we develop

---

sexism
Stereotypes, prejudice, and discrimination based on gender.

interactionism
A theory that explains behavior in terms of the way individuals define themselves, their social relationships, and the world as a whole.

definition of the situation
People's understanding of the conditions in which they find themselves.

about who and what we are, and such an understanding, in turn, tells us what to expect from other people and how to act in a particular social context.

To the interactionist, reality is not something out there in the world waiting to be discovered. Reality is a socially created agreement constructed by the efforts of people acting together in social groups. Meanings are created as we struggle to define ourselves and the world around us and then share those meanings with others. In interactionist theory, human culture is nothing more than a complex system of shared meanings, and those meanings, in turn, determine our behavior.

The work of American philosopher George Herbert Mead was the original force behind interactionist theory.[12] Mead argued that the ability to communicate in *symbols* (principally words and combinations of words) is the key feature that distinguishes humans from other animals. Children develop the ability to think and to use symbols in the process known as **socialization.** At first, young children blindly imitate the behavior of their parents, but eventually they learn to "take the role of the other," pretending to be "mommy" or "daddy." From such role-taking, children learn to understand the relationships among different roles and to see themselves as they imagine others see them. According to Mead, the key to a child's psychological development is the creation of a **self-concept**—the relatively stable mental image we all have of who and what we are. This self-concept is created out of the responses a child receives from the important people in his or her life. For example, if a girl's parents constantly tell her how smart she is, she is likely to formulate a concept of herself as an intelligent person. This concept of self is not a fixed, unchanging structure, however. If later in life her teachers and friends begin to treat her as if she isn't really very bright, her self-concept is likely to change. The concept of self is one of the most important in social psychology, for it influences almost every aspect of our behavior. Another important influence on behavior, according to Mead, is the *generalized other,* the idea we form of what kind of behavior people expect of us—in other words, our conscience.

After Mead's death in 1931, his ideas continued to gain stature among sociologists and social psychologists. Those who adhered most closely to Mead's original ideas became known as *symbolic interactionists.*[13] They have been very active in the study of social problems and have contributed a great deal to our understanding of critical social issues. For example, differential association theory, an important explanation of delinquency and crime, is a direct offshoot of Mead's theories, as is the labeling theory that is used to explain crime and mental disorder (see Chapters 6, 12, and 13). But over the years, interactionist theory has grown far beyond Mead's original vision and has absorbed insights from many other approaches.

Despite its enormous influence, interactionist theory has many critics. The most common complaint is that interactionism is vague and difficult to substantiate scientifically. A more telling criticism is that interactionism has an overly intellectual view of human nature. Classic interactionism sees human behavior entirely in terms of ideas and thoughts; it leaves out feelings and emotions. As a result of such criticism, interactionists have begun to direct more attention to the way our ideas and definitions are linked to emotions and to the role emotion plays in social life.[14]

Other Perspectives

Like sociologists, psychologists have long been involved in the study of social psychology, and they have developed their own perspectives to explain it. One of the most influential approaches is known as **behaviorism.** Originally, behaviorists felt

socialization
The process by which individuals learn the ways of thinking and behaving of their culture.

self-concept
Our image we have of who and what we are.

behaviorism
A theory explaining human actions in terms of rewards and punishments.

science should investigate only observable behavior and that it is a waste of time to explore thoughts, feelings, or anything else that cannot be directly measured. They argued that all behavior is learned as the result of the patterns of rewards and punishments we receive from our environment.[15] Obviously, this approach is quite different from that of the interactionists, with all their emphasis on thoughts and symbols. However, both perspectives see human behavior as learned, not inherited, and more recent behaviorist thinkers who are more willing to look at the subjective side of behavior actually end up with conclusions that are quite compatible with those of the interactionists.[16]

Among the most popular psychological perspectives are the **personality theories. Personality** refers to the stable characteristics and traits that distinguish one person from another. Personality theorists believe it accounts for most differences in individual social behavior. Psychologists usually see personality differences as the result of the child's interactions with parents and other early experiences, although some hold that personality has an inherited component as well. Various ideas about personality have often been used to explain social problems. For example, criminals are sometimes said to break the law because they have "sociopathic personalities" (impulsive, unstable, and immature), and racial prejudice is attributed to an "authoritarian personality" (rigid and insecure, with repressed feelings of guilt and hostility; see Chapter 8).

One of the most basic and long-running disputes in the social sciences is sometimes called the "nature versus nurture" controversy. Those who support the "nurture" side of the debate, including most sociologists, feel that the majority of human behavior is learned. Those on the "nature" side argue that most human behavior is determined by our inherited biological makeup. The **biosocial perspective** comprises a loose grouping of "nature" theories that emphasize the role of biology in determining human behavior. Originally, biological theorists saw virtually all human behavior as caused by inherited patterns of action they called *instincts*. Given the enormous range of human culture and behavior, few contemporary scientists still claim that all behavior is inherited. Contemporary biosocial theorists therefore emphasize the importance of the interaction between biological predispositions and the social environment. For example, many criminologists who argue that there is a hereditary predisposition toward crime see the problem as being as much with society as with genetics. They argue that people with low intelligence, which they hold to be a biological characteristic, are rejected by teachers and more competent students because they do poorly in school. As a result, they are more likely to become rebellious and antisocial (see Chapter 13). Many biosocial theorists focus their studies on the evolutionary process in hopes that an understanding of the forces that shaped the development of humankind will enable us to get a clearer picture of behavioral predispositions that have been passed down from our ancestors.

Applying the Sociological Perspectives: An Example

At first, these abstract theoretical perspectives may not seem to have much to do with all the pressing problems facing our society. If we take a concrete example, however, it is easy to show how these perspectives work to help us build an understanding of the issues at hand. Suppose, for instance, that you often stop at a small market on your way home from class. One day you realize that the woman who is

personality theories
A group of theories that hold that social behavior is determined by differences in personality.

personality
The relatively stable characteristics and traits that distinguish one person from another.

biosocial perspective
A loose grouping of theories that emphasizes the importance of biology in determining human behavior.

sitting in the park across the street with her three children is there every time you come in. You ask the clerk about it, and she tells you that they are all living in their van, which is parked in an alley around the corner. A few weeks later you go to the market and notice that a police car is parked on the street. You see two officers are talking with the woman, and after that you never see her or her children again.

Of course, we would need much more information before we could come to any firm conclusions about why this particular family is in such trouble, but the sociological perspectives can help us learn about the general causes of homelessness and poverty, and that is really the more important question if we are to deal with the roots of the problem. The macro-level approaches lead us to take a broad perspective and to link the family's problem with powerful sociological forces that operate throughout our society. The functionalists see the origins of this kind of problem in the social disorganization that plagues so many parts of modern society. They are particularly likely to see such problems as the product of the weakening of the institution of the family. Some functionalists argue, for example, that the growing strength of the ideals of individualism and freedom are leading us to neglect our community obligations. In the past, people were expected to stay in a marriage, even a difficult one, for the sake of the children and society as a whole. But the weakening of such norms has resulted in more and more husbands and wives splitting up, often leaving a weakened family unit in serious financial straits.

Feminists, on the other hand, see this problem in far different terms. To them, this family's problems are far more likely to be the result of sexism and discrimination. Society expects this woman to assume responsibility for her children and to sacrifice her future for their sake. Yet when a marriage breaks up, the mother is likely to face a job market that discriminates against women, offering only jobs that pay less than the cost of the child care, transportation, food, shelter, and clothing her family requires.

While most conflict theorists are likely to agree with the feminists, they would also point out that this mother also suffers from exploitation by the classes above her in the social hierarchy. The reason there are no decent jobs available is that powerful business interests intentionally work to keep wages low so they can maximize their profits. Similarly, welfare benefits are kept at the lowest possible level: just enough to prevent the underprivileged from rising up and disrupting the system, but far less than would really be needed to lift them out of poverty. When the homeless become a nuisance to affluent neighbors, the police force the homeless to move on.

Interactionists are more likely to seek the origins of this family's plight in the way family members see themselves and their social world. They point out that people from disadvantaged backgrounds often come to define the world in ways that make it difficult to escape poverty. For example, research shows that poor people are more likely to see their lives in fatalistic terms and feel that there is little or nothing they can do to change their situation. Moreover, the way poor people talk, act, and define the world is likely to be very different from the way people from a higher-class background do, and their attitudes and behavior may shut poor people out of many occupational and social opportunities. Interactionists are also likely to see this family as a victim of labeling. The people they interact with near the park are likely to label them as bums or riffraff and then treat them on that basis—excluding them from jobs, social contacts, and support. Eventually, the members of the family are likely to start believing those labels are really true, and they will develop an increasingly negative image of themselves and their place in the world.

Such beliefs soon become a self-fulfilling prophecy as the mother gives up hope of finding a good job and increasingly avoids the company of "respectable" people. As an early interactionist, W. I. Thomas, put it: "If men define situations as real, they are real in their consequences."[17]

If you were interested in taking the next step and actually doing something about the problem of poverty and homelessness, each perspective could also suggest some possible courses of action. For example, some functionalists believe that we must work to strengthen our family system and to reinforce the values that place family obligations ahead of individual self-interest. Liberal feminists call for tough new laws to fight occupational discrimination and for better welfare benefits. Conflict theorists and socialist feminists call for the poor and underprivileged, women, and minorities to band together with their supporters from other groups and demand fundamental structural changes to reduce inequality and make this a more just society. Interactionists advocate education and training programs, not only to teach the disadvantaged new skills but also to help them redefine their world and the way they see themselves. Interactionists would also say that the family needs more supportive contacts with members of the larger community. Of course, these approaches are not mutually exclusive, and just as we can combine their theoretical insights to gain a more complete picture of the problem, so we can combine various proposals for change into a more comprehensive response. Table 1.1 compares the four perspectives.

Quick Review

Briefly describe the main points of the functionalist, conflict, feminist, and interactionist theories.

What are the strengths and weaknesses of each theory?

Doing Sociological Research

The theoretical perspectives discussed so far serve as a guide and a point of reference for the student of social problems. Theories are of little value, however, unless they deal with facts, and in the study of social problems, people often disagree about what "the facts" really are. Because their task is so difficult, sociologists give a great deal of attention to the study of **methodology**—that is, how to do research. Volumes have been written on this subject, yet no one can say that any particular technique is better than all the others. The decision about which research techniques to use must be based on the nature of the problem being studied and the skills and resources of the researcher. Among many possible alternatives, the four most common sources of sociological data are public records and statistics, case studies, surveys, and experiments.

methodology
The study of how to do research.

Public Records and Statistics

Governments and organizations such as the United Nations and the World Bank publish a wealth of statistics and information. A look through the references in this book will reveal numerous citations to data from the Bureau of the Census, the Bu-

Table 1.1	**Sociological Perspectives**

The Functionalist Perspective

- Macro level
- Society is held together by shared norms and values
- Society is a joint effort of many institutions working together for the common good.
- The primary causes of social problems is social disorganization, which often results from rapid social change.

The Conflict Perspective

- Macro level
- Society is held together by power, authority, and coercion.
- Society is a struggle for dominance among competing social groups.
- The primary cause of social problems is the exploitation and oppression of some groups by others.

The Feminist Perspective

- Macro and micro levels
- Gender is a basic organizing principle of contemporary society.
- The social position of women is not only different from that of men but also unequal.
- The primary cause of social problems is the exploitation of women by men.

The Interactionist Perspective

- Micro level
- Individual behavior is based on the symbols and shared meanings we learn.
- This learning occurs during interactions between individuals and other people and groups.
- The primary cause of social problems is the way we define ourselves and our social situation.

reau of Justice Statistics, the United Nations Development Programme, and similar organizations, for such information is vital to sociologists' efforts to understand today's social problems. One of the oldest and most reliable sources of statistics is the U.S. census, which is taken every ten years. The goal of the census is to count all the people in the United States and determine such characteristics as their age, gender, and employment status. Such an effort to get direct information about every person in the country is obviously a massive undertaking, so most of the information we have comes from surveys that question only a sample of the total population. There are periodic government surveys of selected groups, such as the elderly or the unemployed, as well as general surveys designed to measure, for example, the number of people who have been the victims of crime. Other important sources of data are the bureaucracies that register births, marriages, divorces, and deaths; and the official records of government agencies, such as the federal budget and the *Congressional Record.*

Despite their importance to the sociologist, such data still have serious shortcomings. Almost every researcher has had the experience of spending long hours looking through official publications searching for a particular figure that is nowhere to be found. You might, for example, be interested in comparing the income and educational levels of Chinese Americans and Filipino Americans, only to find that the Bureau of the Census lists only whites, blacks, Hispanics, and "others." More serious is the problem of bias and distortion. For example, it has long been known that many African American males from the underclass vanish from census reports in their early years of adulthood only to reappear in middle age. Government statistics may also be biased by political considerations. Such things as the rates of poverty, unemployment, and crime are often hot social issues, and many sociologists have charged that the standards and procedures for calculating those figures are slanted for political reasons.

The Case Study

case study

A detailed examination of specific individuals, groups, or situations.

A detailed examination of specific individuals, groups, or situations is known as a **case study.** There are many different sources of information for such investigations, including the official records just discussed, histories, biographies, and newspaper reports. *Personal interviews* and *participant observation* are two of the most direct ways of gathering information for a case study.

Suppose you were interested in studying juvenile delinquency. To do personal interviews, you might locate a gang of delinquent boys and ask each boy why he became involved in the gang, what he does with the other gang members, what his plans for the future are, and so on. You would then study the replies, put them together in some meaningful way, and draw your conclusions. To do a participant observation study, you would actually take part in gang activities. You might disguise yourself and work your way into the gang as a regular member, or you might tell the boys your purpose and ask their permission to watch their activities. One problem with the interview technique is that we can never be sure the subjects are telling the truth, even if they think they are. Although the participant observation technique avoids this problem, it is difficult and sometimes even dangerous to study people in this way, for they often resent the intrusion of nosy outsiders. Then, too, people often act differently when they know a sociologist is watching them.

When compared with other research methods, the case study has the advantage of allowing researchers to come into close contact with the objects of their study. Interviews and direct observation can provide rich insights that cannot be obtained from statistics, but the case study method has its limitations, especially when the cases selected for study are not typical. For instance, a researcher might unknowingly select a group of delinquents who are strongly opposed to drug use while all the other gang members in the same area are heavy drug users. Another common criticism of the case study method is that it relies too heavily on the ability and insights of the person doing the study. Although this problem is common to all research methods, it is especially troublesome in case studies because all the "facts" that are gathered for examination are filtered by the researcher.

The Survey

survey

A research technique in which a sample of people are asked about their attitudes and/or activities, either in personal interviews or by means of questionnaires.

sample

A cross section of subjects selected for study as representative of a larger population.

Rather than concentrating on an in-depth study of a few cases, the **survey** asks more limited questions of a much larger number of people. It is seldom possible to question everyone concerned with a certain social problem; therefore, a **sample** is used. For instance, suppose you were interested in the relationship between people's age and their attitudes toward the abortion issue. You might select an appropriate city for your study and randomly select a sample of 500 names from the city directory. If the sample is properly drawn (that is, each person in the city's population had an equal chance of being selected), it will usually be representative of all the adults in the city. Each person in the sample would then be interviewed to determine his or her age and attitude toward abortion. Next, you would analyze the responses statistically and try to determine the relationship between the two variables.

The survey, in which a sample of people are asked a series of questions about their opinions or behavior, is one of the most common methods of sociological research.

The survey is an invaluable tool for measuring the attitudes and behaviors of large numbers of people. The Gallup and Harris polls that gauge public opinion about dozens of topical issues are good examples of the way the survey method can be used effectively. However, because most surveys gather answers to only a limited number of fixed questions, they are not as effective as the case study approach in developing new ideas and insights. Another problem is that people do not always answer the questions honestly, particularly if the survey deals with sensitive issues such as sexual behavior or crime. A third difficulty is that surveys are expensive and time-consuming. When conducted properly, however, a survey ensures that the people studied are not misleading exceptions; case studies can seldom provide this assurance.

The Experiment

The **experiment,** in which the researcher performs some activity and watches the results, provides an opportunity for the most carefully controlled type of research. Although there are many types of experimental design, experimenters usually divide their subjects into an experimental group and a control group. Then the experimental group is manipulated in some way, but the other group is not. By comparing the two groups at the end of the experiment, researchers try to discover the effects of what was done to the experimental group. To illustrate, suppose you were interested in the effects of violent programs on television viewers. You might select two

experiment
A research method in which the behavior of individuals or groups is studied under controlled conditions, usually in a laboratory setting.

groups of people and show one, the experimental group, a number of violent television programs and the other, the control group, nonviolent programs. You would then test the two groups to see whether the violent programs caused any increase in violent behavior or attitudes.

A major problem arises because most experimental studies of human behavior must be conducted in laboratory settings. Watching violent television programs in a laboratory is likely to have different effects from watching the same programs at home because the conditions in the two settings differ so greatly. True "social experiments," in which a social change is introduced into real-life settings to determine its effect on a social problem, are rare because few social scientists have the authority or the money to carry out such research. Another problem with experimental research is that the subjects may be inadvertently harmed by the experimental manipulations; many potentially valuable experiments cannot be done for ethical reasons.

Quick Review

Discuss the advantages and disadvantages of the use of the surveys, cases studies, experiments, and public records in doing sociological research.

Interpreting Claims About Social Problems

Even those of us who never do research on social problems sooner or later will have to interpret claims about them. Politicians, journalists, and sociologists, as well as an assortment of cranks and oddballs, constantly bombard the public with opinions and "facts" about these problems. Each person must decide whether or not to believe these claims. Many of them are patently false, but some are presented with impressive-sounding arguments. Reasonable skepticism is an important scientific tool; it should be practiced by anyone who is interested in knowing how social problems arise, persist, and change.

Some people find it easy to believe almost anything they see in print, and they even accept the exaggerated claims of television commercials and newspaper advertisements. In addition, the ability to speak well may be taken as a sign that the speaker is trustworthy and honest. The belief that those who lie in public are usually sued or even put in jail adds to the credibility of public speakers, but there are many ways of telling lies without risking trouble with the law. One technique is to lie about groups rather than individuals. While someone could get in trouble saying that John Jones is a drug addict without some proof, a speaker could say that college students or musicians are addicts. Another technique is to imply guilt by association. Consider, for example, the difference between these two statements:

> Mary Jones, the Communist party, and student revolutionaries agree that there are great injustices in the American economic system.

> Mary Jones, the National Council of Churches, and Supreme Court justices agree that there are great injustices in the American economic system.

Another way of conveying a misleading impression is to quote out of context. This sort of misrepresentation has been brought to the level of a fine art by the merchandisers of paperback books. For example, a reviewer in the *New York Times* might say something like this: "This book is somewhat interesting, but certainly not one of the greatest books of the decade." And the reviewer might end up being quoted like this:

Interesting . . . one of the greatest books of the decade.

—*New York Times.*

It is essential to carefully read claims about social problems and their solutions. Wild propaganda and intentional distortions are usually self-evident. However, most people who are concerned about social issues do not intentionally lie or distort the truth. They may merely be vague, using phrases such as "many people believe" and "it is widely thought" because their knowledge is incomplete. People also tend to unconsciously distort their perceptions to fit their own biases, and misleading statements are hardest to detect when the speaker is sincere. There are a number of standards that can be used to measure the validity of a statement, but none of them is foolproof.

The Author

One of the best places to begin evaluating an article or speech is with the author. What are his or her qualifications? Why should the speaker or writer know anything more about the problem than the audience? Titles and academic degrees in themselves do not mean very much unless they have some clear relation to the problem under consideration. For instance, a professor of physics might be qualified to talk about nuclear power, but her opinion about the influence of international politics on our oil supplies could well be of little value. A professor of sociology might be qualified to comment on the causes of crime but might know little or nothing about how police departments should be organized. An impressive title does not always guarantee authority or expertise.

It is also helpful to know an author's biases. They will often become clear through a look at the author's other work. For example, suppose that an economist who has always supported the Social Security system publishes a study concluding that the system has been a failure. These findings should be given more weight than the same conclusions published by a longtime opponent of Social Security. The same is true of articles published by people with special interests. An article concluding that criminals have been mistreated by the police is more persuasive if it is written by a police officer than if it is written by a burglar.

The Support

Scientific research projects are expensive. If the authors say their assertions are based on research, it is important to know who paid for the research and what, if anything, its supporters stand to gain from its conclusions. Few organizations, including the federal government, will fund a study that is likely to arrive at conclusions harmful to their interests. It is not surprising to find that a study funded by an oil company asserts that oil drilling will produce little environmental damage or to find that a study funded by a tobacco company says smoking cigarettes is as safe as playing badminton. However, a study funded by an oil company that concludes oil drilling will cause serious damage to the environment merits attention.

The Distribution

Where an article is published or a speech is given can be another important clue to the reliability of the statements made. You can usually assume that articles published in recognized journals such as the *American Journal of Sociology* or *Social Problems* meet some minimal professional standards. But an article on race relations published in a newspaper affiliated with the Ku Klux Klan, an article on the minimum wage published in a trade union weekly, or a speech on gun control before the National Rifle Association are likely to contain few surprises.

The Content

There are no firm rules for judging which conclusions are reasonable and which are not. Some research papers are so technical that only an expert can judge their value. But most books, magazine articles, and speeches about social problems are not directed at expert audiences, so readers and listeners need no special qualifications to judge the accuracy of what is said. Asking the following questions is a good way to assess the value of an article or speech.

Does the Article or Speech Make Sense? It is important to get involved with what is being said rather than just passively accepting it. Are the author's arguments logical? If a person says that drug addiction is widespread because enemy agents are trying to weaken the country by enslaving its youth, ask yourself whether it is reasonable to claim that such things could be done in secret. It is also logical to ask why those who are being enslaved by drugs are the least powerful people in the population. Do the author's conclusions seem to follow from the evidence presented? There is good reason to reject an argument that, for example, asserts that college students who smoke marijuana do so because of poverty. Subtler gaps in logic can also be detected by the attentive listener.

Why Does the Writer or Speaker Use a Particular Style? A book or speech need not be boring to be accurate. Nevertheless, there is a difference between a calm, thoughtful analysis and demagoguery. Skillful speakers who give emotion-packed examples of human suffering may only be trying to get an audience's attention, or they may use such examples to cloud the issue. Most articles, speeches, and books necessarily contain some vague claims or assertions. One should always ask whether the vagueness is necessary because some facts are unknown or because the author is trying to obscure the subject or conceal information. Conversely, a collection of numbers and statistics does not guarantee that conclusions are valid. An old saying holds that figures do not lie but liars figure.

Do an Author's Claims Fit In with What Others Say About the Subject? The truth of a proposition is not decided by democratic vote. Majorities can be wrong and minorities right. Even an individual who strays far from what most people—including experts—accept as true is not necessarily wrong. In scientific work, a successful experiment by a lone researcher can challenge truths that have long been accepted; but if an author's claims differ greatly from those of others who know something about the subject, there is reason to be skeptical. The question to be asked is whether the author presents enough evidence to justify rejection of the old ideas and accepted beliefs.

Quick Review

What are the best ways of evaluating the claims people make about our social problems?

Summary

There are two major sociological definitions of the term *social problem*. One says that social problems are created by gaps between a society's ideals and actual conditions in that society. The other defines a social problem as a condition that a significant number of people consider to be a problem.

The public's perceptions of social problems change from time to time. The major forces influencing these changes are social movements that try to bring about social change. These movements usually begin when people who share a common problem communicate with each other and commit themselves to finding a solution. If the supporters of a social movement are powerful, or if they can appeal to popular values and prejudices, the movement has a good chance of success. If the opponents of the social movement have more influence, action is far less likely to be taken. Even if the government takes official action, the agencies that are supposed to deal with the problem may do little or nothing to change it.

Over the years sociologists have developed a body of knowledge, theories, and methods that aid in the study of social problems. Basic concepts used by virtually all sociologists include role, norm, institution, class, culture, subculture, and society.

Sociologists approach the study of social problems from different theoretical perspectives. The two major approaches dealing with large groups and entire societies are the functionalist perspective and the conflict perspective. Functionalists see a society as something like an organism or machine in which all the parts usually work together for the common good. Every society has a set of needs that must be fulfilled if it is to survive, and all the components of a society have functions that they perform to meet these needs. But they may also have dysfunctions or harmful consequences for society. Social problems occur when a society becomes so disorganized that its basic functions cannot be performed as well as they should be. Conflict theorists see social order as a set of power relationships. Coercion, not shared values and beliefs, is the strongest cement holding a society together. Some conflict theorists emphasize class conflict, and others emphasize conflicts between people from different ethnic groups or genders. But they all agree that the oppression of one group by another is a basic cause of social problems. Feminist theory attempts to counterbalance the male-oriented view of the traditional sociological perspectives by describing the world and women's place in it from a woman's viewpoint. They argue that men's and women's lives are not only distinctly different, they are unequal as well, and that contemporary society is a patriarchy that benefits men at the expense of women. The dominant social psychological perspective in sociology is known as interactionism. Interactionists explain our behavior in terms of the patterns of thoughts and beliefs we have. They place particular emphasis on the importance of the way we define ourselves (self-concept) and the way we define our social environment (definition of the situation), both of which are in large measure learned from our interactions with others.

Theory is an important guide, but it becomes effective only when applied to facts. Social scientists use four principal methods to gather data to test theories and uncover the facts. Public records and statistics provide social scientists with a rich source of data so that they do not have to collect it themselves. The case study is a detailed examination of specific individuals, groups, or situations. Surveys put questions to cross sections of the population. Experiments usually try to duplicate the social world in a laboratory so that the various factors being studied can be carefully controlled.

Even those who never do research on social problems should be able to interpret and judge the claims of others. There are at least four commonsense methods for evaluating speeches, books, and articles about social problems: (1) check the qualifications and biases of the author; (2) check the biases of the people who pay the bills of the speaker or author; (3) check the publishers of magazine articles and the special interests of the audience listening to a speech; and (4) check the content of the speech or article and the logic of the arguments the author uses to support a point.

Questions for Critical Thinking

One of the most vital sociological skills is the ability to take a general understanding about the way society operates and apply it to our own personal lives. List the two or three most serious problems facing you in your own life. How do the social forces examined by the different sociological perspectives influence those problems? Is one sociological approach better than the others at helping you to understand those problems? If so, why?

Key Terms

behaviorism	function
biosocial perspective	functionalist perspective
case study	interactionism
class conflict	methodology
conflict perspective	norm
culture	patriarchy
definition of the situation	personality
deviant	personality theories
dysfunction	role
experiment	sample
feminist theory	self-concept

sexism
social class
social disorganization
social institutions
social movements
social problem
social psychological theories

social structure
socialization
society
sociology
subculture
survey

Further Readings

Earl Babbie, *The Practice of Social Research,* 8th ed. (Belmont, CA: Wadsworth, 1998). An introduction to the techniques and goals of sociological research that tries to be as readable as possible.

Randall Collins, *Four Sociological Traditions* (New York: Oxford University Press, 1994). A good introduction to social theory by a well-known theorist.

Seymour Martin Lipset, *American Exceptionalism: A Double-Edged Sword* (New York: Norton, 1996). An insightful analysis of American society from a cross-cultural perspective.

C. Wright Mills, *The Sociological Imagination* (New York: Oxford University Press, 1959). A classic statement of the value of the sociological approach in dealing with the social problems of everyday life.

David R. Simon, *Social Problems and the Sociological Imagination* (New York: McGraw-Hill, 1995). Applies C. Wright Mills's approach to contemporary social problems.

Malcolm Spector and John I. Kitsuse, *Constructing Social Problems* (Hawthorne, NY: Aldine de Gruyter, 1987). An interesting look at the sociology of social problems that focuses on the way particular conditions come to be labeled as social problems.

Notes

1. See Robert K. Merton, "The Sociology of Social Problems," in Robert K. Merton and Robert Nisbet, eds., *Contemporary Social Problems,* 4th ed. (New York: Harcourt Brace Jovanovich, 1976).

2. Herbert Blumer, "Social Problems as Collective Behavior," *Social Problems* 18 (1971): 298–306; Malcolm Spector and John I. Kitsuse, "Social Problems: A Reformation," *Social Problems* 21 (1973): 145–159.

3. See Robert H. Lauer, "Defining Social Problems: Public Opinion and Textbook Practice," *Social Problems* 24 (1976): 122–130.

4. See Howard S. Becker, *Outsiders* (New York: Free Press, 1963).

5. Karl Marx, *Capital: A Critique of Political Economy* (New York: Random House, 1906).

6. Max Weber, *From Max Weber: Essays in Sociology,* ed. and trans. Hans H. Gerth and C. Wright Mills (New York: Oxford University Press, 1946).

7. See Harold R. Kerbo, *Social Stratification and Inequality: Class Conflict in Historical and Comparative Perspective,* 3rd ed. (New York: McGraw-Hill, 1996).

8. See Emile Durkheim, *Division of Labor in Society* (Glencoe, IL: Free Press, 1947). For some classic works on functionalism, see Emile Durkheim, *The Elementary Forms of Religious Life* (New York: Free Press, 1965); Robert K. Merton, *Social Theory and Social Structure,* rev. ed. (New York: Free Press, 1957); and Talcott Parsons, *The Social System* (New York: Free Press, 1964).

9. See Marx, *Capital;* Max Weber, *The Theory of Social and Economic Organization* (Glencoe, IL: Free Press, 1947); and Randall Collins, *Conflict Sociology* (New York: Academic Press, 1979).

10. Karl Marx and Friedrich Engels, *The Communist Manifesto,* ed. Samuel Beer (New York: Appleton Century Crofts, 1955).

11. Patricia Madoo Lengermann and Jill Niebrugge-Brantley, "Contemporary Feminist Theory," in George Ritzer, *Sociological Theory,* 4th ed. (New York: McGraw-Hill, 1996), pp. 436–488.

12. George Herbert Mead, *Mind, Self, and Society* (Chicago: University of Chicago Press, 1934).

13. See, for example, Herbert Blumer, *Symbolic Interactionism: Perspective and Method* (Englewood Cliffs, NJ: Prentice Hall, 1969), and Tamotsu Shibutani, *Society and Personality* (Englewood Cliffs, NJ: Prentice Hall, 1961).

14. For a good summary of contemporary interactionist theory, see John P. Hewitt, *Self and Society: A Symbolic Interactionist Social Psychology*, 6th ed. (Boston: Allyn & Bacon, 1994).

15. See B. F. Skinner, *About Behaviorism* (New York: Knopf, 1974).

16. See, for example, Albert Bandura, *Social Learning Theory* (Englewood Cliffs, NJ: Prentice Hall, 1977).

17. W. I. Thomas, *The Child in America* (New York: Knopf, 1928), p. 572.

PART I

Troubled Institutions

Aneighbor and her family are evicted from their home because she lost her job and can't keep up the payments. A man you know is beaten and robbed by a gang of local teenagers. A girl who used to live down the street gets pregnant and tries to kill herself after her parents berate her and her boyfriend walks out. When such problems arise, we usually explain them in personal terms: "Those boys are a bunch of thugs." "I thought that house was more than Mrs. Jones could afford." "That girl was always a wild one." The goal of the sociological study of social problems is to look behind those personal realities to see the powerful social forces that lie at their roots. An understanding of our social problems must be built on an understanding of society itself. This book therefore begins with an examination of four basic institutions that are fundamental building blocks of our social life. Each institution has its own problems, and each has a major impact on the other problems we will discuss later. We start with an analysis of an institution many sociologists feel is the most basic of all—the family. Next we look at our educational system, and in the last two chapters we explore the problems in the economy and the government—institutions that obviously have an enormous influence on all the other social problems we discuss in this book.

Problems of the Family

How is the modern family changing?

Is divorce a social problem?

What are the causes of family violence?

Are children victims of their parents' problems?

How can the family be strengthened?

31

Donna Oakes works from 8 to 5 as a receptionist at a dental office in Concord, California. Every morning she gets the kids up and dressed, fixes their breakfast and lunch, and drops them off at school on her way to work. Her husband, Randy, is an insurance salesman, so he can usually take time off from work to pick them up and get them over to her mother's house. When Donna gets off work, she picks up the kids, and then it is time to fix dinner, try to help with homework, and drive the kids to their ball games and music lessons. Randy has to work a lot of nights, so they don't get to see much of each other except on the weekends.

Tasha Parker got pregnant when she was 17. Jerome's father was a nice boy, but immature and scared to death of responsibility, so Tasha ended up raising her son as a single mother. She dropped out of high school and was on welfare for a while. Times were hard then. She felt deserted by Jerome's father and ashamed to be getting a public handout. Even with a few odd jobs on the side, she never earned enough to get by on her own. She finally moved back in with her mother and finished high school. After two years as a secretary in the county clerk's office, she is earning enough to start making plans to move out again.

Our family system has been undergoing sweeping changes, and all the old expectations—from the assumption of male dominance to the idea that marriage itself "is forever"—seem open to question. The divorce rate has soared, and more and more women like Tasha Parker are having children without being married at all. With all the economic and social presses of modern life, even two-parent homes like that of Donna and Randy Oakes just aren't the same as they used to be. Some take all this as a sign of the impending collapse of our family system, but that attitude ignores the many strengths of today's families. As we will see in this chapter, the family is certainly changing, but it shows no signs of disappearing. Almost everyone eventually marries, and most who divorce marry again. Although it is easy to idealize the past, there is little reason to believe that families of former years were any happier than families are today.

Families Around the World

family
(1) A group of people who define themselves as a family. (2) A group of people related by marriage, ancestry, or adoption who live together in a common household.

A **family** is usually defined as a group of people related by marriage, ancestry, or adoption who live together in a common household, but like much else about the modern family, even its definition is a matter of debate. Shouldn't two people who have lived together for ten or twenty years be considered a family even if they have never been officially married? What if they were legally forbidden to marry because they are both the same sex? What about people who are legally married but have no emotional bonds, or people who have intense bonds but live separately? The interactionist perspective suggests a more flexible definition, one that seems better suited to today's diverse family landscape. In this approach, a family is simply any group of people that defines itself as a family.

Although some form of family is universal to all human societies, its structure and traditions vary enormously from one place to another. For example, some societies permit only one husband and wife, while others allow more. Anthropologist George P. Murdock's classic study of 565 societies found that about one-fourth followed the pattern of **monogamy** (only one husband and one wife at a time), whereas three-fourths allowed some form of **polygamy** (more than one husband or wife). However, while over 70 percent of all the societies studied allowed a husband to have more than one wife, he found only four societies that allowed a wife to have more than one husband.[1]Another useful classification divides families into two types: nuclear and extended. The **nuclear family** consists of a married couple or single parent and children. Although there are often close ties between the members of the nuclear family and the other relatives, nuclear families are independent, self-controlled units. When two people marry, the couple and their children become a separate family, usually living apart from the families in which the wife and husband were reared.

Although the nuclear family is the most common in the world's industrialized nations, anthropologists have found that the **extended family,** which includes a much wider range of relatives than the nuclear family, is the ideal in most agricultural societies. Life in an extended family is very different from the life most of us know in the nuclear family. For one spouse at least, marriage does not represent a sharp break with the past, as it does in our culture. That spouse continues to live with his or her parents, as before. Although the adjustment is more difficult for the spouse who must move into a new family, husband and wife both remain under the authority of the older generation. They have little chance of controlling their own lives unless they live long enough to take over the responsibility for the entire family. On the other hand, each family member receives far more support and protection from the family unit. For example, many more adults are involved in the rearing of the children, so if something happens to one of the parents, there is always someone else to take over.[2]

monogamy
A family system that allows marriage to only one person at a time.

polygamy
A family system that allows more than one husband or wife at a time.

nuclear family
A married couple—or single parent—and children.

extended family
A family in which other relatives besides a single set of parents and children live together.

Quick Review

What is the best definition of the family?

What different types of families are there?

Understanding Family Diversity

Before the industrial revolution transformed our social world, most cultures had a clear idea of what a "normal" family should be like. Of course, not every family could live up to those expectations, but there was enormous pressure to conform, and the vast majority of people did. In preindustrial societies, the family was the basic unit of economic production, and it was very hard to survive outside family bonds. Marriages were often arranged by parents or other family members, and the needs of the family were supposed to be placed above those of its individual members. Marriage was seen as a family duty, and divorce was often difficult or impossible. The father or oldest male was given authority over the family and its assets. Indeed, the women and children were frequently seen as his property and were expected to respect and obey him.

Over the generations, the industrial revolution transformed family life. As production shifted away from the family farm, individuals gained more economic independence, and it became easier to live without family support. Today, marriage has become

romantic love

The passionate affection toward another that is considered to be the ideal basis for marriage in Western culture.

patriarchal system

A social system based on male domination.

a matter of individual choice. Couples usually marry out of the desire for companionship and personal happiness, not because of duty to their families or economic necessity. The idealization of **romantic love,** which first became popular among the European aristocracy, was originally applied only to extramarital affairs. But with the changes brought by industrialization, it became a primary goal of marriage itself, and the process of mate selection came to focus on finding a compatible person and "falling in love." The underpinnings of the **patriarchal system** (a social system based on male domination) slowly eroded as more and more women took independent jobs outside the home. And family units themselves became smaller as birthrates dropped, the number of single parents increased, and fewer relatives outside the nuclear family lived in the home.

This relentless stream of social and economic change has produced a diverse mosaic of family patterns in modern society. Yet many people still have an idealized picture of the "normal" family handed down from the last period when there was still a strong consensus about family issues. Perhaps best symbolized by the popular television comedies of the 1950s and 1960s, such as *Leave It to Beaver* and *Father Knows Best,* this ideal combines elements of the preindustrial family with many newer developments. The husband is the head of this idealized family, earning the money and making the major decisions. The wife stays home to take care of the house and, most particularly, the children, who are the central focus of family life. The family unit is stable, sex strictly confined to the married couple, and divorce hardly considered as a possibility. This ideal family lives in a large suburban house in a neighborhood filled with people very much like themselves.

Even in the 1950s, this ideal was only that—a goal our culture encouraged us to desire. the ability to live that life-style was always limited: the poor and ethnic minorities were largely excluded, and as time went by, this "typical" family became less common in the white middle class as well. In order to understand the wide diversity of today's families, we must turn our attention to the changing pattern of family life and the way families differ along class and ethnic lines.

Changing Family Patterns

Our family system has undergone rapid change since World War II. While many Americans still live in the kinds of nuclear families idealized in the old television shows, more and more are living in other kinds of family arrangements. One important trend is that people are staying single longer than they did in the past, so there are now more one-person households. In the last four decades, the average age at marriage has increased, and people are waiting longer after a divorce before remarrying. Industrial society's ever increasing demand for education and training is one reason more marriages are delayed, but there are other important factors as well. Greater acceptance of premarital sex makes the single life more attractive, and the public's attitude toward singles has undergone a remarkable change. The nineteenth-century stereotypes of the lonely bachelor and the neglected spinster have been replaced by the new stereotype of affluent, carefree singles who often elicit envy instead of pity. Figure 2.1 shows how rapidly the number of singles has been growing, but this figure should not be misinterpreted. The vast majority (over 90 percent) of Americans eventually get married; they are simply choosing to remain single for a somewhat longer part of their lives.

Another important change in family size concerns the number of children. In the past, it was almost scandalous for a couple to decide that they didn't want to

Figure 2.1

The Growing Number of Singles

The percentage of Americans who are single has steadily increased over the years.

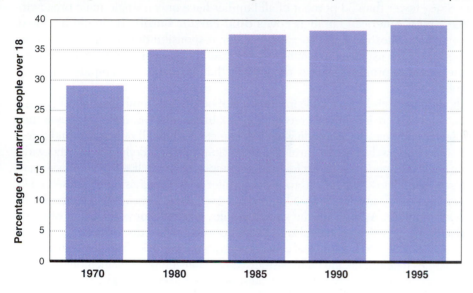

Source: U.S. Bureau of the Census, *Statistical Abstract of the United States, 1996* (Washington, DC: U.S. Government Printing Office, 1996), p. 54.

have any children, but a growing number of couples are now making that choice; and although the vast majority of married couples do eventually have children, they are having fewer than they did in the past. The percentage of families with three or more children is only half as big as it was in 1970, while the percentage of families with no children showed a substantial increase.[3] We will examine the reasons for this more thoroughly in Chapter 15, but there is little doubt that they are closely linked to the process of industrialization. Technology has helped to bring down the death rate, so it is no longer necessary to have many children to ensure that a few survive. And although children were an economic asset in a traditional agricultural society, they are often a financial burden in the industrial world.

One of the most important trends has been rapid growth in the number of **single-parent families.** In 1970, single-parent families made up about 11 percent of all American families, but today one in four families with children has only a single parent in the home, and of those about 84 percent are headed by a woman.[4] Although we will examine single-parent families more fully in the next section, the causes of this increase are not hard to find. The percentage of families headed by widows has declined, but there has been a sharp increase in the number of families with children that are headed by women who have been divorced or have never married.

Another major change has been in the economic role of the wife in families with two spouses. In 1938, a national survey found that 75 percent of all Americans disapproved of a woman working if her husband could support her. But just 40 years later, another survey found a complete reversal of public opinion: 75 percent

single-parent families
Families in which one parent lives with one or more children.

dual-earner family
A family in which both the husband and the wife are employed.

of those surveyed approved of wives holding a job.[5] Statistics also show that behavior has changed along with attitudes. In 1992, 61 percent of all married women were employed outside the home, as were 70 percent of married women with children.[6] Since fewer than 33 percent of all families have only a single male breadwinner, the typical American family is now a **dual-earner family.** It should be noted, however, that males continue to carry greater responsibilities as "breadwinners," both because they usually earn higher wages than their wives (see Chapter 10) and because a greater proportion of working wives than husbands are employed in part-time jobs.

Although there is little reliable information about trends in the number of gay and lesbian couples, there is a growing recognition that they are just as much families as their heterosexual counterparts. According to one estimate, about half of gay men and three-fourths of all lesbians live with a partner.[7] Philip Blumstein and Pepper Schwartz's wide-ranging study of American couples found that homosexuals who live together face many of the same problems as their heterosexual counterparts: the division of household labor, money, power, and love.[8] In addition, however, they must also face deeply entrenched prejudice. Aside from the sneers, insults, and even physical abuse often directed at them, gays and lesbians also confront institutionalized discrimination. The law denies legal marriage to homosexual couples and often shows a strong bias against them when it comes to adoption and child custody cases. Many employers, including the federal government, openly discriminate against gays and lesbians, and few offer fringe benefits such as health insurance or death benefits to their domestic partners.

Despite continuing discrimination in child custody and adoption cases, a growing number of gay and lesbian couples are choosing to raise children.

Class and Ethnic Differences

While these sweeping changes have affected all segments of our society, they have not affected them all equally. Moreover, there have always been significant differences in family structure among the poor, the middle class, and the wealthy and between different ethnic groups. In order to understand the mosaic of the modern family, we must therefore look at the way families differ along class and ethnic lines. Before we do, however, a strong word of caution is needed. The descriptions that follow are only statistical generalizations, and many, many families do not fit the pattern typical of their group. It is important not to let such generalizations harden into fixed stereotypes or to begin passing judgment on whole groups of people because their family patterns do not conform to our own ideals.

Over the years, there has been a considerable amount of research on the ways family patterns differ between the classes, and the general tendencies have been well established.[9] The most easily defined differences concern basic demographics. Poor people and those from the working class generally marry younger than those from higher classes, and they tend to have more children. Numerous studies have shown that there is a negative relationship between income and divorce: the lower the income, the higher the divorce rate. The same holds true of the birthrate among single women, which is much higher for the poor than the affluent. As a result, single-parent families are most common among the poor and decline in frequency as income increases. Over 60 percent of poor children in the United States now live with only one parent, so the single-parent home is now the most common family pattern in the lower class.[10] Although single-parent families are most common among the poor, they have increased significantly among all social classes in recent times.

Although there are many explanations for these differences, most sociologists see economic causes at their root. Poor and working-class people marry earlier because they have far less chance of going to college and therefore less reason to wait. Moreover, they often have more incentive to leave their parents' home, since it is likely to offer less privacy and comfort. The economic problems faced by low-income people are a major contributor to their high rates of divorce. Money is a major source of family conflicts among people from all classes, and the less money there is, the more severe the conflicts are likely to be. Similarly, poor women are more likely to have a child without being married because they are less likely to know men who earn enough money to fulfill the social expectations for a husband and father.

Another important difference concerns the nuclear family's relationship with the wider world. Because of their tenuous economic position, lower-class families pool resources with a wide network of people—lending money, helping with child care, sharing meals. In the working-class family, an extended kinship network involving parents, grandparents, and siblings plays an especially important role in providing financial support and encouragement. Middle-class people receive far more help from outside institutions and are therefore less dependent on friends and relatives. When they are sick, they have health insurance. There are professional therapists for emotional problems, day care and domestic help for the children. Among the upper class, the network of family ties takes on more importance than in the middle class, since it is a great source of prestige, wealth, and social connections.

The African American family has been the focus of a considerable amount of public attention in recent years, most of it centered on a single characteristic: the frequency of female-headed single-parent homes. In 1995, 58 percent of African

American families were headed by a single female, compared to about 21 percent of white families.[11] One of the main reasons for this is that single African American women have a higher birthrate than women from most other ethnic groups. Today, 68 percent of all African American babies are born to single women, compared to 39 percent of Hispanic babies and 23 percent of white babies.[12] This in turn is related to another important demographic fact: African Americans in general, but especially African American women, are less likely to marry than other Americans.[13] In contrast to well-publicized findings about the high incidence of single-parent families, the media have paid far less attention to research that emphasizes the enormous resourcefulness of African American families in the face of racial prejudice and hard economic conditions or the important role that extended families play in African American life.[14]

Although it is still a matter of some debate, several causes stand out for the distinctive demographic characteristics of the African American family. First and foremost, African Americans are much more likely to be poor than whites, and the number of single-parent families is much higher among poor people from all ethnic groups. Second, the prejudice and discrimination that have been aimed at African Americans for so many years have hit particularly hard at males. As William Julius Wilson has shown, a deteriorating labor market for young African American males has produced a significant decline in the number of desirable marriage partners for African American women.[15] Moreover, the high death rate among young African American males and the fact that they are more likely to be incarcerated than members of other groups means that there are simply fewer marriage partners of any kind available to African American women.[16]

Despite their increasing numbers, there has been far less research on Latino families in North America. Although it is widely thought that Latinos tend to have larger extended family networks and a tendency toward traditional gender roles, much more research on these issues is needed. One thing we do know is that there is a major demographic split among different Latino groups in North America. The family pattern of Puerto Rican Americans tends to resemble that of African Americans, with high birthrates among single women and a larger number of single-parent families. However, the demographics of Mexican and Cuban American families tends to more closely resemble the pattern among European Americans.[17]

Quick Review

Describe traditional family structure and how it has changed over the generations. How does the family differ among different classes and ethnic groups?

Family Problems

The modern family is certainly not in as bad shape as some commentators claim, but it is still plagued by a host of serious problems. (See the Debate "Is the Modern Family Decaying?" in this chapter.) In this section we examine five of today's most important family issues: divorce, births outside marriage, violence, child rearing, and the inequalities of family life.

Divorce

This century has seen a dramatic increase in divorce rates. In 1920 there was one divorce for every seven marriages in the United States. Fifty years later the rate had climbed to one divorce for every three marriages, and today there is almost one divorce for every two marriages. The divorce rate in the United States is now the highest of any major industrialized nation, while Canada is in a rather distant second place.[18] There has, nonetheless, been a significant decline in the divorce rate since its peak in 1981.[19] (See Figure 2.2.)

Who Gets Divorced? In the nineteenth century, divorce was mainly for the wealthy. Great Britain and many American states required a special government act for each divorce, and the poor lacked the influence and money necessary for such decrees. Divorce is now most common among the poor, and the divorce rate declines as education and income increase. As we have seen, one reason for this is the intense economic problems low-income families must face. It is possible, too, that divorce is less frequent among the wealthy because the dissolution of a marriage requires complex and costly arrangements for distributing wealth and income among family members. On the other hand, the availability of travel, entertainment, and domestic help allows the wealthy to handle marital problems more easily.

Age is also an important factor in marital instability. A marriage between teenagers is almost three times more likely to end in divorce than a marriage between partners over 30.[20] The divorce rate also varies significantly among different

Figure 2.2

Divorce Rates

The United States has one of the highest divorce rates of any industrialized nation.

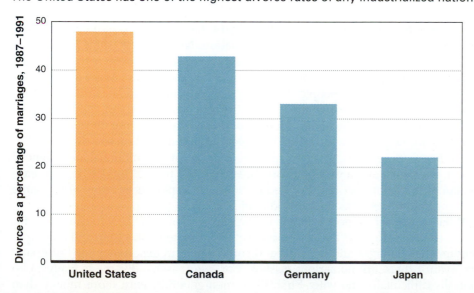

Source: United Nations Human Development Programme, *Human Development Report, 1994* (New York: Oxford University Press, 1994), p. 186.

ethnic groups. African Americans are about 18 percent more likely to be divorced than white Americans.[21]

Most divorces occur fairly soon after marriage. About one in five divorces occurs within the first year of marriage, and the second and third years are the most likely times for a divorce.[22] Considering the length of time it takes to get divorced in many states, this means that many couples begin divorce proceedings shortly after their weddings.

Why the Upward Trend? The increase in divorce has caused considerable alarm among those who consider it a sign of personal failure or moral weakness. Sociologically, the increase in the divorce rate can be explained only by other social forces, not by the vices or virtues of particular individuals. In the past, marriage was considered a social obligation, and great pressure was placed on the partners to stay together. Divorce was seen as an immoral act, an affront to "decent" people. In fact, public sentiment was so strongly against divorce that it was forbidden in some countries and extremely difficult in many others. Today, divorce carries far less stigma. Since romantic love is now the primary reason people get married, it seems to follow that it is better to separate than to continue in an unhappy marriage.

As attitudes have changed, so have the laws. In 1969, California became the first state to pass a "no-fault" divorce law, and its example has been followed by the other states. Instead of the painful process of proving that one partner did not fulfill the conditions of the marriage contract, the no-fault law allows for divorce by mutual agreement, substantially reducing the time and legal costs required.

Another major factor in the increasing divorce rates is economic. In traditional societies, the family was the basic economic unit and people could not easily get by on their own, so divorce was a major economic crisis. As employment moved outside the home, it became far easier to leave an unhappy family situation. These changes have had a particularly strong impact on women. As more and more women are working outside the home, they become less dependent on their husbands and, thus, less likely to stay married to men they have grown to dislike.

Is Divorce a Social Problem? There is no doubt that a divorce is often the only satisfactory solution to an impossible family situation. Nevertheless, some continue to see divorce as a sign of failure—an admission by the marriage partners that they lack the ability, trust, or stamina to continue an intimate relationship. Many of the problems confronting divorced people stem from such attitudes, and because the parties to a divorce often share them, they feel guilty and ashamed about the breakup of their marriage. Despite the high frequency of divorce, we have not developed effective means for helping newly divorced people make the transition to a different lifestyle. When a spouse dies, relatives rally around to provide emotional and financial support. There are also a variety of rituals, such as the funeral service, to help ease the pain of transition. Yet the divorced person, who experiences many of the same problems, seldom receives the same kind of support.

Whatever social support a couple may receive, divorce is likely to cause considerable personal suffering. The termination of an intimate relationship and accompanying feelings of anger and guilt make divorce a painful experience for both partners, even if there are no serious clashes. For two reasons, divorce is likely to be especially difficult for the wife. First, since men generally earn more money than women, a divorce often increases the standard of living of the husband and lowers that of his ex-wife's. Second, if there are children, the woman is likely to assume

Debate   Is the Modern Family Decaying?

Yes

The evidence clearly shows that the family has been eroding throughout the twentieth century. The rates of divorce and illegitimacy have zoomed upward, and more and more people are living alone. Surveys show a shocking decay of sexual morality, with premarital and extramarital affairs at an all-time high. The contemporary family is smaller, weaker, and more unstable than at any other time in our history.

The outlook for the future of the family is dismal. As the children from today's unstable families grow up, they will learn to think of pathological conditions as a normal part of family life. We may thus expect to see increasing family problems in each new generation, until the social fabric of our society finally disintegrates.

We do not, however, need to look to the future to see the harm created by the decay of the family. The damage is all around us. The most obvious victims are the children of broken homes. Such children are more likely to be poor, unloved, and neglected; they do poorly in school and get into more trouble with the police. Children are not the only victims, however; adults suffer as well. Today's small, unstable families cannot provide the emotional support that all family members need. As conflict between husbands and wives has grown, the home has become a battleground rather than a refuge from the pressures of the world.

No

The pessimists who mourn the death of the modern family are confusing change with decay. Today's families are certainly different from those of a hundred years ago, but there is every reason to believe that their members are actually happier than their ancestors were. The rise in the divorce rate does not indicate that people are less satisfied with their marriages than they were in the past. Two hundred years ago it was virtually impossible to get a divorce in most Western nations, and as a result couples stayed together no matter how unhappy they were. The increase in divorces is a healthy trend. It reflects the fact that unhappy marital partners are no longer forced to stay together but are striking out on their own and finding new, more compatible partners. Most people who divorce eventually remarry and return to family life.

The critics of the contemporary family conveniently forget the stifling oppression of the nineteenth-century family. Women were denied the most basic human, political, and economic rights and were considered little more than the property of their husbands. Few people were concerned about child abuse, since parents were given unrestricted authority over their children, and brutal beatings were considered part of good discipline. Those who were unfortunate enough to be caught violating the rigid standards of Victorian sexual morality were mercilessly condemned and excluded from all "decent" company. It is easy to idealize the way things were, but few of us would actually prefer the rigid and oppressive structures of the past to the free and open atmosphere of today's families.

Signs of Hope | The Divorce Rate Levels Off

The divorce rate underwent a major increase in this century. The biggest jump occurred after the mid-1960s, when it doubled in a single decade. Divorce kept rising until reaching its highest point in 1979 and then equaled that level again in 1981. Since then, the divorce rate has declined about 13 percent.* Although it is too early to be sure if these changes represent a long-term trend, there are grounds for optimism that the divorce rate has stopped its steady growth.

*U.S. Bureau of the Census, *Statistical Abstract of the United States, 1996* (Washington, DC: U.S. Government Printing Office, 1996), p. 74.

most of the burden of their upbringing. On the other hand, divorced fathers who want custody of their children often find the courts biased against them. Many divorced fathers may find it difficult to maintain close contact with their children if their ex-wives remarry or move away.

Despite the difficulties divorced couples face, the greatest concern centers on the children. Studies of the children of divorce show high levels of fear, grief, sadness, and anger at what has happened to them. They are significantly more likely to drop out of school, be arrested for a crime, or become pregnant as teenagers. Although most children eventually learn to adjust to their new situation, a divorce can have long-lasting effects. People whose parents are divorced are more likely to become divorced themselves, and young adults from disrupted families are twice as likely to have sought out some kind of psychological counseling than children from intact families.[23]

All this does not necessarily mean that children are better off if conflict-ridden marriages are kept together, however. A recent study of more than 20,000 children by a research team headed by Andrew Cherlin concluded that children whose parents were divorced did indeed suffer significantly more behavioral and psychological problems than other children. However, many of their difficulties actually started long before their parents' divorce as tensions and conflicts built up within the family.[24] Another study of 1400 children found that persistent intense conflicts in the home were just as harmful as the breakup of a marriage.[25]

The debate about the effects divorce has on children is an emotional one, and unfounded claims abound on all sides of the issue. At this point, it seems fair to say that the scientific research points to two conclusions. When there are intense and persistent conflicts in the family or one parent is sexually or physically abusive, the children are likely to be better off after a divorce. However, when the partners are merely frustrated or unfulfilled, evidence indicates that the children are more likely to be harmed than helped by a divorce. Such conclusions are only statistical generalizations, however, and may or may not apply to any unique individual family.

Blended Families The vast majority of people who divorce eventually remarry, and so one result of the increase in divorce has been the creation of a large number of **blended families** in which at least one of the partners lives with the biological children of the other. It is estimated that well over 10 million children live in such families, and many more have a stepparent they don't live with.[26] If these blended fam-

blended family
A family in which at least one of the marital partners brings in children from a previous relationship.

ilies are formed when the children are still young, the difficulties they encounter will probably be minor, but the older the children, the greater the problems are likely to be. If both partners bring children of their own into the family, conflicts and competition between them are almost inevitable, at least during the adjustment period. And whether or not the partners both have children, they often report difficulties disciplining the children of their spouses—a problem that tends to be particularly severe if the children have already entered adolescence. Research shows that there are higher rates of divorce among couples who have children from a previous marriage than among those who do not, and the highest rates are found among blended families with adolescent children.[27]

The question of whether a parent's remarriage is likely to be harmful to the children is another emotional issue that has been the subject of many conflicting claims. Numerous studies have found that when compared to children from intact nuclear families, stepchildren suffer more psychological problems, such as anxiety and depression, and have more behavioral problems and more trouble in school. However, most of the differences found were not large, and the evidence does not show whether stepchildren are worse off than those in single-parent families.[28] One of the most disturbing findings comes from Martin Daly and Margo Wilson, who concluded that children in stepfamilies were far more likely than children from intact two-parent families to suffer physical and sexual abuse.[29] There are numerous possible explanations for these differences. The addition of a new adult to the family can be extremely stressful for a child, especially after the painful breakup of the original marriage. Children often have trouble accepting a new parent when what

Over 10 million children now live in blended families; the effect on children of living with a stepparent is the subject of many conflicting studies and claims.

they wanted was to stay with old ones. Blended families may also carry special financial burdens if the husband is supporting children from a previous marriage who are living with their mothers. Moreover, society as a whole is often unsure how to deal with the blended family; children in the same home not only have different parents but have different sets of aunts, uncles, and grandparents. And part of the problem may come from the stepparents themselves, who favor their biological children over those of their spouse or resent the demands their spouse's children place on them.

Births Outside Marriage

The birthrate among single women has been rising for most of this century, but it soared upward in the last few decades, increasing over 70 percent since 1970. Almost one-third of all births are now to single women.[30]

The rapid increase in the birthrate among single women is ultimately a result of the same social forces that have transformed so many other aspects of family life—weakening both the consensus about what kinds of behavior are acceptable and the mechanisms by which the rules used to be enforced. Among the more immediate causes, a rise in sexual activity among teenagers combined with failure to use appropriate contraceptive techniques stands out as the major contributor (see Chapter 11 for more on changes in our sexual behavior). Although American teenagers have about the same level of sexual activity as teenagers in Western Europe, Americans are less likely to use birth control, and consequently their birthrate is far higher. Another important factor is the growing unwillingness of young couples to marry simply because the woman becomes pregnant. Studies of births in past centuries, when birthrates among single women were low, show that about 20 to 25 percent of all weddings occurred after the conception of a child.[31] Today, the "shotgun wedding" (in which a pregnant woman's father threatens the man if he does not marry the virgin he has "spoiled") has gone out of style. Unwed mothers are still often condemned, but the stigma has decreased over the years.

In some ways, the social position of an unmarried mother in today's society is very similar to her divorced or widowed counterpart; but in other ways, her problems are likely to be more severe. She is more likely to feel deserted by the father of the child and to lack the emotional support she needs during the difficult months of pregnancy. But the greatest problem of unmarried mothers is that many of them are not ready for the responsibilities of parenthood. The vast majority of single mothers are under 25 when they give birth, and about one-third of all such births are to teenagers.[32] These births are seldom planned, and the arrival of an unexpected and often unwanted child may have wrenching consequences for the young mother. Teenagers who become pregnant are more likely than their peers to drop out of school and to either work at low-paying jobs or be unemployed. Their children have a higher rate of infant mortality and more serious health problems than those of other mothers. Moreover, families headed by unmarried women are far more likely to be poor. In 1993, the average income of a married couple with children was $45,548; that of a family headed by a single woman was only $13,472.[33]

Violence

Beatings, stabbings, and other assaults are common events in many families. Family violence ranges in severity from the spanking of a troublesome child (which, though usually socially acceptable, is still a form of violence) to cold-blooded murder. Until quite recently, the problem of family violence remained hidden behind closed doors. Even now, most wife beaters and child abusers escape punishment.

Violence Between Husband and Wife The relationship between husbands and wives is one of the strongest bonds in our society. It is deep, passionate, and often violent. The exact amount of husband-wife violence is difficult to determine, but it is one of the most common forms of violence. More calls to the police involve family disturbances than all other forms of violent behavior combined. In 1993, New York City police alone received 300,000 domestic violence calls.[34] In one of the most comprehensive studies of family violence to date, Murray A. Straus, Richard J. Gelles, and Suzanne K. Steinmetz found that about one-fourth of the husbands and wives they interviewed admitted that there had been violence between them at some time in their marriage. But the researchers themselves feel that their study may have underestimated the rate of husband-wife violence. They estimate that it actually occurs in some form in about half of all marriages.[35]

In many societies, such as those in the Middle East, husbands have traditionally had the legal right to physically punish wives who refuse to accept male authority. Although this practice is no longer approved of in Western culture, it still occurs. Moreover, many victims of spouse abuse find that the police are reluctant to be of much help. Battered women report that abusive husbands are merely given a lecture or taken to jail for the night and are soon back to their threatening ways. There appear to be two major reasons for this leniency. First, most police officers are male, and they tend to hold a traditional view of gender roles. Even assaults that do serious physical harm to the victim are often seen as private matters that should be resolved by the married partners, not the police. Second, unlike the victims of other violent crimes, a significant percentage of the victims of spouse abuse drop the charges against their attackers, so some officers feel that even a vigorous enforcement effort is likely to produce few results. Growing public attention to this problem and increasing pressure from concerned feminist groups, however, are slowly bringing about a change in police behavior. Moreover, as women gain financial and social equality, they also gain greater power in the home, making it easier for them to demand an end to violence or to leave abusive husbands. Straus, Gelles, and Steinmetz found that families that make their decisions democratically have lower rates of both child abuse and husband-wife violence than families in which one member dominates the other.[36]

The effort of husbands to dominate their wives is, however, only one of many causes of family violence. Although their conclusions are highly controversial, several surveys show that wives are about equally likely to initiate a violent episode as their husbands. Most husbands are bigger and stronger, however, and the wives are far more likely to suffer serious injuries. Although wives are almost equally likely to kill their husbands as husbands are to kill their wives,[37] it is widely believed that murderous wives are more likely than murderous husbands to be responding to long-term abuse. There is also a great deal of evidence that a "cycle of violence" can be passed down from one generation to the next. Children raised in violent homes learn that violence is a way to deal with frustration and anger and are therefore much more likely to be violent themselves.[38] (See Chapter 13 for a more complete discussion of the causes of violence.)

Child Abuse No one really knows how many children are abused by their parents each year. For one thing, there is no clear line between "acceptable" punishment and child abuse. The vast majority of parents spank their children at some time or other. These parents are certainly not all child abusers. Yet severe and repeated spankings can be just as cruel as other forms of violence. Straus, Gelles, and Steinmetz found that 8 percent of the married couples with children they surveyed admitted having kicked, bitten, or punched their children, and 4 percent admitted having "beaten up" their children.[39] Estimates of the amount of sexual abuse vary even more widely. One comprehensive review of the literature found that estimates of the percentage of females who were sexually abused as children range from 6 to 64 percent; the range for males was 3 to 31 percent.[40] (See Chapter 11 for more on child molestation.)

Although the figures are shocking, we probably use less violence against our children than our ancestors did. Traditionally, severe physical punishment was considered essential to the learning process. Many parents believed that "if you spare the rod, you spoil the child." In colonial America, a statute even provided for the execution of sons who were "stubborn and rebellious" and failed to follow parental authority. There is, however, no record of such an execution actually taking place. Although the amount of child abuse reported to the authorities has increased significantly, this probably reflects the growing awareness of the problem, not an actual increase in the amount of abuse.[41] A comparison of the rates of child abuse in a survey first done in 1975 and repeated in 1985 found a 47 percent decrease during that ten-year period.[42] Although it is far from certain, it appears that the recent attention given to this problem may be paying off.

David G. Gil's study of officially reported child abuse cases provides some interesting insights into the type of child who is most likely to be mistreated.[43] Contrary to popular opinion, children of all ages are abused. Abused children are much more likely to come from single-parent homes, and fewer than half the abused children in Gil's sample were living with their natural fathers. Children from large families are also more likely to be abused. Gil found that the usual indicators of social class—income, occupational prestige, and education—are all negatively related to child abuse. In other words, the lower the parents' social and economic status, the more they tended to abuse their children. The children in Gil's sample were more likely to be abused by their mothers than by their fathers, in part because the fathers were not present in many homes. Many of Gil's findings, such as those concerning the sex and class differences in child abuse, were also confirmed by Straus, Gelles, and Steinmetz's survey mentioned earlier.

There are many explanations for child abuse. Psychologists tend to picture child abusers as people who have severe emotional problems. The typical child abuser is described as impulsive, immature, and depressed, with little control over his or her emotions. Social workers are inclined to see environmental stress as the most important cause of child abuse. They note that an unwanted pregnancy, desertion by the husband, or unemployment and poverty put special pressures on a parent that may result in child abuse. Social psychologists have found evidence that most child abusers learned that behavior when they were abused during their own childhood (see Chapter 13); that is, they themselves were beaten when they were young.

Many sociologists argue that child abuse is so common in America because the physical punishment of children is condoned and even encouraged. They call for laws that would make it a crime to inflict physical punishment on children, as has already been done in Sweden. It should be remembered, however, that child abuse can be psychological as well as physical—countless parents cause severe emotional damage to their children without ever being physically violent.

Child Rearing

Raising children so they can take over from those who grow old and die is the most critical function of the family. The vitality and even the survival of a society depend on how effectively the family does this job. Thus, every society is only about twenty years from extinction, for if it fails to socialize its children for that length of time, it will cease to exist. Of course, this is extremely unlikely to happen, but it is clear that there are many dysfunctional families in which the relationship between parents and children is disturbed, and even "healthy" families often fail to socialize their children effectively.

Child rearing has never been an easy task, but it is particularly difficult today. Our nuclear family system gives parents almost exclusive responsibility for the support and upbringing of children, and they often receive less assistance from other relatives than parents did in the past. If one parent is unable to perform his or her duties, the family is almost automatically plunged into crisis since there are usually no other relatives in the household to help out. There is, moreover, a growing feeling among parents that our society has turned its back on its children. School lunch programs have been cut back, health care has become more difficult for poor families to get, and welfare benefits for mothers with dependent children have been reduced. Today, more than one American child out of five lives in poverty, and it is estimated that one child out of eight goes to bed hungry at night.[44]

The growing number of single-parent families has made many of the problems of child rearing even more difficult (see Figure 2.3). The percentage of children living with only one parent has more than doubled since 1970, and almost one-third of all American families with children are now single-parent homes.[45] Financially, most single-parent families are always on thin ice, for the majority of them are headed by women, and women on the average earn far less money than men. To make matters worse, they usually have to pay for child care out of their meager earnings. Child support payments may help, but only a little more than half of all single parents have been awarded support payment, and about half of those receive only partial payments or nothing at all.[46] As a result, about one-third of all single-parent families headed by women live below the poverty line.[47] (See the Personal Perspectives in this chapter for a description of some of the problems faced by one single mother.)

Another common child-rearing problem in single-parent families concerns parental supervision and guidance. The plain fact is that single parents often do not have enough time to meet all the demands of their breadwinning and child-rearing roles and still maintain much of a personal life. As a result, their children sometimes do not receive as much guidance and emotional support as they need. After reviewing 50 different studies, L. Edward Wells and Joseph H. Rankin concluded that children from single-parent families are about 10 to 15 percent more likely to become delinquent than children from two-parent families with similar social characteristics.[48] The relationship between discipline and delinquency is not, however, a simple one. Studies show that parental discipline can promote delinquency when it is too strict as well as when it is too lax.[49]

Whatever its causes, there is strong evidence that the children raised by a single mother (there is much less research on father-only homes) are at a disadvantage

Figure 2.3

Single-Parent Families

The percentage of families with children that are headed by a single parent has shown a sharp increase in the last three decades.

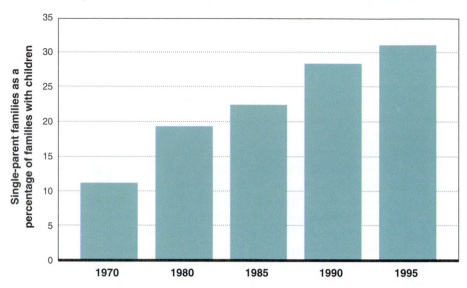

Source: U.S. Bureau of the Census, *Statistical Abstract of the United States, 1996* (Washington, DC: U.S. Government Printing Office, 1996), p. 62.

Personal Perspectives   A Single Mother

The chapter has a lot of statistics about the growing number of single parents, but the following account gives us a more personal picture of the difficulties they face.

What's it like being a single parent? It's probably different for everyone, but for me . . . it's tough. I often feel inadequate because there are so many things to do that I don't have enough time to do them all well. I was raised in a traditional, large family. All six of us sat down to a home-cooked meal together at the same time every night. When I find myself having pizza delivered, or dashing out for burgers, I feel guilty. I feel I should be raising my son the same way I was raised, but time just doesn't allow it.

I'm often lonely, too. I crave companionship, but I feel spending time with my son should always be my first priority. Again, I can't help but compare things to how I was raised. My parents seldom went places without us kids. Everything was family-oriented. I don't feel right about going out and leaving my son with a sitter very often.

Things are pretty tight financially right now, and that makes it a little harder. I seem to worry a lot these days. Really, sometimes it breaks my heart. When my son was born, everything was so good. I thought it would always be that way. I always wanted the best for him, and now I'm having to raise him without his dad and I often can't afford to buy much more than the necessities. And sometimes when he wants to play, I'm just too tired and worn out.

when compared to children from two-parent homes. In addition to the higher rates of delinquency already mentioned, children from mother-only homes score lower on academic achievement tests, get lower grades, and are more likely to drop out of high school. They have lower earnings as young adults and are more likely to be poor. They have higher rates of divorce, and women from mother-only homes are more likely to have a child without being married.[50]

A great deal of concern has also been expressed about the children of families in which both parents work outside the home, but although working mothers often bear extra burdens, the fear that maternal employment somehow harms children is apparently unfounded. After an extremely large number of studies and several comprehensive reviews of the literature, the general conclusion is that there are no major differences between the children of mothers who work and those who don't—at least in terms of the characteristics usually tested, such as intelligence, personal development, school achievement, and social adjustment. There is, however, some evidence of a slight weakening of the mother-child bond.[51]

Dual-earner families do have some special difficulties in raising their children, however. The biggest problem reported by working mothers, whether single or married, is the lack of accessible high-quality child care. According to the Bureau of the Census, almost one-fourth of working mothers with preschoolers are cared for in day-care centers, and about an equal number by family day-care providers or other unrelated persons. The other half of those children are more or less evenly divided between those who are cared for by their fathers and those cared for by other relatives.[52] The data indicate that at least 13 percent of the children from families with working mothers are given no adult supervision during some substantial part of the day, including 8 percent of grade school children.[53] Even for the children who are supervised, however, there are still serious concerns about the quality of the care they receive. The Children's Defense Fund estimates that 43 percent of the day care provided for children outside the home is unregulated (that is, not supervised by a government agency), and other studies show that even licensed day-care centers often provide inadequate care. Not surprisingly, one survey found that about half of all the mothers with children in day-care centers said they would have picked a different center if one had been available.[54] Studies of family day-care providers indicate that they have their own serious problems. One study found that 41 percent of family day-care providers had no planned activities for the children and that only half the children showed signs of trust or attachment to the people who provided their day care.[55] Another serious problem with our current system of child care is the cost. The *average* poor family with a working mother spends almost one-fourth of its total income on child care.[56]

A clear indicators of the difficulties modern families are having with child rearing is the increasing number of **runaways.** The General Accounting Office of the United States estimates that 1 million young people run away from home every year. Although most return within a few days, those who do not are likely to suffer serious hardships. Both males and females may turn to crimes such as prostitution and shoplifting to support themselves. They are also more likely to be the victims of sexual abuse, and their rates of alcoholism and drug addiction are extremely high. In some cases, however, the label of "runaway" that is applied to these young people is quite misleading. A substantial number are actually **pushouts** who are forced to fend for themselves because their families no longer want them.

runaways
Children who move away from their homes without parental consent.

pushouts
Children who are driven out of their family homes because they are no longer wanted there.

Work and Family Inequality

Our ideas about the proper roles of wives and husbands have been undergoing some remarkable changes, and the redefinition of traditional roles has placed considerable stress on the modern family. In the past, each partner in a marriage generally had a clear-cut idea of what to expect from the other, but today a bride and groom can no longer assume that their conceptions of their respective roles coincide, and considerable compromise is required to resolve such differences. More women are working outside the home and demanding an equal share of the decision-making power within the family. Some husbands, socialized to see women as subordinates, consider these demands a threat to their masculinity, particularly if their wives have more success in their careers than they do. Even when both partners accept the ideal of sexual equality, career conflict can still arise. For example, one partner may be offered an important promotion that requires a move that would be disastrous to the career of the other, or one parent may have to miss a critical assignment at work because of a sick child.

The dramatic increase in the number of wage-earning women often leads us to forget about the other essential type of family labor: housework. Although many people assume that having fewer children and the use of modern home appliances have greatly reduced the total amount of housework, that has not proved to be true. New expectations for sparkling dishes and dust-free tabletops have raised the standards that homemakers strive to meet. Some technological "advances" have in fact created more rather than less work. The classic example is the automobile, which produced a new category of household work (driving) that slowly demanded more and more time. As the car became increasingly common, door-to-door peddlers, home delivery by retail stores, and house calls by physicians were sharply curtailed, and automobile-based suburbanization placed schools and jobs farther away from home. These changes transformed the car from a convenience to a costly necessity.[57] Many of the other "laborsaving" devices women went to work to buy actually saved less time than was required to earn the money to pay for them. Despite the dreams of science fiction writers that technology would create a society in which most of us would not have to work at all, a Harris poll found that the amount of leisure time available to the average American has actually declined 32 percent since 1973.[58]

The growing shortage of leisure time makes the division of labor in the family a particularly important issue. In general, men work more hours outside the home and perform automobile and home repairs and other heavy household tasks. Women tend to work fewer hours outside the home but generally do most of the work that needs to be done around the house, including child care, cooking, cleaning, and laundry. How fairly are the family burdens divided? Research shows that when the husband is the only wage earner, the wife works about the same number of hours in the house as he does on the job, but since he also does some work at home, the husband puts in more total hours of work than does his wife. In dual-earner families, however, a sharp increase in the wife's duties reverses this relationship: although the husbands of working wives generally do a little more around the house and more services are purchased from outsiders, the total number of hours the wife must work is greatly increased.[59] Working mothers are especially likely to report feeling heavily burdened by their wide-ranging responsibilities.[60]

Today, more couples are sharing child-rearing responsibilities by allowing each member to perform the tasks he or she does best—regardless of sexual stereotypes.

Quick Review

Describe the trends in divorce and the reasons for them.

Is divorce a serious social problem?

What are the special problems faced by blended families?

Why has the percentage of children born to single women increased so much?

What are the causes of family violence?

What are the most serious problems we face in raising our children?

How have the family roles and responsibilities of women and men changed?

Solving the Problems of the Family

In one sense there are as many responses to family problems as there are families. Because each family is unique, its members respond to their problems in unique ways. In another sense, however, family problems are institutional, and therefore they affect us all. Despite its weaknesses, the nuclear family system is very much in tune with the economic and social institutions of modern industrial society. For this reason, most reformers have chosen to direct their efforts toward strengthening the nuclear family rather than trying to reestablish the larger family units typical of the extended family system.

Better Preparation

One way of strengthening the nuclear family is to see that people are better prepared for marriage. Perhaps the easiest way to achieve this goal is simply to discourage early marriage, so that partners are older and more mature when they do marry. Census Bureau figures show that the average couple is about four years older at marriage now than couples were in 1956.[61] Publicizing the difficulties of early marriage might encourage this trend and stop some young couples from marrying, but it is far from certain that such a campaign would be effective.

Another approach is to prepare the young for marriage through educational programs in high schools and colleges. Although such programs encourage realistic expectations about married life and teach techniques for dealing with marital problems, this approach has not been notably successful. A few hours of classroom instruction are not likely to change long-held attitudes and expectations about marriage.

All educational efforts do not have to change deep-seated attitudes in order to be successful, however. One of the most serious family problems is unwanted pregnancy among teenage girls. More effective sex education programs in the schools could go a long way toward solving this crisis; but to be effective, such educational programs must be combined with a well-publicized effort to provide unrestricted access to birth control services for teenagers who need them (see Chapter 11). Many people, however, advocate restricting rather than expanding young people's access to birth control. Attempts are also being made to restrict the availability of abortion to teenagers and mature women alike. Since about 45 percent of all teenage pregnancies end in abortion, the complete elimination of abortion in the United States could be expected to nearly double the birthrate among American teenagers.[62] (See the Debate in Chapter 6 for arguments for and against the prohibition of abortion.)

An increasing number of young couples are living together before deciding on marriage. While some people feel that this practice promotes stronger marriages and others feel it is harmful, the overall effects of this trend are still unclear. A four-year study by M. D. Newcomb and R. R. Bentler found no differences in marital satisfaction or divorce rates between couples who "cohabited" before marriage and those who did not,[63] and J. Jacques and K. J. Chason found no differences in the way couples described their marriages when they compared couples who had lived together before marrying with those who had not.[64]

Reducing Family Conflict

Ideally, the family is a cooperative, trouble-free unit that shelters its members from the stresses of the outside world, but real families seldom, if ever, achieve this ideal. Periodic episodes of tension and conflict are the rule, not the exception. Indeed, open disagreements and even arguments are an excellent way of resolving the differences that inevitably develop between family members. Families that avoid conflict by avoiding unpleasant subjects or conflict-laden situations are weaker, not stronger, for it. As feelings of resentment build up, such families are likely to break up or deteriorate into an empty shell, in which family members carry out the obligations of their roles but without mutual love, affection, or understanding. Thus, an open and honest airing of disagreements is an excellent way to manage family conflict and keep it within acceptable bounds.

Sometimes, however, differences become so great that they cannot be resolved within the family unit. Friends and relatives can be helpful, but there has also been a significant increase in the number of people seeking professional counseling for family problems. When there are fundamental conflicts between personalities, attitudes, or life-styles, even the best professional counseling may prove futile, but counseling can be extremely helpful for couples with specific, limited marital problems. For example, the sex therapy pioneered by the famous research team of William Masters and Virignia Johnson has proved very effective because it deals with specific problems, such as impotence or frigidity, that respond to straightforward treatment.[65] Counseling programs are also being established to deal with family violence. A number of these programs have apparently achieved significant reductions in violence among their clients, but sufficient scientific evidence has not yet been collected to make a final judgment on their effectiveness.

Changing Social Expectations

Professional help can be beneficial to troubled families, but many of our most serious problems are rooted in the way the family is defined by our society as a whole. Traditional family patterns have often served to subordinate women and deprived

Family counseling has become an increasingly popular response to the problems that arise in contemporary family life.

them of the power to control their own destinies. As a result, many women feel frustrated and angry about their position in the family, while traditional role expectations blind their husbands to the problem. Moreover, the traditional division of labor in the family may require both men and women to do work for which they are poorly suited. Some families that would function more smoothly if the husband stayed home to care for the children continue more traditional arrangements because of our social stereotypes of a "house husband" as a loafer or a "wimp." It therefore seems likely that the nuclear family system will be strengthened by the continuing growth of the new pattern of marriage based on sexual equality. In such families the division of labor is based on the skills and abilities of each partner rather than on their gender, and decision-making power and the work load are shared equally. Many families already function in this manner, but traditional standards lead some people to brand any deviation from the customary patterns as wrong and unnatural, and the entire family system is weakened by this attitude. Public opinion polls show that the ideal of sexual equality is gaining increasing acceptance, although a significant number of people still strongly believe in the traditional standards.

In addition to the contradictions and inequality so common in contemporary culture's view of the family, popular culture also creates unrealistic expectations on the part of both partners. Movies, television, books, and everyday conversation encourage us to look at marriage as a romantic adventure in which two people meet, fall in love, and "live happily ever after." Romantic love is given an almost mystical power to solve our problems and to provide our very meaning for living. Given such towering expectations, it is not surprising that even people in what appear to be successful marriages often feel dissatisfied and unfulfilled. In sharp contrast, cultures based on the extended family see marriage as part of a network of social obligations and commitments, and they view romantic love as a rather subversive force. The solution to our family problems is certainly not to abandon the ideal of romantic love and return to the old views. But we do need to temper our romantic ideals with the realization that a successful family also requires commitment, responsibility, and a lot of hard work.

Helping Parents

Americans have always looked at the family as something private and personal that is none of the government's business. Perhaps for that reason, the United States lags far behind the European nations, and even its Canadian neighbor, in providing basic services for parents and their children. Unfortunately, the changes that have transformed the family—the breakup of the extended family, the huge increase in the numbers of mothers who work outside the home, and the explosive growth in single-parent families—have created serious new problems that demand government attention.

The kinds of birth control programs discussed in Chapter 11 could significantly reduce the number of single teenage mothers if such efforts won vigorous government backing. Whatever measures we take, however, the number of single-parent families is likely to keep increasing in the immediate future, and much more needs to be done to deal with their special problems. Women head most single-parent families, and an effective program to eliminate sexual discrimination in the workplace would go a long way toward reducing the acute financial problems experienced by many of these families. To reach all needy families, the government must also reverse the current trend and begin increasing rather than decreasing the welfare benefits for poor families, whether headed by one or two parents (see Chapter 7 for a discussion of proposals to improve the welfare system).

Families would benefit from the creation of a network of government-supported preschool and day-care programs. In such countries as France, Belgium, Italy, and Denmark, the vast majority of children are already in some kind of state-funded preschool program. Not only could such broadly based programs be a financial lifesaver for low-income families, but increased government supervision could help ensure that the highest possible standards are met for the care of children from all economic backgrounds—thus helping relieve the nagging fears so many parents have about what is happening to their children while they are away at work. Opposition to such a plan has nonetheless been strong. Critics argue that government agencies are poor substitutes for parents and point to the bureaucratic indifference and coldness that are typical of many orphanages, institutions for delinquents, and schools. They fear that day-care centers will harm children by depriving them of parental love. Advocates of government-sponsored day-care centers respond that children in such facilities still have ample contact with their parents and that properly run centers enrich children's lives rather than deprive them. Moreover, they point out that millions of children are already in day care and would benefit from government funding and regulation of the industry.

Rather than restricting their aid to the poorest and most desperate families, 67 countries around the world, including Canada and all of northern and western Europe, provide some kind of direct payment, known as a child or family allowance, to help parents with their heavy financial burdens. In most countries, all families are given a monthly cash payment based on the number of children they have. Typically, the amount is between 5 and 10 percent of the average wage, but it is higher in some nations. Although wealthy families end up paying this money back in taxes, the family allowance can be a significant aid to middle- and lower-class parents.

Quick Review

What are the best ways we can respond to our family problems?

Sociological Perspectives on Problems of the Family

Concern for the "decaying" family is nothing new. Observers dating back as far as ancient Greece have bemoaned the decay of the family, complaining of everything from youthful rebelliousness to a breakdown of traditional moral values. But these age-old complaints have taken on new urgency in our times. The family has even become an issue in national politics, despite the fact that virtually all politicians say they are firm supporters of the family. The rapid change that the family has undergone since the industrial revolution has also led to considerable debate among the proponents of the different sociological theories.

The Functionalist Perspective

Functional analysis of human society has led many sociologists to conclude that the family is *the* most basic social institution. Not only is it found in one form or another in all societies, but no other institution is responsible for performing as many important tasks. Most of us begin and end our lives in the family context, and we are seldom far from its influence during the years in between.

Functionalists agree that the family's most vital function is to provide replacements for members who have died or are disabled. Such replacement has four aspects. First, the family provides for reproduction by creating a stable mating relationship that supports the mother during pregnancy and the children during the critical early years of life. Second, the family socializes the young. It is in the family that the child learns how to think, talk, and follow the customs, behavior, and values of his or her society. The family is therefore an important agency of social control. Third, the family provides support and protection for its children. The family must satisfy a wide range of emotional needs as well as physical needs for food and shelter. Fourth, the family is a primary mechanism of status ascription. Each child is given a social status on the basis of the family into which he or she is born. Thus, children of the wealthy are automatically upper class, while children of low-income families are assigned to the bottom rungs of the social ladder. The family also performs significant functions for adults. As a primary group of great importance, it provides emotional support and reinforcement and physical care in times of illness and old age. The family also transfers wealth from parents to young children and, later, from older children to aging parents.

Functionalists see the historical roots of our family problems in the social disorganization caused by industrialization. The extended family is well suited to the agricultural societies in which it is most commonly found, but it doesn't work very well in modern societies. Economic changes brought on by the industrial revolution broke up the extended family system and forced a shift to the nuclear family. Even cultures that never had a strong tradition of extended families underwent sweeping changes in their family systems. With the declining importance of farming, the family lost its role as the basic unit of economic production. Instead of a social duty and financial necessity, marriage became a voluntary state based on mutual love and emotional support. More recently, the increase in the number of women in the work force and the ideal of sexual equality are bringing about another realignment of family structure. The resultant disorganization and the structural weaknesses caused by the small size of the nuclear family have made it increasingly difficult for the family to perform its functions efficiently. From the functionalist perspective, the present family system is in trouble because it has not had enough time to adapt to these ceaseless social and economic changes.[66]

Functionalists agree that the prosperity and even the survival of contemporary society depend on the strength of its family system. However, functional analysis does not lead to any single proposal for improvement. One possibility calls for other agencies—such as day-care centers and schools—to assume more of the family's functions, permitting the family to handle its remaining functions more effectively. Another approach is to promote trial marriages as a test of compatibility and easier divorce for marriages that fail. However, many functionalists fear that such proposals would contribute to the erosion of the traditional family and the vital functions it performs. These functionalists therefore recommend a return to the values associated with the traditional nuclear family, such as a stronger stigma on divorce and more restrictions on sexual behavior.

The Conflict Perspective

Many conflicts of values and attitudes affect the modern family. People who hold traditional values emphasize the value of a stable family environment for child rearing and thus reject the idea of divorce; modernists see personal happiness as the most important goal of family life and believe that a child will suffer more from an unhappy home than from a broken one. Traditionalists are convinced that sexual relations should be restricted to the married couple; modernists advocate greater sexual freedom. Modernists condemn traditional attitudes toward women as exploitative and unjust, and they support full sexual equality; traditionalists are likely to believe that male dominance is based on innate differences between the sexes and that any other sort of family relationship is unnatural. Traditionalists see the increase in the number of families in which both parents work as a threat to children's welfare; modernists see women's increasing financial power as a positive development that may help create more egalitarian families and a more just society.

Conflict theorists are also concerned about the effects that class conflict has on the family. The poor have significantly higher rates of divorce, illegitimacy, and overall family instability than do other classes, and conflict theorists attribute these conditions to exploitation of the poor by the upper classes. For instance, many men cannot get decent jobs because the financial pressures of a life of poverty and the low quality of local public schools prevented them from learning basic reading, writing, and mathematical skills. Because these men cannot provide their families with the standard of living our society has led everyone to expect, they come to see themselves as failures. This sense of failure may in turn lead to a host of other problems, including the breakup of the family, alcoholism, and violence against other family members.[67]

In the eyes of most conflict theorists, the solution to family problems will come only with greater equality, both within the family and in society as a whole. They recommend that the government undertake a vigorous program to eliminate occupational discrimination against women and minorities and make a serious effort to reduce unemployment and the overall levels of economic inequality in our society (see Chapters 4, 7, 8, 9, and 10 for more details). They also support proposals for a nationwide system of government-funded day-care centers for children and shelters for the victims of physical abuse.

The Feminist Perspective

Friedrich Engels, the German political philosopher who co-authored *The Communist Manifesto* with Karl Marx, long ago wrote that the oppression of women in the family was the original form of human exploitation, and present-day feminists still agree. From the feminist perspective, the traditional family is an exploitative institution organized for the benefit of the husband at the expense of his wife. The husband has the power, prestige, and independence, while the wife has to do the dirty work and carry out the subordinate role. The marriage ceremony commands the wife to love, honor, and *obey* her husband, while no such demands are made on the man. Even the word *family* reflects this fundamental inequality, for it comes from the Latin word *famulus,* which means "servant"—among whom were a man's wife, children, and household workers.[68]

While almost all feminists agree about the exploitative nature of the traditional family, there is considerable disagreement about what we should do about it. A few reject the whole concept of family as an outdated carryover from patriarchal times, but most feminists envision a new kind of family structure based on complete equality between the sexes. Such radical equality might well involve the complete elimination of gender roles. But whether or not that occurred, the division of labor in the family would be based on the individual abilities and inclinations of the people involved and not on a set of stereotyped social expectations. Women would not be expected to be nurturant and compliant, men would be freed of the expectation that they be responsible for the lion's share of the financial burdens, and same-sex marriages would be as accepted as any other kind. Of course, such a family system could flourish only in an egalitarian society committed to eliminating sexism from its culture and discrimination from its economy.

The Interactionist Perspective

Interactionists give particular attention to the process of socialization in the maintenance of any healthy society, and of course it is the family that usually performs that task. Interactionists have linked faulty socialization to problems ranging from mental disorders to juvenile delinquency. Clearly, some families socialize their children to play conformist roles, whereas other families encourage children to behave in ways that others consider indecent and even illegal. Problems in the process of socialization, however, are far more likely to arise from neglect and indifference or, in more extreme cases, from hostility and even violence that parents direct at their children. Interactionists point out that the kinds of responses we receive from our family during early socialization, whether positive or negative, are critical in forming the self-concept that guides our behavior.

For adults, the nuclear family's most critical social psychological role is to provide emotional support and comfort. The family is the only shelter many people have from the relentless demands of modern civilization—the one place where an individual can develop a sense of stability and belonging—and for that reason, dissension and conflict within the family can have devastating psychological consequences for all its members.

Interactionists point to several possible ways to create the kind of stable, emotionally supportive families that do an effective job of socializing their children and providing security and comfort for all their members. One common problem is that the ideal of romantic love is given so much importance in our culture that young people approach marriage expecting more of each other than either can possibly give. Too often they end up bitter and disappointed when their romantic fantasies fail to come true. More realistic expectations, encouraged by schools and the mass media, may be one way of solving the problem. Another approach to building more supportive families is to encourage a wider network of kin and friends to share the emotional burdens of family life. Such family structures might also do a better job of socializing children. With more adults involved in the socialization of each child, the harmful effects of an incompetent or abusive parent could be neutralized more easily.

Quick Review

Examine our family problems from the perspectives of the functionalist, conflict, feminist, and interactionist theories. What do you think are the strengths and weaknesses of each theory?

Summary

The institution of the family is found in all societies, but in many different forms. The two main types of family are the nuclear family, which consists of only a married couple or single parent and children, and the extended family, which usually includes many more relatives.

In the past, there was a strong consensus about what a "normal" family was, and great social pressures upheld those ideals. As the economy changed and the family farm lost its role as the primary unit of economic production, society developed a diverse mosaic of family patterns. The number of single people sharply increased, more wives went to work, and the average number of children declined. Divorce became far more common, and there was a significant increase in the birthrate among single women. As a result, there was also a large increase in the percentage of single-parent families. Moreover, the pattern of family life shows significant differences among different classes and ethnic groups.

Many problems are associated with divorce, including personal stress, family instability, and increased difficulty in child rearing, but it is not at all clear that divorce is worse than the alternative of continuing a conflict-ridden marriage. Unmarried mothers who keep their children have many of the same problems experienced by other single-parent families, but because so many of these mothers are teenagers, they are generally less prepared for the changes a baby brings into their lives.

Although there are no dependable statistics, there is no doubt that violence is a common way of settling disputes between husbands and wives and leads to a substantial number of injuries and homicides every year. Another form of family violence, child abuse, is even more dangerous because the victims are too young to take action to protect themselves. Many explanations of child abuse have been advanced, including emotional disturbances in the parents and the transmission of child abuse from one generation to the next through a process of learning.

Child rearing has always been a difficult task, but the instability of the modern nuclear family and the common lack of sufficient external support make it even harder. The single-parent family is likely to have the most serious problems because only one adult must carry all the burdens traditionally divided among at least two people.

Another source of strain in the modern family is changing expectations about the behavior of husbands and wives. Increasing numbers of women have gone to work outside the home, and because there are now a variety of alternatives to traditional gender roles, the expectations of husband and wife may conflict. One common problem is that the burdens of housework are not fairly reallocated to take into account the time working women must put in on the job.

Many proposals have been made for resolving problems in the family. One approach would strengthen the existing nuclear family system through education, marriage counseling, and a reduction in unwanted births among teenage girls. Sexual equality and greater fairness within the marriage are also frequent suggestions. Many proposals have been made to help parents with the difficult task of child rearing, including greater financial assistance from the government and the creation of a nationwide system of government-sponsored day care.

Sociologists of the functionalist school are convinced that problems of the family are symptoms of social disorganization caused by rapid social change. Industrialization greatly weakened traditional family structure, but no consensus has emerged about what kind of family system should replace it. Conflict theorists note the many conflicting values and beliefs about modern family life and point to them as a major source of tensions. They also stress the notion that many problems, from divorce to family violence, arise because society allows the powerful to profit at the expense of the weak. Feminists believe the problems of the family arise from the suppression and exploitation of women, and they call for a family system based on complete equality of the genders. Interactionists are concerned about the nuclear family's role in socialization and about the long-term impact of the definitions, attitudes, and values we learn during this process.

Questions for Critical Thinking

You don't have to watch TV very long or read a lot of books and newspapers to find out that people are very worried about the future of the family. Why are people so concerned? Look at the history and the current conditions of the family and draw your own conclusions about the future of the contemporary family.

In this chapter we have described many different family patterns—the patriarchal extended family, the traditional nuclear family, the egalitarian nuclear family, and so forth. Evaluate the strengths and weaknesses of each different type of family. Which type of family would you rather live in?

Key Terms

blended family
dual-earner family
extended family
family
monogamy
nuclear family

patriarchal system
polygamy
pushouts
romantic love
runaways
single-parent families

Further Readings

Philip Blumstein and Pepper Schwartz, *American Couples: Money, Work and Sex* (New York: Morrow, 1983). An examination of the lives of American couples based on the results of an eight-year survey of over 6000 heterosexual and homosexual couples.

Alan Booth, ed., *Contemporary Families: Looking Forward, Looking Back* (Minneapolis: National Council on Family Relations, 1991). An excellent compilation of essays reviewing the literature on a variety of family issues.

Scott Coltrane, *Family Man: Fatherhood, Housework, and Gender Equality* (New York: Oxford University Press, 1996). An insightful look at the new roles men are developing in the contemporary family.

Murray A. Straus and Richard J. Gelles, eds., *Physical Violence in American Families: Risk Factors and Adaptations to Violence in 8,145 Families* (New Brunswick, NJ: Transaction, 1990). A collection of papers on family violence edited by two leading specialists in the field.

L. Edward Wells and Joseph H. Rankin, "Families and Delinquency: A Meta-analysis of the Impact of Broken Homes," *Social Problems* 38 (February 1991): 71–93. A comprehensive examination of the research concerning the impact of single-parent families on delinquency.

Notes

1. George P. Murdock, "World Ethnographic Sample," *American Anthropologist* 59 (1957): 664–687.
2. For an analysis of the preindustrial family, see Randall Collins and Scott Coltrane, *Sociology of Marriage and the Family: Gender, Love, and Property,* 3rd ed. (Chicago: Nelson-Hall, 1991), pp. 80–119.
3. U.S. Bureau of the Census, *Statistical Abstract of the United States, 1996* (U.S. Government Printing Ofice, 1996), p. 64.
4. Ibid., p. 65.
5. James C. Coleman, *Intimate Relationships, Marriage, and Family* (Indianapolis: Bobbs-Merrill, 1984), p. 335.
6. U.S. Bureau of the Census, *Statistical Abstract, 1996,* p. 400.
7. Joseph Harry, "Gay Male and Lesbian Relationship," in Eleanor Macklin and Roger Rubin, eds., *Contemporary Families and Alternative Lifestyles* (Beverly Hills, CA: Sage), p. 225.
8. Philip Blumstein and Pepper Schwartz, *American Couples: Money, Work, Sex* (New York: Morrow, 1983).
9. See, for example, Randall Collins, "Women and Men in the Class Structure," *Journal of Family Issues* 9 (March 1988): 27–50; Rayna Rapp, "Family and Class in Contemporary America," in Barrie Thorne and Marilyn Yalom, eds., *Rethinking the Family: Some Feminist Questions* (New York: Longman, 1982), pp. 168–187; Susan A. Ostrander, *Women of the Upper Class* (Philadelphia: Temple University Press, 1984); Lillian Rubin, *World of Pain: Life in the Working-Class Family* (New York: Basic Books, 1976); Collins and Coltrane, *Sociology of Marriage and the Family,* pp. 187–230; and Maxine Bacca Zinn and D. Stanley Eitzen, *Diversity in Families,* 3rd ed. (New York: HarperCollins, 1993), pp. 88–109.
10. U.S. Bureau of the Census, *Statistical Abstract, 1996,* p. 66.
11. Ibid., p. 63.
12. Ibid., p. 78.
13. William L. Rogers and Arland Thornton, "Changing Patterns of First Marriage in the United States," *Demography* 22 (1985): 265–279.
14. Robert Joseph Taylor, Linda M. Chatters, M. Belinda Tucker, and Edith Lewis, "Developments in Research on Black Families: A Decade Review," in Alan Booth, ed., *Contemporary Families* (Minneapolis: National Council on Family Relations, 1991), pp. 275–296.

15. William Julius Wilson, *The Truly Disadvantaged: The Inner City, the Underclass, and Public Policy* (Chicago: University of Chicago Press, 1987).

16. Taylor, Chatters, Tucker, and Lewis, "Developments in Research on Black Families."

17. William A. Vega, "Hispanic Families in the 1980s: A Decade of Research," in Booth, ed., *Contemporary Families,* pp. 297–306.

18. Andrew L. Shapiro, *We're Number One: Where America Stands—and Falls—in the New World Order* (New York: Vintage, 1992), p. 36.

19. U.S. Bureau of the Census, *Statistical Abstract, 1996,* p. 74.

20. Collins and Coltrane, *Sociology of Marriage and the Family,* pp. 457–459.

21. U.S. Bureau of the Census, *Statistical Abstract, 1996,* p. 54.

22. Collins and Coltrane, *Sociology of Marriage and the Family,* p. 454.

23. David H. Demo and Alan C. Acock, "The Impact of Divorce on Children," in Booth, *Contemporary Families,* pp. 162–191; Bacca Zinn and Eitzen, *Diversity in Families,* pp. 383–386; Collins and Coltrane, *Sociology of Marriage and the Family,* 1991, pp. 475–477; Judith S. Wallerstein and Joan Kelley, *Surviving the Breakup: How Children and Parents Cope with Divorce* (New York: Basic Books, 1980); Barbara DaFoe Whitehead, "Dan Quayle Was Right," *Atlantic Monthly,* April 1993, pp. 47–84.

24. Andrew J. Cherlin et al., "Longitudinal Studies of Effects of Divorce on Children in Great Britain and the United States," *Science Journal* 252 (June 1991): 1386–1389.

25. James L. Peterson and Nicholas Zill, "Marital Disruption, Parent-Child Relationships and Behavior Problems in Children," *Journal of Marriage and the Family,* 48 (May 1986): 295–301.

26. Paul C. Glick, "Remarried Families, Stepfamilies, and Stepchildren: A Brief Demographic Profile," *Family Relations* 38 (1980): 24–27.

27. Jean Giles-Sims and Margaret Crosbie-Burnett, "Adolescent Power in Stepfather Families: A Test of Normative-Resource Theory," *Journal of Marriage and the Family* 51 (1989): 1065–1078.

28. Nicholas Zill, "Behavior, Achievement and Health Problems Among Children in Stepfamilies," in E. Mavis Hetherington and Josephine D. Arasteh, eds., *Impact of Divorce, Single Parenting, and Stepparenting* (Hillsdale, NJ: Erlbaum, 1988), pp. 325–368; James Brey, "Children's Development During Early Remarriage," in Hetherington and Arasteh, eds., *Impact of Divorce,* pp. 279–298; Mary Burnside et al., "Alcohol Use by Adolescents in Disrupted Families," *Alcoholism: Clinical and Experimental Research* 10 (1986): 274–278; Elsa Ferri, *Stepchildren: A National Study* (Atlantic Highlands, NJ: Humanities, 1984).

29. Martin Daly and Margo Wilson, *Homicide* (New York: Aldine de Gruyter, 1988).

30. U.S. Bureau of the Census, *Statistical Abstract, 1996,* p. 79.

31. William J. Goode, "Family Disorganization," in Robert K. Merton and Robert Nisbet, eds., *Contemporary Social Problems,* 4th ed. (New York: Harcourt Brace Jovanovich, 1976), p. 519.

32. U.S. Bureau of the Census, *Statistical Abstract, 1996,* p. 79.

33. Ibid., p. 468.

34. Andrea Dworkin, "Trapped in a Pattern of Pain Where No One Can Help," *Los Angeles Times,* June 26, 1994, pp. M1, M6.

35. Murray A. Straus, Richard J. Gelles, and Suzanne K. Steinmetz, *Behind Closed Doors: Violence in the American Family* (New York: Doubleday, 1980), pp. 37–60, 148.

36. Ibid., pp. 190–197.

37. Jan E. Stets and Murray A. Straus, "Gender Differences in Reporting Marital Violence and Its Medical and Psychological Consequences," in Murray A. Straus and Richard J. Gelles, eds., *Physical Violence in American Families* (New Brunswick, NJ: Transaction, 1990), pp. 151–166; Collins and Coltrane, *Sociology of Marriage and the Family,* pp. 417–418.

38. Joan Kaufman and Edward Zigler, "Do Abused Children Become Abusive Parents?" *American Journal of Orthopsychiatry* 57 (1987): 186–192; Byron Egeland, Deborah Jacobvitz, and Kathleen Paptola, "Intergenerational Continuity of Abuse," in Richard J. Gelles and Jane Lancaster, eds., *Child Abuse and Neglect: Biosocial Dimensions* (Hawthorne, NY: Aldine de Gruyter, 1987), pp. 255–276; J. Ross Eshleman, *The Family: An Introduction,* (New York: Allyn & Bacon, 1997), pp.

573–577; for a dissenting view, see Mildred Daley Pagelow, *Family Violence* (New York: Praeger, 1984), pp. 67–68, 223–257.

39. Straus, Gelles, and Steinmetz, *Behind Closed Doors,* pp. 190–197.

40. Stephanie D. Peters, Gail E. Wyatt, and David Finkelhor, "Prevalence," in David Finkelhor, ed., *A Sourcebook on Child Sexual Abuse* (Beverly Hills, CA: Sage, 1986), pp. 15–59.

41. Richard J. Gelles and Jon Conte, "Domestic Violence and Sexual Abuse of Children: A Review of Research in the Eighties," in Booth, ed., *Contemporary Families,* pp. 327–360.

42. Murray A. Straus and Richard J. Gelles, "Societal Change and Change in Family Violence from 1975 to 1985 as Revealed by Two National Surveys," *Journal of Marriage and the Family* 48 (August 1986): 465–479.

43. David G. Gil, *Violence Against Children: Physical Child Abuse in the United States* (Cambridge, MA: Harvard University Press, 1970), pp. 98–99, and "Violence Against Children," *Journal of Marriage and the Family* 33 (1971): 644–648.

44. U.S. Bureau of the Census, *Statistical Abstract, 1996,* p. 472; Scripps Howard News Service, "Study: Hunger Hits 1 in 8 American Kids," *San Luis Obispo Telegram-Tribune,* March 26, 1991, p. C5.

45. U.S. Bureau of the Census, *Statistical Abstract, 1996,* p. 63.

46. Ibid., p. 385.

47. Lawrence Mishel, Jared Bernstein, and John Schmitt, *The State of Working America, 1996–97* (New York: Sharpe, 1997), p. 322.

48. L. Edward Wells and Joseph H. Rankin, "Families and Delinquency: A Meta-analysis of the Impact of Broken Homes," *Social Problems* 38 (February 1991): 71–93.

49. Larry J. Siegel and Joseph J. Senna, *Juvenile Delinquency: Theory, Practice, and Law,* 3rd ed. (St. Paul, MN: West, 1988), p. 246.

50. For a good review of this literature, see Sara McLanahan and Karen Booth, "Mother-Only Families: Problems, Prospects, and Politics," in Booth, ed., *Contemporary Families,* pp. 405–428.

51. Melissa Healy, "Study Says Day Care Affects Bonding But Not Learning," *Los Angeles Times,* April 4, 1997, pp. A1, A27; Glenna Spitze, "Women's Employment and Family Relations," in Booth, ed., *Contemporary Families,* pp. 381–404; Suzanne M. Bianchi and Daphne Spain, *American Women in Transition* (New York: Russell Sage, 1986); Cheryl D. Hayes and Sheila B. Kamermann, eds., *Children of Working Parents: Experiences and Outcomes* (Washington, DC: National Academy, 1983); Thomas C. Taveggia and Ellen M. Thomas, "Latchkey Children," *Pacific Sociological Review* 17 (1974): 27–34.

52. O'Connell Marin, *Who's Minding the Kids? Child Care Arrangements: Fall 1991* (Washington, DC: U.S. Government Printing Office, June 1994).

53. Harris, *Inside America,* p. 95; Susan Leach, "1.6 Million Kids in US Are Alone at Home," *Christian Science Monitor,* May 20, 1994, p. 8.

54. Mishel and Bernstein, *The State of Working America 1992–93,* pp. 413–415.

55. Susan Chira, "Broad Study Says Home-Based Day Care, Even if by Relatives, Often Fails Children," *New York Times,* April 8, 1994, p. A9.

56. Mishel and Bernstein, *The State of Working America, 1992–93,* p. 414.

57. Joan Smith, "Transforming Households: Working-Class Women and Economic Crisis," *Social Problems* 5 (December 1987): 416–436.

58. Harris, *Inside America,* p. 19.

59. Janice Peskin, "Measuring Household Production for the GNP," *Family Economics Review* (Summer 1982): 10.

60. Harris, *Inside America,* pp. 39–40.

61. Sam Roberts, *Who We Are* (New York: Times Books, 1995), p. 45.

62. See Theodore Caplow, *American Social Trends* (San Diego: Harcourt Brace Jovanovich, 1991), pp. 55–56.

63. M. D. Newcomb and R. R. Bentler, "Cohabitation Before Marriage," *Journal of Marriage and the Family* 41 (February 1980): 597–602.

64. J. Jacques and K. J. Chason, "Cohabitation: Its Impact on Marital Success," *Family Coordinator* 28 (January 1979): 35–39.

65. William Masters and Virginia Johnson, *Human Sexual Inadequacy* (Boston: Little, Brown, 1970).

66. See Nancy Kingsbury and John Scanzoni, "Structural-Functionalism," in Pauline G. Boss et al., *Sourcebook of Family Theories and Methods: A Contextual Approach* (New York: Plenum, 1993), pp. 195–217.

67. Keith Farrington and Ely Chertok, "Social Conflict Theories of the Family," in Boss et al., *Sourcebook of Family Theories and Methods,* pp. 357–381.

68. Roberts, "Who We Are," p. 33.

Problems of Education

Why is an educated population so important to modern societies?

Does our educational system favor middle-class children?

Do our schools do a good job of educating minority students?

Why don't our students score better on standardized achievement tests?

How can we improve our educational system?

There was nothing very special about it. As in thousands of other cash-strapped school districts, New York City school officials recently decided to lay off a fourth-grade teacher from Public School 41 in Greenwich Village. The parents, of course, were shocked and upset, especially when they found out that Lauren Zangara's layoff would force a big increase in the average class size—from 26 to 32 students. What was different was that the parents banded together and quickly raised $46,000 to pay Zangara's salary. This seemingly generous offer raised a furor on the school board and left many difficult questions for us to ponder. Most of us would agree that there is nothing more important to the future of society than the education of our children, so why do so many of our schools always seem to be teetering on the edge of financial disaster? Most people would also agree that all children should get an equal chance for a good education whether their parents are rich or poor, so why is it that the wealthier kids always seem to get all the advantages? Is it fair for the parents of P.S. 41 to pay for an extra teacher when the parents in many other city schools can't afford to do the same? The school board solved the problem at P.S. 41 in the most politically expedient way. They refused the parents' offer of financial support but found enough of their own money to return Zangara to her classroom. Most conflicts of this kind are not, however, resolved so easily, and the troubling question this case raises remains unresolved.[1]

One thing is clear—we place tremendous faith in education. We expect it to provide a guiding light for the young and to pass on the democratic traditions of our society. Education is seen as a path out of the slums for new immigrants and a ladder out of poverty for the sons and daughters of the disadvantaged; but it is also essential for the "good life" and professional careers so highly valued by the middle class. As technology becomes more sophisticated, even our hopes for our economic future are coming to rest on the quality of our educational system and its graduates.

While our goals and aspirations continue to grow, however, our educational institutions seem to be mired in one crisis after another. Several national reports have issued stinging attacks on the quality of American education, and some corporate leaders complain that our work force is not as well trained as those of nations like Germany and Japan. Every year we lose tens of thousands of good teachers like Laura Zangara, and many of our students become alienated and rebellious. The poor and minority groups charge that the system has shut them out, while many in the middle class have growing doubts about how well it is serving their needs.

The picture is not really so bleak, however. Although our high school students often do not score as well on standardized achievement tests as students in some other industrialized nations, it is generally agreed that American universities are the best in the world, and North Americans are far more likely to receive a higher education than the citizens of other industrialized countries. The history of our educational institutions is, moreover, one of continual expansion. In 1890, only 7 percent of children of high school age in the United States were in school; today, more than ten times that percentage actually graduate.[2] This growth has transformed education into a big business. Virtually every American receives some formal education, and most people spend a good portion of their lives in school.

What are the reasons for this enormous growth? In small traditional societies, education took place in the home and in children's informal day-to-day association with adults. Training for the few specialized occupations that existed was the responsibility of those who held the jobs, usually members of the same family. Customs and traditions were passed along from one generation to the next without the assistance of schools or professional teachers. In more complex societies, specialized organizations developed for the transmission of knowledge. In the beginning, these schools were mostly for the training of priests and other religious officials, but secular education soon followed. Until the nineteenth century, however, education was reserved for aristocrats and a few of their important servants. The masses had little need to read or write, and some aristocrats saw any attempt to develop these skills in the lower classes as a threat to their power. It was only a little more than two hundred years ago that the British governor of the colony of Virginia condemned all popular education: "Thank God there are no free schools or printing; . . . for learning has brought disobedience and heresy into the world, and printing has divulged them. . . . God keep us from both."[3]

It was not until the end of the eighteenth century, when democratic revolutions took place in America and France, that the idea of education for the common people began to catch on. Education for the lower classes became more important as the masses began to share in important government decisions, and technological advances created the demand for a more highly skilled work force. Another contribution to the growing popularity of mass education came from Protestant religious groups, which placed increasing emphasis on the need for everyone to be able to read the Bible. Yet progress toward equality has been slow, and the children of the wealthy continue to receive more and better education than the children of the poor.

Quick Review

Why have our educational institutions expanded so much in the last two centuries?

Equal Educational Opportunity for All?

In the past, the keys to economic success usually involved such things as the ownership of good farmland or the canny skills of the small-business owner. As formal education and professional training have gained in importance, so has the issue of educational equity. Many have charged that our educational system fails to provide equal opportunity for all, and as a result, the poor, immigrants, women, and minorities don't get a fair shot at economic success. To understand this significant issue, we will first examine the role that social class plays in a student's academic achievement, then look at how good a job the educational system does meeting the needs of minority and female students.

Social Class and Achievement

Grade school teachers and university professors alike can easily see that the children of affluent parents do better in school than the children of the poor. In fact, numerous studies have found social class to be the single most effective predictor of achievement in school. As Robert James Parelius and Ann Parker Parelius put it:

> Whether we look at scores on standardized ability or achievement tests, classroom grades, participation in academic rather than vocational high school programs, involvement in extracurricular activities, number of years of schooling completed or enrollment in or completion of college and professional school, children from more socioeconomically advantaged homes outperform their less affluent peers.[4]

There are two principal explanations for this difference. One focuses on the advantages higher-status children have because they come from home environments in which books, a large vocabulary, and an emphasis on achievement are common. The other holds that the schools themselves are often organized in ways that ignore the educational needs of the poor.

Family Background Lower-class children live in a very different world from that of middle-class children. The homes of the poor tend to have fewer books, newspapers, and magazines, and the parents have less education. People with low incomes are less likely to read for entertainment; thus, children in low-income homes are less likely to be encouraged to learn that vital skill. Lower-class families are also larger and are more often headed by only one adult. Children in such families frequently receive less parental contact, guidance, and educational encouragement. Another factor is health: poor children are more likely to be undernourished than their middle-class counterparts, and they are sick more days a year.[5] And unhealthy children simply do not learn as well as healthy ones. On the other hand, some of the academic success of children from affluent homes stems from the fact that their parents have higher expectations. A number of surveys have shown that children from wealthy families have higher educational aspirations than children from poorer backgrounds.[6] One reason is that middle-class homes are more likely to define the world in a way that sees a college education to be essential for future success and happiness. Some of this difference also reflects a realistic adjustment by poor children to the fact that they have less chance of getting a good education.

Children whose first language is something other than English face obvious obstacles in most North American schools, but language differences among different social classes also have an important impact on educational achievement. **Standard English** is more commonly spoken by African Americans with middle-class backgrounds, while those from the lower class are more likely to speak Black English dialects. Similar language differences are found among Americans from European backgrounds. People from the lower class tend to use short, simple sentences, while middle-class people use longer, more complex sentences containing more abstract concepts and a larger vocabulary. These differences give middle-class students, whatever their ethnic backgrounds, a big head start in their schoolwork and make it easier for them to understand their teachers.

The Schools In addition to the obstacles in the home environment of many lower-class students, the school system itself favors the education of middle- and upper-

standard English
The English dialect spoken by the middle and upper classes.

class students. This fact is obvious, first of all, in the way schools are financed. Even a brief examination of the American system of school finance reveals glaring inequities both in how taxes are levied and in how they are spent. For one thing, there are great differences among the various states in the importance placed on education and in their ability to pay for it. For example, New Jersey spends almost three times as much money per pupil as Utah.[7] Moreover, the differences between local school districts within the same state can be even greater. Because property taxes are a major source of school funding, districts with expensive homes and other valuable real estate often receive much more revenue than poor districts. In Illinois, for example, the richest districts spend about six times as much per student as the poorest districts, and in New York, they spend almost eight times as much.[8] Moreover, such inequities can occur even when the rich school districts have a lower tax rate than the poor ones.

Defenders of the present system of financing point to studies that conclude that the amount of money spent per student has little direct effect on educational achievement.[9] There is certainly little doubt that a badly run school can spend a great deal of money and still achieve poor results, but such findings hardly justify the practice of making the disadvantaged pay higher property taxes than the rich while their children languish in understaffed and underfunded schools.

There have been some serious efforts to correct this inequitable system through the courts. Twenty-nine different states have had legal challenges to their systems of school finance, and fourteen state supreme courts have ruled the existing systems unconstitutional and ordered basic reforms.[10] But because the U.S. Supreme Court has refused to get involved in this issue, the process of reform is a hit-or-miss affair. Some courts have upheld the method their state uses to fund public education even when it allocates more money to educate rich than poor children, and no challenge has yet been made in many other states. Moreover, such cases do nothing to rectify the great imbalance in school funding among different states.

Family finances also have an important effect on educational achievement. Despite the fact that public education itself is free, children from poor families simply cannot afford as much education as those from more well-to-do backgrounds. Students from poor homes are more likely to drop out of school and go to work. At the college and university level, the cost of tuition, books, and transportation puts extra pressure on poor students. Many highly qualified lower-class students must attend local community colleges that emphasize technical careers because they cannot afford a university education. Less qualified upper- and middle-class students may go to expensive private universities to prepare for professional careers. Moreover, the financial pressure on college students has gotten substantially worse in recent years. Even after adjusting for inflation, the cost of a college education has more than doubled since the 1960s, and the last decade has also seen large cuts in the financial aid available to college students.

Of course, colleges and universities are not the only educational institutions that charge their students. Compared to other industrialized nations, the United States devotes a far higher percentage of its educational spending to private schooling.[11] In 1996, about 13 percent of American children attended private schools.[12] The quality, the cost, and the philosophical orientation of these schools vary enormously, however. The most prestigious of them are the so-called **prep schools,**

prep schools
Private schools that focus on preparing their students for college.

which offer a much higher quality of education than most public schools, but only to the children of families who can afford to pay the price (or the gifted few who receive scholarships). Thus, many of the finest primary and secondary schools are largely closed to poor, working-class, and even most middle-class children. Even less prestigious and less affluent private schools have a major advantage over the public schools: it is far easier for them to exclude troublemakers and low achievers and thereby isolate their students from disruptive influences. Public schools must try to meet the needs of *all* the young people in their communities, even those having social or academic problems.

Because children from upper-class families generally receive a better secondary education, they have easier access to the elite universities that lead students to top positions in government and corporations. Moreover, some less qualified students from upper-class families are able to attend elite universities because of admission programs that favor the children of alumni and the children of big contributors to fund-raising campaigns.

Aside from differences in the quality of schools, achievement is also affected by the expectations that teachers have for their students. Considerable evidence indicates that teachers expect less from lower-class students, in terms of both academic achievement and behavior, and that for some students those exceptions become a self-fulfilling prophecy.[13] Robert Rosenthal and Lenore Jacobson performed an interesting experiment to demonstrate this.[14] Experimenters gave a standard IQ test to pupils in 18 classrooms in a neighborhood elementary school. However, teachers were told that the instrument was the "Harvard Test of Inflected Acquisition" (which does not exist). Next, the experimenters arbitrarily selected 20 percent of the students' names and told their teachers that the test showed these students would make remarkable progress in the coming year. When the students were retested eight months later, those who had been singled out as intellectual bloomers showed a significantly greater increase in IQ than the others. As you might expect, these findings created quite a controversy when they were first published, and many similar studies have since been done. Most of them supported Rosenthal and Jacobson's findings, but some did not, and it is still not clear under exactly what conditions teachers' expectations are most likely to become a self-fulfilling prophecy.[15] One thing we do know is that lower-class and minority students are the ones most likely to be harmed by this process, for they are the ones for whom teachers hold the lowest expectations. For example, when D. G. Harvey and G. T. Slatin gave teachers pictures of students and asked them to evaluate their chances for success in school, the teachers reported the highest expectations for white students who appeared to be from middle- and upper-class backgrounds.[16]

Chances are, however, that lower-class students will not be in the same high school classes as middle-class students even if they attend the same school. Most high school students are placed in one of several different "tracks" or "ability groups." The "most promising" are put into college preparatory courses, while others go into vocational or "basic" classes. There is considerable evidence that lower-class students are more likely to be placed in the vocational or basic track.[17] Tracking is supposed to be based on such criteria as academic record, performance on standardized tests, and the students' own feelings about college, but there is little doubt that the schools themselves have lower expectations for students from the lower classes. Even when there is no bias, a serious problem remains: once students have been placed in a lower track, they will be exposed to less challenging material and teachers will have lower expectations of them. When isolated from college-bound students, even the best students in the lower tracks are less likely to want to go to college. Karl Alexander, Martha Cook, and Edward L. Dill found that students in a college preparatory track were 30 percent more likely to plan to go on beyond high school than equally motivated and able students in nonacademic tracks.[18]

Minority Education

The history of minority education has not been a bright one (see Chapter 8), and African Americans have been the victims of particularly harsh treatment. During the era of slavery, they were seldom given any education at all. Only fifty years ago, most African Americans in the South were forced to attend **segregated schools** that were clearly inferior to those attended by whites. A landmark Supreme Court decision in 1954 recognized the fact that segregated schools were inherently unequal and declared them unconstitutional. In the turmoil that followed, intentional legal segregation was ended, but unlike **de jure** (legal) **segregation, de facto** (actual) **segregation** has been resistant to change. Although African Americans and whites were assigned to the schools nearest their homes regardless of race, most schools remained segregated because most neighborhoods were segregated.

To deal with this problem, the Court ruled that school districts must aim for racial balance in their schools, even when it is necessary to bus students long distances. Intense opposition from whites made school busing an inflammatory racial issue for two decades, but public interest in this controversy has been declining in recent years. Polls show that a large majority of Americans now support integrated schools even if they still dislike the school busing that is often required to achieve it. At first, busing and other court-ordered **desegregation** programs proved effective, and the segregation of ethnic minorities sharply declined. But because of the migration of the middle class to the suburbs, the fact that many urban whites send their children to private schools, and a heavy influx of new immigrants, in many big cities too few white children remain to create truly integrated schools. As a result, many city schools have become **resegregated.** According to a 1993 study by the Harvard Project on School Desegregation, two-thirds of African American students in the United States now attend schools in which most of the students are from minority backgrounds—the highest level since 1968. Moreover, Latino students are even more segregated than African Americans. Almost three-fourths of Latino students in the United States attend predominantly minority schools.[19]

The debate over school integration has generated a great deal of concern about the effects of integration on students. The Coleman report, published in 1966, found that the quality of schools attended by African Americans and by whites was similar when measured by such factors as physical facilities, curriculum, and the qualifications of teachers.[20] The greatest influence on achievement was found to be the students' class background. Middle-class students did much better than students from the lower class. However, Coleman found that disadvantaged students did better when they were in the same classes with middle-class students. He concluded, logically enough, that the performance of lower-class African American children would improve if they were integrated in the same classes as middle-class white students. The effects of desegregation on academic performance have been

segregated schools

Schools in which students are separated according to their racial, ethnic, or class background.

de jure segregation

A system in which the law requires the separation of different ethnic or racial groups.

de facto segregation

A system in which different ethnic or racial groups are in fact separated from each other even though the law does not require it.

desegregation

The attempt to eliminate school segregation.

resegregation

A return to racial or ethnic segregation that occurs after official desegregation problems have started.

the subject of dozens of studies since the Coleman report was first published. These studies vary widely in methodology and overall quality and have reached contradictory conclusions. Rita E. Mahard and Robert L. Crain reviewed 93 different works on this topic, and after eliminating the poorly designed studies, they analyzed the others and came to some interesting conclusions. Desegregation did indeed improve the academic performance of African American students, but mainly in the primary grades, not in junior high or high school. Moreover, there seems to be an optimum ratio of white students to African American students, which varied in the different studies from 3 to 1 to 9 to 1. Finally, the most successful approach to desegregation was the so-called metropolitan plan, which integrated inner-city and suburban schools.[21]

In addition to the academic benefits, school integration may help reduce racism and create understanding among the nation's many diverse ethnic groups. Unless school administrators modify some of their traditional policies, however, minorities may be resegregated into different classes within an integrated school. For example, academic tracking often results in predominantly white college preparatory classes and predominantly minority vocational classes. Well-intentioned bilingual and compensatory education programs may also result in the removal of minority students from regular classrooms for a large part of the day.[22] Thus, to realize the full benefits of an integrated education, it is necessary to do more than just integrate the schools. Administrators, teachers, and concerned parents must work to create an integrated and supportive environment within individual schools as well.

How well are minority groups doing in today's educational system? The answer is a complex one. Some Asian groups have done extremely well and now have a higher level of education than European Americans. The gap between Americans of European and African descent has also narrowed considerably in the last 30 years, but white Americans still have more education: 83 percent currently have a high school diploma compared to 74 percent of African Americans.[23] The educational achievement of Latinos remains below both groups. In 1995, only a little more than half of all Hispanics in the United States were high school graduates.[24] (See Figure 3.1.) There are two main reasons for this. The first is language. Many Latinos come into English-speaking schools with little knowledge of that language, and many others are less proficient in English than their classmates who grew up speaking it. The second is immigration. There has been a heavy influx of new immigrants from Latin America, and they frequently come from low-income groups that have received an inadequate education in their own country. (See Chapter 7 for more details on these problems).

Gender Bias

In the past, our educational system openly discriminated against women and girls in much the same way it discriminated against minorities. The traditional attitude held that it was far more important to educate sons, who would have to go out and find jobs, than daughters, who would just stay home and take care of the house, and our educational system clearly reflected this bias. Boys were given more and better education than girls, and many of the top universities did not even admit women. While today's students may think this kind of blatant discrimination is a thing of the distant

Figure 3.1

High School Graduates

African Americans and Latinos are less likely to finish high school than European Americans.

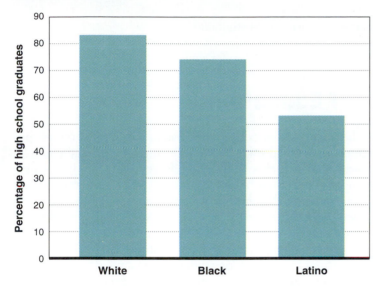

Source: U.S. Bureau of the Census, *Statistical Abstract of the United States, 1996* (Washington, DC: U.S. Government Printing Office, 1996), p. 159.

past, such practices actually continued until quite recently. Harvard University, for example, excluded women from its law school until 1950 and from its graduate business program until 1963.

Important progress toward gender equality has unquestionably been made since then. The most blatant barriers to equal educational opportunities for female students have been removed, and today more females than males actually graduate from both high school and college.[25] However, many more subtle forms of **sexism** remain. The attitudes and behavior of teachers reflect the same gender stereotypes that are found among other groups, and girls are often subtly discouraged from pursuing "masculine" interests in subjects such as science and math. At least partially as a result, while more females graduate from college, they are far less likely to be in the technologically oriented majors that often lead to the highest-paying jobs. Research also shows that elementary and secondary teachers focus more attention on male students, who tend to be more disruptive, than on female students.[26] Teachers' expectations reinforce traditional gender roles in other ways as well. Good male students are expected to be active, adventurous, and inventive, whereas the qualities of good female students include conscientiousness and sensitivity.[27] The result is that our educational system often limits the expectations placed on female students rather than challenging them to achieve their highest potential. (See Chapter 10 for more on gender inequality.)

sexism
Stereotyping, prejudice, and discrimination based on gender.

Quick Review

How does social class affect student achievement?

Discuss the history of ethnic discrimination in education and how we have tried to correct it.

How are our schools biased against female students?

The Quality of Education

The controversy about the quality of our educational system has jumped out of specialized journals and onto the political stage. Several prestigious national commissions have been highly critical of our schools, and there is a growing fear that American students are falling behind their counterparts in other countries. Such attention is certainly long overdue, but before we can go very far to make the schools more effective, we must first decide what they are supposed to do. Should they teach students to do well on standardized tests of academic achievement? Teach the skills of critical, independent thinking? Essay writing? Higher mathematics? Public citizenship? Or should they focus on students' social needs, such as preventing delinquency and drug abuse? In this section we will discuss some of the main issues in the current debate about our educational system; but because the parties to this debate do not agree about the system's underlying goals, they tend to see its problems very differently.

Authority and Rebellion

Our leaders are fond of talking about the need to teach children democratic principles and the ability to think for themselves. Most schools, however, are large bureaucracies that demand obedience to a rigid set of rules over which the students, and even most teachers, have little influence. Our schools have been compared to factories in which workers (teachers) turn raw materials (students) into finished products (educated citizens) under the strict supervision of the management (school administration); they have even been likened to prisons, with principals as wardens and teachers as guards. Although such comparisons can easily be taken too far, it is hard to see most schools as places that encourage creativity or individual initiative.

authoritarianism

A extreme belief in the importance of authority and in the individual's responsibility to submit to it.

goal displacement

The substitution of a new goal or goals for the officially stated objectives of an organization.

In one sense, the bureaucratic structure of our schools both reflects and requires **authoritarianism.** Students are required by law to go to school, where they are compelled to spend large amounts of time in classrooms and truancy is considered a form of delinquency. All bureaucracies require strict rules and regulations if they are to coordinate the activities of large numbers of people. Without such rules, school life would quickly degenerate into chaos; however, some observers believe that schools carry the emphasis on authority and obedience to harmful extremes. They argue that many schools are experiencing a problem common to bureaucracies—**goal displacement** (see Chapter 5). In this case, there has been a shift from education to the maintenance of order and authority as the primary goal of the schools. Many conflict theorists charge that there is thus a **hidden curriculum** in our schools: that along with reading, writing, and arithmetic, students are taught conformism and obedience to authority. Those who do not learn this lesson are doomed to failure in the educational bureaucracy, no matter how academically talented they may be.

While some criticize the authoritarianism of schools, others condemn what they see as chaos in the classroom. Numerous opinion polls have shown that the public believes "lack of discipline" to be the biggest problem in schools today. To most people this lack of discipline conjures up images of lazy or disrespectful students refusing to do their work. Of courses, this is hardly a new problem, and students have been getting in fights as long as there have been schools. Unfortunately, there have been frequent reports of far more serious problems: drug dealing, students carrying weapons, and vicious assaults and rapes directed against students and even teachers. A survey of Los Angeles high schools in 1995 and 1996 found that 14 percent of their students had taken a weapon to school at least once, and 2.5 percent admitted taking a gun onto campus.[28]

hidden curriculum
Things students must learn in order to succeed in school that are not part of the formal curriculum, such as obedience to authority.

The problem of maintaining order is a particularly serious one in poor inner-city schools. In this photograph, a school official is using a metal detector to check students for weapons.

In 1994, the federal government passed the Gun-Free School Act, which required schools receiving federal aid (which is almost all public schools) to expel for at least a year any student who brings a gun to school. But many states have gone well beyond the federal mandate and adopted "zero-tolerance" policies for all forms of weapons and drugs. While the supporters of these policies claim they are starting to bring down the rate of school violence, their inflexibility has produced many extreme reactions. For example, an 8-year-old Louisiana girl was suspended for a month because she brought her grandfather's gold pocket watch to school—and on the same chain was a one-inch knife he used to clean his fingernails. A 13-year-old in Ohio who was suspended for nine days for bringing a bottle of Midol to school.[29] Some schools in high-crime areas have even taken to using metal detectors to check students for weapons before entering campus. However, 64 percent of the students in the Los Angeles survey mentioned above said that metal detectors don't keep weapons off campus.[30]

Declining Achievement?

functionally illiterate

People whose skills in reading and writing are so poor that they cannot perform many of the basic tasks necessary to daily life in an industrial society.

It is estimated that at least 3 million Americans cannot read or write at all. Moreover, more than 10 times that number are **functionally illiterate**—that is, their skills at reading and writing are so poor that they cannot perform many of the basic tasks necessary to daily life in an industrial society.[31] The demand for a more educated work force has made the problem of illiteracy an increasingly serious one. The long-range trends have actually been toward an increase in the number of years the average person spends in school and a decline in illiteracy among native-born Americans (see the Signs of Hope box "Rising Achievement Among Minorities"). On the other hand, however, the recent influx of poorly educated immigrants has caused an overall decline in literacy among people between the ages of 21 and 25.[32]

Despite the fact that people are getting more years of education, there is growing concern that educational achievement has declined among secondary school students. One of the most worrisome statistics has been the poor performance of American students on standardized tests of academic achievement; for example, scores on the Scholastic Aptitude Test (SAT)—the most widely used college admission examination—declined about 7 percent from their peak in the mid-1960s until 1980, and they have stayed more or less the same since then (although there has been a slight improvement since 1992).[33] Moreover, American students often do poorly in comparisons with students from other nations. Although American fourth graders score near the top in science and are above average in math, by the time they reach the eighth grade they have fallen below average in math and are only slightly above average in science. America is consistently outscored on these tests by such poor nations as Bulgaria and Slovenia.[34] In tests of geographic knowledge, young Americans again rank dead last among the citizens of the industrialized nations. In fact, in one study, young people (ages 18 to 24) from Sweden, Mexico, Canada, Germany, Japan, and France knew more about the U.S. population than young Americans did.[35] Sadly, American adults don't do any better. In a 1994 poll of knowledge of international current events, Americans scored lower than the citizens of any other industrialized nation tested.[36] Not surprisingly, this poor educa-

The Japanese students shown in this photograph are likely to go to school more hours a day, do more homework, and score higher on standardized tests of academic achievement than their American counterparts.

tional performance has a major impact on the American economy. It is estimated that American business loses between $25 and $30 billion a year because of poor literacy among workers, and the National Association of Manufacturers recently concluded that about one-fourth of American firms have trouble reorganizing work activities and upgrading products because employees can't learn the necessary skills.[37]

There are three common explanations for these educational problems. The first attacks the tests themselves, arguing that test scores don't accurately reflect how much students are actually learning; the second holds the schools responsible; and the third blames the problem on changes in students' social environment. Critics of the validity of these tests point out that some (but not all) of the decline in scores on college entrance examinations can be attributed to the increasing number of poor and minority students who are taking the tests. The critics also raise a more fundamental issue; such tests, they assert, focus on only one or two types of educational skills and should not be used to make an overall evaluation of educational achievement. The other side generally agrees that these tests do not measure all aspects of educational achievement, but they argue that the tests are a valid indicator of some critical skills. Moreover, they argue that there is no reason to believe American students do any better in the kinds of skills that are not tested than in the ones that are.

Those who blame the schools for the drop in test scores attribute much of it to a decline in academic rigor. As more and more students come into school from unstable families, the schools have taken on numerous new tasks, from teaching about AIDS and family life to preventing drug abuse. A two-year study by the National Commission on Education and Learning, published in 1994, concluded that Ameri-

Debate   Is the Quality of Public Education Deteriorating?

Yes

The decay of public education is obvious to anyone who cares to look. The cheap, run-down buildings that house so many public schools are the most visible signs of trouble, but inside those walls lie much greater problems. Year after year, our schools are given more responsibility to solve social problems. We now expect our schools to combat racism, stop drug abuse, prevent unwed pregnancies, help the handicapped, and reduce delinquency; yet at the same time, we are cutting away at already inadequate school budgets instead of providing the additional money necessary to deal with the demands of our technological age. Teachers are paid less than cocktail waitresses, and positions in math, science, and engineering go begging. Our schools often lack basic supplies, much less the expensive computer systems that are necessary if students are to learn the skills contemporary society demands.

Not only are our schools failing to meet the technological challenges of the 1990s; considerable evidence shows that they are not even teaching the basics of reading, writing, and arithmetic very well. Many classrooms exhibit a kind of educational paralysis. Students are unruly, attendance is sporadic, the use of drugs and alcohol is common, and an atmosphere of violence prevails. Too many teachers have given up on discipline, and too many administrators allow students to dodge academic classes and take trivial electives instead. The private schools aggravate these already serious problems by skimming off the wealthiest and most motivated students. Not only does this situation tend to lower classroom standards even further, but it also deprives the public schools of the support of parents who would be effective in pushing demands for reform. The tragic fact is that a growing number of students are emerging from high schools illiterate and uneducated.

grade inflation
The tendency to assign steadily higher grades to work of the same quality.

can students now spend only 41 percent of their school day on academic subjects such as math, science, and history. In their four years of high school, American students spend less than half as many hours studying academic subjects as students in France, Germany, or Japan.[38] Moreover, many critics also charge that increasing pressure not to flunk out disadvantaged poor and minority students has led to a watering down of academic standards and lower overall expectations. For example, surveys show that fewer than 40 percent of twelfth graders do an hour or more of homework a night.[39] Such softening of standards has often been covered up by the practice of **grade inflation:** assigning grades of *A* or *B* to students who have barely learned the subject at hand.

Whatever the shortcomings of the schools, experts agree that students' home environment has an enormous influence on how well they master their studies, and there are good reasons to believe that the environment of today's students is less conducive to educational achievement than it was in the past. For example, the average high school senior now spends almost three hours a day watching television.[40]

No

Determining the quality of public education is not like weighing a cabbage. There are enormous disagreements about the ends that a good education ought to achieve, and there are few effective ways to measure how well those ends are met. It is easy to point to the decline in scores on standardized tests as proof that our educators are not doing a good job. But the realities are much more complex. The fact is that the explosive growth of electronic communication and the ever increasing number of children living in single-parent homes have changed students in a fundamental way. If our students are given less family support and less exposure to the written word, how can we expect them to earn higher marks than their predecessors? Moreover, there is reason to doubt the validity of standardized tests as a measure of educational achievement. At best, these tests, which ask students to fill in hundreds of little bubbles, measure only the narrowest of educational skills. What about the appreciation of good literature and music, a knowledge of world affairs, the ability to communicate verbally, and the countless other skills that sound education should impart?

The growing emphasis on equipping our students to deal with social problems they will encounter in the real world makes today's education more relevant and more valuable for the average student than it ever was in the past. Aren't students better off gaining the knowledge that helps them prevent an unwanted pregnancy and an early marriage than learning calculus? Our schools are reaching out to meet the emotional and social needs of a generation that lacks the family support that was assumed by traditional education. All in all, our educational system is doing a better job of meeting the needs of students; those needs have simply changed.

A survey by the Educational Testing Service found that 13-year-old Americans were more likely to report watching a great deal of television and failing to do their homework than the 13-year-olds in any of the other countries studied.[41] Obviously, children who sit in front of television sets instead of playing basketball will not become good basketball players. Just as obviously, children who watch television instead of reading books will not become good readers and, consequently, will not learn to write very well either.

Teachers often complain that their students have been growing more rebellious and less interested in their studies, but it is difficult to determine whether such comments reflect a real change in students or just an idealization of the "good old days." There is, however, one good reason to believe that these complaints are accurate—the huge increase in the percentage of families in which there is only one parent or in which both parents work outside the home. These changes in family structure often reduce the amount of time and energy parents have to devote to their children, and it seems reasonable to assume that some students' behavior at school

Signs of Hope   Rising Achievement Among Minorities

Despite the obstacles still faced by minority children, their educational achievement has shown remarkable improvement in the last three decades. For one thing, there has been a sharp increase in the percentage of minority students who complete high school. For example, in 1960 only one-fifth African American adults had a high school diploma, but today more than two-thirds do. Equally important is the fact that the academic performance of minority children has also improved. In just two decades, the percentage of 17-year-old African American high school students who can do at least basic math increased from 70 to 86 percent, and those with basic reading skills increased from 82 to 97 percent. Moreover, while the SAT scores of white students declined slightly during the last two decades, the scores of Latinos and African Americans actually increased.[*]

[*]U.S. Bureau of the Census, *Statistical Abstract of the United States, 1996* (Washington, DC: U.S. Government Printing Office, 1996), p. 159; Christopher Jencks, "Is the American Underclass Growing?" in Christopher Jencks and Paul E. Peterson, eds., *The Urban Underclass* (Washington, DC: Brookings Institution, 1991), p. 70; Lawrence Mishel and Jared Bernstein, *The State of Working America, 1992–93* (New York: Sharpe, 1993), p. 360.

suffers as a result. These structural changes in the family may also mean that parents are not able to spend as much time assisting their children with their studies or getting involved in the educational programs of their schools.

Quick Review

Are our schools too authoritarian or too lenient?

What are the causes of low student achievement?

Solving the Problems of Education

The problems of education are economic and political problems as well. Some proposals for change call for a sweeping restructuring of society that goes far beyond our educational institutions. But educational problems are also bureaucratic problems, and other proposals for change call for improved efficiency in the existing school system and its teaching methods. Proposals to upgrade the educational system fall into two broad categories: recommendations for providing more equal educational opportunities for everyone and suggestions for improving the quality of education itself.

Toward Equal Educational Opportunity

Almost everyone agrees that there should be equal educational opportunity for all, but there is widespread disagreement about what equal opportunity means and how it can be achieved. Integration of students from different ethnic backgrounds into the same schools is often proposed as a solution to educational inequality. Another approach is to set up **compensatory education programs** to provide special assistance to disadvantaged students or programs to help fight gender inequality. Finally, many propose that we change the way education is financed so that the same amount of money is spent on both rich and poor students.

Effective Integration For years the American government, particularly the judicial branch, has been trying to achieve racial and ethnic integration in the schools. Despite many advances, this goal has still not been met. Following court-ordered integration, unofficial resegregation often occurred as whites moved to the suburbs or enrolled their children in private schools. The metropolitan plan reduces resegregation by merging suburban school districts with inner-city school districts and then busing children within each district. One difficulty with this proposal is distance. Some suburban communities are so far from city centers that bused students spend a large part of their school day in transit. Another difficulty is prejudice. The proposal does nothing to discourage white parents from putting their children in private schools, and in fact it might encourage more prejudiced whites to do so.

As an alternative, some districts have created voluntary desegregation plans that give students the right to attend any school they wish, provided it does not have a higher percentage of students of their ethnic group than their neighborhood school. A related idea is creation of **magnet schools** with unique educational programs that attract students from all ethnic groups. The goal of these plans is to reduce "white flight" while still allowing minority and lower-class students to attend integrated middle-class schools if they wish. Critics of such plans argue that they are not likely to significantly reduce segregation because most students choose to attend their neighborhood schools, and most neighborhoods are still segregated to one degree or another.

Another approach encourages the integration of residential areas so that neighborhood schools are automatically integrated. In many ways this is the most appealing solution, for it provides the broadest possible opportunity for development of interracial friendships and cooperation. However, daunting obstacles stand in the way of efforts to create truly integrated communities. For one thing, a long history of prejudice and suspicion makes many Americans prefer to live in neighborhoods in which the residents have similar economic and ethnic backgrounds. Moreover, the poor and minorities simply cannot afford to live in affluent neighborhoods. One possible solution is to create more subsidized housing for low-income families in wealthy neighborhoods, along with tax incentives for affluent families who refurbish and live in older homes in lower-income neighborhoods. Specific proposals often run into intense opposition from wealthy homeowners who fear that low-cost housing will decrease their property values and from residents of low-income neighborhoods who fear they will be displaced by more prosperous newcomers.

Compensatory Education Another way to boost the educational achievement of the poor and minorities is to provide them with special programs and assistance. The most popular and widely known compensatory program of this kind is Project Head Start, which gives preschool instruction to disadvantaged children. The original

compensatory education programs
Programs designed to help make up for the educational difficulties that disadvantaged students experience.

magnet schools
Schools with special enriched programs designed to attract students from diverse ethnic groups in order to encourage integration.

research on the Head Start program indicated that it produced significant educational gains among its students, but follow-up studies found that most of the early benefits faded away by the time the children reached the second or third grade.[42] However, research on the Perry Preschool Program, which is very much like Project Head Start except that it spends about twice as much per student, has shown real long-term benefits. A study that followed a group of students from age 3 to age 27 found that those who attended the Perry Program earned more money, had more stable marriages, and were less likely to use illegal drugs than those in a matched control group. The researchers estimated that because of these benefits, the Perry Preschool Program saved taxpayers $7.16 for every dollar spent.[43] A related program under Title I of the Elementary and Secondary Education Act provides federal money to give extra help to disadvantaged students who are already in school. Over 5 million elementary school students are aided under this program, and its supporters credit it with reducing the gap between the achievement scores of African American and white students in recent years. But critics point to studies showing that the benefits of elementary school programs do not carry over into high school.[44]

Research on both Head Start and Title I programs thus reaches much the same conclusion: these programs significantly improve the performance of the underprivileged students who are enrolled, but after they finish the program, the benefits tend to diminish.[45] The solution to this problem is obvious: Don't stop the programs after only a few years. Disadvantaged students should continue to receive extra help as long as they need it, which in many cases would probably be until their final years of high school. The difficulty with this proposal is, of course, money. Today, despite the growing popularity of Head Start, only about 40 percent of the eligible students participate in the program,[46] and even for those lucky students, funding remains inadequate when compared to more successful programs such as the Perry Preschool Program. It would certainly take a lot more money to provide help for all the students in all grades who need it, but such an investment would pay enormous dividends in terms of a healthier, more competitive economy; lower rates of crime and welfare dependency; and, most important, a more just society.

A variety of educational opportunity programs have also been established at the college level. Generally, these programs make special provisions for the admission of disadvantaged and minority students who do not meet standard admissions requirements. They also provide tutoring and assistance to help these students stay in school. Although these programs have their critics, they have become an accepted part of most colleges and universities. One common problem is that such programs often fail to provide enough academic help after the disadvantaged students are admitted, so their graduation rate remains significantly lower than it is for other students. However, the greatest conflicts have arisen over special admissions programs for graduate and professional schools. Competition for places in these schools is intense, and white students complain that they are the victims of "reverse discrimination" because some whites are rejected in favor of less qualified minority students. Supporters of special admissions programs argue that minorities have already been subjected to a great deal of discrimination and that **affirmative action programs** merely attempt to compensate for some small part of it (see Chapter 8). The majority of the American public, however, is generally opposed to any kind of preference based on race or ethnic group,[47] and recent legislation and court rulings have been undermining affirmative action in

affirmative action program
A program designed to make up for past discrimination by giving special assistance to members of the groups that were discriminated against.

Compensatory education programs, such as the Head Start class shown in this photograph, are one of the best hopes for improving the educational achievement of disadvantaged students.

college admissions. A 1996 initiative in California banned such preferences, and the result has been a precipitous drop in the number of African Americans and Latinos attending the University of California and its prestigious graduate schools.

Fighting Gender Inequality Although our schools have made significant progress in providing more equal opportunity for both genders, much remains to be done before full equality is achieved. The funding and attention given to male and female athletics, for example, remains highly unequal. Many schools, moreover, continue to tailor their curricula to reflect traditional gender stereotypes: nutrition classes for the girls and auto shop for the boys. More effort also needs to be made to convince girls that math and sciences aren't just "boys' classes" and that they too should get involved. The biggest challenge, however, is the teachers. Like most other people in our society, teachers have many stereotypes about what kinds of behavior are appropriate for girls and for boys and about how girls' and boys' abilities and interests should differ. A comprehensive training program that sensitizes teachers to the negative effects of such stereotypes and teaches them how to keep such biases out of the classroom could help transform our schools from institutions that reinforce gender inequality to ones that actively promote equality.

Reforming School Finance As was pointed out earlier, schools in rich districts often receive much more money per student than do schools in poor districts. Although this problem could be dealt with by reforming the system of school finance in individual states, such an approach does nothing to rectify the huge inequalities among states. The only solution to that dilemma is much more federal funding. For example, if the federal government paid for all primary and secondary education, it could provide equitable funding for all schools. There is, however, a strong tradition of local control of the schools in the United States, and many people fear that national financing would mean federal control that would be unresponsive to the needs of local communities.

Although such concerns are certainly well grounded, there appear to be few alternatives to increased federal aid to education, even if it stops far short of complete financial support. When economic distress causes troubled school districts and financially strapped states to cut back on education, the result may be a vicious cycle in which poorer education creates a less competent work force that, in turn, causes more economic problems. Federal money is needed to break this cycle. There is, moreover, another important reason for the federal government to get more involved: it is the only level of government that has the resources to significantly increase overall funding for education. Although critics of proposals to increase spending for education point out that the amount of money spent per student actually rose during the last decade and a half (largely as a result of declining student enrollments), the American government still ranks near the bottom in its financial commitment to education. Of the 18 major industrialized nations, the United States ranks next to last in the percentage of its gross domestic product the government spends on education (see Figure 3.2).[48]

Improving the Schools

The original Coleman report created a furor when it was first published in 1966 because it found that none of the measures of school quality it used—funding, teacher qualifications, or physical facilities—had much effect on the educational achievement of the students. These results were widely interpreted to mean that "schools don't make any difference." Subsequent research has shown that those results were largely a product of the extremely narrow questions the researchers asked; in truth, their conclusions were highly misleading. For instance, Michael Rutter's study of London high schools found that they had a critical impact on student achievement. Not surprisingly, the best schools were those that maintained high standards, required more homework, and had clear and well-enforced standards of discipline yet still created a comfortable, supportive atmosphere for students.[49] Coleman himself later acknowledged that schools do make a substantial difference. In a comparison of private and public schools, Coleman and his colleagues wrote that "the indication is that more extensive academic demands are made in the private schools, leading to more advanced courses, and thus to higher achievement."[50] In addition to the idea of requiring more work, reformers also propose reorganizing the school system and hiring better teachers.

Requiring More Work One obvious way to improve academic performance is to raise the schools' requirements and make students work harder. In the 1960s, schools were heavily criticized for their bureaucratic rigidity, and the curriculum was loosened to allow more individual choice. Now, with the increasing concern about

Figure 3.2
Education Spending
When compared with other industrialized nations, the United States spends a rather small percentage of its gross domestic product on public education.

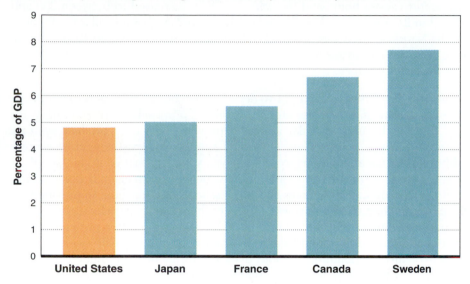

Source: Lawrence Mishel and Jared Bernstein, *The State of Working America, 1992–93* (New York: Sharpe, 1993), p. 374.

scholastic achievement, electives are being replaced with tougher requirements for more academic courses. A related proposal is to increase the amount of homework so that students must meet higher standards in the courses they do take. A criticism sometimes heard from minority leaders is that tougher requirements force disadvantaged students who cannot compete to leave school and go out on the streets. Efforts to make our schools more rigorous must therefore be accompanied by the kinds of compensatory educational programs discussed in the last section; otherwise, the result is likely to be lower, not higher, academic performance among some groups. In a different kind of attempt to get students to work harder, several cities, including San Jose, Atlanta, St. Louis, and Philadelphia, have launched tough antitruancy programs in which the schools and local police work together to pick up and detain truants.[51]

Programs to raise academic standards, require more homework, and crack down on truancy win at least verbal support from teachers and school administrators, but those groups often oppose another fundamental change that needs to be made—an increase in the amount of time students spend in school. The United States has one of the shortest school years of any major industrialized nation, and things are not much better in Canada. The average student in the United States goes to school about 180 days a year, while in Japan schools are in session for 244 days and in Germany about 210 days. Moreover, the average school day is only six hours in North America, while eight-hour days are common in other nations.[52] It is unrealistic to expect American students to compete with their counterparts abroad who have as many as 30 percent more school days a year. In 1983, the National Commission on Excellence in Education recommended that the average school day be increased to seven hours and the school year be increased to between 200 and 220 days, but its conclusions have been largely ignored. So has a similar recommendation the National Commission on Education and Learning made in 1994.[53] But in the long run, it is hard to see how North American students can remain competitive without this kind of reform.

Restructuring the Schools   The last two decades have been a time of ferment in our educational system, and there are literally dozens of proposals for restructuring our schools. One of the most popular among conservatives is the **voucher system.** Under most versions of this plan, automatic support for existing public schools would be withdrawn, and parents would be given vouchers that could be "spent" at any school, public or private. Advocates of the voucher system claim it would stimulate competition among the schools and force schools and teachers to provide top-quality education or go out of business. Critics of these proposals, who include many of the nation's leading educators, say that such changes would create educational chaos: tens of thousands of independent schools would spring up with enormous differences in quality, curriculum, and objectives. California's superintendent of public instruction described the voucher proposals as "dangerous claptrap" that would produce the same disastrous results as the deregulation of the savings and loan industry, and Wisconsin's superintendent likened this approach to "nuking" the public school system.[54]

A less radical proposal is to open the enrollment of public schools so that students can attend any school they want. The idea is that such programs cause a mass exodus from weak schools and force them to improve in order to get their students back. Left unanswered are the questions of how the good schools could physically accommodate all the students who would want to come and what would happen to the teachers and facilities at the weaker schools. One of the most best-known success stories among school choice programs is in the East Harlem section of New York City. Starting in the 1970s, the district slowly developed a network of alternative elementary and junior high schools, each using its own unique educational approach. By the mid-1980s, reading scores in East Harlem had risen from the lowest in the New York City school system to about average. Improvements in other districts have caused the position of East Harlem schools to slip a bit since then, but they continue to produce impressive results for a district in which the overwhelming majority of students come from poor and minority backgrounds.[55]

The Chicago school district that some called one of the worst in the nation has attempted to solve its problems through a sweeping decentralization program that gives control to local councils elected for each of its 553 schools. The idea was to cut out the numerous bureaucratic rules and requirements that come from central school administrators and give decision-making power directly to principals, teachers, and parents at the local schools. But after six years, these reforms seem to have produced only minor gains. Test scores have shown only sporadic improvement, the truancy rate has been increasing, and about 1,000 positions on the local councils are unfilled due to a lack of interested candidates.[56] But whether or not the Chicago experiment works, many educators support more "school-based management." To be

voucher system

A program in which the government gives vouchers to pay for children's education at any school their parents choose.

successful, however, such a policy must make local schools accountable for their results, as measured by such indicators as dropout rates or student performance on standardized achievement tests.

Baltimore tried an even more radical approach by turning nine public schools over to a private company to run them for a profit. The company claimed that by cutting administrative overhead and staff salaries (but not teacher salaries) it could increase the amount of money actually reaching the classroom. After a year of operation, the company claimed that it had raised test scores in its schools by nearly a whole grade level. But when the National Federation of Teachers commissioned its own study, it was discovered that test scores had actually gone down, and Baltimore ultimately canceled the company's contract and reclaimed control of the schools.[57]

A proposal for educational reform that has been tried throughout North America calls for public schools to get "back to basics." According to this concept, schools should create a more rigorous curriculum that focuses on the basic skills of reading, writing, and mathematics, while both teacher and student performance should be continually evaluated by standardized tests. Despite the increasing popularity of this approach, troubling questions remain. As more and more importance is given to standardized tests, teachers have been accused of "teaching to the test," that is, sacrificing the broader goals of education and focusing exclusively on the skills that improve test scores. Moreover, many educators reject the idea that successful education involves nothing more than teaching students to excel at basic skills. Is it better, they ask, to produce creative, well-adjusted children or to turn out neurotic overachievers who ace standardized tests but lack essential social skills? Obviously the matter is not that simple, but there are many alternative approaches that hold out a much broader ideal for education. The famous Summerhill "free" school, for example, encourages open expression and democratic principles among its students and allows them to focus their studies on whatever subjects interest them most,[58] and the rapidly growing Waldorf schools place as much importance on art and personal development as on basic academic skills.[59]

Finally, the most radical approach to restructuring our schools is advocated by supporters of the **home schooling** movement, who recommend that parents keep their children home and teach them themselves. Supporters of home schooling are generally critical of the quality of public education and feel that children's parents are likely to give them far more attention and concern than a professional teacher can. These parents also worry about the negative influence that close contact with other schoolchildren may have on their own child, and they object to some of the public school curriculum. Critics of home schooling point out that while some parents can do an excellent job of educating their own children, others cannot. Moreover, even the best home schooling is likely to provide only a narrow perspective that reflects only the personal viewpoints of the parents. These critics say that every child should have the right to hear a much broader range of views and perspectives and that social contact with other schoolchildren is essential for normal social development in our diverse society.

home schooling
Educating students at home rather than in public or private schools.

Better Teachers In the long run, nothing is more important to the schools than the quality and dedication of teachers. Recruiting and keeping the best possible faculty is therefore a vital task facing our schools. Unfortunately, we have not been doing a very good job of it. A 1996 report by the National Commission on Teaching and America's Future concluded that one-fourth of the nation's classroom teachers were not fully qualified and called the current state of teacher training a "national shame."[60] There is less prestige in being an elementary or secondary teacher than there was in the past; one way to improve the quality of our teachers is to offer a substantial increase in pay to attract and retain high-quality professionals. In 1993, the average starting salary for a teacher in the United States was $22,505, while accountants started at $28,020 and engineers at $35,004.[61] America ranks last among major industrialized nations in how generously it compensates its teachers.[62] One proposal already implemented in some school districts provides additional merit pay for superior teachers. A related approach is to create "master teacher" programs in which a school's best teachers are given extra pay to provide counseling and assistance to other teachers. (See the Personal Perspectives for a firsthand account of some of the problems our teachers face.)

Too little money, however, is not the only problem. Teachers also complain about the frustrations of working within a bureaucracy that is often more concerned about the smooth functioning of its schools than about education. Other sources of discontent are excessive paperwork and the conflict between the demand that they be classroom police officers and the need to be educators. It is no surprise, then, that teachers suffer such a high burnout rate. Fewer than one in five new teachers is still in the profession after ten years.[63]

Even streamlining the bureaucracy and increasing pay will not guarantee that schools can recruit enough top-quality teachers. Success will depend largely on society's attitude toward education. As Tom Hayden, chair of the California Assembly's Subcommittee on Higher Education, put it:

> The desire to teach is fostered in a social climate that supports the personal mission of helping others grow, of creating and sharing knowledge and pur-

Personal Perspectives A Junior High School Teacher

Teaching is a rewarding profession. But as we can see from the following account by a male teacher in his thirties, it can also be extremely frustrating.

I love teaching. It's something I've always done and always will do. But the restrictions and expectations and frustrations you have to put up with to be a teacher here are horrific. The lack of support that the students get at home and the lack of support that the teachers get in the system makes it so that whatever pleasure you get in a student's progression is overshadowed by the frustrations.

Kids who don't have consistent discipline at home cause problems at school. . . . The more the parents are involved in a child's education, the more everyone can learn. Then teachers don't have to spend all their time on discipline problems. Ideally, a child should come to school ready to learn. Another problem is that the school system doesn't necessarily know how to parent. Some teachers and administrators do the wrong thing. It's a tightrope between doing what's needed, and not doing what will get you into trouble. For example, some children who desperately need hugs don't get them because teachers are afraid it could be construed as sexual abuse.

suing a higher quality of life. Such values are not promoted in a climate of self-serving shortsightedness that lures people toward the quick fix, the fast buck, and the easy answer. Until a new emphasis on public service and social responsibility arises to balance narrow self-interest, the teaching crisis will remain difficult to resolve.[64]

Valuing Learning A strange paradox in American culture underlies many of the educational problems we have discussed in this chapter. Americans place tremendous faith in education in general, but at the same time they don't seem to value learning itself very highly. In European countries like France and Germany, intellectuals and scholars not only have great prestige but are a powerful political force. The same is often true in poor Third World countries as well—the last two presidents of Mexico, for example, have both had a Ph.D. degree. In the United States, intellectuals are viewed with far more suspicion and kept on the margins of political life. But the problem goes far deeper than just politics. A student who scores at the top of the class in Japan is some kind of a celebrity in school, but the brilliant student in the United States is often seen as something of a "nerd." For the boys, it is the star athletes who win the most admiration, and for the girls it is often those with the knockout good looks. International polls also show that Americans read fewer books and newspapers than people in other industrialized nations and are less informed about global events.[65]

In addition to the kinds of new programs and policies we have just discussed, the revitalization of American education will require cultural changes as well. The idea that there is some kind of contradiction between those who think and study and those who take action in the "real world" is nothing but an unfounded prejudice. Most of the world's greatest revolutionary leaders, from Thomas Jefferson to Mao Tse-tung, have been intellectuals as well. Earning a top score in the SAT is at least as difficult a task as winning a football game, and it is far more likely to lead to a successful career. But aside from any external benefits we may derive from an education, it is vital to recognize the intrinsic rewards of learning itself in enriching our lives and the lives of those around us.

Quick Review

What can we do to give everyone more equal educational opportunities?

How can we improve the quality of the education our children receive?

Sociological Perspectives on Problems of Education

There seems to be a virtually endless debate about the deficiencies of our educational system and what to do about them, and since the opposing sides do not even agree about the goals of a good education, the discussion often produces more confusion than consensus. A look at the problems of education from each of the major

Schools do much more than teach reading, writing, and arithmetic. One of their most important functions is to provide for students' social and recreational needs.

sociology perspectives can clarify the situation by linking criticisms of the educational system and proposals for change with the broader vision of society from which they arise.

The Functionalist Perspective

Functionalists see education as a basic institution that must meet a growing list of social needs. Originally, the two principal functions of education were to teach students a body of skills and knowledge and to grade them on how well they had mastered their studies. Education also became an important channel for social mobility for talented students from disadvantaged backgrounds. As industrial societies became more diverse and education became virtually universal, the schools took on an increasingly important role in transmitting values and attitudes as well as skills. They also assumed the important **latent** (hidden) **function** of reducing unemployment by keeping many young people out of the labor market. Finally, as the traditional family unit became more unstable, educational institutions were asked to take up some of the slack by launching programs to prevent delinquent behavior and to help deal with students' social and psychological needs. Many functionalists believe our schools have been given so many conflicting tasks that they are unable to do any of them very well, and as a result, their efforts to achieve one goal often conflict with other goals. For example, the time spent on drug education or "teen skills" can detract from the schools' academic programs, and attempts to modify the curriculum to prevent disadvantaged students from getting discouraged may lower the achievement of more gifted students. Functionalists also complain that many

latent function
A hidden function performed by a social institution or agency.

schools have become disorganized because of poor management and a lack of sufficient concern on the part of parents and the community.

All functionalists do not agree on how to make schools more effective. Many advocate the elimination of some of the new programs that have been introduced in recent years. Although such changes might well improve fundamental education, they are also likely to disrupt efforts to deal with other pressing social problems. Proposals for employing more effective teaching methods are also compatible with the functionalist perspective, but most functionalists argue that such reforms can work only if accompanied by a reorganization of the schools. For example, teachers must be rewarded for good teaching rather than for being efficient bureaucrats or for the length of time they have spent on the job. Finally, many functionalists advocate better planning and coordination with other social institutions in order to reduce the problem of unemployment and underemployment among the educated. But such a program must be combined with an effort to reduce the instability of our economic institutions, since it is extremely difficult to train students to meet the needs of an economy that is in a state of rapid and unpredictable flux.

The Conflict Perspective

Conflict theorists are not convinced that providing equal opportunity and encouraging upward mobility for the poor have ever been goals of our educational system. Rather, they argue that the schools are organized to do the opposite: to keep members of subordinate groups in their place and prevent them from competing with members of more privileged classes. They point to the fact that free public education for all children is a relatively new idea and that even today many poor children must drop out of school to help support their families. Moreover, expensive private schools provide a superior education for children from the upper classes, whereas the public schools that serve the poor are underfunded, understaffed, and growing worse. Conflict theorists also argue that the old system of officially segregated education and the current system of de facto segregation serve to keep oppressed minorities at the bottom of the social heap. Their general conclusion is that the social and cultural biases in the educational system are not an accident but rather reflect a social system that favors the powerful.

Conflict theorists also see the schools as powerful agents of socialization that can be used as a tool for one group to exercise its cultural dominance over another. For example, they argue that by demanding all students learn English, American schools serve to perpetuate the domination of those from one linguistic background over those from all the others.

From the conflict perspective, the best and perhaps the only way to change these conditions is for the poor and minorities to organize themselves and reshape the educational system so that it provides everyone with equal opportunity but does not indoctrinate students in the cultural values and beliefs of any particular group. All children must be given the same quality of education that is now available in private schools; cash subsidies must be provided for poor students who would otherwise be forced to drop out of school; and special programs must be set up to provide extra help for children whose parents have a weak educational background. Nevertheless, most conflict theorists probably agree with Christopher Jencks, who concluded that the educational system can do little to reduce inequality without changes in the broader society. Even if there were complete educational equality and everyone were given a college education, social and economic disparities would remain. Such changes would not produce more interesting, highly paid professional jobs or reduce the number of menial, low-paying ones. Thus, educational and social change must be carried out together.

The Feminist Perspective

Feminists are deeply concerned about the role of the schools in perpetuating gender stereotypes and failing to encourage the highest possible academic achievement from female students. From a feminist standpoint, an effective school system needs to do more than just eliminate obvious gender and ethnic discrimination; it needs to be an active agent for social change—encouraging full gender equality not just in academic performance but in our social relationships as well.

But many feminists also view the schools in the context of our broader social problems, and they see a vital role for the schools in helping relieve some of the enormous pressures on today's families. The standard of a six-hour school day for nine months of the year fit well with the rhythms of the farm, when children were needed as laborers during the summer harvest season and there was always somebody home after school. But in most of today's families, either both parents work or there is only a single parent in the home. So some feminists call for a new style of school that stays open 12 or 14 hours a day year-round, providing not only more academic work but also recreational and social programs. Feminists argue that such a program could improve the stability of our families, the security of our parents, and the academic achievement of our children.

The Interactionist Perspective

Interactionists are concerned with the vital role the schools play in shaping the way their students see reality. Many have commented on the possibility that the authoritarianism so common in our schools impedes learning and encourages undemocratic behavior in later life. Moreover, schools create serious difficulties for students who for one reason or another do not fit into the educational system. The schools show their students a world in which individual competition and achievement is of central importance, and this heavy emphasis on competition and the consequent fear of failure are disturbing to those students who are already anxious and insecure. Students who do not do well in school are often troubled by feelings of depression and inadequacy, and the failure to live up to the academic expectations of parents and teachers is a major contributor to teenage suicide. Many alternative schools, such as Summerhill and Waldorf, attempt to improve this socialization process by deemphasizing competition for grades and placing more importance on enhancing self-esteem. Of course, some children do poorly in such an environment and benefit from a great deal of discipline and an emphasis on obedience to authority. Authoritarian environments may, however, impede the ability of other children to learn and to function effectively; thus, it seems logical to provide the greatest possible range of educational alternatives so that the needs of each student can be met.

The finding that teachers' expectations have a huge influence on student achievement comes as no surprise to interactionists. Interactionists have long known that our behavior is shaped by the way we define the world, so if students are made to feel like high achievers, they will act like high achievers. Interactionists therefore call for teacher training programs to encourage teachers to understand the critical importance of their role in influencing a student's view of the world, and they urge teachers to avoid branding students with negative labels that oftentimes become a self-fulfilling prophecy.

Quick Review

What would a functionalist, a conflict theorist, a feminist, and an interactionist say about the problems of our educational system?

Which approach do you think is most useful?

Summary

Education was originally reserved for the elite. Today, however, it has become a big business, employing millions of teachers and administrators. Children from the lower classes generally do not do as well in school as children from the middle and upper classes. Poor children usually come to school with a variety of economic and cultural handicaps, and the school system discriminates against these children in a number of ways. Racial and ethnic discrimination in the American educational system goes back to the days of slavery. Since the Supreme Court's decision outlawing school segregation, most legal (de jure) discrimination has been abolished. However, de facto (actual) segregation arising from segregated housing patterns is still widespread. In the same way that schools have helped to perpetuate ethnic inequality, they have often served to promote gender inequality.

Schools are always struggling to deal with the twin problems of authority and rebellion. If schools lack discipline, students run wild and education suffers; but if discipline is too strict, students learn antidemocratic values and attitudes, and rebellion and delinquency may increase. There is great concern about the quality of our educational system because of the decline in scores on college entrance examinations and because of North American students' relatively poor showing in international comparisons of academic achievement. Some critics argue that those tests are not a good measure of educational quality; others claim that the problem lies in the changing family environment of today's students; and still others hold the schools themselves responsible.

Many proposals for creating more equal education have been offered. These include programs to achieve more effective integration, to give special assistance to poor and minority students, and to promote gender equality, as well as reforms in school financing. Suggestions for improving the educational process itself include raising academic standards and requiring more homework, lengthening the school year, restructuring the schools to give teachers and local administrators more power, making education a more attractive career so that schools can hire better teachers, and increasing the cultural value we place on learning.

Functionalists argue that the educational system is not running smoothly and that solving the problems of education is mostly a matter of reorganizing schools so that they will operate more efficiently. Conflict theorists are prone to look beyond the stated goals of the educational system and argue that economic and political elites use the schools to help maintain the status quo and the privileges those groups enjoy. Feminists argue that the schools need to actively promote gender equality and institute programs to help relieve some of the pressure on today's families. Interactionists are concerned with the way the schools help shape their students' view of reality and with the harmful impact that negative labeling and an excessive emphasis on competition can have.

Questions for Critical Thinking

Take a critical look at your own education. Were you one of the privileged students, or did you suffer from some kind of educational disadvantage? How good an education do you think you have received so far? How would you compare the quality of your education with that of a typical American student? This chapter discussed many different problems in our educational system. Which ones did you encounter in your own education?

Key Terms

affirmative action program	home schooling
authoritarianism	latent function
compensatory education programs	magnet schools
de facto segregation	prep schools
de jure segregation	resegregation
desegregation	segregated schools
functionally illiterate	sexism
goal displacement	standard English
grade inflation	voucher system
hidden curriculum	

Further Readings

Peter W. Cookson, Jr., and Barbara Schneider, eds., *Transforming Schools* (New York: Garland, 1995). A good collection of articles exploring the ways to improve our schools.

John Devine, *Maximum Security: The Culture of Violence in Inner-City Schools* (Chicago: University of Chicago Press, 1996). An examination of violence in the schools.

Helen Lefkowitz Horowitz, *Campus Life: Undergraduate Cultures from the End of the Eighteenth Century to the Present* (Chicago: University of Chicago Press, 1987). An interesting historical look at the subculture of college undergraduates and how it has changed.

Jonathan Kozol, *Savage Inequalities: Children in America's Schools* (New York: Crown, 1991). A comprehensive work by a longtime critic of American education.

National Center for Education Statistics, *The Condition of Education* (Pittsburgh, U.S. Government Printing Office, 1995). A good general source of information on American education.

Jeannie Oakes, *Multiplying Inequalities: The Effects of Race, Social Class, and Tracking on Opportunities to Learn* (Santa Monica, CA: Rand Corporation, 1990). A report on the way schools promote social inequality.

Notes

1. Romesh Ratnesar, "Class-Size Warfare," *Time,* October 6, 1997, p. 85.
2. U.S. Bureau of the Census, *Statistical Abstract of the United States, 1996* (Washington, DC: U.S. Government Printing Office, 1996), p. 158.
3. Quoted in Mavis Hiltunen Biesanz and John Biesanz, *Introduction to Sociology,* 2nd ed. (Englewood Cliffs, NJ: Prentice Hall, 1973), p. 616.
4. Robert James Parelius and Ann Parker Parelius, *The Sociology of Education,* 2nd ed. (Englewood Cliffs, NJ: Prentice Hall, 1987), p. 265.
5. See S. Leonard Syme and Lisa F. Berkman, "Social Class, Susceptibility and Sickness," in Howard D. Schwartz, ed., *Dominant Issues in Medical Sociology,* 2nd ed. (New York: Random House, 1987), pp. 643—649.
6. Parelius and Parelius, *The Sociology of Education,* pp. 280–282.
7. U.S. Bureau of the Census, *Statistical Abstract, 1996,* p. 170.
8. William Celis III, "Michigan Votes for Revolution in Financing Its Public Schools," *New York Times,* March 17, 1994, pp. A1, A9; Bob Secter, "Gaps Between Rich, Poor Schools Ignite Legal Fights," *Los Angeles Times,* November 26, 1990, pp. A1, A20.
9. James S. Coleman et al., *Equality of Educational Opportunity* (Washington, DC: U.S. Government Printing Office, 1966); Christopher Jencks et al., *Inequality: A Reassessment of the Effects of Family and Schooling in America* (New York: HarperCollins, 1972); Harvey A. Averch et al., *How Effective Is Schooling: A Critical Synthesis and Review of Research Findings* (Englewood Cliffs, NJ: Prentice Hall, 1974); Samuel Bowles and Herbert Gintis, *Schooling in Capitalist America* (New York: Basic Books, 1976).
10. Elizabeth Ross, "A Leveling of Granite State Schools," *Christian Science Monitor,* March 14, 1994, p. 10.
11. Lawrence Mishel and Jared Bernstein, *The State of Working America, 1992–93* (New York: Sharpe, 1993), p. 374.
12. U.S. Bureau of the Census, *Statistical Abstract, 1996,* p. 153.
13. See Parelius and Parelius, *The Sociology of Education,* pp. 293–296.
14. Robert Rosenthal and Lenore Jacobson, *Pygmalion in the Classroom* (New York: HarperCollins, 1969).
15. See Roy Nash, *Teacher Expectations and Pupil Learning* (London: Routledge & Kegan Paul, 1976); Parelius and Parelius, *The Sociology of Education,* pp. 293–296.
16. D. G. Harvey and G. T. Slatin, "The Relationship Between a Child's SES and Teacher Expectations," *Social Forces* 54 (1975): 140–159.
17. See Jeannie Oakes, *Multiplying Inequalities* (Santa Monica, CA: Rand Corporation, 1990).
18. Karl Alexander, Martha Cook, and Edward L. Dill, "Curriculum Tracking and Educational Stratification," *American Sociological Review* 43 (1978): 47–66.
19. William Celis III, "Study Finds Rising Concentration of Black and Hispanic Students," *New York Times,* December 14, 1993, pp. A1, A11; William J. Eaton, "Segregation in U.S. Schools on Rise, Study Finds," *Los Angeles Times,* December 14, 1993, pp. A1, A22.

20. Coleman et al., *Equality of Educational Opportunity.*
21. Rita E. Mahard and Robert L. Crain, "Research on Minority Achievement in Desegregated Schools," in Christine H. Rossell and Willis D. Hawley, eds., *The Consequences of School Desegregation* (Philadelphia: Temple University Press, 1983), pp. 103–125.
22. See Janet Eyler, Valerie J. Cook, and Leslie E. Ward, "Resegregation: Segregation Within Desegregated Schools," in Rossell and Hawley, *The Consequences of School Desegregation,* pp. 126–162.
23. U.S. Bureau of the Census, *Statistical Abstract, 1996,* p. 159.
24. Ibid., p. 159.
25. Ibid., pp. 180, 191.
26. Myra Sadker, David Sadker, and Susan S. Klein, "Abolishing Misconceptions About Sex Equity in Education," *Theory into Practice* 25 (Autumn 1986): 220.
27. Beverly A. Stitt, *Building Gender Fairness in Schools* (Carbondale: Southern Illinois University Press, 1988), pp. 29–32.
28. Richard Lee Colvin, "14% of Students Have Carried Weapon to School, Study Says," *Los Angeles Times,* March 10, 1997, pp. B1, B3.
29. Tamar Lewin, "School Codes Without Mercy Snare Pupils Without Malice," *New York Times,* March 12, 1997, pp. A1, A13.
30. See John Devine, *Maximum Security* (Chicago: University of Chicago Press, 1996).
31. Irwin S. Kirsch, Ann Jungeblut, Lynn Jenkins, and Andrew Kolstad, *Adult Literacy in America: A First Look at the Results of the National Literacy Survey* (Washington, DC: Department of Education, 1993).
32. Kirsch et al., *Adult Literacy.*
33. U.S. Bureau of the Census, *Statistical Abstract, 1996,* p. 177; U.S. Bureau of the Census, *Statistical Abstract, 1993,* p. 170.
34. James Bennet, "Fourth Graders Move Near Top on Science Test," *New York Times,* June 11, 1997, pp. A1, A21; Richard Lee Colvin and Elizabeth Shogren," U.S. 4th-Graders Score Strongly in Science, Math," *Los Angeles Times,* June 11, 1997, pp. A1, A23; Peter Applebome, "U.S. Gets Average Grades in Math and Science Studies," *New York Times,* November 21, 1996, pp. A1, A21; Richard Lee Colvin, "Global Study Finds U.S. Students Weak in Math," *Los Angeles Times,* November 21, 1996, pp. A1, A24.
35. William Celis III, "International Report Card Shows U.S. Schools Work," *New York Times,* December 9, 1993, pp. A1, A8; Andrew L. Shapiro, *We're Number One: Where America Stands and Falls in the New World Order* (New York: Vintage, 1992), pp. 64–69.
36. Stanley Meisler, "Americans Get No Gold Stars for Current Events Answers," *Los Angeles Times,* March 16, 1994, p. A9.
37. Louis B. Gerstner, Jr., "Our Schools Are Failing. Do We Care?" *New York Times,* May 27, 1994, p. A15.
38. National Commission on Education and Learning, *Prisoners of Time* (Washington, DC: U.S. Government Printing Office, April 1994).
39. Robert J. Samuelson, "Why School Reform Fails," *Newsweek,* May 27, 1991, pp. 62, 68.
40. Applebome, "U.S. Gets Average Grades in Math and Science Studies."
41. Shapiro, *We're Number One,* p. 71.
42. Parelius and Parelius, *The Sociology of Education,* pp. 334–335.
43. William Celis III, "Study Suggests Head Start Helps Beyond School," *New York Times,* April 20, 1993, p. A9; see also John R. Berrueta-Clement et al., *Changed Lives: The Effects of the Perry Preschool Program on Youths Through Age 19* (Ypsilanti, MI: High/Scope, 1984).
44. David G. Savage, "U.S. School Aid: Looking for Results," *Los Angeles Times,* April 11, 1985, sec. 1, p. 1.
45. For an exception to this rule, see John R. Berrueta-Clement et al., *Changed Lives.*
46. Angela E. Couloumbis, "New Targets for Head Start: Children in Diapers," *Christian Science Monitor,* March 17, 1994, pp. 1, 4.
47. Seymour Martin Lipset, *American Exceptionalism: A Double-Edged Sword* (New York: Norton, 1996), pp. 125–131.

48. Shapiro, *We're Number One*, p. 56; also see Mishel and Bernstein, *The State of Working America, 1992–93*, p. 374.

49. Michael Rutter, *15,000 Hours: Secondary Schools and Their Effect on Children* (Cambridge, MA: Harvard University Press, 1979).

50. James S. Coleman, Thomas Hoffer, and Sally Kilgore, *High School Achievement: Public, Catholic and Private Schools* (New York: Basic Books, 1982), p. 178.

51. Michael de Couracy Hinds, "Philadelphia Adopts Tough Truant Policy, with Handcuffs, Too," *New York Times,* February 9, 1994, p. A14; Michael de Couracy Hinds, "In San Jose, Reaching Out to the Truant," *New York Times,* February 9, 1994, p. A14.

52. Shapiro, *We're Number One,* p. 60; Michael J. Barrett, "The Case for More School Days," *Atlantic,* November 1990, pp. 78–106.

53. Dennis Kelly, "Panel: Extend School Year," *USA Today,* May 5, 1994, p. 1A.

54. Tom Morganthau, "The Future Is Now," *Newsweek,* Special Edition on Education, Fall–Winter 1990, pp. 72–76.

55. David L. Kirp, "What School Choice Really Means," *Atlantic Monthly,* November 1992, pp. 119–132.

56. Peter Applebome, "Chicago School Decentralization Provides Lessons, But No Verdict," *New York Times,* November 8, 1995, pp. A1, B6.

57. Associated Press, "Baltimore Ends School Privatization Experiment," *San Luis Obispo Telegram-Tribune,* Novermber 23, 1995, p. A6; George Judson, "Improved Schools at a Profit: Is a Private Effort Working?" *New York Times,* November 14, 1994, pp. A1, A12; William Celis III, "Hopeful Start for Profit Making Schools," *New York Times,* October 6, 1993, pp. A1, B3.

58. A. S. Neill, *Summerhill: A Radical Approach to Child Rearing* (New York: Hart, 1960).

59. Ronald E. Kotzsch, "Waldorf Schools: Education for Head, Hands, and Heart," *Utne Reader,* September–October 1990, pp. 84–90.

60. Elaine Woo, "Study Calls Poor Teacher Training a 'National Shame,'" *Los Angeles Times,* May 26, 1997, pp. A1, A5.

61. U.S. Bureau of the Census, *Statistical Abstract, 1996,* p. 167.

62. Shapiro, *We're Number One,* p. 63.

63. Jonathan H. Mark and Barry Anderson, "Teacher Survival Rates: A Current Look," *American Journal of Educational Research* 15 (1978): 379–383.

64. Tom Hayden, "Running Short of Good Teachers," *Los Angeles Times,* June 24, 1983, sec. 2, p. 5.

65. See Shapiro, *We're Number One*.

4

Problems of the Economy

What is the "world economy"?

What are the different types of capitalist economies?

Who controls corporations?

Is the "work ethic" dead?

Why have things gotten harder for average people?

What can the government do to solve our economic problems?

Don Snyder used to be an assistant professor of English at Colgate University. He had a comfortable six-bedroom house, a $36,000 salary, and 18 weeks of paid vacation a year that left him plenty of time to write. Like many Americans, he thought he had it made. "I was very popular with the students, and my peers didn't hate me. I thought I was safe." Snyder soon found out he was dead wrong. His colleagues, it turned out, were not impressed with the novels he had been publishing, and he was given his pink slip. At first he denied the seriousness of his situation, and he even tried to hide the truth from his pregnant wife, Colleen. But finally, after 93 rejection letters, reality began to sink in, and he entered a two-and-a-half year path of self-destruction that included a bonfire, in which he melodramatically burned his academic books, and a near overdose of sleeping pills. Times were tough for the rest of the Snyder family too, and sometimes they had to manage on little more than a stack of food stamps. Fortunately, Don Snyder's story has a happy ending. He eventually found employment and a surprising degree of satisfaction as a construction worker. He even wrote a book about his experiences and sold the rights to the Disney movie studios.[1]

Our economy may seem a vast and confusing system, but it is made up of countless simple stories like that of Don and Colleen Snyder. Of course, few of the millions of people who lose their jobs every year are likely to have their experiences turned into a movie, but otherwise theirs is a common story. Too often when we hear about the growing economic insecurity of the middle class, the latest figures on unemployment, or a decline in factory wages, such news seems like nothing more than dry abstractions divorced from the flesh-and-blood realities of life. So it is important to keep in mind the impact that the economic problems we are going to be discussing in this chapter have on average people. On the other hand, however, it is equally essential to realize that the economic difficulties most average people face are not just their own doing but are deeply rooted in the social and economic forces that shape our world. The first place to look to try to understand those forces is the world economy.

The World Economy

When economic problems crop up, we tend to seek an explanation by looking at familiar events close to home. Although some problems can be understood in terms of a single nation or even a single city, today's economic woes are world problems. No one can understand the causes of inflation, unemployment, or economic stagnation by looking only at a single nation in isolation from the complex international network of trade, production, and finance known as the **world economy.** So we will start our exploration of today's economic problems from a global perspective.

world economy
The system of international economic relationships in which all countries participate.

Although all nations are part of the world economy, all countries do not have equal roles. The principal dividing line in the modern world is between the wealthy industrialized nations and the poor nations often known as the **Third World** or the **less developed countries.** Although most of the world's products are manufactured in the industrialized nations, almost 80 percent of the world's people live in the poor nations.[2] Most of them make their living from agriculture and the export of raw materials. Although there is a growing industrial sector in many less developed countries, their industries pay low wages and are often owned and operated by foreigners. In contrast to the poverty of the Third World, industrialized nations such as the United States have accumulated huge reserves of wealth, not just in terms of money but also in terms of the things it can buy: highways, buildings, factories, power plants, public facilities, and, of course, an educated populace and a well-trained work force. In between these two extremes are nations like Thailand and South Korea, which have a higher standard of living and are more industrialized than most Third World countries but are still far behind such nations as the United States and Japan (see Chapter 17 for a discussion of the problems of the Third World).

While most Third World nations have struggled to improve their position within a world economy dominated by rich capitalist countries, some have followed a different road and rejected the capitalist system altogether. Under communism, inspired by the ideology of Marx and Lenin, governments took direct control of all their major economic institutions. They created planned economies in which there was little competition and the important decisions were made by government officials. Originally, the communist nations sought to keep out the influence of foreign corporations and the capitalist world economy they dominate, and to industrialize themselves by following their own step-by-step development plans. While the Soviet Union and some of the other communist nations had considerable success in completing the early stages of industrialization, none reached the same level of affluence enjoyed by rich capitalist countries. Furthermore, in the last decade, most communist countries have made a radical shift in their economic direction—either abandoning **communism** altogether or mixing it with a strong dose of capitalism.

It may sound as if wealthy capitalist nations such as the United States and Canada have few economic problems, but that is hardly the case. To understand their problems, we must examine the nature of **capitalism** more closely. Although difficult to define precisely, capitalist economic systems display three essential characteristics. First, there is private property. Second, a market controls the production and distribution of valuable commodities. Third, privately owned businesses compete with one another in the market, each aiming to make the greatest possible profit. The classic statement of the principles of free-market capitalism was set forth in Adam Smith's book *The Wealth of Nations*, first published in 1776.[3] Smith argued that individuals will work harder and produce more if allowed to work for personal profit. Private greed will be transformed into public good through the workings of a free market regulated only by supply and demand. The profit motive will drive manufacturers to supply goods that the public demands, and competition will ensure that the goods are reasonably priced. The market will regulate itself in the most efficient possible way—as though guided by an "invisible hand"—if the government does not interfere with the free play of economic forces.

Although some economists and politicians still fervently believe in the principles set forth in Smith's writings, it is clear that no real economic system operates the way Smith said it should, and no nation has completely "free" markets. Smith himself realized that businesses can reap large profits by restricting free competition and raising prices: "People of the same trade seldom meet together, even for merriment and diversion, but the conversation ends in a conspiracy against the public, or in some contrivance to raise prices."[4] Since those words were written, the major corporations have grown to a colossal size that Smith could hardly have imagined, and as a result, their ability to artificially control the marketplace has become a far greater problem. Moreover, markets are now restricted in many other ways as well. Governments in the capitalist nations have all enacted numerous economic regulations and restrictions, sometimes to protect powerful special interests, sometimes to protect the public as a whole, and sometimes even to protect competition itself. Governments have also created welfare programs to help the most disadvantaged, and workers themselves have joined together into unions to demand higher wages and better treatment from their employers.

Even though no nation lives up to Adam Smith's ideal of the perfect capitalist economy, some countries are much stronger believers in the principles of **laissez-faire capitalism** than others. On one side are nations such as the United States, which practice what is sometimes called **individualistic capitalism.** As the name implies, these nations tend to stress the importance of the individual over the group or community. The government's role in their economies is far greater than Adam Smith envisioned, but it is still significantly less than in other countries, and welfare benefits are generally lower. The government tries to encourage competition through the use of antitrust laws that restrict cooperation between the giant corporations, and the principal goal of the corporations themselves is making a profit for their individual shareholders.

In contrast, the **communitarian capitalism** practiced in Germany and Japan is quite different. Those nations are more skeptical about the value of unregulated competition, and protecting the long-term interests of the corporations and the people who depend on them is given greater priority than big profit margins. Corporations are allowed, and even encouraged, to cooperate with each other and to link themselves into large corporate interest groups such as the Japanese *keiretsu.* The government itself plays a much larger role in directly guiding the economy of these nations: coordinating the actions of large corporate groups, supporting various business activities, and trying to shape the overall direction of the economy. Workers also have a greater involvement in shaping corporate policy than is typical in the United States, through a slow process of consensus building in Japanese corporations and through powerful unions and "codetermination laws" (which require corporations to bring the workers into the decision-making process) in Germany. Underlying the structural differences between these two systems is an important cultural divide. As Lester Thurow puts it, "The essential difference between the two forms of capitalism is their stress on communitarian versus individualistic values as the route to economic success—the 'I' of America or of the United Kingdom versus 'Das Volk' and 'Japan Inc.'"[5]

laissez-faire capitalism
An economic ideology that argues that the government should stay out of economic affairs and allow the free market to regulate itself.

individualistic capitalism
A capitalistic economic system that emphasizes the importance of the individual over the group or community.

communitarian capitalism
A capitalist economic system that emphasizes the importance of the group or community over the individual.

Quick Review

What is the world economy?

What are the differences between communitarian and individualistic capitalism?

Understanding Our Economic System

The first step in understanding our economic system is to see its role in the world economy. But we cannot get very far in our efforts without also looking at its internal structures and the way they operate. In this section we examine the four most important players in the contemporary economy—corporations, government, small businesses, and workers.

The Corporations

If all the world's largest organizations—including its governments—were listed in order of size, half would be corporations. Such giants as General Electric, Exxon, and Ford have hundreds of thousands of employees, and their assets are worth billions of dollars. Moreover, the largest corporations keep growing, both in absolute size and in the percentage of the economy they control. The 100 largest industrial corporations in the United States now have about $1.7 trillion in yearly sales, and $2 trillion in assets, and they make over 16 percent of all the profits earned by incorporated businesses in the United States.[6] This staggering concentration of wealth obviously gives these corporation enormous power to influence the government and to shape the way average people live their lives.

When the United States was first industrializing, several of the new corporate giants that sprang up seized monopolistic control of entire industries and were able to charge exorbitant prices unrestrained by any serious competition. As a result, the federal government and many individual states passed **antitrust laws** that forbid **monopolies** (the control of industries by single firms) and any arrangements among competitors to work together to keep prices artificially high. While these laws did prevent most American industries from falling under the control of a single firm, they have failed in a number of other important ways.

Few of today's markets are controlled by outright monopolies, but the markets for many important products and services, ranging from automobiles and gasoline to aspirin and broadcasting, are dominated by a few enormous firms—an arrangement known as **oligopoly.** About 60 percent of all the goods and services produced in the United States (not counting those produced by the government) are made in industries dominated by such oligopolies. Even in these restricted markets, one giant is often larger and stronger than any other, thus allowing it to have a considerable degree of market control. Although antitrust laws forbid collusion among the members of these oligopolies to rig prices or restrict competition in other ways, these laws have never been effectively enforced, and there is little doubt that such activities are still common.

At best, antitrust laws have been only modestly successful at encouraging open competition, and in recent years they seem to be creating a new kind of economic difficulty for American firms competing in the world economy. While these laws have discouraged American firms from linking themselves together into cartels and corporate interest groups, their foreign competition faces no such restrictions. Not only do these corporate groups provide many foreign firms with financial and technical support for their ventures, but they also relieve a great deal of the pressure for short-term profits that plagues many American companies. For example, most of the stock in major Japanese corporations is held by the other firms in their corpo-

antitrust laws
Laws designed to protect free competition in the marketplace.

monopoly
The control of a market or an entire industry by a single firm.

oligopoly
The control of a market or an entire industry by a few large companies.

rate groups, while private individuals hold a much larger share of American firms. Although the American system may sound like a better arrangement, private stockholders are primarily concerned with a corporation's quarterly profits and the dividends it allows them to pay out, while corporate stockholders are likely to take a much longer view of successful management.[7]

Who Runs the Corporations? The modern corporation is a vast financial network. The relationships between a given corporation and its competitors, banks, subcontractors and suppliers, stockholders, directors and managers, workers, unions, and various local and national governments are extremely complex and may change without warning. Moreover, researchers who try to determine who, or what, controls this network rarely have the cooperation of corporations. Because researchers must rely on secondhand data on this politically charged issue, their conclusions are often contradictory.

Supporters of the system claim that corporations are democratic institutions owned by many different people, and they point to the fact that tens of millions of citizens own stock in American corporations. However, critics note that although many people own some stock, most is owned by a small group of wealthy individuals.[8] Institutional stockholders such as banks, insurance companies, and pension and investment funds also hold large blocks of stock. In fact, most of the public trading on the New York Stock Exchange is conducted for institutional stockholders, not private individuals. Although many of these financial institutions issue their own stock, which may be held by individual investors, their directors nevertheless have considerable influence on the affairs of the corporations whose stock their company owns. Moreover, banks and other financial institutions exercise great influence over corporate decision making through their power to grant or reject loans.[9]

Most economists agree that there is a significant separation between ownership and control in most corporations; because there are so many stockholders, most of them simply vote for or against the current management and have little influence on individual corporate decisions. The technical complexity of modern business is so great that many stockholders do not even understand the key issues facing management. Economist John Kenneth Galbraith calls the group of managers who make the important decisions the "corporate technostructure." He points out that most national and international corporations are no longer run by a single powerful person, such as Andrew Carnegie or John D. Rockefeller. Decisions are made by anonymous executives and managers who spend their entire careers gaining the technical skills and knowledge needed to manage a modern corporation. However, the managers of American corporations must still serve the primary interest of their stockholders—making profits—or they risk losing their jobs. David R. James and Michael Soref, for example, found that declining profits were the single major reason that corporate presidents lost their jobs, regardless of whether the firm was owned by a large number of stockholders or by a single individual.[10]

Corporate managers do not make their decisions simply on the basis of their knowledge and skills, however. High-level corporate managers are a distinct social class, and they act to promote their own self-interest. For example, from 1989 to 1995, the average worker's pay was almost unchanged, but top executives increased their own pay almost 42 percent.[11] If young managers are to get to the top, they must have more than just technical skills, ability, and drive. They must also accept the ideology and worldview of the corporate elite and support its interests. As

C. Wright Mills put it, "In personal manner and political view, in social ways and business style, [the new manager] must be like those who are already in, and upon whose judgments his own success rests."[12]

The Multinationals In recent years most large corporations have expanded across national boundaries, setting up a complex web of sales, manufacturing, distribution, and financial operations. Although these firms are usually based in a single country and run by people of that nationality, they are often transnational in organization and perspective. Jonathan Schell argues that the contemporary corporate executive is "not dependent on the labor, capital or technical knowledge of any particular country. He can pick and choose from anywhere in the world. . . . [He] is not an 'American' businessman or a 'Japanese' businessman. He belongs to no country."[13] While Schell may be overstating the case a bit, this transnational perspective is clearly growing stronger year by year. Furthermore, those who invest in corporations are developing the same transnational orientation as the managers as more and more investors buy stock in foreign nations.[14]

The growth of powerful **multinational corporations** has generated tremendous controversy. Some people see their rise as the first step toward world unity. They are convinced that by linking the economies of the world's nations, the multinationals are laying the foundation for a global government that will usher in a new era of peace and prosperity. In contrast, the critics of the multinationals see them as international bandits that exploit small countries and play large ones against one another.

The expansion of multinational corporations among the industrialized countries has created many problems of international control and regulation. Canadians, for example, are extremely concerned about the economic power of American multinationals, which hold 80 percent of all foreign investment in Canada.[15] Even though the Canadian government has made repeated efforts to promote economic independence, more of Canada's economy is in foreign hands than is true of any other industrialized nation; for instance, despite the creation of Petro-Canada, a government-owned petroleum company, foreigners still control about 60 percent of the Canadian gas and oil industry.[16] Many Canadians have come to see foreign economic domination as a grave threat to their national independence. Even in the United States, many people are concerned about the growing influence of foreign capital. Not only do foreign multinationals own hundreds of billions of dollars' worth of assets in the United States, but the U.S. government depends on foreign investors to buy the bonds it sells to finance the government debt.

The worst abuses of the multinational corporations have, however, resulted from their expansion into the less developed countries of Africa, Asia, and Latin America. Although the multinationals bring advanced technology and encourage some types of economic development, the "host" nations must pay a heavy price. Foreign corporations wield tremendous political power in the poor countries in which they invest, and too often, critical economic decisions are made by foreign corporate executives who have little concern for the welfare of the local people. Moreover, there are grounds for questioning how much economic benefit poor nations actually reap from foreign investment. Although there is considerable controversy about the issue, a number of studies have concluded that foreign investment produces only short-term economic rewards. These studies indicate that once the initial investment is made and the multinationals begin taking home their profits, the economies of nations with large foreign investment begin to fall behind those of

multinational corporation
A corporation that has manufacturing, service, and sales operations in many countries around the world.

The symbols of powerful multinational corporations can be seen all over the world, and their expansion into weak and impoverished nations often brings with it the fear of foreign domination.

nations that rely on their own resources for their economic development. Thus, in the long run, more self-reliant nations have greater economic growth.[17]

Corporate Crimes The business world is sometimes described as a lawless jungle in which profits rule and those who let ethics stand in their way are considered foolish and quaint. Although this is an exaggeration, there is ample evidence that the crime rate is high in the business world.

Everyone has had the experience of buying an article of clothing or an appliance that seemed to fall apart after hardly any use. Although the manufacture and sale of such merchandise do not violate the law, knowingly making false claims for a product is a type of **fraud.** There are countless examples of fraud in industries ranging from cosmetics to automobiles, but some of the most costly come from the savings and loan scandal that first came to light in the late 1980s. The virtual collapse of the savings and loan industry is estimated to have cost as much as $500 billion, much of it paid for by the taxpayers. Although estimates vary about what percentage of those staggering losses was caused by corporate crime, the evidence indicates that some kind of fraud or other illegal activity was involved in the majority of the savings and loan failures.[18] Fraud is not just a matter of money, however; some

fraud
Deceit or trickery used to gain some unfair economic advantage.

fraudulent claims endanger the health or even the life of the consumer. The major pharmaceutical companies have, for example, frequently been caught making fraudulent claims about their products or concealing information to cover up their hazards. Two well-known examples are the painkiller known as Oraflex, which is thought to have killed 49 people and injured almost a thousand more, and the Dalkon shield contraceptive device, which is believed to have caused the deaths of at least 17 women and about 200,000 injuries.[19]

price-fixing
Collusion by several companies to cut competition and set uniformly high prices.

Price-fixing—collusion by several companies to cut competition and set uniformly high prices—is another common corporate crime. A survey of the heads of the 1000 largest manufacturing corporations asked whether "many" corporations engaged in price-fixing. Among those heading the 500 largest corporations, a surprising 47 percent agreed that price-fixing is a common practice. An overwhelming 70 percent of the heads of the remaining 500 corporations agreed.[20] It is quite possible that price-fixing costs consumers more than any other kind of crime.

Many companies also use illegal practices to drive their competitors out of business. One technique is for a big company to sell certain products at a loss in order to bankrupt a small competitor. The company recovers its loss and increases profits by selling the products at much higher prices after the competition has been eliminated. Another technique is for a giant corporation to buy out producers of key raw materials and cut off supplies to its smaller competitors. As with most corporate crimes, the damage extends far beyond the immediate victims to the general public, who in one way or another end up footing the bill.

The Government

Although everyone recognizes the power and importance of corporations in our economic life, many people in countries that practice individualistic capitalism underestimate the economic importance of the government. Although supporters of Adam Smith's laissez-faire ideology argue that governments should simply stay out of economic affairs and allow the free market to regulate itself, the governments of all industrialized nations are deeply involved in directing their economies. Actually, government plays two key economic roles in contemporary capitalist societies. First, as a major employer, government provides jobs and paychecks for millions of people who do everything from sweeping streets to flying bombers. Second, government regulates the economic activities of the private sector.

Some regulation is done directly through the legal system—for example, when the courts decide civil suits involving private businesses or when the government brings legal action for the violation of antitrust laws. U.S. government agencies such as the Federal Trade Commission and the Food and Drug Administration play a major role in regulating economic activities in a variety of different industries. But the operation of these regulatory agencies has been the focus of considerable debate in recent years. Consumer groups charge that although these agencies were set up to protect the public interest, they often end up serving the interests of the industries they regulate: "The regulatory agencies have become the natural allies of the industries they are supposed to regulate. They conceive their primary task to be to protect insiders from new competition—in many cases, from any competition."[21] One problem is that the directors of these agencies often come from the industries they are supposed to regulate and return to those same industries when they leave the government. This "revolving door" between business and government obviously undermines the public interest. It brings in many people who are more sympathetic to the interests of the corporations than the public, and it makes many regulators fearful of risking their economic future by offending corporations that might some-day offer them a high-paying position. Moreover, even when officials try to do their best, the power of the corporations is so great that these small, underfunded agencies are often too weak to get the job done.

On the other hand, business groups often make the opposite criticism, charging that government regulation damages the economy by requiring a mountain of costly and time-consuming paperwork and placing unnecessary restrictions on their activities. As a result of these criticisms, a number of important industries have been **deregulated** since the 1980s. Unfortunately, the results of deregulation have often been disappointing. Deregulation of the airline industry, for example, not only produced a drop in ticket prices but also brought a decline in the safety and quality of service. Moreover, it touched off a wave of mergers, buyouts, and bankruptcies that has reduced competition and may once again lead to higher prices. Deregulation of the savings and loan industry had even more serious consequences. Once freed from government controls, many managers pursued speculative high-risk investments or fraudulent schemes to enrich themselves at their companies' expense, and the result was the virtual collapse of the entire industry.

> **deregulation**
> The termination of government economic regulations and controls.

In addition to direct regulation, the government also has a variety of indirect means it can use to influence the economy. If the government wants to stimulate the economy to grow more rapidly, it can increase the size of its **budget deficit** (the difference between what the government earns in taxes and other revenue and how much it spends) or use its financial power to push down the interest rates charged on loans. As great as it is, however, the government's power is not unlimited. If it stimulates the economy too much, the result is likely to be a higher rate of **inflation** (price increases) and a greater danger of a severe economic downturn in the future. If the inflation rate gets too high or the economy appears to be growing too rapidly, the government can reverse those policies and push up interest rates or reduce the deficit. But then the likely result is more **unemployment.** Tax policies also have a tremendous impact on the economy, influencing the general rate of economic growth and providing special benefits or problems for specific industries. Whatever techniques the government uses, the average citizen now expects it to do everything possible to ensure economic prosperity. When the economy is in decline, the government is blamed and politicians have a difficult time getting reelected, but a prosperous economy is a boon to incumbent politicians.

> **budget deficit**
> The difference between what the government earns in taxes and other revenue and how much it spends.

> **inflation**
> An increase in prices.

> **unemployment**
> The problem suffered by those in the work force who want jobs but are unable to find them.

Small Business

Although overshadowed by the huge corporate and government bureaucracies, small businesses nonetheless play a key role in the economy. Numerically, small businesses have always been the majority. With the current limitations in the growth of government employment and the "downsizing" of many big corporations, small businesses have played a key role in creating new jobs for the growing work force. The share of the work force that is self-employed has grown over 11 percent since 1973.[22] Estimates of the total number of American workers who are self-employed vary widely depending on the definitions and techniques used, but they range from about 8 to 13 percent of the work force.[23] Of course, most people in the small-business sector are not self-employed but work for someone else.

Although there may be more job opportunities in small business, working conditions are very different from those in the government or corporations. The main attraction of small business is the independence it offers to its many owner-operators; but most new businesses go bankrupt in their first year or two, and many of the entrepreneurs who succeed work long hours for a modest return. The employees of many small businesses share their boss's economic insecurity, but without the compensation of greater independence. In comparison with corporate workers, the employees of small businesses are less unionized and receive lower pay and fewer fringe benefits.

Although small businesses and corporations are often lumped together as part of the private sector, there are fundamental differences in the economic environment they face. As we have seen, the large corporations are often able to restrict competition among themselves, thus safeguarding their profitability. Even when they face stiff competition, most major corporations have accumulated huge financial assets that can help see them through rough times. In contrast, small businesses generally struggle against a host of competitors and have very limited financial reserves to fall back on. Another important difference is political. Major corporations wield enormous political power and as a result can obtain many benefits and special favors from the government. Small businesses are much less influential, and therefore they pay higher taxes, receive fewer government benefits, and cannot expect a government bailout when they run into financial trouble. For these reasons, some economists refer to the corporations as the monopoly sector of the economy and to small businesses as the competitive sector.

Although the owners of small businesses, such as the man shown in this photo, create many new jobs, they lack the political power and financial resources of big corporations.

Perched between the corporate giants and the legions of "mom-and-pop" businesses are the medium-sized firms that are at the center of much economic innovation and technological development. Unlike small companies, these firms have the size and economic resources necessary to develop new products and market them effectively. Compared with the giant corporations, medium-sized firms have less cumbersome bureaucracies and are more subject to the competitive pressures of the marketplace. Because medium-sized firms are not large enough to dominate their principal markets, they face the same choice as small businesses: be efficient and competitive, or go under.

The Workers

Not only are workers the heart of the economic system, but their work is often a central focus of their lives. People's self-concepts—their ideas of who and what they are—are profoundly affected by their occupations and their place in the occupational hierarchy. Our jobs bring us into contact with specific social worlds and specific groups of people. If we consider, for example, the differences between the social world of a police officer and that of a ballet dancer, it becomes obvious how deeply people are influenced by their work.

The Work Force Both the types of jobs and the kinds of people who work at them have changed radically in this century. Three major trends are apparent in the changing job market. First, the numbers of workers, owners, and managers of farms—once the largest job category—has steadily declined. Mechanization and technology have enabled a handful of workers to feed millions, so fewer people are needed on the farm. Farmers now make up only 1.9 percent of the work force, and the Department of Labor expects their numbers to keep declining.[24] Second, because of automation and increasing competition from foreign products, there has been a shift of workers away from higher-paying manufacturing and production jobs and into lower-paying **service occupations** (jobs that provide a service to someone else rather than making a product or extracting a natural resource). Just since 1989, the United States has lost over 1 million jobs in manufacturing, mining, and construction while creating 10 times that number of new service jobs.[25] In addition to the growing number of self-employed workers we have already discussed, there has been an even sharper increase among temporary workers, whose numbers have more than tripled in the last decade and a half.[26]

> **service occupations**
> Jobs that provide a service to someone else rather than making a product or extracting a natural resource.

These changes have brought great hardship to people from all walks of life but especially to the working class (see Figure 4.1). Although a service job may sound more attractive than working in a factory, the reality is often quite different. Service work can be just as dull, menial, and repetitive as most factory work, and on the average the pay is only 70 percent as high. The result has been a growing income gap between the working class and more highly trained managers and professionals, along with the deterioration of entire towns that depend on failing manufacturing concerns.

The third and perhaps most important of these trends involves the sweeping changes in the role of women in the work force. For one thing, unprecedented numbers of married women have been taking jobs outside the home. In 1900, only 5 percent of married women were part of the work force; today, over 61 percent of all married women hold jobs.[27] Another key development has been the entrance of women into occupations that used to be reserved almost entirely for men. (See Chapter 10 for a full discussion of these trends.)

It is easy to overlook the unemployed, but it should be remembered that those who are out of work are still part of the work force. Although the amount of unemployment goes up and down from one year to the next, since 1989 the official unemployment rate has averaged about 6.2 percent of all workers.[28] Moreover, official unemployment statistics do not count **discouraged workers** who have given up looking for jobs and those who are the victims of **underemployment**—that is, those who take part-time jobs when they want full-time work. If those two groups were added in, the unemployment figures would almost double. Although government unemployment insurance provides some help, only people officially defined as unemployed are eligible, and even among that group the number who actually receive unemployment benefits has steadily declined as eligibility standards have been raised and the average length of unemployment has increased. Moreover, the severe financial problems created by the loss of jobs are only part of the problem, as we can see from this chapter's Personal Perspectives from an unemployed logger.

To make matters worse, the use of part-time workers has grown increasingly popular with employers. Since 1973, the percentage of workers holding part-time jobs has increased more than 11 percent.[29] The reason for this trend is clear: part-time workers are cheaper. On the average, women who work part time earn 23 percent less per hour than full-time workers, and men receive almost 40 percent less; and they are both far less likely to receive medical or retirement benefits. Not surprisingly, more than one-fifth of part-time workers really want full-time work.[30]

discouraged workers
Workers who have given up looking for work; not counted in unemployment figures.

underemployment
The situation of workers who want permanent full-time work but can find only part-time or temporary work.

Figure 4.1

Poverty-Level Jobs

The percentage of full-time workers in the United States who do not earn enough to keep a family of four above the poverty line has steadily increased over the years.

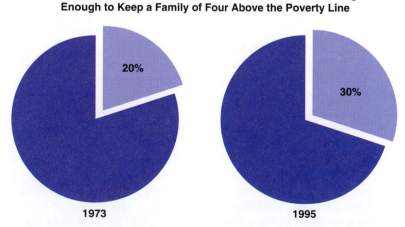

The Percentage of Full-Time American Workers Not Earning Enough to Keep a Family of Four Above the Poverty Line

20%

30%

1973

1995

Source: Lawrence Mishel, Jared Bernstein, and John Smitt, *The State of Working America, 1996–97* (New York: M. E. Sharpe, 1997), p. 339.

Personal Perspectives   An Unemployed Logger

A job is more than just a way to make a living. The loss of a job can have traumatic psychological effects. This is especially true for people like this unemployed logger, who sees little chance of getting another job as good as the one he lost.

There was a disbelief among the workers that we would ever be permanently laid off. We believed the United States needed building materials, and it had to come from somewhere. When I found out the day before Christmas that I was permanently laid off, I wasn't too worried. After 16 years, I felt I had valuable job skills in the timber industry and that I wouldn't have any problem getting another job. It didn't work out that way, though, and after awhile fear of the future set in. There weren't many job prospects, and I had to lower my sights on wages.

About this time, my marriage started coming apart. I had been paying all the bills, and suddenly my wife had to start contributing to paying the bills. Her paycheck used to be just for her. This caused a problem. Arguments happened more often. About four months after I was laid off, she told me she wanted a divorce. This was a pretty low time for me. The marriage stuff was more of an emotional downer than the job stuff. All the cornerstones of my life came tumbling down.

In retrospect, it was a growth experience. You get middle-aged, have a job, relationship, home . . . you coast. When it all gets taken away from you . . . well, it was a growth experience.

Worker Alienation Mechanization of the workplace during the industrial revolution led to a progressive dehumanization of workers as they were forced to change their patterns of work to meet the demands of the machines they operated. Although work hours may not be as long as they were a century ago, many of today's factory workers still find their jobs tedious and trivial and see themselves as little more than cogs in a machine. Such feelings of **alienation** are so common that they have been given a name: the blue-collar blues. David J. Charrington's survey of worker attitudes found that "feeling pride and craftsmanship in your work" was one of the most highly desired characteristics of a job.[31] Yet technology is rapidly eliminating skilled craftspeople and replacing them with complex computer-controlled machinery. People displaced from such jobs often drift into low-skilled service industries; but even those who are retrained to repair and maintain the new equipment often lose the sense of pride that came from being directly responsible for producing a high-quality product.

> **alienation**
> (1) A feeling of estrangement from society and social groups. (2) A feeling of the loss of control over one's activities, especially one's labor.

A number of programs have been created to help blue-collar workers gain greater satisfaction on the job. Some corporations, for example, give a group of workers responsibility for assembling a finished product rather than give each individual responsibility for only one small part of it. Other companies encourage workers to rotate from one job to another in order to vary their tasks. Some managers allow employees to set up their own work procedures and schedule their own hours. Allowing workers to participate in management decisions that affect their jobs also reduces alienation. However, conflict theorists argue that worker alienation will not be reduced significantly until workers receive a greater share of the profits of the companies using their labor.

Ironically, just as the corporations are discovering the problem of worker alienation among the shrinking blue-collar labor force, the computer revolution is creating similar problems among the growing numbers of clerical workers. Computers were supposed to liberate office workers from the drudgery of performing the same tasks again and again, but so far that hasn't been the result. As in the early days of factory automation, computers have been used to break down jobs into smaller and simpler tasks. The use of computers has also tended to isolate workers from other employees, and at the same time, new technology has increased employers' ability to scrutinize the actions of their workers. For example, workers who deal with the public on the phone often find that computer-generated reports show how many calls they answer and how long they spend with each customer, while supervisors randomly audit calls that exceed a given length. Moreover, repetitive movements required by some computerized equipment, such as cash registers that read bar codes, have caused a seven-fold increase in repetitive-strain injuries, such as strained wrists, since 1981.[32]

Death on the Job Boredom and alienation are not the only problems workers have to face on the job. Working for the wrong company or in the wrong industry can have fatal consequences. The Centers for Disease Control and Prevention estimate that about 17 workers a day were killed on the job during the last decade.[33] In addition to the thousands of workers who die from workplace accidents, a much larger number die more slowly from the effects of occupationally caused diseases. The U.S. government estimates that there are 100,000 such deaths a year, but that figure is only an educated guess. Many workers who die from occupational diseases never know the source of their condition. Besides this huge death toll, at least 2.2 million workers a year are injured in occupational accidents, and many more are probably made ill by the work they do.[34]

It is clear that some employers simply do not care about the deaths and injuries they cause their workers. New procedures and techniques are constantly being developed by industry, but few employers take time to test them adequately before bringing them into the workplace. Over half a million chemicals are used in industry, but only a few thousand have been thoroughly tested to see if they are dangerous. And even when tests do show a chemical to be hazardous, some firms try to keep the results secret. For example, when an Italian scientist discovered that vinyl chloride (a popular plastic) causes a rare form of cancer that had been found among

Signs of Hope   Jobs Are Getting Safer

A day on the job is a difficult and dangerous affair for many workers, but there are signs that things are getting better. In 1960, about 14,000 Americans were killed on the job, or about 21 of every 100,000 workers. In 1994, in contrast, only about 5,000 people died on the job, and because the work force had grown considerably, the occupational death rate was less than one-fifth as high. Moreover, there was a similar drop in the number of workers who suffered disabling injuries on the job.*

One reason for this improvement was the decline in the percentage of the work force employed in heavy manufacturing jobs (which tend to be the most dangerous). Tighter government regulations, a growing concern about worker safety, and the threat of lawsuits against negligent employers also played a major role.

*Statistical Abstract of the United States, 1996, p. 433.

workers exposed to it, the Manufacturing Chemists Association joined with the European firm that sponsored the research in a coordinated effort to keep the findings secret. Confidential memos indicate that the manufacturers of asbestos followed the same policy and intentionally concealed the dangers of asbestos exposure from their workers. The ultimate death toll among these men and women is expected to be well over 200,000.[35] Nonetheless, there are signs that things have been getting better in recent years, as we see in the box "Jobs Are Getting Safer."

Labor Unions The early period of industrialization created misery among workers. Entire families labored in mines and factories. Industrialists paid subsistence wages, claiming that workers were lazy and would stop working if they were better paid. Working conditions were terrible, and deaths from occupational accidents were common. Workdays were long, often 14 hours or more, and holidays were few and far between. Conditions were so bad that Karl Marx proclaimed the workers would soon destroy capitalism in a violent revolution. But the workers did not respond with revolution; they responded with unionization.

Early labor unions faced bitter struggles with employers and the U.S. government, which supported employers' interests. In many places, unions were outlawed and organizers jailed; even when unionization became legal, organizers found themselves harassed at every turn. Unions gradually gained official recognition and acceptance, and as they won power, the conditions of the average worker improved.

Traditionally, the threat of a strike has been the unions' most effective weapon in their struggle for better pay and better working conditions. In today's anti-union climate, however, the number of successful strikes is far lower than it was in the past.

Unions eventually became a major economic and political force that was often critical to the success of politicians and business enterprises alike.

Yet despite the successes of the past, unions are in a serious decline. In 1996, only 15.5 percent of the work force (excluding the self-employed) was unionized; that figure was more than twice as large in 1955. With dwindling membership has come timidity and ineffectiveness. The average number of strikes a year has dropped to a fraction of what it was in earlier decades, and the wage settlements unions win are also far smaller than in the past.[36] Indeed, a growing number of strikes has resulted in the permanent replacement of the strikers with nonunion labor.

What caused this erosion of union membership and union power? Since union membership is highest in manufacturing and among **blue-collar workers,** a significant part of the decline in union membership resulted from a decrease in the importance of those occupations. Unions are now directing more efforts toward organizing government employees and **white-collar workers,** but resistance remains strong. Today's unions face other serious problems as well: on one side are the increasingly sophisticated industrial robots that threaten more and more union jobs; on the other are the masses of the world's poor who will eagerly work for a fraction of union wages. Ironically, increasing their output through automation is one of the few ways workers in high-wage countries such as the United States and Canada can continue to compete with low-wage workers in the less developed countries. As a result, the unions are often faced with the unpleasant choice of losing jobs to automation or to foreign labor. To make matters worse for the unions, their declining numbers have reduced their political clout, which has made it easier for business interests to win government bureaucrats and policymakers to their side.

blue-collar workers
Workers who perform manual labor.

white-collar workers
Workers who peform nonmanual labor.

Quick Review

Who runs the corporations?

How have corporations shaped the modern economy?

What role does the government play in the economy?

How are conditions different for small businesses and big corporations?

How has our work force changed in the twentieth century?

Why has union membership declined?

The New Economic Realities

Some voices in the media have been telling us that these are the best of economic times and that long-term prosperity is at hand. Unemployment and inflation are down, and the stock market is reaching record highs. But if things are so good, why do people feel so insecure about their jobs? Why have the wages of most workers been going down, not up? To answer these puzzling questions, we have to look at long-term trends in the American economy. But measuring economic trends is no easy task. For one thing, when you compare average wages or income between one year and another, your conclusions don't mean much unless you correct for inflation (the increase in average prices), but experts disagree about how much inflation there really is. Comparisons between individual years also are misleading because all capitalist economies go through a **business cycle**—alternating periods of "boom" and "bust" in which the economy swings from growth and prosperity to stagnation and recession. During downturns in the cycle, unemployment generally goes up while **real wages** stagnate or go down, and during the upswings these trends are reversed. Inflation is usually lower in the downward part of the cycle and higher during the upswing. What is important, then, is not what happens in any particular year but long-term trends.

Three Economic Eras?

If we look at the American economy since the end of World War II, we can see two distinct eras and what looks like the beginning of a third. From the end of the war until 1973 were what might be called the "golden years." The nation was experiencing record economic growth, and both inflation and unemployment were low. Worker **productivity** (the value of the goods or services an average worker produces in a given period of time) was increasing rapidly; American products were the most competitive in the world; and the standard of living was head and shoulders above any other nation. The oil crisis of 1973 marked the beginning of a new and unsettling era in the American economy. An embargo by the Arab oil producers caused the price of oil to increase 400 percent that year, and the world economy went into shock. Inflation skyrocketed while unemployment increased and real wages plummeted. But America's economic problems did not disappear when the price of oil started to decline again. (The real price of oil is lower today than it was before the oil crisis). For the next two decades, the yearly increase in productivity dropped to less than half its earlier levels, average wages continued to decline, and unemployment and inflation remained far higher than they had been in the past. For the first time, key American industries seemed unable to compete with products being pumped out by Japan and the newly industrializing nations. American manufacturers were virtually driven out of the home electronics business, and they lost a sizable share of the market for such vital products as automobiles and machine tools.

The government responded to this economic crisis with conservative economic policies. It forced a huge increase in interest rates, which slowed the economy, in hope of bringing down inflation. Taxes were cut for the wealthy, and many regulations designed to control business activity were stripped away. Big corporations slashed their labor costs by attacking unions and laying off ("downsizing") millions of workers. Pressed by economic troubles on all sides, average families were still able to win a small increase in their income, but only because a flood of women who had been staying home to raise their families entered the job market.

Although it is too early to tell for sure, it appears that we are now entering another new era. Unemployment and inflation have gone down. Corporate profits have skyrocketed, and while American products do not seem markedly more competitive than they were in the 1980s, the drop in American competitiveness seem to have stopped. But while some people are trumpeting the dawning of another golden age, the reality of the situation is far different. Unlike the case during the postwar boom, today's economic gains have been won at the cost of the workers and much of the middle class. Corporate profits (and the stock market) are up because wages and corporate employment are down. While times are great for the rich, for the average American this new era seems likely to be a difficult one.

business cycle
The ups and downs that characterize the economies of all capitalist nations.

real wages
The actual value of wages after a correction for inflation has been made.

productivity
The value of the goods or services an average worker produces in a given period of time.

Figure 4.2

Wages and Debt

The real average wage (after controlling for inflation) has declined significantly since 1973, while the nation's debt has exploded.

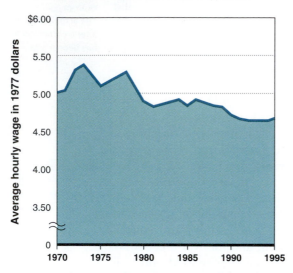
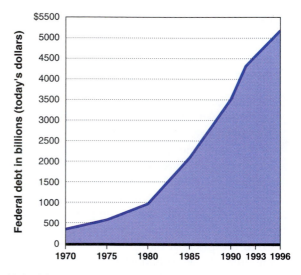

Source: U.S. Bureau of the Census, *Statistical Abstract of the United States, 1996* (Washington, DC: U.S. Government Printing Office, 1993), pp. 332, 424.

Measuring the Changes

Current trends in the economy include declining wages, increasing inequality (the rich are getting richer and the poor are getting poorer), and greater insecurity, but how large have the changes actually been? From their peak in 1973 until the beginning of 1997, the average hourly wage of workers in private industry declined about 13 percent. (See Figure 4.2.) But such a broad generalization conceals many important facts. While the average man's wage dropped by a little over $2.00 an hour (in today's dollars), the average woman's pay increased by $0.34 an hour. On the average, however, a woman still earns only about three-fourths as much as a man. The same trends are apparent in fringe benefits. In 1979, 79 percent of all private sector workers had employer-provided health insurance, but today that figure is only about 64 percent. Another important trend was the growth in inequality. The wages of the lowest-paid workers dropped the most, but the top 10 percent of workers actually saw their pay increase.[37] The growing gap between the rich and the poor can be seen in numerous other statistics as well. For example, take family wealth. In the last decade, the richest 1 percent of Americans saw their total wealth *increase* by about 28 percent, while the 40 percent of the population at the bottom *lost* almost half their total wealth.[38] The growing sense of economic insecurity is not as easy to measure in economic statistics, but we know that the average worker's chance of losing his or her job was about 5 percent higher in the early 1990s than in the early 1980s. About 15 percent of all male workers and 11.4 percent of female workers can expect to lose their jobs within the next three years. Although blue-collar workers are *much* more likely to be fired than their bosses, the corporate downsizing of the last decade produced a much higher increase in job insecurity among managers than any other category of workers.[39]

The Causes

To deal with these new economic problems, we must understand their causes, and the first place to look is the changing world economy. At the end of World War II, all the major industrialized nations—except the United States and Canada—lay in ruins. Because the factories of North America emerged from the war undamaged, their products were sometimes the only ones available. As Europe and Japan began to recover from the war, they were hungry consumers of North American goods. The United States became the world's dominant economic power, and the American dollar was virtually an international currency. But that era is over. Europe and Japan now have vigorous industries of their own that compete with American firms in the world market. But all the new competition for American workers did not come from foreign companies alone. As we have seen, the big American corporations have become truly international organizations with little allegiance to the interests of their home country. Because the United States was the most prosperous country in the world during the postwar period, its workers received the highest wages. The availability of cheaper labor in the poor nations led large American corporations to shift many of their manufacturing operations to other countries. Thus, the increasing competition faced by American workers drove wages down and unemployment up, while wealthy investors often saw their profits increase as the cost of labor fell.

The increase in world competition was an inevitable result of the recovery of nations such as Germany and Japan from the devastation of World War II. It is also true, however, that many American industries have failed to keep up with that foreign competition. The key to maintaining a high standard of living and competitiveness in the world market lies in high productivity. If workers make more products per hour, businesses can pay higher wages without raising the price of the products they make. The shift to a service-based economy makes it harder to measure productivity accurately, but it is generally agreed that although the American work force remains among the most productive in the world, many other nations have been improving their productivity considerably faster.

The most obvious cause of this faltering productivity is that the United States has reinvested a significantly lower percentage of its national income in new plants and equipment than its most successful competitors. On the average, Japan invests twice the proportion of its national economy in new plants and equipment as the United States does, and Germany about 50 percent more.[40] Much the same picture comes from a look at another major key to a healthy economy: investment in research and development. Expressed as a percentage of the gross domestic product, private corporations spend about 25 percent more on civilian research and development in Germany and about 50 percent more in Japan.[41] Moreover, U.S. spending for other things that produce long-term improvements in productivity, such as transportation, and education, has been slashed since 1980. Federal investment in building projects has dropped 34 percent (as a percentage of the national income), and its investment in education has declined 27 percent.[42]

There are many reasons why the United States has failed to reinvest enough money to keep its industries leaders in the world market. Part of the problem is psychological: Americans became complacent about their technological edge and decided to enjoy the fruits of their labor instead of investing for the future. Americans save less of their income than the people of any other major industrialized nation, and that means there is less available to invest. The huge overseas investments made by American companies in the last few decades are also important because the flow of money out of the country reduced the pool of capital available for domestic investment. One of the biggest drains on investment comes from the heavy military burden carried by the United States. The enormous cost of the American defense establishment siphons off billions of dollars that might otherwise be used for more economically productive ventures. Although some nations, such as North Korea and Israel, spend a greater percentage of their income on the military, it is no coincidence that America's strongest economic competitors carry a far lighter military burden (see Figure 4.3).

Accentuating these other problems is the fact that the United States is facing competition from a new style of capitalism that developed in such countries as Japan and West Germany after World War II. Their "communitarian" approach emphasizes group cooperation and national coordination to a far higher degree than in the United States, and the individualistically oriented American system has had a difficult time adjusting to this new challenge. In America, the interests of the individual stockholders are given priority over the long-term good of the corporation,

Figure 4.3

The Military Burden

The United States spends far more on its military than its major economic competitors.

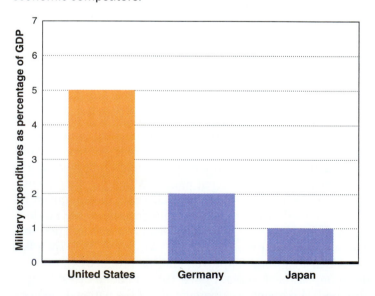

Source: U.S. Bureau of the Census, *Statistical Abstract of the United States, 1996* (Washington, DC: U.S. Government Printing Office, 1996), p. 858.

while in communitarian capitalism the opposite is true. Consequently, American corporations pay out a far higher percentage of their profits in stock dividends (about 80 percent) than do Japanese corporations (about 30 percent),[43] which obviously leaves the Japanese with more money to invest in the future of their firm. Similarly, top Japanese executives are often shocked by what they see as the personal greed of their American counterparts, who often raise their own salaries even when their companies are losing money. In 1990, the average **chief executive officer (CEO)** of a large Japanese company made 18 times more than the company's workers, while an average American CEO made 119 times the salary of an average worker.[44] By 1995, the U.S. ratio had shot up to 173 to 1![45]

chief executive officer (CEO)
The head of a corporation.

One final factor in our current economic problems must be mentioned: the environment. One reason North Americans traditionally enjoyed a higher standard of living than the rest of the world was that the continent's vast stores of natural resources were easily put to use—productive farmlands, timber, coal, iron, and petroleum, to name just a few. But North Americans were foolish and shortsighted in their exploitation of these natural treasures. The environment was seen as an endless horn of plenty; whole forests were razed, farmlands overworked, and petroleum reserves pumped dry. Moreover, the dizzying growth in population has meant that the resources that remain must serve the needs of more and more people every year. (See Chapter 16 for a more complete discussion of this issue.)

Quick Review

What are the three economic eras since the end of World War II?

Why has the U.S. economy stagnated?

Solving the Problems of the Economy

There are a staggering number of proposals for dealing with our economic problems, but most of them can be grouped into two broad categories. The first includes ideas about ways to improve the economy, and the second includes proposals for adjusting to the new economic environment and improving the quality of life regardless of the ups and downs of the economy. Advocates of the first type of proposal often claim that their programs can restore the vigorous economic growth of the past, whereas advocates of the other approach are more likely to feel that those days are gone forever. Despite such disagreements, both kinds of responses can be used at the same time. Most North Americans, however, are reluctant to accept the idea that we must lower our economic expectations in order to have a more stable and sustainable society, despite a great deal of convincing evidence pointing to that conclusion (see Chapter 16 on the environment). So the proposals that aim to revitalize the economy are far more common than those that seek to help us adapt to our new economic realities.

The Role of the Government: Bystander or Planner?

Some strategies to revitalize the economy cut across ideological lines. For example, proposals to reduce the budget deficit or to improve our educational system gain supporters across the political spectrum (although liberals and conservatives often disagree about how to achieve those objectives). The overall approach of those on the political right and left, however, differs markedly.

The conservative approach is based on the free-market laissez-faire ideology that has traditionally been so strong in the United States. Conservatives generally want to cut back on the size of government in order to free more money for private investment and to sharply reduce the government's role in regulating the economy to avoid the inefficiency they feel regulation produces. They often advocate cuts in social welfare spending, which in their view encourages people not to work, and support a reduction in the minimum wage (or allowing it to be slowly eroded by inflation) in order to reduce the cost of labor for American business. But the proposal dearest to the hearts of most conservatives is a sharp cut in taxes. Supporters of *supply-side economics*—an economic theory that focuses on increasing the supply of goods instead of the more usual approach, which emphasizes increasing the demand for them—argue that tax cuts create so much economic growth that they make up for lower tax rates. More traditional conservatives feel that deep reductions in spending are needed to bring the federal budget back into balance. Both groups agree that tax cuts stimulate investment by putting more money into the hands of the wealthy than they are likely to spend. Conservatives argue that the economic benefits those investments produce then "trickle down" to the average citizen. Thus, conservatives advocate an individualistic approach to solving economic problems: the government should cut back on all the programs and policies, whether welfare or business regulations, that restrict the free individual struggle for gain. If a big corporation is driven to the edge of bankruptcy by foreign competition, let it go under; when successful entrepreneurs make a fortune, let them enjoy their wealth without excessive taxation.

Critics argue that such policies are cruel and misguided: they rip the social safety net out from under millions of hardworking Americans, increase homelessness and malnutrition, and create an intolerable level of economic insecurity. In their view, cutting back the government's role in regulating the economy does not create more competition but less, because the wealthy and powerful are free to use their advantages to lock everyone else out of the economic game. These critics point out that in the past, tax breaks for the wealthy have often spurred spending on luxuries or such things as gold and antiques and have therefore produced few benefits for anyone else.

The U.S. government has been following this conservative road since the 1980s, and progressive critics charge that the results have been just as they predicted. Although inflation and unemployment finally seem to have declined, wages have dropped, employment has become more insecure, and poverty has increased, while the rich have grown ever richer. In their view, the push to cut back on government regulation created serious economic problems, including a financial crisis in the airline industry and the near collapse of the savings and loan industry. The conservatives respond that whatever problems there may be in our current economy, they are the result of our failure to go far enough with the conservative prescription for change.

In contrast to the individualistic approach of the conservatives, those on the left call for more socially oriented policies to foster great economic cooperation. One of their principal recommendations is for more **ecnomic planning** on the part of the

economic planning
The active involvement of government in directing the economy.

government. Advocates of economic planning point out that the governments of America's most successful economic competitors are deeply involved in planning and directing the economies of their nations. They therefore argue that representatives of the U.S. government, major corporations, unions, and environmental groups should work together to develop a comprehensive economic plan that identifies areas of economic strength and weakness and outlines a coherent strategy to improve the economic environment. Then, all these diverse groups must be motivated to work together for the good of the entire nation.

Although it remains to be seen what kind of policies such a cooperative effort would produce, many suggestions have been made. One proposal is to create a federal bank or finance corporation to provide low-interest loans to high-growth industries and to help older industries become more competitive. Others propose government grants or joint research efforts between government and private businesses to develop new technologies in key industries facing intense foreign competition. Many advocates of economic planning argue that we need to create a comprehensive strategy to reduce our military spending to about the same level as that of our main economic competitors. Such a plan would need to include such things as a program to assist military contractors in putting their skills to productive civilian use, as well as retraining for the workers no longer needed for military purposes. Almost all supporters of economic planning also like the kinds of proposals for increasing our investment in the future discussed in the next section.

Critics of the government's role in the economy point to the damage done by some government programs in the past. They argue that, as in the communist countries, deep government involvement in the economy causes waste and inefficiency. Supporters of economic planning respond that the conditions here are completely different and that we should seek a healthy balance that avoids both the anarchy and exploitation that come from unregulated capitalism and the oppressive centralized control of the communist system.

Investing in the Future

As we have seen, the United States invests far less in its economic future than Germany or Japan, and there is a growing consensus that Americans need to take a much longer-term perspective when making key economic decisions. While it is easy to say that we need to increase our investment in the future, there seems to be little will actually to do it. The fact is that we cannot have our cake and eat it too: the only place to get the money for those investments is to reduce our consumer spending, in other words, to lower our current standard of living. Perhaps we should learn from the long-range perspective taken by Native Americans, who considered a major decision by asking themselves what impact it would have seven generations in the future.

Once we have committed ourselves to take a longer-term view and invest more in the future, there are several possible ways to do it. To start with, we could reform the tax structure to reduce taxation on investment and increase it on spending. For example, we could increase the tax rate on corporate profits and use the money to provide tax credits and other incentives to companies that invest in more research and new plants and equipment. Another idea would be to increase the tax rate on speculative investments such as buying and selling commodities or real estate and

Debate   Is Freer World Trade the Way to Economic Prosperity at Home?

Recent years have seen some important steps toward freer world trade. In 1993, the U.S. Senate ratified the North American Free Trade Agreement (NAFTA), which allowed Mexico to enter the free-trade zone that already existed between the United States and Canada. The next year saw the signing of the Uruguay Round of the General Agreement on Tariffs and Trade (GATT), which lowered many tariffs (taxes on imports) and subsidies (payments governments make to support their industries) among trading partners around the world. But are such agreements really beneficial to our own economy?

Yes

The record is clear. Free trade is good for the world economy, and it is good for the individual nations that participate in it. When the United States passed the Smoot-Hawley Tariff Act in 1930, the ensuing trade war established new barriers to world commerce that were a major cause of the Great Depression. After World War II, however, the industrialized nations worked together to bring down their trade barriers, and the world economy flourished.

The reasons for this are simple. Freer trade gives the businesses of each nation larger potential markets, but also many more competitors. Thus, well-run businesses flourish while the incompetent go under. The result is a more efficent and more productive economy that benefits everyone.

Some people claim that freer world trade will help the Japanese, the Germans, or the Third World nations more than it will us, but there is no reason to believe that is true. Each nation has its own unique economic strengths and weaknesses. And it makes good sense to let each nation make the products it makes best and buy from someone else the products it is not good at making. Although some nations may be hurt if they can't produce anything that anyone else wants to buy, does anyone really think that is true of the United States or Canada? We will prosper in an open world market, and we should do everything we can to encourage its growth.

reduce the rate for productive investments such as building an environmentally sound factory that creates new jobs. More money and effort should be spent on education to improve the quality of our work force and teach the growing population of poor and immigrant children the skills needed in a high-tech economy (see Chapter 3 for more details). Another pressing need is to create better systems of mass transit and rebuild our decaying highways and railroads. The rate of American investment in basic infrastructure (roads, bridges, etc.) is less than half what it was in the 1960s, and we are outspent by all our major economic competitors.[46] In addition to their long-term benefits, many of these kinds of investments are also likely to

No

The world has changed, and the old answers simply don't work anymore. In the past, freer trade always benefited the most industrialized nations because their products were cheaper and better than those from other places. After World War II, for example, North American products were the best in the world, and the fewer restrictions there were on trade, the more money our businesses made.

But today things are different. There is far greater competition from such places as Germany and Japan, but the more critical problem is the Third World. In the past, Third World industries weren't much of a problem because they operated with inefficient management and outdated technology. But now multinational corporations bring the latest technology and management techniques to whatever country has the lowest labor costs. There are literally billions of workers in the Third World willing to work for a few dollars a week, and their numbers and their desperation are growing every day. Free trade is a boon to the multinational corporations and their stockholders, but it will drive millions of our workers into poverty and unemployment.

Free trade can flourish only in a free world. Until we can break the Third World nations' chains of poverty and despair and help them bring their runaway population growth under control, we must protect our workers with strong tariff barriers. We have no other choice!

create a considerable number of the kind of well-paying jobs that are currently in such short supply.

Restructuring the Workplace

Many proposals have been made to improve our productivity by restructuring workplaces and the corporations that organize and create them. One Japanese idea that is gaining growing popularity is known as **lean production.** Firms using this approach cut back their overlapping layers of management, use a smaller but more

lean production
An approach to manufacturing that attempts to use the smallest possible amount of labor.

flexible work force, and strive to develop a closer working relationship with parts and equipment suppliers. Another successful Japanese idea is to give workers more responsibility in the decision-making process. This approach not only fosters a greater commitment to the organization, but also takes advantage of the workers' intimate knowledge of day-to-day problems they face on the job. In the long run, however, workers are unlikely to show more commitment to their companies unless companies also demonstrate greater commitment to them by avoiding layoffs and showing a genuine concern for their welfare.

economic democracy
A program to give workers control over the decisions that affect their lives.

Advocates of **economic democracy** take such ideas a step further and propose programs to give workers more power over the decisions of top corporate officials as well. Past experience has shown that employees have a more cooperative attitude, accept necessary cuts in wages, and work harder when they own a part of the company and share directly in its profits (or losses). It therefore seems logical that the government assist workers to take over the ownership of financially troubled firms and help workers start new cooperative enterprises. In fact, the trend toward greater employee ownership is already under way. The number of employees participating in stock ownership plans increased from fewer than 2 million in 1976 to almost 11 million in 1992.[47] Although most of these plans fall far short of owning a controlling interest in the firm, several major corporations have been acquired by their employees in recent years—one of the most successful examples being the Avis car rental company. A bolder approach would be to pass legislation as Germany has to require that worker representatives be included on the boards of directors of all major corporations. Another useful addition to corporate boards would be a public representative who could speak for the interests of the nation as a whole. However it is implemented, advocates of economic democracy argue that a fairer and more efficient system would give workers a strong voice in controlling their own occupational lives.

Adjusting to Economic Change

Increasing international competition and dwindling natural resources have convinced many social scientists that there is nothing we can do that will create a new economic boom comparable to that of the golden era after World War II. They argue that we must therefore take measures to adjust to slower growth and longer periods of recession.

Most nations depend on economic growth to create enough new jobs for their expanding work forces; thus, economic stagnation threatens millions of people with permanent joblessness or underemployment. Moreover, efforts to improve productivity may actually make unemployment worse. When an employer buys more efficient machines to increase workers' output, fewer people are needed on the assembly line and surplus workers are laid off. Western European nations have responded to this problem with large-scale job-retraining programs. The idea is to train unskilled workers for new occupations as well as to retrain skilled workers who have lost jobs in declining industries. Such a program would clearly be beneficial in the United States; however, even if all unemployed workers were retrained, there would still not be enough jobs to go around. Either workers must put in fewer hours to spread the work around, or new jobs must be created. Prodded by the unions and growing public concern, several European nations are experimenting with a reduction in the workweek in order keep more people employed (albeit with a lower income). A different response to this problem is the call for government to create jobs for those who are unable to find any other work. Critics charge that such "make-work" programs are wasteful and inefficient, but it is difficult to see how they could be more wasteful than unemployment itself. Nonetheless, it is important that new job programs be effectively managed and targeted to meet pressing social needs, such as building railroads and mass transit systems and providing top-quality day care for our children. If these goals are met, such a program could provide a major boost for the economy and especially for those at the low end of the economic scale.

It is also important to remember that the quality of life is not measured solely by the economist's computations of average income or the standard of living. The quality of life can be improved regardless of the economic climate. Numerous suggestions for such improvements are discussed in this book, including proposals to make the workplace safer, reduce crime, improve the lives of the elderly and the poor, clean up the environment, and upgrade the educational system so that people can better understand the complexities of the world around them. Of course, all these things are expensive, but their overall cost is small compared to the benefits they bring.

Building a Sustainable Economy

If we stand back and take a hard look at the global economy, it seems shockingly irrational. Every year we are using up more and more of our limited natural resources

Environmentalists argue that conversion to more environmentally sound technologies can create many new jobs, such as the one for the installer of this solar panel.

and pouring out ever increasing amounts of toxic pollutants in order to produce a flood of consumer goods that add little or nothing to the quality of our lives. In fact, the relentless materialism of our consumer culture is more likely an overall source of suffering than satisfaction.

Spurred by the ideals of the environmental movement, many people are coming to believe that the economy should be restructured to make it more environmentally sustainable. From a theoretical standpoint, it seems clear that we must find a more harmonious way to live with our environment, yet we often fail to take even the most obvious steps toward building a more **sustainable society.** For example, it has been over two decades since the first "energy crisis," yet the United States is still so dependent on foreign oil that a new crisis in the Middle East could have the same or even worse consequences. If we wanted to reduce this danger and cut the enormous environmental damage cause by our heedless consumption of petroleum, we could raise gasoline taxes and use the money to help communities develop local hydroelectric and solar resources, and we could conserve energy by implementing programs for such things as better insulation and more effective systems of mass transit.

One underlying problem is that our economic system is structured to reward individuals who seek immediate short-term profits, while the costs of the long-term harm they cause are passed on to our entire society. But an even more fundamental difficulty lies in the values of our consumer culture that tell us that we can never have enough. The more riches we have, the happier we will be. Chapter 16 explores many proposals for building a more stable, sustainable society, but we will have to take a long, hard look at our economic values before we will be willing to carry them out.

sustainable society
A stable society that does not exceed the carrying capacity of its environment.

Quick Review

What are the best ways of dealing with our economic problems?

Sociological Perspectives on Problems of the Economy

Shrinking wages, foreign competition, the hardships of unemployment, and similar difficulties seem to be matters for technically trained economists. Indeed, some economists devote their lives to the study of these problems. Sociologists, however, generally feel that a "dollars and cents" approach cannot, by itself, yield genuine understanding of our economic difficulties. To the sociologist, economic ills can be understood only in their social context. It makes no more sense to study economic problems apart from their social background than it does to try to solve social problems without understanding their economic basis. Sociologists therefore use the theoretical perspectives discussed in Chapter 1 to analyze economic problems in relationship to society as a whole.

The Functionalist Perspective

Functionalists see the economic system as a machine that produces and distributes the commodities a society needs. If the system functions efficiently to give the society what it wants, there are few economic problems; but sometimes the machine balks or strains. One part may run faster or slower than others, throwing the whole system out of balance; for example, distribution may not keep up with production, or we may produce too many goods of one kind and not enough of another. Such maladjustments may correct themselves through the operation of the free market, or they may be corrected through government action. Economic crises occur when the whole machine becomes disorganized and coordination throughout the system falters.

Functionalists blame contemporary economic problems on the rapid changes that have thrown the traditional economic system out of balance. It took hundreds of years for Western society to develop and perfect an economic system based on open competition among private individuals in a free market, but as the system became larger and more complex, its problems multiplied. As we have seen, huge corporations sprang up and gained control of many vital markets, the government stepped in to regulate the economy, and powerful unions began to control the labor market. Thus, these new cogs destabilized the old machinery. Then, just as we were struggling to bring the system back into balance, major shifts occurring in the world economy threw North American business into intense competition with dynamic new economies around the world. Under these conditions, many of the old economic ideas no longer worked as they had in the past, and dysfunctional economic decisions followed. The breathtaking pace of economic change made it impossible to resolve old economic problems before new ones arose.

Most functionalists shy away from radical, far-reaching proposals for solving economic problems, principally because they know that change brings problems as well as solutions. Disruptive change in an unbalanced system makes a new balance even more difficult to achieve. Functionalists favor specific, limited cures for specific, limited problems, such as education and training for the unemployed and better law enforcement to deter corporate crime. The basic goal of the functionalist is to reduce the disorganization in economic institutions and to improve the coordination between them and other social institutions. Only when this goal has been reached will the economic system function smoothly and efficiently.

The Conflict Perspective

Conflict theorists take a very different view of the economic system. Unlike functionalists, they do not consider society a unified whole based on a consensus about norms and values. Consequently, they do not say that the economic system performs either well or badly for the entire society. Rather, they believe that it benefits certain groups at the expense of others and that who benefits, and to what degree, changes from time to time.

From the conflict perspective, society is composed of many different groups, each trying to advance its economic interests at the expense of the others. Most economic problems arise because one group—or a coalition of groups—seizes economic power and acts in ways that advance its own interests at the expense of the rest of society. Thus, conflict theorists say that recent changes in the economic system reflect competition among different groups. They each work for their own selfish interests, as Adam Smith said they should. But conflict theorists do not, like Smith, assert that this competition brings advantages to everyone. They say it benefits only the most powerful competitive groups. Conflict theorists charge that ever since businesspeople and industrialists seized power from the landed nobility, they have busily enlarged their power and their affluence at the expense of everyone else.

According to the conflict perspective, the underlying cause of most economic problems is the exploitation of workers by their employers and other members of powerful elites. If these problems are to be solved, the workers must somehow gain enough control to make the elites give up their advantages and create a more just economic order. The first step, according to Marxists, is for oppressed workers to develop **class consciousness,** a sense of unity based on the realization that they are being exploited. Then the workers must organize themselves for political action and achieve change either through peaceful struggle—elections, protests, and strikes—or, if need be, through violent conflicts. Conflict theorists, whether Marxist or not, see the widening gap between the income of the "haves" and the "have-nots" as a direct result of the decline in the power of the unions and the failure of political organizations to represent the interests of working women and men. They feel that these trends must be reversed if most people are ever going to see their economic situation improve.

class consciousness
A sense of unity and awareness among the members of a social class.

The Feminist Perspective

When feminists look at recent developments in our economy and the role women have played, they see two important stories. The first is the enormous flexibility women have shown in adapting to a historic change in their economic role. In earlier years, women's primary economic contribution was in the home: doing housework and taking care of the children. But with the economic crisis of the 1970s, millions of women poured into the work force in order to help their families make ends meet. As a result, the position of women in our society underwent a fundamental transformation, and both women and men are still struggling to adjust. Today, the average mother not only handles most of the traditional homemaking and child-care responsibilities, but she puts in many long hours working outside the home as well.

The second story is one of continuity, not change. Unfortunately, that continuity lies in the economic exploitation of women. Although record numbers of women have entered the work force and many have entered traditionally male jobs, the fact remains that on the average, a woman is still paid only 75 cents for each dollar her male counterparts earn.

The solution to this problem lies in an attack on the barriers of prejudice and discrimination that still keep women second-class economic citizens. Changes in the educational system to encourage women to enter the highest-paying fields of study, tougher enforcement of antidiscrimination laws, and changes in the hostile attitudes many male workers have toward their female co-workers are just a few of the suggestions commonly made. In addition, the workplace needs to be made more "woman-friendly." The fact of the matter is that women still bear the major share of the responsibility of child rearing, and employers need to create more on-site day-care centers, allow more flexible working hours, and in general take a more supportive attitude toward their employees' families' needs.

The Interactionist Perspective

Because interactionists are concerned mainly with individuals and small groups, they rarely address large-scale economic problems directly. Instead, they are more interested in the impact of the economic system on an individual's psychological makeup, attitudes, and behavior patterns. They also examine the impact of these ways of behaving on the larger economic system. Interactionists and other social psychologists have found, for example, that unemployment has devastating psychological consequences for many workers. Feelings of boredom, uselessness, and despair are common, and some frustrated workers suffer much more serious difficulties. Studies show that the rates of such stress-related problems as high blood pressure, alcoholism, mental disorders, and suicide are significantly higher among the unemployed. Unemployed workers are also more likely to lash out at those around them. Research shows that a rise in unemployment increases the rate of child abuse and other family violence.[48]

But the psychological damage caused by the economic system is not limited to the unemployed. Our competitive economy encourages a strong achievement motivation that often leads to dissatisfaction and anxiety. When a large percentage of a population is oriented toward individual competition, the culture they share is likely to show many forms of innovation and creativity; but this system also promotes insecurity, fear, and aggression. Interactionists have observed, however, that these burdens are not equally shared by everyone in a society. On the average, the unskilled and downwardly mobile have far more social and psychological problems than other people. They are more likely to be hostile and withdrawn and to suffer from low self-esteem and bouts of intense anxiety.

Effective solutions to the psychological problems created by our economic system are not easy to find. One possibility would be to deemphasize the values of competition and achievement and to emphasize instead cooperation and mutual support. But despite the fact that such values have long been stressed in family and religious institutions, their application to society at large meets strong resistance. This opposition seems to be based on the fear that reducing competitiveness will destroy initiative and creativity. Perhaps this is why more emphasis is placed on the clinical treatment of psychological disorders than on changing the economic and social conditions that produce them. Many interactionists nonetheless continue to argue that reducing economic insecurity, even in a competitive society, would improve the mental health and well-being of our entire population.

Quick Review

What are the differences in the ways a functionalist, a conflict theorist, a feminist, and an interactionist would explain our economic problems?

Summary

Change has come so rapidly to our economic system that many people have difficulty seeing things as they really are. One common mistake is to look only at familiar events close to home and ignore the web of international relationships that make up the world economy. The principal dividing line in the modern world is between the wealthy industrialized nations and the poor agricultural nations. Although some poor nations have attempted to pull out of the capitalist world economy and rely on a centralized state plan to industrialize themselves, most of the nations that followed this communist system have now given it up or greatly modified it. All the rich industrialized nations practice one version or another of capitalism—although no nation adheres very closely to the ideals of the completely open free-market system advocated by Adam Smith. The economies that come closest to that ideal, such as the United States, are sometimes said to practice individualistic capitalism while the systems that emphasize more economic cooperation and government involvement practice communitarian capitalism.

The corporation is a major force in the modern economic system. Some corporations have grown so large that they control dozens of different companies in many countries. Although antitrust laws no longer permit most markets to be controlled by a monopoly (one corporation), many industries are dominated by an oligopoly (a few large corporations). There is considerable debate over who runs the corporations. Some people see stockholders as the owners and controllers, while others argue that power rests with corporate managers, who have the special technical skills needed to make effective decisions. Most sociologists hold that high-level corporate decision makers represent the interests of a small elite, but others suggest that the decision makers represent a wide variety of conflicting interests.

Most large corporations are multinationals; that is, they have offices and facilities in many different nations around the world. These big multinationals are tied in to the world market, and they often have little allegiance to the interests of their home country. Some think the multinationals are laying the foundation for a new era of world peace and cooperation, but others see them as exploiters of the poor and the powerless. Moreover, corporations often engage in criminal activities such as fraud and price-fixing in their own countries as well.

The government, like the corporations, has come to play a key role in the economic system. The government is not only a major employer but also is deeply involved in managing the economy.

With the "downsizing" of many corporations in recent times, small businesses have come to play an increasingly important role in the creation of jobs. However, conditions are difficult for many small businesses. Competition is generally much more intense than in the corporate sector, financial reserves are often inadequate, and unlike the corporate giants, small businesses seldom get a government bailout when they get into trouble.

Workers are at the heart of any industrial economy. Recent times have seen a sharp decline in the number of workers in farming and the old manufacturing industries, while service jobs have been on the increase. Unfortunately, most of the new jobs have been low-paying ones, and there is a growing shortage of attractive employment opportunities. Unemployment and underemployment remain significant problems. Another important trend is that women, especially married women, have been entering the work force in ever increasing numbers.

The United States is faced with several worrisome economic trends: a decline in average wages, growing economic insecurity, and a big increase in the gap between the haves and have-nots. Numerous explanations for this stagnation have been offered, including increased competition in the world economy, faltering American investment and productivity, and less abundant natural resources. Many proposals have also been made for dealing with this crisis, most of which focus on either rebuilding and improving the economy or adapting to the changing economic realities of our times. Functionalists seek to reduce economic disorganization. Conflict theorists call for the common people to ban together to demand a bigger share of the economic pie. Feminists see the need to end discrimination against women and make the workplace a friendlier place for mothers with children. Interactionists call for a greater concern with the personal problems caused by our competitive economic system.

Questions for Critical Thinking

There are many different ways we can evaluate our economic system. Economists tend to take the narrowest view and look simply at how much wealth it produces. Most sociologists think the question of how fairly wealth is distributed is often more important than how much wealth there is. Environmentalists focus their attention on the sustainability of the economic system: how much damage does it do to the environment, and does it consume resources faster than they can be replaced? Finally, from the broadest perspective, we might ask whether our economic system contributes to the overall sense of well-being and happiness of the people or whether it leaves them frustrated and unfulfilled. Do your own evaluation of our economic system in terms of each of these four viewpoints.

Key Terms

alienation
antitrust laws
blue-collar jobs
budget deficit
business cycle
capitalism
chief executive officer (CEO)
class consciousness
communism
communitarian capitalism

deregulation
discouraged workers
economic democracy
economic planning
fraud
individualistic capitalism
inflation
laissez-faire capitalism
lean production
monopoly

multinational corporations
oligopoly
price-fixing
productivity
real wages
service occupations
sustainable society

Third World, less developed countries
underemployment
unemployment
white-collar job
worker alienation
world economy

Further Readings

David Bensman and Roberta Lynch, *Rusted Dreams: Hard Times in a Steel Community* (New York: McGraw-Hill, 1987). An analysis of what happened in a Chicago neighborhood when its major employer closed its doors.

Jeffry A. Frieden and David A. Lake, *International Political Economy: Perspectives on Global Power and Wealth* (New York: St. Martin's Press, 1995). A comprehensive reader focusing on economic problems from a global perspective.

Beth Mintz and Michael Schwartz, *The Power Structure of American Business* (Chicago: University of Chicago Press, 1985). A careful analysis of the power structure of the United States that emphasizes the dominating role of banks and other financial institutions.

Lawrence Mishel, Jared Bernstein, and John Schmitt, *The State of Working America, 1996–97* (New York: Sharpe, 1997). An extremely comprehensive and well-organized presentation of facts and figures that paints a disturbing picture of the current conditions of working Americans.

Lester Thurow, *Head to Head: The Coming Economic Battle Among Japan, Europe, and America* (New York: Morrow, 1992). An insightful analysis of the economic differences among the world's leading industrialized nations and the conflicts they produce. Also contains some interesting proposals to help North Americans deal with this new economic environment.

Notes

1. Curtis Rist and Mark Dagostino, "Handy Lesson," *People*, October 6, 1997, pp. 79–80.
2. *World Population Data Sheet, 1997* (Washington, DC: Population Reference Bureau, 1997).
3. Adam Smith, *An Inquiry into the Nature and Causes of the Wealth of Nations* (New York: Random House, 1937 [originally pub. 1776]).
4. Ibid., p. 128.
5. Lester Thurow, Head to Head: *The Coming Economic Battle Among Japan, Europe, and America* (New York: Morrow, 1992), p. 32.
6. U.S. Bureau of the Census, *Statistical Abstract of the United States, 1996* (Washington, DC: U.S. Government Printing Office, 1996), pp. 554, 555.
7. See Thurow, *Head to Head.*
8. Lawrence Mishel, Jared Bernstein, and John Schmitt, *The State of Working America, 1996–97* (Armonk, NY: Sharpe, 1997), p. 10.
9. See Beth Mintz and Michael Schwartz, *The Power Structure of American Business* (Chicago: University of Chicago Press, 1985).
10. David R. James and Michael Soref, "Profit Constraints on Managerial Autonomy: Managerial Theory and the Unmaking of the Corporate President," *American Sociological Review* 46 (February 1981): 1–18.

11. Mishel, Bernstein, and Schmitt, *The State of Working America, 1996–97*, p. 7.

12. C. Wright Mills, *The Power Elite* (New York: Oxford University Press, 1956), p. 141.

13. Jonathan Schell, "Capital Is No Respecter of Ideologies," *Los Angeles Times,* June 17, 1991, p. B5.

14. Robert B. Reich, "The REAL Economy," *Atlantic,* February 1991, pp. 35–52.

15. Wayne D. Thompson, *Canada 1986* (Washington, DC: Stryker-Post, 1986), p. 106.

16. Ibid.

17. Volker Bornschier and Christopher Chase-Dunn, *Transnational Corporations and Development* (New York: Praeger, 1985).

18. James William Coleman, *The Criminal Elite: Understanding White Collar Crime,* 4th. ed. (New York: St. Martin's Press, 1998), pp. 80–85.

19. Ibid., pp. 76–77.

20. For a review of this and other studies on price-fixing, see Coleman, *The Criminal Elite,* pp. 51–53.

21. Morton Mintz and Jerry S. Cohen, *America, Inc.* (New York: Dial, 1971), p. 70.

22. Mishel, Bernstein, and Schmitt, *The State of Working America, 1996–97,* pp. 271–273.

23. Ibid., p. 271; Louis Uchitelle, "Newest Corporate Refugees, Self-Employed But Low-Paid," *New York Times,* November 15, 1993, pp. A1, C2.

24. U.S. Bureau of the Census, *Statistical Abstract, 1996,* p. 407.

25. Mishel, Bernstein, and Schmitt, *The State of Working America, 1996–97,* p. 185.

26. Ibid., p. 268.

27. U.S. Bureau of the Census, *Statistical Abstract, 1996,* p. 400.

28. Mishel, Bernstein, and Schmitt, *The State of Working America, 1996–97,* p. 243.

29. Ibid., p. 258.

30. Ibid., pp. 257–261.

31. David J. Cherrington, *The Work Ethic: Working Values and Values That Work* (New York: AMACOM, 1980).

32. Bob Baker, "Assembly Line Stress in Offices," *Los Angeles Times,* June 13, 1991, pp. A1, A28–A29.

33. Associated Press, "17 American Workers a Day Died on the Job During the 80s," *New York Times,* April 15, 1994, p. A8.

34. Coleman, *The Criminal Elite,* p. 10.

35. Ibid., pp. 70–71.

36. Steven Greenhouse, "Strikes Decrease to a 50-Year Low," *New York Times,* January 29, 1996, pp. A1, A10.

37. The most current data on wages come from Allen R. Myerson, "In Era of Belt-Tightening, Modest Gains for Workers," *New York Times,* February 13, 1997, pp. C1, C4; for much more detailed analysis of the trends, see Mishel, Bernstein, and Schmitt, *The State of Working America, 1996–97,* pp. 131–239. For data on health coverage, see p. 7.

38. Mishel, Bernstein, and Schmitt, *The State of Working America, 1996–97,* p. 285.

39. Ibid., pp. 253–257.

40. Thurow, *Head to Head,* p. 127.

41. Robert B. Reich, "The REAL Economy."

42. Ibid.

43. Thurow, *Head to Head,* p. 126.

44. Ibid., p. 138.

45. Mishel, Bernstein, and Schmitt, *The State of Working America, 1996–97,* p. 7.

46. Thurow, *Head to Head,* p. 161.

47. Adam Bryant, "Can Unions Run United Airlines?" *New York Times,* December 9, 1993, pp. C1, C5; Stuart Silverstein, "Wave of Employee Buyouts Due?" *Los Angeles Times,* December 17, 1993, pp. D1, D4.

48. M. Harvey Brenner, *Estimating the Cost of National Economic Policy,* U.S. Congress, Joint Economic Committee, 1976.

Problems of Government

Who runs the government?

How do the media influence the political process?

What are the threats to our civil liberties?

How big a problem is government corruption?

How can government be made more democratic?

Katherine Hicks broke into tears when she testified at the recent Senate hearing into the abuses of the Internal Revenue Service. The IRS, she said, had harassed her for 14 years because of an error in her master file, charged her thousands of dollars in interest for its own mistakes, and financially ruined her and her husband. "It was physically exhausting. We almost never slept. There were the visits to the attorneys and the accountants, their bills and their depressing advice: 'Pay it; it's cheaper than fighting.' My credit is completely destroyed. The IRS is judge, jury, and executioner— answerable to no one."[1] (IRS commissioner Michael Dolan, who was grilled relentlessly by the same committee, would be unlikely to agree with that last statement.)

Power is the essence of politics—the power to determine what is a criminal act and what is not, the power to start or avoid wars, the power to collect vast sums of money and spend them on everything from ballpoint pens to nuclear bombs. Those who wield that power regulate thousands of aspects of our daily lives—deciding how fast we can drive, what drugs we may take, even determining whom we may or may not marry. When that power is misused, innocent people like Katherine Hicks can suffer horrible consequences. But at the same time, that government power is an essential part of almost any serious effort to deal with our social problems. Even such personal issues as divorce and mental disorder have their political side, and it is hard to imagine any solution to such diverse problems as crime, poverty, environmental pollution, or urban decay without effective government action.

The critical question is therefore "Whose interests does the government serve?" Does it serve the narrow interests of its employees and officials, the interests of the wealthy and powerful, or the interests of society as a whole? There are almost endless examples of powerful special-interest groups that have blocked policies that are in the best interests of the nation and the vast majority of its citizens. Yet a government that truly represents the interests of the people is the key to mounting an effective response to the numerous problems discussed in the pages of this book, and the bedrock upon which all our civil liberties are built.

The Growth of Government

Governments throughout the world have been growing rapidly since the beginning of this century. In 1929, the year of the great stock market crash, there were a little more than 3 million government employees in the United States; today there are over 19 million. Of course, the country's population was also increasing, but the percentage of the total work force employed by the government still rose from 6.5 to around 16 percent. The often heard accusation that there has been runaway growth in the size of the government in recent years is false, however. There has actually been a small decline in the percentage of the labor force employed by the government since 1980,[2] and although there is some variation from year to year, the share of our national income that funds state and federal government hasn't changed much since the early 1970s.[3]

The influence of government on the daily lives of its citizens has grown along with its size. In past centuries, most centralized governments were distant and ineffective. Important decisions were made locally and were based on long-standing customs and traditions. Today, governments are much stronger, and they are less tightly bound by traditional restraints. Most of this growth in size and influence has been a response to changes in other social institutions. For example, as the family became smaller and less stable, the government had to assume some of the functions that families once performed, such as ensuring some minimum financial support for the poor and the elderly. Similarly, as the contemporary system of industrial capitalism developed, it proved to be highly unstable, swinging from times of booming prosperity to deep depression. Even in the United States, with its deep suspicion of centralized authority, the federal government has been forced to get involved in regulating and directing the economy.

bureaucracy
A form of social organization characterized by a division of labor, a hierarchy of authority, a set of formal rules, impersonal enforcement of rules, and job security.

When most people think about the growth of government, they think about the growth of **bureaucracy.** The huge labyrinth of federal offices and bureaus in the United States is certainly one of the largest bureaucracies that ever existed; but from a sociological standpoint, most private corporations are just as bureaucratic. In fact, one researcher concluded that over 90 percent of all American workers are employed in some kind of bureaucratic organization.[4] What, then, is a bureaucracy? A bureaucracy is simply a formal organization in which the members perform specialized tasks and are regulated by a hierarchy of authority and a set of formal rules.[5]

Everyone seems to complain about bureaucratic waste. However, Max Weber, the great German sociologist, argued that because bureaucracies are based on rational rules that treat everyone with the same impersonal objectivity, they are actually

Both public and private bureaucracies have grown rapidly in the last century, and many people complain about their inefficiency and rigidity.

the most stable and efficient form of organization.[6] The very strengths of a bureaucracy can also be its weakness, however. The formal rules that permit a government agency to function smoothly can also drown it in a sea of red tape. No system of rules is perfect. When unusual cases occur, it may be necessary to bend the rules to meet an organization's goals, but meeting those goals is not the only concern of employees. Most workers place a higher priority on holding on to their jobs, and because they can be fired for breaking rules, the tendency is to play it safe. Employees try to give at least the appearance of following all the rules, regardless of the consequences for the organization. For example, a welfare worker may know that a family is needy and deserves government assistance but is ineligible because of some technicality. An employee who is afraid to violate the rules "passes the buck" by sending the applicant to another office. At the next office, the applicant may be referred to someone else, and so on through the bureaucratic maze—while the family goes hungry. Such **goal displacement** is extremely common in bureaucracies, both in the government and in private industry.[7] Moreover, bureaucracies often become a powerful political force in themselves, lobbying for programs and policies that may not be in the public interest. Even Max Weber was concerned about the depersonalizing effects of bureaucratization. He came to fear that the unending drive for bureaucratic efficiency would imprison people in what he called the "iron cage" of reason, with little room for human emotions.

goal displacement
The tendency of bureaucracies to substitute informal goals for the official objectives of the organization.

Quick Review

Why has the government grown so large?

What is a bureaucracy, and how does it operate?

Who Runs the Government?

There is no more controversial topic in the social sciences than the question of who really runs the government, and its enormous growth only makes that issue more important. Most governments say they are democratic; but does power really reside in the people, or is it in the hands of special-interest groups, an exclusive power elite, or the government bureaucrats and officeholders themselves? An enormous amount of research has been done on this critical issue over the years, and we will begin our discussion with a look at the major theories these researchers have developed.

elitists
Those who believe that industrial nations are ruled by a small elite class.

Three Theoretical Approaches

Sociologists who have studied this issue generally fall into one of three theoretical camps. Perhaps the most popular theory is that of the **elitists,** who hold that government policy is shaped by a small and relatively unified power elite. A second group sees the government as being far more democratic. These **pluralists** feel that the key government decisions are determined by competition among many different interest groups and that no single group predominates. The newest approach is

pluralists
Those who believe that decisions in industrialized nations are made by a democratic process involving changing coalitions among many different interest groups.

structuralists
Those who believe that the structure of capitalist society forces the government to support and protect the interests of a privileged few.

that of the structuralists. Like the elitists, the **structuralists** take the view that government decisions reflect the interests of the privileged few, but they see the government as having far more independent power than do the elitists.

The Elitists   Radicals have long argued that America is dominated by a small group of powerful men, but it was C. Wright Mills's book *The Power Elite,* published in the 1950s, that started much of the current debate about who runs the government. According to Mills, the power elite is a coalition of people in the highest ranks of the economy, the government, and the military who together form a unified and self-conscious social class:

> There is no longer, on the one hand, an economy and, on the other hand, a political world, containing a military establishment unimportant to politics and to money-making. There is a political economy numerously linked with military order and decision. This triangle of power is now a structural fact, and it is the key to any understanding of the higher circles in America today. For as each of these domains has coincided with the others, as decisions in each have become broader, the leading men of each—the high military, the corporation executive, the political directorate—have tended to come together to form the power elite of America.[8]

According to Mills, one of the major sources of the unity of the power elite is its members' common social background. They tend to come from upper-class and upper-middle-class white families living in urban areas. They attend the same Ivy League colleges and, by and large, share the same attitudes toward the world and their position in it. In addition, the social networks that they represent are closely interconnected, with many common interests. Finally, although the power elite does not represent some great conspiracy, its members meet both socially and professionally and often coordinate their activities.

Below the power elite, Mills saw two other levels of power in American society. At the bottom of the heap are the great masses of people—unorganized, ill-informed, and virtually powerless. Between these masses and the elite are the "middle levels" of power, where some true competition between interest groups still exists. Mills saw the U.S. Congress as part of these middle levels of power. Although Congress decides some minor issues, the power elite ensures that no serious challenge to its control is tolerated in the political arena.

The work started by Mills has been carried on by G. William Domhoff and other contemporary elite theorists.[9] These researchers all accept Mills's conclusion that power is concentrated in the hands of the few, but they question his inclusion of the military leadership in the power elite. Although they recognize the importance of the military, they are convinced that the most critical decisions, even in the field of international relations, are made by an economic-political elite. This elite is not, however, an equal partnership between top corporate and top government officials. The lion's share of the power is held by those in key positions of corporate power. Not only do they greatly outnumber powerful government officials, but they also possess far more wealth, and their careers are not dependent on the uncertainties of the electoral process.

The Pluralists   Pluralists believe that democratic societies are indeed democratic. Although they recognize that there is a large apolitical mass with little power, they argue that critical political decisions are not made by a single power elite but are decided in a contest among many competing groups. David Riesman, a pluralist writing at about the same time as Mills, arrived at some very different conclusions. He called interest groups "veto groups" because he thought their main objective was merely to block policies that might threaten their interests.[10] Where Mills saw common interests among powerful groups, Riesman saw divergence; where Mills saw growing concentration of power, Riesman saw growing dispersion of power.

Current pluralist thought runs along the lines taken by Riesman. However, his idea that interest groups are mainly concerned with stopping legislation they dislike is no longer widely accepted. Arnold M. Rose, a sociologist who was also a state legislator, pointed out the obvious fact that interest groups also take action on their own behalf. According to Rose:

> [The pluralist] conceives of society as consisting of many elites, each relatively small numerically, and operating in different spheres of life. . . . While it is true that there are inert masses of undifferentiated individuals without access to each other (except in the most trivial respects) and therefore without influence, the bulk of the population consists not of the mass but of integrated groups and publics, stratified with varying degrees of power.[11]

The pluralists emphasize the importance of the role of government officials in transforming all those diverse interests into some kind of coherent public policy. Competing interest groups argue, negotiate, and compromise. At critical points in the decision-making process, public opinion and the common values shared by the citizenry and participants in the political process often tip the scales in favor of the public interest. Thus, though it is far from perfect, the pluralists still see the political system as a truly democratic process.[12]

The Structuralists   The newest theory about who runs the government comes from a group of thinkers known as the structuralists. Like the elitists, they take a conflict perspective on society, and they too believe that key government decisions are made to serve the interests of the few, not the many. However, the structuralists differ from the elitists on two important points. While many elitists have focused their work on the ways members of the elite work to influence government policy, structuralists such as Nicos Poulantzas argue that the upper class does not need to be involved in the political process.[13] They believe that the structure of capitalist societies forces the government to protect the interests of the upper class or risk the collapse of the whole system.

The structuralists criticize the elitists' view of the relationship between the government and the upper class in another way as well. They charge that the elitists see the government as nothing more than a passive instrument used by the power elite to advance their own interests. To the structuralists, the government and its officials are an independent power group in their own right. Theda Skocpol's analysis of three of the most important revolutions in recent world history, for example, concluded that before each of those revolutions, government leaders became involved in a costly international quest for power and prestige that was harmful to the economic interests of the upper class.[14] Although the structuralists see the government as capable of taking autonomous action independent of the upper class, it is only a *relative autonomy.* In the short run, the government may move against the desires of the upper class in order to stave off popular discontent or to advance its own interests; but in the long run, it must work to promote the interests of the capitalist system and those in its key positions of economic power, or it risks being over-thrown or seeing the collapse of the whole system.

The Political Process: Citizens and Special Interests

In order to evaluate these theories, we must turn our attention to the concrete operations of the political process. As most of us learned in our high school government classes, in an ideal democracy political power is shared equally by all citizens. Virtually no sociologists or political scientists feel that we actually have such a system, however. One of the major problems of any would-be democracy is the apathy of its citizens (see Figure 5.1). The number of Americans who vote has never been high, and it has declined significantly since the 1960s.[15] Only about 49 percent of the voting-age population actually voted in the 1996 presidential election, and less than 40 percent voted in the congressional election two years before.[16] Other forms of political participation, such as working in a political campaign or taking part in a political rally, are even less common than voting.

Of course, it is not necessary for all the citizens in a democracy to participate if those who do are representative of those who do not; but this is not the case. Studies of citizen participation reveal a strange paradox. Those who most need the government's help are least likely to take part in the political process. People with higher incomes and more education are much more likely to be politically active,

Figure 5.1

Voter Turnout

Although the United States has a long history of democratic government, its voters tend to be more apathetic than those in other industrialized nations.

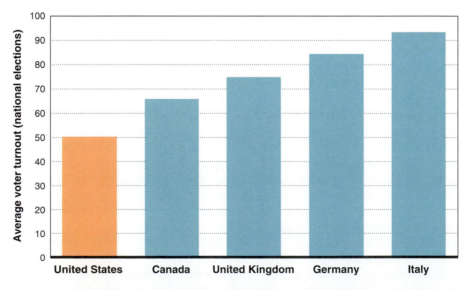

Source: Andrew L. Shapiro, *We're Number One: Where America Stands—and Falls—in the New World Order* (New York: Vintage, 1992), p. 106.

while minorities and the poor are less likely to get involved.[17] Thus, it seems that wealth and education create the interest and the resources necessary for political participation. Another source of voter apathy is distrust of the government and a general feeling of powerlessness. Many people do not think their votes or opinions count for much against the powerful special-interest groups and the huge number of other voters. A single vote, the argument goes, is almost never decisive in even the closest election.

Even citizens who are interested in politics often find it difficult to decide where a particular politician stands on the issues (see Personal Perspectives below). For one thing, politicians often try to conceal their opinions about controversial matters. In addition, the voters seldom get a chance to talk directly with candidates, relying instead on the mass media for information. Effective campaigners try to project a positive image in their advertising and television speeches, which often have little to do with the issues. Advertising agencies sell candidates in the same way they sell soap or deodorant. In a 30-second television commercial, there is little time for serious consideration of political issues. Moreover, candidates of minor political parties and those without strong financial backing have little access to the media and are thus frozen out of the arena of serious political debate.

The media have influence, however, far beyond their role in political advertising. As Thomas R. Dye, a well-known political scientist, puts it: "The media determine what the masses talk about. . . . Political issues do not just 'happen.' The media decides what are issues, problems, even crises, which must be acted upon."[18] Moreover, control of the media is concentrated in relatively few hands. Four huge media corporations account for 80 percent of the news and entertainment broadcasts on television. Most of America's 1700 or so daily newspapers receive news from the Associated Press wire service, and the 15 largest newspaper conglomerates account for over half the total newspaper circulation in the country.[19]

Personal Perspectives   A Member of the House of Representatives

Politics is like any other profession. The longer you stay in the profession, the better you learn how to do your job. In this excerpt, a former Republican congressman lets us in on some of the conventional wisdom among elected officials that may help explain some of the problems of today's government.

> The name recognition factor alone, coupled with the apathy and disinterest of most voters, should be sufficient to ensure the incumbent congressman's reelection year after year—with one exception. Here lies the rub. The exception to success in my profession occurs when an incumbent takes a position or casts a vote which a competent opponent can use to stir public apathy by creating strong feelings *against* the incumbent. As several elderly congressmen are wont to tell newly elected colleagues, "No man has ever been defeated on the basis of what he *didn't* say." The penalties in the profession of politics are applied to those who attempt to lead, take controversial positions and, most of all, allow those controversial positions to become known to their constituents.*

*Former Representative Paul N. McCloskey, Jr., *Truth and Untruth: Political Deceit in America* (New York: Simon & Schuster, 1972).

Despite all the obstacles, average citizens do sometimes band together into a social movement that wields significant power. One good example is the environmental movement. Although factory owners, land developers, and automobile manufacturers saw nothing wrong with their polluting activities, a growing environmental crisis was obvious to average citizens when they looked around their communities. Activists began forming organizations and planning protests, meetings, and demonstrations. They eventually won sympathetic media attention and came to wield significant influence on the political process.

One of the most important forces influencing legislators and other government officials is the so-called **special-interest group**—an organized group that has a stake in a particular piece of legislation. Physicians, real estate developers, small businesses, big businesses, labor unions, and numerous others are all special-interest groups. The most common concern of such groups is financial; they actively promote legislation that will help make them money and oppose legislation that will increase their costs. People who feel strongly about a particular issue also form organizations on more idealistic grounds, for example, civil rights and peace groups. The influence of these groups depends to a large extent on their size, their degree of organization, and the money at their disposal. Big business is clearly the most powerful of all interest groups because it has command of more of those resources.

The effort of special-interest groups to influence lawmakers is known as **lobbying,** and it is one of their principal activities. Lobbyists aim to convince lawmakers to pass the kind of legislation the groups desire. One of their most effective tools is information: because individual legislators are seldom well informed about all the bills they must consider, and because legislative bodies lack the funds to make independent investigations of all the issues before them, the facts and figures supplied by lobbyists can often sway lawmakers' votes. Lobbyists also try to influence legislation by cultivating the friendship of individual legislators. Many well-heeled lobbyists are notorious for their lavish parties and their ingratiating manner. Moreover, a lobbyist's promise of political support from a powerful special interest often determines an elected official's decisions. Threats by a special-interest group can be effective too. Opposition by a powerful labor union or an important corporation has resulted in the defeat of many politicians.

Money is one of the special-interest groups' main resources. Political campaigns are becoming more and more expensive, and the special interests are supplying the money. As recently as 1960, the price tag of an average congressional campaign was only about $25,000, but in the 1996 election, the average race for the House of Representatives cost about $550,000 and the average Senate rate cost almost $3 million (see Figure 5.2). If you add up all the money spent by the candidates, the parties, and other political groups, it came to $2.2 billion![20] One of the main sources of funding is the political action committees (PACs) set up to represent various special-interest groups. And, of course, many individual contributions come from people with a particular interest in a specific policy or program.

Politicians inevitably claim that such contributions are merely a sign of support from those who favor their policies and that money has no influence on their votes, but few outside observers find such statements convincing. It is too simplistic to say that most politicians overtly sell favors and influence for campaign contributions (although periodic corruption scandals show that some certainly do), but those millions of dollars often exert a dominating influence on the political process.

In theory, the ability of special interests to hire lobbyists and make campaign contributions that help elect sympathetic politicians wouldn't make much differ-

special-interest group
An organized group of people who have a stake in a particular area of public policy.

lobbying
The activities of special-interest groups intended to influence government decision makers.

Figure 5.2
Running for Office
The cost of running for public office increased enormously in recent years.

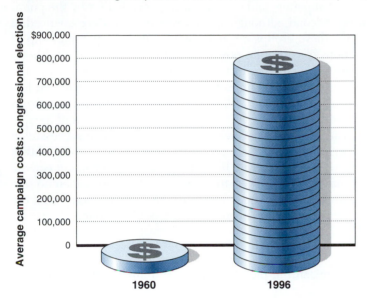

Source: New York Times, November 25, 1997, p. A12; Theodore Caplow, *American Social Trends* (San Diego: Harcourt Brace Jovanovich, 1991), p. 114.

ence as long as supporters on both sides of important issues had roughly the same amount of money to spend; but that is clearly not the case. Corporations give far more than labor unions, polluters give more than environmentalists, big businesses more than small businesses, and Republicans more than Democrats.[21] Obviously, the poor and the underprivileged will never be able to spend as much money to advance their political interests as the wealthy do, just as broadly based "general-interest" groups such as environmentalists and consumer advocates are unable to match the financial power of the big corporations whose policies they oppose.

The general public is largely unaware of another important influence on government policy—the major foundations and civic associations. Large foundations such as the Ford Foundation and the Kellogg Foundation receive their money from donations by corporations and individuals of great wealth, and they use it, among many other things, to fund research on various social issues. The most influential policy-planning groups, such as the Council on Foreign Relations and the Business Roundtable, also generally represent the viewpoint of the established elites, and together with researchers from major universities who are funded by the foundations, they analyze public issues and make policy recommendations to the government. Because these groups provide much of the brainpower behind government policy, they exert a significant influence over its long-term direction.[22]

An Appraisal

As we have seen, the political process is a complex and multifaceted one. None of the major theoretical approaches offers all the answers, but some basic conclusions about the way the process operates do seem justified. First, numerous competing interest groups, including government officials themselves, take part in the struggle to shape government policy. These groups form shifting patterns of alliances on different issues, cooperating, competing, and compromising as called for by the political realities of their times. Second, although many diverse groups are involved in shaping political decisions, these groups are not equals. One group—made up of those who hold key positions of corporate power and/or great personal wealth—is far more powerful than any of the others. In normal times, this elite dominates the decision-making process on most of the important questions of economic and foreign policy. Third, despite all this, it would still be wrong to say that average citizens have no political power. In times of crisis, catastrophe, and mass discontent, people often band together in social movements, which on occasion have been successful in forcing fundamental changes in government policies and even in the political process itself. And fourth, there are concrete limits to what the government can do. In times of crisis, government may be forced to carry out policies for which no sector of society has much enthusiasm, and the demands of the world economy limit the choices available to any individual nation, even a rich and powerful one.

Quick Review

Describe the differences between the pluralist, elitist, and structuralist theories of government.

Which theory do you think is most convincing?

The Dilemmas of Government

The most basic problem of democratic government is democracy itself: how to fairly represent the will of the people. As we have just seen, contemporary government does not do a very good job with this fundamental task. In this section, we will examine some of the other major problems of government—preventing scandals and corruption, maintaining civil liberties, dealing with military issues, and deciding who is to bear the burden and receive the benefits of government policies. The fundamental need for a more democratic government underlies all these other issues, however, and will appear again and again in our discussion.

Scandals and Corruption

Most people see the problem of government corruption in personal terms: crooked politicians getting rich or getting reelected by dishonest means. But it is far more than that, for government corruption strikes at the heart of democracy itself. The more control the influence peddlers and the corrupt interests have over government policy, the less control the people have.

Government officials can be corrupted in many ways that are completely legal. The biggest problem comes from the system of campaign financing we have already discussed. It is clearly a crime to pay a politician to vote for a certain bill or to perform some other political favor, but it is perfectly legal to give large campaign contributions to that same politician and then to ask her or him to vote in the way you want—as long as no one acknowledges that the contributions were made in exchange for the vote. The fact that our politicians must carry on a continual quest for financial gifts to pay for their election campaigns creates a built-in **conflict of interest** every time a bill favored by one of their major contributors comes up for a vote.

Another way successful politicians can reward their campaign workers and contributors is with a government job. In the nineteenth century, most government jobs were handed out in exchange for contributions and support in what came to be known as the **spoils system.** Since then, civil service reforms have sharply reduced the number of jobs officeholders can give out as political patronage, but the practice still continues. A new president, for example, must appoint thousands of people to government positions, and it is accepted practice to give most of those jobs to friends and political supporters.

A different kind of conflict of interest occurs when officeholders decide an issue in which they have a personal financial interest. For example, the House of Representatives recently reprimanded one of its members for concealing his investment in an industrial company and then voting for a bill that granted it a lucrative government contract.[23] But the issues are not always that clear-cut. Most established politicians have considerable personal wealth, and it is almost inevitable that some of the wide-ranging decisions they are called on to make will influence their investments in one way or another. This dilemma could be avoided if officeholders would place their financial investments in a "blind trust" managed by a third party, but few politicians actually do so.

Most conflicts of interest fall into the gray area between the unethical and the illegal. There is no question, however, that outright **bribery** is still a serious problem. In earlier times, when only a small group of landholders could vote, the main problem was the bribery of the voters by politicians. In the 1757 race for the Virginia House of Burgesses, for example, George Washington was accused of giving out 50 gallons of rum, 24 gallons of wine, 46 gallons of beer, and 2 gallons of cider in a district that had only 391 voters![24] Today, of course, the bribe money normally flows in the opposite direction. Political bribery is probably most widespread at the state and local level, often involving zoning changes or the award of government contracts. But no one really knows how common bribery at any level really is. There have, of course, been numerous scandals over the years, but how much bribery goes undetected is anybody's guess. Some even claim that investigators sometimes inadvertently create the crimes they are supposed to prevent. For example, in the so-called Abscam case, FBI agents claimed to be working for an Arab sheik in need of some Washington favors. The agents handed out bribes to eight officeholders and subsequently arrested them. Critics of such operations (which are more commonly carried on against state and local officials) claim the agents are simply creating crime by tempting honest officeholders to break the law; others feel that the relative ease with which they find officials who will take their bribes indicates a high level of government corruption.[25]

Although conflicts of interest from campaign fund-raising are as much of a problem as they have ever been, other forms of government corruption are probably less common than they were in the past. New laws requiring fuller financial disclosure by officeholders, a new interest among law enforcement officials in investigating and prosecuting corruption cases, and most importantly, ever more stringent media scrutiny have made it harder for elected officials to get away with illegal schemes.

conflict of interest
The ethical dilemma that occurs when an officeholder's official duty and his or her personal interests conflict.

spoils system
A political system in which government jobs and favors are handed out in exchange for political support.

bribery
Giving officials money or some other reward in order to influence the way they carry out their duties.

But there has been a heavy price to pay for the media's growing interest in political misbehavior. Some of the famous corruption cases of recent years, such as Watergate and the Iran-Contra scandal, involved important issues concerning the misuse of government power, but an insatiable appetite for scandal has led the media to focus more and more attention on politicians' sex lives and other personal matters that have little or nothing to do with their performance in office. An increasing number of elections seem to turn on the success the two sides have in digging up and publicizing dirt about their opponents. Political contests driven by scandal instead of real differences over the issues can hardly be expected to produce a representative government that truly reflects the will of the people. Moreover, the media's willingness to splash every detail of a politician's private life across the headlines and the increasingly negative stereotypes about government leaders in general are discouraging many talented people from pursuing careers in public service.

Growing Public Cynicism

A closely related problem is the rise in public cynicism. The opinion polls, for example, show that Americans' confidence in their government has plummeted in recent years. In 1995, only 1 in 10 Americans queried by pollsters said that they had a great deal of confidence in Congress or the presidency—yet only about two decades earlier those numbers were twice as high.[26] Today, many Americans look at their

The media used to respect the privacy of political figures, but now even the most intimate details about their sex lives are often splashed across the headlines. As a result, more and more elections are being decided by scandals and sensational accusations instead of the political issues, and many people are deciding against entering careers in public service.

government as unresponsive, bureaucratic, and inefficient and see those who work in it as self-serving and often corrupt. Antigovernment feelings have reached a frenzied pitch among some extreme conservatives who engage in outright terrorism such as the bombing of a federal government office building in Oklahoma City, killing over a hundred people.

Of course, a reasonable skepticism about the government and its policies is a healthy thing in a democracy. As we have seen, government corruption *is* a serious problem, and more importantly, the wealthy and powerful *do* often trample over the interests of the majority. But when skepticism turns into the kind of corrosive cynicism that sees no possibilities for improvement, the result is likely to be a growing sense of apathy and indifference that only makes those problems worse.

Why has the public's opinion of government fallen so dramatically in the last few decades? There is no reason to believe that the government has gotten less democratic or more corrupt; in fact, just the opposite is probably true (see, for example, the Signs of Hope box in this chapter). The changes seem to be less in what the government is doing as in the way the public perceives it, and much of that can be attributed to the media. In the past, the media had a much cozier relationship to the government and were usually content to present the official version of the news. President Roosevelt was virtually never shown in his wheelchair or on his crutches for fear it might make the nation's leader look weak, and although numerous reporters knew about extramarital affairs carried on by various national leaders, such as Presidents Eisenhower and Kennedy, they never mentioned these affairs in the press. A new era of investigative reporting has shed valuable light on numerous corrupt and undemocratic practices, but it has also fanned the flames of public cynicism. It would, however, be unfair to lay the whole problem on the media, for in many ways they merely reflect changes in our overall society, which is far more educated, more sophisticated, and more skeptical than at any time in the past.

The Military Dilemma

The military poses a dilemma in all democratic societies: it is essential but at the same time extremely dangerous. With its traditions of command, authority, and unquestioning obedience, the military often responds when disorganization and confusion paralyze an elected government. The list of struggling democracies that have been taken over by their military is a long one, particularly in the less developed countries of Asia, Africa, and Latin America. Developed countries with long democratic traditions—such as Great Britain, Canada, the United States, and Switzerland—are in little danger of a direct military takeover, but even these nations face the danger of growing too dependent on the military, both politically and economically.

A military force is, of course, necessary for national defense. The critical question is how much of the government's budget should be spent for this purpose. Different nations answer this question in different ways. The United States spends a high percentage of its income on its military, while Japan and Germany, with similar economic and political systems, spend comparatively little.

One point is clear, however. Although military spending can give a temporary boost to a lagging economy, serious long-range damage results. Most military products have no practical use unless there is a war: you can't eat them, wear them, or live in them. Moreover, military research and development take scientific talent away from more productive civilian research. As noted in Chapter 4, the military burden borne by the American economy is often cited as an important part of the reason the United States has grown less competitive with such nations as Germany and Japan. Many historians believe that the heavy military burden borne by Great Britain in the nineteenth century was a major cause of its economic decline and that the same thing may be happening to the United States today.

Why does the United States spend so much on its military? The prolonged struggle of World War II, closely followed by the Cold War with the Soviet Union and the Korean and Vietnam conflicts, left the United States with enormous military commitments and a vision of itself as the world's military and political leader. After each of those conflicts was resolved and draftees returned to civilian life, the military establishment ended up larger and more expensive. Even after we control for inflation, the United States now spends more on its military than it did at the height of the war in Vietnam. Today, after the collapse of the Soviet Union decimated the only military force capable of challenging U.S. global dominance, America's military outlays are still over $300 billion a year. Almost 3 million Americans are on active duty or in the military reserves,[27] and millions of others work in civilian industries supplying the military with the goods and services it requires.

Given the enormous size and economic strength of the American military, it is not surprising that many observers have expressed concern about its influence in a democratic society. One of the most unexpected warnings came from President Dwight D. Eisenhower, a career army officer. In his farewell address, President

The military always poses a dilemma in a democratic society. On the one hand, it is essential for the protection of society, but on the other, its traditions of obedience and conformity can pose a threat to democratic institutions.

Eisenhower warned against the influence of the **military-industrial complex** and the growing interdependence between the military and the giant corporations. Such companies as United Technologies and Lockheed Martin are not owned by the military, but their profits come largely from military contracts. Hundreds of other companies also sell a substantial percentage of their products to the military, so corporations and the armed forces have many interests in common. The military has its own lobbyists, who wield tremendous influence in Washington. They are often assisted by lobbyists for organized labor, which sees military spending as an important source of jobs, and by lobbyists for corporations, which see military spending as good business. Even if there were no military lobbyists, senators and representatives from states with high concentrations of military bases or defense industries would still be vigorous supporters of military appropriations. Although all this does not add up to military control of the American government, the military-industrial complex obviously has enormous influence and power.

> **military-industrial complex**
> The powerful interest group formed by the military and the civilian corporations that supply it with services, materials, and equipment.

Now that the Cold War is over, many new questions about the American military role in the world must now be faced. Supporters of the military-industrial complex argue for continuing military spending at current or even higher levels, claiming that the world is just as dangerous a place as it was before the collapse of the Soviet Union. However, many people find it hard to see how nations such as Iran or North Korea, with little technological sophistication and even less money, can pose a realistic threat to the United States—a nation shielded by two enormous oceans, with the world's largest economy and its most devastating nuclear arsenal. Since the Cold War is over, common sense would seem to tell us that America's military burden must be reduced to something more similar to that of its major economic competitors, but that is no easy task. Not only has the military-industrial complex gained enormous political power over the last fifty years, but a large sector of the American economy has come to depend on military spending. If the U.S. military were suddenly slashed back to a size comparable to the military of Germany or Japan, there would be a devastating economic shock.

Many social scientists therefore believe that what is necessary is a carefully thought out program of **defense conversion** to redirect corporations and workers from military to civilian work. Some military technologies are already being put to civilian purposes. For example, the global satellite system the U.S. military created to enable its soldiers to instantly find their location anywhere in the world is now forming the basis for a whole new industry that will be putting computer navigation devices in passenger cars. Advocates of defense conversion argue that the federal government must make a more concerted effort to encourage such transfers of technology, fund retraining programs for defense workers, and provide financial subsidies to help defense contractors find new civilian markets in the global economy. By itself, however, such an effort will still not be enough to head off major economic damage to local communities when a military base must be closed or the production of a expensive weapon system stopped. Any effective program to redirect national resources from military to civilian purposes must therefore provide help for such beleaguered communities as well.

> **defense conversion**
> Changing corporations and workers from military to civilian work.

Freedom or Oppression?

Of all the dilemmas confronting modern government, none is more important than the issue of how to protect personal freedom while still maintaining social order.

The fear that the government and the big corporations want to control every aspect of our lives and strip us of our basic human rights is shared by people from many walks of life. The nightmare that could come from a fusion of technology and totalitarianism, depicted in such books as George Orwell's *1984* and Aldous Huxley's *Brave New World*, has haunted the Western world for fifty years.

Lists of human rights usually include freedoms of speech, assembly, and movement and the right to privacy, autonomy, and political expression. The ideas embodied in these noble generalizations are, however, difficult to put into practice. The expression of one person's rights may interfere with the rights of another and the needs of the entire society, and there is always someone to claim that "the common good" or "the general welfare" requires the suppression of all individual freedom.

The list of systematic violations of individual liberties is tragically long, even in democratic countries. One famous example is the anticommunist "witch-hunts" that took place in the United States in the 1950s. The hysterical search for communist subversives led to the **blacklisting** and professional ruin of many people whose only offense was belonging to the "wrong" political organization or holding an unpopular opinion. A more recent example comes from Canada, another country with a long democratic tradition. When two prominent Canadians were kidnapped in 1970 by members of a group seeking independence for the province of Quebec, the national government invoked the War Measures Act, thereby suspending civil liberties. Membership in or support for the group responsible for the kidnapping was forbidden, and about 490 "separatist sympathizers" were rounded up and jailed. Of these, 435 were eventually released without ever being charged with a crime. Polls indicated that the Canadian people clearly approved the use of the War Measures Act, just as the American people had approved of the anticommunist crusades.[28]

Watergate, one of the biggest political scandals in American history, involved a different sort of violation of civil liberties. President Nixon's White House was not riding a wave of popular fear and resentment but rather was working behind a cloak of official secrecy to harass and silence its political opponents. Among other crimes, the Watergate scandal involved burglaries of the offices of political groups, including the Democratic party, and the use of illegal wiretaps and listening devices, tax audits, and false rumors against those on the "enemies list" put together by the White House. Once the scandal began to come to light, administration officials perjured themselves, paid bribes, and destroyed evidence in order to obstruct the investigation.[29]

Similar tactics were used by several presidential administrations to try to undercut the civil rights movement and crush opposition to the war in Vietnam. Evidence that came to light years later shows that the FBI and other government agencies used burglaries and a variety of illegal surveillance techniques to gather information. They even engaged in a direct campaign of political harassment and repression. Phony letters were sent to the friends and families of political activists, accusing them of everything from embezzlement to cheating on their spouses; false stories were planted in the media; police were urged to arrest activists on minor charges; utilities were encouraged to shut off their services; and some activists were attacked and even killed by people acting under government sponsorship. Such illegal activities tapered off after the end of the war and the collapse of the militant organizations the government had targeted. But the bits and pieces of information that occasionally leaked out show that the government's surveillance and harassment of American citizens continued long after the end of the Vietnam war.[30]

blacklisting
The practice of denying employment and economic opportunities to people because of their political views.

Along with the government, many private corporations now pose their own threat to civil liberties. For one thing, many companies are using a host of new techniques to peer into the private lives of their employees. This trend began with the use of the polygraph machine (lie detector) to screen job applicants and ferret out employee theft. In 1988, when a new law banned most involuntary polygraph tests,[31] corporations jumped on a new bandwagon—drug testing. A study by the American Management Association found that 63 percent of the companies surveyed had some kind of drug-testing program,[32] and other research has found that 70 percent of companies do background checks on new employees, about 50 percent examine their police records, and around 20 percent administer some kind of psychological test.[33] Supreme Court decisions have also given employers almost unlimited freedom to eavesdrop on their workers' conversations, and one study by *MacWorld* magazine found that 22 percent of the firms surveyed admitted carrying on searches of employees' computer files, voice mail, or other electronic records.[34] A different sort of invasion of workers' privacy comes from employers' attempts to avoid the rising costs of health care benefits. Not only do some companies refuse to hire smokers (who have more health problems than nonsmokers), but current employees have actually been fired for off-the-job smoking. There is also increasing job discrimination against the overweight (who are presumed to have more health problems) and homosexuals (who are seen as more likely to fall victim to AIDS).

Private firms pose a threat to more than just their employees, however, and with the proliferation of new technologies for gathering and retrieving information, privacy seems to be in danger of becoming a thing of the past. Private database firms now have cross-referenced lists of the U.S. population that include everything from the value of a family's home to their children's ages. Open databases with names such as Sleuth, Asset Locator, and People Finder allow the curious to search out the private details of their friends' and neighbors' lives. And while the convenience and portability of the cellular phone has made it a worldwide success, cellular calls are far easier for a nosy outsider to monitor. One expert estimated that 60 percent of cell-phone calls in California's Silicon Valley were being taped. With the proliferation of video surveillance cameras, it has become more and more difficult to be anonymous even in public places. Denver's new international airport, for example, has no fewer than 1500 surveillance cameras. Such equipment is now in common use in bank lobbies and parking lots and near automatic teller machines.[35]

It is hardly surprising that people of all political persuasions are becoming concerned about the threat that the use of technology may pose to civil liberties. The federal government maintains 910 different databases that contain billions of entries about its citizens.[36] They range from files on "subversives" and criminals, kept by investigative agencies such as the FBI, the CIA, and military intelligence agencies, to the files in the massive record-keeping systems of the Internal Revenue Service and the Social Security Administration. The Department of Justice alone keeps lists of persons involved in civil disturbances, members of criminal syndicates, narcotics addicts, criminal defendants, individuals wanted by the police, passers of forged checks, and resident aliens. Clearly, government agencies need many of these files if they are to do their work efficiently, but is such efficiency dangerous? What about the growing number of private firms that are keeping their own lists and selling them to whoever pays the price? The prospect that all these files might be centralized is a frightening thought to anyone who values our civil liberties. It is now possible to establish a system that could, with the entry of an identification number, reveal all the significant events in an individual's entire life. The power available to the controller of such a system would obviously be immense.

The Privacy Act of 1974 was supposed to prevent the indiscriminate sharing of files between government agencies, but it has failed to do the job. A loophole exempts routine sharing that is "compatible" with the purpose for which the information was collected, and it has been used to justify virtually any kind of exchange of information. An additional concern is the fact that some of the information in government and private data files is false or misleading. People have lost their jobs, or have been unable to find new ones, because of false information included in a file. The Freedom of Information Act was intended to solve this problem and prevent government agencies from covering up their mistakes by giving everyone more access to the information the government collects about itself and its citizens, but the bureaucracy has proved ingenious in developing ways to obstruct the public's access. Every year, for example, the federal government creates millions of new secrets that are exempt from the Freedom of Information Act. Even if all the information in the files were accurate, the prospect of untold numbers of hapless men and women being haunted for their entire lives by a single mistake is not a pleasant one. Clearly, the totalitarian nightmares of such authors as Orwell and Huxley are now technologically possible. The problem facing all free people is to prevent them from coming true.

Burdens and Benefits

More than any other social institution, the government is concerned with social justice. In theory, at least, it is supposed to right social wrongs through the legal codes—for example, by prohibiting discrimination against women and minorities—and by creating programs to help the disadvantaged and the deprived. In addition, the government has numerous other programs intended to help more privileged groups. But none of this comes free; someone must bear the cost of these programs. The continuing battle over who is to receive the benefits of government action and who is to pay for them is the central feature of modern politics.

Taxation is one of the most difficult issues our political leaders must face. The voters constantly demand more and more government services, yet they do not want to pay more taxes in order to get them. Despite all the political rhetoric of recent years, the United States has one of the lowest overall tax rates of any industrialized nation. In Denmark, taxes total about half of the gross domestic product; in France, about 44 percent; in Germany, 39 percent; and in Canada, 36 percent. But in the United States, the tax burden is less than 30 percent (see Figure 5.3).[37] Of course, along with lower taxes goes a much lower level of social services. For example, the United States is the only industrialized nation without some kind of national health care program for all its citizens.

In addition to the question of how much revenue must be raised is the critical issue of who is to bear the tax burden. In recent years, the overall level of taxation has remained relatively constant, but there have been some important changes in who bears it. During the 1980s, taxes on the wealthiest citizens were slashed while taxes were increased for other Americans. The tax reforms of 1993 were more favorable to middle- and low-income taxpayers, but the wealthy came our far ahead of where they started. Between 1977 and 1996, the top 1 percent of American families

Figure 5.3

Taxes

Despite many public complaints, taxes in the United States are actually lower than in most other industrialized nations.

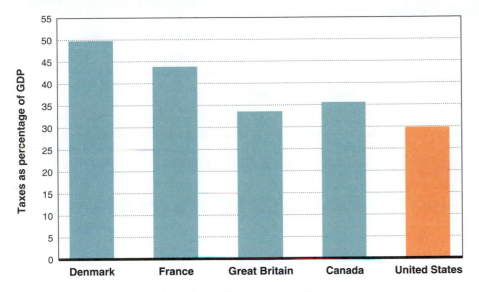

Source: *Statistical Abstract of the United States, 1996,* p. 840.

saw their tax burden decline by 18.5 percent while the bottom 80 percent saw their federal taxes drop only 2.5 percent.[38] Moreover, this trend continued with the tax reforms of 1997, which doubled the amount of inherited wealth that is exempted from taxes and reduced the tax rate on the profits that are made on investments. A second important shift in the tax burden has been from older to younger citizens. The huge increase in the federal deficit caused by tax cuts in the 1980s has forced the government to borrow vast sums of money, and future generations must pay the interest on this debt. According to federal calculations, the net lifetime tax rate for someone born in 1900 was 24 percent; for someone born in 1950 it will be 33 percent; but for today's teenagers it is likely to be around 37 percent.[39] Although much of that increase is due to the higher level of government services provided since 1900, the growing debt burden on future generations is also a major factor.

In addition to shifting the tax burden away from the wealthy and the elder generation, the U.S. government has also made significant changes in its spending priorities. In the second half of 1980s, military spending increased by 46 percent (after controlling for inflation), while social programs for such things as housing and child nutrition were slashed. Another big loser was the programs designed to make long-term investments for the future. From 1980 to 1990, the percentage of the gross domestic product the federal government invested in public infrastructure, such as highways and mass transportation, declined by 34 percent, and spending for education fell by 27 percent.[40] In the 1990s, big increases in military spending stopped, but the extra money did not go into neglected social programs. They continued to be cut while payments skyrocketed for the huge debts the government ran up during the 1980s, and the aging of the population has required more and more money to go into Social Security and Medicare payments.

Quick Review

How serious a problem are conflicts of interest, bribery, and corruption in our government?

Why has the public grown more cynical about its government?

What dilemma does the military pose in a democratic society?

What are the most serious threats to our civil liberties?

Are the burdens and benefits of government fairly distributed in our society?

Solving the Problems of Government

Practically all social problems are in part governmental problems. But *the* problem of government is the need to create a political system that is truly democratic: a government "of the people, by the people, for the people." Democracy is not just a system of government; it is a constant struggle to protect and expand the power of the people. The current system is clearly far from the democratic ideals we espouse, and there have been different proposals to solve its problems.

Reforming Campaign Finance

As we have seen again and again in the pages of this chapter, the political deck is stacked in favor of wealth and against people who would challenge those already in positions of power. One of the most important reasons for this corruption of democracy is the current system of campaign financing. In the elections of 1994, for example, the *average* incumbent raised five times more money than his or her opponent.[41] The obvious reason for this enormous imbalance is that those in office are in a far better position to offer political rewards to big contributors than are the challengers. Political action committees, for example, contribute seven times more to incumbents than to challengers.[42]

Current laws regulating campaign financing look good on paper, but they do virtually nothing to limit the ability of the wealthy to use their money to frustrate the will of the majority. The law limits direct contributions to a candidate's election committee, but the wealthy can still spend all the money they want to help a candidate as long as they do so as individuals or give the money to PACs that support their views. Presidential candidates are eligible for federal funds if they agree to a fixed spending limit, but there are no spending limits on federal money for other candidates. Even in presidential elections, individuals and PACs are once again allowed to spend an unlimited amount to support a candidate so long as they do so independently of the candidate's election committee. Moreover, there are virtually no limits on the donations to the Republican and Democratic parties, and this so-called soft money can also be spent for their presidential candidates. In 1996, the Democrats raised $124 million in soft money and the Republicans $138.[43]

The fact is that the current system forces politicians to sell their powers of office to the highest bidder and creates grossly unequal contests between candidates running for the same office. The best solution to this problem is to provide federal financing in *all* campaigns for national office, not just in presidential elections. This law would have to be written so that third-party candidates would be eligible for government financing along with candidates of the two major parties. If properly drawn, such a law could eliminate the injustices of the current system of campaign financing. A related idea, intended to counteract the slick professional television commercials that tell so little about the real political issues, is to require the media to provide free time for all candidates to discuss their views in depth.

Restructuring Government

Many social scientists believe that the sheer growth in the size of modern nations has made governments more distant and less responsive to the will of their citizens. In a huge country with millions of citizens, most people have never even met their legislative representatives, much less the president or prime minister. Many see government policies as decisions made in distant places by officials who are not aware of or concerned with their interests—and oftentimes they are right. In response to this problem, some suggest that government power be decentralized—in other words, they want to reduce the power of the central government and transfer it to local government. Advocates of decentralization claim that local governments are closer to the people and therefore more responsive to their needs. Further, they are convinced that if local governments were given more self-determination, many more citizens would become involved in the political process. There is, however, another side to this issue. Some political scientists argue that local governments are too close to the people to be given unrestricted power, contending that local passions and prejudices often lead to the oppression of defenseless minorities. Whether or not that actually occurs, it is clear that small local governments are too weak and divided to cope with such huge problems as pollution, warfare, and the demands of the contemporary world economy.

A different kind of reform that is already being tried in some states is to limit the number of times a person can be reelected to the same office. Supporters of such **term limits** argue that they are the only way to break the power of entrenched incumbents who enjoy built-in advantages over their challengers. In a 1994 Gallup poll, 61 percent of the respondents agreed that members of Congress should be limited to 12 years in office.[44] Critics of such ideas, however, feel that term limits will make matters worse, not better. They argue that legislators, like people in any other business, need time to learn their job and that turning out everyone with any experience would cripple the government's decision-making process. Moreover, they claim that legislatures with many inexperienced members would have to rely even more heavily on lobbyists and special-interest groups.

term limits
Legislation that limits the time an elected official may serve.

Limiting Government Secrecy

There are good reasons for government secrets. National governments must keep military and sometimes even economic information from potential enemies; local governments must not let speculators know that a certain piece of land is about to be purchased for public use. But the "secret" stamp used for these purposes can also be used to cover up official incompetence and, worse yet, crimes and violations

Debate   Should the Government Finance Our Election Campaigns?

Countless political commentators have complained about the corrupting influence of politicians' constant need to collect money for their election campaigns. The most far-reaching proposal for change would have the government, instead of private contributors, provide most or all of the money necessary for election campaigns.

Yes

Imagine you are an American senator, and you need to raise $12,000 a week to pay for your next election campaign. Unless you get that money, you will probably lose your job. Now imagine that the only place you can get that kind of money is from the special-interest groups and lobbyists who want your vote when their issues come before the Senate. Don't you think you would listen more carefully to contributors who gave you tens of thousands of dollars than to an average citizen who disagreed with them but couldn't give any money?

The current system of campaign finance is based on a kind of legal bribery in which the rich and the well-financed special-interest groups give millions of dollars to politicians in order to buy political influence. Of course, in some cases supporters on both sides of an important issue have equal amounts of money to spend and therefore balance each other out, and in other cases a courageous politician might take a risk and go against the powerful special interests. The fact remains, however, that huge campaign contributions buy political influence, and as a result we do not get a government of the people but a government of the highest bidders.

There are many proposals about how to correct this shameful state of affairs, but the only way to really do the job is to completely end politicians' dependence on gifts from contributors in order to finance their campaigns, and that means the government must provide serious candidates with the money they need to run for office. Critics claim that public financing would be a big burden on the taxpayers, but that assertion is just a smokescreen erected by politicians and special interests who have profited from the current system. Actually, the amount of money needed is a minute sum compared with the overall federal budget. If we really believe in the principles of democracy, then we must end the corrupt influence of wealthy campaign contributors once and for all.

of civil liberties. The cold light of publicity can do a great deal to restrain overzealous government officials, and that is the reason the Constitution prohibited Congress from making any law that abridges the freedom of the press. In effect, the press was given the duty of uncovering government secrets.

Making sure government bureaucrats inform the public about their behavior is not easy. One of the first attempts came in the Freedom of Information Act. This act requires U.S. government agencies to hand over any information they have about an individual citizen if that person requests it. Many government bureaucracies, however, respond to requests with months of stalling, and some charge fees for

No

Our current system of government has served us well over the years, and we shouldn't change it now. What other nation has been more prosperous, more stable, and more democratic than the United States? Why fix what isn't broken?

Although the critics are always making wild claims that our political leaders sell the powers of their office in exchange for campaign contributions, there isn't a shred of evidence that this is a common practice. Popular politicians can easily raise the money they need to run their campaigns, no matter how they vote on the issues that affect big campaign contributors, and unpopular politicians are not going to be re-elected anyway. Besides, it is clearly against the law to sell votes in exchange for campaign contributions or anything else, and only very foolish politicians would take the risk of going to jail just to get a few more dollars for their campaign funds. The fact that several well-known political leaders have been convicted on bribery charges in recent years shows that the enforcement effort really works.

Placing limits on private campaign contributions may seem to be a democratic step, but it is actually just the opposite. How can a free nation tell its citizens that they cannot spend or give away their own money in order to support a cause they believe in? Moreover, government financing of election campaigns will only lead to new and serious problems. You can be sure that any legislation to create such a system would be written to favor incumbents and the candidates of the two major parties and that everyone else would be hurt. But even if that problem could be avoided, these proposals raise other troubling questions. What right do we have to take money from taxpayers to support the campaign of a politician they disagree with? Why should any taxpayers be burdened with what are really politicians' business expenses? Our current political system is working well the way it is, and these so-called reforms would only make things worse.

the information they furnish. Other agencies protect information they do not want the public to see by classifying it as secret. In response, Congress has added amendments to the bill, establishing a deadline for responding to requests for information, limiting the fees that can be charged, and providing for judicial review of classified material. This legislation gave the public much greater access to government records, but the bureaucracies continue to put up a determined resistance. The fact of the matter is that no bureaucrats or public officials want their activities subject to close public scrutiny, and that is doubly true when it comes to the domestic surveillance and **covert operations** that are the biggest threat to civil liberties. There is

covert operations
Secret operations carried out by government agencies such as the CIA.

Signs of Hope Letting More People In

Despite the failings of our political system, which we have examined in this chapter, and the ways it favors the wealthy and the well connected, there is no doubt that it has been growing steadily more democratic. This nation was originally ruled by a foreign king, and the elections that were allowed were restricted to white male property owners. Over the years, the vote was extended to more and more people. First, the property restrictions were dropped. Then, after the Civil War, the vote was officially extended to freed male slaves, although the southern states soon devised a variety of schemes that placed formidable barriers in the way of African Americans who wanted to exercise their new right. Next, the male establishment gave in to the demands of the "suffragettes," and women too obtained the right to vote. Another phase of this long process came as a result of the demands of the civil rights movement of the 1950s and 1960s, when Supreme Court rulings and new federal laws broke down the last official barriers to African American voting rights. Yet another group gained representation during the Vietnam war, when the legislature conceded that if 18-year-olds were old enough to be drafted, they were old enough to vote. The right to vote is only a first step toward true political representation, but there is no doubt that it is a critically important one.

clearly a compelling need for stronger laws to limit government secrecy and protect the right of free political expression.

Getting Politically Involved

Despite the range of complex political problems facing modern democracies, one response can help resolve them all: increased involvement of ordinary citizens in the process of government. While that sounds simple enough, there are enormous obstacles to that goal. Some sociologists argue that in politics, as in sports, the media have transformed the average citizen into a passive spectator rather than an active participant. Although there is some truth to such assertions, political apathy has many other causes as well. The sheer increase in total population has meant that each elected official represents more and more people and, as a result, is less responsive to any single individual. The growing anonymity of the modern metropolis has eroded the sense of social responsibility and shared community so essential to the political life of traditional small-town America. And as we have seen, the political deck is stacked against the average citizen, who has little influence compared with the powerful and the privileged.

There is, however, reason for optimism. It is easy to idealize the political life of bygone small-town America, but in many important respects the United States is far more democratic today than it was in the past. In the early days of the republic, only white males who owned property could vote; but step by step, the poor, minorities, and women were let into the political process, even if they still do not enjoy equal representation. Today's society presents daunting obstacles to individual citizens who want to influence government, but history has shown us that those individuals can have an impact when they band together in political organizations to press for change.

Quick Review
What are the best ways to respond to the problems of government?

Sociological Perspectives on Problems of Government

Practically everyone agrees that the government has serious shortcomings. Indeed, pointing out these weaknesses has become a career for some public figures. Yet there is considerable disagreement over exactly what the problems are. Conservatives are usually concerned about government inefficiency and waste, military preparedness, and what they consider excessive interference with the economy. Liberals and progressives are more worried about violations of civil liberties, protection of minority rights, erosion of the democratic process, and the government's effectiveness in dealing with society's other problems. An examination of the different sociological perspectives helps clarify the situation by pointing out the ways these diverse problems are linked to wider social forces.

The Functionalist Perspective

The government performs at least five basic functions essential to modern society. First, government enforces society's norms when other methods of social control fail. This responsibility is usually carried out by the police and the other parts of the criminal justice system, but other government agencies occasionally serve these ends as well. Second, government maintains order by acting as the final arbiter of disputes arising between individuals and groups in the thousands of lawsuits settled by the courts every year. Third, government is responsible for the overall planning and direction of society and the coordination of other social institutions. Fourth, government must deal with social needs that are left unmet by other social institutions, for example, maintaining roads and caring for homeless children. Finally, government is responsible for handling international relations and, if necessary, warfare.

According to functionalists, the rapid social changes of the past century have made it very difficult for many governments to perform these functions effectively. Government has accepted more and more responsibilities but has been ill prepared for its new tasks. Many governments are saddled with old-fashioned systems of organization that were adequate in the eighteenth and nineteenth centuries but are ineffectual today. Government officials often fail to understand their duties, or they pursue their own interests rather than the public's. High offices are given out to reward the supporters of victorious candidates, and bribery and corruption are everyday occurrences. Another problem is created when technological changes take place so rapidly that government officials are unable to control their application. As a result of all this, government fails to function effectively.

Functionalists suggest that steps be taken to reduce this disorganization by reshaping the government. The tasks of government bureaucracies should be spelled out in detail, and each bureau should be organized to achieve them. The decision-making mechanism should be revamped to eliminate awkward traditional structures that impede efficiency. For example, the U.S. Congress should reform its committee system so that more effective laws can be enacted. Tougher laws to reduce unnecessary secrecy and to protect civil liberties should also be passed. Finally, functionalists recommend that law enforcement agencies launch a more vigorous effort to root out bribery and corruption.

The Conflict Perspective

Conflict theorists see the government as a source of tremendous political power that is used to advance the interests of those who control it. Government works to repress conflict rather than to resolve it. That is, the groups in control of the government (the upper class) use their power to smother opposition. Vagrancy laws, for example, have been used to force the poor to work in dangerous, low-paying jobs. Tax laws with loopholes that benefit the rich are another example of the expression of class interests through legislation. When there are strong conflicts of values about the morality of a particular kind of behavior, such as homosexuality, the power of the state is often used as a tool to try to impose the standards of the dominant group.

According to the conflict perspective, control of government is a prize that is won through political conflict. Once a group gains such control, it uses the power of the government to maintain its position, and thus the group becomes difficult to dislodge. The law and its administration become tools of the power elite and are used to exploit the masses. The solution to this problem is to give a stronger voice to the "common" man and woman. Such measures as providing government financing for political campaigns, restricting lobbying, and requiring full disclosure of all government deliberations and proceedings are steps in this direction. Conflict theorists believe that greater economic and social equality is the real key to achieving a true democracy and that the way to win a more equal distribution of both wealth and power is through greater political activism and better organization of those who are not being represented in government. The government will change only when those groups gain enough power to force it to change.

The Feminist Perspective

When feminists look at the political system, the first thing they see is the gross underrepresentation of women at all levels of government. In the United States, no woman has ever been president, vice president, speaker of the house, or chief justice of the Supreme Court. Only one woman has ever been the prime minister of Canada, and then for only a few months. A few European countries have better records, but there isn't a single country around the world in which women have an equal share of government power. Moreover, whether we look at top officials, elected representatives, or only middle-level bureaucrats, the story is still the same.

From the feminist perspective, this situation is a real tragedy, not only because it deprives women around the world of their basic human rights but, perhaps as important, because it deprives the decision-making process of the wisdom and common sense the world's women have to offer. Many feminists feel that this would be a more peaceful planet with more caring governments if women had their full political rights.

At least in the Western democracies, the official, legal barriers to women's political participation have been removed (although feminists point out that former slaves got the vote in the United States before women did). Today, feminists call for women and sympathetic men to ban together and force open the doors of the "old boys' club" that still dominates the political system. The majority of eligible voters in most industrialized countries are women, and feminists urge them to seize the power their numbers give them and work to create fundamental improvements in the way old system operates.

The Interactionist Perspective

Interactionists hold that the political system, like all other social processes, is guided by the ideas, definitions, and beliefs we hold about it. If a nation values the political participation of average citizens and defines democratic rule as the only legitimate source of power, it is likely to be democratic. If, on the other hand, average citizens come to see political participation as futile, hopeless, or just boring, the very foundations of democracy are threatened. Thus, interactionists are concerned about the everyday cynicism that has crept into our view of the government, and they urge citizens to actively support what is good in our government and to work constructively to change what needs to be changed. In their view, the long-term health and even the survival of democratic institutions depend on such seemingly simple everyday attitudes and beliefs.

Political socialization—the way in which people learn their political values and perspectives—is another major concern of interactionists. Children learn most of their political attitudes from their parents early in life as they form their ideas about the political system and develop attachments to such symbols as the flag, patriotic slogans, and well-known public figures. As they grow older, their views are affected by their peer groups and teachers, among others. A democratic society can do little to change the home environment of its children without threatening basic civil liberties. Schools, however, can teach children to respect the rights of others, to understand how governments actually operate, and to work for the equality of all people. Another important aspect of political socialization is what we learn about political activity itself. Is it the duty of every citizen or a waste of time? Once again, the schools and the media can help encourage or discourage positive political attitudes.

political socialization
The process by which people learn their political values and perspectives.

Other Perspectives

Personality theorists focus on the relationships between political systems and individual personality. Some suggest that the character of a nation's people affects its political system; others assert that political systems affect personality just as economic systems do. The citizens of some nations seem to accept their leaders with almost unquestioning obedience, while other cultures breed rebellious individualists who are suspicious of all higher authority. One of the most famous psychological studies of fascism concluded that many of the followers of totalitarian leaders have **authoritarian personalities.**[45] Such persons are said to be rigid, extremely conformist, and uncomfortable with ambiguity and uncertainty. As a result, this type of individual favors strong leadership that provides order and conformity at the expense of individual liberty. Personality theorists therefore urge parents to avoid excessive authoritarianism in their child-rearing practices. They would encourage children to think for themselves, advise parents not to just order their children around but to explain why children need to do what their parents ask, and teach

authoritarian personality
A personality type that is characterized by rigidity and an unquestioning obedience to authority.

Children usually pick up their parents' political values and attitudes at an early age, in a process known as political socialization.

children about the importance of compromise and that even people they disagree with may well have something important to say. In the view of the personality theorists, the future of democracy depends on the way each new generation develops, and it is vital to encourage the growth of the right kind of attitudes and personality characteristics.

Quick Review

What are the differences among the main sociological perspectives about the problems of government and their solutions?

Summary

Governments and their bureaucracies have expanded rapidly in the last century as they have struggled to meet the needs of a changing society. Social scientists have exerted much effort trying to determine who really controls modern governments, and there are three principal theoretical approaches. The elitists believe that the government is run by a small, unified power elite. The pluralists see many different groups competing for power and are not convinced that a single ruling class exists.

Like the elitists, the structuralists also feel that the government works primarily in the interests of the privileged few—not because of the direct involvement of individual members of the elite, but because the structure of capitalist societies forces the government to support the interests of the upper class.

Government corruption is a serious threat to the ideals of democracy. Our current system of campaign financing creates many completely legal ways to win corrupt influence over elected officials, and personal conflicts of interest and outright bribery are also common problems. The ever increasing media interest in government scandals has probably made politics more honest, but it also frequently helps to shift national attention away from political issues to irrelevant details of politicians' personal lives.

The military poses a basic dilemma in a democratic society. Its traditions of unquestioning obedience and authoritarianism can be a real threat to democratic institutions, yet its power seems essential to national survival. With the end of the Cold War, many governments now face the task of reducing the size of their military forces without causing unnecessary economic disruption.

Protection of civil liberties is a critical task in every nation aspiring to democratic principles. There are many recent examples of governments violating individual rights and interfering with democratic processes. The use of modern technology by private and pubic organizations to collect, store, and retrieve information about individual citizens is another growing threat to civil liberties.

Local, state, and national governments have been caught in a financial dilemma caused by the demand for lower taxes combined with a continued insistence on a high level of government services. In the last twenty years, the tax burden has been shifted away from the wealthy and from the older generation to the younger. Overall, the American tax rate is one of the lowest among industrialized nations.

Many responses to these problems have been proposed, including federal financing of election campaigns, decentralizing government, limiting government secrecy, and encouraging the political participation of average citizens.

Functionalists see the problems of government as signs of disorganization; the political institution has failed to work correctly and must be adjusted so that it runs smoothly again. Conflict theorists are more likely to feel that the political system creates social problems because it was intentionally designed to favor the elite and the organized special interests. They argue that if our political problems are to be resolved, this dominance must end. Feminists note the great underrepresentation of women in the political process and call for women to work together to win more political power. Interactionists place great importance on the way citizens define the government and the political process, and they emphasize the need for political socialization that recognizes the importance of democratic institutions.

Questions for Critical Thinking

We have repeatedly described the average citizen as rather apathetic and uninvolved in government issues. How involved are you? Can you name the elected officials who represent you? What are their positions on the issues that affect you the most?

Why is it that we all talk about how important democracy is, but few of us ever get involved in the political process? Is it just a matter of personal choice, or is there something about the way our political system is structured that discourages the participation of average citizens?

Key Terms

authoritarian personality

blacklisting

bribery

bureaucracy

conflict of interest

covert operations

defense conversion

elitists

goal displacement

lobbying

military-industrial complex

pluralists

Political socialization

power elite

special-interest group

spoils system

structuralists

term limits

Further Readings

Robert Dahl, *Dilemmas of Pluralist Democracy: Autonomy vs. Control* (New Haven, CT: Yale University Press, 1982). An analysis of the American political system by an influential pluralist.

Thomas R. Dye, *Who's Running America? The Clinton Years* (Englewood Cliffs, NJ: Prentice Hall, 1995). An analysis of the American power structure by a leading political scientist.

Seymour Martin Lipset, *American Exceptionalism: A Double-Edged Sword* (New York: Norton, 1996). A look at American government and society from a cross-cultural perspective.

C. Wright Mills, *The Power Elite* (New York: Oxford University Press, 1956). The classic work that gave rise to contemporary elite theory.

Michael Parenti, *Land of Idols: Political Mythology in America* (New York: St. Martin's, 1994). A challenge to many of the beliefs and assumptions that underlie American political culture, by a well-known conflict theorist.

Notes

1. Michael Hirsh, "Behind the IRS Curtain," *Newsweek*, October 6, 1997, p. 29.

2. U.S. Bureau of the Census, *Statistical Abstract of the United States, 1996* (Washington, DC: U.S. Government Printing Office, 1996), pp. 419, 421; U.S. Bureau of the Census, *Statistical Abstract of the United States, 1991* (Washington, DC: U.S. Government Printing Office, 1991), pp. 400–401.

3. Lawrence Mishel, Jared Bernstein, and John Schmitt, *The State of Working America, 1996–97,* (New York: Sharpe, 1997), p. 102.

4. Theodore Caplow, *American Social Trends* (San Diego: Harcourt Brace Jovanovich, 1991), p. 92.

5. Max Weber, *From Max Weber: Essays in Sociology,* trans. Hans H. Gerth and C. Wright Mills (New York: Oxford University Press, 1946), pp. 196–244.

6. Max Weber, *The Theory of Social and Economic Organization,* trans. A. M. Henderson and Talcott Parsons (New York: Free Press, 1947), p. 337.

7. See Francis Rourke, *Bureaucracy, Politics and Public Policy,* 3rd ed. (Boston: Little, Brown, 1984).

8. C. Wright Mills, "The Structure of Power in American Society," in *Power, Politics and People: The Collected Papers of C. Wright Mills* (New York: Ballantine, 1963), p. 288.

9. See, for example, G. William Domhoff, *The Power Elite and the State* (New York: Aldine de Gruyter, 1990); G. William Domhoff, *Who Rules America Now?* (Englewood Cliffs, NJ: Prentice Hall, 1983); Thomas R. Dye, *Who's Running America? The Clinton Years* (Englewood Cliffs, NJ: Prentice Hall, 1995); Leonard Silk and Mark Silk, *The American Establishment* (New York: Basic Books, 1980).

10. David Riesman, *The Lonely Crowd* (New York: Doubleday, 1953).

11. Arnold M. Rose, *The Power Structure: Political Process in American Society* (New York: Oxford University Press, 1967), p. 6.

12. See Robert A. Dahl, *Dilemmas of Pluralist Democracy: Autonomy vs. Control* (New Haven, CT: Yale University Press, 1982).

13. Nicos Poulantzas, "The Problem of the Capitalist State," in Robin Blackburn, ed., *Ideology in the Social Science* (London: Fontana, 1972), pp. 238–253.

14. Theda Skocpol, *States and Revolutions: A Comparataive Analysis of France, Russia, and China* (New York: Cambridge University Press, 1979).

15. Caplow, *American Social Trends,* p. 113.

16. Federal Election Commission, August 1997, ⟨http://www.fec.gov⟩.

17. U.S. Bureau of the Census, *Statistical Abstract, 1996,* p. 286.

18. Dye, *Who's Running America?* p. 125.

19. Ibid.

20. Federal Election Commission, August 1997, ⟨http://www.fed.gov⟩.

21. Federal Election Commission, *Record,* 19:2 (Feburary), (Washington, DC: U.S. Government Printing Office, 1993), p. 4.

22. Dye, *Who's Running America?* pp. 127–149; Domhoff, *The Power Elite and the State.*

23. James William Coleman, *The Criminal Elite: Understanding White Collar Crime* (New York: St. Martin's, 1998), pp. 32–33.

24. Ibid., pp. 102–103.

25. Ibid., p. 45.

26. Kathleen Maguire and Ann L. Pasatore (eds.), *Sourcebook of Criminal Justice Statistics,* (Washington DC: Bureau of Justice Statistics, 1995), p. 145.

27. Ibid., p. 352.

28. James William Coleman, *The Criminal Elite: The Sociology of White Collar Crime,* 2nd ed. (New York: St. Martin's Press, 1989), pp. 55–72.

29. Ibid.

30. Brian Glick, *War at Home: Covert Action Against U.S. Activists and What We Can Do About It* (Boston: South End Press, 1989).

31. Associated Press, "Most Polygraph Use by Employers Banned," *San Luis Obispo Telegram-Tribune,* October 22, 1988, p. D1.

32. Marcia Staimer, "Do Workers Have Private Lives?" *USA Today,* May 13, 1991, pp. A1–2A.

33. Elys A. McLean, "Working to Avoid Violence," *USA Today,* April 27, 1994, p. B1.

34. Thomas B. Rosenstiel, "Someone May Be Watching," *Los Angeles Times,* May 18, 1994, pp. A1, A12.

35. Ibid.

36. Ibid.

37. Mishel, Bernstein, and Schmitt, *The State of Working America, 1996–97,* p. 103.

38. Ibid.

39. *Budget of the United States: Analytical Perspectives Fiscal Year 1995* (U.S. Government Printing Office, 1994), pp. 21–31.

40. Robert B. Reich, "The REAL Economy," *Atlantic,* February 1991, pp. 35–52.

41. Stephen Labaton, "On the Money Trail, Most 'Insiders' Had the Advantage," *New York Times,* November 9, 1994, p. B1.

42. Caplow, *American Social Trends,* p. 114.

43. Doyle McManus, "President Proposes End to 'Soft Money' Donation Loophole," *Los Angeles Times,* June 4, 1997, pp. A1, A16.

44. Nick Galifianakis and Marty Baumann, "How USA Feels About Terms Limits," *USA Today,* June 28, 1994, p. 1A.

45. T. W. Adorno, E. Frenkel-Brunswick, D. J. Devinson, and P. N. Sandord, *The Authoritarian Personality* (New York: Harper & Row, 1950).

CHAPTER 6

Health and Illness

What are the most frequent causes of physical and mental disorders?

Why is American health care so costly?

How does the American system of health care differ from the Canadian and British systems?

What are the ethical dilemmas posed by modern medicine?

How can our health care system be improved?

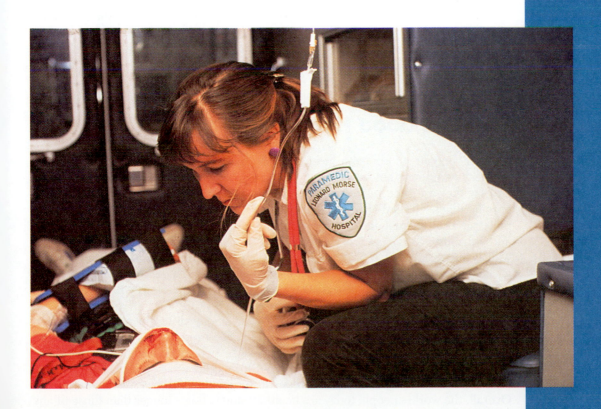

Gene Hays made a big mistake when he retired. He gave up his health insurance because he just couldn't afford the $500 monthly payments. Six months later his wife had a heart attack, and she has been in a coma ever since. Gene became one of those unlucky people who "fall between the cracks" in the health care system. Too young to qualify for Medicare (the government health care program for the elderly) and not eligible for Medicaid (the medical welfare program for the poor), the Hayses were on their own. Mr. Hays who suffers from Parkinson's disease, and his 93-year-old father had to take care of his wife when she came home from the hospital, managing the complicated medical equipment necessary to keep her alive. The costs were staggering. He soon used up all the savings they had accumulated for retirement, and he started selling off their other assets one by one.[1]

Illness and death are, of course, an unavoidable part of human life. Society nonetheless has a profound influence on our health and on the ways we cope with our illnesses. Countless people like Gene Hays are financially ruined by the cost of today's high-tech medical care, and millions more simply don't get the kind of health care they need. But our society has a great impact on our health before we ever get to the doctor. Society helps determine what kind of diet we eat, how many dangerous pollutants we are exposed to, how much stress we feel, and even how much we smoke and drink. Although most people don't realize it, our social groups even tell us when we are sick and when we are healthy. The visions that modern psychiatry interprets as a symptom of mental illness, for instance, may be seen as a special religious insight by some tribal people. The diarrhea and upset stomach that send us to the doctor are often accepted as normal conditions by people in poor countries. And of course, when we do get sick, the availability, quality, and organization of health care help determine how quickly we recover, or whether we recover at all.

What Is Good Health?

To many people, good health means simply that they have no obvious illnesses or physical symptoms; but what about those people who are depressed, lack vitality, and say they are "not feeling well," even though they cannot be shown to have any specific illness? The World Health Organization defines **health** as "a state of complete physical, mental and social well-being and not merely the absence of disease and infirmity."[2] It is clear that health involves social and psychological conditions as well as biological ones. For example, some people who suffer from a variety of medical symptoms still maintain a positive mental outlook and a definition of themselves as basically healthy, while others who see themselves as seriously ill have literally created symptoms where no organic cause exists.

The way we define good health also varies among different nations and even among different classes within the same nation. The tired, listless feeling associated with inadequate nutrition is considered normal by poor people in most parts of the world, but it is seen as a sign of illness by the middle and upper classes. Even in poor countries, the standard of what constitutes good health has steadily increased. Overall, the world's people today are healthier and will live longer than those of any

health
A state of physical and mental well-being.

other generation in history. In the eighteenth century, the average life span in even the most prosperous nations was no more than 35 years. Dramatic declines in infant mortality and in deaths from contagious diseases have helped extend the average life expectancy in the industrialized nations to 75 years.[3]

Although it is much harder to measure historical changes in mental health, the standards by which we judge it have certainly grown much higher, too. Only a century ago, conditions that would warrant serious medical concern today, such as depression or severe anxiety, were usually just ignored. Only those who were unable to carry on a normal life were considered to be mentally disordered. Thus, the difference between health and illness is a relative one that changes from time to time and place to place.

Quick Review

How can we define good health?

Physical Illness

The great improvement in living conditions in the twentieth century is the main reason people live longer today than they did in the past. A rising standard of living and increased agricultural production have meant better food, shelter, and clothing for the average person. The construction of sewer and water purification systems has sharply reduced waterborne disease. Although sophisticated and expensive medical procedures such as open-heart surgery have added little to the average life span, some medical breakthroughs, such as antibiotics and immunizations against contagious disease, have been extremely important.

Not all the changes that have transformed the twentieth-century world have been beneficial to our health, however. Stress, overindulgence, and environmental pollution can cripple and kill as effectively as typhoid or tuberculosis, and the ancient scourges of poverty, malnutrition, and warfare still plague humankind. We will begin our examination of contemporary health problems with a look at the way our life-style contributes to ill health; then we will explore the problems caused by physical injuries, environmental hazards, contagious diseases, and poverty.

Unhealthy Life-styles

Most North Americans are far less active than their ancestors were. Laborsaving devices ranging from the automobile to the electric toothbrush have reduced the amount of physical effort required for daily living, and automation has created an increasing number of "thinking jobs" that demand no harder work than picking up a pencil or making a phone call. Medical research shows that regular exercise is essential to good health. Not only do people who exercise regularly report that they feel better, but exercise has been shown to reduce significantly the risk of heart disease—the leading cause of death in North America. In fact, a study of Boston men by Charles Rose and his associates found that the amount of exercise a person gets is one of the best predictors of longevity.[4]

Diet is another aspect of life-style that has a profound impact on health. Although there are many disagreements about what type of diet is most conducive to good health, there is a growing consensus among nutritionists about what is wrong with the way we eat. As the surgeon general's *Report on Nutrition and Health* concluded, North Americans eat too many fatty foods, such as red meat, and not enough fruits, vegetables, and whole-grain products. Our sugar consumption should be reduced and the fiber in our diet increased. Despite repeated warnings, however, North Americans' love of high-calorie food and our tendency to overeat have caused obesity to become a serious problem. Research shows that heart disease, high blood pressure, and diabetes are all associated with obesity, and the National Center for Health Statistics now estimates that one-third of all American are obese.[5]

Despite heated denials from the tobacco industry, there is no longer any doubt that smoking is a serious health hazard. It has been linked to a long list of diseases, including lung cancer, emphysema, ulcers, and heart disorders. The surgeon general's yearly reports on smoking state that, among other things, the death rate of smokers is 70 percent higher than that of nonsmokers the same age, and the death rate of heavy smokers (two or more packs a day) is double that of nonsmokers. A study in the *Journal of the American Medical Association* that looked at the underlying causes of fatal illness recently concluded that tobacco smoking causes almost one in every five deaths in the United States, making it America's *number one* cause of death.[6] Although there are some disagreements among researchers about the criteria for addiction, many feel that tobacco is more addictive than heroin, cocaine, or any other commonly used drug (see Chapter 12).[7] Growing concerns are also being raised about the effects of nonsmokers' exposure to tobacco. A report to the Environmental Protection Agency estimates that 53,000 Americans die because of "passive smoking" every year, and the EPA has declared secondhand smoke a "group A" carcinogen.[8]

Smoking is a personal choice, but stress seems to be an almost unavoidable part of modern life. The initial symptoms of stress, such as irritability, insomnia, and a queasy stomach, are usually minor, and a certain amount of stress may even be nec-

Signs of Hope   Healthier Life-styles

Concern about what we eat and how healthy our life-styles are seems to be paying off. Nutritionists have long recognized that the high fat content of the North American diet is a major contributor to heart disease, cancer, and other health problems. The National Center for Health Studies found that the percentage of our calories derived from fat has declined 14 percent since the mid-1960s. As a result, the average level of blood cholesterol has declined, and so has the death rate from heart disease.* Nutritionists have also been urging us to eat more fruits and vegetables and less red meat, and statistics show that we are doing so. Between 1970 and 1992, the consumption of fresh vegetables increased 19 percent and the amount of fruit we eat went up 14 percent, while the average consumption of red meat declined by 15 percent. Even more important is the decline in smoking, which most experts believe to be the leading preventable cause of death in North America. Since 1974, smoking has decreased 38 percent among 18- to 25-year-olds and 37 percent among those 26 and older.†

*Jane E. Brody, "Study Shows Americans Are Cutting Fat in Diet," *New York Times,* March 8, 1994, p. B8.
†U.S. Bureau of the Census, *Statistical Abstract of the United States, 1996* (Washington, DC: U.S. Government Printing Office, 1996), p. 144.

essary to good mental health; but high levels of stress over long periods of time can lead to serious health problems. One study found that two-thirds of all air traffic controllers in the United States have peptic ulcers, probably as a result of the demands of a job in which a mistake may mean death for hundreds of people.[9] Stress is also associated with heart disease. A study of lawyers, dentists, and physicians found a strong correlation between the amount of stress associated with their specialty and their rates of heart disease; thus, general-practice lawyers had less heart trouble than trial lawyers, who had less trouble than patent lawyers. Interestingly, a study conducted by Columbia University found that workers such as waiters and telephone operators, who face heavy demands but have little decision-making control, are the most likely to have heart and circulatory problems.[10]

Physical Injuries: Suicide, Accidents, and Violent Crimes

Accidents are the leading cause of death among Americans from the time they are born until they reach middle age.[11] Common household accidents cause a huge number of injuries every year, but the most frequent type of fatal accidents involves motor vehicles. Fortunately, our society has become increasingly aware of these dangers. Legislation now requires automobile manufacturers to include such safety features as seat belts and air bags, and stronger efforts to combat drunken driving have also had considerable success (see Chapter 12). Lawsuits and consumer pressure have also forced the manufacturers of other products to improve their safety, and better educational efforts have taught people how to reduce their risks of harm. Overall, the death rate from accidents declined by more than one-third between 1970 and 1994.[12] Although accidents account for more deaths than suicides and homicides combined, the death rates from such intentional violence have shown some significant increases in recent years. (The causes of violent crime are discussed in Chapter 13.) Suicide, which is actually more common than homicide, has very different causes and usually strikes a different type of victim. Unlike homicides or accidents, suicide is most common among elderly people and among whites rather than members of ethnic minorities. With the exception of some relatively rare acts of self-sacrifice, most people kill themselves because their lives seem so painful and unpleasant that they no longer want to continue living. What makes people feel that way? Emile Durkheim, the famous French sociologist, argued that the lack of supportive social groups leaves people aimless and unhappy, and he mustered an impressive battery of statistics to show that suicide rates are higher among those who are not part of such groups.[13] Psychologists, on the other hand, tend to focus on more individual characteristics, for example, a disturbed childhood or a mental disorder such as acute depression. Although they often seem irrational to others, suicidal individuals may actually be trying to achieve concrete goals by their attempts at self-destruction. A suicide attempt may be a way of calling for help or an effort to punish relatives or loved ones the victims believe have let them down.[14]

Environmental Hazards

The pollutants that industries dump into the environment are more than just an ugly nuisance; they are killers. Air pollution has been found to be related to deaths from bronchitis, heart disease, and emphysema as well as several types of cancer. An

American Lung Association study concluded that between 50,000 and 120,000 deaths a year are linked to the air pollution caused by trucks and cars.[15] A sharp rise in deaths from breast cancer, leukemia, and brain tumors over the last two decades has also led many researchers to suspect environmental causes.[16] The Environmental Protection Agency estimates that exposure to radon gas causes 7,000 to 30,000 deaths a year.[17] And there is little doubt that the depletion of the ozone layer caused by atmospheric pollution is a major factor in the increase in skin cancer (see Chapter 16). The contamination of water with poisonous wastes, such as lead and mercury, has already taken many lives, and the list of new dangers grows daily. Over a thousand new chemicals are placed on the market every year, and most of the tens of thousands of chemical compounds already used by industry have never been thoroughly tested to find out how dangerous they are.

Not surprisingly, laborers who work directly with dangerous substances are at greatest risk. Steelworkers are 7.5 times more likely to die of cancer of the kidney and 10 times more likely to die of lung cancer than people in other occupations—but steelworkers are lucky compared with asbestos workers. Almost half of the 500,000 workers who were exposed to high doses of asbestos will die as a result: 100,000 are expected to die of lung cancer, 35,000 of asbestosis (another lung disease), and 35,000 of mesothelioma (an otherwise rare cancer of the linings of the lungs and stomach).[18] The Centers for Disease Control and Prevention estimate that about 17 workers a day were killed on the job during the last decade. A much larger number—perhaps 100,000 persons a year—die more slowly from the effects of occupationally caused diseases.[19]

Contagious Disease

Cancer and diseases of the heart and circulatory system are the most frequent causes of death in wealthy industrial societies, but such killers are seldom the causes of ordinary health problems. Most common difficulties result from the relatively minor **contagious diseases** that are a seemingly inevitable part of daily life. A ten-year study of families in Cleveland, Ohio, found that common respiratory and intestinal diseases (colds, bronchitis, flu, and the like) accounted for 76 percent of all illnesses. The average person in this study had 5.6 respiratory and 1.5 intestinal diseases a year.[20]

contagious disease
A disease spread from one person to another.

Although these relatively minor ailments remain a continuing problem, great progress has been made against the death-dealing epidemics that once threatened humanity. Improvements in sanitation and water treatment have all but eliminated such waterborne diseases as cholera and typhoid from the industrialized nations and have sharply reduced their incidence in many poor countries. Vaccinations have had even greater success against other dread diseases such as polio and smallpox.

For a while it actually seemed that we were on the way to eliminating most of the contagious diseases that had threatened the human race for countless centuries. The tide has shifted, however, and it is obvious that the battle against these killers is far from over. Some of our current problems stem from simple neglect. For example, more than one in five American preschoolers have not been vaccinated against polio, one in ten have not been vaccinated against measles and tetanus.[21] Although conditions in the Third World have improved, the struggle against contagious disease has never been as successful there as in the industrialized nations. Over 1 billion people in the world today lack safe drinking water; almost 2 billion have no access to proper sanitary facilities; and on the average there is less than one doctor for

Personal Perspectives   Putting Their Lives on the Line

Helen Miramontes is a 66-year-old grandmother and a professor of nursing, and she wants to be injected with the HIV, the virus that causes AIDS. So does Jose Zuniga, a 28-year-old AIDS activist from Chicago. They are part of a group of physicians, nurses, and health activists who have stepped forward to volunteer to be tested with an AIDS vaccine.

Scientists generally agree that the best hope for stopping a deadly epidemic like AIDS is to develop an effective vaccine. But there is simply no way to know if a vaccine really works except to test it on humans. Unfortunately, the safest AIDS vaccines in which the subject is injected with a dead form of the virus do not seem to work very well on animals, and unproven vaccines made from a weakened but still living form of the virus run the risk of infecting the patient with the deadly disease or causing other long-term health problems.

So far the government has not approved any of the experimental AIDS vaccines for testing on humans, but people like Miramontes and Zuniga hope that by publicly stepping forward to volunteer as subjects they will be able to speed up the process. Whether or not they ever participate in these tests, no one can ever question their courage. "I am a little fearful," Zuniga admits, "but I have lost too many friends and loved ones to the disease."*

*Christine Gorman, "None but the Brave," *Time,* October 6, 1997, p. 76.

every 6000 people.[22] As a result, diseases such as hepatitis, measles, malaria, and cholera take millions of lives a year. In addition, medical researchers have paid much closer attention to the diseases that affect people in rich countries. One study concluded that in 1996, about $3274 was spent on AIDS research for every person who died from the disease, but only $65 was spent on malaria research for each fatal case of that disease.[23]

Another blow to our efforts to control contagious disease has come from the development of new strains of viruses and bacteria. One major problem is that many diseases eventually develop a genetic resistance to the antibiotics that are used against them. New strains of tuberculosis, malaria, and other contagious diseases are resistant to drugs that used to be highly effective against them. As a result, physicians must rely on more expensive medications that may not be as effective as the ones they replaced. This is a particular problem in the less developed countries, where there is seldom enough money even for the most inexpensive drugs.

In addition to the antibiotic-resistant strains of old diseases, several entirely new (or at least previously unknown) viruses have also emerged in recent years. The most dangerous of these is **human immunodeficiency virus,** or **HIV**, which causes **acquired immune deficiency syndrome,** or **AIDS.** Virtually unknown as recently as 1980, there were over 100,000 new cases of AIDS reported in the United States in 1993.[24] The disease attacks the body's immune system, leaving it vulnerable to a host of other diseases. AIDS often lies dormant without symptoms for years, but once it becomes active, it is usually fatal. Current treatments can extend the life of the patient, but at present there is no known cure.

Fortunately, AIDS is not easily transmitted from one person to another; a direct exchange of body fluids is usually necessary. The most common forms of transmission in the industrialized nations are sexual intercourse and needle sharing among

human immunodeficiency virus (HIV)
The virus that causes AIDS.

acquired immune deficiency syndrome (AIDS)
A fatal disease that attacks the body's defenses against illness.

Because the AIDS epidemic first began among groups that were unpopular with large segments of the public, its victims and their supporters have had to band together and demand greater public attention to the problem.

sexually transmitted disease
A disease that is transmitted from one person to another during sexual activity.

intravenous drug users. Almost two-thirds of U.S. AIDS victims are homosexual men, and one-third are intravenous drug users.[25] In contrast, most AIDS cases in Africa (where the infection rates are the highest in the world) are transmitted through heterosexual activities such as prostitution. This is probably because Africans are in poorer overall health and are much more likely to be infected with other **sexually transmitted diseases.** (HIV is more easily transmitted to someone who already has another sexually transmitted disease). In the last few years, the number of new cases of AIDS transmitted through homosexual contact has decreased in Western countries, although homosexual activity is still the most common way the disease is spread, while infection through intravenous drug use and heterosexual contacts has increased. The chances of contracting AIDS heterosexually remain extremely low unless one partner is a bisexual male or an intravenous drug user.[26]

Like many other diseases, AIDS is most widespread among the poor and minorities. The rate of infection among Latinos is more than double the rate for European Americans, and the rate for African Americans is almost five times higher. Moreover, the differences are even greater among women and children from those groups.[27]

One of the most frightening things about the AIDS epidemic is the projection of how many people it will strike. The World Health Organization estimates 20 million people are already infected with HIV, and although the spread of the virus seems to be slowing in the industrialized nations, it is continuing unabated in the Third World. Unless a cure or an inexpensive treatment is found soon, the vast majority of those people can be expected to die from the disease, and the human impact of such an occurrence would obviously be staggering. Even the health care systems of the rich countries are ill prepared to deal with the flood of desperately sick AIDS patients, and things are far worse in the poor countries. Moreover, most poor nations have no social welfare systems capable of coping with the growing number of orphans the epidemic is likely to leave.

There have been some significant new strides in treating AIDS sufferers, but until medical researchers can find a cure or an effective vaccine, the best way to combat this epidemic is by changing behavior. The two steps most likely to be effective are the use of condoms by all sexually active people who are not in a strictly monogamous relationship and an end to needle sharing by intravenous drug users.

As serious as the AIDS epidemic is, it is important to keep it in perspective. Pneumonia, which is caused by several different organisms, kills more than twice as many people in the United States as AIDS does every year.[28] On a global scale, AIDS still ranks far down the list of fatal diseases. Worldwide, over 4 million people die of acute respiratory infections every year, over 3 million from various forms of diarrhea, and 3 million more from tuberculosis; AIDS causes around 1 million deaths a year.[29]

Poverty

There is overwhelming evidence that poor people have more health problems than those who are better off. The effects of poverty are obvious in the overpopulated agricultural nations. Lack of clothing, housing, and food takes a frightening toll; epidemic disease is commonplace; and 10 to 20 million people simply starve to death every year (see Chapter 17). The infant mortality rates in such countries as Iraq, Nigeria, and Pakistan are at least 10 times higher than in the United States, even though the United States itself has the highest infant mortality rate of any major industrialized nation.[30]

The problems of the poor are less visible in the industrialized nations, but they are no less real. They include lower life expectancies, higher rates of infant death, and more contagious disease, heart ailments, arthritis, and high blood pressure. African American children in the United States are twice as likely as white children to die in their first year of life, and a number of studies show that poor people and members of the ethnic minorities are sick more days a year than the wealthy. African Americans are 39 percent more likely to die from cancer, 45 percent more likely to die from heart disease, and 150 percent more likely to die from diabetes than other Americans. An African American man in Harlem now has a shorter life expectancy than the impoverished citizens of Bangladesh. When asked about their health, poor people are about three times more likely to say that it is only fair or poor or that they have some serious chronic illness.[31]

Poverty is the indirect cause of most of these problems. About 25 million Americans cannot afford to keep themselves adequately fed and are therefore particularly susceptible to illness and disease. Their diet contains more cheap, fatty foods, and poor people are more likely to be overweight. Lack of proper sanitation and protection from rain, snow, cold, and heat also take their toll. Reports of rat bites in slum areas number in the thousands each year, and contaminated water is a hazard for many Native Americans. Moreover, daily life for the poor is stressful as they struggle to pay their bills and buy groceries. As Leonard Syme and Lisa Berkman put it, the poor have "higher rates of schizophrenia, are more depressed, more unhappy, more worried, more anxious, and are less hopeful about the future."[32] Finally, as we will see, the poor receive inferior care when they are sick.

Quick Review

How do unhealthy life-styles contribute to physical illness?

How serious a health problem are accidents and environmental hazards?

What are the most deadly contagious diseases?

Why is poverty a health hazard?

Mental Disorders

mental disorder

(1) A condition that makes it difficult or impossible for a person to cope with everyday life. (2) A label for those who violate certain kinds of social rules.

Although there are deep disagreements about what is good mental health and what is **mental disorder,** there is no question at all that serious psychological problems are extremely common in our society. The best evidence we have on this issue comes from the National Comorbidity Survey headed by Ronald C. Kessler. The researchers asked a broad sample of 8098 Americans aged 15 to 54 detailed questions about their mental health, and they reached some startling conclusions. Close to half the sample (48 percent) had experienced a mental disorder at some time in their lives, and in any given year, almost one-third suffer from a mental disorder. The most common problems were major depression, alcohol dependence, and various kinds of phobias.[33]

American men between the ages of 14 and 45 spend more time in the hospital for mental disorders than for any other cause, and only childbirth accounts for more days in the hospital for women of that age.[34] Yet most people who have mental problems never get to a hospital or receive professional help of any other kind. The National Comorbidity Survey found that only four of every ten persons who had had a serious mental problem received any professional treatment.[35] The others turn to friends or to one of the dozens of new "pop psychology" books published every year, or simply they ignore their problems and hope that somehow they will go away.

What Are Mental Disorders?

Few things are more frightening than the thought of "going crazy," but what does that expression really mean? Terms like *mental illness* or *insanity* may bring to mind images of a madman foaming at the mouth, struggling to break free of his straitjacket, or a disheveled woman babbling incoherently while she wanders the streets. Most mental disorders are neither bizarre nor dramatic, however; instead, they involve the common experiences of anxiety or depression.

Speaking generally, a person may be said to have a mental disorder if he or she is so disturbed that coping with routine, everyday life is difficult or impossible—but this definition, like most others, is vague. Exactly how do we determine whether individuals can or cannot cope with their everyday affairs? Or, for that matter, how can we tell if their circumstances are "normal" or so difficult that most people would have trouble dealing with them? Although many social scientists have attempted to define mental disorder more precisely, none of the definitions has received universal acceptance.

Mental Illness In the past, mental disorders were commonly believed to be caused by demons and spirits. "Treatments" such as flogging, starving, prayers and chants, and dunking the sufferer in boiling water were used to drive the devils out. As the scientific way of thinking gained strength, serious psychological disorders came to be seen as mental illnesses caused by the same natural forces as physical illnesses. Thus, the concepts and methods of modern medicine came to be used to diagnose and treat mental illness in the same fashion as, for instance, a sprained knee or the measles.[36]

The use of this "medical model" to explain and treat mental disorders was a great advance over the old superstitious beliefs, but some observers charge that it has outlived its usefulness. Thomas Szasz, a psychiatrist and harsh critic of the medical model, argues that the whole idea of mental illness is a myth used to make the values and opinions of the psychiatric establishment resemble scientific fact.[37] He believes that although everyone knows what it means to be physically healthy and there is general agreement among doctors about the causes and treatment of most physical illnesses, there is no similar agreement about the nature of mental health or the causes and treatment of mental illness.

Personal Maladjustment A major alternative to the medical model holds that mental disorders represent problems of personal maladjustment. According to this perspective, mental disorders arise when someone is unable to deal effectively with his or her personal difficulties, and disturbed behavior is therefore caused by the same forces that govern other behavior. Therapists who use this approach do not look for symptoms of a specific disease; instead, they examine their patients' overall adjustment to their environment.

Supporters of the personal-maladjustment approach point to several advantages it has over the medical model. First, it does not consider individuals in isolation from their environment, as a physician would when treating a broken leg or a "mental illness." Second, because abnormal behavior is seen to be produced by the same processes as normal behavior, this perspective discourages the assumption that mentally disturbed people are freaks or lunatics. Third, it accepts the fact that any diagnosis of mental problems is a highly uncertain affair and, therefore, that there are no specific cures for these conditions. The personal-maladjustment approach also has its shortcomings, however. Although it does not ignore the individual's environment, it still assumes that the individual—not the social order—is responsible for psychological disturbance. Some problems stem from an unlivable environment rather than an individual's deficiencies. In some circumstances, the healthiest individuals may actually be the ones who are not well adjusted to their social environment.

Social Deviance The newest approach to mental disorders derives from the **labeling theory,** which is discussed in Chapter 13. The idea is that there are really no objective standards by which to judge someone's mental health. From this perspective, the determination that someone is or is not mentally disordered is strictly a cultural matter, and what is considered mental illness in one culture may be perfectly normal in another. Thus, mental "illness" is really a form of social deviance. However, mental illness differs from other kinds of deviance in one important way—the

labeling theory
A theory that sees crime, mental illness, and other types of deviance as labels applied to those who break social norms, and which holds that branding someone as deviant encourages rather than discourages further deviant behavior.

rules that the mentally ill violate are so commonly accepted that most people don't even realize they are social rules. If a man stabs his wife to death while she is sleeping, he is labeled a murderer; if a woman sells sex, she is branded a prostitute. Most people condemn such behavior, but they still feel they understand why those people did what they did. People who do something we can't understand—refuse to come out of their room for months at a time or declare that they are Joan of Arc or Hitler—we label mentally ill.[38]

Because the social deviance approach places responsibility for mental disorders on the environment rather than on the individual, the stigma of mental illness is removed. Therapists are encouraged to deal with the patient's family and personal environment rather than assuming that the patient is suffering from a personal defect or disorder. However, this approach has been severely criticized by experts who hold more traditional ideas about mental health and mental illness. These experts point out that the labeling approach neglects the disturbed individuals themselves and says nothing about the causes of the behavior that resulted in their labeling. Even if no one were labeled "mentally ill," people would still suffer from the same problems: their hallucinations, delusions, intense depressions, and anxieties would still be there. Further, the critics argue that labeling people who have mental problems is the only way we can identify those who are in need of help.

Classifying Mental Disorders

Mental problems are as diverse as the people who suffer from them. In one way or another, every individual problem is unique; but those who work with the mentally disturbed have long sought a standardized system to help make sense out of these diverse problems. The most widely accepted classification (see Table 6.1) is the American Psychiatric Association's *Diagnostic and Statistical Manual of Mental Disorders* (DSM). First published in 1952, this manual has been revised over the years, and critics charge that the changes have been motivated as much by political pressure and trends in public opinion as by new scientific knowledge. Changing public attitudes and pressure from gay activists resulted in the removal of homosexuality from the list of mental disorders in 1974, but less well-organized groups, such as sadomasochists, remain on the list. Similarly, as the antismoking movement gained power, tobacco dependence was included as a mental disorder for the first time. Critics also point out that psychiatrists often use these diagnostic categories in inconsistent and contradictory ways. For example, in one study, 131 patients were randomly selected from a large mental hospital and rediagnosed by a team of evaluators. In the majority of cases, the new diagnosis did not agree with the old one. Only 16 of the 89 patients originally diagnosed as schizophrenic were given the same diagnosis by the research team.[39] Despite its weaknesses, however, the DSM is still the best classification system we have. Although 15 major categories of mental disorders are listed in the current DSM, 3 are far more common than the others (see Figure 6.1). The **mood disorders** most commonly involve some kind of depression. Of course, everyone feels sad at one time or another, but "major depression" involves not only a deep sadness but such things as fatigue, loss of appetite, low self-esteem, and a feeling of hopelessness. **Substance abuse disorders** include problems resulting from the use of alcohol, tobacco, or the illegal drugs. By some measures, the most common disorders of all are the **anxiety disorders.** Like sadness, anxiety is certainly a normal part of daily life. Anxiety disorders, however,

mood disorder
A mental disorder involving severe disturbances in mood and emotion.

substance abuse disorder
A category of mental disorder applied to people who use excessive amounts of alcohol or other drugs.

anxiety disorder
A mental disorder involving severe and prolonged anxiety, irrational fears, panic attacks, obsessive thoughts and rituals, or the debilitating consequences of some traumatic event.

Table 6.1

Major Mental Disorders According to the American Psychiatric Association

1. Disorders first evident in infancy, childhood, or adolescence
Includes such things as mental retardation and stuttering.

2. Delirium, dementia, and amnestic and other cognitive disorders
Disorders with organic causes such as senility and brain damage.

3. Substance-related disorders
The abuse of alcohol and/or other drugs.

4. Schizophrenic and other psychotic disorders
Symptoms include such things as withdrawal from ordinary social contacts, bizarre thought processes, and hallucinations.

5. Mood disorders
Emotional disorders such as depression or exaggerated mood swings.

6. Anxiety disorders
Phobias, panic attacks, extreme anxiety, and stress from traumatic experiences such as battle shock.

7. Somatoform disorders
Psychological problems that manifest themselves as symptoms of physical disease, such as hypochondria.

8. Factitious disorders
Disorders involving the intentional feigning of a mental problem.

9. Dissociative disorders
Problems in which part of the personality is dissociated from the rest, such as multiple personalities and amnesia.

10. Sexual and gender identity problems
Sexually related problems such as transsexualism, exhibitionism, and inhibited sexual desire.

11. Eating disorders
Includes such problems as anorexia and bulimia.

12. Sleep disorders
Insomnia and other problems with sleep.

13. Impulse control disorders
The inability to control certain undesirable impulses, such as kleptomania, pyromania, and pathological gambling.

14. Adjustment disorders
Difficulty in adjusting to the stress created by such common events as unemployment or divorce.

15. Personality disorders
Includes various kinds of maladaptive personality traits that impede normal psychological functioning. Examples include the paranoid and antisocial personality types. (The DSM groups the personality disorders on a different "axis" than the other disorders listed above.)

Source: American Psychiatric Association, *Diagnostic and Statistical Manual of Mental Disorders IV* (Washington, DC: APA, 1994).

Figure 6.1

Mental Disorders

The most common mental disorders involve anxiety, depression, or substance abuse.

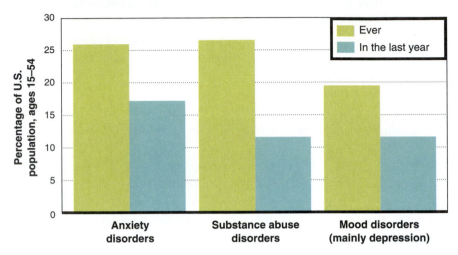

Source: Ronald C. Kessler, et al., "Lifetime and 12-Month Prevalence of DSM-III-R Psychiatric Disorders in the United States," *Archives of General Psychiatry* 51 (January 1994): 8–19.

schizophrenia

A mental disorder involving extreme disorganization in personality, thought patterns, and speech.

involve severe and prolonged anxiety as well as irrational fears (phobias), panic attacks, obsessive thoughts and rituals, and posttraumatic stress syndrome (the debilitating consequences of a traumatic event such as being raped or being in a vicious military battle). One of the most severe and persistent mental disorders is **schizophrenia.** Its symptoms include delusions, hallucinations, and disturbances in the thought process. Schizophrenia is, however, relatively rare. The National Comorbidity Survey found that less than 1 percent of the American population had ever suffered from this problem.[40]

The Distribution of Mental Disorders

Sociologists have long been interested in the way mental disorders are distributed throughout society, both because of the inherent importance of the issue and for the clues it might offer about the causes of psychological disturbance. Starting in the 1930s with the research of Robert E. L. Faris and H. Warren Dunham[41] and followed by numerous others, including August B. Hollingshead and Frederick C. Redlich[42] and Leo Strole and colleagues,[43] sociologists have been particularly interested in the relationship between social class and mental health. After reviewing 44 studies on this subject, Bruce P. Dohrenwend and Barbara Snell Dohrenwend concluded that "analysis of these studies shows that their most consistent result is an inverse relation between social class and reported rate of psychological disorder."[44] In other words, the less money someone has, the more likely he or she is to have a mental disorder. The National Comorbidity Survey found that class differences were much more marked for disorders involving anxiety and fear than those involv-

The difference between being labeled a prophet and being labeled mentally disturbed depends on the reaction of the audience. This photograph shows the removal of the bodies of some of the 39 people who committed suicide at the urging of a flying saucer cult in San Diego, California. The members of the cult considered their leader a great prophet, but others said his role in encouraging this carnage was the act of a deranged mind.

ing depression.[45] Thus, it appears that a good-paying job and higher social status help reduce stress and anxiety but are less effective against feelings of sadness and depression. Many studies also show that even though mental disorder is more widespread among poor people, the poor are less likely to receive any treatment.

Many sociologists also expected to find higher rates of mental disorders in the cities than in rural areas, but it did not turn out that way. For example, a study of the Hutterites—a religious group that lives in close-knit farming communities—concluded that their rate of severe mental disorder was roughly equal to the rate of hospitalization for mental disorder in New York State.[46] The most important difference was that the Hutterites usually cared for disturbed people in their homes rather than in hospitals. A comparative study by Eleanor Leacock found a high rate of psychosis in some decaying rural areas and a low rate in some relatively well-off urban areas.[47] It therefore appears that the characteristics of an individual's immediate community have more to do with mental health than does the number of people who live in it.

Men and women have roughly the same chance of experiencing some kind of mental disorder in their lifetimes, but there are some significant differences between the genders. A considerable body of research shows that women are more likely to suffer from disorders involving anxiety or depression, while men are more likely to have substance abuse problems. The National Comorbidity Survey also found that women are significantly more likely to have had three or more serious disorders during their lifetimes.[48]

Some researchers believe that these differences are the result of the physiological differences between women and men, but such figures are also influenced in several important ways by our gender role expectations. The elevated rates of anxiety and depression among women probably reflect the frustrations that come from the subordinate role many women are expected to play in the family and the workplace, as well as the conflicting demands modern society places on them. The difficulties men experience with alcoholism reflect, in part, the greater acceptability of heavy drinking among men. Moreover, the fact that men feel more pressure to conceal their emotional problems and "keep up a front" to the world may make drugs or alcohol seem to be the only way to cope with their psychological difficulties.

Marital status also has a bearing on one's likelihood of experiencing a mental disorder. Married people have the lowest rates of treatment for psychiatric problems, while rates for those who have never married are considerably higher for men but only slightly higher for women. Among the divorced, widowed, or separated, however, the rates are high for both sexes. Age is significant too. The National Comorbidity Study found that the rates of serious mental disorders were highest among 15- to 24-year-olds and declined steadily with age.[49] Although the survey did not include the elderly, it is generally recognized that they are much more likely to suffer from mental disorders that involve organic damage or deterioration, such as senility or **Alzheimer's disease.**

Alzheimer's disease
A disease that causes mental deterioration in older people.

The Causes of Mental Disorder

Considering the amount of disagreement over the definition and classification of mental disorders, it is not surprising that there are many arguments about their causes as well. Although there are numerous theories, we will consider four of the most important—those based on biology, early childhood development, social stress, and labeling.

Biology Most psychologists and psychiatrists agree that some people have an inherited predisposition that makes them more likely to experience certain kinds of mental disorders, but there are enormous disagreements about the relative importance of heredity and environment. Some hold with the old axiom that "biology is destiny," while others argue that biological influences are of minor importance and the real origins of most mental disorders lie in environmental factors.

Most of the earlier work by the biological theorists came from the study of schizophrenia. The most famous of these early studies was by Kallmann and Roth. They studied 17 pairs of identical twins (who have much greater genetic similarities than fraternal twins) and found that if one twin had schizophrenia, the other had the same problem 88.2 percent of the time.[50] However, the rate of concordance (if one has it, both have it) was only 22.9 percent for the 35 pairs of fraternal twins they studied. More recent studies have also concluded that close genetic relationships between identical twins are reflected in higher concordance rates. However, the differences found were not nearly as great as those reported by Kallmann and Roth. For instance, Hoffer and Polin found a concordance rate of 15.5 percent for identical twins and 4.4 percent for fraternal twins in a sample of almost 16,000 twins in the U.S. armed forces.[51] Of course, the concordance rate among identical twins may result from the fact that the physical similarity of identical twins leads their family and friends to treat them alike; but other research shows a higher concordance rate among identical twins even when they have been raised apart. Other research shows that a child is at greater risk of developing schizophrenia if one parent is schizophrenic and that the child's risk is significantly greater if both parents are schizophrenic. Moreover, such children are more likely to be schizophrenic even if they are raised away from their schizophrenic parents.[52]

There has also been a considerable amount of research into the biological roots of depression and related mood disorders. One team of researchers focused on a large Amish family in Pennsylvania with a very high incidence of **bipolar disorder.** After a careful analysis of blood samples, the researchers discovered genetic makers that indicated a difference in the DNA between those who had the disease and those who did not.[53] However, studies of people with the same problem from other groups have not found those same genetic markers.[54] Animal studies have led some researchers to believe that depression is linked to the deficiency of certain neurotransmitters, especially serotonin.[55] This conclusion is supported by the fact that drugs such as Prozac, which increase the body's level of serotonin, often relieve the symptoms of depression.

bipolar disorder
A mood disorder characterized by extreme emotional swings from depression to hyperactivity and back again.

Critics of the biological approach nonetheless remain unconvinced. They point out that antidepressant drugs are often ineffective and that even when biological treatments do work, there is no proof that the problem was biological. For example, antidepressant drugs are often effective in treating depression caused by such social factors as the death of a child or the loss of a job. The critics have also raised numerous questions about the validity of procedures used in conducting twin studies, and they point out that nearly 90 percent of diagnosed schizophrenics have no close relatives with the disorder.[56]

Developmental Theories Few experts doubt that social environment plays a major role in determining whether someone develops a mental disorder, but there are many different theories about how this influence is expressed. Details vary from one theory to another, but many of them borrow extensively from Sigmund Freud and his **psychoanalytic theory.** Freud held that the unusual behavior of the mentally disturbed is merely a symptom of deeper unresolved conflicts locked in the unconscious mind of the patient. Freud believed that an individual's personality is formed during the early years of childhood and that the family is therefore the major force in personality development. If children experience serious emotional trauma, their psychological development may be impaired, leading to difficulties later in life. For example, traumas caused by the parents' negative reaction to infantile sexual behavior may create unconscious conflicts between the desire for sexual gratification and the desire for approval from parents and society. Freud treated mental disorders with psychoanalysis, a slow, detailed analysis of the patient's mental history. Freud's theories have been attacked on numerous grounds, from their lack of empirical scientific support to their seeming obsession with sexuality and their denigration of women, but they have nonetheless been extremely influential.

psychoanalytic theory
A theory of personality created by Sigmund Freud, which emphasizes the role of unconscious desires in human behavior.

Many contemporary developmental theories see parental love and affection as the key to the normal maturation of a child. Children who are rejected by their parents may display a variety of psychological problems, including anxiety, insecurity, low self-esteem, and hostility. Parental standards of discipline are also important for proper development. Harsh, rigid standards may produce either a hostile and rebellious child or a passive, guilt-ridden one. Lack of discipline is thought to encourage antisocial and aggressive tendencies. Others feel that the children of overprotective parents develop "passive-dependent personalities."[57] Notice, however, that most of these conditions would not really qualify as mental disorders by most psychiatric standards.

Gregory Bateson and his associates developed a theory of schizophrenia based on what they called the **double bind.** This occurs when a parent gives a child two conflicting messages at the same time—for example, when a mother tells her son "I love you" but flinches or pulls away every time he touches her. Children who receive such conflicting messages are in a double bind; they desperately want to believe what their parents are saying, but they are constantly exposed to evidence that what is said is false. Thus, they may come to mistrust and misinterpret normal communications and eventually become seriously disoriented.[58]

On the whole, critics have not been kind to those who hold early parental influences responsible for major mental disorders. For one thing, they say that this approach is too vague about the exact conditions that cause mental disorders. Almost every family has some conditions that developmental theorists consider conducive to psychological disorder, but most children do not develop mental disorders. Moreover, many contemporary critics feel that this approach unfairly blames parents for everything that goes wrong with their children and that it produces unnecessary parental guilt and anxiety.

Traumas and Social Stress While there is a great deal of skepticism about the old idea that differences in child-rearing practices play a major role in the development of mental disorders, there is a growing recognition that traumatic events such as physical abuse or sexual molestation lie at the root of many serious psychological problems. In one study of female patients hospitalized for depression, over half acknowledged being sexually abused during childhood. A history of abuse was also correlated with the number and severity of depressive symptoms.[59] Similar results have been found in research on noninstitutionalized subjects. For example, a community survey of 3125 women found that anxiety, depression, and phobias were significantly higher among those who had been sexually abused as children.[60]

A related approach known as **stress theory** is based on commonsense ideas about psychological problems. Simply put, the theory holds that each individual has a breaking point and that if stress builds up beyond this level, the individual will experience serious psychological problems. This theory is used by military psychiatrists to explain the symptoms of "battle fatigue"—a kind of mental breakdown that occurs among troops during periods of combat. It can also be used to account for the behavior of harried parents, pressured executives, and overworked students. Since sociologists have found that social stress is much greater among the poor than among the affluent, it is not surprising to find a higher rate of serious mental disorder in the lower classes.

The relationship between stress and mental disorder is, however, more complex than our simple illustrations suggest. A certain amount of stress is actually beneficial because it provides a challenge that motivates an individual to respond in new and creative ways, but too much stress over too long a period seems to exhaust the individual's resources. The problem is to determine how much stress is appropriate and how much is harmful. Individuals have different tolerance levels, so something that

double bind
A situation conducive to the development of mental disorder, in which a parent gives a child two conflicting messages at the same time.

stress theory
A theory which holds that an individual will experience serious psychological problems if exposed to excessive levels of stress.

constitutes a healthy challenge to one person may cause serious psychological consequences in another.

Labeling Theory Interactionists look at mental "illness" not as a medical condition but rather as a social role that is learned like any other role. Playing the role of being mentally ill offers many rewards to people who have trouble coping with their "normal" life or want to escape from unwanted personal or social responsibilities. Interactionists do not say that most mentally disturbed people are "faking it" but only that their behavior is based on the social expectations of their society. According to labeling theory, which was created by the interactionists, people who have been declared mentally ill experience great pressure to act out that role. Their opportunities to play "normal" roles are reduced as friends shun them, prospective employers turn them away, and even their efforts to shed the label are taken as evidence of their instability. Everyone behaves as though the labeled person is sick; therefore, he or she eventually comes to believe it and act that way. The "sick" role may even become attractive to some victims of labeling. It allows them to escape from responsibilities, stop worrying about other people's reactions to their behavior, and relax their battle against the label. The late British psychiatrist R. D. Laing went a step further, claiming that the individuals we consider disturbed are in fact the sanest ones among us and that it is really our society that is sick. To Laing, schizophrenia was a healthy attempt to deal with the sickness of everyday life: "Can we not see that this voyage (schizophrenia) is not what we need to be cured of, but that it itself is a natural way of healing our own appalling state of alienation called normality?"[61]

Not surprisingly, most traditional therapists and mental health experts vigorously deny the idea that mental illness is just a social label and argue that people who aren't unbalanced don't act in ways that everyone knows will get them labeled as mentally ill. Whatever labeling theory's weaknesses, however, there is increasing recognition that the labeling process does indeed have harmful effects on many mental patients. For example, a study by Bruce Link found that labeled mental patients ended up with lower incomes and lower occupational status than people with the same background and the same psychological symptoms who had not been labeled.[62]

Quick Review

What are the three views about the nature of mental disorder?

What are the most common types of mental disorder?

Among which groups is mental disorder most common?

What are the main theories about the causes of mental disorder?

Health Care in the United States

The organization of America's health care system remains unique among the industrialized nations. In response to ever rising costs and the demand that competent health care be available to everyone, the other industrialized countries have all adopted broadly based systems of government-supported health care. The United States, however, took a different course, creating a medical welfare system for the poor and the elderly but leaving the rest of the health care system in private hands.

Doctors and Nurses

Physicians command more respect and admiration than people in practically any other profession, and, as is so often the case, high income accompanies high prestige. There is, nonetheless, a growing discontent with their performance. Many patients now see themselves as "health care consumers," and complaints that physicians are more concerned about their income than about their patients are becoming increasingly common. As medical technology has grown more complex and the health care system more bureaucratic, the doctor-patient relationship has become depersonalized. The old general practitioner who was a family adviser and friend has been replaced by an army of narrow specialists. As late as 1931, general practitioners outnumbered specialists by 5 to 1. Today that ratio is reversed: fewer than 1 in every 9 American physicians practices general medicine.[63] Currently, there is only about 1 pediatrician for every 1350 children in the United States. To make matters worse, there has been a significant decline in the number of medical school graduates going into internal medicine in recent years, and fewer than 40 percent of the internists surveyed by the American College of Physicians said they would pursue the same career again. Part of the problem is that internists make less money than most other medical specialists. In 1993, the average general practitioner had an income of about $117,000, compared with $263,000 for surgeons.[64] Another difficulty is the growing demand that internists and general practitioners be the "gatekeepers" of the health care system. Many cost-conscious insurance companies are now providing financial incentives for these primary-care providers to limit the services they give to patients and are requiring them to decide whether patients should be allowed to see specialists. Many of these physicians feel that these restraints compromise their ability to care for their patients.

While there is a shortage of primary-care physicians, there are too many doctors in prestigious and highly paid specialties such as surgery. Moreover, the surplus of surgeons has encouraged many unnecessary and potentially dangerous operations. For example, a 1987 Rand Corporation study found extremely high rates of unneeded surgery for three types of operations. The most overused of these three procedures was the carotid endarterectomy, intended to reduce the risk of stroke. The Rand study concluded that only about one-third of those operations were clearly in the interests of the patient.[65] A 1990 study in the *New England Journal of Medicine* reached similar conclusions about several other kinds of operations and found that physicians who specialized in a particular operation were more likely than other surgeons to perform it unnecessarily.[66]

American physicians are also poorly distributed in terms of ethnic group and gender. Like the members of other lucrative professions, most physicians have traditionally been white males. Although the last two decades have seen a significant increase in the number of female doctors, they still make up only about 20 percent of the profession and are particularly underrepresented in the most prestigious specialties. Members of most ethnic minorities are even more scarce. Currently only 4.9 percent of physicians in the United States are African American and 4.3 percent Latino.[67] It may appear that the personal background of well-trained physicians makes little difference to the quality of care they give, but imagine the difficulties of a Spanish-speaking patient whose physician cannot understand what he is saying, or the embarrassment of a female patient who would rather not discuss the intimate details of her sex life with a male physician.

Physicians are also far too heavily concentrated in the affluent neighborhoods of big cities and suburbs, leaving many low-income and rural areas with a critical shortage. Wealthy states such as Massachusetts and Connecticut have twice as many physicians per person as poor states such as Alabama or Arkansas. As Howard D. Schwartz puts it, "Two-thirds of American physicians treat the one-third of the population that is most able to pay."[68]

When a patient gets to see a doctor, his or her problems may be just beginning, for patients are often hurt rather than helped by their physicians. A study at a major university hospital found that more than one-third of its patients suffered from some sort of physician-caused disease—most commonly an adverse reaction to medication. When a group of researchers from the Harvard Medical School analyzed a survey of the drugs taken by elderly Americans, they found that one-fouth took at least one inappropriate prescription drug. Others estimate that 5 to 15 percent of hospital patients develop medically induced infections unrelated to their original health problem.[69] And the numerous deaths are caused by the unnecessary surgery already discussed.

Why do such problems occur? No matter how well trained they are, doctors and nurses are only human, and some make mistakes that cost patients their health or their lives. In addition to the inevitable errors, some physicians and nurses are simply incompetent, and because neither patients nor government officials are as well qualified as physicians to judge professional competence, the burden of protecting the public has fallen on the medical profession itself. Unfortunately, physicians have failed to live up to this important responsibility. The subculture of their profession strongly discourages physicians from criticizing each other, and the medical boards charged with regulating the profession bar only the most grossly incompetent doctors. There are hundreds of thousands of physicians in the United States, but only a handful of medical licenses are revoked each year. Even then, the most common reason for revoking a medical license is not malpractice but violations of narcotics laws. Another source of serious trouble is that our health care system provides too few doctors, nurses, and hospitals to care for the poor and the uninsured, so medical personnel who do take on that task are often rushed and overworked.

In many ways, the relationship between doctors and nurses mirrors the relationship between men and women in our society. Doctors, who are mostly male, make the important decisions and enjoy most of the prestige, while nurses, who are usually women, work under the authority and control of the doctors. Thus, physicians are the elite of the medical profession while nurses are its "working class." Doctors make the diagnoses and prescribe the treatments, but the nurses generally carry out those instructions and do the other work necessary for the day-to-day operation of the hospitals and other treatment facilities.

Many nursing jobs require long hours and entail enormous responsibilities that may mean life or death to a patient. Nurses are also the ones who must try to meet the emotional needs of patients who are away from home under unpleasant and often frightening circumstances. Yet nurses seldom receive the recognition or the pay that such important work warrants. On the average, a physician makes about four times more than a nurse practitioner (a highly trained nurse who often performs some of the same duties as a physician) and enjoys better working conditions and far higher prestige.[70] There is already a serious shortage of nurses, and the situation is expected to get far worse as our population ages and the concern with exploding medical spending makes the lower-cost care provided by nurses increasingly attractive.

The Hospitals Hospitals were originally hospices, places of refuge where the poor could go to die. Not until modern times did the hospital become a place where sick and injured people were given medical treatment. Today hospitals are the nerve centers of the medical profession. A hospital determines which physicians will be allowed to use the hospital and thus which patients will be admitted. Some hospitals are deeply involved in teaching and research, and an increasing number offer a wide range of outpatient services through clinics and emergency rooms.

In most industrialized nations, hospitals are either owned directly by the government or are operated under tight government controls. In the United States, the ownership and control of hospital services rests in many different hands. The federal government has special hospitals for military personnel and veterans, and many counties operate their own hospital systems, which often carry a heavy share of the burden of providing health care for the poor. Most hospitals, however, are owned by such diverse private groups as universities, religious organizations, physicians, health plans, and charities.

Of all types of hospitals, the fastest growing are large corporate hospital chains. This trend toward corporate ownership has had some beneficial effects. Hospital chains often provide more comfort and convenience for patients and have introduced computerized billing facilities and other efficient management practices. Yet on the whole, this trend is a worrisome one. One fear arises from the shift in control that goes with corporate ownership. Traditional hospitals are usually run by their physicians, but the corporate chains are controlled by professional managers who are likely to have far less understanding of medical practice and the needs of patients. The greatest concerns, however, center on finances. Although corporate hospitals provide more services to patients, they also charge higher rates than the traditional nonprofit hospitals. Moreover, corporate hospitals have tended to ignore the enormous health care needs of the poor; instead, they focus on people with good health insurance who are already well cared for. These hospitals have often been charged with performing "wallet biopsies" before admitting any patient who does not have a dire need for emergency care. Even their lower-cost emergency-care centers often take credit cards but not **Medicaid** (the government health care program for the poor). Defenders argue that corporate hospitals have no more responsibility to provide free services to the poor than any other business and that it is up to the nonprofit hospitals to carry the cost. The problem with that argument is that the corporate hospitals are skimming off the lucrative business that nonprofit hospitals once used to cover their losses from treating the poor. As a result, more and more nonprofit hospitals are going bankrupt—often to be bought by the corporate chains and closed to the poor.

Medicaid
A medical welfare program for the poor, blind, and disabled.

But the growth of corporate medicine is not the only reason many hospitals are having financial troubles. Another major problem is that the cost of medical technology has continued to escalate while cost-containment efforts by the government and private insurers have made it more difficult for less efficient hospitals to pass along all their expenses. Government restrictions on payments by **Medicare** (a medical welfare program for the elderly) and Medicaid, for example, have meant that nearly half of U.S. hospitals lose money treating the elderly and the poor.

Medicare
A medical welfare program for the elderly.

Mental institutions have always been different from other hospitals, and they deserve some special attention. Most hospitals focus on short-term treatment for people with acute medical conditions, but because physicians are unable to "cure" most mental disorders, mental hospitals, like nursing homes, provide long-term treatment and custodial care for chronic patients. Moreover, sociologists have long questioned the wisdom of sending psychologically troubled people to large, impersonal institutions in order to help them resolve their problems. For example, Erving Goffman's classic study of life in the "asylum" uncovered a host of difficulties that beset the institutionalized mental patient.[71] For one thing, patients often come into the institution with a sense of betrayal, believing that they have been tricked and manipulated by their friends and family. Upon admission, they are subjected to a variety of what Goffman called "degradation rituals" that strip them of their dignity and their identity. Familiar clothing and personal possessions are taken away; they are poked, prodded, and classified by medical personnel; and, worse of all, they are locked up and denied the freedom to move about as they please.

As a result of such stinging criticisms and the desire of politicians to reduce the costs of supporting these institutions, a widespread movement to deinstitutionalize mental patients developed. The goal was to treat people with mental disorders in community facilities and get them out of the large mental institutions, and the number of patients in mental facilities soon plummeted.[72] Critics of **deinstitutionalization** argue that it is merely a convenient justification for ignoring the problems of the mentally disturbed. It is estimated that about one-third of the nation's growing body of homeless men and women suffer from serious mental disorders. Former mental patients are commonly seen aimlessly wandering city streets, eating food from garbage cans, and sleeping in alleys and parks. Although there seems little doubt that these people need more help than they are receiving, defenders of deinstitutionalization point out that the original intent of the reforms was never carried out. The idea behind deinstitutionalization was to treat fewer mental patients in hospitals and more in the community, but most of the mental patients who were released from hospitals never received adequate treatment on the outside. Only a fraction of the community centers needed to support deinstitutionalized mental patients were ever built, and the majority of state and local funding still goes to large mental hospitals.

deinstitutionalization
Removing patients from mental hospitals and placing them in the community.

Paying the Cost   Traditionally, Americans bought medical care the way they buy beans, pork chops, and cars: purchasing what they desire and could afford. Direct payments by patients have been supplemented by government programs and private insurance, which now pick up most of the tab; but these changes were carried out in a haphazard way, and as a result, the current system is highly inequitable.

Government pays the biggest share of the health care bill—currently about 43 percent. Insurance companies pay about one-third, and consumers pay about one-fifth of the cost directly.[73] The critical problem with this system of financing is that while some people are almost entirely shielded from the potentially crushing costs of medical care, others have only spotty protection, and over 15 percent of Americans have no insurance at all.[74] Moreover, the financial contribution demanded by insurance companies, and the number of people who must pay for their medical care entirely out of their own pockets, have both been growing rapidly in recent years. It is not surprising, then, that a survey published in the *Journal of the American Medical Association* in 1994 found that one-fifth of American families had problems paying their medical bills.[75]

Those lucky enough to have good insurance coverage pay little or nothing for even the best medical care. While most Americans have some kind of private insurance, there are usually significant gaps in coverage. Some policies have little or no coverage for office visits or preventive care, while others require patients to make large deductible payments before the insurance company contributes. Most policies also limit the total amount the insurer will pay for any illness. Thus, people with serious medical conditions may find that their coverage has run out or that their insurance company has canceled their policy and refuses to pay for any future treatment.

Aside from this inadequate coverage, the private insurance system has another critical fault: it is extremely wasteful and inefficient. Estimates of how much the insurance companies spend on overhead and administration vary from source to source, but all the figures indicate that private insurance companies are far less efficient than government programs. A report by one consumer group estimated that private insurance companies spend $.033 on administration, marketing, commissions, and other overhead for every $1 they pay for medical care, while Medicare's administrative costs were only $.02 and the administrative costs of national health care in Canada were about $.03 per $1. *Consumer Reports* estimates the administrative cost of the Canadian system at 1 to 2.5 percent and that of private insurance at 10 to 11 percent.[76] Whichever estimate is most accurate, the conclusion is clear.

The government's health care payments come primarily from two programs: Medicare and Medicaid. Medicare buys medical services for people 65 and older, while Medicaid is designed to help the poor, the blind, and the disabled. The Medicare program is relatively uniform throughout the nation. Medicaid, however, is administered by the states, and each state has its own standards of eligibility and levels of benefits.

There are major gaps in the coverage of these programs, and they are growing wider year by year. The worst off are increasing numbers of the poor and near poor who are not eligible for Medicaid and cannot afford private insurance. When Medicaid was first established in the mid-1960s, it covered about 70 percent of those with incomes below the poverty line. Today, only about 45 percent of the poor are covered.[77] In addition, state and federal governments have been placing tighter limits on the assistance the poor receive. Some states have been creating more restrictive lists of the kinds of treatment they are willing to pay for, bringing charges that they are rationing health care for the poor. For example, the state of Oregon recently decided that medical procedures such as organ and tissue transplants were too expensive and that poor people who needed them would either have to get them from charity or do without. The most common approach has been to limit access to care informally by making it difficult and unattractive for physicians and hospitals to treat welfare patients. For one thing, the states pay far less for most medical procedures than physicians and hospitals usually charge. On top of that, states often impose a bewildering array of bureaucratic barriers that must be overcome before a physician can actually be paid. As a result, physicians simply refuse to accept Medicaid patients.

Medicare coverage for the elderly is far less restrictive than Medicaid—almost everyone 65 and over qualifies. But Medicare still requires the elderly to make a substantial financial contribution of their own and completely excludes coverage for the costs of care in a nursing home. In 1994, a study by the American Association of Retired Persons estimated that despite Medicare coverage, older Americans spend about 23 percent of their total family income on medical care and that their out-of-pocket medical expenses had doubled since 1987.[78] Another problem is that the government's efforts at cost control have made Medicare payments fall further and further behind those of private health insurance companies. In the 1970s, Medicare paid about 85 percent as much as private insurers for the same medical procedures; today it pays only about 60 percent as much.[79] As a result, physicians and hospitals are becoming increasingly reluctant to treat Medicare patients.

Quick Review

Why does medical treatment actually harm some patients?

What are the differences in the roles of physicians and nurses in our health care system?

What are the problems faced by today's hospitals?

Who pays the cost of health care in America?

The Crisis in American Health Care

How well does the American system work? Despite the efforts of some of the most dedicated and capable health care workers in the world, the problems of the American system remain serious and deep-seated, and many trends seem to be pointing in the wrong direction. Not only does the United States spend far more money per person than any other nation, but it also spends a much larger share of its total national income—45 percent more than Canada, 65 percent more than Germany, and double the percentage spent by Great Britain or Japan.[80] (See Figure 6.2.) Yet despite spending almost $1 trillion on health care every year, the United States does rather poorly in a comparison of international health statistics. Although the United States is the world leader in many branches of medical research, its infant mortality rate is the highest of any major industrialized nation, and so is its percentage of low-birthweight infants. Overall, the United States ranks only fifteenth in average life expectancy. It would be wrong to attribute all these differences to the health care system alone; variations in life-style, diet, and environment are also important. Nonetheless, it is clear that the American system often fails its neediest patients, and at the same time its overall cost continues to escalate out of control.

Failing the Patients: Unequal Access The American health care system's most glaring defect is its failure to meet the needs of our low-income citizens. As we have seen, access of the poor and minorities to health services is often severely restricted even when they are lucky enough to be covered by Medicare or Medicaid programs. Research shows that older whites are 3.5 times more likely to have heart bypass surgery than older African Americans and that African American kidney patients are only half as likely to receive a kidney transplant as white kidney patients.[81] A study of patients on Medicaid found that they were less than half as likely as those with private insurance to receive several common surgical treatments and that the gap between the two groups has increased as the relative value of Medicaid payments decreased over the years.[82] In many ways, the problems with our system of dental care are even worse. A minority child is three times more likely than a white child to lose a tooth by the age of 17. The percentage of minority children with unfilled cavities is twice as high as it is for whites, and among adults the percentage is three times higher.[83] One recent poll found that almost one-fourth of Americans had put off some medical treatment in the last year because they could not afford it.[84] This

Figure 6.2

Comparing Health Care Costs

The United States has the most expensive system of health care in the world.

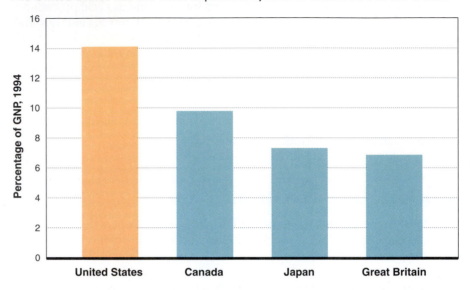

Source: U.S. Bureau of the Census, *Statistical Abstract of the United States, 1994* (Washington, DC: U.S. Government Printing Office, 1996), p. 834.

situation is not only unjust; it is also foolishly shortsighted. When people delay medical treatment until their problems are so severe that they have no choice but to seek help, the total cost is likely to be far greater than that of timely preventive care. The cost of the prenatal care denied to many poor women, for example, is far less than the hundreds of thousands of dollars often necessary to help their gravely ill infants.

Lack of prenatal care is only one of the ways the medical system neglects women's health needs. Until recently, women were denied entry into the upper levels of the medical profession, and as we have noted, the vast majority of physicians and medical researchers are still men. This male bias is reflected in many other aspects of the health care system as well. Medical researchers have often excluded women from studies, leaving physicians unsure whether new medical findings apply to female patients. Most clinical research on heart disease, for example, has used only male subjects. This practice is often justified on the grounds that heart disease is more common in men—although it is the leading cause of death in American women as well. Moreover, the same male-only approach to medical research was used for conditions that clearly affect women as much as men. For example, in 1958 the National Institute on Aging began a major study of the problems of aging, but women were not included among the subjects until 20 years later.[85] On the other hand, advocates for men's health needs also have significant grounds for complaint. They point out that research on breast cancer, the second most lethal cancer among women, receives four times more money than research on prostate cancer, the second most lethal cancer among men. While the National Institutes of Health spends

13.5 percent of its research budget on diseases unique to women, it spends only 6.5 percent of its budget on diseases unique to men. Moreover, because women live longer, go to the doctor more frequently, and receive more medical treatment; two out of every three health care dollars are spent on women.[86]

To stem the ever rising costs of health care, insurance companies have been exercising tighter and tighter controls on the kinds of treatments and services patients can receive. Over half of all Americans are now enrolled in some system of **managed care,** and it appears that it has met with some success in slowing the rate of medical inflation. The cost to the patients has, however, been enormous. In most systems of managed care, the patient's general practitioner acts as a health care gatekeeper, and many complain that they are denied access to the specialists who know the most about treating their particular illnesses. Moreover, there have been numerous reports of insurance companies denying patients treatments they need when the costs are high. Some insurance companies, for example, classify established therapies as "experimental" in order to refuse coverage, or demand that physicians use less costly treatments when the more expensive ones are known to work better.

> **managed care**
> A system of health care in which the treatments and services available to patients are tightly controlled to hold down costs.

Runaway Costs Not only is the American health care system the most expensive in the world, but the overall cost of health care has exploded in the last four decades (see Figure 6.3). In 1950, the United States spent 4.4 percent of its gross national

Figure 6.3

Rising Costs

Health care now takes twice as big a piece of the American economy as it did 25 years ago.

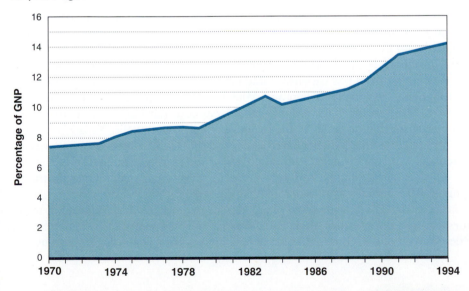

Source: David R. Francis, "Rising Health Costs Limit Other Programs," *Christian Science Monitor,* December 12, 1993, p. 9; U.S. Department of the Census, *Statistical Abstract, 1991* (Washington, DC: U.S. Government Printing Office, 1991), p. 92; *Statistical Abstract, 1993,* p. 849; *Statistical Abstract, 1996,* p. 834.

product on health care; by 1994, that figure was 14.2 percent.[87] The specter of runaway medical inflation has led to a host of new measures by the government and the private insurance companies to institute stricter cost controls, and the rate of medical inflation has dipped in the last few years.[88] But many experts believe that much of the cost savings from managed care have already been achieved, and they feel we can expect sharp increases in the years ahead.

There are at least three reasons health care is so expensive in the United States. The first is the way the health care industry is organized and financed. Unlike the case in most other countries, medicine in the United States is largely a private business organized for individual profit. As we have seen, the inefficient system of competing private health insurance companies wastes billions of dollars in unnecessary overhead costs. Most physicians also operate like private businesses aiming to maximize their profits. For example, University of Arizona researchers found that physicians who owned diagnostic imaging equipment ordered four times more imaging examinations than other physicians.[89] Because most physicians are paid on a **fee-for-service** basis (that is, they are paid for each individual service they perform), there are strong financial incentives to perform as many medical procedures on each patient as possible. Another study found that government employees covered by Blue Shield insurance, which pays doctors on a fee-for-service basis, had more than twice as much surgery as employees with group medical plans offering doctors no financial incentives for unnecessary operations.[90] Moreover, the fact that less than one-fourth of health care costs are paid directly by patients means that they have fewer incentives to look for the least expensive care or take other steps to hold costs down. *Consumer Reports* estimates that the United States could save $200 billion a year by cutting down on administrative inefficiency and unnecessary medical procedures.[91]

A second important cause of increasing costs has been the development of expensive new drugs and medical techniques. Such procedures as organ transplants and renal dialysis (the use of artificial kidney machines) are extremely costly and tend to drive up the overall price tag for health care. Moreover, the fact that there are huge profits to be made in developing new drugs and medical procedures has diverted attention from less expensive, and often more effective, techniques of preventive medicine. As Jeffrey Klein and Michael Castleman put it, "The processes that drive medical research toward expensive treatments also turn it away from preventive measures that do not hold the promise of corporate profit."[92]

A third factor is that patients have discovered that they can sue doctors for **malpractice** and win; as a result, the number of those suits has quadrupled since the late 1970s. All doctors—competent or not—now must pay high malpractice insurance premiums. The increasing number of malpractice suits has indirectly driven up health care costs. The fear of being charged with malpractice has also forced many doctors to practice "defensive medicine"—that is, they may order costly tests because they do not want to be accused in court of having forgotten something important.

fee-for-service
A form of compensation in which a health care professional receives a fixed fee for each service rendered.

malpractice
Incompetent or negligent practice by a physician or other professional.

Quick Review

Why do some groups of Americans have less access to health care than others?
Why has the cost of health care increased so much?

The development of complex and expensive new techniques has been a major factor in the rapid increase in the cost of medical care.

National Health Care: Britain and Canada

In all the industrialized nations except the United States, the government has created a system of **national health care** with some form of universal coverage. The fact that the government pays most of the cost of health care does not make it "free," as is sometimes claimed. Obviously, citizens must be taxed or pay some other charge to finance those services. National health care nonetheless has three major advantages over the American system. First, it is usually more fair, since the wealthy can be made to pay for the health care of those who cannot afford it. (Medicaid and Medicare help the very poor and the elderly, but other needy Americans are ignored.) Second, these systems provide far better service for the less fortunate. Third, they are cheaper. It would be a mistake, however, to look at all national health care systems as if they were basically the same. Every nation takes its own approach to providing health care for its citizens. A look at two other industrialized nations—Britain and Canada—shows us two different ways of organizing a national health care system.

national health care
A system of health care that is directed by the government.

Britain

In England, Northern Ireland, Scotland, and Wales, most medical care is provided at very little direct cost to the patient. The government owns the hospitals and pays most of the physicians. It also pays most of the costs of dental care and drugs. The National Health Service operates a two-tiered system of health care. Everyone signs up with a general practitioner, who is the one patients go to first with any ailment. Most general practitioners have about 2000 patients. They are paid on the basis of how many patients they have on their list, not how many procedures are performed, and as a result there is no financial incentive for "overdoctoring." When patients need special services, they are referred to a consultant in a hospital. The consultants are paid a fixed salary that does not depend on the number of patients or the procedures performed. Many consultants work only part time for the National Health Service and also have a private practice in which they charge fees directly to their patients.

In many ways the British system is more efficient than the American one. Britain spends only about half as large a share of its total economy on health care, and in terms of the actual amount spent per person, the gap is even larger. Yet the death rates for most age groups in the two countries are very similar.[93] The British system is clearly superior in providing health care for the poor, since everyone has equal access to the National Health Service. On the other hand, financial restraints mean that expensive procedures are often informally rationed, so there may be delays in receiving some kinds of treatment that can be safely postponed. Moreover, Britain, like all other industrialized nations, is having trouble meeting the needs of an aging population and coping with the exploding costs of medical technology. In the last decade and a half, the government has failed to provide sufficient funding to meet these new expenses. As a result, there are increasing delays before a patient can receive a needed operation, and a growing number of the British people have now taken out private insurance to supplement the public system. Thus, the gap between the quality of health care for the rich and the poor has grown wider in recent years.

Canada

Although the Canadian and American cultures are similar, Canadians have always been more enthusiastic about government social programs than their neighbors to the south. As a result, Canada became involved in government-supported health care much earlier and to a much greater extent than the United States. As far back as 1914, the province of Saskatchewan established a hospital insurance program, following it with comprehensive health insurance in 1948. By the end of the 1950s, hospital insurance had gone nationwide, and in 1966, the Medical Care Act provided government-funded medical care for all Canadians. At the same time, Canada also outlawed all private insurance for services covered by the government plan.

The Canadian system of national health care is quite different from the British one. For one thing, it is more decentralized, with the federal and the provincial governments sharing in the control and the financial responsibility. Another difference is that although Canadian hospitals are funded by the provinces, their ownership remains in private hands. One of the most important contrasts is in the way physicians are paid. Like their American counterparts, most Canadian physicians are paid on a fee-for-service basis rather than a fixed salary, but unlike the case in the United States, there is only a single fee schedule for each province, which is negotiated between the provincial government and the local medical association. Although physicians' incomes are somewhat lower than in the United States, doctors are still among the highest paid of all Canadians. The average Canadian physician earns 4 to 5 times more than the average industrial worker, while that ratio is 5 or 6 to one in the United States.

The growing cost of health care is a problem in Canada, as it is in the United States, but Canadian officials have been far more effective in containing it. Twenty-five years ago, before the start of national health care, Canada and the United States both spent about 6 percent of their gross domestic product on health care. By 1994, that figure had grown to 9.8 percent for Canada but to 14.2 percent for the United States.[94] There are several reasons for Canada's success. Physicians' fees and hospital budgets must be negotiated directly with the provincial governments; therefore, governments have far more leverage to hold down prices. Another major saving is in the reduction in paperwork: because all the costs are paid by the government, physicians and hospitals do not have to worry about collecting bills from patients, and the duplication of services and high executive salaries typical of the private insurance industry are eliminated. One estimate holds that a Canadian-style national health system would save the United States more than $21 billion a year in overhead alone.[95]

The Canadian system clearly costs less, but how good is the care? Critics point out that provincial restrictions on hospital budgets have slowed the purchase of the equipment needed to handle expensive new procedures such as heart transplants. But even if the Canadian system does not do quite as well in providing the most expensive medical innovations, it does a far better job of supplying the everyday health care most people need. Medical services are provided without cost to the patients; therefore, low-income Canadians get far better care than they would in the United States. Equally important is the fact that Canadians are free to go to their doctors for minor problems or preventive care before they develop serious complications. Infant mortality is significantly lower in Canada than in the United States, and overall life expectancy is higher.[96] The final proof of the superiority of the Canadian system lies in the opinions of its clients. In one poll, 9 out of 10 Americans felt that their health care system needed "fundamental changes," while in a different poll, a similar number of Canadians agreed that their health care system is "one of the things that makes Canada the best country in the world in which to live."[97]

Quick Review

How do the health care systems in Britain and Canada differ from the one in the United States?

Ethical Dilemmas

To most outsiders, the moral responsibility of the medical profession seems clear: to save lives and help patients be as healthy as possible. The increasing power of medical technology has created perplexing ethical dilemmas for which we have yet to find satisfactory answers, however. One such issue concerns the so-called heroic efforts physicians use to extend the lives of dying patients. Medical costs mount

Debate   Should Abortion Be Legal?

Yes

To deny a woman the right to have an abortion is to deny her control of her own body. The government has no right to force a woman to have a child she does not wish to bear. Those who demand that the government stop all abortions are urging us down the road to a totalitarian society in which the police and the courts control our most personal decisions.

Those who oppose abortion claim that a fetus is a fully formed human being and to abort it would be murder. Such claims lack any scientific support. A fetus is not an independent living creature and can survive only as long as it is attached to its mother's body. If it is murder to abort a fetus that cannot live on its own, then it is murder to practice birth control and cut off the unfertilized egg's chance of survival.

In addition to the obvious danger of giving the state authority over the private workings of our bodies, there is another important reason to keep abortion legal. The laws prohibiting abortion never stopped such operations. What they did do was to force hundreds of thousands of women to go to incompetent, untrained abortionists, and many of them paid with their lives. If the antiabortion crusaders are successful, the black-market abortionists will be back in business, and thousands of women will be their victims.

No

Abortion is murder, plain and simple. When a fetus is aborted, a human life is ended. An aborted fetus dies just as surely as a baby shot with a gun. A society that claims to respect human life cannot allow the continuation of this slaughter.

The supporters of abortion claim that the old antiabortion laws created a flourishing business in illegal abortions that injured or killed many of its customers. They are certainly right in pointing out the harm the illegal abortionists did to many of these women; but they ignore the harm that abortions—legal or illegal—do to innocent fetuses. The way to stop the black-market abortion business is not to legalize it but to demand tougher law enforcement to stamp it out.

There is another important reason to make abortion illegal again: to preserve the sanctity of the family and to reinforce our society's support of the fundamental value of human life. When society permits a mother to take the life of her unborn child, it tells us all that human life is a cheap commodity to be thrown away for the sake of mere convenience. Mothers should be required to carry their babies the full term necessary for their survival. Unborn babies have a right to life.

rapidly in the final weeks of a patient's life. One-third of Medicare's entire budget is spent on people in the last year of life. Most of us would say that cost should not be the standard to decide who lives or dies—but in a world in which millions of people starve to death every year, the money we use to keep one dying patient alive for another month could save a thousand hungry babies in the Third World. Is this fair? What about all the American babies who die because their mothers never received a few hundred dollars' worth of prenatal care?

Even if we ignore the costs, serious ethical issues remain. When people die, all their life-sustaining systems usually fail at about the same time, but medical equipment can take over the functions performed by the heart and lungs, thus keeping some gravely ill patients alive almost indefinitely. Although such patients are alive, the quality of their life is often pitifully low. They lie trapped in a hospital bed, connected by wires and tubes to a machine they totally depend on. If the patient wishes to continue under such conditions, there appear to be few ethical problems. In many cases, however, the patient is unconscious and unable to make any sort of decision. Some people now make out "living wills" that spell out how far they wish their physicians to go in using heroic means to extend their lives if they become gravely ill.

Yet even the principle of self-determination implied in such wills is not universally accepted in our society. Many hospitals refuse to turn off patients' life-support machines even if they request it. In fact, in most states a physician who helps a dying patient end a life of pain can be charged with murder. Yet there is growing support for legalizing "physician-assisted suicide"—that is, allowing physicians to assist patients to end their life if the patients are too ill to do it by themselves. A 1994 Harris poll found that 73 percent of the Americans polled agreed with the statement "The law should allow doctors to comply with the wishes of a dying patient in severe distress who asks to have his or her life ended."[98]

Just as many perplexing ethical questions surround the beginning of life as its end. One of the most controversial ethical issues of our time is abortion. This difficult matter revolves around two separate issues that are often confused. On a personal level, the question is wheather a woman is morally justified in deciding to have an abortion; and on the sociological level, the question is the role the government should play. (See the Debate "Should Abortion Be Legal?")

The abortion debate has been going on for decades, but advances in medical technology are also creating new dilemmas about human reproduction. The technique for artificially inseminating a woman without sexual contact has been used for decades to help women with infertile husbands become pregnant. In contrast, the practice of **surrogate mothering,** in which a woman is hired to bear someone else's child, has raised a storm of protests. Although the surrogate mother signs a contract agreeing to give the child to its biological parents, bitter legal battles have arisen when surrogates have attempted to void those contracts and claim legal custody of the child. Obviously, there are no simple answers to these troubling ethical questions, yet society must somehow formulate social policies to guide the medical profession in making these ethical decisions.

surrogate mothering
One woman bearing a child for another.

Quick Review

What new ethical dilemmas are faced by today's health care system?

Solving the Problems of Health Care

There are two approaches to the problems of the sick. The first is to try to prevent health problems by changing life-styles and eating habits, reducing pollution, and increasing the use of preventive medicine. The second aims at improving care for people after they become sick. The latter approach includes proposals designed to create equal access to health care regardless of income and to improve the overall quality of these services at less cost.

Preventive Medicine

The old saying "an ounce of prevention is worth a pound of cure" is as true today as it was a hundred years ago. As we noted earlier, improvements in sanitation and nutrition have saved more lives than all hospitals combined. Yet our health care system continues to emphasize treatment rather than prevention of disease. A delicate heart operation is much more dramatic than the dull business of educating people to avoid heart trouble through proper diet and regular exercise. Yet the second approach is both cheaper and more effective. In its broadest sense, **preventive medicine** includes a wide range of programs to encourage healthier living, including school courses in nutrition, personal hygiene, and driver training as well as campaigns against excessive use of tobacco, alcohol, and other drugs.

This approach has a long history in non-Western medical traditions. Wealthy Chinese commonly placed a practitioner of traditional medicine on a monthly salary to overlook the welfare of their families. The physician would make regular visits to check dietary and personal habits, dispense advice and medicines to help prevent illness, and generally keep abreast of the state of health of each family member. If anyone fell seriously ill, the payments were *stopped* until the physician had nursed the patient back to health.[99]

There is no question that Western medicine has made enormous progress in curing disease. Many critics charge, however, that today's physicians focus so intently on the symptoms of disease that they have forgotten the patients who suffer from them. Drawing heavily from the approach of traditional Chinese and Indian physicians, practitioners of **holistic medicine** focus on the patient's overall mental, emotional, and physical condition. The goal is not to cure the symptoms of disease but to improve the general state of the patient's health. Whether or not most medical practitioners follow the holistic approach and adopt specific techniques borrowed from non-Western traditions, they clearly need to pay more attention to their patients' life-style and mental outlook and not just to the symptoms of disease.

Medical Personnel

Although a recent national report recommended cutting medical school admissions by 20 percent to reduce the supply of physicians, the United States clearly needs to train more general practitioners, pediatricians, and nurses. By restricting the number of students in overcrowded specialties such as surgery, medical schools could help move physicians into fields in which they are badly needed, particularly general practice. Medical schools could also train more **physician's assistants** and **nurse practitioners,** medical personnel who, although less broadly trained than medical doctors, are qualified to perform many services that are now restricted to physicians. Significant progress has nonetheless been made in one area: today almost 40 percent of medical school graduates are women, compared with only 5 percent in 1960.[100]

One way to cut costs in our health care system would be to offer higher pay and more professional authority for nurses. Not only would this attract more people into the profession, but costs would be lower if nurses were allowed to do more of the services now carried out exclusively by physicians. During the last two decades, the medical profession has been moving in this direction with the development of the new field of advanced practice nursing, which includes nurse practitioners in fields

preventive medicine
An approach to health care that attempts to prevent health problems.

holistic medicine
A medical approach that focuses on the overall health of the patient and not on individual symptoms.

physician's assistants
Medical personnel trained to carry out particular medical services traditionally performed by physicians.

nurse practitioner
A nurse trained to take full charge of patients' basic health care.

Regular exercise is an important component of healthy living, and growing numbers of people are making an effort to incorporate more physical activity into their lives.

such as pediatrics and women's health, who see patients very much as physicians do; nurse midwives; and nurse anesthetists. Their numbers have been increasing rapidly in recent years, but regulations concerning nurse practitioners vary greatly from state to state, and they have had to fight numerous battles with physicians some of whom see advanced practice nurses as a threat to their professional status.[101]

Restructuring the Health Care System

As we have seen, America's health care system is in the midst of a deep crisis. Most Americans agree that reforms are necessary, and there seem to be two objectives that must be met: controlling costs and providing universal coverage. A 1994 poll, for example, found that 8 in 10 Americans agreed that universal health insurance was "very important," and although this survey didn't ask about reducing costs, that objective is undoubtedly supported by an even larger proportion of the population.[102] Unfortunately, this consensus quickly breaks down when it comes to specific proposals to achieve those goals. In an industry that accounts for roughly one-seventh of the economy, every proposal that would achieve significant improvements has run into intense opposition from powerful special interests.

All proposals for reform must come to terms with two fundamental issues: how to organize the health care system and how it pay for it. From an administrative standpoint, the most efficient approach is a "single-payer system" in which one government agency pays all the bills, as in Great Britain or Canada. As we have seen, the overhead costs in such systems are far lower than in the current American approach, with its hundreds of competing insurance companies and numerous government programs. Not surprisingly, however, the insurance industry has put up intense opposition to any effort to create a single-payer system, and, at the present time at least, such an efficient system seems to have no realistic chance of enactment in the United States. A second approach, put forth by President Clinton in his unsuccessful health care reform proposals, would be to encourage the existing insurance companies to band together in large "health care alliances" that would then compete with each other under general cost and procedural standards set by the government. Some supporters of this idea claim it would be even more efficient than a single-payer plan, but there is no hard evidence since it has never been tried in any other country. Moreover, the insurance industry mounted a very effective attack on this proposal as well. A third possibility would be to leave the current system as it is and just expand existing medical welfare programs or provide subsidies to enable more low-income people to afford private insurance. This approach, however, does little or nothing to contain the exploding cost of medical care.

Some of the most bitter battles in the health care debate have concerned the best way to pay for universal coverage. There are three possible sources of money: direct payments by individuals, payments from employers, and general tax revenues. Not surprisingly, all the proposals for funding universal health coverage have run into strong opposition from one quarter or another. The Clinton administration proposed an "employer mandate" that would require all employers to provide insurance for their workers. That proposal was fiercely attacked by small-business owners, who claimed they could not afford it even with the help of various subsidies that were also being proposed. A second approach is simply to require everyone to have some form of health insurance. If their employers don't pick up the tab, individuals would be required to pay for it themselves. Even if the government provided a basic package of coverage at a fairly low cost, however, this approach still doesn't solve the problems of those too poor to afford insurance payments. A third approach is to use tax revenues to finance all health care or to subsidize those who can't afford it. The advantage of this approach is that it would place the burden of financing the health care system on those who are best able to pay. However, it would obviously require a major increase in taxes, and proposals to create such a system have run into the same kind of heated opposition as efforts to increase taxes for other proposes.

It should be clear from this discussion that the most difficult part of improving the health care system is political. None of the proposals is perfect, but there are several reasonable approaches that would almost certainly provide more universal coverage and more effective cost controls than the current American system, which after all does very poorly in terms of cost and coverage in comparison with the health care systems of other industrialized nations. The critical task is to break through the logjam of opposition from the powerful special-interest groups—the insurance industry, pharmaceutical companies, the medical profession, and hospitals, among others—in order to create a system that serves the interests of society as a whole.

Community Mental Health Treatment

Despite the problems created by the movement to deinstitutionalize mental patients, well-run community-based care is still the best way to treat all but the most severely disturbed individuals. Patients who remain in their communities during treatment avoid the shock of being taken out of their normal environment. They also escape the labeling, humiliation, and feelings of powerlessness that are bound to accompany institutionalization, as well as the painful readjustment period that follows it.

Community mental health centers usually offer five basic services: short-term hospitalization, partial hospitalization that allows patients to return home at night or on the weekends, outpatient therapy, emergency care for special problems, and consultations and educational services for the community at large. These centers thus provide a broad range of services, many of which are likely to be unavailable from other sources. The major problem with today's centers is simply that there are not enough of them, and those that do exist are too often underfunded and understaffed.

Other kinds of community programs can also help deal with the problems of the mentally disturbed. For example, physicians, teachers, police officers, and others who are likely to come into contact with people who need mental health care should be taught the best ways of working with those individuals and should be familiarized with agencies that can provide help. Many private organizations can also help meet community mental health needs. Citizens working without pay for hotline agencies answer phone calls from people in need of help, refer them to appropriate agencies, try to head off suicides, or merely lend a sympathetic ear.

Quick Review

What are the best ways to improve the health care system?

Sociological Perspectives on Problems of Health and Illness

Concern about ever rising costs and the increasing gap between the high-quality health care that modern medicine can provide and the care that many people actually receive has made health care an important social problem. Social scientists of every persuasion have tried to explain why the social organization of health care is not better, given the fact that it is now a multibillion-dollar business. We should have the knowledge and technology necessary to provide excellent services for everyone.

The Functionalist Perspective

Viewed functionally, the jumbled health care system is a result of the rapid development of medical technology combined with changes in public attitudes about medical care. In the nineteenth century, medical knowledge was so limited that private doctors could handle almost all demands for health care. Rapid growth of medical knowledge and techniques greatly increased the kinds of services doctors could offer; because these services were effective, the demand for them boomed. People came to see good health care as a fundamental right, but the American system of health care was unable to adapt efficiently. The idea that health care is a commodity, to be bought the way one buys a sack of potatoes or hires a carpenter, is still with us, as is the conviction that medical care should be provided by a private practitioner and not by a corporation or a government bureau.

It is because of this lag, functionalists say, that the U.S. health care system is failing to do its job efficiently. Health care services are still sold privately. This individualistic "free-enterprise" system has been supplemented, in patchwork fashion, by a great variety of cooperative organizations: clinics, hospitals, group practices, and health maintenance organizations. It has also been supplemented by many new sources of funding: employers, unions, insurance companies, and a host of government agencies.

In short, the U.S. health care system is disorganized because it has grown rapidly and haphazardly, without proper planning. Obviously, the solution to this problem is reorganization, but functionalists do not agree on the form this reorganization should take. Some would have us return to complete free enterprise in the health care business. Such a system would allow physicians to sell their services at whatever price the market will bear, and those too poor to pay that price could turn to private charity or go without. Most functionalists, however, feel such a system would be too harsh and uncaring. Other functionalists believe that we should stick with the present system and work to streamline it and make it more efficient. They call for reallocating medical personnel, reducing fraud and malpractice, lowering costs, and training more nurses and other medical personnel in short supply. Still other functionalists argue that the best way to reduce the disorganization in the current system of health care is to create a centralized government-run system like the ones in Britain and Canada.

The Conflict Perspective

Conflict theorists see the U.S. health care system in a different light. They argue that its problems and deficiencies stem from the fact that it is designed to serve the needs of the rich and powerful (including doctors themselves) and thus neglects the needs of low-income groups. Health care is dominated by businesspeople with medical degrees who try to sell their services at the highest price. Because physicians have a legally enforced monopoly on medical services, they are in a position to rig prices. They sell their services at inflated prices that only the rich or well insured can pay, and they oppose programs that would reduce profits or require physicians to provide cheap health care for the poor. Further, conflict theorists claim, physicians have created an aura of mystery about their profession in order to boost their occupational prestige and cover up their shortcomings. In this atmosphere, patients are not expected or allowed to judge the quality of their medical care—"the doctor knows best." Incompetents and profiteers are not weeded out because patients are kept in the dark about the true nature of the medical care they are receiving.

Sociologist Paul Starr's research has shown that the U.S. health care system's reliance on unrestricted fee-for-service payments by insurance companies and government agencies was created by powerful interests in the medical industry itself.[103] According to Starr, the largest, most important health insurance company, Blue

Cross/Blue Shield, was created to protect the interests of hospitals and physicians. Blue Cross, which originally covered only hospital expenses, was started in response to the financial crisis of U.S. hospitals during the Great Depression and was directly controlled by the hospital industry. Blue Shield, which originally covered doctors' expenses, was created and controlled by physicians. Starr also argues that the generous system of medical payments in the original Medicare legislation was put there as a result of pressure from the medical lobby.

Conflict theorists would resolve the health care problem by reducing the medical profession's control over the financing and organization of the health care system. This power would then be transferred to the government to ensure good medical care for all citizens regardless of their ability to pay. Most conflict theorists call for government-financed health care that is available without charge to individual patients. They also argue that such changes will come about only if those who receive inadequate health care organize themselves to counter the tremendous power of the health care establishment.

The Feminist Perspective

Most feminists are more receptive to the conflict perspective than to the functionalist analysis of the health care system. But in addition to the exploitation of the poor and the working class by wealthy professionals, feminists also see a systematic repression of women. Until recently, women were grossly underrepresented in medical school, and they were excluded from many of the highest-paying and most prestigious medical positions. No only is this unfair to the women who work in the medical profession, but the whole system has functioned to reinforce and support traditional gender stereotypes. The male doctors became powerful symbols of power and authority while the female nurses they directed carried out the subordinate roles. Generations of women went to male doctors and psychiatrists with their most intimate problems, and those medical professionals became a primary source of the male control of women's bodies and women's lives. In addition, feminists argue that the current system of health care and medical research is focused more on needs of men than on those of women.

Feminists obviously applaud the trends toward an increasing number of female physicians, but they argue that much more needs to be done. For one thing, women are still underrepresented in most of the highest-paying and most prestigious positions, and nurses are still paid far less than the physicians who give them orders. So in addition to reforms to provide better medical care for the poor, feminists call for an end to the discrimination against women in medical careers and for new concern for the special health care needs of women and children.

The Interactionist Perspective

Although interactionists rarely deal directly with the organization of health care services, they have made significant contributions to our understanding of the health care field. They have shown, for example, that the socialization process in medical schools often has unanticipated consequences, making doctors into something less than the humanitarians many medical students aspire to be. A crushing burden of work and isolation from people in other walks of life create a powerful sense of group solidarity among physicians that has made it difficult for outsiders to exercise proper scrutiny of their behavior. Interactionists have shown that people learn to be "sick" (to play the role of sick people) just as they learn to be parents, factory workers, or lawyers. It follows that health care services sometimes make people sick rather than well.

Interactionists are also concerned with the ways we develop unhealthy habits and life-styles. Attitudes toward exercise, diet, smoking, and drinking are learned from our primary groups and reflect the attitudes of our culture as well. Further, interactionists point out that unhealthful behavior is often encouraged by the mass media, business, and even the government. Expensive advertising campaigns designed to sell junk food, cigarettes, and alcohol are good examples. The competitive pressures of our economic system are also a major factor in the numerous health problems resulting from stress and tension.

Many interactionists believe that significant improvements can be made in public health through a concerted campaign of education and social change. First, there must be greater awareness of the damage caused by unhealthy life-styles and poor diet. Second, there must be social changes that will encourage everyone to follow the principles of good health. The ideal of the successful, hard-driving achiever will have to be modified to permit a new emphasis on cooperation and mutual support. It is also important that businesses take greater social responsibility for the products they sell. A new social climate must be created in which it is no longer acceptable for corporations to spend millions of dollars advertising children's breakfast cereals that are mostly sugar, developing new cigarettes with more "sex appeal," or promoting other dangerous products.

Quick Review

How do the functionalist, conflict, feminist, and interactionist theories explain the problems of our health care system?

Summary

In the past century, there has been a tremendous drop in the death rate. Though improved health care and new treatments for deadly diseases contributed to this decline, it was largely due to improvements in living conditions—better food, housing, and sanitation. While industrialization and technology have helped increase food supplies and reduce epidemic disease, they have also created new health problems. The stress of modern-day living and a decline in physical exercise have increased the frequency of a variety of heart and circulatory diseases, and our diet is often unhealthy. Suicide, accidents, and violent crime are major health problems of a different kind. Occupational hazards, smoking, and environmental pollution are now major causes of death and injury. As the AIDS crisis has shown us, even the

problem of epidemic disease is far from over. On the average, poor people have
more health problems and a shorter life span than others. Many factors contribute
to these problems, including stress and worry, dangerous occupations, poor diet,
and inadequate medical care.

There are significant disagreements about the true nature of mental disorder.
Some see it as mental illness, others as a problem of personal maladjustment, and
still others as a label given to deviant behavior. The *Diagnostic and Statistical Manual of Mental Disorders* (DSM) is the most widely used classification system for
mental disorders; its most commonly used diagnoses include mood disorders, substance abuse disorders, and anxiety disorders. Like physical illnesses, mental disorders are more common among the poor. There are many different theories about
the causes of mental disorders, including the notions that they stem from an inherited biological predisposition, that they result from difficulties in early childhood
development, and that they come from problems in the individual's environment.

The American system of health care is unique among all the industrialized nations because it is organized and run as a private business. Despite medical welfare
programs, poor people receive inferior care, and almost 40 million Americans are
not covered by welfare programs or private insurance. At the same time, the inefficiency and high overhead costs of this system make it the most expensive in the
world. Physicians practicing in the United States are poorly distributed among the
various specialties and geographic regions, and there is a shortage of nurses. Critics
charge that it is too difficult to stop incompetent physicians from practicing. Traditionally, most American hospitals were privately owned but operated as nonprofit
businesses. In recent years, however, hospital chains run by large corporations have
grown rapidly. Another important change has been the deinstitutionalization of
mental patients since the 1950s. American medicine is financed by an inefficient
combination of private health insurance, government welfare programs (Medicaid
and Medicare), and direct payments by patients.

The main alternative to this approach is some kind of government-funded national health care system. In Britain almost all health care costs are paid directly by
the government. Citizens sign up with the general practitioner of their choice, and
the physician is paid based on the number of patients served, not the number of
tests or treatments performed. In Canada, most health care services are also financed by taxpayers rather than by individual patients; however, the Canadian
health care system is much more decentralized than the British system. Each
province directs its own health care program, and the federal government under-
writes part of the cost. Hospitals remain in private hands, and physicians are paid on
a fee-for-service basis.

There are two general ways of dealing with the problems of the sick. One is to
prevent health problems before they start. Another approach is to improve the
quality of health care services for people who have become ill. This includes proposals for improving medical personnel and for restructuring the health care system
to hold down costs and provide universal coverage for all Americans.

Functionalists contend that the health care system is disorganized because the
ways and means of delivering medical services have not adjusted to changes in the
medical services themselves. Conflict theorists argue that because the U.S. health
care system is controlled by medical professionals and the rich, it serves their interests and neglects the poor. Feminists point out that the health care system discrimi-

nates against women and perpetuates traditional gender stereotypes. Interactionists point out that unhealthful life-styles are learned, and they call for a program of education and social change to improve our way of living.

Questions for Critical Thinking

Many sociologists believe that our economic and political institutions are critical forces in both causing and resolving our social problems. Is this true of our problems of health and illness? How have economic and political forces shaped our health care system? Does the system favor the rich at the expense of the poor and the uninsured?

Key Terms

acquired immune deficiency
  syndrome (AIDS)
Alzheimer's disease
anxiety disorder
contagious disease
deinstitutionalization
double bind
fee-for-service
health
holistic medicine
human immunodeficiency virus (HIV)
labeling theory
malpractice
manic depression

Medicaid
Medicare
mental disorder
mood disorder
national health care
nurse practitioner
physician's assistant
preventive medicine
psychoanalytic theory
schizophrenia
sexually transmitted disease
stress theory
substance abuse disorder
surrogate mothering

Further Readings

Erving Goffman, *Asylums: Essays on the Social Situation of Mental Patients and Other Inmates* (New York: Doubleday, 1990) [originally pub. 1961]. A classic exploration of the social psychological effects of life in a "total institution" (mental hospital, prison, etc.).

"The Health Care Crisis," *Consumer Reports* 57 (July–September 1992). An excellent three-part report on the deficiencies of the American health care system from a strong advocate of consumer rights.

David Mechanic, *Mental Health and Social Policy: The Emergence of Managed Care,* 4th ed. (Boston: Allyn & Bacon, 1998). An examination of the problems of mental health and mental disorder by a well-known medical sociologist.

Pauline Vaillancourt Rosenau (ed.), *Health Care Reform in the Nineties* (Thousand Oaks, CA: Sage, 1994). A collection of articles exploring the best ways to reform the American system of health care.

Paul Starr, *The Social Transformation of American Medicine* (New York: Basic Books, 1982). An extremely influential book tracing the origins and development of the American health care system.

Carol Wekesser (ed.), *Health Care in America: Opposing Viewpoints* (San Diego: Greenhaven, 1994). An interesting collection of pieces arguing different viewpoints in the current health care debate.

Notes

1. Jerry Bler, "Man 'Hit Cracks' in Wife's Care," *Fresno Bee,* March 2, 1994, p. A1.
2. Quoted in Paul I. Ahmed and Aliza Kolker, "The Role of Indigenous Medicine in WHO's Definition of Health," in Paul I. Ahmed and George V. Coelhi, eds., *Toward a New Definition of Health* (New York: Plenum, 1979), p. 113.
3. Population Reference Bureau, *World Population Data Sheet, 1997* (Washington DC: Population Reference Bureau, 1994); John B. McKinlay and Sonja M. McKinlay, "Medical Measures and the Decline of Mortality," in Howard D. Schwartz, ed., *Dominant Issues in Medical Sociology,* 2nd ed. (New York: Random House, 1987), pp. 691–702.
4. See P. H. Fentem, "Benefits of Exercise in Health and Disease," *British Medical Journal* 308 (May 1994): 1291–1295; Gregory D. Curfman, "The Health Benefits of Exercise: A Critical Reappraisal," *New England Journal of Medicine* 328 (February 1993): 574–576; William L. Haskell, "Overview: Health Benefits of Exercise," in Joseph D. Matarazzo et al., eds., *Behavioral Health: A Handbook of Health Enhancement and Disease Prevention* (New York: Wiley, 1984), pp. 409–423.
5. Melinda Beck, "An Epidemic of Obesity," *Newsweek,* August 1, 1994, pp. 62–63; D. M. Hegsted, "What Is a Healthful Diet?" in Matarazzo et al., *Behavioral Health,* pp. 552–574.
6. Sheryl Stolberg, "Mortality Study Finds Tobacco Is No. 1 Culprit," *Los Angeles Times,* November 10, 1993, pp. A1, A33; Oakley Ray, *Drugs, Society and Human Behavior,* 3rd ed. (St. Louis: Mosby, 1983), pp. 183–205; U.S. Department of Health and Human Services, *Smoking and Health: A Report of the Surgeon General* (Washington, DC: U.S. Government Printing Office, 1979).
7. Philip J. Hilts, "Is Nicotine Addictive? It Depends on Whose Criteria You Use," *New York Times,* August 21, 1994, p. B6; Associated Press, "Koop: Tobacco Like Heroin, Cocaine," *San Luis Obispo Telegram-Tribune,* May 16, 1988, p. A1.
8. John Schwartz, "Secondhand Smoke Increases Health Risk, Study Finds," *Los Angeles Times,* May 20, 1997, p. A10; Sheryl Stolberg, "Science Stokes the Tobacco Debate," *Los Angeles Times,* May 26, 1994, pp. A1, A22, A23; Associated Press, "EPA Official Tries to Bury Smoking Report," *San Luis Obispo Telegram-Tribune,* May 30, 1991, p. B8.
9. Sidney Cobb and Robert M. Rose, "Hypertension, Peptic Ulcer, and Diabetes in Air Traffic Controllers," *Journal of the American Medical Association* 224 (1973): 489–492.
10. *New York Times,* April 3, 1983.
11. U.S. Bureau of the Census, *Statistical Abstract of the United States, 1996,* p. 95.
12. Ibid., p. 94.
13. Emile Durkheim, *Suicide* (New York: Free Press, 1951).
14. See George Howe Colt, *The Enigma of Suicide* (New York: Summit Books, 1991).
15. Marlene Cimons, "Car Fumes Linked to High Medical Costs," *Los Angeles Times,* January 20, 1990, p. A18.
16. U.S. Bureau of the Census, *Statistical Abstract, 1993,* p. 91; Susan Okie, "Some Cancer Rates Rising Rapidly, Study Finds," *Los Angeles Times,* August 24, 1990.
17. Associated Press, "Radon Tied to 30% Rise in the Risk of Cancer," *New York Times,* January 25, 1994, p. B8.

18. James William Coleman, *The Criminal Elite: Understanding White Collar Crime*, 4th ed. (New York: St. Martin's 1998), pp. 70–71.

19. Associated Press, "17 American Workers a Day Died on the Job During the 80s," *New York Times,* April 15, 1994, p. A8; Coleman, *The Criminal Elite,* p. 10; Lawrence White, *Human Debris: The Injured Worker in America* (New York: Putnam, 1983), pp. 15–23.

20. John H. Dingle, "Ills of Man," in *Life and Death and Medicine* (San Francisco: Freeman, 1973), p. 53.

21. U.S. Bureau of the Census, *Statistical Abstract, 1996,* p. 141.

22. United Nations Development Programme, *Human Development Report, 1994* (New York: Oxford University Press, 1994), pp. 134–135, 152–153.

23. Nicholasa D. Kristof, "Malaria Makes a Comeback, and Is More Deadly Than Ever," *New York Times,* January 8, 1997, pp. A1, A7.

24. Centers for Disease Control and Prevention, "Heterosexually Acquired AIDS—United States, 1993," *Morbidity and Mortality Weekly Report 9* (March 11, 1994): 155.

25. William A. Rushing, *The AIDS Epidemic: Social Dimensions of an Infectious Disease* (Boulder, CO: Westview, 1995), p. 18.

26. Ibid., pp. 106–118.

27. Ibid., p. 38.

28. U.S. Bureau of the Census, *Statistical Abstract, 1996,* pp. 91, 96.

29. Terence Monmaney, "World Facing Disease Crisis, Report Warns," *Los Angeles Times,* May 20, 1996, pp. A1, A19.

30. Population Reference Bureau, *World Population Data Sheet, 1997.*

31. U.S. Department of the Census, *Statistical Abstract, 1996,* p. 96; Colin McCord and Harold P. Freeman, "Excess Mortality in Harlem," *New England Journal of Medicine* 322 (1990): 173–177; "Forgotten Americans," *American Health,* Special Report, November 1990, pp. 41–42; Leonard Syme and Lisa Berkman, "Social Class, Susceptibility, and Sickness," in Howard Schwartz, ed., *Dominant Issues in Medical Sociology,* 3rd ed. (New York: McGraw-Hill, 1994), pp. 643–699.

32. Syme and Berkman, "Social Class, Susceptibility, and Sickness," p. 644.

33. Ronald C. Kessler et al., "Lifetime and 12-Month Prevalence of DSM-III-R Psychiatric Disorders in the United States: Results from the National Comorbidity Survey," *Archives of General Psychiatry* 51 (January 1994): 8–27.

34. U.S. Department of the Census, *Statistical Abstract, 1993,* p. 126.

35. Kessler et al., "Lifetime and 12-Month Prevalence of DSM-III-R Psychiatric Disorders in the United States."

36. Robert C. Carson, James N. Butcher, and James C. Coleman, *Abnormal Psychology and Modern Life,* 8th ed. (Glenview, IL: Scott, Foresman, 1988), pp. 28–43.

37. Thomas Szasz, *The Myth of Mental Illness* (New York: Harper & Row, 1974).

38. See Thomas Scheff, ed., *Labeling Madness* (Englewood Cliffs, NJ: Prentice Hall, 1975).

39. Alan A. Lipton and Franklin S. Simon, "Psychiatric Diagnosis in a State Hospital: Manhattan State Revisited," *Hospital and Community Psychiatry* 36 (1985): 368–373.

40. Kessler et al., "Lifetime and 12-Month Prevalence of DSM-III-R Psychiatric Disorders in the United States."

41. Robert E. L. Faris and H. Warren Dunham, *Mental Disorders in Urban Areas* (Chicago: University of Chicago Press, 1939).

42. August B. Hollingshead and Frederick C. Redlich, *Social Class and Mental Illness: A Community Study* (New York: Wiley, 1958).

43. Leo Strole, T. S. Langer, S. T. Michael, M. K. Opler, and T. A. L. Rennie, *Mental Health in the Metropolis: The Midtown Manhattan Study* (New York: McGraw-Hill, 1962).

44. Bruce P. Dohrenwend and Barbara Snell Dohrenwend, *Social Status and Psychological Disorder: A Causal Inquiry* (New York: Wiley, 1969), p. 165.

45. Kessler et al., "Lifetime and 12-Month Prevalence of DSM-III-R Psychiatric Disorders in the United States."

46. Joseph W. Eaton and Robert J. Weil, *Culture and Mental Disorder* (New York: Free Press, 1955).

47. Eleanor Leacock, "Three Variables in the Occurrence of Mental Illness," in Alexander Leighton, John Clausen, and Robert Wilson, eds., *Explorations in Social Psychiatry* (New York: Basic Books, 1957), pp. 308–340.

48. Kessler et al., "Lifetime and 12-Month Prevalence of DSM-III-R Psychiatric Disorders in the United States."

49. Ibid.

50. Franz Kallmann and B. Roth, "Genetic Aspects of Preadolescent Schizophrenia," *American Journal of Psychiatry* 112 (1956): 599–606.

51. A. Hoffer and W. Polin, "Schizophrenia in the NAS-NRC Panel of 15,909 Twin Pairs," *Archives of General Psychiatry* 23 (1970): 469–477.

52. Irving Gottesman, Peter McGuffin, and Anne E. Farmer, "Clinical Genetics as Clues to the 'Real' Genetics of Schizophrenia," *Schizophrenia Bulletin* 13 (1987): 23–47.

53. Janice A. Egeland et al., "Bipolar Affective Disorders Linked to DNA Markers on Chromosome 11," *Nature* 325 (February 26, 1987), pp. 783–787.

54. Miron Baron et al., "Genetic Linkage Between X-Chromosome Markers and Bipolar Affective Illness," *Nature* 326 (March 19, 1987), pp. 289–292; Stephen Hodgkinson et al., "Molecular Genetic Evidence for Heterogeneity in Manic Depression," *Nature* (February 26, 1987), pp. 805–808.

55. Paul Wender and Donald F. Klein, *Mind, Mood, and Medicine: A Guide to the New Biopsychiatry* (New York: Farrar, Straus & Giroux, 1981).

56. Ibid.

57. For a review of this literature, see Carson, Butcher, and Coleman, *Abnormal Psychology and Modern Life,* pp. 115–124.

58. Gregory Bateson, Don D. Jackson, Jay Haley, and John Weakland, "Toward a Theory of Schizophrenia," *Behavioral Science* 1 (1956): 251–264.

59. Jeffrey Bryer et al., "Childhood Sexual and Physical Abuse as Factors in Adult Psychiatric Illness," *American Journal of Psychiatry* 144 (1987): 1426–1430.

60. M. Audrey Burnam et al., "Sexual Assault and Mental Disorders in a Community Setting," *Journal of Counseling and Clinical Psychology* 56 (1988): 843–850.

61. R. D. Laing, *The Politics of Experience* (New York: Ballantine Books, 1967), p. 127.

62. Bruce Link, "Mental Patient Status, Work, and Income: An Examination of the Effects of Psychological Labeling," *American Sociological Review* 47 (April 1982): 202–215.

63. U.S. Department of the Census, *Statistical Abstract, 1996,* p. 123.

64. Ibid., p. 125.

65. Robert Steinbrook, "Thousands of Surgeries Called Unnecessary," *Los Angeles Times,* November 13, 1987, sec. 1, pp. 1, 30.

66. "Rate High on Unneeded Surgeries," *Los Angeles Times,* October 29, 1990, p. B3.

67. U.S. Department of the Census, *Statistical Abstract, 1996,* p. 405.

68. Schwartz, "Irrationality as a Feature of Health Care in the United States," p. 477.

69. Sharon M. Wilcox, David U. Himmelstein, and Steffie Woolhandler, "Inappropriate Drug Prescribing for the Community Dwelling Elderly," *Journal of the American Medical Association* 272 (July 1994): 292–296; K. Steel, P. M. Gertman, C. Crescsenzl, and J. Anderson, "Iatrogenic Illness on a General Medical Service at a University Hospital," *New England Journal of Medicine* 304 (1981): 638–642.

70. Sara Fritz, "Nurses Expand Roles as Debate Grows Over Care," *Los Angeles Times,* January 1, 1994, pp. A1, A18, A19; Bob Herbert, "Nurses on the Advance," *New York Times,* December 15, 1993, p. A17.

71. Erving Goffman, *Asylums: Essays on the Social Situation of Mental Patients and Other Inmates* (New York: Doubleday, 1961).

72. U.S. Department of the Census, *Statistical Abstract, 1996,* p. 129.

73. Ibid., p. 111.

74. Robert A. Rosenblatt, "Number of Americans Lacking Health Insurance on Rise," *Los Angeles Times,* September 11, 1996, p. A21.

75. Elisabeth Rosenthal, "Patients Share Bigger Burden of Rising Health Care Costs," *New York Times,* May 12, 1994, pp. A1, A16.

76. Consumers Union, "The Crisis in Health Insurance," *Consumer Reports* 55 (September 1990): 608–617; Associated Press, "Health Insurers' Efficiency Is Questioned," *Los Angeles Times,* October 19, 1990, p. D6.

77. Consumers Union, "The Crisis in Health Insurance," p. 82; U.S. Department of the Census, *Statistical Abstract, 1996,* p. 118.

78. Rosenthal, "Patients Share Bigger Burden of Rising Health Care Costs."

79. Robert Pear, "Medicare Paying Doctors 59% of Insurers' Rate, Panel Finds," *New York Times,* April 5, 1994.

80. U.S. Department of the Census, *Statistical Abstract, 1996,* p. 834.

81. Sonia Nazario, "Treating Doctors for Prejudice," *Los Angeles Times,* December 29, 1993, pp. A1, A36, A37; Douglas P. Shuit, "Black, Poor Medicare Patients Get Worse Care," *Los Angeles Times,* April 20, 1994, pp. B1, B4.

82. Thomas H. Maugh II, "Surgery Study Finds Poor at a Disadvantage," *Los Angeles Times,* December 9, 1993, pp. A3, A36.

83. Associated Press, "Millions of Americans Can't Afford Dental Care," *San Luis Obispo Telegram-Tribune,* November 29, 1993, p. D1.

84. Janny Scott, "The *Times* Poll: Many Believe They Can't Afford Good Health Care," *Los Angeles Times,* February 5, 1990, pp. A1, A23.

85. Mary Lake Polan, "Medical Researchers, Heal Thyselves of Gender Bias," *Los Angeles Times,* February 24, 1991, p. M1.

86. Andrew G. Kadar, "The Sex-Bias Myth in Medicine," *Atlantic Monthly,* August 1994, pp. 66–70.

87. U.S. Department of the Census, *Statistical Abstract, 1996,* p. 834.

88. Milt Freudenheim, "Health Care Costs Edging Up and a Bigger Surge Is Feared," *New York Times,* January 1, 1997, pp. A1, C20.

89. Consumers Union, "Wasted Health Care Dollars."

90. See Coleman, *The Criminal Elite,* pp. 36–38.

91. Consumers Union, "The $200 Billion Dollar Bottom Line," *Consumer Reports,* July 1992, p. 436.

92. Jeffrey Klein and Michael Castleman, "The Profit Motive in Breast Cancer," *Los Angeles Times,* April 4, 1994, p. B7.

93. U.S. Bureau of the Census, *Statistical Abstract, 1993,* pp. 848, 849.

94. U.S. Bureau of the Census, *Statistical Abstract, 1996,* p. 834.

95. Mary Williams Walsh, "Socialized Medicine Cuts Canada's Costs—and Care," *Los Angeles Times,* April 9, 1990, pp. A1, A12.

96. Population Reference Bureau, *World Population Data Sheet, 1997.*

97. Ernest Conine, "Canada's Sensible Approach," *Los Angeles Times,* March 26, 1990, p. B1; Walsh, "Socialized Medicine Cuts Canada's Costs—and Care."

98. Brad Knickerbocker, "Assisted-Suicide Issue More Active as Citizens Appear to Change Mood," *Christian Science Monitor,* May 2, 1994, p. 6.

99. Daniel P. Reid, *The Tao of Health, Sex and Longevity* (New York: Simon & Schuster, 1989), p. 233.

100. U.S. Bureau of the Census, *Statistical Abstract, 1996,* p. 194.

101. Howard D. Schwartz, Peggy L. DeWolf, and James K. Skipper, "Gender, Professionalization, and Occupational Anomie: The Case of Nursing," in Schwartz, *Dominant Issues in Medical Sociology,* pp. 559–569; Fritz, "Nurses Expand Roles as Debate Grows over Care."

102. Maureen Dowd, "Strong Support for Health Plans," *New York Times,* July 20, 1994, pp. A1, A8.

103. Paul Starr, *The Social Transformation of American Medicine* (New York: Basic Books, 1982).

The Problems of Inequality

Most people say they believe in equality. Political leaders around the world never tire of calling on this value to rally support for one program or opposition to another. In North America, the ideal is not so much that everyone have a college education, a high income, and a position of political influence, but that they have an equal *opportunity* to achieve those things. But even when stated in this more qualified way, there is a huge gap between our ideals and the realities of our daily life. Each of the chapters that follow focuses on a different kind of inequality, exploring the ways our society is structured to favor the members of one group over those of another. We begin with the problem of poverty because the issue of economic inequality is critical to understanding all the other problems discussed in this section.

The Poor

CHAPTER 7

Who are the poor?

Why is the gap between the rich and the poor growing wider?

What is the underclass?

Are the poor to blame for their poverty?

What can we do to reduce poverty?

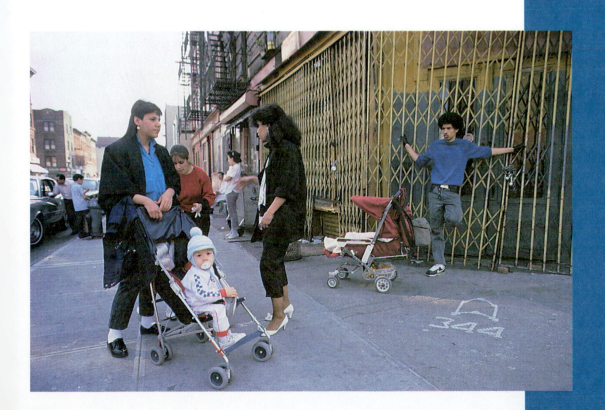

Ruth Acosta lives on the sixth floor of a crowded New York apartment building with her three sons, teenage daughter, and 3-year-old grandson. She is used to her small apartment; what worries her is that the refrigerator is nearly empty and there are only 10 cans of food left in her kitchen cabinet—some sweet peas, instant potatoes, peaches, and kidney beans are about all there is to eat. It's not much to feed a family when you are out of money for the month and you won't get any more food stamps for another eight days. Ms. Acosta doesn't panic—at age 37, she has been in this situation many times before. Like a lot of welfare recipients, she finds that her life follows a predictable rhythm. At the beginning of the month, when her cupboards are full, she feels pretty good about things, but as the weeks go by, her worries mount as dinner becomes less and less predictable.[1]

Our industrial economy has produced fantastic wealth for the privileged few, and even middle-class Americans have luxuries that were undreamed of in past centuries. The world we see in television shows, movies, and books is one of affluence and comfort, but there is an underside to our material well-being, for millions of people like Ruth Acosta and her family do not share in the abundance.

The poor in North America may not look like the starving masses in famine zones of the Third World, but their misery is just as real. In fact, poverty can be more difficult in a rich country than in a poor one. There is less shame in poverty in a nation like India because so many people are poor. In North America, poor people are not only constantly confronted by the wealth they are denied; they are also often blamed for their own suffering. Despite the appearance of widespread affluence, North America has some of the worst slums in the industrial world. Poor nutrition, nagging hunger, shabby clothing, and a crowded room or two in a deteriorating old building are all that many families can hope for. Yet when compared with the people of the European countries, Americans appear to have a remarkably callous attitude toward the poor, as if people were poor simply because they didn't want to work.

Although the poor are a minority in every sense of the word, they are a sizable one. According to government estimates, there are almost 40 million poor people in the United States—over 14 percent of all Americans.[2] Such figures should, however, be viewed with a skeptical eye, for as we will see, there is considerable debate about how to determine whether someone is poor. Although the experts may not agree about how many poor people there are, there is no doubt that the problem is an enormous one.

The Rich and the Poor: A Widening Gap

When news commentators and politicians talk about the problem of poverty, they seldom have much to say about those at the other end of the economic ladder, but wealth and poverty are two sides of the same coin. The deprivation of some creates abundance for others. To understand the problem of poverty, it must be seen in the context of the social and economic inequality between those at the top and those at the bottom of society.

All the data show that there is a gap between the haves and the have-nots and that it has been growing steadily wider. There are two general ways of determining how great this gap actually is. One approach attempts to measure differences in income, and the other focuses on wealth. Although these two yardsticks are related, there are important differences between them. **Income** refers to the amount of money a person makes in a given year. **Wealth** is the total value of that person's assets: real estate and personal property, stocks, bonds, cash, and so forth.

The requirement that everyone report their income to the Internal Revenue Service makes it fairly easy to examine the distribution of income (except for the income people hide from the tax collectors). IRS data show a society deeply divided along class lines. To get an idea, suppose that a sample of 20 average families perfectly mirrors the national distribution of income. In an average year, the family with the highest income earns about as much as the 10 lowest-income families combined.[3] These differences become even clearer when we look at actual dollar figures. In 1995, the average pay for a chief executive officer of a major American corporation (including stock options and other benefits) was $4,367,000, 173 times an average worker's salary.[4]

Examining the distribution of wealth is more difficult. For one thing, it is not always clear how much a particular asset, such as a painting or a mansion, is actually worth; in addition, those with great wealth often conceal many of their assets from

income
The amount of money a person earns or receives from other sources in a given year.

wealth
A person's total economic assets (e.g., cash, real estate, stocks and bonds, etc.).

Wealth and poverty are two sides of the same coin. The more equally income is distributed, the less there is of both.

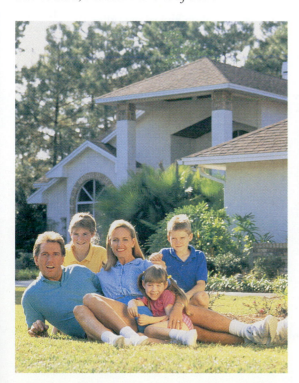

the scrutiny of outsiders. The U.S. Bureau of the Census does not even attempt to publish yearly reports on the distribution of wealth as it does for income. However, the Federal Reserve Board and the IRS occasionally do a joint study of the distribution of wealth in America, and they find that wealth is far more unequally distributed than income. Picture those 20 families again. The federal study shows that the single richest family has more wealth, not than just the 10 poorest families, but than *all the other families combined.*[5]

Why is wealth distributed so much more unequally than income? There appear to be two principal reasons. First, lower-income people usually have to spend everything they make just to get by and are therefore less able to build up savings accounts, investments, or other assets. The debts of the bottom 20 percent of American families equal or exceed their assets, so they have zero net worth.[6] Second, wealth tends to be passed on from one generation to another. Poor people usually have poor parents and start out with nothing. Wealthy people, on the other hand, usually have wealthy parents and are much more likely to come into a substantial estate.

Although many Americans see their country as the land of opportunity and equality, international comparisons do not bear out this view (see Figure 7.1). There is certainly far more economic inequality in the poor nations than in any of the industrialized countries (see Chapter 17). But the research indicates that the United States has by far the highest poverty rate and the biggest gap between those on the top and those on the bottom of any developed nation, while Canada is in the middle of the pack and the Scandinavian countries and Japan have the least inequality.[7] The

Figure 7.1

Poverty

The United States has a much higher poverty rate than any of the other industrialized nations.

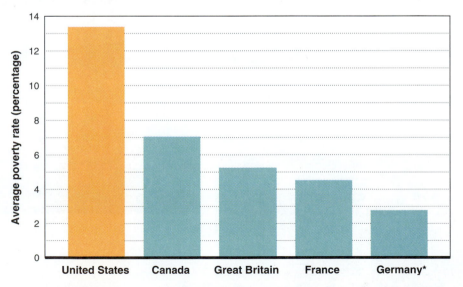

Source: Lawrence Mishel and Jared Bernstein, *The State of Working America,* 1996–97 (New York: Sharpe, 1997), p. 402.
*Data represent West Germany only.

infant mortality rate—a common indicator of the amount of poverty in a nation—is also substantially higher in the United States than in Japan, Canada, and most western European nations.[8]

The old saying "The rich get richer and the poor get poorer" has not always proved to be true, but since the late 1970s there has clearly been a significant widening of the gap between the haves and the have-nots. For example, between 1973 and 1995, our highest-income family saw its share of all income go up almost 30 percent while our eight low-income families saw their share drop about 17 percent, and there was a similar trend in the concentration of wealth as well.[9]

Many complex forces contribute to the growing inequality of American society, but four stand out as particularly important. First, the economy has stagnated in recent years, so the poor can no longer benefit from a steady improvement in the overall standard of living (see Chapter 4). A second factor, strongly related to the first, is foreign economic competition. Increasing industrial development in poor countries has placed the North American worker in direct competition with workers who receive far lower wages. The result has been a decline in real (after-inflation) wages for the average American worker. Of course, the managers and stockholders of multinational corporations actually benefit from the profits made possible by lower labor costs, and the incomes of engineers, scientists, and other professionals have continued to increase, since few people in the less developed countries have the training necessary for such jobs. A third factor has been the use of technology to reduce or eliminate well-paying jobs for skilled laborers, as well as the corresponding increase in low-paying service jobs. The fourth cause of the growing inequality in American society is a political one. Since 1981, taxes on the rich have been substantially reduced, while government programs that benefit the poor and the working class have been cut to help make up the loss in revenue (see Chapter 5).

Quick Review

What are the differences between the distribution of wealth and the distribution of income?

Why has the gap between the rich and poor increased?

Measuring Poverty

Even though everyone has a general idea of what **poverty** is, it is a difficult term to define precisely. Certainly, poor people lack many of the goods and services that others enjoy. They may have insufficient food, shelter, clothing, or entertainment, but how much is "insufficient"? Are people poor if they have no shoes, no bicycle, no car, only one car?

Poverty is usually defined in one of two ways: absolute or relative. The **absolute approach** divides the poor from the nonpoor by using some fixed standard, usually the lack of money to purchase a minimum amount of food, shelter, and clothing. The **relative approach** holds that people are poor if they have significantly less income and wealth than the average person in their society. Supporters of the relative approach argue that what is really important is not the fact that the

poverty
(1) Having insufficient resources to provide a minimum standard of living. (2) Being significantly worse off financially than the average person in one's society.

absolute approach
Defining poverty by dividing the poor from the nonpoor on the basis of an objective standard (e.g., income).

relative approach
Dividing the poor from the nonpoor on the basis of the wealth and income of the average person.

poor have a low standard of living but that they are psychologically and sociologically excluded from the mainstream of society. Despite the appeal of such arguments, the absolute approach is nonetheless far more widely used both by government agencies and social scientists—perhaps because what most concerns the public is not the relative deprivation of the poor but their lack of basic necessities.

Every year the U.S. government sets a "poverty line" for families of different sizes. If a family's income falls below the line, they are officially considered to be poor. The poverty line was originally based on studies showing that the average low-income family spent about one-third of its budget on food. The Department of Agriculture's Economy Food Budget was then multiplied by 3 to calculate the poverty line. Beginning at $3,000 in 1964, the poverty line for a family of four reached $15,569 by 1995.[10]

Although such numbers make the poverty line sound precise and objective, it is actually a rather arbitrary figure. A different approach to these computations could easily lead to a very different figure, and there is considerable debate over whether the poverty line is too high or too low. Some conservatives feel that it is too high (thus overestimating the amount of poverty) because welfare benefits that are not given in cash, such as food stamps and Medicaid, are not counted as income. Advocates for the poor counter that the original calculation that a poor family spends one-third of its income on food did not include such benefits either (although it is true that benefits are higher now than they were in 1964). They argue that if we are going to count such welfare benefits as income, we must also deduct the taxes the poor must pay. Furthermore, they point out that the Department of Agriculture itself admits the Economy Food Budget was intended only as a temporary or emergency budget; it does not meet long-term nutritional needs. In 1969, the government stopped adjusting the poverty line on the basis of the rising cost of food and used a measure of overall inflation instead. Since then, the cost of necessities, especially housing, has gone up much faster than the consumer price index as a whole, and families living at the poverty line are unable to buy as much of the things they need as they could in the past. In 1995, the National Research Council examined the way the poverty level was calculated and recommended an alternative measure that adds noncash welfare benefits, subtracts out-of-pocket child-care and medical expenses, and adjusts for changing consumption patterns (Americans now spend proportionately less on food and more on other expenses such as housing). The result was that about 9 million more people were counted as poor than in the official figures.[11]

Who Are the Poor?

One of the major reasons for trying to define who is poor and who is not is to discover which segments of our society experience the greatest poverty. Single-parent families, for example, have a much higher than average poverty rate, and their growing numbers have had a major impact on the problem of poverty. From 1970 to 1995, the percentage of all families with children that were headed by a single woman more than doubled, from 10 to 24 percent, and single mothers with children are now the fastest-growing segment of the poverty population.[12] In fact, the majority of poor families with children are now headed by single women, and the poverty

Signs of Hope   Poverty Drops Among the Elderly

We have all heard the claims that government is hopelessly inefficient and that its programs to deal with our social problems are just a waste of money, but such charges are clearly false when it comes to Social Security. The use of a more generous formula for calculating Social Security benefits has had a dramatic impact in reducing poverty among the elderly. In 1970, those age 65 and older had the highest poverty rate of any group in the country: 24.6 percent. The decision to index Social Security benefits (provide an automatic adjustment for inflation) led to steadily rising benefits and a sharp decline in poverty among the aged. By 1994, the poverty rate for the elderly was only half as high as it was in 1970, and it was actually *lower* than the national average.*

*U.S. Bureau of the Census, *Statistical Abstract of the United States, 1996* (Washington, DC: U.S. Government Printing Office, 1996), p. 473.

rate of such families is almost five times greater than that of married couples (see Chapter 2 for more details).[13]

As a result of this trend and higher birthrates among the poor, children under age 16 are more than 50 percent more likely to be poor than the average American. Interestingly, while poverty has been rising among the young, the Social Security program has helped bring it down among the elderly, and as the Signs of Hope box in this chapter shows, their poverty rate is now lower than the national average.[14]

Contrary to popular stereotypes, most poor people in the United States are white, not African American or Latino; U.S. census figures indicate that about two-thirds of all poor people are white. However, the *percentage* of whites below the poverty line is considerably lower than it is for most minorities. For example, in 1995 about 11 percent of all whites were poor, compared to about 30 percent of African Americans and Latinos.[15] Income figures show the same disparity—$24,698 for the average African American family, $28,658 for a Latino family, and $40,884 for the average white family.[16] (See Chapter 8 for an explanation of these differences.)

When we think about where the poor live, it is the crowded urban ghettos that come most quickly to mind, but the percentage of people below the poverty line is almost as high in rural areas.[17] The vast majority of poor people do live in cities, but that is simply because our population as a whole is so highly urbanized. The suburbs, in contrast, have the lowest poverty rate—less than half that of the central cities or rural areas—but as our original suburbs have aged, they too have developed growing pockets of poverty (see Chapter 14).[18]

The Trends in Poverty

Another important use for the statistics on poverty is to measure changes in the poverty population. As we have seen, there is little agreement about where to draw the poverty line, so statistics giving the exact percentage of the population living in poverty are not very meaningful. If the same standards are applied consistently, however, they ought to measure trends accurately. Official statistics indicate that poverty declined sharply in the 1960s from over 22 percent of the total population at the start of the decade to around 11 percent in the early 1970s. The two main reasons for this improvement were the economic prosperity of the times and a strong government commitment to what was known as the War on Poverty. As both economic prosperity and the government's efforts to reduce poverty faded, the improvements stopped and poverty began to grow. Today, the poverty rate is back around 14 percent.[19]

Although studies indicate that there is less poverty now than there was forty years ago, they also show that problems associated with poverty have gotten far worse in recent years. For one thing, there has been a sharp increase in the percentage of poor people who live in **extreme poverty.** In 1975 about 30 percent of poor people had incomes that were less than half the poverty line, but by 1995 that figure had risen to 38 percent.[20] Moreover, these general figures obscure the steady growth of poverty among the most vulnerable members of society—its children. More than one-fifth of American children now live in poverty, and that figure represents a 27 percent increase since 1979.[21]

extreme poverty
The poorest of the poor. Often defined as those whose income is less than half the poverty level.

Quick Review

What are the two different ways of measuring poverty?

What type of person is most likely to be poor?

What are the current trends in poverty?

The Life of Poverty

Being poor in a rich country has profound psychological and sociological consequences. In our materialistic society, people are judged as much by what they have as by who they are. Children of poverty lack so many of the things everyone is "supposed" to have that they often feel there is something wrong with them or their families. Poor people of all ages are constantly confronted by things they desire but have little chance to own.

The poor are deprived of more than just material possessions. In contrast to the rich and even the middle classes, those brought up in poverty often appear to speak crudely, with heavy accents and a limited vocabulary. They have less education, are less informed about the world, and are less likely to vote. Significant numbers of poor people cannot even read or write and so are cut off from much of mainstream culture. Under these conditions, poor people can hardly avoid feelings of inadequacy, frustration, and anger. Some bottle up those feelings, contributing to psychosomatic illnesses and aggravating problems such as high blood pressure and ulcers. Others express hostility and anger in violent crime. The rates of murder, assault, and rape are all much higher among poor people than among the rest of the population (see Chapter 13).

Economic uncertainty is another important part of being poor. Even poor people who are lucky enough to have a permanent job ordinarily work in low-paying, dead-end positions that are the first to be cut in bad times. Others can find only temporary work or are unemployed. Welfare sometimes helps out, but, as we shall see, the benefits are meager and the bureaucracy demeaning. To make this insecurity worse, the poor have far higher rates of family instability than others. The poor marry younger and have the highest rates of divorce, separation, family violence, and out-of-marriage childbirth. This pattern of inequality even carries over into matters of life and death. Although we hear a great deal about medical miracles such as organ transplants, most of these "miracles" are reserved for people with good health insurance. As a rule, the poor receive second-rate health care, a deficient diet, and inadequate shelter. Consequently, they catch more contagious diseases and have a higher rate of infant mortality and a shorter life span.

While these generalizations apply to all the poor to one degree or another, it is important to recognize that people who live in poverty are as diverse as those in any other class. While some are so desperately poor they starve or freeze to death, for others poverty is a short-term condition that is soon overcome. Among this diverse population, we will devote some special attention to three overlapping groups: the homeless, the underclass, and the working poor.

The Homeless

We have all seen them—the bag ladies who push around everything they own in a rusty shopping cart, the disheveled men sleeping on park benches or over heating grates to keep warm, an entire family living in an abandoned car. Lack of protection from the elements is the most obvious hardship they face. In the summer they swelter, and in the winter some freeze to death. Even getting enough food to eat is a continual concern for many of the homeless. Because they are almost always on the streets, they are easy targets for criminals and thugs. Aside from a few overworked charity and welfare agencies, the homeless confront a society that seems indifferent to their plight. The police, to whom most of us would turn for protection, see the homeless as a nuisance who must be moved out or arrested when their numbers become too great. (See the Personal Perspectives box in this chapter.)

No one is really sure how many Americans are homeless on any given day. The Census Bureau counted 228,621 homeless people in its last nationwide tally, but that figure is generally believed to be far too low, and even the bureau itself says it never set out to count every homeless person.[22] The Urban Institute estimates that there are about 600,000 homeless; the Department of Health and Human Services says 2 million; and advocates for the homeless put the figure at about 3 million or more.[23] The one thing virtually everyone agrees about is that the number of homeless men and women has grown substantially in recent years.

Who is most likely to be homeless? According to a survey of 26 major cities by the U.S. Conference of Mayors, over half of all homeless people are African American, about one-fourth European American, and 13 percent Latino. Almost half of the homeless have some kind of alcohol or drug problem. Yet one in five has a full- or part-time job but simply can't afford a steady place to live. Perhaps the most disturbing finding of this survey was the sharp increase in the number of homeless

Personal Perspectives   A Homeless Man

What is it like not to have a home? The following account from a homeless man in his late twenties may give you some ideas.

> Before I was homeless, I thought [the people] on the streets were losers—drug and alcohol abusers or mental cases. I was fairly judgmental. I remember telling one panhandler to get a job. I thought he was just lazy.
>
> Now I'm homeless and jobless. I'm willing to work, but once people see your backpack, they're scared off. People generally don't trust homeless people. They think we're flakes and don't feel safe hiring us. That makes it hard to break the cycle.
>
> I don't eat good because I don't have much money, so my health isn't real good. I don't get medical help when I need it, also because I have no money. And I don't sleep well because I always need to have one eye open. I usually sleep behind homes or churches. They feel safer to me.
>
> I just don't want people to prejudge me. After all, there are far more substance abusers and "flaky" people with homes than there are people who are homeless.

families. While single men used to make up the vast majority of the homeless population, a year-long survey conducted in late 1992 and 1993 found an equal number of people in families among the homeless. (Each group made up 43 percent of the total homeless population.[24])

There are several reasons why homelessness appears to have risen even in years when poverty has not. The most popular explanation is that the deinstitutionalization movement, which sharply reduced the population of state mental hospitals, has left many severely disturbed patients to wander the streets (see Chapter 6). Although there is little doubt that this policy has been a major contributor to the ranks of the homeless, it is not the only factor. Articles in magazines such as *Time*, *Newsweek,* and *People* have claimed that the majority of the homeless are mentally disturbed, but several studies have put the figure much lower than 50 percent. Most research suggests that somewhere around one-third of the homeless have mental problems.[25] A study of homeless adults in Texas concluded that "the most common face on the street is not that of the psychiatrically-impaired individual, but one caught in a cycle of low-paying, dead-end jobs that fail to provide the means to get off and stay off the streets."[26] The federal government has contributed to the problem by sharply reducing the amount of money spent on subsidized housing programs over the last three decades. (See the Debate in this chapter.) Equally important is the fact that large increases in the cost of rental housing have simply priced many poor people out of the market. Over 1 million flophouse rooms have been torn down since 1970, and the average cost of rental housing has grown twice as fast as the average income of renters.[27]

underclass

Those in the lower part of the poverty class who are excluded from the economic and cultural mainstream of society.

The Underclass

Originally coined by sociologist Gunnar Myrdal in the early 1960s, the concept of the **underclass** was picked up in series of articles published in *New Yorker* magazine in 1981, and from there it jumped into the daily vocabulary of educated Americans. Like most such terms, it is defined differently by different people. Common to most of these definitions is the idea that the underclass comprises the bottom of the poverty class and the implication that its members are excluded from the economic and cultural mainstream of society.[28] The disagreements arise over the standards that define who is in the underclass and over how large a group it is. The broadest standard holds that the underclass consists of those who are trapped in long-term poverty. By that definition, the underclass would include between 40 and 60 percent of all poor people.[29] Another approach defines the underclass as the "poorest of the poor"—that is, those who have the lowest incomes. If we define extreme poverty as living on less than half the poverty-level income, then almost 4 in 10 poor people were in the underclass in 1995.[30] Finally, the most restrictive standard would include only those who live in neighborhoods that are overwhelmingly poor. Rough estimates based on the data from census tracts (which do not follow the boundaries of actual neighborhoods) place that number at a little under 10 percent of the poor.[31] Despite its usefulness, some sociologists have become uncomfortable with the concept of the underclass because of the sensationalistic way many journalists use the term. Herbert J. Gans, for example, writes that it is an "increasingly pejorative term that seems to be becoming the newest buzzword for the *undeserving* poor."[32]

However the term is defined, the underclass is, in the words of William Julius Wilson, "the heart of the problem of poverty."[33] Members of the underclass are much more likely to have been raised in poverty than the population of poor people

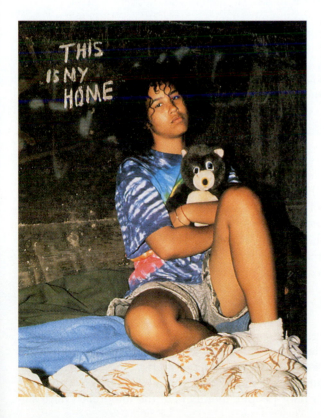

The problem of homelessness has grown much more severe in recent years, and the sharpest increases have been among women and children.

Debate   Should the Government Provide Free Housing for the Homeless?

Many cities and towns provide temporary shelter for the homeless, but there are many more homeless people on the streets than the shelters can accommodate. Some people therefore propose that federal funds be provided to guarantee every homeless person a place to sleep if he or she wants one.

Yes

A new wave of homeless men, women, and children is flooding the nation, and we must do something more than just pick up the bodies after they freeze to death. Some people say that we should rely on churches and other private charities to handle the problem. Although such an approach may have worked in a nation of small, tightly knit farming communities, it is hopelessly inadequate in a complex urban society. The charities themselves openly admit that they do not have the money or the resources to solve this problem.

The government is the one organization that can provide adequate housing for our most needy citizens. The only question is whether or not these people deserve to be helped, and the answer is a resounding yes. More fortunate people often look down their noses at the homeless and blame them for their own misery. But no one chooses to be born into the underclass, to have a mental disorder, or to fall victim to the disease of alcoholism. And even the most zealous ideologue would have a difficult time finding a reason to blame homeless children for their plight. The real reason so many wealthy people oppose aid to the homeless is simple greed. They would rather see these unfortunates die on the streets than pay another $25 a year in taxes. Surely we are a more generous and public-spirited people than that. Our values and our traditions demand that we take forceful action to solve this tragic problem, and it is time we stopped talking and got the job done.

as a whole. They are also far more likely to come from ethnic minorities, especially if we define the underclass as those living in overwhelmingly poor neighborhoods. By that definition, 65 percent of the underclass are black and 22 percent Latino.[34] Members of the underclass tend to come from single-parent families with a poor educational background and a history of welfare dependency. A substantial proportion of the people in the underclass can't read or write and lack other job skills. In the past, such people could at least get menial work as manual laborers, but changes in the job market have left many of them without any hope of meaningful work. (See Chapter 4 for a discussion of those changes.)

As a result of these factors, many members of the underclass are trapped in a self-perpetuating cycle of poverty that is extremely hard to break. The fact is that mainstream society no longer has a use for them, and many people would rather they just disappeared. Of course, they are not going to do that, and the frustration and hopelessness of life in the underclass extract a heavy toll. Compared with other Americans and even most other poor people, members of the underclass have sig-

No

As soon as we hear about a new social problem, the first thing some people want to do is rush in and start throwing money at it. But a gigantic new government program to house the homeless would inevitably prove as wasteful and ineffective as other welfare programs have been. For one thing, the government is so inefficient and hamstrung by political pressures that most of the money is likely to be wasted before it ever gets to the homeless. Even if enough free housing were created to put a roof over their heads, that would do nothing to solve the underlying problems that made them homeless in the first place. The alcoholics and the mentally disturbed would simply be suffering from the same conditions indoors rather than on the streets.

A free housing program for the homeless would be a financial monster. It would grow bigger year by year, and eventually we would be forced to abandon it. We might begin by providing housing only to those who are now homeless, but what about the poor people who are working at low-paying jobs and still paying rent? They would soon walk away from their old apartments so that they too could become "homeless" and claim a free place to live.

The solution to the problem of the homeless is for individual citizens to give more to the private charities that have already proved they can do an efficient job dealing with the problem. Setting up another huge government bureaucracy would only make things worse.

nificantly higher rates of mental disorder, alcoholism, drug abuse, and suicide, and they are far more likely to fall victim to violent crime.

The Working Poor

Many people assume that the solution to the problem of poverty is simply to find jobs for the poor, but statistics from the Bureau of the Census show that nearly one-fifth of poor people work year-round, and half work at least part time.[35] Furthermore, the working poor make up one of the fastest-growing groups in the poverty population. Since 1978, the number of full-time workers living in poverty has risen twice as fast as the overall poverty population.

How can so many people hold full-time or nearly full-time jobs and still be poor? The answer is simple: low wages. A study by the Bureau of the Census found that nearly one-fifth of American workers did not earn enough money to keep a family of four above the poverty line. And that was a 50 percent increase since

1979—a development the usually understated bureau termed "astounding."[36] Clearly, such low-wage jobs have been the fastest-growing segment of the labor market in recent years, and the employment prospects for young workers without high school degrees have been growing progressively worse (see Chapter 4).

Despite laboring long hours for little pay, the working poor do have some important advantages over other poor people. Psychologically, they have the self-respect that comes from knowing that they are working and contributing to society. They also have far better prospects of eventually moving out of poverty. Unfortunately, a great many poor people do not really have the option of working, even if they could find a job. About one-third are under age 15, and substantial numbers are elderly or in bad health. Even the welfare mothers who bear the brunt of so much criticism cannot realistically be expected to take minimum-wage jobs without continued public assistance, since medical and child-care expenses would eat up most of their take-home pay.

Quick Review

Why has the number of homeless people increased so much?

What is the underclass?

Why are so many working people still below the poverty line?

Understanding the Welfare System

Before we examine the general causes of poverty, we must first take a look at the welfare system, which has become so much a part of the phenomenon of poverty in the twentieth century. The first step in understanding the welfare system is to understand the public's attitudes toward the poor.

Attitudes Toward the Poor

Attitudes toward poverty are remarkably different in North America than in European societies. Rejection of the European class system and the availability of a vast new land to conquer helped create a tremendous faith in the value of hard work and competition among North Americans. In this way of thinking, each individual is responsible for his or her own economic destiny. Most people believe that even in a period of economic depression and high unemployment, anyone who works hard enough can be successful. It is also generally held that "there is always room at the top" for capable and hardworking people, no matter how humble their origins.

Despite its attractiveness, this belief in individual responsibility has a negative side. If the rich are personally responsible for their success, it follows that the poor are to blame for their failure. "Poor folks have poor ways," the old saying goes. Joe R. Feagin has summarized the principal points in this **ideology of individualism** as follows.

ideology of individualism
The belief that each individual is personally responsible for his or her own economic success or failure.

1. Each individual should work hard and strive to succeed in competition with others.
2. Those who work hard should be rewarded with success (seen as wealth, property, prestige, and power).

3. Because of widespread and equal opportunity, those who work hard will in fact be rewarded with success.
4. Economic failure is an individual's own fault and reveals lack of effort and other character defects.[37]

Surveys show that this ideology is still a potent force in American life. When asked about the causes of poverty, most people respond with individualistic explanations that blame the poor themselves rather than with structural explanations that hold society responsible or with fatalistic explanations that blame such things as bad luck or illness. In one survey, for example, 58 percent of the respondents said that lack of thrift and proper money management is a significant cause of poverty, and 55 percent said that lack of effort by the poor is a very important cause of poverty.[38]

The History of the Welfare System

The ideology of individualism has had an enormous impact on the response to poverty in the United States. People receiving government assistance are often stigmatized as lazy or incompetent even when they are recognized as "truly needy." Frances Fox Piven and Richard A. Cloward argued that the growth of the modern welfare system resulted more from an attempt to silence the political discontent of the poor than from a desire to improve their living conditions, and their findings have been supported by several more recent studies.[39]

The origins of today's welfare system are to be found in the Great Depression of the 1930s, when unemployment rose dramatically and armies of the newly impoverished demanded assistance: "Groups of men out of work congregated at local relief agencies, cornered and harassed administrators, and took over offices until their demands were met."[40] Despite such determined protests, reforms were made grudgingly. Relief for the poor was still largely a local matter, but cities and counties proved unable to shoulder the financial burden. The federal government began to give small direct payments to the unemployed, but it soon shifted to work relief programs, which were more in tune with the ideology of individualism. With the coming of President Franklin D. Roosevelt's New Deal, a host of new government agencies were created to put unemployed Americans to work. Public opposition to these and other welfare programs nonetheless remained strong through the Depression. The most popular New Deal program that still survives, Social Security, is often seen more as a form of insurance than welfare.

The 1950s brought only modest increases in welfare support for the poor, but a "welfare explosion" occurred in the 1960s. From December 1960 to February 1969, the number of recipients of **Aid to Families with Dependent Children (AFDC),** the main welfare program providing direct financial aid to poor mothers, increased by 107 percent.[41] Daniel Patrick Moynihan laid the blame for this increase on the deteriorating black family and on the general increase in female-headed families.[42] Piven and Cloward disagreed, maintaining that family deterioration made only a minor contribution to the growing welfare rolls and that the real cause was increased activism among the poor, who began to demand greater social support.

The 1960s also saw the launch of President Lyndon Johnson's War on Poverty, which included such programs as the Job Corps, the Neighborhood Youth Corps, VISTA, and Head Start. These programs have often been criticized because they were inefficiently organized and because some of them were aimed primarily at

Aid to Families with Dependent Children (AFDC)
A welfare program providing direct financial aid to poor mothers. Now called Temporary Aid to Needy Families (TANF).

young urban males and neglected females, the rural poor, and the elderly. Yet despite all its faults, most researchers agree that the War on Poverty did help to reduce poverty significantly in the United States.

The 1970s did not bring any new initiatives against poverty comparable to those introduced in the 1960s, but progress continued to be made. There was, however, a sharp reaction against welfare programs for the poor in the early 1980s, which was spearheaded by the newly elected Reagan administration. Between 1981 and 1985, federal welfare spending dropped by 19 percent, about 400,000 families were cut from AFDC rolls, food stamp rolls were reduced by about 1 million people, and 3 million children were cut from school lunch programs.[43] The continuing growth in the number of single-parent families and the proliferation of poverty-level jobs have once again forced up the number of welfare recipients. By 1994, nearly 11 percent of American families received food stamps,[44] and despite tougher eligibility standards, even the number of AFDC recipients had increased substantially. Yet welfare benefits were far less generous than they had been twenty years earlier, and many states had begun experimenting with time limits and work requirements to try to force mothers with dependent children off the welfare rolls. (See Figure 7.2).

The Attack on Welfare

The ideology of individualism has always fostered a tendency for Americans to blame the poor for their own poverty. In the last two decades of hard economic times and growing anxiety about the future, the welfare system became a scapegoat

Figure 7.2

Welfare

The United States spends much less on welfare programs than most other industrialized nations.

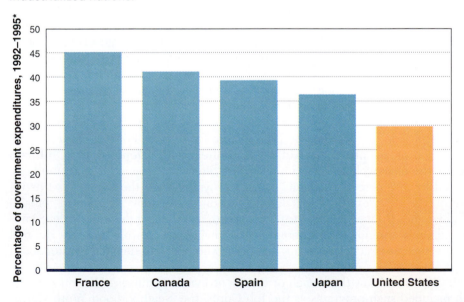

Source: United Nations Human Development Programme, *Human Development Report, 1997* (New York: Oxford University Press, 1992), p. 212.
*Includes Social Security.

for a wide host of perplexing national problems. Critics charged that welfare does everything from encouraging sexual promiscuity to undermining the economy. In one televised debate, a well-known conservative even blamed the welfare system for his lack of success in hiring a maid. Ignoring the complex sociological forces that trap so many people in poverty, these critics often present a simplistic and unfair stereotype of welfare recipients as loafers who are living high at taxpayers' expense. This tendency to "blame the victims" for their misfortune reached new heights in a highly publicized book by Charles Murray and Richard Herrnstein. In *The Bell Curve,* they argued that poor people are biologically inferior to the affluent and that because their average intelligence is so low, government training or welfare programs for the poor are unlikely to do them any good.[45]

Ironically, those who attack the welfare system usually ignore the largest welfare program, **Social Security,** because most of the benefits go to wealthier and more politically powerful recipients. (Social Security was supposed to be a kind of pension fund in which workers' contributions would be invested and the money returned to them when they retired, but the benefits are actually paid for directly by our taxes like any other welfare program.) Instead, the most bitter attacks have been focused on AFDC—perhaps because it was created with the intention of assisting children whose fathers had died or been disabled, yet the vast majority of recipients are single women who are divorced or have never been married. Or perhaps it is simply hostility toward members of ethnic minorities, who are more likely to receive family assistance.

The fact that there are so many unfair and unfounded attacks on the welfare system does not, however, mean that there are no reasonable criticisms. One of the biggest problems is that the current welfare system is far too complex, too bureaucratic, and too wasteful. The government actually spends more administering welfare programs (paying for welfare offices, case workers, and so on) than it pays out in benefits to the poor.[46] Another problem is that the old AFDC program tended to discourage welfare mothers from getting jobs: the money they earned was often deducted from their welfare checks, and they ran the risk of losing their Medicaid benefits if they earned too much. Another common criticism was that AFDC encouraged the breakup of families because it denied them assistance if an unemployed man was in the home. A third concern is that welfare programs help perpetuate the "cycle of poverty" because children who grow up in welfare families may fail to learn the basic work habits and attitudes necessary for success in the job market.

The Current Welfare System

The result of all this criticism was a sweeping welfare reform program enacted in 1996. The principal target of this new legislation was to get AFDC recipients off the welfare rolls and into a job. The new law eliminated the 60-year-old guarantee of cash assistance for the nation's poorest children; required able-bodied adults to work after two years on welfare; and placed a strict five-year cap on the lifetime benefits any family can receive. AFDC was even given a new name: **Temporary Aid to Needy Families (TANF).** The individual states were given broad new power to organize their own programs but required to meet new targets for getting their welfare recipients into jobs. Changes were also made in other welfare programs, the most controversial being the elimination of benefits for legal residents who are not citizens of the United States.

Social Security
A government-administered program providing pensions for older Americans.

Temporary Aid to Needy Families (TANF)
A welfare program providing temporary financial aid to poor mothers.

Welfare programs have never been as popular in the United States as they are in Europe. But in recent years, welfare recipients have endured an unprecedented wave of political attacks.

At the time of this writing, the full effects of these drastic changes have yet to be felt. The individual states are still struggling to meet the new requirements, and no one has yet reached the five-year benefit limit. There is, however, great concern about what will happen to the millions of mothers and children who will have their welfare payments cut off and about whether there will be enough jobs for all the poorly qualified women forced out into the market.

Despite all the attention paid to programs that provide cash assistance to needy families, there are also several other important welfare programs. The other major cash program is **Supplemental Security Income (SSI),** which gives financial assistance to poor people who are blind, disabled, or elderly. The federal government also has a variety of "noncash" programs that provide goods or services instead of money. The **food stamp program** gives recipients coupons that can be exchanged only for food, and **Medicaid** helps pay its recipients' health care bills. (Medicaid is only for poor people; **Medicare** is a more generous program for everyone over age 65.) Housing assistance is sometimes provided through rent subsidies and public housing projects that offer low rents to those poor enough to qualify. The states make a financial contribution to most of these programs, and state and local governments also supplement federal programs with short-term emergency aid and other benefits.

Whatever the effect of these most recent changes, we know that the real (after-inflation) value of welfare benefits in the United States has been falling for more than two decades, and the U.S. tax and welfare system already provides less help for the poor than any other industrialized nation.[47] The United States is the only indus-

---

Supplemental Security Income (SSI)
A government program that provides financial assistance to poor people who are blind, disabled, or elderly.

food stamp program
A welfare program that gives people coupons to exchange for food.

Medicaid
A U.S. program designed to help the poor, the blind, and the disabled pay for medical care.

Medicare
A U.S. program that pays for medical care of people over 65 years old.

trialized country without a comprehensive national health system or some kind of **family allowance.** Moreover, if current trends continue, we can expect even more cutbacks and reductions in the years ahead.

Quick Review

What is the ideology of individualism?

Briefly describe the history of the American welfare system.

How did the 1996 reforms change the welfare system?

What are the main types of welfare assistance available in the United States?

Explanations of Poverty

The economic base of some societies is so fragile that hunger is a daily reality for most people. Such extreme scarcity of food, clothing, and shelter is not characteristic of modern industrial societies or even most traditional ones. The poverty problem in these societies is one of distributing wealth rather than one of producing it. There are many explanations of economic inequality, but most fall into three overlapping categories: explanations based on an analysis of economic structures, explanations based on an analysis of political relationships among power groups, and explanations based on an analysis of the culture of the poor.

Economic Explanations

Much poverty can be traced to simple economic causes: low wages and too few jobs for those at the bottom of the social hierarchy. We have already seen that even a full-time job at the minimum wage doesn't pay enough to keep a family out of poverty, and a growing number of people are forced to take part-time or temporary jobs because they cannot find full-time work. In technologically advanced societies such as Canada and the United States, people without education and skills are finding it increasingly difficult to secure any kind of employment, and those who find work are likely to be employed in low-paying jobs. After controlling for inflation, the average earnings of men who did not finish high school have declined by almost one-fourth in the last two decades.[48]

As we saw in Chapter 4, the average wage of all American workers has declined significantly since 1973, but the biggest decrease has been for those who get the lowest wages. For example, if we compare the 10 percent of American workers who are the highest and lowest paid, we find that in real terms, the average wage earned by the lowest-paid workers has declined by 17 percent since 1973, while at the same time the wages of the highest-paid workers increased by 5 percent.[49] As a result of these changes, nearly one-third of all American workers received poverty-level wages in 1995—a 26 percent increase since 1973.[50]

Although the unemployment rate goes up and down with the business cycle (see Chapter 4), it has seldom dropped below 5 percent in the last two decades. Moreover, the official unemployment rate is not a very good measure of joblessness since it doesn't count those who have given up looking for work or those forced to take part-time jobs when they want full-time work. When those workers are added in, the picture gets far worse—in fact, the unemployment rate almost doubles.

In addition to the overall national problem, many areas have a particularly high unemployment rate because of local conditions. For example, some regions depended on industries that are no longer competitive in the world economy. The slums of the central cities are especially vulnerable to a variety of forces that combine to create an unhealthy economic climate. Low income in these areas makes it tough going for businesses that depend on local residents for their customers. A high crime rate, a lack of local services, and a significant measure of fear and racism keep the wealthy away and discourage outside investment. At the same time, inadequate transportation and the long commuting distances to prosperous areas make it difficult for residents of inner-city slums to find work in other neighborhoods. For example, a study by James E. Rosenbaum and Susan J. Popkin found that poor women assigned to public housing in middle-class suburbs were much more likely to find jobs than those given housing in the central city.[51]

To add to their other problems, the poor often get less for their hard-earned dollars than other consumers do. Slum dwellers, for example, may pay more rent for a run-down apartment than people living in a small town pay for a house with a yard. More generally, because the poor are not mobile, it is difficult for them to shop around for sales and special values. They are obliged to patronize local merchants, who usually charge higher prices than those in affluent areas. Many stores in slum areas actively solicit sales on credit because the interest charges are more profitable than the sale itself. If the customer cannot meet the installment payments, the merchandise is repossessed and sold to another poor customer.[52] When unexpected expenses occur, the poor must borrow money; but because they are not considered good credit risks, it may be impossible for them to get bank loans at standard interest rates. Instead, they must go to loan companies, which charge much higher interest rates, or to loan sharks, who charge exorbitant illegal rates.

It is easy to look at all these difficulties as separate individual problems, but deeper roots in the basic structure of our economy link them all together. In an open capitalist society, the operation of the competitive market inevitably creates a huge gap between the rich and the poor. On the one hand, the market demands that employers pay the lowest wages and hire the fewest workers they can, or they run the risk of being driven out of business by more ruthless competitors. On the other hand, this same competitive struggle also stimulates the creation of enormous amounts of wealth, much of which goes to those who own and operate businesses. Although some workers who have skills or strong union organizations can demand better treatment, many others are inevitably left behind and sink into poverty. Of course, no capitalist economy operates in this completely unrestricted way. Governments in every capitalist nation have stepped in to help relieve some of the suffering caused by the harsh realities of the marketplace, both for humanitarian reasons and to prevent those at the bottom from rising up and threatening the whole system.

Political Explanations

Poverty is as much a political problem as a problem of economics or culture. How much poverty a country has (at least in the relative sense) is largely determined by the policies of its government. For example, the United States has the highest poverty rate of any industrialized country, yet it actually starts off with one of the most equal distributions of income. How can that be? The U.S. government redistributes less of that income from the wealthy and the middle class to the poor.[53] This high degree of inequality persists in the United States because many Americans seem to have little concern about the poor, and those who do care are not politically organized. Politicians win votes by promising to eliminate crime and cut taxes, but few votes are won by promising to eliminate poverty. The ideology of individualism has convinced most Americans that the world is full of opportunities and that the poor deserve to be poor because they are too lazy or incompetent to seize those opportunities. As long as the poor are seen to be responsible for their poverty, effective political action to change the conditions that cause poverty is unlikely.

Furthermore, as Herbert Gans has pointed out, poverty is valuable to the wealthy, and many powerful groups do not want it eliminated.[54] First, it ensures that society's dirty work gets done, for without poverty few people would be willing to do low-paying, unpleasant, and dangerous jobs. Second, the low wages the poor receive for their work subsidize the wealthy by keeping the prices of goods and services low and profits high. Third, poverty creates jobs for the many people who service the poor (such as welfare workers) or try to control them (such as police officers and prison guards). Fourth, the poor provide merchants with last-ditch profits by buying goods that otherwise would be thrown away: stale bread, tainted meat, out-of-style clothing, used furniture, and unsafe appliances. Fifth, the poor guarantee the status of the people above them in the social hierarchy. The poor provide a group that "respectable" people can brand as deviants—examples of what happens to those who break social rules. Thus, the fact that poverty helps make the middle and upper classes more comfortable creates powerful opposition to any program that is likely to significantly reduce it.

Cultural Explanations

There are clear cultural differences among the social classes in all modern societies, and some scientists see these differences as a major cause of poverty. The foremost advocate of this position has been Oscar Lewis, who argued that some poor people share a distinct **culture of poverty**.[55] Lewis did not ignore the economic basis of poverty; his thesis was simply that a separate subculture has developed among the poor as a reaction to economic deprivation and exclusion from the mainstream of society. Once a culture of poverty has taken hold, it is passed down from generation to generation. Children who grow up in poverty acquire values and attitudes that make it very difficult for them to escape their condition.

culture of poverty
A theory that holds there is a self-perpetuating subculture among some (but not all) poor people that helps trap them in poverty.

According to Lewis, the family in the culture of poverty tends to be female-centered, with the mother performing the basic tasks that keep the family going. The father, if present, makes only a slight contribution. Children have sexual relations and marry at an early age. The family unit is weak and unstable, and there is little community organization beyond it. Psychologically, those who live in the culture of poverty have weak ego structures and little self-control. Although Lewis did not use the term, most people living in the culture of poverty would clearly be part of the underclass.

Lewis studied a number of societies and concluded that the culture of poverty is international. It develops in societies with capitalist economies, persistently high

Conflict theorists argue that the wealthy want poverty to exist so they can be assured of a plentiful supply of cheap labor.

unemployment rates, low wages, and an emphasis on accumulation of wealth and property. However, Lewis found a number of societies that have a considerable amount of poverty but no *culture* of poverty. India and Cuba, for example, have no culture of poverty because the poor are not degraded or isolated. Even in the United States, most poor people do not live in the culture of poverty. Lewis estimated that because of the influence of the mass media and the relatively low level of illiteracy, only 20 percent of the poor live in a culture of poverty.[56]

Most social scientists agree that poor people are more likely to have some of the characteristics described by Lewis, but there is much skepticism about claims that they have any special personality type or that they value work less than other groups. Some of Lewis's critics are not even so sure that a distinct life-style is passed from one generation to the next. Rather, it is argued by **situationalists** that each generation of the poor exhibits the same life-style because each generation experiences the same conditions: poor housing, crowding, deprivation, and isolation. Charles A. Valentine, for example, argued that the conditions Lewis described are imposed on the poor from the outside rather than being generated by a culture of poverty.[57]

situationalists

Those who believe that the life-style of the poor is the product of their social situation and not a culture of poverty.

Quick Review

Explain the economic, political, and social causes of poverty.

Solving the Problems of Poverty

No one knows whether it is possible to create a classless society in which all people are economically equal in an industrial nation. Certainly no such society exists to-day. It does, however, seem possible to eliminate poverty in an absolute sense, even if some people remain richer than others. Many societies have made much greater progress toward this goal than the United States has, and some of the approaches to reducing poverty are discussed in this section.

More and Better Jobs

Reducing unemployment and creating better-paying jobs is a continuing concern of governments around the world. The easiest approach is to stimulate the national economy by cutting taxes and interest rates or by increasing the amount of money the government spends. The problem with this kind of "quick fix" is that it drives up inflation and the national debt, and if carried on too long it may actually cause economic harm. Long-term improvements in the economy require the kind of basic structural changes described in Chapter 4. Unfortunately, reforms that aim to increase the rate of saving and investment, improve the educational system, and provide better government planning often have little political appeal because they are expensive and seldom produce results quickly enough to influence the next election. Such fundamental reforms are essential, however, if we are ever to make significant progress in the struggle against poverty, for an effective antipoverty program must do more than just create jobs: it must create good jobs that pay a living wage.

New education and job-training programs are likely to be another essential part of any effective effort to return the poor to the mainstream of our economic life. European countries, for example, have much larger programs for **job retraining** than in North America. The idea is a simple one: teach unemployed workers skills that are in demand so that they can find new jobs. While this approach is reasonable in this age of rapidly changing technology, it has basic limitations. If the millions of unemployed and low-wage workers were all taught the latest skills, there still wouldn't be enough jobs to go around under current economic conditions. Such programs can therefore be effective only if they are combined with an effort to create more jobs.

job retraining
 A program to teach workers new skills.

For that reason, many countries have attacked unemployment by increasing the number of government jobs. It is often suggested that government work programs should be greatly expanded to give a job to anyone who is unable to find one in the private sector. Making government an "employer of last resort" could virtually end unemployment. Critics have repeatedly charged that such programs are wasteful and inefficient, and funding for job programs of all types has been greatly reduced in the last two decades. Yet despite such criticisms and cutbacks, there is little doubt that in the long run, the cost of a well-run government job program would be far less than the cost of the lives and productive energy wasted by unemployment. Moreover, some kind of major jobs program will probably be necessary if we are going to meet the ambitious goals for getting welfare mothers to work set in the 1996 welfare reform legislation.

Improving Welfare

The welfare system has been attacked from all points of the political spectrum, and at least the conservatives feel that the new welfare reforms with their strong emphasis on getting welfare mothers into a job will be a big improvement. While few object to the goal of getting mothers off welfare and into gainful employment, progressives feel that the way those reforms are likely to be carried out will be harsh and uncaring and that the overall objectives of the program are highly unrealistic. For one thing, a large number of welfare mothers are poorly educated and lack basic job skills. If they are going to have any chance to get a decent job, they will need education and training. That means that in the short run, an effective program will cost considerably more to set up and run than it saves. Yet the reform legislation actually *cuts* welfare spending. The second difficulty is providing enough good, low-cost day care for the participants' children while the mothers are in training or at work. Once again, this is going to cost more money than welfare programs are likely to be able to spend. The third problem is that the reform proposals are far too optimistic about the chances of these poor welfare mothers finding permanent jobs. In the past, even the most successful programs failed to find jobs for about one-third of the participants, and those who did find work often did not make enough money to get off welfare. For example, a study of 6467 AFDC mothers who volunteered for a job-training and employment program found that only about half were still employed a year after the program was completed, and of those, only about one-fifth rose above the poverty level after two years.[58] A final drawback is that this approach is too negative. Although welfare mothers are threatened with the loss of their benefits if they do not participate in employment programs, their benefits are cut back or eliminated when they start earning money, so they receive few positive rewards for holding down a job. Particularly troublesome is the fact that many of these women will lose their Medicaid coverage, while few of the low-paying jobs they can get are likely to provide health insurance.

Despite these difficulties, a well-designed employment program for welfare mothers could be a positive step if it avoids a punitive approach based on stereotypes and misunderstanding. However, such a program must provide comprehensive job training and placement, and even more important, it must make sure that poor children receive health care, proper nutrition, and good-quality supervision while their mothers are at work.

Another popular proposal for reform is to improve the system for keeping track of absent fathers in order to force them to contribute more to the support of their children. The advocates of such ideas claim that they can save taxpayers billions of dollars in welfare costs. Such an effort seems more likely to benefit mothers from more affluent backgrounds, however, since the fathers of children on welfare usually have few financial resources to contribute. A different program, which is now being tried in New Jersey, is to deny additional welfare benefits to mothers who have another child while on welfare. A more positive approach to achieve the same objective would be to provide a small cash incentive for welfare mothers to use a long-acting contraceptive such as Norplant, or at least to provide effective contraceptive services free of charge.

A different way to improve America's welfare system is through administrative reforms. As currently structured, welfare programs are administered by a patchwork of federal, state, and local agencies, and a tremendous amount of time and money that might be used to help poor people is spent on determining who is eligible for assistance. Such administrative waste would be drastically reduced if more welfare services were provided to all citizens, not just to those who can demonstrate special needs. Most other industrialized nations have taken this approach, relying far more heavily on **noncategorical programs**—social programs for which everyone is eligible. Canada, for example, provides all its citizens with medical care, a small retirement pension, and a family allowance for each dependent child, and similar programs exist in all the western European countries. Such an approach has three major advantages. First, the poor are not discouraged from working by the threat of losing their welfare benefits when they start to earn some money; second, welfare fraud is almost completely eliminated; and third, bureaucratic overhead is greatly reduced.

noncategorical program
A welfare program with no restrictions on eligibility.

Distributing the Wealth More Fairly

One of the most important sociological functions of the welfare system is to transfer wealth from the middle and upper classes to the poor people who need it most. But even a well-funded welfare program is still likely to leave a tremendous gap between the haves and have-nots. Is a day's work by the CEO of an average U.S. corporation really worth 173 times more than a day's work by an average employee? The pay gap is far less in the other industrialized nations, as is the overall gap between the rich and the poor. There is no secret about how to create a more egalitarian society: change the tax structure. As we saw in Chapter 5, the United States has the lowest overall rate of taxation of any major industrial power, and its taxes are particularly light on those with the highest income and the greatest wealth. For example, the first $1 million in inherited wealth is tax free. If we increased the taxes on those with the most wealth and highest incomes, we could reduce the taxes on those in the lower brackets and provide more government services (such as the system of national heath care discussed in Chapter 6), thus reducing the overall level of social inequality.

Organizing the Poor

Any effective program to deal with the problems of poverty is likely to have a high price tag. Although we often give lip service to the ideal of equality, the government has usually been unwilling to put that ideal into practice with the kind of financial support it requires. As we have seen, most programs to help the poor were created only when the poor organized themselves and demanded a bigger piece of the economic pie. Amid the activism of the 1960s, for example, a number of poor people's organizations sprang up to press such demands and were able to win support from more broadly based groups. As a result, the welfare system was improved and poverty decreased. If the government is once again to take new action to deal with the plight of the poor, new organizations and new coalitions will have to be formed to push for change.

Quick Review

Discuss some of the best ways to deal with the poverty problem.

Sociological Perspectives on Problems of the Poor

Poverty has not always been seen as a social problem. Although concern for poor people has a long history, until quite recently poverty was considered an inevitable part of social life or the fault of the poor themselves—a lowly status deserved by the lazy and incompetent. The Great Depression of the 1930s, tragic though it was, helped show social scientists that the conditions of poverty are institutional matters determined by large-scale economic, political, and social processes. Social scientists now agree that poverty is a social problem rather than a collection of personal problems, even though they still have different views about its causes and solutions.

The Functionalist Perspective

Functionalists consider the extremes of poverty and wealth common in most nations to be a result of malfunctions in the economy. In many parts of the world, rapid industrialization has disrupted the economic system, leaving it disorganized and unable to perform many of its essential functions. At first, people who lack job skills are forced into menial work at low wages, and later, with the coming of automation, they are not needed at all. Industrial products become outdated (horse carriages, steam engines, milk bottles), and unless rapid adjustments are made, people who manufacture those products lose their jobs. Training centers and apprenticeship programs may continue to produce graduates whose skills are no longer in demand. Discrimination, whether it is based on sex, age, race, or ethnic status, also wastes the talents of many capable people, and society is the loser.

Functionalists point out that the welfare system intended to solve the problem of poverty is just as disorganized as the economy. Administrators often show more concern for their own well-being than for their clients, and the first priority of many welfare workers has become the protection of their own jobs. Legislative bodies establish programs without enough funds to operate efficiently, and sincere welfare workers are drowned in a sea of rules, regulations, and paperwork. Inadequate communication systems fail to inform the poor about benefits to which they are entitled. Job training and educational programs are not coordinated with the needs of agriculture, commerce, and industry.

The best way to deal with poverty, according to the functionalist perspective, is to reorganize the economic system and the social service agencies so they operate more efficiently. The poor who have been cast out and neglected must be reintegrated into the mainstream of economic life. Members of the underclass must be provided with training and jobs so that they can resume their roles as productive citizens. They must also be given a new sense of hope based on the knowledge that the rest of society cares about them and is willing to help them overcome their poverty. Functionalists also recommend reforms to help stabilize the economic system so that it will not produce new poor people as others escape from poverty.

In general, however, functionalists are much more concerned about absolute poverty than about relative poverty. Many of them doubt that relative poverty (economic inequality) can or should be eliminated. Kingsley Davis and Wilbert E. Moore, for example, argued that economic inequality is actually beneficial for society.[59] Their main point is that the desire for more money motivates people to work hard to meet the standards of excellence that are required in many important jobs. Without inequality of reward, the most capable people would not be motivated to train for or perform the demanding jobs that are essential to the economic system. It should not be concluded, however, that functionalists are convinced that the social system should remain unchanged or that the amount of economic inequality should not be reduced. The functionalist conclusion is simply that *some* inequality is necessary for the maintenance of society as we know it.

The Conflict Perspective

Conflict theorists start with the assumption that because there is enormous wealth in industrialized nations, no one in such societies need be poor. Poverty exists because the middle and upper classes want it to exist. Conflict theorists argue that the working poor are exploited: they are paid low wages so that their employers can make fatter profits and lead more affluent lives. The unemployed are victims of the same system. Wealthy employers oppose programs to reduce unemployment because they do not want to pay the taxes to support them. They also oppose such programs because the fear of unemployment helps keep wages down and workers docile. Thus, conflict theorists argue that the economic system of capitalist countries operates to create and perpetuate a high degree of economic inequality.

Conflict theorists also note that wealthy and middle-class people are more likely than the poor to say that poverty stems from a lack of effort rather than from social injustice or other circumstances beyond the control of the individual. This application of the ideology of individualism enables the wealthy to be charitable to the poor by giving some assistance freely, while ignoring the economic and political foundations of poverty. Charity, including the government dole, blunts political protests and social unrest that might threaten the status quo. Moreover, some poor people come to accept the judgments passed on to them by the rest of society and adjust their aspirations and their self-esteem downward.

Conflict theorists view these adjustments to poverty as a set of chains that must be broken. They believe that the poor should become politically aware and active, organizing themselves to reduce inequality by demanding strong government action. In other words, political action is seen as the most effective response to inequality and, thus, to the problem of poverty. Most conflict theorists doubt that economic inequality can be significantly reduced without a concerted effort by poor people that gains at least some support from concerned members of the upper classes.

The Feminist Perspective

Feminists were among the first to point out what has been termed the "feminization of poverty"—that is, the long-term trend in our society for poverty to be more and more concentrated among women and children. While there are many causes for this trend, the most important factor is the growing instability of the family and the huge increase in the number of single mothers raising their children alone. Feminists argue that in addition to the kinds of general approaches advocated by the functionalists and conflict theorists, special attention must be given to the problems of single mothers if we are to create an effective program to deal with poverty. There is, for example, a crying need for a nationwide system of government-supervised and subsidized day care so that working women can be assured that their children are being properly cared for in their absence. A system of national health care in which basic medical services are seen as a right, not a privilege, would be another major step that would provide enormous benefits for poor families (see Chapter 6). Finally, more effort must be made to end occupational discrimination against women so that working mothers can earn wages high enough to keep their families out of poverty.

The Interactionist Perspective

Interactionists study the effects of attitudes and beliefs on behavior, pointing out that poor people learn to behave in the ways society expects of them. The values of those who live in the culture of poverty are passed on to their children, thus directing them into lives of poverty. For example, some claim that the children of the poor learn to seek immediate gratification and that, unlike middle-class achievers, they are not inclined to defer small immediate rewards so that long-run goals, such as a college education, can be reached. More generally, interactionists point to cultural differences in the ways poor people and wealthy people define their worlds. They note that even when new economic opportunities arise, poor people are often unaware of them or are psychologically and socially unprepared to take advantage of them. Thus, the differences in the ways the rich and poor see the world keep the poor at the bottom of the social ladder.

Interactionists also study the psychological effects of being poor in a wealthy society. The easy availability of television and other media encourages the poor to compare themselves with more fortunate people in a fantasy world. When they do so, many come to define themselves as failures. Some blame personal shortcomings rather than social forces that are beyond their control, and the outcome is likely to be low self-esteem, which in turn precipitates a variety of personal problems, ranging from drug addiction and mental disorders to delinquency and crime. Poor people may also come to define themselves as the victims of an unjust society. On the one hand, this attitude may contribute to a healthy social activism; on the other, it may create a sense of hopelessness or a desire for revenge against those who have taken advantage of them.

The interactionist perspective implies that poverty traps poor people psychologically as well as economically and socially. We could eliminate this trap by eliminating absolute poverty (the lack of adequate food, shelter, and clothing) and by opening up more opportunities for the children of the poor, thus reducing overall inequality. Interactionists also agree that the poor must be encouraged to redefine their social environment. Even if avenues for upward mobility are created, little change will occur as long as the poor are convinced that they can expect no better than a life of poverty. Before they will be able to take advantage of any new opportunities, many poor people will also need help to change a self-image shaped by defeat and rejection.

Quick Review

How would a functionalist and a conflict theorist disagree about the causes of poverty?

What suggestions do feminists make for dealing with the problem of poverty?

How can poor people's definition of themselves trap them in poverty?

Summary

Whether economic inequality is measured by income or wealth, there are large gaps between the rich, the middle class, and the poor that have grown much wider in recent years. Significant differences also exist in the cultural perspectives and lifestyles of these different groups. In cities the poor are trapped in run-down, crime-ridden neighborhoods, while the affluent have a multitude of opportunities from which to choose. Psychologically, the poor have to cope with feelings of inadequacy and inferiority because they lack the money and goods that everyone is "expected" to have. The families of the poor are more unstable, and poor people have more health problems and shorter life spans.

There are two common ways to measure poverty. The relative approach holds that people are poor if they are significantly less well-off than the average person in their society. The absolute approach, which is used by most government agencies, defines poverty as the lack of the essentials of life, such as sufficient food, shelter, and clothing. According to the official figures, the poverty rate has decreased since the early 1960s but has gone up since the early 1970s. A look at the distribution of poverty shows that the young are more likely to be poor than the middle-aged or the elderly, as are children from single-parent families and members of ethnic minority groups. The poverty rate is highest in the inner city and in rural areas and lowest in the suburbs.

There are many important differences among poor people. At the very bottom of the social heap are the homeless, who lack almost all the essentials of the lifestyle expected in our society. The underclass is composed of the long-term poor who are shut out of the mainstream of society. The working poor are those who hold down jobs but earn too little to be above the poverty line.

The ideology of individualism, which stresses personal responsibility and self-reliance, has made Americans far more likely than citizens of other industrialized nations to blame the poor for their own condition. Nonetheless, the Great Depression of the 1930s forced the government to deal with the acute problems of poverty. Programs and benefits generally kept increasing until the 1980s, when there was a sharp conservative reaction against the welfare system. The welfare reforms enacted in 1996 are the latest in a series of efforts to cut the welfare rolls and force welfare mothers to get jobs.

There are many explanations for poverty. In some societies the economic base is so weak that many people must go hungry, but in modern industrial societies there is more than enough to go around. The immediate causes of poverty in industrial societies are such problems as unemployment and low wages, which can in turn be traced back to the basic economic structure and the competitive demands of the capitalist marketplace. In order to relieve such economic problems, governments all over the world have programs to reduce poverty and redistribute wealth to their less fortunate citizens, but because the rich and the powerful oppose effective measures to eliminate poverty, the government's actions inevitably fall short of that goal. Another explanation for poverty is based on Oscar Lewis's idea that some nations develop a "culture of poverty" with distinctive characteristics.

There are numerous proposals for reducing poverty. First, more and better jobs could be created by improving the economy, providing job training, raising the minimum wage, and increasing government employment. Second, welfare programs could be improved by eliminating bureaucratic waste and inefficiency, providing day care and education to help welfare mothers find employment, encouraging the use of family planning, and providing basic necessities such as health care to all citizens regardless of income. Third, the poor could organize themselves to push for government programs that really meet their needs.

Functionalists see extremes of poverty and wealth as the result of a breakdown in social organization. Conflict theorists are convinced that poverty thrives because the wealthy and powerful benefit from it. Feminists point to social changes that have forced more and more women and children into poverty. Interactionists are concerned with the problems created by being poor in an affluent society, and they note that the socialization of the poor often encourages them to develop attitudes and behavior patterns that make upward social mobility difficult.

Questions for Critical Thinking

The problem of poverty and the welfare system necessary to help deal with it has been one of the most controversial issues in American politics in the last two decades. Most Americans say they believe that everyone should have an equal opportunity to succeed in life, but they also believe that people who work harder or are more capable deserve to be wealthier than others. So it comes down to questions of fairness: Do you think American society provides equal opportunities for all its citizens, whether their families are rich or poor or whether they are male or female, black, white, or brown? Are people who work at low-wage jobs paid enough for their labor? Are those at the top paid too much? What about the issue of inheritance? Is the present system fair, or should the government tax inherited wealth at a higher rate? (Currently, the first $1 million of inherited wealth is tax free.)

Key Terms

absolute approach
Aid to Families with Dependent
    Children (AFDC)
culture of poverty
extreme poverty
family allowance

food stamp program
ideology of individualism
income
job retraining
Medicaid
Medicare

noncategorical program
poverty
relative approach
situationalists
Social Security

Supplemental Security Income (SSI)
Temporary Aid to Needy Families
    (TANF)
underclass
wealth

Further Readings

Dennis Braun, *The Rich Get Richer: The Rise of Income Inequality in the United States and the World,* 2nd ed. (Chicago: Nelson-Hall, 1997). An up-to-date examination of the growing gap between the haves and have-nots.

Barbara Ehrenreich, *Fear of Falling: The Inner Life of the Middle Class* (New York: HarperCollins, 1991). An insightful look at today's middle class by one of America's most thoughtful social critics.

Christopher Jencks, *The Homeless* (Cambridge, MA: Harvard University Press, 1995). One of the best available analyses of homelessness in America.

Christopher Jencks and Paul E. Peterson, eds., *The Urban Underclass* (Washington, DC: Brookings Institution, 1991). A first-rate collection of essays stimulated by Wilson's work on the underclass.

Harold R. Kerbo, *Social Stratification and Inequality: Class Conflict in Historical and Comparative Perspective,* 3rd ed. (New York: McGraw-Hill, 1996). An excellent text on social stratification that puts the problem of poverty into its larger context.

William Julius Wilson, *The Truly Disadvantaged: The Inner City, the Underclass, and Public Policy* (Chicago: University of Chicago Press, 1987). A penetrating look at the causes of the deteriorating conditions of the American underclass. Probably the most influential work on poverty of the last decade.

Notes

1. Donna St. George, "For Food-Stamp Families, a More Uncertain Furture," *New York Times,* September 10, 1997, pp. C1, C8.

2. U.S. Bureau of the Census, *Statistical Abstract of the United States, 1996* (Washington DC, Government Printing Office, 1996), p. 472.

3. Lawrence Mishel, Jared Bernstein, and John Schmitt, *The State of Working America, 1996–97* (Armonk, NY: Sharpe, 1997), p. 53.

4. Ibid., p. 226.

5. Ibid., p. 283.

6. Ibid., p. 278.

7. See ibid., p. 402; Harold R. Kerbo, *Social Stratification and Inequality: Class Conflict in Historical and Comparative Perspective,* 3rd ed. (New York: McGraw-Hill, 1996), pp. 27–33.

8. Population Reference Bureau, *World Population Data Sheet, 1997* (Washington, DC: Population Reference Bureau, 1997).

9. Mishel, Bernstein, and Schmitt, *The State of Working America, 1996–97,* pp. 53, 283.

10. Ibid., p. 298.

11. Ibid., p. 299.

12. U.S. Bureau of the Census, *Statistical Abstract, 1996,* p. 63; U.S. Bureau of the Census, *Statistical Abstract, 1993,* p. 61.

13. Mishel, Bernstein, and Schmitt, *The State of Working America, 1996–97,* p. 317.

14. U.S. Bureau of the Census, *Statistical Abstract, 1996,* p. 473.
15. Mishel, Bernstein, and Schmitt, *The State of Working America, 1996–97,* p. 313.
16. U.S. Bureau of the Census, *Statistical Abstract, 1996,* pp. 48, 51.
17. Paul E. Peterson, "The Urban Underclass and the Poverty Paradox," in Christopher Jencks and Paul E. Peterson, eds., *The Urban Underclass* (Washington, DC: Brookings Institution, 1991), pp. 3–27.
18. Ibid.
19. Mishel, Bernstein, and Schmitt, *The State of Working America, 1996–97,* p. 297.
20. Ibid., p. 307.
21. Ibid., p. 314.
22. Associated Press, "Count of Homeless Useless, Official Says," *Los Angeles Times,* May 10, 1991, p. A27.
23. Anna Mulrine, "Self-Help Urged for Homeless," *Christian Science Monitor,* December 7, 1993, p. 6; Mitchel Levitas, "Homeless in America," *New York Times Magazine,* June 10, 1990, pp. 44–45, 82–91.
24. Elizabeth Shogren, "Families Total 43% of Homeless, Survey Reports," *Los Angeles Times,* December 22, 1993, pp. A1, A16.
25. James D. Wright, "The Mentally Ill Homeless: What Is Myth and What Is Fact?" *Social Problems* 35 (April 1988): 182–191.
26. David A. Snow, Susan G. Baker, Leon Anderson, and Michael Martin, "The Myth of Mental Illness Among the Homeless," *Social Problems* 33 (June 1986): 407–423.
27. Ibid.; Marta Elliott and Lauren J. Krivo, "Structural Determinants of Homelessness in the United States," *Social Problems* 38 (February 1991): 113–131.
28. Wilson, "Studying Inner-City Social Dislocations"; Christopher Jencks, "Is the American Underclass Growing?" in Christopher Jencks and Paul E. Peterson, eds., *The Urban Underclass* (Washington, D.C.: Brookings Institution, 1991).
29. Kerbo, *Social Stratification and Inequality,* p. 256.
30. Mishel, Bernstein, and Schmitt, *The State of Working America, 1996–97,* p. 307.
31. Wilson, "Studying Inner-City Social Dislocations."
32. Herbert J. Gans, "Deconstructing the Underclass: The Term's Danger as a Planning Concept," *Journal of the American Planning Association* 56 (Summer 1990): 271.
33. William Julius Wilson, *The Truly Disadvantaged: The Inner City, the Underclass, and Public Policy* (Chicago: University of Chicago Press, 1987), pp. 6–8.
34. Wilson, "Studying Inner-City Social Dislocations."
35. U.S. Bureau of the Census, *Statistical Abstract, 1996,* p. 476.
36. U.S. Bureau of the Census, "The Earnings Ladder: Who's at the Bottom? Who's at the Top?" *Statistical Brief* (Washington, DC: U.S. Government Printing Office, March 1994).
37. Joe R. Feagin, *Subordinating the Poor: Welfare and American Beliefs* (Englewood Cliffs, NJ: Prentice Hall, 1975), pp. 91–92.
38. See Kerbo, *Social Stratification and Inequality,* pp. 257–262.
39. Frances Fox Piven and Richard A. Cloward, *Regulating the Poor: The Functions of Public Welfare* (New York: Vintage, 1971); Michael Betz, "Riots and Welfare: Are They Related?" *Social Problems* 21 (1974): 345–355; Larry Isaac and William Kelly, "Racial Insurgency, the State and Welfare Expansion," *American Sociological Review* 45 (1980): 1348–1386.
40. Piven and Cloward, *Regulating the Poor,* pp. 61–62.
41. Ibid., pp. 184–185.
42. Daniel Patrick Moynihan, *The Politics of a Guaranteed Income: The Nixon Administration and the Family Assistance Plan* (New York: Random House, 1973).
43. Bob Drogin, "True Victims of Poverty: The Children," *Los Angeles Times,* July 30, 1985, pp. 1, 10–11; Kevin Roderick, "Case History of a 20-Year War on Poverty," *Los Angeles Times,* July 31, 1985, pp. 1, 8–9.
44. David Holmstrom, "Food Stamp Use—and Abuse—Reaches All-Time High in US," *Christian Science Monitor,* March 15, 1994, pp. 1, 4.

45. Charles Murray and Richard Herrnstein, *The Bell Curve: Intelligence and Class Structure in American Life* (New York: Basic Books, 1994).

46. Michael Harrington, *The New American Poverty* (New York: Holt, Rinehart and Winston, 1984), pp. 81–87.

47. Mishel, Bernstein, and Schmitt, *The State of Working America, 1996–97,* p. 403.

48. Ibid., p. 169.

49. Ibid., p. 143.

50. Ibid., p. 150.

51. James E. Rosenbaum and Susan J. Popkin, "Employment and Earnings of Low-Income Blacks Who Move to Middle Class Suburbs" in Jencks and Peterson, *The Urban Underclass,* pp. 342–358.

52. See Paul Jacobs, "Keeping the Poor Poor," in Jerome Skolnick and Elliott Currie, eds., *Crisis in American Institutions,* 5th ed. (Boston: Little, Brown, 1988), pp. 134–140.

53. Mishel and Bernstein, *The State of Working America, 1996–97,* pp. 328–331.

54. Herbert J. Gans, "The Uses of Poverty: The Poor Pay All," *Social Policy* 2 (1971): 21–23.

55. Oscar Lewis, *La Vida* (New York: Random House, 1965).

56. Ibid.

57. Charles A. Valentine, *Culture and Poverty: Critique and Counter-Proposals* (Chicago: University of Chicago Press, 1968).

58. Elizabeth Shogren, "Welfare-Job Study Indicates Tough Task for Reform Plan," *Los Angeles Times,* April 26, 1994, p. A14; David Whitman, "The Key to Welfare Reform," *Atlantic,* June 1987, p. 25.

59. Kingsley Davis and Wilbert E. Moore, "Some Principles of Stratification," *American Sociological Review* 10 (1945): 242–249.

8 The Ethnic Minorities

What are the most common patterns of ethnic relations?

What are the problems shared by ethnic minorities in North America?

What are the special problems unique to each different minority group?

Why do most minority groups have such a high poverty rate?

What are the best ways to deal with the problem of ethnic inequality?

Laurencie Nyirabeza lives in the highlands of central Rwanda—a small African country that has been ripped apart by ethnic conflict in the last decade. She is angry and upset because one of her former neighbors, Jean Girumuhatse, has just returned from exile and moved back into her neighborhood. In the mid-1990s, there was a genocidal bloodbath in Rwanda in which the majority ethnic group, the Hutus, slaughtered somewhere between 500,000 and 1 million members of the Tutsi minority. It was during that explosion of hatred and violence that Mrs. Nyirabeza says that Girumuhatse beat her with a stick and hacked at her neck with a machete. Finally, she says, "This man threw me in a ditch after killing off my whole family." Mr. Girumuhatse admits killing a total of six people, but he claims that he was not responsible for his actions because he was only following the orders of his superiors in the Rwandan government. Mrs. Nyirabeza's granddaughter, however, says that he killed 27 people in her extended family alone. Mr. Girumuhatse may eventually be put on trial by Rwanda's overwhelmed legal system, but until then these neighbors will have to live side by side in a climate of ethnic hatred and fear.[1]

The violent face of ethnic relations—riots, beatings, and even outright murder—is familiar to anyone who watches the evening news. From Albania to Zimbabwe, ethnic conflict is a burning issue around the world. Virtually every nation with more than one ethnic group has had its clashes. Some have managed to achieve long-term stability; others have been ripped apart in an explosion of violence and hatred; but most have just muddled through with alternating periods of conflict and cooperation. Today, most of the wealthy industrialized nations have a relatively stable system of ethnic relations, and each one claims to treat all ethnic groups fairly. But just below the surface there is a seething caldron of ethnic injustice. For Muslims in France, Koreans in Japan, and African Americans, Latinos, and other minorities in the United States, society is often a hostile place. Jobs are scarce, pay is low, and people from the dominant groups tell you in a thousand different ways that they think they are better than you. Of course, things are far better now than they were a century ago, but that is small consolation to those who face a wall of hostility and discrimination because of the color of their skin or the way they talk.

Ethnic Groups

We often watch in horror and amazement when the news brings us the bloody spectacle of ethnic violence from around the world. Long-simmering hatred in the Middle East and Northern Ireland are bad enough, but the disintegration of Yugoslavia into a bloodbath of ethnic violence and the genocide and mass exodus in Rwanda seem almost incomprehensible. The sad fact is that the same forces that caused these tragedies are at work in our own society as well. It is essential to understand what these forces are and how they operate; we will start with some basic terminology.

An **ethnic group** is usually defined as a body of people who share a common set of cultural characteristics or at least a common national origin.[2] What sets an ethnic group apart is its sense of being a common group and the belief that its members

ethnic group
A group whose members share a sense of togetherness and the conviction that they form a distinct group or "people."

share a unique social and historical experience. As we can see from even a quick look at the evening news, people often form an intense loyalty to their ethnic group, and many are even willing to die for it. Part of the reason is that in an ethnically divided society, individuals' economic and social destinies are often tied up with those of their ethnic group. If their ethnic group is powerful, they are likely to reap economic rewards. If they come from a disadvantaged minority, they are likely to face a host of economic and social barriers. People often form a strong psychological identification with their ethnic group as well. Thus, any slight or injustice toward their group is seen as a personal attack on them, and the victories and achievements of their group are likewise a source of personal pride and psychological satisfaction.

ethnic minority

An ethnic group that suffers prejudice and discrimination at the hands of a larger dominant group.

The term **ethnic minority** is used in two different ways. Sometimes it simply refers to a small ethnic group that is outnumbered by the majority group in a society, but sociologists use the term in a more relative sense. To the sociologist, how many people there are in the group is less important than how they are treated. In this sense, an ethnic minority is an ethnic group that suffers prejudice and discrimination at the hands of the dominant group in a society.

race

A group of people thought to have a common set of physical characteristics and a common ancestry.

Although a racial group is often an ethnic group as well, the two are not the same. A **race** is usually defined as a group of people with a common set of physical characteristics, but the members of a race may or may not share the sense of identity that holds an ethnic group together. The concept of "race" as it is used in everyday speech is more a social idea than a biological fact. Physical characteristics are biological in origin, but the way they are classified and the meanings they are given are socially determined. Among the more than 5 billion people in the world, there is a wide range of skin colors, body builds, hair types, and other physical features, and even the scientists who study racial types do not agree on a single classification system.[3] Compared to the similarities, the biological differences among racial groups actually are minor and would be of little importance except for the fact that they are used to define membership in a particular social group.

ethnocentrism

The tendency to view the norms and values of one's own culture as absolute and to use them as a standard against which to measure those of other cultures.

racism

A belief in the superiority of one racial group over another that leads to prejudice and discrimination.

People from all ethnic groups tend to see their own culture as the best and most enlightened. This attitude is known as **ethnocentrism.** Because values and behavior patterns differ from one culture to another, one's own culture naturally appears superior when judged by its own standards. Thus, ethnocentrism seems to be universal. All cultures show some prejudice against foreigners, who are commonly viewed as heathens, barbarians, or savages. **Racism** is usually defined as a belief in the superiority of one racial group to another, which leads to prejudice and discrimination. The main difference between racism and ethnocentrism is that the former is concerned with the physical differences among people and the latter with their cultural differences. Although racism is common throughout the world, it is not as universal as ethnocentrism. In many societies, people who share a culture and a religion do not consider the racial differences among themselves important. Where racism does exist, though, it is often more vicious and divisive than ethnocentrism. Two chilling examples are Hitler's mass executions of European Jews and Gypsies and the nearly successful European and American attempts to wipe out the native population of much of North America.

Patterns of Ethnic Relations

It is easy to see from the world news that relationships between ethnic groups take a bewildering variety of forms. To help us make sense of this confusing picture, sociologists have constructed three models of the general patterns ethnic relations usually take. When one ethnic group holds all the power and keeps the others under its economic and political control, the pattern is known as **domination.** Societies based on ethnic domination often impose varying degrees of **segregation** (the separation of the ethnic groups) in order to protect the privileges of the favored groups. In contrast, the ethnic groups in a system of **integration** are basically equal. They go to the same schools, work in the same businesses, and live in the same neighborhoods. In **pluralism,** different ethnic groups are still equal, but they are more separate and distinct. Children are likely to go to a school that places emphasis on teaching the traditions of their group, families live in their own ethnic neighborhoods, and adults work in businesses run by other members of their ethnic group. It is important to note that these are only general models, however. In real life, conditions of domination, integration, and pluralism occur together. It is the sociologist's job to figure out how strong each of these patterns really is in an actual society.

When two ethnic groups come into close contact for the first time, ethnocentrism and competition for resources often stimulate conflict. One group usually emerges as the winner, monopolizing political and economic power and discriminating against the subordinate group. The domination of African slaves by white Americans is an example. Politically, the displaced Africans were powerless, sharing none of the rights of other Americans. They had no weapons or organizations with which to fight their oppressors. Their work produced riches for plantation owners, but their lowly condition was far beneath mere poverty. They were isolated, rejected, and considered more animal than human. Although American slavery is an extreme case of ethnic domination, the same pattern is found again and again throughout the world.

When competing ethnic groups are evenly matched, a more pluralistic system is likely to emerge. The ethnic groups in a pluralist society maintain a high degree of independence. They identify with the larger society but control some of their own social and political affairs. Oftentimes they live in different neighborhoods or different parts of the country and are therefore able to control their local schools, governments, and economic institutions. In actual practice, the relationships among many ethnic groups have elements of both domination and pluralism. For instance, French Canadians are usually considered part of a pluralistic system, but though they maintain a distinct identity and have a strong cultural tradition, they are dominated in some ways by English-speaking Canadians. Anglo-Canadians (and Americans) control the Canadian economy, and the English and American cultural influence is very strong throughout Canada.

An integrated society, like a pluralistic one, strives for ethnic equality, but the interests of one ethnic group are not balanced against those of another. Rather, ethnic backgrounds are ignored, and, ideally, all individuals are treated alike. In a truly integrated society, all people attend the same local schools, go to the same houses of worship, and vote for political candidates on the basis of merit alone. Of course, complete integration never occurs in an actual society, any more than does completely equal pluralism. As long as people living together define themselves as members of different ethnic groups, some degree of prejudice and discrimination will remain. Most societies that encourage ethnic equality through integration have therefore enacted various laws that prohibit discrimination and try to compensate its victims.

Each of these three systems of ethnic relations has its own sources of instability. A system of domination must keep minorities weak and divided. If the victims of exploitation organize themselves to demand justice, the balance of power is likely to

domination
A social system in which one ethnic group holds power and uses it to keep other groups in a subordinate position.

segregation
The separation of two or more racial or ethnic groups.

integration
A social system in which an individual's ethnic background is considered unimportant and people from different ethnic groups live in the same neighborhoods, attend the same schools, work in the same businesses, and so on.

pluralism
A social system in which there are distinct and separate ethnic groups that nonetheless maintain equal social, economic, and political relationships.

change. Sometimes the result is a civil war filled with the kind of bloodshed and brutality that ethnic hatred is so good at bringing out. However, peaceful reforms are sometimes possible if the dominant groups can be persuaded to look at the situation realistically. A pluralistic system can also lead to ethnic conflicts, especially if one group decides it is not treated fairly. In the extreme, separatist movements may divide the pluralist nation into two or more independent countries. This was the case in the division of India and Pakistan and later of Pakistan and Bangladesh. A similar process is even possible in Canada, where some French Canadians want to create separate French- and English-speaking nations.

Just as pluralism can lead to ethnic conflicts and the eventual partition of a society, integration may lead to the gradual reduction or elimination of distinctive ethnic characteristics. Groups that live in close contact, watch the same television shows, eat at the same fast-food stands, and even intermarry are bound to grow increasingly similar as time passes. Today, many North Americans with European backgrounds have given up their separate ethnic identities and simply see themselves as Americans. Even racial differences may begin to fade after years of intermarriage, as they have in Mexico.

Melting Pot or Salad Bowl?

So far we have been describing the kinds of relationships that actually exist among different ethnic groups. Aside from what is, people are naturally concerned about what ought to be. In North America, it was traditionally assumed that minority groups should take on the culture of the dominant group in a process known as **assimilation.** Because immigrants were expected to conform to the standards of Anglo-American culture, this ideal is often known as Anglo-conformity. To be accepted, the immigrant had to learn English, convert to Protestantism, and adopt Anglo-American values and ways of life. African Americans and Native Americans, as well as whites who refused to adopt Anglo-American ways, were condemned to be permanent outsiders. They were not "real Americans."

Although there is still considerable pressure to conform to Anglo-American standards, it has weakened over the years. As more and more different ethnic groups came to North America, people began proposing ideals that were less one-sided. The most influential was the **melting pot theory,** which holds that the different immigrant groups that came to the United States have blended into a distinctively new culture. To this way of thinking, the assimilation of ethnic minorities is still a good thing but should be a two-sided process. Immigrants should be encouraged to adopt the culture of their new home, but the majority group should learn from the newcomers and change their cultural expectations accordingly. Critics of this view often complain that while the ideal of the melting pot may be fine, in actual practice it has been used as a justification for the continued demand for conformity to Anglo culture.

A third ideal, which is sometimes called the **salad bowl theory,** holds that North America works best as a diverse blend of "unmelted" subcultures. Although Mexicans, Jews, Africans, Chinese, Puerto Ricans, Koreans, Europeans, Indians, Cubans, and other groups all share in many common elements of American culture, they are not all the same. These groups remain equally American, but each retains its own distinctive traditions. Advocates of the ideal of the salad bowl hold that melding together these diverse groups would not only destroy valuable ethnic traditions but would make the United States a far less interesting place to live. However,

---

assimilation
A process by which a person takes on a new culture.

melting pot theory
The belief that the different ethnic groups in a nation should learn from each other and merge together to create a single new culture.

salad bowl theory
The belief that a society should encourage its ethnic groups to maintain their distinctive cultural characteristics.

8

Signs of Hope — Prejudice Declines

It is always a difficult thing to measure personal attitudes such as ethnic prejudice. The best data we have come from the public opinions polls, and as Seymour Martin Lipset puts it, they show "a vast improvement in white Americans' attitudes toward blacks, women, and other minorities since the 1950s."* A 1994 NBC/*Wall Street Journal* poll found that four-fifths of African Americans and seven-tenths of European Americans say that they have a close friend whose race is different than their own, and another poll found that the majority of people in both groups say that they would prefer to live in a neighborhood that had an even mix of racial groups. As recently as 1987, only 43 percent of white Americans agreed that "it's all right for blacks and whites to date each other," but by 1994 that figure was 65 percent, and there were similar increases among African Americans. Of course, people are not always honest with the pollsters, but their findings do provide real grounds for optimism.†

*Seymour Martin Lipset, *American Exceptionalism: A Double-Edged Sword* (New York: Norton, 1996), p. 129.
†Ibid., pp. 129–131.

critics of this view argue that it is unrealistic to think that immigrants, who often come from poor nations, can keep their traditional cultures alive in the middle of an alien industrialized society. At best, they might hang on to a few of their traditional ways in segregated ethnic subcultures, but, the critics charge, the discrimination and conflict such a system breeds is far too high a price to pay for its meager benefits.

Quick Review

What is an ethnic group?

What is the difference between racism and ethnocentrism? Compare and contrast the systems of integration, pluralism, and integration.

What ideals do the theories of the melting pot and the salad bowl hold out for American society?

Ethnic Minorities in North America

Historical Background

The Indians were the first Americans, and for that reason they are often referred to as Native Americans, although that term also usually includes Eskimos and Pacific Islanders (residents of other Pacific islands that are part of the United States). Contrary to popular stereotypes, not all Native Americans were nomadic warriors. In fact, there were many different native cultures. Some Native Americans were wandering hunters, but many others lived in stable farming villages. In some areas, Native Americans had highly advanced civilizations. In North America alone the native peoples spoke about 300 different languages.[4]

Three major groups of European colonists settled in North America: French, British, and Spanish. In the beginning, relations between the European immigrants and Native Americans were generally peaceful, and a lively trade developed, but the continued influx of colonists disrupted this early system of pluralism. Europeans came to dominate the eastern tribes and then slowly moved westward, first driving the native peoples from their lands at gunpoint, then restricting them to isolated reserves, and finally requiring even reservation Indians to obey their laws.

Conflict was not restricted to whites and Native Americans, for the European powers also were bitter enemies, fighting among themselves for power, money, and land. The British emerged as the victors in the lands north of what is now the U.S.-Mexico border. The boundaries of the newly independent United States steadily expanded, moving westward as Americans took over vast sections of land formerly held by Spain, France, and Mexico. This westward conquest meant, of course, that sizable European and non-European minorities were brought under the domination of the English-speaking majority.

The two North American nations took very different approaches to the problems of their native minorities. The treaties Canada signed with Native Americans were usually honored, and the government attempted to minimize stealing, looting, and pillaging by the white settlers. In tragic contrast, the U.S. government repeatedly agreed to treaties and then broke them as soon as white settlers demanded more land.[5] The loss of their land, the disruption of their economy, and the spread of European diseases almost led to the annihilation of the native peoples of North America. In 1500, between 12 and 15 million Indians lived in North America (excluding Mexico), but by 1850, only about 250,000 survived.[6]

After the resistance of the Native Americans was broken, they were subjected to cruel domination. Most Indian people were denied the vote, had to obtain passes to leave their reservations, and were prohibited from practicing their own religions, sometimes by force. Children were dragooned off to boarding schools where they were severely punished if they were caught speaking their own language.[7]

The French minority in Canada and the Spanish minority in the United States took divergent paths after they fell under Anglo domination. French Canada had a substantial population at the time of the English conquest, and it has maintained itself as a self-perpetuating community with little new immigration. Quebec has become an island of French in an English-speaking sea. In contrast, the Spanish-speaking population in most of the areas taken from Spain and Mexico was quite small. After the Gold Rush and the building of the transcontinental railroad, these people were overwhelmed by waves of English-speaking immigrants. However, later immigration from Mexico and other Latin American countries eventually led to significant increases in the Latino population of the United States.

In the first century following the American Declaration of Independence, most immigrants to the United States came from the Protestant countries of northern Europe, but from 1870 to 1920, immigrants increasingly arrived from the Catholic areas of Europe: Italy, Ireland, and eastern Europe, especially Poland. At first it was assumed that these immigrants would quickly assimilate into British Protestant culture; when they failed to do so, ethnic tensions and hostilities grew. In addition, nonwhite immigrants, principally from China and Japan, arrived on the West Coast to be greeted with even more prejudice and discrimination. A federal law passed in 1924 severely restricted immigration from southern Europe and stopped all immigration from Asia. This restrictive policy remained in effect until the Immigration Act of 1965 eliminated the quota system that favored people from European counties, and as a result, a new wave of Third World immigrants has come to the United States during the last two decades.

The history of the Africans in North America is unique because they were brought in chains against their will. Slaveholders intentionally tried to extinguish their native culture: the African family system was broken up, and fathers were routinely separated from their children. Slaves who shared common cultural roots were systematically separated and forbidden to speak their own language. They were even forced to abandon their native religions and to become Christians.

After slavery had been abolished, African Americans continued to be plagued by racism. Black political power blossomed briefly after the Civil War, but this fragile flower was soon uprooted. African Americans were systematically murdered, terrorized, and subjugated. Terrorist organizations such as the Ku Klux Klan and the Knights of the White Camellia drove African Americans back into their subordinate status. Slavery was replaced by a system of segregation that once again denied Americans of African ancestry their civil rights. The goal of segregation was to separate African Americans from the rest of society and force them to accept second-class citizenship. African Americans were required to attend separate schools, swim at different beaches, use different restrooms, and even sit in the back of the public buses; and a variety of ruses were used to deny them the right to vote and to participate in the political process.

Unlike other immigrants, Africans were forced to come to North America against their will. Most were put to work as slaves on southern plantations.

The rigid segregation system in the southern states and the more informal segregation practiced in the rest of the country thrived for a hundred years. It was not until the 1950s and 1960s that the civil rights movement finally broke the back of legal segregation. With a new sense of political awareness, thousands of African Americans and their supporters from other ethnic groups, backed by Supreme Court decisions, organized, demonstrated, and demanded equal rights. Although the system of official discrimination has ended, racial prejudice and discrimination continue to be a fact of life for African Americans.

The new sense of black pride and political awareness that developed out of this struggle had an impact on other ethnic groups as well. Militant Latinos, Asians, and Native Americans organized and began echoing demands for "black power" with calls for "brown power," "yellow power," and "red power." In Canada, the Quebecois (French Canadians) also began to assert their cultural identity, and some demanded a new nation separate from Canada. The ethnic conflicts that were simmering in the 1960s quieted in the following years, but the grievances that caused them remain very much alive.

Institutional Inequality

To understand the problems ethnic minorities face today, the first thing most sociologists do is look at such questions as "What kind of jobs do they have?" "What is their average income?" and "What is their educational background?" The answers reveal a high degree of institutional inequality in North American society—in other words, members of most ethnic minorities are much more likely to be at the bottom than the top of our institutional hierarchies.

Education North American culture puts tremendous faith in education. Numerous studies have shown that people with more education are likely to have higher-paying and higher-status jobs. But African Americans, Latinos, and Native Americans receive significantly less education than others. In 1995, almost 83 percent of adult whites had finished high school, but fewer than 74 percent of African Americans and about 53 percent of Latinos had finished. Asians are exceptions to this pattern; taken as a whole, they actually have a slightly higher level of educational achievement than white Americans, but such broad generalizations obscure the fact some Asian groups, such as Laotians and Cambodians, are far below the U.S. average.[8]

The sources of this educational inequality are rooted in economic and cultural domination. For example, during the period of slavery, few African Americans received any schooling, and after emancipation they were put into separate schools of decidedly inferior quality. The civil rights movement and the Supreme Court eventually ended legal segregation. Although there is no longer a separate system of schools for blacks and whites, many students still attend segregated classes as a result of the segregated housing patterns of American cities (see Chapter 3 for more details).

In many ways the history of Native American education is even more dismal. Many of the early Indian schools were run by missionaries who were determined to "civilize" and Christianize the "heathen savages." The government-run boarding schools that eventually replaced the missionary schools were no better:

The young Indian, torn from his family, was shipped to the school where his hair was immediately cut and where he was given a military uniform and taught close order drill. One of the prime objectives of the system was to teach him the English language as rapidly as possible. He was given demerits for speaking in his native language. Since the incoming student could speak no other language, great personal tragedies resulted, leading to high suicide rates.[9]

Many young Native Americans returning from boarding school were adrift: they did not fit into the white world, yet they were no longer comfortable in the traditional world of their parents.

The cultural assumptions of the white middle class are still built into today's schools, and that creates behavioral as well as learning problems for some minority students. For example, success in school depends largely on the student's ability to meet middle-class standards of discipline and self-control. Students from homes that allow free emotional expression and place few controls on behavior are therefore at a disadvantage. In addition, textbooks and other course materials are often culturally biased. Imagine Native American children's reaction on reading that traitors in their ancestors' struggle to keep their land are to be called "friendly Indians." Only recently have American textbooks acknowledged the contributions of ethnic minorities to U.S. society. Cultural biases are also institutionalized through language. Immigrant children are often required to do their schoolwork in English whether or not they are fluent in that language. Obviously, children who must struggle to learn mathematics, science, and history in a language they do not fully understand are less likely than native speakers of English to get good grades or even to finish high school.

It should not be concluded, however, that most of the differences in educational achievement between ethnic minorities and the dominant group stem from the cultural biases built into the school system. For one thing, regardless of their ethnic group, poor children do not do as well in school as children from wealthier families, and ethnic minorities are more likely to be poor. Further, ethnic groups differ significantly in the value they place on education and in their family structure, and these differences affect achievement. Japanese Americans, as well as several other Asian groups noted for their cohesive family structure, have been very successful in school despite the barriers of language and racial prejudice.

Employment Statistics show that members of minority groups are far more likely to have low-status and low-paying jobs. Whites are more than twice as likely as African Americans or Latinos to work as managers or professionals, and similar patterns are found in the distribution of income. In 1995, the average African American family earned only about 60 percent as much as the average white family, down slightly from a high of 61 percent in 1970. The average earnings of Latino and African American families were just about the same, but the larger size of Latino families meant less money per person.[10] A look at the unemployment figures shows much the same story. In 1995, 4.9 percent of white workers were unemployed, while that figure was 9.3 percent for Latinos and 10.4 percent for African Americans (see Figure 8.1).[11]

Much of this inequality can be explained by the educational differences already discussed: because minorities have less education, they are less likely to qualify for high-paying jobs. Education is not the whole story, however, for minority employees tend to receive less pay than whites with the same level of education. On the average, an African American family headed by a high school graduate has about the same income as a white family headed by someone with only eight years of education.

Figure 8.1

Income and Unemployment

African Americans and Latinos have significantly lower incomes and more unemployment than European Americans.

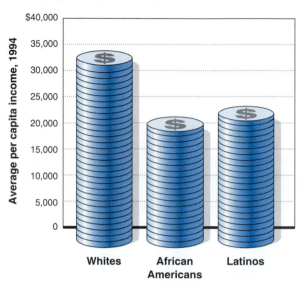

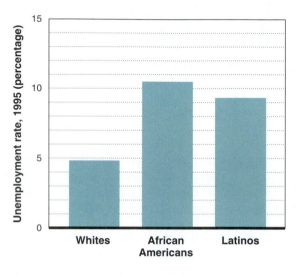

Source: U.S. Bureau of the Census, *Statistical Abstract of the United States, 1996* (Washington, DC: U.S. Government Printing Office, 1996), pp. 394, 461.

One cause for this difference was clearly shown in an experiment conducted by the Urban Institute. When equally qualified groups of whites and blacks applied for jobs in Chicago and Washington D.C., most applicants were treated equally regardless of race. But 20 percent of the time, whites were given preferential treatment over blacks, while blacks were given preferential treatment only 7 percent of the time.[12]

A related problem arises from cultural discrimination. Despite the talk about equal opportunities for those with equal ability, many people are hired and promoted because of their personal relationship with an employer or manager. Generally speaking, it is mutual understanding and a common background that promotes such friendships. If the personnel manager and boss are white (which is likely to be the case), members of a minority group may be at a distinct disadvantage even if company policy prohibits job discrimination. A survey of America's 24 largest corporations found that 8 out of 10 African Americans and about half the members of other ethnic minorities felt that women and minorities were excluded from informal networks and work groups in their companies.[13]

Law and Justice Discrimination has a long history in the American legal system. The U.S. Constitution did not explicitly mention race or slavery, but it nonetheless provided for the return of escaped slaves and held that a slave should be counted as two-thirds of a person for congressional apportionment and tax purposes. In 1857 the Supreme Court ruled that constitutional rights and privileges did not extend to African Americans:

We think . . . that they [African Americans] are not included, and were not intended to be included, under the word "citizen" in the Constitution, and can therefore claim none of the rights and privileges which that instrument provides for and secures to the citizens of the United States. On the contrary, they were at that time considered as a subordinate and inferior class of beings, who had been subjugated by the dominant race, and whether emancipated or not . . . had no rights or privileges but such as those who held power and the government might choose to grant them.[14]

Even though such racist ideas are no longer part of the law, numerous studies have shown that African Americans are more likely than whites to be arrested, indicted, convicted, and committed to an institution. An analysis of Justice Department data, for example, shows that the racial difference in incarceration rates is huge and getting bigger. Today, about 1 in every 3 young African American men is either in prison or on probation or parole.[15]

Some criminologists say that these differences occur because African Americans are more often involved in serious and repeated offenses than whites. There is little doubt that the urban underclass has an extremely high crime rate and that its members are disproportionately drawn from the ranks of African Americans (see

The deep racial divide in the United States was reflected in the sharp differences of opinion among black and white Americans about the trail of former sports hero O. J. Simpson for the murder of his ex-wife. Polls showed that most African Americans believed Simpson's claims that he was framed by the police, while most whites were equally convinced of his guilt.

Chapter 13). Other social scientists hold racial prejudice to be more important. They argue that the expectations of police officers, prosecutors, and judges that African Americans are more likely to be criminals become a self-fulfilling prophecy. Because African Americans are expected to commit more crimes, they are watched more closely, and therefore they are arrested and prosecuted more often.

Whether or not members of ethnic minorities are more likely to be arrested for their crimes, minority leaders are nearly unanimous in their complaints about excessive force and police brutality in their communities. The most infamous case of police brutality in recent times was that of Rodney King. The case began when several Los Angeles police officers were videotaped beating Mr. King as he lay helpless on the ground. As this shocking footage was shown again and again on television, this case quickly became a national issue. In 1992, the officers involved were acquitted of the criminal charges against them by a jury without a single African American member; their acquittal touched off the bloodiest rioting in the history of urban America. Although the officers involved were later convicted on federal charges, this case remains a symbol of the failure of the American system of justice.

Problems and Prospects

As we have seen, ethnic minorities in North America have many difficulties in common, but all ethnic groups have their own unique concerns and problems. In order to understand the mosaic of North American life, it is necessary to examine the largest ethnic groups separately.

Native Americans Although they were the original residents of North America, native peoples are now far outnumbered by other groups. There are only about 2 million Native Americans in the United States, amounting to less than 1 percent of the total population.[16] They nonetheless have a special status among the minorities of North America. While they share the economic problems experienced by most minority groups, no one else has signed legal treaties with the governments of the United States and Canada, and no other groups have reservations (lands granted to individual tribes by those treaties).

Indians who live on reservations have higher rates of poverty and unemployment and less education than other Indians. Moreover, many of the reservations offer inadequate housing, poor health care programs, and a lack of public facilities. Figures from Canada indicate that life expectancy for Native Americans is 8 years less than the national average, largely as a result of poverty and deprivation on the reservations. Yet the reservations give native peoples more political autonomy than other minorities have. Elected tribal governments have wide political and economic authority to regulate the affairs of their own people. Despite the fact that native peoples were given only the worst land in the most undesirable locations, many of these remote reservations have turned out to have considerable natural resources. One estimate holds that while native people own about 5 percent of the land in the United States, they have one-tenth percent of the known gas and oil reserves, one-third of the strippable coal, and half of the uranium reserves.[17] This situation has led to large economic disparities among the tribes that have rich natural resources and those that do not, as well as some bitter disputes among tribes over the control of reservation lands. Many tribes are also engaged in legal battles over lands they believe were given to them in treaties and then illegally taken away.

The biggest victory for native rights in recent times came in Canada. In November 1992, after years of negotiations, the Inuit people (often known as Eskimos) won voter approval for the creation of a new Canadian territory that they will dominate. The new territory, which will officially be established in April 1999, will be known as Nunavut and will contain almost one-fifth of all the land in Canada. Although this northern land is sparsely populated, over 80 percent of its residents will be Inuit. The Inuit were also given direct title to some 136,000 square miles of land and a multimillion-dollar cash settlement.[18]

Despite the popular stereotype, most Native Americans now live in cities, not on reservations. While still considerably below the nation's average income, these urbanites are better off economically than those who remain behind, but at the price of growing separation from their traditional culture. Urban Indians are, for example, considerably less likely to speak a native language or practice a native religion than those who live on reservations.[19]

Europeans Descendants of the European immigrants are, of course, the majority in North America, but within this large group there are many different ethnic traditions. Some writers divide the Europeans into two main groups: the Anglo-Protestants (Protestants of British descent) and the **white ethnics,** such as the Irish, Italians, Jews, and Polish. However, the term *white ethnic* is misleading, since Anglo-Protestants are obviously as much an ethnic group as any other. Over the years, religion has become one of the primary focuses of ethnic identity among European Americans, and the distinctions among Protestants, Catholics, and Jews are often more important than those based on the country from which their ancestors came.

> **white ethnics**
> American of European descent who maintain a distinct ethnic identity.

Recent years have seen two contradictory trends among these groups. On the one hand, many European Americans responded to the minority activism of the 1960s and 1970s with an increased interest in their own ethnic traditions and a renewed identification with their ancestral homeland. On the other hand, the differences among European groups have sharply declined as immigrants have assimilated into the mainstream of American culture. Richard D. Alba's research shows, for example, that successive generations of Italian Americans have fewer and fewer distinctive cultural characteristics that set them off from other European Americans and that they have grown increasingly likely to marry outside their group.[20] Stanley Lieberson and Mary C. Waters find the same trends among other European ethnic groups as well.[21] Such data led Alba to conclude that these groups are in the "twilight of ethnicity." While it is unlikely that identification with different European nationalities is going to disappear any time in the near future, this kind of ethnic identity has become a voluntary personal choice, and a growing number of people descended from those groups see themselves simply as Americans.

It is a mistake, however, to look at this merely as a process of assimilation that has left the dominant group unaffected. Research by Andrew M. Greeley shows that many "white ethnic" groups now actually have higher educational achievement and income than white Protestants. Greeley found that the average income of Jews and of Italian, Irish, and Polish Catholics exceeded the income of Presbyterians, who were the most affluent white Protestants.[22]

There is, however, one group of Europeans in North America that has not followed this pattern of assimilation. Perhaps because of their long history on this continent or because they are heavily concentrated in the province of Quebec, where they are the majority, French Canadians continue to maintain a very different linguistic and cultural tradition from Anglo-Canadians. In fact, separatist feelings run so high in Quebec that the survival of a unified Canada has been in doubt several times in the last two decades.

Jews Although the vast majority of Jewish immigrants to North America came from Europe, their special historical experience sets them apart from the European groups mentioned in the previous section. Jews have lived in Europe since ancient times, but their religious differences and distinct culture always distinguished them from the Christian majority. Through the centuries, they remained a distinct minority group that frequently suffered at the hands of the majority. European Jews were routinely discriminated against in both economic and social life, and on occasion they were the victims of violent assaults and even systematic attempts at mass extermination. Although many Jewish immigrants came to North America looking for a land of opportunity and a chance to escape European anti-Semitism, they encountered the same kind of prejudice they had always faced. Racist organizations such as the Ku Klux Klan condemned Jews along with African Americans; Jews were often stereotyped as greedy and clannish, and many prestigious universities established quotas to keep Jewish enrollment from growing too large. Nonetheless, the treatment of Jews in the United States has generally been better than in Europe. Research shows a decline in American anti-Semitism in recent decades, and some Jewish leaders, like those of many other ethnic groups, now worry about the loss of ethnic identity to assimilation and intermarriage.

The roughly 5.5 million Jews in the United States account for about 44 percent of the world's Jewish population. American Jews are heavily concentrated in the big cities of the Northeast, especially New York, and in California. Although the Bureau of the Census does not collect systematic data on Jewish Americans as it does on most other ethnic groups, evidence shows that Jews have been remarkably successful in conquering the barriers of prejudice and discrimination. They now have the highest educational level and the highest income of any white group in the United States. One analysis of a list of the 400 richest Americans found that 23 percent were from Jewish backgrounds.[23] Their success has not ended the problem of anti-Semitism, however, and in some ways it may have intensified the tendency for frustrated and hostile individuals to blame their problems on Jews.[24]

African Americans According to the Bureau of the Census, about 12.6 percent of all Americans are of African descent, making them the largest minority in the United States.[25] (See Figure 8.2.) For that reason and because they have always been singled out as the targets of special prejudice and discrimination, African Americans have come to symbolize the problems all ethnic minorities face in the United States. Not surprisingly, African Americans have often led the way in the struggle for ethnic justice in the United States.

But the African American community itself is now deeply divided between a growing middle class and the increasingly desperate poor. Since 1950, the number of African Americans holding white-collar jobs has risen much faster than their population as a whole, and the number of elected African American officials has shown even larger gains. African Americans moved into professional and managerial jobs in unprecedented numbers; they became increasingly important in the entertainment business; and they came to dominate several highly paid professional sports.

Figure 8.2

America's Ethnic Population

African Americans are the largest minority group in the United States, but Latinos are not far behind.

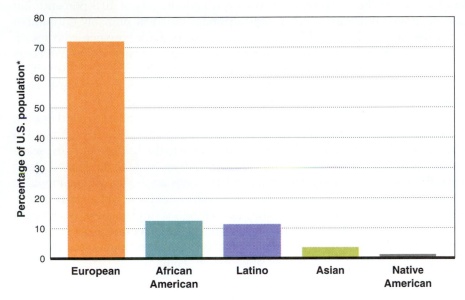

Source: U.S. Bureau of the Census, *Statistical Abstract of the United States, 1996* (Washington, DC: U.S. Government Printing Office, 1996), p. 19.
*Estimate for the year 2000.

Real family income and educational achievement went up, and infant mortality went down.

Yet as more affluent African Americans left the ghettos for the suburbs, conditions deteriorated for the poor who remained behind. Since the late 1970s, the percentage of African Americans living in extreme poverty (defined as family income of less than half the poverty line) grew from one-third of all poor African American people to almost half.[26] At least in part as a result of the "war on drugs," the already high rate of incarceration for African Americans has skyrocketed, increasing almost 30 percent since 1990.[27] Even more disturbing, the *majority* of African American children are now born to single women, and only about one-third live with both their parents, a lower percentage than for any other ethnic group in the United States.[28]

The explanation for the crisis of the black underclass is not entirely clear, but William Julius Wilson argues that there are two major reasons.[29] First, there has been a major shift in employment away from the lower-skilled jobs many poor African Americans depended on. Second, the exodus of more successful African Americans to the suburbs led to what Wilson terms "concentration effects" that worsened the already serious problems in the ghettos. Wilson argues that the concentration of poor urban African Americans in homogeneous neighborhoods without a significant middle class intensified their social isolation and encouraged the decay of community institutions. In addition, many observers lay part of the blame on cutbacks in welfare benefits and other social programs that have been made in the last decade and a half and on the indifference of more wealthy Americans to the plight of the urban poor.

Latinos Latinos are the second-largest American minority (about 10.3 percent), but because of heavy immigration and a high birthrate, they will probably outnumber African Americans in the near future.[30] Many outsiders think everyone who speaks Spanish is part of the same culture, but Latinos are actually a diverse group. Well over half of all Latinos in the United States are of Mexican origin. Most of them live in California, Texas, and the other states of the Southwest. Puerto Ricans are the second-largest group; their population is centered in New York City and the Northeast (and, of course, on the island of Puerto Rico, which is a commonwealth of the United States). The third-largest Latino group is the Cubans, who are most heavily concentrated in Florida. Many well-educated middle-class Cubans came to the United States to escape the Cuban revolution, and as a result, middle-class Cubans came to the United States to escape the Cuban revolution, and as a result, Cubans are better off economically than other Latino groups in North America. However, more recent Cuban immigrants, often known as "boat people" because they arrived by sea in precarious small boats, tend to be from more disadvantaged backgrounds. On the other end of the economic scale are the Puerto Ricans. Their poverty rate is about 50 percent higher than for Mexican Americans, as is their percentage of single-parent families.[31]

The constant influx of newcomers, who are often poorly educated and unfamiliar with the ways of American society, creates some serious problems for the Latino community. Many of these immigrants come illegally and are subject to exploitation by unscrupulous employers who violate minimum wage and safety laws, knowing that their workers dare not turn them in. The problems of overcrowding, poverty, and lack of proper health care are also especially severe among new immigrants.

Spanish is the second most commonly spoken language in the United States. The large and rapidly growing Latino community has given rise to everything from Spanish-language newspapers and television networks to Spanish billboards and traffic signs. These changes have produced concern among some other groups that the nation will be permanently divided into separate English-speaking and Spanish-speaking societies. Such fears are unfounded: Latinos, like other immigrants, are certainly helping to reshape American culture, but there is no evidence that they are any less interested in moving into the mainstream of American life than the immigrants who preceded them.

Asians Asians are the fastest-growing ethnic group in North America. The Asian population of the United States more than doubled between 1980 and 1990, and Asians now make up about 3 percent of the population.[32] But it is even more misleading to talk about Asian Americans as if they were a single cultural group than it is for Latinos. At least Latinos share a common language and some general similarities in cultural background. Today's Asian immigrants come from dozens of different countries that in many cases have little or nothing in common. A cross section of recent Asian immigrants might, for example, include everything from a Hong Kong shipping tycoon seeking a more stable economic climate to a refugee from an isolated hill tribe of Southeast Asia or a poverty-stricken peasant from Bangladesh.

As a group, Asian Americans have gained a reputation for being a kind of "model minority"—hardworking, well disciplined, and highly successful. While there is some truth to this image, such generalizations mislead as much as they inform. Studies do indeed show that Asians have a higher educational level, higher family income (although not necessarily a higher income per person), and lower rates of infant mortality than white Americans. Yet the largest Asian American groups tend to have a "bipolar" occupational structure. In other words, Asian workers are clustered either in relatively high-paying professional jobs or in low-paying service jobs, with few in the middle of the occupational hierarchy.[33] Such generalizations also ignore the plight of the many new Asian immigrants and those from less successful Asian groups. For example, a study by researchers from the University of California at Los Angeles found that while Asians as a whole have a relatively low level of welfare dependency, almost one-third of Southeast Asians in the United States receive welfare assistance. Among some groups, such as Cambodians and Laotians living in California, the welfare rate reaches as high as 77 percent.[34]

Many fear that the stereotype of Asian Americans as workaholic superachievers is also fanning the flames of racism and prejudice. Asian leaders complain that informal quotas are being used to restrict their admission to the most prestigious universities, that movies stereotype them in more blatant ways than any other minority, and that they often bear the brunt of the anger and frustration of workers who suffer from foreign economic competition. Japanese Americans have a special reason to fear such racism. Not only were they singled out for internment in concentration camps during World War II, but Japan's recent economic success has also made them easy targets for those seeking a scapegoat for America's economic problems. One study found that in 1993, 30 Asian Americans were killed in crimes that apparently had a racial motivation.[35]

Mixed Backgrounds The traditional attitude among almost every ethnic group in North America is that their ways and their people are better than everyone else and that their children should marry only people "of their own kind." The strongest prohibitions have always applied to interracial relationships. Until relatively recently, interracial marriages were illegal in most states, but neither the law nor fierce social intolerance prevented millions of mixed-race babies from being born.

Traditional taboos about marrying outside one's ethnic group have slowly weakened but have not disappeared. Whether one's ancestors came from Italy, Germany, Ireland, or England has taken on less and less importance among white Americans over the years, and the vast majority of European Americans now have ancestors from several different countries. Although Jews maintain a more distinct ethnic identity, one survey found that half the marriages involving Jews are now interfaith marriages—compared to fewer than 1 in 10 a generation ago.[36] Similar trends are occurring among Asian Americans. About one-fourth of Chinese Americans under age 24, for example, marry someone from a different ethnic group. Even the marriage barriers between blacks and whites have shown signs of weakening. Although the total percentage of mixed-race couples remains small, it has quadrupled since 1970,[37] and interracial marriages are clearly growing more acceptable to the public. The Gallup poll found that 64 percent of those from age 18 to 29 approved of interracial marriages, while only 27 percent of those over age 50 did.[38]

Their mixed ethnic heritage doesn't usually pose much of a problem for the millions of Americans with ancestors from different European countries—provided their parents did not have unresolvable religious differences over their upbringing. People from mixed racial backgrounds, on the other hand, often run into much more serious difficulties. In some societies, they are in the unenviable position of being rejected by both racial groups. In America, children with a black and a white parent were traditionally considered black and were subject to the same discrimination and prejudice as other African Americans. Even today, most children of such mixed marriages identify themselves as African American, but that, of course, entails rejecting the ethnic identity and heritage of one parent. Children from other kinds of racially mixed marriages often find that society doesn't know quite how to deal with them. As a result, there has been a growing movement to recognize people from mixed racial backgrounds as a distinct group. Advocates recently attempted to get the Bureau of the Census to list a "mixed" racial category along with its more traditional ones for the census in the year 2000. However, some African American leaders objected, fearing that the addition of a new category would reduce their overall numbers in the census count. The Bureau of the Census refused to add the new category, although in the next census it will allow people to check more than one racial group.

The Impact of Immigration

No other force has had a greater impact on the changing face of ethnic relations in North America than immigration. Recent years have seen not only a big increase in the number of immigrants but also a major shift in the countries from which they come. In the past, most immigrants came from European countries, but since the Immigration Act of 1965, things have changed. As recently as the 1950s, three-fourths of the immigrants to the United States were from Europe or Canada, but now about 85 percent come from Asia or Latin America.[39] Although exact figures are impossible to come by, there has also been a sharp increase in the total number of immigrants, and the last decade saw the largest number of new immigrants in American history.[40] In 1996 alone, over 1 million immigrants were granted U.S. citizenship.[41] However, because the population of the United States is so much bigger than in the past, today's immigrants are still a smaller proportion of the total than they were at the peak of European immigration in the early decades of the twentieth century.

Unless there are major changes in government policy, this heavy influx of immigrants seeking to escape the poverty of the Third World is likely to continue. By the end of this decade, it is expected that 1 in 10 U.S. residents will have been born in another country. The Bureau of the Census estimates that whites will shrink from 83 percent of the population today to about 79 percent in the year 2020. Latinos will be the largest minority by then, making up over 16 percent of the population; African Americans will be next at about 14 percent; and the percentage of Asians will have more than doubled to over 6 percent.[42]

The impact of this new wave of immigration is one of the most hotly debated issues in the whole field of ethnic relations. On the positive side, these new immigrants bring willing hands and many skills that are needed in today's economy. Their distinctive cultural perspectives and overseas ties have proved vital to many businesses that compete in the global economy. On the other hand, however, new immigrants often come into conflict with already established groups, and in hard economic times they may drive down wages and may take jobs from citizens who want them. Such problems are aggravated by the fact that the new immigrants are not evenly dispersed throughout the country but concentrated in only a few areas.

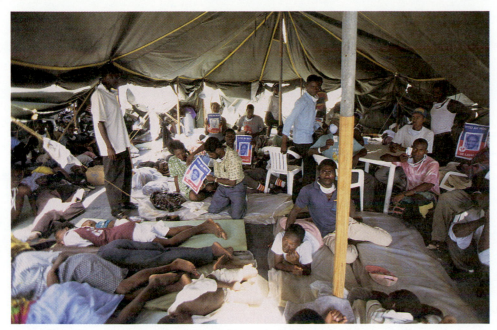

As these Haitians found out, the United States is becoming increasingly reluctant to accept refugees seeking to escape desperate conditions in their own countries.

Three-fourths of all foreign-born Americans live in just seven states, and even within those states they are heavily concentrated in major cities such as Los Angeles, New York, and Miami.

Quick Review

Briefly describe the history of ethnic relations in North America.

Describe the ways ethnic inequality is built into our educational, economic, and legal institutions.

What are the special problems faced by each of the major ethnic groups in our society?

What impact has immigration had on the problem of ethnic relations?

Explaining Ethnic Inequality

The first job of the sociologist facing an important social problem is to describe it as precisely as possible. Although that is usually a lot harder than it sounds, the second task—explaining the causes of the problem—is harder still. In the last section we described the pervasive problem of ethnic inequality, and now we examine its causes. We will focus our attention on three major factors that are the keys to solving this riddle: conflict and competition, prejudice and discrimination, and class.

Conflict and Competition

If we go back far enough into the history of the relationship between different ethnic groups, we almost always find a period of open conflict as the groups compete for control of resources, power, and prestige. If the groups are roughly equal in strength, there will probably be some equitable solution to their differences. If one group enjoys significant advantages over the other, however, the weaker group is likely to be stripped of its resources and forced into a position of subordination. For example, the European settlers who came to North America had a far more technologically developed culture than the native peoples they encountered. The immigrants used that superiority to take Indian land and force Native Americans into a subordinate role in the new European-style society they created.

Although the initial competition between ethnic groups often takes a military form, it is likely to become more peaceful over the years. The military advantage of one group is transformed into economic and political advantages. Members of the stronger group seize resources from the weaker and then pass that wealth down to their descendants. They also create political and economic systems that favor members of their own group. As time goes by, people may forget the origins of this inequality and come to see it as the natural order of things. Of course, things do not always happen this way. There are many examples of ethnic conflicts that result in seemingly endless rounds of bloodshed and military strife, and others in which the groups ultimately come to some equitable solution or forget the ethnic differences that once set them apart.

Prejudice and Discrimination

prejudice

An unsupported negative attitude toward a group as a whole or toward an individual because he or she is a member of that group.

discrimination

An action that penalizes someone because of such characteristics as ethnic group, religion, or gender.

Prejudice and discrimination are closely associated, but they are not the same. **Prejudice** refers to attitudes; **discrimination** refers to actions. Gordon Allport used the following definition in his classic study *The Nature of Prejudice:* "Ethnic prejudice is an antipathy based upon a faulty and inflexible generalization. It may be felt or expressed. It may be directed toward a group as a whole, or toward an individual because he is a member of that group."[43] Discrimination involves actual behavior: favoring one person or penalizing another because of that individual's ethnic status. It usually surfaces when members of a dominant group deny equal treatment to a subordinate group, but even the oppressed may discriminate against others when they have the chance. Although prejudice and discrimination usually occur together, this is not always so.[44] Sometimes we are prejudiced toward a person but reject discrimination because of moral conviction or the fear of legal penalties. On the other hand, economic and social pressures may lead us to discriminate against someone without feeling any prejudice.

Like other types of human behavior, prejudice and discrimination are not easily accounted for. Many influences come together to create them, and their origins cannot be found entirely in individual psychology or oppressive social institutions. Rather, psychological and social processes blend together, like prejudice and discrimination themselves.

authoritarian personality

A person who is rigid and inflexible, has a very low tolerance for uncertainty, and readily accepts orders from above.

Psychological Theories Many psychologists believe that people with an **authoritarian personality** are the most likely to be prejudiced.[45] Such people are rigid and inflexible and have a low tolerance for uncertainty. They place a high value on conventional behavior and feel threatened when others do not follow their standards. Indeed, their prejudices help reduce the threat they feel when confronted by uncon-

Violence and terrorism, such as that practiced by the Ku Klux Klan, are common techniques used to protect the domination of one ethnic group over another.

ventional behavior. By labeling others as "inferior," "immature," or "degenerate," authoritarians avoid any need to question their own beliefs and attitudes. The notion that this personality type is responsible for prejudice and discrimination has come under severe attack, however. Critics charge that the characteristics said to make up an authoritarian personality are not a unified whole but a number of unrelated traits given a single name, and that the concept of the authoritarian personality is just another label we can use to stigmatize people we dislike.

Another common psychological theory focuses on the use of minority groups as **scapegoats** for other people's problems—when people are frustrated and unhappy, minority groups can provide a safe target for their rage. The term *scapegoat* originates from a Jewish tradition. On Yom Kippur, the Day of Atonement, a goat was set loose in the wilderness after the high priest had symbolically laid all the sins of the people on its head. Ironically, the Jews themselves often became scapegoats in Western history. When plagues swept through medieval Europe, killing millions of people, rioters stormed into Jewish ghettos and burned them down, believing that Jews were somehow responsible for the epidemics. Six centuries later, when the Nazis set up their death camps, Jews were still being blamed for the troubles of Europe.

scapegoat
A person or group that is unjustly blamed for the problems of others.

Cultural Theories Prejudice and discrimination may be fueled by the desire to blame others for our problems, but both are learned. People do not need to have authoritarian personalities to have strong racial prejudice when they live in a culture in which such attitudes are the norm. Most prejudice is learned early in the socialization process. Children often adopt their parents' prejudices as naturally as they adopt their parents' language, and discrimination follows prejudice as regularly as night follows day.

ethnic stereotype
The portrayal of all the members of a particular ethnic group as having similar fixed, usually unfavorable, traits

contrast conceptions
The strong stereotypes that ethnic groups often develop about each other.

institutional discrimination
Discrimination against minority groups that is practiced by economic, educational, and political organizations rather than by individuals.

Some of the most common prejudices are taken from **ethnic stereotypes** that portray all the members of a particular group as having similar fixed, usually unfavorable, characteristics. The "happy-go-lucky Mexican," the "lazy Negro," and the "cunning Jew" reflect ethnic stereotypes that most of us have heard at one time or another.[46] In situations of ethnic conflict, **contrast conceptions** often develop; that is, people from two ethnic groups develop strong negative stereotypes about each other. For instance, while white racists in the United States perpetuate vicious anti–African American stereotypes, African American racists have developed their own stereotypes that depict all whites as greedy, selfish, and bent on subjugating African Americans.

Although the prejudice expressed in ethnic stereotypes is usually obvious, it can be quite subtle; for example, a white schoolboy living in an integrated neighborhood learns prejudice when he hears his mother say that it is all right for him to sleep overnight at the home of an African American friend because "that house is so clean you could eat right off the floor." An unspoken but potent prejudice is at the base of the mother's praise: African Americans are crude and dirty, but this family is an exception.

Structural Theories Another important source of prejudice and discrimination can be found in the way a society structures its economic, political, and social activities. This form of bigotry is often termed **institutional discrimination** because inequality is built into the social structure and occurs whether or not the individuals working in that system are themselves prejudiced. For example, when Latino immigrants take civil service examinations, they are often at a severe disadvantage because English is their second language and it is hard for them to do as well on a test written in English as those who grew up speaking that language.

There is ample evidence that the realities of economic competition lie beneath much prejudice and discrimination. If members of minority groups are excluded from elite colleges and professional schools, they obviously will not be able to compete with members of the dominant group in occupations requiring a high degree of training. In times of high unemployment, members of the dominant group can protect their jobs by making sure that minorities are the first to be fired and the last to be hired. It has long been noted that racial prejudice is highest among white working-class men who compete with African Americans for low-paying, unskilled jobs.

Members of the dominant group are not necessarily aware of the exploitation, however, because their stereotypes of ethnic and racial inferiority justify the inequalities in their society. Members of minority groups are seen to be poor because they are lazy or stupid, not because of the discrimination against them. Those in subordinate groups, of course, realize that they are being victimized, and their anger and resentment find expression in their own prejudices or may ultimately lead to revolutionary violence.

Racism and prejudice can also play an important part in class conflict. Racial animosities between African American and white workers in the United States have often been used to divide and weaken the working class. Many employers intentionally encourage racial conflicts to keep workers from forming a united front in their demands for higher wages and better working conditions. In the early part of this century, when most unions excluded African American workers, it was common for employers to bring them in as strikebreakers to end union disputes. The unions eventually realized that all workers were being hurt by these racial divisions and began recruiting African American members, although a more subtle racism still remains in many unions.

Class

In the late 1970s, William Julius Wilson published an influential book, *The Declining Significance of Race,* in which he argued that racial prejudice and discrimination are no longer an important cause of the problems of African Americans.[47] The principal source of today's problems is, according to Wilson, the fact that African Americans are trapped in a self-perpetuating cycle of poverty. Minority children are more likely to live lives of poverty because they are more likely to be born into poverty. Thus, the historical effects of the racism and discrimination that originally forced minorities into a subordinate position in the class system are seen to be more important than the discrimination they currently encounter. And just as the class system passes along the burdens of past discrimination to minority children, so the benefits of past favoritism are passed along to the descendants of the dominant groups.

The supporters of this theory can cite considerable evidence for their conclusion that class is now the key factor. Surveys show that racial and ethnic prejudice have been declining in recent years, and explicit laws have been passed against occupational discrimination. There is, as we noted, a vigorous and expanding African American middle class that seems to have been able to overcome the barriers of racism. There are also a substantial number of whites in the underclass who seem every bit as disadvantaged as the minorities (see Chapter 7). It is nonetheless important to recognize that although progress has been made in the fight against prejudice and discrimination, it is still a powerful force in American life. The members of minority groups must still deal with economic obstacles and social bigotry that European Americans seldom have to face.

Quick Review

What role does conflict and competition play in ethnic relations?

What are the different theories about the causes of prejudice and discrimination?

What role does social class play in the problem of ethnic inequality?

Solving the Problems of Ethnic Relations

Although true equality remains a distant goal, the history of this century shows significant progress toward racial and ethnic justice. Elimination of the oppressive segregation system in the United States was a major step forward, as was legislation outlawing discrimination in housing and employment. At least partially as a result, minorities have gained access to numerous high-level business and professional careers that used to be closed to them. Illiteracy rates among minorities have dropped, and their level of education has increased (see Chapter 3). Although racism and ethnic stereotypes remain, these prejudices are seldom publicly voiced by business and political leaders, as they once were; and public opinion surveys show that prejudice against minorities has significantly declined.[48]

Disturbing signs over the last decade, however, indicate that hard economic times have led to a deterioration of ethnic relations and that a new crisis may be brewing. Whites have grown increasingly resentful of affirmative action programs designed to help win equality for minorities, and some politicians have used attacks on welfare recipients and street crime in thinly veiled attempts to make minorities the scapegoats for the nation's troubles. Factors including the loss of millions of manufacturing jobs in North America, the new influx of Third World immigrants, the exodus of middle-class African Americans from the cities, and over a decade of government neglect have all contributed to ever worsening conditions in the inner cities.

Even the many people working to solve these serious problems often disagree about the ultimate goals of their efforts. Should we work toward a melting pot that merges us all into a single new group, or should the goal be to achieve true equality among a salad bowl of distinct ethnic groups? While this is a significant philosophical issue, it is important to remember that no matter which approach we prefer, the goal is the same—justice and fair treatment for all—and the proposals that follow all aim to achieve it.

Political Activism

civil rights movement
The social movement in the United States that brought an end to the segregation system.

Most of the government's actions to help minorities have come about only because of organized political pressure. The segregation system that denied those of African descent the rights enjoyed by other Americans was not declared unconstitutional until almost a hundred years after the Civil War. Even then, a tremendous political effort was necessary to win the implementation of that decision. The **civil rights movement**—a coalition of activist African Americans and liberal whites—used nonviolent demonstrations, marches, and sit-ins to demand an end to segregation. Despite their eventual success, many African Americans became increasingly frustrated with their failure to win full equality. The black power movement came to reject integration as just another form of domination and demanded separation of the races, but on an equal basis. As the movement turned increasingly violent, it was repressed by force, and most of its leaders were killed or jailed.

The spirit of minority activism nonetheless lives on. However, the activists, many of whom now hold government office, are generally working within the system. Native American activists have been particularly successful in using legal actions to win back the rights granted in government treaties. They won the right to fish in Puget Sound and Lake Michigan and won legal title to lands in North Dakota, Maine, and Rhode Island. In the last decade, Native Americans have also been among the most militant of all ethnic groups in directly confronting the political system. This militancy is perhaps best symbolized by armed confrontation between Mohawk warriors and army troops near the small town of Oka, Quebec, in the early 1990s. Although this incident began as a conflict over an attempt to put a golf course on a tribal burial ground, it soon escalated into a direct challenge to the authority of the government. However, violent confrontation has not proved to be the most successful tactic in their struggle. Inuit people won the creation of their huge new territory through 15 years of methodical negotiation with the Canadian government.[49]

The success of black political activism can be seen in the growing representation of African Americans among the nation's officeholders. The number of African Americans holding elected office was more than five times higher in 1994 than it was in 1970.[50] Yet despite such advances, an increasingly conservative political climate has meant that efforts of minority leaders have been largely devoted merely to defending the victories won in the past.

Political activism has proved to be the most effective tool for winning social justice for minority groups. Here, the late Dr. Martin Luther King, Jr., is shown leading a protest march in Boston. Such protests were part of the civil rights movement that brought an end to legal racial segregation in the United States.

Reforming the Educational System

Many people feel that the best way to compensate for the lingering effects of past discrimination and to help break the vicious cycle of poverty is through better education. In the early 1970s, the hottest issue in the field of education was whether to pursue that goal through integration, as the advocates of mandatory school busing proposed, or though pluralism, as favored by supporters of neighborhood schools. Today, the focus has shifted to finding the best ways to improve the academic performance of poor and minority children regardless of the makeup of their school's student body. Many different proposals have been made, and many experimental programs have been carried out, but the most promising approach is probably the most obvious one—to provide extra tutoring and other special programs to help overcome the barriers poverty and prejudice place in the way of a good education (see Chapter 3).

Another important issue concerns education's responsibility to help reduce prejudice and discrimination. Until the wave of minority activism in the 1950s and 1960s, textbooks and teaching materials often contained blatantly racist stereotypes or simply ignored ethnic minorities altogether. Great improvements have been made since then, but critics charge that our educational system still presents a **Eurocentric** view of the world. In other words, they charge that the curriculum and the general orientation of our schools and universities still have a European slant and largely ignore the perspectives of those from Africa, Latin America, and Asia.

Eurocentric
A view of the world or an educational curriculum that takes an exclusively European perspective.

multicultural education

Education that includes the perspectives and experiences of different ethnic groups.

These critics therefore call for **multicultural education** to reflect the background and perspectives of all Americans. Such proposals have met strenuous opposition from those who see them as a threat to European cultural traditions, and teachers who are not trained in the new approach see it as a threat to their jobs. A related proposal calls for secondary schools and universities to require students to take classes in ethnic studies in order to help them understand the perspectives, problems, and concerns of people from other groups.

Fair Employment

affirmative action

A policy of positive effort to rectify the effects of past discrimination.

The idea that everyone deserves an equal opportunity to make a living has a great deal of popular support, but implementing this idea has been difficult. Civil rights activists of the 1960s succeeded in winning the passage of a broad Civil Rights Act, which forbids discrimination by unions, employment agencies, and businesses employing more than 25 workers, but the problems in enforcing the law have been immense, for it is extremely difficult to prove why someone was not hired or promoted. The laws forbidding discrimination have now been supplemented by **affirmative action** programs, which require a positive effort to recruit and promote qualified members of minority groups. Employers can no longer defend themselves by claiming that a decision not to hire someone was based on some criterion other than ethnicity: they must prove they are not discriminating. If the percentage of minority employees is significantly lower than their percentage in the work force, companies must accept a goal for minority employment and set up a timetable stating when these goals are likely to be met.

white backlash

The negative response of whites to affirmative action or other programs designed to assist disadvantaged minorities.

These procedures have created a powerful **white backlash.** Conservative critics charge that the ratios are not goals but quotas and that affirmative action programs really call for **reverse discrimination** (discrimination against white males). Some more liberal critics also charge that the benefits of affirmative action have mainly gone to minorities from the middle and upper class because the members of the underclass who need the most help lack the necessary qualifications for most jobs. Resolution of these conflicts will be extremely difficult. It is true that affirmative action programs give preferential treatment to some members of minority groups and that therefore some whites are discriminated against; but it is also true that minorities still face far more discrimination than whites do.

reverse discrimination

Discrimination against white males.

The Supreme Court has yet to resolve these difficult legal issues. Originally, the Supreme Court upheld the constitutionality of most affirmative action programs. But as more conservative judges have been appointed to the Court, it has become more skeptical of affirmative programs that are not intended to rectify a proven history of past discrimination, and one federal circuit court in the Southwest even ruled against the constitutionality of all affirmative action. Overall, it is still not clear which kinds of affirmative action programs are constitutional and which kinds are not. In 1996, California voters waded into this issue, passing an initiative that banned affirmative action for the state government and its contractors. The federal government, especially the executive branch, has continued its support for most affirmative action programs. Laws that merely prohibit employment discrimination against minority groups do not seem able to do the whole job; therefore, some affirmative action procedures must be continued if equality of opportunity is to be achieved, but there is considerable disagreement about how to do so fairly. Opinion polls show that the public is deeply divided about this whole issue. Even among whites, about two-thirds of the people tell pollsters that they support "affirmative action programs provided there are no rigid quotas." But if you ask those same people whether women or minorities should be given preferences to make up for past discrimination, large majorities say they are opposed. There is, nonetheless, overwhelming support for laws that ban discrimination based on ethnic groups or gender.[51] (See the Debate in this chapter.)

Economic Justice

No social problem stands alone. The dilemmas of ethnic relations are interwoven in complex ways with other social problems. Solutions to the problems discussed in other chapters in this book would go a long way toward alleviating ethnic conflicts as well. Perhaps the foremost issue among them is the lack of economic equality. As we saw in Chapter 7, the gap between the rich and the poor has been growing significantly wider in recent times. When the problem of poverty gets worse, minorities are most strongly affected, since they are most likely to be poor. Thus, programs to reduce unemployment, retrain unskilled workers, provide good-quality health care, reduce poverty, and shift the tax burden to those best able to carry it are as essential to achieving ethnic justice as programs specifically attacking prejudice and discrimination.

Quick Review

How can our educational system deal more effectively with the problems of ethnic inequality?

What is affirmative action, and why is it so controversial?

Sociological Perspectives on Problems of Ethnic Minorities

Public concern about ethnic inequality waxes and wanes with the political climate. Interest in equality is particularly intense in times of change, when old patterns of ethnic relations are breaking up and there is conflict over what direction to take in the future. In the United States, ethnic relations raised the most public concern during the Reconstruction period after the Civil War and during the era of the civil rights and black power movements that marked the end of the segregation system a hundred years later. At both times, ethnic inequality became a pressing social problem because an old system of ethnic relations was deteriorating and a new pattern was taking shape. Even during the most stable periods, however, the problem of fairly managing ethnic relations in so diverse a society is never far below the surface.

The Functionalist Perspective

Functionalists believe that shared values and attitudes are the cement that holds a society together. The more disagreement there is over basic values, the more unstable and disorganized a society is likely to be. Although the various ethnic groups in

Debate Are Affirmative Action Programs Fair?

Affirmative action programs are designed to encourage employers to hire and promote women and minorities if they are underrepresented in the work force. Under such programs, women and minorities are hired instead of equally qualified white males in order to compensate for past and present discrimination.

Yes

In a perfect world, we would not need affirmative action. Personnel decisions would be made on the basis of each individual's abilities and qualifications, without regard to ethnic group or gender. But we all know that things don't really work that way. Centuries-old prejudices will not simply vanish because the law tells everyone to stop discriminating. Even with current affirmative action programs, women and minorities still get lower pay and have fewer chances for advancement than white males. Without the government's pressures to meet affirmative action goals, the situation would be far worse. Affirmative action merely provides a small counterweight to a system that still treats women and minorities as second-class citizens.

Critics claim that laws prohibiting discrimination are all we need to ensure fair treatment for all. Unfortunately it is extremely hard to prove to a court that you were the victim of discrimination, for employers can always think of some excuse to explain their decision. All affirmative action does is to shift the burden of proof to the employers to show that they are *not* discriminating. After all, the employers are the ones with the money to hire lawyers to make their case in court.

Even if we could wave a magic wand and end all discrimination tomorrow, we would still need affirmative action programs to compensate for the effects of past discrimination. Remember that Africans were brought to this land in chains. For generations they were brutalized, tortured, and even killed at the "master's" whim; their family structure was shattered and their culture destroyed. Women from all ethnic groups were themselves in a slavelike position. Traditionally, a woman was considered to be the property of her husband, whom she must "love, honor, and obey." She couldn't vote, she couldn't hold a responsible position, and her husband had complete control of all her property (if she was even allowed to own any). The effects of this kind of brutality and discrimination are passed on from one generation to the next. Their consequences will never go away unless we take affirmative action to correct them, and fairness demands that we do.

North America have come to share many values over the years, significant differences remain, and these differences are an important source of conflict. North America lacks the unity, consensus, and organization essential to a harmonious society. Although efforts of the largest ethnic groups to dominate the others have become less and less successful, neither pluralism nor integration has replaced domination. Society is disorganized, unable to muster its people to work together for the common good.

From the functionalist perspective, ethnic discrimination is both a cause and an effect of contemporary social disorganization. The failure to give minorities full

No

Two wrongs do not make a right. It was wrong to discriminate against women and minorities in the past, and it is wrong to discriminate against males with a European background today. Of course, supporters of affirmative action claim that such programs are not discriminating against white males but just correcting for past discrimination, but what else do you call it when an employer refuses to hire the most qualified candidate because of his race and gender? Racism is still racism even when the victims are white. Sexism is still sexism even when the victims are males.

Under current affirmative action laws, the daughter of a black television star with $100 million in the bank would be given *preference* in employment over the son of a homeless alcoholic who happened to be white. How can you call that fair?

The supporters of affirmative action say that simply banning discrimination is not enough to bring about true justice in our society, but society cannot fight racism and sexism by means of a law that requires employers to discriminate on the basis of race and sex. There are many far better ways to correct social injustices—for example, the government could work to improve the terrible schools in the urban slums, provide job retraining for the unemployed, and create jobs. Of course, such projects cost money, and it is far easier for politicians simply to pass a law requiring employers to give special preferences to the groups that are pressuring them to act. Programs that seek to aid the poor and disadvantaged make this a stronger society by helping to bring those people (the majority of whom are minorities and women) into the mainstream of social life. Programs that give special privileges to someone only because of race or sex make this a weaker society by fostering a sense of injustice and feelings of hostility among members of different groups. Fairness demands that the law resolutely condemn all forms of discrimination, including that against white males. Affirmative action laws are based on pure hypocrisy and must be repealed.

equality wastes valuable human resources and generates ethnic hostilities that reduce economic production and undermine political authority. These hostilities, in turn, contribute to prejudice and discrimination as different ethnic groups come to see one another as enemies.

To functionalists, the best response to these problems is to reduce discrimination by reorganizing our social institutions. Unity is the objective, whether it is achieved through domination, pluralism, or integration. Integration is the ideal, however, because an integrated society is likely to have the fewest conflicts. Functionalists ask for an attack on discrimination in housing, education, criminal justice, and elsewhere, arguing that an effective reform movement must increase support for "the system" among ethnic minorities while at the same time maintaining the allegiance of the majority.

The Conflict Perspective

Conflict theorists see the history of ethnic relations in North America as one of conflict and oppression. European colonists fought with each other and with the Native Americans. Eventually English-speaking whites conquered most of the continent, but conflict did not end there. As new groups settled in the "promised land," some were assimilated. Those who refused to give up their ethnic identity were shunted into inferior positions: employees rather than employers, police officers rather than judges, farmhands rather than landowners, blue-collar workers rather than white-collar workers, and so on. (See the Personal Perspectives for an account of the way the schools discouraged one famous African American from pursing a professional career.)

From the conflict perspective, the history of all ethnic relations is the history of a struggle for power. When one group is more powerful than others, a system of domination develops in which weaker groups are exploited for the political, social, and economic advantage of the dominant group. When power is more equally distributed, pluralism develops. Whether ethnic groups are in a relationship of domi-

Personal Perspectives   A Victim of Racism

The history of racism in America has left many deep psychological scars. The following account of racism in the schools in the 1940s comes from the autobiography of Malcolm X, who later went on to become one of the best-known advocates of black power. Try to imagine yourself in his place as you read this.

> Somehow, I happened to be alone in the classroom with Mr. Ostrowski, my English teacher. . . . I was one of his top students, one of the school's top students—but all he could see for me was the kind of future "in your place" that almost all white people see for black people.
>
> He told me, "Malcolm, you ought to be thinking about a career. Have you been giving it thought?"
>
> The truth is, I hadn't. I never have figured out why I told him, "Well, yes, sir, I've been thinking I'd like to be a lawyer." Lansing certainly had no Negro lawyers—or doctors either—in those days to hold up an image I might have aspired to. All I really knew for certain was that a lawyer didn't wash dishes, as I was doing.
>
> Mr. Ostrowski look surprised, I remember, and leaned back in his chair and clasped his hands behind his head. He kind of half-smiled and said, "Malcolm, one of life's first needs is for us to be realistic. Don't misunderstand me, now. We all here like you, you know that. But you've got to be realistic about being a nigger. A lawyer—that's no realistic goal for a nigger. You need to think about something you *can* be. You're good with your hands—making things. Everybody admires your carpentry shop work. Why don't you plan on carpentry? People like you as a person—you'd get all kinds of work."*

The Autobiography of Malcolm X (New York: Ballantine Books, 1964), pp. 35–36.

nation or equality, there is no guarantee that the system will remain stable. Social change is primarily a process by which one group grows stronger at the expense of others. Those who have power want peace and stability; those who are out of power want conflict and change. Institutionalized discrimination is thus a technique for keeping the dominant group in power and protecting it from its competitors.

Conflict theorists assert that ethnic equality can be achieved only through struggle. A group that has improved its status is by definition a group that has seized more political and economic power. Conflict theorists argue that political change is often necessary to bring about economic change in such things as employment, education, housing, and health care. The key to increased power is organization for political action. A small ethnic group that is unified can wield much greater power than its numbers would suggest. In a democratic society, political change can be achieved by outvoting and outmaneuvering one's opponents according to the established rules of the game. Political change can also be achieved by attacking the established rules in demonstrations and protests that may threaten—or provoke—violence. Both techniques are being used in ethnic struggles in North America and around the world, and conflict theorists counsel those who would change the system to study the historical record of the successes and failures of such efforts.

The Feminist Perspective

Feminists have often commented on the similarities in the social position of women and minorities in our society. Both groups have been put down in derogatory stereotypes, subject to widespread occupational discrimination, and often excluded from the mainstream of our cultural life. Women's groups also share a common interest with minority activists to protect the affirmative action programs that have benefited both groups over the years. Many feminists are nonetheless starting to recognize that white women still hold a privileged position relative to women of color and that there are important differences in perspectives and opinions between the two groups. White women are, for example, far more likely to be born into wealth and privilege than women of color, and they are also more likely to have the kinds of social connections that are often vital to economic success. So while strongly opposing discrimination of all sorts, many contemporary feminists are calling for special attention to the problems of women of color, who suffer from the double discrimination of sexism and racism.

The Interactionist Perspective

Interactionist theory holds that individuals develop their concept of personal identity from their interactions with the people around them. When members of a minority group are constantly insulted, demeaned, and harassed, they are bound to be affected. Some internalize these feelings, resulting in low self-esteem and feelings of personal inadequacy. The victims of such prejudice are also more likely to develop other personal problems, such as alcoholism and drug addiction. For example, the rates of addiction to heroin and crack cocaine among African Americans and Latinos are much higher than the national average, and alcoholism is an especially severe problem among Native Americans. Another common response by members of minority groups is to reject forcefully such ethnic stereotypes and those who believe in them and to assert their own value and importance. Still others try to avoid the effects of prejudice and discrimination by isolating themselves in segregated ethnic communities.

The interactionists' proposals for reducing ethnic discrimination and prejudice fall into two broad categories. Those in the first category are based on the fact that whatever is learned can be unlearned. Included here are recommendations for more ethnic contact and communication and for a direct attack on ethnic stereotypes in the media and in schools. By showing people from different ethnic groups as they actually are, and not as stereotypes depict them, we can break down the barriers to communication and understanding.

The second category includes proposals that attempt to go to the roots of the problem by recommending long-term changes to reduce ethnic competition and conflict. More contacts and communication among ethnic groups will enable people to overcome their prejudices, but research shows that these contacts must be among ethnic groups of relatively equal social status that are working together for a common goal rather than competing with one another for survival. In other words, interactionists say that prejudice and discrimination will decrease as the fear of economic competition decreases.

Interactionists also point out that grouping people into common categories on the basis of such characteristics as skin color and type of hair is simply a cultural tradition, and one that has caused enormous social problems. It therefore follows that the best solution to the "racial problem" is to abandon those traditional attitudes and adopt the more scientifically supportable view that all people are members of a single human race.

Quick Review

What are the differences between the ways conflict theorists and functionalists look at the problems of ethnic relations?

What solutions do interactionists propose for our problems of ethnic relations?

Summary

Throughout history, tension and conflict have existed between ethnic groups that live in close contact. People who share a sense of identity and togetherness tend to be ethnocentric, believing that their ways of doing things are better than those of other groups. Ethnocentrism becomes racism when it is based on the idea that people with certain physical traits are superior to others and deserve special privileges.

The relationship among ethnic groups usually follows one of three general patterns. Domination exists when one ethnic group holds power and exploits another group or groups. When two or more ethnic groups have roughly equal power so that each controls its own affairs, a system of pluralism exists. Finally, when two or more ethnic groups blend together and share power, customs, and social institutions, the relationship is known as integration.

North American society has promoted several different ideals for ethnic relations. Originally, all other ethnic groups were expected to assimilate and conform to the Anglo-American cultural pattern. A second, more recent, ideal is that of the melting pot, which holds that different ethnic groups should merge together to form a single new culture. Finally, there is the ideal of the salad bowl, which encourages ethnic groups to retain their cultural distinctiveness.

Historically, North America has seen the conquest and domination of the Native Americans, French, Spanish, and Mexicans by English-speaking peoples. Domination also characterized relations with African slaves and with most immigrant groups. That domination has met increasing challenges. Some ethnic groups have won more equal status with the old dominant group, while the differences between other groups have slowly decreased as they have become more integrated. Nonetheless, our society still shows a high degree of inequality. Whether in education, jobs, or housing, the members of most minority groups still lag behind the national average. Each of the ethnic groups in North America—Native Americans, Europeans, Jews, African Americans, Latinos, and Asians—also has its own special characteristics and problems, and each contains several distinct subgroups.

There are many possible explanations for the problem of ethnic inequality. The historical cause is the competition among ethnic groups in which one group wins a dominant position and forces the others into a subordinate status. A second major factor is prejudice and discrimination, which, in turn, have psychological, cultural, and structural causes. Finally, there is the influence of class and the fact that a life of poverty or of privilege tends to be passed down from one generation to the next.

Many suggestions have been made to deal with the problems of ethnic relations. Greater political activism by members of minority groups and their supporters is often considered an important starting point for reform. Changes in the schools to include the perspectives of ethnic minorities is a common suggestion, as is a greater commitment to compensatory education programs designed to correct the damage done by poverty and discrimination. An end to bias in employment and promotion is another obvious need. Finally, many programs designed to help poor people can do a great deal to foster greater ethnic justice as well.

According to functionalists, North American society is disorganized and unable to muster its many ethnic groups to work in harmony for the common good; but conflict theorists see institutionalized discrimination as an intentional way of protecting the economic and political power of the dominant groups. The key to increasing the power of minority groups, in their view, is political activism. Feminists see many similarities to the position of women and minorities in our society and call for special attention to the needs of women of color. Interactionists point out that prejudice and discrimination are learned and that both are associated with the fear of competition. They recommend more contacts and communication among ethnic groups and a reduction of economic competition.

Questions for Critical Thinking

Back in 1944, the famous Swedish sociologist Gunnar Myrdal called ethnic relations "the American dilemma" because of the fundamental contradiction between the American creed of justice and fair play for all and the realities of a society rife with prejudice and discrimination.[52] Myrdal was convinced that in the long run, the higher values of the American creed would win out over the forces of hatred and bigotry. Do you think he was right? How much progress have we made since 1944? How much further do we have to go?

Key Terms

affirmative action
assimilation
authoritarian personality
civil right movement
contrast conceptions
discrimination
domination
ethnic group
ethnic minority
ethnic stereotype
ethnocentrism
Eurocentric
institutional discrimination

integration
melting pot theory
multicultural education
pluralism
prejudice
race
racism
reverse discrimination
salad bowl theory
scapegoat
segregation
white backlash
white ethnics

Further Readings

Ellis Cose, *The Rage of a Privileged Class* (New York: HarperCollins, 1993). An examination of the frustrations of the black middle class in the United States.

Malcolm X, *The Autobiography of Malcolm X* (New York: Ballantine, 1964). The autobiography of one of America's most influential black activists.

Richard T. Schaefer, *Racial and Ethnic Groups,* 7th ed. (New York: Longman, 1997). A good comprehensive text on ethnic relations in the United States.

Ilan Stavans, *The Hispanic Condition: Reflections on Culture and Identity in America* (New York: HarperCollins, 1995). A Mexican-born novelist looks at the condition of Hispanics in North America today.

Ronald Takaki, *Strangers from a Different Shore: A History of Asian Americans* (Boston: Little, Brown, 1989). An excellent history of Asians in the United States.

William Julius Wilson, *The Declining Significance of Race: Blacks and Changing American Institutions,* 2nd ed. (Chicago: University of Chicago Press, 1980). The controversial book in which Wilson argues that class is now more important than racial prejudice as a cause of the disadvantaged economic position of African Americans.

Elisabeth Young-Bruehl, *The Anatomy of Prejudices* (Cambridge, MA: Harvard University Press, 1996). A look at the nature of prejudice from a psychological perspective.

Notes

1. Philip Gourevitch, "The Return," *New Yorker,* January 20, 1997, pp. 44–54.
2. Richard T. Schaefer, *Racial and Ethnic Groups,* 5th ed. (New York: HarperCollins, 1993), pp. 7–10.

3. Ibid., pp. 10–14.
4. Ibid., pp. 148–184.
5. Nancy Oestreich Lurie, "The American Indian: Historical Background," in Norman Yetman and C. Hoy Steel, eds., *Minority and Majority: The Dynamics of Racial and Ethnic Relations,* 4th ed. (Boston: Allyn & Bacon, 1985).
6. Schaefer, *Racial and Ethnic Groups,* p. 150.
7. Lurie, "The American Indian," p. 179.
8. U.S. Bureau of the Census, *Statistical Abstract of the United States, 1996* (Washington, DC: U.S. Government Printing Office, 1996), p. 159.
9. Joseph H. Cash, "Indian Education: A Bright Path or Another Dead End?" in Editors of the Winston Press, *Viewpoints: Red and Yellow, Black and Brown* (Groveland Terrace, MN: Winston Press, 1972), p. 14.
10. U.S. Bureau of the Census, *Statistical Abstract, 1996,* pp. 48, 51.
11. Lawrence Mishel, Jared Bernstein, and John Schmitt, *The State of Working America, 1996–97* (Armonk, NY: Sharpe, 1996), p. 243.
12. Seymour Martin Lipset, *American Exceptionalism: A Double-Edged Sword* (New York: Norton, 1996), p. 138.
13. Jim Schachter, "Unequal Opportunity: Minorities Find That Roadblocks to the Executive Suite Are Still in Place," *Los Angeles Times,* April 17, 1988, sec. 4, p. 1.
14. Quoted in Charles E. Reasons and Jack E. Kuykendall, eds., *Race, Crime and Justice* (Pacific Palisades, CA: Goodyear, 1972).
15. Fox Butterfield, "More Blacks in Their 20s Have Trouble with the Law," *New York Times,* October 5, 1995, p. A8.
16. U.S. Bureau of the Census, *Statistical Abstract, 1996,* p. 50.
17. Richard T. Schaefer, *Sociology* (New York: McGraw-Hill, 1989), p. 253.
18. David Pelly, "Birth of an Inuit Nation," *Canadian Geographic,* 116: 4 (April 1994), pp. 23–25.
19. S. Dale McLemore, *Racial and Ethnic Relations in America,* 3rd ed. (Boston: Allyn & Bacon, 1991).
20. Richard D. Alba, "The Twilight of Ethnicity Among Americans of European Ancestry: The Case of Italians," in Richard D. Alba, ed., *Ethnicity and Race in the U.S.A.* (Englewood Cliffs, NJ: Prentice-Hall, 1988), pp. 134–158.
21. Stanley Lieberson and Mary C. Waters, *From Many Strands: Ethnic and Racial Groups in Contemporary America* (New York: Russell Sage, 1988).
22. Andrew M. Greeley, *Religious Change in America* (Cambridge, MA: Harvard University Press, 1989).
23. Lipset, *American Exceptionalism,* pp. 151–152.
24. See Schaefer, *Racial and Ethnic Groups,* pp. 395–426.
25. U.S. Bureau of the Census, *Statistical Abstract, 1996,* p. 14.
26. William Julius Wilson, "Studying Inner-City Social Dislocations: The Challenge of Public Agenda Research," *American Sociological Review,* 56 (February 1991): 1–14.
27. Ronald J. Ostrow, "Sentencing Study Sees Race Disparity," *Los Angeles Times,* October 5, 1995, pp. A1, A 17.
28. U.S. Bureau of the Census, *Statistical Abstract, 1996,* p. 65.
29. Wilson, "Studying Inner-City Social Dislocations."
30. U.S. Bureau of the Census, *Statistical Abstract, 1996,* p. 14.
31. Theodore Caplow, *American Social Trends* (San Diego: Harcourt Brace Jovanovich, 1991), pp. 191–193.
32. U.S. Bureau of the Census, *Statistical Abstract, 1993,* p. 18.
33. Schaefer, *Racial and Ethnic Groups,* pp. 303–394.
34. Nancy Rivera Brooks, "Study of Asians in U.S. Finds Many Struggling," *Los Angeles Times,* May 19, 1994, pp. A1, A25; Ashley Dunn, "Southeast Asians Highly Dependent on Welfare in U.S.," *New York Times,* May 19, 1994, pp. A1, A17.
35. Katherine Imahara, Stanley Mark, and Phil Tajitsu-Nash, *Audit of Violence Against Asian Pacific Americans: Anti-Asian Violence, A National Problem* (Los Angeles: National Asian Pacific American Consortium, 1994).

36. Barry A. Kosmin, *Highlights of the CJF 1990 National Jewish Population Survey* (New York: Council of Jewish Federations, 1991).

37. Richard T. Shaefer, *Racial and Ethnic Groups,* 5th ed. (New York: HarperCollins, 1993), pp. 27–28, 367–369.

38. Lynell George, "Cross Colors," *Los Angeles Times,* March 27, 1994, pp. E1, E2.

39. Ronald Brownstein and Richard Simon, "Hospitality Turns Into Hostility." *Los Angeles Times,* November 14, 1993, pp. A1, A6–A7.

40. Peter Skerry, "Has Immigration Collided with the Welfare State?" *Los Angeles Times,* May 1, 1994, pp. M1, M6.

41. Patrick J. McDonnell, "A Renewed Debate in Red, White, and Blue," *Los Angeles Times,* July 4, 1997, pp. A1, A28, A29.

42. U.S. Bureau of the Census, *Statistical Abstract, 1996,* pp. 18, 19.

43. Gordon W. Allport, *The Nature of Prejudice* (New York: Doubleday, 1956), p. 10.

44. Robert K. Merton, "Discrimination and the American Creed," in Robert M. MacIver, ed., *Discrimination and National Welfare* (New York: Harper & Row, 1949).

45. T. W. Adorno, E. Frenkel-Brunswik, D. J. Devinson, and R. N. Sandord, *The Authoritarian Personality* (New York: Harper & Row, 1950).

46. See Judith Andre, "Stereotypes: Conceptual and Normative Considerations," in Paula S. Rothenberg, ed., *Racism and Sexism: An Integrated Study* (New York: St. Martin's Press, 1988), pp. 257–262.

47. William Julius Wilson, *The Declining Significance of Race: Blacks and Changing American Institutions* (Chicago: University of Chicago Press, 1978).

48. See Lipset, *American Exceptionalism,* pp. 129–130.

49. Julie Gozan, "Land to the Inuit," *Canadian Geographic,* 13: 9, (September 1992), pp. 7–8.

50. U.S. Bureau of the Census, *Statistical Abstract, 1996,* p. 284.

51. Lipset, *American Exceptionalism,* pp. 125–127.

52. Gunnar Myrdal, *An American Dilemma* (New York: Harper, 1944).

The Old and the Young

CHAPTER 9

How does society respond to the process of aging?

Is there an "erosion of childhood"?

Why is adolescence such a difficult time of life?

What problems do the elderly face in today's society?

How should society respond to the problems of the young and the old?

285

Gavin and Frances are sitting next to each other at the Children's Wonderland Day Care Center in Oxnard, California, while the children around them play a spirited game of balloon volleyball and sing a few nursery rhymes. Gavin is 4 years old and is in day care because his parents are both away at work. Frances is in her eighties and is there because she has Alzheimer's disease and often forgets what she is doing. About 120 of the center's clients are under age 6, but 15 are some seven decades older. The very young and the very old often face surprisingly similar problems, and they can help each other if given the chance. Frances and her contemporaries teach the children new games and tell them stories, and the children are a continuous source of enjoyment for the elderly.[1]

From the time we are born until the time we die, we are constantly aging. Most people see this only as a biological process, but aging is a social phenomenon as well. The problems of aging are rooted in the physiological changes we all undergo. But society tells us what these changes mean and how people of different ages should act, and how well our social institutions respond to those problems has a profound effect on us all. Without the Wonderland Center, for example, Frances might easily have ended up sitting at home without proper care or cheerful social contacts. Thus, the problems of aging are social problems. There is little doubt that many of the most serious difficulties the elderly face today have little to do with the aging process itself, but stem from the fact that they no longer receive the respect and consideration that older people enjoyed in the past. In colonial times, Americans dressed to make themselves look as old and dignified as possible; today there is a multibillion-dollar industry devoted to making us look younger than we really are. Yet at the same time as we idolize youthful beauty, we seem to be indifferent to the real needs of the young. Compared with older people, the younger are far more likely to be poor. They are also far more likely to suffer from a deep confusion about who they are and where they are going. Society cannot eliminate the need to adjust to the changes brought on by such things as sexual maturity or the physical deterioration of old age, but we can do a far better job of dealing with the social and biological realities of aging.

Aging and the Life Cycle

Everyone is familiar with the biological changes we experience as we age. They occur most rapidly in our earlier years, as we grow from babies to children to sexually mature adults. The changes occur more slowly after physical maturity, but they never stop. As we grow older, most of our physical abilities eventually decline. The most obvious signs of aging are external ones—graying of the hair and wrinkling of the skin—but the changes are much more far-reaching than that. Hearing, eyesight, muscular strength, reaction time, and heart and lung capacity all decline.

Although aging produces continual changes in our bodies and minds, those changes are profoundly affected by such social factors as diet, exercise, medical care, and life-style. Improvements in diet and public health made us taller and healthier than our ancestors, and today's children also reach their full height and mature sexually at an earlier age than they did in past generations.[2] The physical problems often associated with advancing age are subject to the same social influences. For example, a study of 1300 men and women in their seventies found that those who had a lifelong habit of intellectual activity and regularly participated in strenuous physical activity suffered the least decline in mental abilities.[3] Research shows that new opportunities and new stimulation actually increase the IQ scores and mental abilities of elderly people.[4] Our social environment can have the opposite effect as well: skid-row alcoholics and homeless transients, for example, often appear to be ten or fifteen years older than they actually are.

In addition to its influence on the physical process of aging, society tells us what we have to do to "act our age." Every society is divided into what anthropologists call **age grades:** groups of people of similar age. The **life cycle,** then, consists of a series of passages between the social roles expected of people in different age grades. As we progress from one age grade to another, we are presented with a predictable set of new social expectations and a new set of problems that go with them.

Such transitions may also present a difficult challenge of their own. On the one hand, people entering a new age grade must cope with the feeling of loss at seeing an end to a major period of their lives. On the other, they must face the difficult task of learning new roles. Young adults must conquer their fears and learn how to shoulder the new responsibilities expected of them. The elderly must learn how to reorganize their lives after the stability of child rearing and employment is torn away.

Most cultures have what are known as **rites of passage** to mark transitions from one stage of life to another. These ceremonies provide individuals who are in transition with group support and symbolic confirmation of their new status. Although our culture still maintains a few rites of passage, such as marriage, confirmation, and bas mitzvah ceremonies, most of the time we don't receive much social support when we make critical transitions from one age grade to another.

Age grades and the behaviors associated with them vary tremendously from one society to another and even within a single society over the course of history. Our current ideas about age and what it means are very complex, and experts see the stages of aging in different ways. Four broad age grades are recognized in most contemporary industrial societies—**childhood, adolescence, adulthood,** and **old age**—but each of these can also be subdivided into two or more smaller categories.

Most of the remainder of this chapter will focus on the problems of those at the two ends of the life cycle: the young and the old. By most sociological standards, those in their middle years are a relatively advantaged group. Yet despite the fact that they have higher incomes, more prestige, and more power than people in other age grades there is growing recognition that these advantages do not necessarily translate into personal happiness. For one thing, those in midlife are often responsible for the care and support of both their children and their parents, and they often find their responsibilities to be a heavy burden. The cost of raising a family and supporting aging parents leaves many midlife adults with little to show for the higher wages they earn. About three-fourths of those caring for the elderly are women, and the demands on their time and their emotional reserves can be overwhelming. A report to the U.S. House of Representatives concluded that the average American woman will spend 17 years raising children and 18 years helping to care for aged parents.[5] Thus, many women spend all their middle years looking after other people, while still somehow trying to find the space to meet their own financial and psychological needs.

age grades
Groups of people who share a common social status because of their age.

life cycles
A series of passages between the social roles expected of people in different age grades.

rites of passage
Rituals that mark the transition from one stage of life to another.

childhood
The earliest age grade, lasting from birth to the onset of puberty.

adolescence
The age grade of persons who have reached puberty but have not been given full status as adults.

adulthood
The age grade of persons who are considered to have reached full social and physical maturity.

old age
The last age grade, usually considered to start around age 65.

midlife crisis

A psychological predicament commonly experienced by persons in their middle years when they face the passing of their youth and the limitations on their future.

Another common problem is the psychological predicament that has come to be known as the **midlife crisis.** This crisis typically occurs in the late thirties or the forties, when people begin grappling with the reality that their youth is gone and that death is the inevitable end of their journey. Those devoted to a career may need to come to terms with the fact that their dreams of success may never come true. Others may be faced with the even more difficult realization that success itself was an empty goal that has left them frustrated and unhappy.[6] Thus, the problems of midlife can be as difficult as those of any other age grade, even if they are less likely to be aggravated by economic and social restrictions.

Quick Review

What is the life cycle?

What are the main age grades in Western society?

Problems of the Young

Childhood

To most of us, childhood conjures up memories of a carefree time that we would love to relive. Although adolescence is usually the most difficult period of a young person's life, children face some very real problems as well. Child abuse and molestation have been the subject of increasing national concern (see Chapters 2 and 11), but the economic problems faced by our children have received far less attention. In 1991, the poverty rate for children under 16 was more than 50 percent higher than the national average and double the rate for people in their middle years. More than one-fifth of American children now live in poverty.[7] At the same time as the poverty rate was soaring among the young, the government seemed to turn its back on their needs. School lunch programs were slashed, eligibility requirements for welfare assistance were tightened, and federal support for education was cut. The fact is that unlike the elderly, the young cannot vote and have virtually no political power.

The sweeping changes in the family life examined in Chapter 2 have caused serious problems for many children. The birthrate among single women increased more than 70 percent just in the last decade, and children born to single mothers have an extremely high poverty rate.[8] This trend, combined with a significant increase in the divorce rate, means that more than 25 percent of today's children live in single-parent homes. The changes have not been confined to single-parent families, however. Over 60 percent of married women with children under age 6 now work outside the home, so even children who live with both parents may have less contact with them than they would have had in the past.[9] These trends have made the problem of finding adequate child care a critical issue in many families. A recent study found that 8 percent of grade school children with working mothers came home to an empty house without adult supervision.[10]

A different kind of trouble for today's children comes from their parents' abuse of alcohol and other drugs. It is estimated that 300,000 babies a year are born with serious neurological damage because their mothers used drugs during pregnancy, and there has been a sharp rise in the number of children placed in foster homes because of their parents' drug use and overall family instability. The foster care system, which was already inadequate, simply cannot keep up with rising need.[11] Nonetheless, as the Signs of Hope box in this chapter shows, the overall health of our infants has been improving.

Many researchers studying the lives of today's children have expressed concern about what is termed the **erosion of childhood**—that is, the deterioration of the specially protected status accorded our children. There are still strong restrictions on child labor (as much to protect the jobs of older people as the welfare of children); but the ever increasing importance of education and the relentless materialism of our culture often make children's lives highly competitive ones, while changes in family structure have forced many children to take on adult roles and responsibilities at an earlier age than they did in the recent past. (See the Debate "Are We Turning Our Backs on the Problems of the Young?")

Another important contributor to the breakdown of the protective barrier around the world of childhood is television. It is estimated that the average child has watched 5,000 hours of television before entering the first grade, 19,000 hours by the end of high school.[12] In the past, parents controlled their children's access to information about such things as sex, crime, and social injustice; but the media now bring the harshest adult realities to the television screen and thereby into the world of childhood. In the early days of television, programs were carefully scrutinized to make sure that they were appropriate for family viewing. The results may often have been bland and boring, but television did strive to protect the sheltered world of childhood. Today, however, the media are straining to win the lucrative "baby boom" market, and even early evening programs are often filled with sex and violence.[13] The evening news, moreover, is as much a contributor to the problem as entertainment programming. One study found that 48 percent of all television news stories about children concerned crime and violence, and 50 percent of the 11- to 16-year-olds questioned said they feel angry, afraid, or depressed after watching the news.[14]

erosion of childhood
The deterioration of the specially protected status accorded our children.

Signs of Hope   Healthier Infants

Although financial insecurities and a growing instability in the family have created many problems for infants and young children, there is one area in which they are clearly better off than they were in the past: their health. The most widely accepted measure of this variable is the infant mortality rate (the percent of children who die during their first year of life). The good news is that the infant mortality rate in the United States has dropped by almost two-thirds since 1970.* Although there is no single cause for this dramatic improvement, better health care was certainly a major factor. Increasing educational levels among the general population and greater media attention also contributed to a growing awareness of the importance of good nutrition and prenatal health care for pregnant women. New laws requiring warning labels on alcohol, cigarettes, and medications that might be harmful to unborn infants may also have helped.

*U.S. Bureau of the Census, *Statistical Abstract of the United States, 1996* (Washington, DC: U.S. Government Printing Office, 1996), p. 90.

Debate   Are We Turning Our Backs on the Problems of the Young?

Yes

We were far more concerned about the problems of our children a generation ago than we are today. Television was tightly regulated to make sure its programs were suitable for even the youngest viewers. The movies contained only the tamest sex and far less graphic violence than they do today, and pornography was banned from all respectable newsstands. Even parents seemed more willing to sacrifice their own happiness and stay together for the sake of their children.

Perhaps some of the changes in our society were the inevitable result of long-term historical trends, but even the government seems to have forgotten about the needs of our children. Funding for education is grossly inadequate. Federal programs to provide such things as free school lunches and welfare benefits to poverty-stricken families have been slashed, parks and playgrounds in hundreds of cities have been shut down, and nothing is being done to stop advertisers' shameless exploitation of the young. Commercials tell our children that processed breakfast cereals laden with sugar are part of a nutritious breakfast and urge them to buy everything from ice cream and candy bars to war toys, and the government just looks the other way.

The babies that used to be considered a "bundle of joy" are now more often seen as a noisy, messy nuisance. Parents are glared at when they bring their infants into a movie or a restaurant, "adults only" apartment buildings have sprung up across the country, and the birthrate itself has plummeted as more and more young couples decide that extra spending money is more important than children. Today's children are the forgotten Americans. Their needs clearly come last on our list of national priorities.

Adolescence

No other age grade must face such contradictory social expectations as adolescents. No longer children but not yet adults, adolescents live in a kind of limbo. On the one hand, they are told that they must act their age and behave in a responsible and mature manner; but at the same time, they are told that they are not old enough to get married, have sex, drink, vote, or hold down a well-paying job. It is therefore hardly surprising that psychologist Erik H. Erikson concluded that the **identity crisis**—the pressing need to figure out who we are and how we fit into the scheme of things—is the central problem of adolescence.[15]

identity crisis
The personal crisis, typical of adolescence, in which people try to define who they are and how they fit into society.

Children have most of their decisions made for them, and later in life we are likely to be following a long-established course; but adolescents face a host of difficult decisions that are likely to shape the rest of their lives. Every day they must make critical decisions about relationships with the opposite sex, marriage, school, and careers, with little previous experience to fall back on. It might appear that confronting such difficult problems would at least give adolescents a sense of autonomy and self-control, but just the opposite is true. It is a sense of powerlessness, not in-

No

Today's society is a far better place for children than it ever was before. Improvements in public health, sanitation, and medicine have slashed the infant mortality rate and allow more children to grow into healthy adults. The number of years an average child attends school has gone up, and illiteracy has gone down. Children are now more likely to have braces on their teeth and vaccinations against serious diseases, and their parents generally keep a much closer watch on their diet and their physical safety than they ever did in the past.

The increase in sexually oriented material in the media has nothing to do with our attitudes about children. It is a result of changing attitudes about sex. Similarly, the increase in divorce is not the result of a lesser concern for children but a decline in the belief that keeping an unhappy marriage together is really good for children.

Far from turning its back on children, the government is much more involved in protecting their welfare than it ever was before. The safety of toys, for example, is much more tightly regulated, and many popular toys from the 1950s and 1960s can no longer be sold at all. We used to all but ignore the problems of child abuse and molestation, but today they are major social concerns. The public is more vigilant, the police are more willing to investigate, and the courts are more likely to send offenders to prison than at any time in the past. A hundred years ago, children commonly worked long hours in dirty sweatshops and dangerous factories, and severe beatings were accepted as normal discipline; but today all that is against the law. There simply is no doubt that we are more, not less, concerned with the welfare of our children than we were in the past.

dependence, that is most characteristic of adolescent life. Although they feel themselves to be physically mature and capable of running their own lives, teenagers are constantly under the authority of their elders, whether parents, teachers, or the local police.

Because adolescents have so many unique problems and experiences, they tend to create their own distinct subculture apart from the adult world. Many of the characteristics of this **youth culture** can be seen as a reflection of teenagers' pressing need to create a viable identity.[16] Constantly changing fashions in speech, clothing, and music provide a sense of belonging and a way to gain status and feel a part of an "in-group." These symbols also allow teens to see themselves as separate and somehow "cooler" than the adults that exercise such power over their lives.

youth culture
The distinctive subculture created by adolescents in industrial society.

This symbolic rejection of the adult world becomes more direct and violent in the delinquent subculture that flourishes within the overall youth culture. This subculture, along with the closely related drug culture, contributes to the fact that the arrest rate for 16- to 21-year-olds is higher than for any other age group. One survey found that more than 1 in 10 high school juniors admitted stealing from a store or being in trouble with the police two or more times in the previous year. Moreover, there is evidence of a sharp rise in both crime and criminal victimization among teenagers.[17]

The use of alcohol and other drugs is another serious issue. One survey found that 2 of every 5 high school seniors acknowledged having had a "drinking binge" (five or more drinks in a row) in the last two weeks, 1 of 5 smoked daily, and, perhaps most disturbing of all, 1 in 3 admitted drinking and driving in the last year.[18] Of course, all these problems are not the result of deviant subcultures or even a sense of youthful rebellion. Adolescence is a time of exploration and experimentation, and it is hardly surprising that young people try out as many options as they can. If nothing else, they are less likely to have the responsibilities of a well-paying job or a family to support and therefore have far less to lose if caught breaking society's rules.

While some teenagers respond to their difficulties with delinquency and rebellion, others give in to depression or other mental disorders. A report by the Institute of Medicine concluded that as many as 12 percent of young people suffer from some form of psychological illness.[19] One of the most disturbing manifestations of this problem is the sharp increase in suicide. One study found that 15 percent of high school students admitted making at least one suicide attempt. A different study found that even success in school offered no guaranteed protection, for one-third of the top students surveyed reported having considered suicide.[20] While most suicide attempts are unsuccessful, the suicide rate among teenagers has more than tripled since 1960.[21]

One of the most difficult problems adolescents must face is coming to terms with their sexuality. If anything, society's norms and expectations for adolescent sexual behavior are even more confusing than they are for other aspects of their lives. Teenagers are bombarded with books, movies, and advertising emphasizing the importance of being sexy and attractive. Everything from soft drinks to jeans is given the sexual sell. Yet at the same time, parents, teachers, and religious leaders tell young people that they are not ready for sex and the complications it involves. And unlike young people in most European countries, American teenagers are often discouraged from using birth control. As a result, unmarried teenagers in the United States have the highest birthrate of any country in the industrialized world (see Chapter 11).

Finally, something must be said about the serious economic problems faced by many adolescents. Most teenagers are economically dependent on their families, and because poor people have larger families, a disproportionate number of teenagers are trapped in poverty. The poverty rate for teenagers is higher than for any other age group in the United States except those under 13. Teenage males who work full time still make less than one-third as much as men in their peak earning years. Despite their low wages, those working teenagers are the lucky ones: the unemployment rate for teenagers was more than three times higher than the national average in 1995 (see Figure 9.1).[22] In many ghetto neighborhoods, teenagers looking for work are more likely to end up unemployed than with a job.

Quick Review

What are the most difficult problems faced by American children?

What is the erosion of childhood, and why are people so concerned about it?

Why is adolescence such a difficult period of life?

What is the youth culture?

Teenagers have a higher unemployment rate than any other age group, and when they can find a job, it is usually menial and low-paying.

Figure 9.1

Unemployment

Unemployment is highest among teenagers and declines sharply with increasing age.

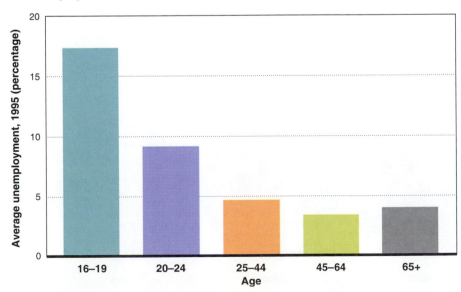

Source: U.S. Bureau of the Census, *Statistical Abstract of the United States, 1996* (Washington, DC: U.S. Government Printing Office, 1996), p. 413.

Problems of the Elderly

In traditional societies with extended family systems, increasing age is usually accompanied by increasing prestige; but with the breakup of the extended family, the status of the elderly has suffered a severe decline. No longer are old men and women the respected heads of an ongoing social unit. Rather, they are increasingly isolated and alone. Youth and vigor are cultural ideals in North America, and there is widespread belief that older people have little or nothing left to contribute. In a common phrase, the elderly are said to be "over the hill."

The problems of the elderly have drawn considerable attention in recent years, probably because there are more old people than ever before. Since 1900, the average life expectancy in the United States has risen by 24 years, and the percentage of the population over age 65 has more than doubled. There are now over 33 million people age 65 or older, which is 12.7 percent of the U.S. population, and projections indicate that the elderly population will continue to grow rapidly in the years ahead (see Figure 9.2).[23]

Health

Of all the problems that trouble older people, health seems to concern them the most, and with good reason. The elderly have more severe health problems than any other age group. Most Americans over age 65 have at least one chronic illness, such as arthritis or heart disease. Elderly people actually have fewer acute illnesses (such as colds and infectious diseases) than others, but their recovery time tends to be much longer than that of younger adults. Most elderly people say that they are in reasonably good health, perhaps because they have learned to put up with illness and physical impairment as an inevitable part of the aging process.[24]

Many elderly people have trouble getting the care and treatment they need for their ailments. Most hospitals, designed to handle injuries and acute illness that are

Figure 9.2

The Graying of America
The population of the United States is rapidly aging.

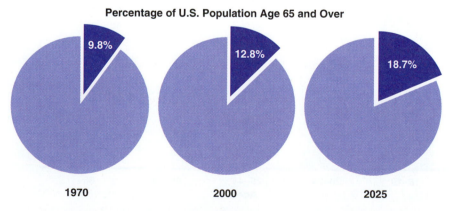

Percentage of U.S. Population Age 65 and Over

9.8%   12.8%   18.7%

1970   2000   2025

Source: U.S. Bureau of the Census, *Statistical Abstract of the United States, 1993* (Washington, DC: U.S. Government Printing Office, 1993), pp. 15, 24.

common in the young, do not have the facilities or personnel to treat the chronic degenerative diseases of the elderly. Many doctors are also ill-prepared to deal with such problems. As Fred Cottrell points out, "There is a widespread feeling among the aged that most doctors are not interested in them and are reluctant to treat people who are as little likely to contribute to the future as the aged are reputed to."[25] Even with the help of Medicare, the elderly in the United States often have a difficult time paying for the health care they need. (See Chapter 6 for an examination of the problems of the health care system.)

Physical and Psychological Abuse

The problem of child abuse began receiving public attention in the 1960s, as spouse abuse did in the 1970s (see Chapter 2), but it was not until much more recently that the public began to become aware of the problem of **elder abuse.** Hearings by a subcommittee of the House of Representatives helped focus concern on this issue when it reported such shocking cases as that of a 74-year-old woman who was raped by her son-in-law and then threatened into silence by her daughter and that of a 75-year-old man whose son attacked him with a hatchet. But as dramatic as such incidents are, elder abuse involves much more than just physical violence. Psychological threats, verbal attacks, and social humiliation are probably more common than outright violence. Many elderly persons are also financially victimized by their caregivers; some caregivers intimidate an older relative into turning over their savings or pension checks, and others simply take their property without permission.

elder abuse
The physical or psychological mistreatment of the elderly.

Studies shows that the elderly are most likely to be abused by the people with whom they live, thus in many cases elder abuse is *also* spouse abuse. Some research indicates that elderly men are more likely to be abused by their wives than the other way around. Perhaps this is because women tend to live longer and marry older men, and so they are less likely to be physically dependent on their husbands. However, elderly women who are abused by husbands are more likely to suffer serious injuries than abused men.[26]

Elder abuse has many similarities to child abuse. When elderly people become frail and unable to care for themselves, they tend to take on a dependent family role similar to that of a child. The stress of added responsibilities, overcrowding, and lack of privacy that often results from living with an aged parent can cause a strong sense of resentment among other family members. Like the victims of child abuse, frail elderly people are often too frightened to go to the authorities when they are victimized, either because they depend on the care an abusive relative gives or because of what might happen to them if they speak out.

Money

For most of this century, the elderly were much more likely than other people to be poor. Recent statistics reveal a remarkable turnaround in the general financial condition of older people. In 1994, 11.7 percent of persons 65 or older were below the poverty line, while that figure was 14.5 percent for the entire population and 21.8 percent for children under 18.[27] One of the main reasons for this improvement is that since 1970, Social Security benefits have automatically been adjusted for inflation. In the late 1970s and early 1980s, when prices were rising at a record pace, the income of Social Security recipients was growing considerably faster than the income of wage earners. Inflation helped more affluent elderly people in another way as well. Unprecedented increases in the cost of real estate produced enormous profits for older people who had purchased a home in the days when prices were low. Households headed by someone over age 60 have more than 10 times the average net worth of households headed by someone under age 35.[28] The financial condition of the elderly is not as rosy as these figures might suggest, however; poverty among the elderly is still higher than it is for those in their middle years, and there are some serious pockets of poverty among older people, especially among widows and members of minority groups. Government statistics underestimate the amount of poverty among the elderly because such data do not acknowledge the fact that older persons need more money than younger persons to enjoy the same standard of living. Medical bills increase, and as the elderly grow more feeble, they must hire others to do many of the chores they once did themselves.

One source of these financial problems is that as people grow older, they are less likely to be employed. Most older people look forward to retirement and the escape it offers from the pressures of the working world, but some find they must retire because they no longer have the stamina their jobs require. Another problem arises when technological changes suddenly make the skills that older workers have acquired over a lifetime obsolete. Older people who know how to bake bread, build fine cabinets, or repair shoes are bound to have a tough time when bakeries become

Discrimination and a lack of the latest technological skills force many elderly people who don't have a pension plan or enough savings to work at menial jobs.

bread factories, cabinets are made of plastic, and cheap shoes are imported in huge quantities. They cannot even get unskilled jobs because employers want the energy of youth. Employee training programs that might lead to new skills are often closed because training directors believe that older men and women will not work long enough to repay the cost of the training.

Discrimination in hiring and promotion is a fact of life for the elderly. Employers give a variety of reasons for their reluctance to hire senior citizens. They fear that older workers will take longer to learn a new job, will work fewer years on the job, will demand higher pay, will be less willing to accept the authority of supervisors younger than themselves, and will be sick more often than their younger counterparts. Although such fears are not entirely groundless, they certainly do not apply to all older workers. Yet all older workers are potential victims of age discrimination.

Retired men and women receive income from a variety of sources, including pensions, Social Security, and personal savings. Most workers dream of retiring on a "fat pension," but only a minority of the elderly receive any pension at all, and such pensions are seldom "fat." Moreover, the number of workers covered by pension plans has shown a significant decline in recent years. In 1979, almost half the employees in the private work force were covered by pension plans, but by 1993 that figure had dropped to 45 percent.[29] The single most important source of income for elderly people in the United States is Old Age and Survivors' Insurance, commonly called Social Security. About 60 percent of the elderly in the United States would be living in poverty if they did not receive Social Security. Still, despite the automatic cost-of-living adjustments, Social Security benefits are hardly extravagant. The average retiree now receives only about $697 a month.[30]

Housing

Decent housing is especially important to the elderly because they spend so much time at home. For personal comfort, the elderly need higher room temperatures than the young require, but housing for the elderly often lacks proper heating. Those who are physically handicapped or disabled also need wheelchair ramps, elevators, and other special facilities. Even owning a home is not easy for many elderly people. There may still be mortgage payments to meet, and rising taxes and insurance premiums must also be paid. Many of the homes in which the elderly live were built before World War II, and they are old by U.S. standards. New roofs and other needed repairs may be left undone because many elderly people are unable to do the work themselves and cannot afford to hire outside help.

So-called **retirement communities** can be a very effective way to meet an elderly person's special housing needs; unfortunately, most of these are private, and the better ones are available only to people with substantial means. Often built in sunny climates, these complexes of houses or apartments are designed for the elderly and usually include special recreational facilities. Some are run like hotels or make hotel-like arrangements for residents who can afford them. Retirement communities have often been criticized because they weaken the ties between generations and create a kind of "old people's ghetto." Nevertheless, many older people move to retirement communities precisely because they seek the companionship of others who share their interests and experiences.

Only a small percentage of people over 65 live in institutions, but that percentage increases sharply with advancing years. Most of these institutions are profit-making businesses. Many that charge high fees give excellent service, but some of

retirement communities
Planned communities for elderly people.

these, and most of the less expensive ones, do not do much "nursing" and are in no sense "homes." The worst of these facilities are old, overcrowded, unsanitary fire-traps. There are not enough toilets, the plumbing backs up, and the light switches don't work. Residents complain that they are served only the cheapest foods and they do not get a balanced diet. Even those who live in good nursing homes may face serious psychological problems, for many people feel that entering a nursing home is a disgrace—a sign of final rejection by friends and family and proof that no one really cares.

Problems of Transition

Like adolescents and young adults, elderly people must learn to adjust to the profound role changes that are thrust on them. The transition to old age is an especially difficult one, however, because it usually involves the loss of status, while role changes for younger people are likely to involve increasing prestige and responsibility. The three most significant personal transitions that the elderly must face are retirement, the loss of friends and loved ones, and their own death.

After a person has been employed for decades, the transition to retirement can be painful. The daily routine that has given direction to the worker's life is suddenly yanked away. This transition is not just a matter of finding new things to do; it requires major psychological adjustments. Retirement demands a new answer to the first question strangers are likely to ask each other: "What do you do?" An old saying held, "It is better to wear away than to rust away." People who are perceived to be rusting away on park benches and shuffleboard courts are seen as useless and perhaps a little immoral as well. To make matters worse, retirees usually suffer a drop in income and can no longer afford many of the things that they were used to buying—another sign of "failure." Despite these problems, however, studies show that most retired people are satisfied with their lives. When a Harris poll asked a sample of retired people, "Has retirement fulfilled your expectations for a good life or have you found it less than satisfactory?" 61 percent of the respondents said that retirement had fulfilled their expectations, while only one-third felt that it was less than satisfactory.[31]

The social world of the elderly tends to shrink as the years go by. There are fewer social contacts as friends and relatives die, and moving from place to place becomes increasingly difficult. Old social roles are dropped, and even sex differences decline. Old people look and behave differently and are often shunned by the young. If they have children or sisters and brothers, they are fortunate, for ties with surviving family members normally remain strong. Those without close living relatives find their world growing smaller and smaller.

Sooner or later, old people die. When one member of a married couple dies, the survivor must cope without a partner. Most survivors are women, both because most wives are younger than their husbands and because women tend to live longer than men. Normlessness, isolation, and loneliness can be particularly severe in widowhood. The older the widow, the greater the problems. There is often no sex, no love, no help with daily tasks, and less income. The problems of transition begin immediately after the husband's death. The woman who may have depended on her husband to make the decisions and handle financial affairs must, in the midst of her grief, work her way through a maze of medical bills, insurance claims, funeral expenses, and tax payments. She is likely to discover that she is eligible for little or

Personal Perspectives   Caring for a Mother with Alzheimer's Disease

Alzheimer's disease causes a progressive deterioration in the mental functioning of its victims as they age. As the symptoms of the disease grow progressively worse, the victims slowly lose their ability to function normally or care for themselves. The following account of the problems faced by someone caring for a victim of Alzheimer's disease comes from a man in his fifties.

The first year that I took care of Mother I thought I was going to the nuthouse. I had to get used to the fact that she asks the same questions over and over again and that she constantly argues with me. She also follows me around the house like a puppy dog. What finally helped me to deal with her when she was especially argumentative and difficult was a tip I got from the Alzheimer's support group I go to. I picture a sign around her neck that says "Ill." It really helps me to increase my patience with her.

Taking care of Mother is, in many ways, like being a housewife. I take care of everything. I do all the cooking, cleaning, laundry, gardening, and take care of all the money matters. I'm constantly on the lookout for things that can be dangerous to her, and I recently put a monitor in her room so I can hear if she has any problems. I had to take the knobs off the gas stove because I caught her starting to cook something, then she wandered off and forgot what she was doing. I have to make sure I pick up the mail before she does because she forgets where she puts it, then denies she ever got it. Just the other day I heard her bumping around in her bedroom. When I went back to see if everything was O.K., I found her groping around in the dark. The light bulb had burned out and she couldn't figure out that all she had to do was walk back down the hallway and get me to fix it for her. I'm constantly afraid she's going to hurt herself, so I seldom leave her alone. So I'm on duty 24 hours a day, 7 days a week.

The biggest challenge, without a doubt, is the role reversal. It's very difficult emotionally to be taking care of my mother as though she were a young child. Another difficult thing is that Mother doesn't know she is ill. She's in her eighties, but she thinks she's in her sixties and she doesn't need me. When she gets upset, she yells at me to go back to Los Angeles, that she doesn't need me. Sometimes she doesn't recognize me.

nothing from her husband's pension benefits, and she may have to choose between looking for a job, trying to live on Social Security, or remarrying. Remarriage is not likely to be easy, however, for there are not enough eligible older men. Moreover, after living with one man for most of a lifetime, the idea of taking up with another may not be attractive.

Becoming a widower has its problems too. Should the elderly widower desire to remarry, his chances of finding a mate seem brighter because there are more elderly women than men; but if he does not remarry, his life is likely to become more difficult. In most families it is the wife who keeps up contacts with friends and relatives, arranges parties, and runs the household. Consequently, a man who loses his wife is likely to lose touch with many of his friends as well. Further, although some widows can fall back on their maternal roles, widowers generally have weaker ties to their children and are therefore more likely to be lonely and isolated.

Whether married or not, all elderly people must come to terms with their own mortality. In the rich industrialized nations where death rates are low, we often pretend that death is an accident. When it occurs we grieve, but we imagine that it is avoidable, like automobile collisions or flunking out of college. The dying pay the price for this denial of reality, for they are avoided as deftly as our thoughts of death. Most people in the industrialized nations die in a hospital or other institution, shut away from the familiar surroundings of home. As a result, feelings of rejection and loneliness are common among the dying. Even the friends, relatives, and medical personnel who have contact with the dying engage in a kind of "conspiracy of silence." Everyone tries to avoid the subject of death and to pretend that nothing is really going to happen to the patient.

Quick Review

Why is health such an important problem for elderly people?

What is elder abuse?

What are the most serious financial problems faced by elderly people?

What problems do elderly people face in finding good housing?

What are the problems of transition faced by older people?

The Graying of America

So far we have been focusing on the problems individuals face during the different stages of the process of aging, but we are also undergoing some profound changes in our demographic structure that pose a major challenge for society as a whole. Simply put, the populations of the industrialized nations are growing old. In 1997, they had 42 percent fewer children (as a percentage of their total population) than the Third World countries and almost 3 times more people over 65.[32] In the United States, 12.7 percent of the population is currently over 65, and the U.S. Bureau of the Census projects that as the **baby boom generation** ages, that proportion will continue to swell. In 30 years, over 18 percent of the U.S. population is expected to be over 65.[33]

baby boom generation
The large generation of Americans born after World War II.

What impact will this profound change have on our society? Although many people have groundless fears based on false stereotypes about older people, there are some legitimate reasons for concern. The number one issue is probably the health of the Social Security system, which is so vital to the financial well-being of our older citizens. The original idea behind Social Security was that all workers would contribute part of their income to a pension fund, and those contributions would be matched by the employer. When workers retired, they would be entitled to regular payments from these savings. In practice, however, the contributions of workers have not been saved—they have been paid out as needed. Thus, the increase in the number of retirees (see Figure 9.3) means that today's workers must pay higher Social Security taxes than in past decades. There are currently about four workers supporting every Social Security recipient, but that number is expected to shrink substantially in the years ahead.[34]

Another concern is with those in extreme old age who are frail and in need of constant help. The number of Americans over age 84 is expected to increase by 65 percent in the next thirty years,[35] and that will pose a major challenge to our health care system. Nursing home care is already costly, inefficient, and in short supply, and a concerted effort will be needed just to keep things from getting worse.

Figure 9.3

Social Security Recipients

The number of people receiving Social Security benefits has increased enormously since 1950.

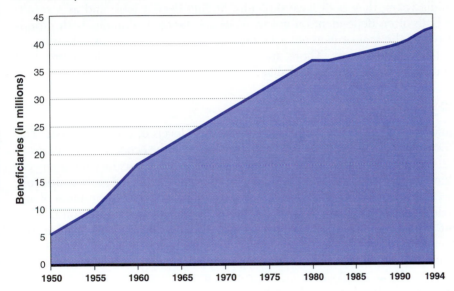

Source: U.S. Bureau of the Census, *Statistical Abstract of the United States, 1993* (Washington, DC: U.S. Government Printing Office, 1993), p. 374; *Statistical Abstract, 1996,* p. 375.

It is, however, easy to exaggerate the problems we can expect from the aging of our population. One important reason our population is aging is that people are healthier and live longer than then did in the past. Thus, we can expect older people to be in better physical shape than the old were in the past. That not only means savings in health care costs, but also that people are likely to work longer before they retire, thus reducing the projected shortfall of the Social Security system.

Quick Review

What is the "graying of America," and what problems is it likely to create?

Solving the Problems of the Young and the Old

The needs of our younger and older citizens are often played off against each other in the political arena. When politicians create programs to help one group, they often pay for them by cutting benefits for the other or by borrowing the money and running up the government's debt. (This shifts the cost to the younger generation, since they are the ones who will have to pay off the debt.) When our younger and older citizens are pitted against each other in this way, the young almost inevitably lose because they are less organized and less wealthy and in most cases can't even vote. The interests of these two groups are not necessarily opposed, however. Both groups share many common problems: they both have lower incomes than those in their middle years; they both have difficulty finding decent jobs; and as a result, they are both often dependent on government assistance. Culturally, both groups are shut out of the mainstream of social life, and both are seen to be a burden on those in their middle years. There are therefore many proposals for action that could benefit the young and the old alike.

Employment

Both aging workers and adolescents suffer from high levels of unemployment. The most effective way to deal with this problem is to improve the economic conditions of all workers. When the unemployment rate is low, more employers hire the many capable older workers who are available and give teenagers a chance at their first job.

The United States, like other nations, has tried to deal with the problem of age discrimination by passing laws against it. The Federal Age Discrimination in Employment Act of 1967 prohibits many types of age discrimination. As a result, the most blatant signs of such bias have decreased significantly; but more subtle forms of discrimination continue. Laws of this type are difficult to enforce because it is hard to prove why an employer hired or promoted one person rather than another. In actual practice, the law is enforced on a hit-or-miss basis because there isn't enough money to enforce it across the board. Moreover, the current laws are far too narrow and do not prohibit discrimination against young workers. Although legislation of this kind can never be a complete answer to the problem, a revision of the law to include all kinds of age discrimination and a significant increase in the funding to enforce the law would certainly be steps in the right direction. In France, where about one in four young people in the labor force is unemployed, the government pays a temporary subsidy of about $200 a month to employers who create jobs for youths.[36]

Social Welfare

As we have seen, the government substantially reduced its commitment to young people during the two decades. Although such shortsighted policies may achieve some immediate saving, in the long run their social and financial costs are likely to be staggering. The problems of neglected youth do not simply go away but grow progressively worse and more costly as the years go by. For example, the cost of a measles shot is only $8, but hospitalization for a child with complications from measles runs about $5000.[37]

The obvious way to reaffirm our commitment to the young is to increase the government's support for children and their families. A school lunch program to provide at least one nutritious meal to every child every day, free health care for any child who needs it, an increase in the tax exemption allowed for dependent children, and a national system of top-quality day care at no cost to middle- and low-income parents would contribute enormously to the welfare of our children; but a real commitment to the young must go beyond providing the necessities for survival. Our young people desperately need a better system of education, and that will require the kinds of costly reforms discussed in Chapter 3. We also need to take more interest in the social needs of the young. The financial problems of local governments have resulted in the closing of many parks and the elimination of sports programs. A new commitment to the young would mean a reversal of this trend and a greater effort to see that young people are given positive, healthful outlets for their energies.

Although government programs designed to help the elderly are different from those for the young, their goals are much the same: to assist a group of people who cannot always provide for themselves. Social Security is the major source of income for most elderly Americans. Although it is one of the most popular and widely accepted social programs in the United States, Social Security is experiencing some serious difficulties. As we have seen, benefits are too low to support some elderly people, yet the system is having trouble meeting its financial commitments to an aging population. Similar problems are also occurring in the other industrialized nations. The Canada Pension Plan, for example, is expected to run out of money early in the next century unless contributions are significantly increased.[38]

The current burden of Social Security falls disproportionately on low- and middle-income people. Unlike the income tax, the Social Security tax rate does not decrease with decreasing income, and those with high incomes do not pay taxes on their entire earnings but only on the portion below a fixed level. Thus, one way to ensure adequate benefits and keep the system on sound financial footing is to institute a progressive Social Security tax that goes up as income increases.

The elderly could benefit from a variety of other programs as well. One of the most pressing needs is for more government-subsidized housing for those who are too poor to own their own homes or live in retirement communities. To help middle-income retirees squeezed by inflation and health care costs, several states allow the elderly to defer their property taxes until after their death, when the equity in their house is used to pay the taxes due. Finally, a universal program of national health insurance that contained effective cost-control measures would help the elderly, the young, and many of those in their middle years as well (see Chapter 6).

Cultural Change

The problems of the elderly and the young are rooted in the cultural traditions of our society. There is, for example, a strong negative stereotype of elderly people. A public opinion survey sponsored by the National Council on Aging found that older people consistently described themselves in more positive terms than those used by the general public. For instance, people over 65 were almost three times as likely as those under 65 to say that the elderly are "very open-minded and adaptable." The general public also saw the elderly as much less active and more bored than the elderly saw themselves. Those under 65 were more than twice as likely to believe that the elderly spend a lot of time sleeping or doing nothing, and they were four times as likely to say that "not having enough to do" is a serious problem for the elderly.[39] Such stereotypes become self-fulfilling prophecies that lead to the exclusion of the elderly from employment opportunities and other forms of social involvement.

The most effective way to change this situation is to encourage the elderly to participate in community life, putting their wealth of wisdom and experience to work for the good of others. A number of programs are aimed toward these ends. For example, the Foster Grandparent Program helps the young and the old at the same time by paying older people to work part time at child-care centers and institutions. The elderly get meaningful work and additional income, and the children

Many in our culture view old people as useless and incompetent, but few of the elderly actually fit this stereotype. The store of information and wisdom accumulated by the elderly is especially useful to the young as they are growing up.

receive the benefits of personal attention and concern. Senior citizens' centers, which are funded by public and private sources, also employ older people in community projects. Perhaps more important, these centers provide a place where the elderly can congregate, make new friends, and get a hot meal.

The problems of adolescents stem less from the negative stereotypes about them—although these certainly abound—than from the contradictory demands and expectations of the adult world. If we are to reduce juvenile delinquency, drug and alcohol use, suicide, and the general sense of boredom and aimlessness among the young, we must provide a more clear-cut set of expectations for their age grade, along with more rewarding and worthwhile things for them to do. In the past, teenagers were considered adults and given adult responsibilities. If industrial society continues to deny adolescents full adult status, young people must at least be encouraged to see themselves as respected and worthwhile members of their community. Providing jobs for young workers who need them would certainly make a big difference; but adolescents need something more than just a regular source of income. Of all age grades, they are the most idealistic, and they need to feel that they are contributing to the world around them. It is up to society to tap this youthful idealism and channel it into worthwhile projects. Not only can such endeavors give purpose and meaning to those involved; they can produce real benefits for society as a whole.

Quick Review

What are the best ways to deal with the problems of the young and old?

Sociological Perspectives on Problems of the Life Cycle

Each of us must come to terms with the realities of growth, aging, and death as we pass through the stages of the life cycle. This may appear to be a lonely struggle, but it is not. Although the major sociological perspectives focus on different issues, they all show us how such seemingly individual problems are inextricably bound up with the social order in which we live.

The Functionalist Perspective

Functionalists see much confusion in the institutions and agencies that are supposed to meet the special needs of the young, the middle-aged, and the elderly. At the root of the problem are the changes that continue to transform Western culture. In the past, death came at an early age, and there were relatively few elderly people. Most of those who did grow old were cared for by their families. With improvements in sanitation and food supplies brought about by industrialization, the percentage of elderly people in the population has increased enormously. At the same time, economic changes have caused a breakdown in the traditional extended family, leaving many older people alone and unable to support themselves.

These developments are, moreover, having just as profound an effect on children and young adults as on the elderly. The weakening of the family has created severe problems for the growing number of children who come from broken or conflict-ridden homes. At the same time, changes in the economic system that slashed the demand for unskilled workers have fundamentally transformed the social role of teenagers as they have been squeezed out of the mainstream of the labor force and into a marginal position. The creation of the new age grade of adolescence stemmed, at least in part, from an attempt to deal with the special problems of this group, yet society continues to hold highly contradictory expectations for its young people.

From the functionalist perspective, it is necessary to reorganize the social institutions that traditionally cared for the young and the elderly or to develop new agencies that can do so more effectively. The fact that the government has been taking increased financial responsibility for the elderly can be seen as an attempt to get the machinery of society running smoothly again; but there is a great deal of disorganization in the administration of government programs for the elderly, just as there is in the far smaller programs for the young. These programs are often cumbersome and inefficient, and they spend far too much on administrative costs; but the most serious problem is that these agencies often do not have enough money to meet the needs of the people they serve.

There are signs that society is at least beginning to come to terms with the problems of the elderly. Stereotypes about the elderly are beginning to change, and senior citizens' centers, retirement communities, and other organizations designed to meet the needs of the elderly are becoming more common. Our efforts to deal with the problems of the young, however, seem to be less successful. Some of the functions formerly performed by the family have been shifted to the schools and the criminal justice system, but generally these institutions remain a poor substitute for a supportive family environment. Moreover, at the present time at least, there seems to be little willingness on the part of society to make the financial and psychological commitment to take effective action.

The Conflict Perspective

Many social scientists are convinced that the government's seeming indifference to the problems of the old and the young is no accident but a product of class conflict. They argue that the wealthy and powerful have blocked efforts to help these groups. The wealthy do not need government assistance for their children or in their old age, and they do not care to pay for such help for others.

Value conflicts also play an important part in these problems. Our ideals about the importance of competition, self-reliance, and personal responsibility clash with the effort to care for people who are not economically productive. Thus, the ideology of individualism (see Chapter 7) blames the elderly for their poverty, assuming that they deserve to suffer because they have failed to provide for their future. Similarly, single parents are blamed for their failure to follow traditional family patterns. Ignoring their complex financial and social problems, society tells single mothers to simply go out and get a job. On the other side of this conflict are those who hold to the values of community and collective responsibility. These people see the problems of the life cycle as the product of social forces beyond the control of any individual; and if these problems are created by society, it follows that society should do something to resolve them.

From the conflict perspective, the most effective response to the problems of the life cycle is political action. Senior citizens have already organized themselves into an effective lobby. Acting through such organizations as the American Association of Retired Persons, senior citizens have been able to protect Social Security from the cutbacks that hit most other social programs in the 1980s and early 1990s. Children and adolescents are, however, in a much weaker position. They lack political experience, have little money, and cannot vote. Their only hope for political representation lies with concerned adults who are willing to fight for their interests.

The Feminist Perspective

A feminist analysis points directly to the critical role women play in the problems facing the young and the old. For one thing, women live longer than men, so when we discuss the problems of the elderly, we are talking largely about the problems of *elderly women*. But equally important is the fact that women are assigned a disproportionate share of the responsibility for dealing with the problems of the young and old. Traditionally, women have always been given the lion's share of the responsibility for the care and protection of our children, and opinion polls show that on the average, women are more concerned with the problems of children and families than men are. Research shows that women also shoulder the majority of the burden of caring for the elderly in need.

Feminists advocate two kinds of solutions for problems discussed in this chapter. First, they would like to see men pitch in and provide more help in child rearing and the care of elderly relatives (see Chapter 2). But feminists recognize that many men are as overburdened as their wives, so they also call for the government to lend a bigger hand. Financially, the government could increase welfare support for poor families with dependent children and provide tax breaks for those caring for children or the elderly. But equally important, the government needs to create institu-

Conflict theorists are convinced that political activism is the most effective way to solve the problems of both our youngest and oldest citizens.

tional structures—such as day-care centers and nursing homes—to lift some of the weight off these hard-pressed families.

The Interactionist Perspective

Interactionists have long been concerned with the social process of aging and with the ways the social definitions we hold for people of different ages shape their attitudes and their behavior. As people reach different age levels, society's expectations and their group memberships change, and they assume new roles. The key to negotiating these role transitions lies in the nature of the new groups. If a person entering a new phase of the life cycle is accepted by his or her new peers and given some positive ideal to emulate, the transition is likely to be an easy one. Those entering adolescence, however, are often confronted with a confusing barrage of competing groups with conflicting ideals and expectations, and as a result they find it difficult to discover their own direction. On the other hand, people entering old age find that their previous roles disappear, along with many friends and loved ones, but that their new role is poorly defined. There are far fewer expectations of any kind placed on them and fewer goals to pursue. Although this can be a liberating experience, feelings of aimlessness and apathy are another common result.

Most interactionists recommend the same general solution to the problems of young and old alike: help integrate them into supportive social groups that offer a constructive role to play in society. Though this conclusion is almost universally accepted for adolescents, there are some who feel that it is less appropriate for the elderly. The majority of social psychologists adhere to what is known as **activity theory,** which urges older people to remain active and involved in community life

activity theory
A theory of aging which holds that older people are happiest when they continue to be actively involved in social life.

disengagement theory
A theory of aging which holds that older people are best off when they slowly disengage from social activities as they age.

as they age. However, **disengagement theory** rejects this recommendation and holds that old age is best handled by accepting the inevitable contraction of one's social world and gradually disengaging from social involvements and responsibilities as death comes nearer. While the idea of disengagement clashes with the activist bent of Western culture, it is the ideal of many Asian cultures that the elderly should withdraw from everyday activities and focus their attention on spiritual pursuits.

Quick Review

What is the difference between activity theory and disengagement theory?

What responses do feminists recommend to the problems of the young and old?

What role does class conflict play in the problems of the young and old?

What do functionalists see as the cause of the problems of aging in our society?

Summary

Aging is a social as well as a biological process. All societies divide their members into age grades—groups of people of similar age—and the members of the various age grades have different rights and duties. Sociologically, the life cycle is a series of transitions from one set of social roles to another, and such role transitions are often difficult. The individual making such changes must adapt to a new set of expectations and leave behind the rewards and security of earlier roles. The four principal age grades in industrial societies are childhood, adolescence, adulthood, and old age.

Although childhood is seen as a carefree time, children still face significant problems in today's society. There is a great deal of concern about child abuse and molestation, and the poverty rate is higher for children than for any other age group. Moreover, the sheltered status children have enjoyed during most of the twentieth century seems to be eroding. Changes in family structure have forced many children to assume adult responsibilities at an earlier age, and television and the other mass media are bringing adult attitudes and problems into the world of childhood.

Adolescents are seen neither as children nor as adults, and society's expectations are probably more contradictory for them than for any other age grade. Adolescents face many difficult problems, including constructing a viable personal identity, dealing with their awakening sexuality, and making critical decisions about education and jobs. To make matters worse, adolescents have a higher poverty rate than any other age group except young children. The youth culture provides many adolescents with a group identity and supplies some common answers to the perplexing questions they face.

Western culture puts a high value on beauty and vigor and fails to give the elderly the prestige they receive in many other cultures. Elderly people have more chronic diseases and poorer overall health than the general population, but most elderly people say that they are in reasonably good health. The problems arising from the psychological and physical abuse of the elderly have been gaining increasing attention in recent years. Money worries are also common among the aged. Most elderly people are not eligible for a private pension, and those that they do receive are usually inadequate. Many elderly people live mainly on Social Security payments or public assistance. As the elderly lose old friends and relatives and many of the social roles they once performed, they are more likely to be lonely and isolated. The death of a spouse makes matters worse. After a brief period of support and sympathy, the new widow or widower must take up a new life. Widows have some special problems of adjustment because their incomes are often greatly reduced and their chances for remarriage are slim; and all elderly people are faced with the reality that their own death is drawing near.

Many different responses to the problems of our youngest and oldest citizens have been suggested. A program to create more jobs would help all workers regardless of age. A broader prohibition against age discrimination, a reform of Social Security financing, free school lunches, and a comprehensive national health insurance program are common suggestions, as are making cultural changes that give both the old and the young a more positive role to play in our society.

Functionalists see the problems of the old and the young as one more product of the disorganization that follows rapid economic and social change. Conflict theorists are convinced that those groups suffer because the wealthy and powerful profit from their misery. They advocate stronger organization for political action by these groups and their supporters. Feminists focus on the central role women play in dealing with the problems of the young and the old. Interactionists study how age-graded roles are learned and emphasize the need of all people to be integrated into supportive social groups.

Questions for Critical Thinking

The age grades in traditional cultures are all clearly (if somewhat rigidly) defined, and there are shared rituals marking the transition from one stage in life to another. Elders are given respect for their wisdom and experience, and young people assume adult responsibilities at a much earlier age. How has our society changed from those traditional patterns? What are the advantages and disadvantages of our more individualistic approach to aging? Do we need to change our approach, or are things good as they are?

Key Terms

activity theory	erosion of childhood
adolescence	identity crisis
adulthood	life cycle
age grades	midlife crisis
baby boom generation	old age
childhood	retirement communities
disengagement theory	rites of passage
elder abuse	youth culture

Further Readings

Georgia M. Barrow, *Aging, the Individual and Society,* 5th ed. (St. Paul, MN: West, 1992). A good general text on the problems of aging.

Karen A. Conner, *Aging America* (Englewood Cliffs, NJ: Prentice Hall, 1992). An examination of the issues posed by the aging of the American population.

S. Shirley Feldman and Glen R. Elliott, *At the Threshold: The Developing Adolescent* (Cambridge, MA: Harvard University Press, 1993). A comprehensive study of adolescence.

Joseph M. Hawes and N. Ray Hiner, eds., *American Childhood: A Research Guide and Historical Handbook* (Westport, CT: Greenwood, 1985). A good resource for those interested in taking a closer look at childhood in American society.

Elisabeth Kübler-Ross, *Questions and Answers on Death and Dying* (New York: Macmillan, 1985). A general work by the most influential student of the process of dying.

Matilda White Riley, "On the Significance of Age in Sociology," *American Sociological Review* 52 (February 1987): 1–14. A discussion of the sociology of aging by a highly respected gerontologist.

Notes

1. Lisa Gubernick, "Granny Care and Kiddie Care," *Forbes,* December 30, 1996, p. 74.
2. See Vern L. Bullough, "Age at Menarche: A Misunderstanding," *Science* 213 (1981): 365–366.
3. Warner K. Schaie, "The Course of Adult Intellectual Development," *American Psychologist* 49 (April 1994): 304–313.
4. P. B. Baltes and S. L. Willis, "Enhancement of Intellectual Functioning in Old Age: Penn State's Adult Development and Enrichment Program," in F. I. M. Craik and S. E. Trehrib, eds., *Aging and Cognitive Process* (New York: Plenum, 1982).
5. Melinda Beck, "Trading Places," *Newsweek,* July 16, 1990, pp. 48–54.
6. See Daniel J. Levison, *The Season of a Man's Life* (New York: Knopf, 1978).
7. U.S. Bureau of the Census, *Statistical Abstract of the United States, 1996* (Washington, DC: U.S. Government Printing Office, 1996), p. 472.
8. Arlene F. Saluter, "Marital Status and Living Arrangements: 1994," *Current Population Reports* (Washington DC: U.S. Government Printing Office, 1995).
9. U.S. Bureau of the Census, *Statistical Abstract, 1996,* p. 400.
10. O'Connell Marin, "Who's Minding the Kids?" (Washington, DC: U.S. Government Printing Office, June 1994).
11. Susan Chira, "Study Confirms Worst Fears on U.S. Children," *New York Times,* April 12, 1994, pp. A1, A12; Barbara Kantrowitz, "Children Lost in the Quagmire," *Newsweek,* May 13, 1991, p. 64; Ron Harris, "Youth Isn't Kid Stuff These Days," *Los Angeles Times,* May 12, 1991, pp. A1, A20.
12. Richard Zoglin, "Is TV Ruining Our Children?" *Time,* October 15, 1990, p. 75.
13. Elizabeth Douvan, "The Age of Narcissism, 1963–1982," in Joseph M. Hawes and N. Ray Hiner, eds., *American Childhood: A Research Guide and Historical Handbook* (Westport, CT: Greenwood, 1985), pp. 587–617.
14. Marilyn Gardner, "Media's Message to Children Is, 'You're the Problem,'" *Christian Science Monitor,* March 10, 1994, p. 13.
15. Erik H. Erikson, *Childhood and Society,* rev. ed. (New York: Norton, 1964).
16. Hans Sebald, *Adolescence: A Social Psychological Analysis* (Englewood Cliffs, NJ: Prentice Hall, 1984).
17. Angela E. Couloumbis, "New Report Finds Youth Deaths By Homicide Doubled Since 1985," *Christian Science Monitor,* April, 25, 1994, p. 18; Sonia Nazario, "Many Teen-Agers Facing Harder Lives, Study Finds," *Los Angeles Times,* April 25, 1994, pp. A1, A3.

18. Harris, "Youth Isn't Kid Stuff These Days."

19. Anastasia Toufexis, "Struggling for Sanity," *Time,* October 8, 1990, pp. 47–48.

20. Elizabeth Shogren, "Survey of Top Students Reveals Sex Assaults, Suicide Attempts," *Los Angeles Times,* October 20, 1993, p. A22.

21. Sonia Nazario, "Schools Struggle to Teach Lessons in Life and Death," *Los Angeles Times,* March 10, 1997, pp. A1, A12, A13.

22. U.S. Bureau of the Census, *Statistical Abstract, 1996,* p. 413.

23. Ibid., p. 15.

24. Arthur N. Schwartz, Cherie L. Snyder, and James A. Peterson, *Aging and Life,* 2nd ed. (New York: Holt, Rinehart & Winston, 1984), pp. 37–38.

25. Fred Cottrell, *Aging and the Aged* (Dubuque, IA: Brown, 1974), p. 19.

26. Karl Pillemer and David Finkelhor, "The Prevalence of Elder Abuse: A Random Sample Survey," *Gerontologist* 28 (1988): 51–57.

27. U.S. Bureau of the Census, *Statistical Abstract, 1996,* p. 473.

28. Theodore Caplow, *American Social Trends* (San Diego: Harcourt Brace Jovanovich, 1991), pp. 141–142.

29. Lawrence Mishel, Jared Bernstein, and John Schmitt, *The State of Working America, 1996–97* (New York: Sharpe, 1997), p. 160.

30. U.S. Bureau of the Census, *Statistical Abstract, 1996,* p. 374.

31. See Walter R. Cunningham and John W. Brookbank, *Gerontology* (New York: HarperCollins, 1988), pp. 228–245.

32. Population Reference Bureau, *World Population Data Sheet, 1997* (Washington DC: Population Reference Bureau, 1997).

33. U.S. Bureau of the Census, *Statistical Abstract 1996,* pp. 15, 25.

34. Ibid., pp. 373, 375.

35. Ibid., p. 25.

36. Howard LaFranchi, "France Decides to Pay Companies to Hire Youths," *Christian Science Monitor,* April 4, 1994, p. 6; Richard Thau, "French Youths Serve Warning," *Christian Science Monitor,* April 11, 1994, p. 22.

37. Gibbs, "Shameful Bequests to the Next Generation."

38. Kaye Fulton and Nancy Wood, "A Reasonable Limit," *Maclean's,* December 17, 1990, pp. 20–21.

39. See Jon Hendricks and C. David Hendricks, *Aging in Mass Society: Myths and Realities,* 2nd ed. (Cambridge, MA: Winthrop, 1981), pp. 14–18.

Women and Men

What are the differences between male and female gender roles?

Are the differences in the behavior of females and males caused by biology or culture?

How do we learn gender roles?

What forms does gender discrimination take?

How can gender inequality be reduced?

W hen the guerrilla army known as the Taliban first marched into Afghanistan's capital a few years ago, it seemed like just one more turn in the endless wars that had been raging in that country for two decades. But for the women of Afghanistan, it was anything but business as usual. Fueled by an extremist interpretation of their Islamic faith, these young and often illiterate soldiers imposed a virtual reign of terror on the women in the territories they controlled. In a country where women often had to keep the economy running while their husbands fought the wars, the Taliban suddenly decreed that no women could work outside their homes. Girls were thrown out of school and denied an education, and even adult women who were veiled from head to foot in the traditional Afghani costume were forbidden to leave their homes without a male relative to accompany them. Finally, the Taliban decided it was immoral for male doctors to see female patients. They decreed that no female patients could be treated at any of the major hospitals—leaving thousand of desperate women without proper medical care.

This is, of course, an extreme example of the repression so often directed against women. Most Westerners see these events as something foreign and incomprehensible. But it wasn't all that long ago that women lived in similar conditions in the Western nations. Of course, Western women were never required to wear veils or forbidden to leave their houses, but many women often feared to venture very far from their homes without company. Women were far less likely to get an education than men, and they were denied the right to vote or even to manage their own financial affairs. It was not until the sweeping changes brought on by the industrial revolution that those traditional roles began to change and **gender inequality** came to be seen as a social problem. Today, of course, even popular magazines and daily talk shows discuss the problem of **sexism** and debate the proper role of women and men in our society, but too much of this dialog is carried out in a sociological and historical vacuum. To understand this issue more deeply, we must first explore the nature and origins of gender roles and the ways gender inequality is built into our social institutions.

gender inequality
The differences in the economic, social, and political conditions of females and males.

sexism
Stereotyping, prejudice, and discrimination based on gender.

Gender Roles

Like actors, each of us plays many roles. The list is almost endless—parent, child, student, worker, pedestrian, automobile driver, shopper, consumer. **Gender roles** are assigned to us on the basis of our biological sex. (Although the terms are not always used consistently, *sex* usually refers to biological characteristics and *gender* to social characteristics.) These roles contain sets of expectations for both what we are supposed to do and what we are not supposed to do. A woman who spends hours coloring her hair and applying just the right makeup before going out meets our gender role expectations; a man who does the same thing violates those expectations.

Gender roles are assigned early in life. Children quickly learn that they are girls or boys and act accordingly. Nevertheless, adult gender roles are complex, involving both personality and behavioral characteristics. Women are traditionally expected to be passive, warm, and supportive. In contrast to men, who are expected to suppress their feelings, women are encouraged to express emotions openly. Men are

gender roles
Social roles assigned on the basis of biological sex.

supposed to be active, independent, and self-controlled, while women are thought to be more dependent and in need of emotional support. A man's role centers around his work and his responsibilities as breadwinner and provider of financial security. The traditional role of women, on the other hand, is to run the home and rear the children.

The movement of women out of the home and into the workplace has shaken the old notions about the natural differences between the sexes. In the past, people who did not fit the expectations for their gender were shunned and ridiculed. Today, some argue that the healthiest individuals display both strong masculine and strong feminine characteristics and that the new ideal should therefore be a single **androgynous** one combining traits traditionally assigned to the two genders.[1] Others hold that the distinction between masculine and feminine characteristics is harmful and should be abandoned altogether.[2] Nonetheless, these traditional roles and stereotypes are still a powerful force in our society, and their consequences will be with us for a long time to come.

androgynous

Having the characteristics traditionally ascribed to both males and females.

Nature or Nurture?

Where do gender roles come from? Why do we see such differences in the way men and women act? As with so many other issues in the social sciences, the answers to such questions reflect the long-running debate about the relative importance of nature (biology) and nurture (learning) in human behavior.

The two most significant biological differences between the sexes are clearly the greater size and strength of the male and the female's ability to bear and nurse children. In most physical contests, males have a clear advantage. Not only is the average male taller than the average female, but testosterone, a male sex hormone, promotes muscular development and strength. The female, of course, has a much closer biological tie with the process of reproduction. Childbearing is the exclusive domain of the female; and before the development of baby bottles, only the mother could feed a child for the first months of its life. Because a sexually active woman in an agricultural society will become pregnant about once every two years without the use of contraceptives, the average woman in such societies was either pregnant or nursing a small child during most of her adult life.[3]

Despite the male's advantage in physical strength, females are clearly the healthier sex. Males are subject to a variety of sex-linked genetic defects, including hemophilia and color blindness. They are also more susceptible to some diseases, and they mature more slowly than females. Although slightly more male infants are born, their rate of death is significantly higher, and females have longer life spans in all modern societies.[4]

The relationship between sex hormones and behavior is a complex and controversial issue. Numerous researchers have attempted to show that male hormones are linked to such things as aggression and dominance, female hormones to mothering and nurturant behavior. Studies have been made of children exposed to high levels of male hormones in the womb because of a hereditary defect in the function of the adrenal gland (adrenogenital syndrome) and of children exposed to high levels of a female hormone (progesterone) given to mothers because of difficulties in pregnancy. In general, these studies have found girls exposed to male hormones to be more "masculine" and males exposed to female hormones to be more "feminine." However, the interpretation of these results is far from clear. The cause of

Changes in life-style have significant effects on physique. Muscular strength used to be considered "unfeminine," but such attitudes are now changing.

the lower levels of aggression and physical activity in the "feminized" boys may have been their mothers' problems during pregnancy and not the drug prescribed to deal with those problems. Similarly, the "masculinized" behavior of girls with adrenogenital syndrome may have been the result of cortisone (a drug that can cause hyperactive behavior in adults) given these girls by their physicians, or it may have been the result of the expectation of parents and friends that they will be more masculine than other girls (at birth their genital organs may appear to be those of a male).[5]

Other researchers have sought to demonstrate a causal link between high levels of the male hormone testosterone and aggressive behavior in adult men, but such studies have produced mixed results. Some have shown a significant relationship between high levels of testosterone and aggression and hostility, but most have not. Even if a correlation between the two were clearly established, however, it would not prove that the hormone causes aggression. Numerous studies have indicated that testosterone levels are strongly affected by an individual's environment and emotional state. For example, researchers have found that a man's testosterone level goes up after he wins a tennis match and goes down after he loses one. Moreover, the practice of castrating prisoners or giving them drugs that neutralize male hormones has proved to have little effect in preventing violence.[6]

One of the most recent areas of interest is the difference in structure in female and male brains. Although there is a slight difference in average brain size and weight, most of the attention has focused on a difference in neural pathways originally discovered by two anthropologists who conducted autopsies on 14 human brains.[7] What they found was that a portion of the corpus callosum that connects the two hemispheres of the brain is, on the average, larger in women's brains than in men's brains. Although some scientists have used this structural difference to explain various differences in behavior between the sexes, at this point there is not enough evidence to say what, if any, impact differences in brain structure may have on actual behavior.

If gender roles are determined solely by biology, it is logical to assume that they should be the same in all cultures. Researchers agree that some degree of male dominance is a characteristic of most known societies.[8] Anthropological studies have shown, however, that there are enormous differences in the gender roles of different cultures, and historians have found that gender roles change within the same culture over time. For example, in many foraging societies (small societies in which people make their livings by foraging from the land), both men and women are peaceful and cooperative. In other societies, such as the Mundugumor of New Guinea, both men and women are highly aggressive and competitive.[9] Further evidence against the biological determination of gender comes from the study of people who have been raised as members of the opposite sex. This usually occurs because of a physical abnormality of the genitals, but it occasionally happens for other reasons as well. The general conclusion from this research is that a woman raised as a man will act like a man and that a man raised as a woman will act like a woman.[10] In other words, people act the way they are taught to act; their behavior is not predetermined by a biological program.

Two conclusions seem justified from the evidence. First, gender roles themselves are social creations. The gender roles we learn are determined by society, not by biology. Second, the gender roles that society creates are nonetheless strongly influenced by biological considerations. Men tend to be stronger and larger than women, and only women can bear and nurse children, so it is not surprising that men are assigned more activities that involve strength and travel or that women are more concerned with child rearing and the responsibilities of the home. The typical pattern of male dominance can be seen as a result of the greater physical strength of the male. The typical "family-oriented" female pattern can be seen as a consequence of childbearing and breast-feeding. As we will see in the next section, however, the influence of these biological considerations has been greatly diminished in modern industrial societies.

The Historical Development of Gender Roles

Throughout human history, the roles of women and men have been shaped by the demands of their environment and their economic system. In the earliest societies, people lived in nomadic bands and got their food by gathering edible plants and by hunting animals. Judging by the foraging societies that still survive today, it appears that these early human cultures were highly egalitarian, with few fixed distinctions of status or wealth. Leaders would emerge in response to specific problems and then be absorbed back into the groups when the problems were solved. The economic contribution of both men, who did most of the hunting, and women, who fo-

*There are wide variations in gender roles among the various cultures of the world.
Foraging societies, such as the one pictured here, generally have egalitarian
relationships between the sexes.*

cused more on gathering and child care, were essential to the survival of the group.
Although some anthropologists feel that men's monopoly on the hunting of large animals gave them a source of prestige not available to women,[11] others hold that
women provided other services of equal social value.[12] Despite such disputes, anthropologists generally agree that the relationships between the sexes, like other relationships in foraging societies, tend to be egalitarian.

A major change in human society occurred with the discovery that plants could
be grown specifically for human use. In the earliest farming societies, women and
men often shared the work of cultivating the fields, while women did most of the
child rearing and men fought the wars (foragers generally do not engage in warfare). As farming technology was improved by irrigation and the use of the plow,
men's responsibility for agricultural labor increased, and the status of women generally declined. The growth of the state further strengthened male dominance as men
came to monopolize government and religious bureaucracies.[13]

The industrial revolution once again brought profound changes in human society and in the relationship between the genders. The ideal of the large extended
family declined, and the nuclear family became the norm (see Chapter 2). Economic changes that made children a financial burden instead of an asset led to lower
birthrates and a smaller number of children. Industrialization reduced the importance of physical labor, and women joined the work force in increasing numbers.

This transformation of the family and the economic system had a significant impact on gender roles. Technological and social development sharply reduces the importance of the biological differences between the sexes; therefore, gender roles

change as societies industrialize. The male's greater size and strength mean much less in an age of machines and automation. The qualities necessary for economic success are now related more closely to personality and intelligence than to physique and are possessed equally by women and men. At the same time, birth control, smaller families, bottle feeding for babies, and the great increase in life span mean that child rearing no longer takes up most of a woman's adult life. Though there have been significant improvements in the status of women in industrial societies, cultural change lags behind technological change. The ideal of equality between men and women has gained increasing acceptance in the industrialized nations, yet the realities of women's lives still often include subordination and oppression.

Gender Socialization

gender socialization

The process by which a person learns the behaviors and attitudes that are expected of his or her gender.

sexual stereotyping

The portrayal of all females or males as having similar fixed traits.

Socialization is the process by which we learn the essentials of life in our culture. Customs, behavior, mores, values, how to speak, even how to think—all these are learned in the course of socialization. **Gender socialization** is part of this process. It is the way we learn the behavior and attitudes that are expected of the members of our sex. **Sexual stereotyping** starts almost from the moment of birth, when boys are wrapped in blue blankets and girls in pink ones. Girls' and boys' bedrooms are often decorated differently and contain different kinds of toys. Researchers have found that boys are given a wider variety of toys than girls and that boys' toys are more likely to encourage activities outside the home.[14] The most important differences, however, are learned as children begin to master a language. For one thing, most languages require the speaker to make frequent distinctions between the sexes. The use of the words *he* and *his* or *she* and *hers* continually draws the child's attention to the importance of gender differences. In addition, the structure of languages conveys social assumptions about the nature of the differences between the sexes. The English-speaking child quickly learns that the male is given first-class status, while the female takes second place. For example, masculine pronouns and adjectives are traditionally used to describe people whose gender is unknown ("No person shall be compelled in any criminal case to be a witness against himself"). The term *man* or *mankind* is often used to refer to the entire human race. The male is primary in our language, the female a vaguely defined "other."[15]

homophobia

The fear of homosexuality.

As children get older, the different expectations for boys and girls become even more obvious. The male role is more narrowly defined, and young boys come under intense pressure not to be "sissies" and not to "act like a girl." A boy who playfully puts on a dress and lipstick is likely to receive a hostile and even panicky reprimand from his parents. One root of these attitudes is the deep-seated **homophobia** (fear of homosexuality) in Western culture; another is the general devaluation of women's roles. Some argue that the training boys receive to repress their feelings of love for other males eventually leads to a repression of all emotional expression, and there is little doubt that most boys learn at an early age to reject and even fear the feminine.[16] With the coming of adolescence, however, it is girls who find their lives increasingly restricted by the demands of their gender role. While boys are allowed and even encouraged to "sow some wild oats," girls are usually denied such freedom. Not only are girls far more closely watched, but they quickly learn that appearing too assertive is believed to make them less attractive to the opposite sex and threaten their prospects for marriage and a traditional family life.

From their earliest years, girls are taught the vital importance of personal relationships, and they are encouraged to develop the traits that promote them: empathy, expressiveness, and sensitivity to others. Boys, on the other hand, are urged to be self-reliant, assertive, and achievement-oriented. The results of this differential socialization are reflected in the relationships that girls and boys create. Girls tend to have fewer, more intense friendships, whereas boys form larger, less intimate groups.[17]

Boys generally have more trouble adjusting to school than girls. Boys mature more slowly, so they are often less able to live up to the expectations of the school than girls of the same age. Since boys are given more encouragement to be independent and assertive, they also tend to find the docile, cooperative behavior expected of schoolchildren far more frustrating. As a result, boys are more likely to get into trouble in school.[18] Perhaps for this reason, studies of teacher-student interaction have found that boys get more attention, both positive and negative, than girls. As Myra Sadker and her associates put it, "Boys are the central figures . . . and girls are relegated to second-class participation."[19]

Research shows that teachers' expectations have a powerful influence on the way students perform in the classroom (see Chapter 3). This fact creates a serious problem for girls because most teachers accept the gender stereotypes so common in our society. Teachers expect a good male student to be active, adventurous, and inventive, whereas they expect a good female student to be calm, conscientious, and

Gender role socialization begins almost from the moment of birth. As children grow older, boys are encouraged to develop "masculine" attributes while girls are taught "feminine" qualities. By the time most people reach adulthood, gender role socialization has produced significant differences between women and men.

sensitive.[20] Several studies have concluded that teachers pose more academically challenging questions to boys, are more likely to praise them for the intellectual quality of their work, and are more likely to encourage their classroom participation.[21] Researchers have found that the content of books and classroom materials has improved considerably in the use of gender-neutral language and in the inclusion of more female characters, but boys are still more likely to be given the active, adventurous roles.[22]

The mass media also have a profound effect on the definition of our gender roles. Many studies show that television, motion pictures, radio, books, and magazines all tend to reinforce gender stereotypes. Children's television programs, which are particularly important in the early socialization process, reflect the same stereotyped attitudes. Male characters are shown in such active and prestigious occupations as physicians, lawyers, and police officers, while women are more likely to be relegated to secondary roles such as mother, secretary, or helper. Commercials also reflect these biases. J. H. Feldstein and S. Feldstein found that boys are overrepresented in advertisements for every type of toy except dolls and that the girls who are shown are far more likely to be given only passive roles.[23] Even children's cartoons are stereotyped. One study found that male cartoon characters outnumbered female characters by three to one;[24] but beyond simply showing more males, the cartoons depict males as being more powerful and having a greater impact on their environment than females do.[25]

Of course, sexist stereotypes are not limited to children's television. The advertising aimed at adult audiences reveals the same bias. Women are used to attract attention to the sales pitch—perhaps wearing a bikini while sipping a drink, wearing a silk gown while slithering into a sports car, or staring seductively at a man who uses the right brand of shaving cream. The prime concern of the "good housewife" is the whiteness of her wash and whether she can see her face reflected in her dinner plates. In contrast, male voices are often used to convey authority and importance.[26]

The same stereotypes are found in prime-time entertainment as well. Despite an increasing number of well-placed female characters, a long-term study by the Annenberg School of Communications found that women are still greatly underrepresented on television.[27] On the average, the characters played by women are younger and therefore less authoritative than male characters.[28] Research shows that in addition to being young, female characters are disproportionately likely to be thin, attractive, and blonde. One study found that women on television were twice as likely to be blonde as the average American woman.[29]

Music videos, which have become so popular in recent years, are a new subject of research interest. In the mid-1980s, researchers agreed that music videos reflected the "chauvinism of rock culture."[30] Women were shown primarily as sex objects—often scantily dressed and acting provocatively. The videos were also full of violence, usually by men against other men. One break from the usual stereotypes was that when women were involved in violence, they were more often shown as the aggressors than the victims. Nonetheless, the overwhelming message was that women are sexual objects, not complete human beings. The recent popularity of a new style of band with strong, independent female members has led to a new approach in music videos as well. Although still containing a heavy sexual content, this alternative style shows women controlling their lives and sexuality and depicts women's experiences in a more positive light.[31] The alternative video remains just that, however, and most videos continue to focus on women as sex objects. It seems clear that despite some serious efforts at reform, the media—children's programs, prime-time entertainment, movies, and music videos—still play a powerful role in socializing both women and men into traditional gender role expectations.

Quick Review

What are gender roles?

What part do biology and learning play in creating our gender roles?

How do gender roles differ in different types of societies?

What forces shape gender socialization?

Gender Inequality

In Western society, traditional male and female roles are not only substantially different but also highly unequal. As we have seen, the male is given the dominant position. In a sense he is the star actor, whereas the female often plays only a supporting role. The male is expected to have superior strength, greater stamina, higher intelligence, and better organizing ability. Psychologically, the male is trained to play the role of decision maker, whereas the female is encouraged to be submissive and obedient. This same gender inequality is reflected in our basic institutions. In education, employment, and politics, women clearly are treated as inferiors. They are victims of sexism (sexual stereotyping, prejudice, and discrimination) in much the same way as African Americans are victims of racism.

Education

In the past, women faced open discrimination in almost every aspect of our educational system. Far more boys than girls were enrolled in primary and secondary schools, and most of the best colleges did not admit women at all. Changing cultural expectations and new antidiscrimination laws broke down most of these barriers, and great progress has been made. Today, more females than males graduate from high school and from college.

Yet men still retain some important educational advantages. For one thing, men receive 60 percent of professional degrees and doctorates.[32] There are also important differences in the majors women and men pursue. More women major in the liberal arts and humanities, while more men major in such fields as science, mathematics, and engineering, which are most likely to lead directly to high-paying careers. Although the reasons for these differences are not entirely clear, several factors appear to be important. It seems that traditional gender role stereotypes no longer stop females from pursuing an education, but women are discouraged from going into academic areas that are overwhelmingly dominated by males. For example, one recent study shows that the lack of female role models among faculty members in mathematics, science, and engineering subtly conveys the message to young women that those fields are not for them.[33] Women's preference for a more general liberal education may also reflect the fact that because women expect to carry more child-rearing responsibilities than their male counterparts, they may shy away from majors leading to demanding careers that would interfere with those responsibilities (see Chapter 3).

Employment

Women's role in the work force has undergone a remarkable change. Sixty years ago, fewer than one-fourth of all adult women in the United States worked outside the home. Today, that figure has almost tripled, and the number of working women continues to increase.[34] In the next decade, 6 of every 10 new workers in the United States will be women, and a similar trend is evident in Canada, where 44 percent of all workers are now women. Both countries are behind such European nations as Denmark, Finland, and Sweden.[35]

Although the gap between men's and women's pay has narrowed in recent years, it is still large (see Figure 10.1). In 1975, women earned only about 60 percent as much as men, but by 1995, that figure was around 75 percent.[36] Unfortunately, the gap has closed mainly because of a decline in men's earnings rather than an increase in women's pay. An analysis by the Economic Policy Institute concluded that about two-thirds of that improvement was caused by a drop in men's wages and only one-third by rising women's wages.[37]

Many women receive smaller paychecks than men because women enter lower-paying occupations and hold lower-ranking jobs within their fields. Yet there are substantial differences in pay even among men and women who do the same type of work. Women in sales earn only 58 percent as much as salesmen, and women professionals earn about 70 percent as much as their male counterparts.[38] A *Business*

Figure 10.1

Income

Working women still earn significantly less than men.

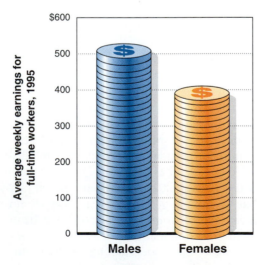

Source: U.S. Bureau of the Census, *Statistical Abstract of the United States, 1996* (Washington, DC: U.S. Government Printing Office, 1996), p. 426.

Week survey found that among graduates of the best MBA programs in the United States, the starting salaries of men are 12 percent higher than the starting salaries of women.[39] Even when workers break out of the traditional occupational stereotypes, women still come up short. Although 94 percent of all registered nurses are female, male nurses earn about 10 percent more than their female co-workers. Women who cross the gender barrier to join the building trades, on the other hand, earn about 25 percent less than male construction workers.[40]

Employers traditionally justified this inequality by claiming that men need higher pay because they must support their families and that women just work for "extra" money. Few employers openly use such rationalizations anymore, but they nonetheless persist in paying women lower wages. Some economists explain this income gap by pointing out that the average male worker has more years of experience than his female counterpart. Others argue that women are more likely to put the demands of their families ahead of their jobs. A *Time* magazine poll, for example, found that a happy marriage was the single most important goal for most young women, while young men rated career success as their number one objective.[41] Although such factors are significant, sexism and discrimination are still of central importance as causes of the income gap. Employers pay women less for the same work because they can get away with it: they know that the prevailing wages are lower for women and that their female workers probably cannot get other jobs at "men's wages."

Many occupations are clearly "sex-typed"; that is, they are considered either men's jobs or women's jobs. About 55 percent of all university faculty are men, as are 86 percent of police officers and 92 percent of engineers. In contrast, 75 percent of primary and secondary teachers, 83 percent of librarians, and 98 percent of all secretaries are women.[42] "Women's jobs" almost always have lower pay and lower status than comparable "men's" positions. The nurse (usually female) is subordinate to the doctor (usually male), just as the secretary (usually female) is subordinate to the executive (usually male). Jobs that are relatively autonomous are usually typed as male, as in the case of truck drivers or traveling sales personnel.

"Women's jobs" also offer less chance for advancement (see Figure 10.2). The secretary seldom becomes a top executive or the nurse a doctor. Although there are now far more women in middle management, they remain more likely to be in dead-end positions (such as administering affirmative action programs or supervising the hiring process) than in the production and financial posts that lead to the top corporate jobs. After years of progress at other levels, women still hold only 2 percent of top corporate positions in the United States[43] and 6 percent of the seats on corporate boards of directors.[44] Many successful women complain about an invisible "glass ceiling"—a kind of unseen barrier that seems to block them from rising to the top levels of power. A survey of female attorneys in the Los Angeles area, for example, found that 60 percent felt they received less desirable case assignments than their male colleagues, and 75 percent felt they were held to a higher standard than the men.[45]

There are, nonetheless, some hopeful signs. There has been a slow but steady decrease in occupational segregation since the 1960s, and many women have managed to breach the walls that kept them out of better-paying "men's jobs." In 1960, only about 6.5 percent of U.S. physicians were women; today, it is almost a quarter. Women have made similar strides in the legal profession: in 1960, fewer than 1 in 20 lawyers and judges was a woman, but today, the ratio is more than 1 in 4.[46]

Figure 10.2

Work

Although the percentage of women in the professions has been increasing, most female workers are still concentrated in the lower-paying, less prestigious jobs.

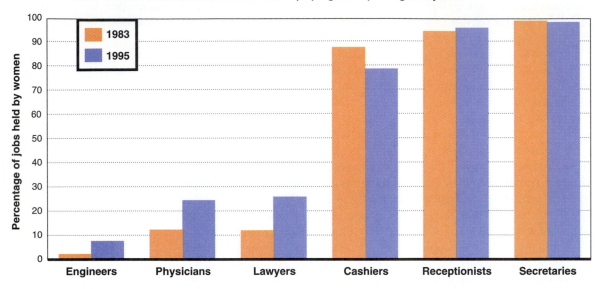

Source: U.S. Bureau of the Census, *Statistical Abstract of the United States, 1996* (Washington, DC: U.S. Government Printing Office, 1996), pp. 405–407.

Political Power

Politics has traditionally been considered a man's business. Women were not even allowed to vote in most democracies until this century. The few women who have gained top positions of power have often had the benefit of family connections to overcome objections to their sex: Pakistan's Benazir Bhutto, Sri Lanka's Chandrika Kumaratunga, and the hereditary European monarchs such as Britain's Queen Elizabeth II are good examples. The United States has never had a female head of state, and Canada's only woman prime minister, Kim Campbell, held that office for only about six months.

In 1997, only about 10 percent of the members of the U.S. Congress were women, while women's representation in the Canadian parliament was only slightly better.[47] No woman has ever held a key position of power in the U.S. Congress, such as majority leader or speaker of the House, and women are still largely locked out of the inner circles of power in the White House—including, of course, the presidency itself. In the judicial branch, only two women in the history of the United States have ever been on the Supreme Court. Moreover, the story is much the same in other democratic nations. Women have the greatest representation in the Scandinavian countries and the lowest in Great Britain, the United States, and Japan, but they are greatly underrepresented in the legislative bodies of all the industrialized

Figure 10.3

Lawmakers

Although the number of women lawmakers varies from year to year, the United States has never been among the leaders.

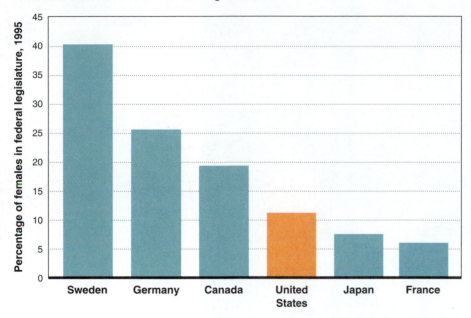

Source: United Nations Human Development Programme, *Human Development Report, 1997* (New York: Oxford University Press, 1997), p. 152.

nations (see Figure 10.3). Things are somewhat better in America's state legislatures, where women make up about 22 percent of the members.[48]

Women nevertheless have enormous political potential. Most of the volunteer workers essential to political campaigns are women. Even more significant is the fact that women outnumber men and could outvote them if they voted as a block. Until recently, women voted much as their husbands did, but in the last decade, a significant "gender gap" between the voting patterns of men and women has developed. Polls show that women look more favorably on welfare programs and environmental protection and are more likely to oppose military spending and an aggressive foreign policy. In the last three presidential elections, substantially more women than men voted for the Democratic candidate. So far, the gender gap has not been a decisive factor in U.S. politics, but the potential is certainly there.

Social Life

Sexism in education, employment, and politics is obvious to anyone who cares to look. But women are also victims of less conspicuous forms of discrimination that are woven into the fabric of our daily lives.

In the entire history of the United States, only two women have ever sat on the Supreme Court, and no woman has been president or vice president.

The Devaluation of Women Women in our society are told in countless subtle ways that they are second-class citizens. Women are taught from childhood that beauty and sex appeal are the keys to happiness. Success comes not from their own efforts but from the ability to appeal to the right man. Women are more likely to be admired as the wives and mothers of important people than as significant individuals in their own right.

Women are routinely expected to repress their desires and ambitions in ways that are seldom demanded of men. Studies of dual-earner families (in which both husband and wife work) reveal that it is usually the wife who must sacrifice her career if it interferes with that of her spouse. The working woman is also expected to carry more of the homemaking and child-rearing responsibilities in addition to her job (see Chapter 5).

Women are expected to repress their sexuality just as they are expected to repress their career ambitions. During the Victorian era, women's sexuality was almost entirely denied. Women were expected to keep themselves covered from their feet to their necks in what were often highly uncomfortable clothes. The "good" woman would never mention sex, and in fact, she was not even expected to enjoy it, but merely to put up with it for her husband's sake. Recent research shows that although the **double standard** for sexual behavior has weakened in recent years, it is still very much with us. Young men are expected to gain sexual experience before marriage, but women who do the same thing are condemned as "sluts." And those who berate an unfaithful wife often condone a husband's infidelities with a wink (see Chapter 11).

double standard
A set of norms requiring different behavior for women and men, especially in regard to sexual activity.

Language and Communication Until a few decades ago, no one seemed to pay much attention to the obvious inequity of calling the human race "mankind" or always using the masculine pronoun to refer to someone whose gender they did not know. Since then, feminists have made considerable progress in changing some of the most blatant linguistic inequalities. The use of gender-neutral terms such as *police officer, humankind,* and *spokesperson* has become far more common, and books are now more likely to use both masculine and feminine pronouns together. Nonetheless, our language continues to reflect (and thereby reinforce) the sexual inequalities of our society. Words associated with men tend to take on connotations of strength and power, while words associated with women are more likely to be linked with sex or family. Consider, for example, the difference between having a mistress and having a master or the difference between a governess and a governor.

More important than the words themselves, however, is the way they are used, and research on our patterns of communication reveals some striking gender differences. Studies of conversations between women and men reveal a clear pattern of male dominance. Men do more of the talking and interrupt women more often, and they are more likely to be successful in focusing the conversation on the topics they introduce.[49] Deborah Tannen argues that men and women also have different styles of communication and different objectives.[50] Women's conversations tend to have a more cooperative, social character, while men are likely to be more competitive and individualistic. According to Tannen, men seek to dominate, while women seek to connect—a fact that she sees as underlying much of the misunderstanding between the genders.

Research shows that these same gender differences are also reflected in nonverbal communications. A man is more likely to invade a woman's personal space by touching her and standing close than the other way around. A man is more likely to stare at a woman, while the woman's response is often to avert her eyes. Research shows that, whether stared at or not, women smile at others more often than men.[51]

Sexual Harassment The entry of women into the work force in ever greater numbers has focused attention on another kind of problem—**sexual harassment** (see the Personal Perspectives box, "A Victim of Sexual Harassment," for a famous example of this problem). Since 1975, when the term was first used, a flood of complaints has come in from women who were the victims of unwanted sexual pressures at work.[52] A survey of 13,000 federal employees found that 42 percent of the women reported experiencing some kind of sexual harassment on the job.[53] Even women in top executive jobs are not immune: one survey of women executives, whose salaries averaged almost $200,000 a year, found that 58 percent had faced sexual harassment on the job.[54] Sexual harassment has also become a major issue on campus; a growing

sexual harassment
Unwanted sexual comments, gestures, or physical advances, especially in the workplace.

Personal Perspectives   A Victim of Sexual Harassment

One famous case of sexual harassment involves charges brought by Anita Hill against her former boss, Judge Clarence Thomas, during the Senate hearings on his nomination to the Supreme Court. Judge Thomas denied Hill's charges and eventually won confirmation by the Senate. The following excerpts come from Hill's sworn testimony before the Senate.

I declined the invitation to go out socially with him, and explained to him that I thought it would jeopardize what at the time I considered to be a very good working relationship. I had a normal social life with other men outside the office. I believed then, as now, that having a social relationship with a person who was supervising my work would be ill advised. I was very uncomfortable with the idea and told him so.

I thought that by saying "no" and explaining my reasons, my employer would abandon his social suggestions. However, to my regret, in the following few weeks he continued to ask me out on several occasions. He pressed me to justify my reasons for saying "no" to him. . . .

My working relationship became even more strained when Judge Thomas began to use work situations to discuss sex. On these occasions, he would call me into his office for reports on education issues and projects or he might suggest that because of the time pressures of his schedule, we go to lunch to a government cafeteria. After a brief discussion of work, he would turn the conversation to a discussion of sexual matters. His conversations were very vivid.

He spoke about acts that he had seen in pornographic films involving such matters as women having sex with animals, and films showing group sex or rape scenes. He talked about pornographic materials depicting individuals with large penises, or large breasts involved in various sex acts.

On several occasions Thomas told me graphically of his own sexual prowess. Because I was extremely uncomfortable talking about sex with him at all, and particularly in such a graphic way, I told him that I did not want to talk about these subjects. I would also try to change the subject to education matters or to nonsexual personal matters, such as his background or his beliefs. My efforts to change the subject were rarely successful.*

*Hearings Before the Committee on the Judiciary, United States Senate, October 11, 12, and 13, 1991, p. 37.

number of students who have been the victims of unwanted sexual advances are recognizing their right to stand up and protest.[55]

Although definitions of sexual harassment vary, it includes everything from unwanted sexual comments and gestures to direct physical assaults. There are two generally recognized types of sexual harassment. The first, which lawyers term *quid pro quo harassment,* includes sexual comments and advances aimed directly at a particular individual. This kind of harassment involves an implicit or explicit threat, such as loss of a job, or a reward, such as a better grade, if the victim goes along. Obviously, a woman whose boss makes sexual advances is in a very difficult position. She must often choose between a physical relationship she does not want and a job she cannot afford to lose. The second type of sexual harassment is known as *hostile environment harassment.* This offense involves unwelcome sexual comments, gestures, explicit photographs, and other things that create an offensive or intimidating environment for female employees. This kind of harassment may be unintentional, or it may be part of an explicit effort by male employees to drive women out of jobs that they consider to be men's work.

Men's Problems

Women are not alone in suffering from gender stereotypes. Although the male role often has higher status, it is also more narrow and restrictive, and many men find the demand to repress natural "feminine" behavior a heavy burden. While women frequently complain about being only sex objects in the eyes of men, an increasing number of men are complaining that they are only "success objects" for women. Three-fourths of the young women, but only one-fourth of the young men, polled by *Time* magazine said that a well-paying job was an essential requirement for a spouse.[56] Obviously, three-fourths of all men do not have well-paying jobs. In fact, the income of the average man has dropped significantly in recent years, and the income of young men has been declining faster than that of any other group in our society. Since 1979, the median wage for women increased by about $0.35 an hour (after controlling for inflation), while the average wage for men declined about $2.00 an hour.[57] Of course, men's incomes are still higher on the average, but these changes have placed enormous psychological pressure on many men that is not felt by women. Success as a man has traditionally been defined by the ability to "bring home the bacon." The erosion of their incomes and their growing dependence on their wives' earnings to help make ends meet are therefore a serious blow to the self-esteem of many men. Not surprisingly, the suicide rate among men has shown a steady increase, and men are now more than four times more likely than women to commit suicide.[58]

Another common complaint among men is that although they are being encouraged to take a greater role in child rearing, the deck is still stacked against them when it comes to child custody after a divorce. When both parents seek custody, many courts assume that the mother will make the better parent. Yet although the mother is usually given custody of the children, the father still has to pay to support them and is given only limited visitation rights. The average divorced man in the United States is able to spend only two days a month with his children.[59] In addition, when the separation is a bitter one, many husbands complain that their wives have tried to turn their children against them.

Signs of Hope   Men Are Getting More Involved with Their Kids

Feminists have long urged men to get more involved in raising their children, and there is statistical evidence that it is finally starting to happen. One study found a sharp increase in the percentage of fathers who take care of preschoolers while their mothers are at work. Although that percentage had remained fairly steady for over a decade, it jumped from 15 to 20 percent between 1988 and 1991.* Another indication that men are taking on greater child-rearing responsibility is the increasing number of single-parent families that are headed by men. In 1980, about 10 percent of single-parent families were headed by a man, but by 1995, about 17 percent were.†

*Susan Chira, "Census Data Show Rise in Child Care by Fathers," *New York Times,* September 22, 1993.

†U.S. Bureau of the Census, *Statistical Abstract of the United States, 1996* (Washington DC: U.S. Government Printing Office, 1996), p. 63.

Finally, there are the increasingly negative stereotypes of men that have become a staple of the contemporary media. A study of 1000 television commercials in which there was a negative portrayal of one side of a male-female interaction found that the male was cast as the "bad guy" in every case.[60] Today's media repeatedly stereotype men either as violent, sexually aggressive, and emotionally distant or as fumbling nerds who are good for a laugh but not much else.

Quick Review

How does our educational system discriminate against women?

Why do women receive lower pay and hold fewer political offices than men?

What kinds of sexism do women face in social life?

What problems do contemporary gender roles create for men?

Solving the Problems of Gender Inequality

Like other social problems, an effective response to the problems of gender inequality must have many dimensions. On one level, we need to develop an understanding of the problems involved, and then we have to decide what needs to be done to improve things. But that is of little use unless we also join together and take political action to achieve those ends. Thus, sociological analysis and social action are intimately related. Effective social action must be based on an understanding of the problem at hand, and the results of that action in turn provide information we can use to reformulate our plans and improve our understanding.

Political Activism

The problem of gender inequality has been the subject of intense debate in recent decades, but to understand the current controversy, we need to understand the history of the political struggles that created it. The beginnings of the women's movement in North America are usually traced to the nineteenth century and the drive to free the slaves. Many women who were involved in the abolitionist movement came to realize that they too were part of an oppressed group. These early feminists made wide-ranging demands for sexual equality, but the movement they created eventually came to focus on a single issue: women's right to vote. After years of struggle, these "suffragettes" built themselves into a powerful political force and won their battle for the vote; but after that success, the women's movement began to fade. It was not until the 1960s, when the civil rights movement was once again calling attention to the racial injustices of North American society, that the feminist movement was reborn.

The modern feminist movement has scored some remarkable successes. Women's liberation and sexual equality are now widely discussed, and more and more women are entering occupations that were formerly closed to them. Through effective court and legislative action, feminists have successfully attacked employment and promotion practices that discriminate against women. Government-

The feminist movement has a long history in North America, dating back to the struggle for women's suffrage (the right to vote). Today's feminists are seeking complete equality between the sexes.

sponsored affirmative action programs now require employers to hire and promote more women and members of minority groups, and the overall gap between men's and women's pay is declining. Feminists have even made some inroads on the sexual biases built into the English language. Women now often identify themselves as *Ms.* rather than *Miss* or *Mrs.*, and new sexually neutral words such as *chairperson* and *humankind* are replacing the traditional masculine terms. As we have seen in this chapter, however, we are still a very long way from full equality. The victories of the past have been won against the most obvious and direct forms of discrimination, and feminists must now face much more subtle forms of bias.

Although still much smaller and weaker, there is also a growing "men's movement" that has its own critique of today's gender problems. In general, the men's movement is sympathetic to the feminist perspective and its call to redefine gender relations. Advocates of the men's movement argue that current gender roles are just as harmful to men as they are to women, but in different ways. They particularly object to the ideal of masculinity that holds that "real" men must always be strong, self-controlled, and successful. The effort to live up to this impossible ideal (or at least to appear to live up to it) leaves many men feeling anxiety-ridden and isolated. However, the men's movement does voice one major criticism of the feminists— what they see as their tendency toward "man bashing." That is, some supporters of the men's movement feel that feminists perpetuate negative stereotypes of men and blame men for problems that are actually created by historical forces beyond the control of any person or group.

Debate Should We Crack Down on Sexual Harassment?

Yes

The problem of sexual harassment has reached crisis proportions, and we must take action before things get even worse. Sexual harassment is more than just the demeaning comments, the leering stares, and the snide remarks—although those are certainly bad enough. Every day countless women are pressured by their bosses, their male colleagues, or their teachers to engage in a sexual relationship against their will. Nobody knows how many women succumb to this pressure, but we do know the horrible consequences: anxiety, depression, fear, and plummeting self-esteem. Those women who hold out may not suffer as much psychological damage, but many pay for their integrity with the loss of a job or some other serious punishment.

Some claim that sexual harassment is inevitable in any society that allows free individuals to guide their own sexual behavior, but in fact just the opposite is true. Allowing people the freedom to make their own choices about their sexual behavior *requires* that we take strong action to end sexual harassment and coercion. Our society can never be free until women are free from this kind of degrading assault. We must end sexual harassment now, and only strong new laws and tough enforcement that treats the offenders like common criminals can do the job.

No

All the talk about sexual harassment is just the latest media fad. Of course, men sometimes say or do things that offend women, and women sometimes offend men. The fact of the matter is that in dating and sexual relationships, people inevitably have different goals, objectives, and dreams. Sometimes we experience unwanted sexual advances, and other times our own advances are rebuffed. Short of separating the genders from all public contact and going back to arranged marriages, there is simply nothing we can do about it.

Of course, the government has a critical role to play in punishing rapists and other sex offenders, but it has already gone too far in trying to legislate away "sexual harassment." The current maze of rule and regulations in the workplace has already created an atmosphere of fear and suspicion. Male and female co-workers are often afraid to make a joke or to give a compliment or even a pat on the back. After all, how can one ever be sure that a friendly gesture won't be interpreted as an unwelcome sexual advance? One third grader was even suspended from school for giving an innocent kiss to a classmate! The government has a vital role to play in many social problems, but when it intrudes into the most personal and private part of our lives, it is time to draw the line. Do we want to live in a free and open society or in a police state?

Fighting Gender Discrimination

Proposals for eliminating obvious discrimination often win wide support. Few people openly approve of such practices as paying women less money than men for the same work, refusing to grant them financial credit, or denying them jobs and promotions simply because they are women. The values of democratic society make it very hard to justify such practices, and many of the feminists' most important victories have been against this kind of discrimination.

As the most obvious forms of sexism are eliminated, however, the movement for social change must challenge more entrenched institutional structures, and further progress becomes increasingly difficult. For example, the law has long required employers to pay men and women the same wage for the same work, yet it remains perfectly legal to pay secretaries, nurses, and others in "women's jobs" far less than comparable jobs that are filled mainly by men. Proposals to require comparable pay for comparable work have run into fierce opposition because they threaten the interests of businesses that benefit from the low cost of women's labor. Although affirmative action programs, which force employers to take positive action to compensate for past injustices, have done much to combat gender discrimination in the last three decades, they too are meeting with increasing political opposition (see Chapter 8). There are, nonetheless, several other useful ideas that have a wide base of support. Proposals to give tougher sentences to rapists and other sex offenders are extremely popular with the voting public, and the last two decades have already seen some significant increases in the average terms served by such offenders. The public is also far more aware of the physical abuse many women suffer from their spouses and boyfriends, and as public attitudes have changed, the approaches and priorities of the criminal justice system have shown some significant improvements. Much more, however, remains to be done (see Chapter 13).

In today's political climate, women's greatest ally in the fight against gender discrimination is probably their own success. So many women hold key corporate and government positions that it is getting harder to practice the open discrimination that was the norm only a few decades ago. Many women are now banding together to form "old girls' networks" that in some cases rival or even surpass the "old boys' networks" from which women were traditionally excluded.

Changing Gender Roles

Many feminists feel that despite its importance, fighting discrimination simply isn't enough to create real gender equality. As long as women and girls are socialized to be more supportive and compliant than men, they are likely to remain in a subordinate position with or without gender discrimination. Yet proposals for restructuring gender roles have run into far greater opposition than those aimed at overt discrimination. Our attitudes and expectations about gender are formed early in life, and many people feel threatened when such basic assumptions are challenged. Many of the most vicious attacks on feminism can be seen as a response to this kind of insecurity. Despite the fear and hostility produced by rapid change, gender roles in industrial societies are nonetheless undergoing a revolutionary transformation.

The attitudes and assumptions parents bring with them into the family are one of the greatest forces shaping our gender role expectations, but social institutions such as the schools and the media also play a critical role, and they are much more subject to social pressure. Although both institutions have made great strides in presenting powerful role models for women and girls, many of the old stereotypes still remain side by side with those new images. Stronger efforts to eliminate sexism in those two social institutions are therefore critical to future success.

While it is impossible to say what roles will finally develop, there is no reason to suppose that sexual equality would mean that men and women would become socially identical. Some of the differences in behavior between men and women already have diminished, but the development of a "unisex" remains a prospect for the distant future, if at all. What does seem possible, perhaps even likely, is a further weakening of the rigid gender role expectations of the past, allowing both women and men to act in ways that suit them as individuals instead of compelling them to conform to the stereotyped expectations for their genders.

Quick Review

What are the best ways of responding to the problems of gender inequality?

Sociological Perspectives on Problems of Gender

Every society assigns different roles to women and to men. In the past, these social arrangements were usually accepted as the will of God or an inevitable result of biological differences, but such justifications are no longer as convincing as they once were, and there is a significant gap between the ideal of equality and the reality of male domination over females. The major sociological theories provide us with different perspectives on why this gap exists and what should be done about it.

The Functionalist Perspective

Functionalists say that the problems with contemporary gender roles stem directly from the historical changes discussed earlier in this chapter. Traditionally, gender roles were based on biological differences between the sexes: women were concerned primarily with child rearing and men with providing economic support. The changes brought on by the industrial revolution threw this arrangement out of balance, however. The decline in infant mortality and the spread of effective methods of birth control made it possible to depart from traditional roles. It was no longer necessary for women to devote most of their adult lives to the raising of children, and automation wiped out the importance of the male's greater strength for most types of work. However, attitudes and expectations about the proper role of women have changed much more slowly than social and economic conditions. This cultural lag is therefore the principal source of today's problems.

To resolve such difficulties, most functionalists suggest that expectations be made to conform more closely to actual conditions. Some advocate a return to the stable past, believing that too great a shift toward sexual equality is dysfunctional.

They argue that the traditional division of labor between men and women was highly efficient, enabling society to train people for specialized roles that meshed together in stable families. Other functionalists, however, advocate a redefinition of gender roles to bring them into line with current social conditions. Although these functionalists do not all agree on the exact form the proposed changes should take, they do generally accept the need for a shift toward full sexual equality and a reconstruction of women's roles to encourage economic competition and achievement. Along with this change, basic institutions would also have to be modified to eliminate sexual discrimination. The current family system, for example, would have to undergo extensive changes to accommodate new roles for both women and men.

The Conflict Perspective

Prejudice and discrimination against women come as no surprise to conflict theorists, since they see exploitation and oppression as universal human problems. Conflict theorists say that men first used their greater size and strength to force women into a subordinate position. Then, like any other dominant group, men created institutions that served to perpetuate their power and authority. Men gain economic advantages by paying women low wages and excluding them from positions of economic control and political power. Men also benefit from women's subordinate role in the family. The "good" woman, we are told, blindly serves her husband and obeys his will in the same way a domestic servant would. The traditional wedding vows reflect the strong social support for the subordination of women. Only the bride had to pledge to love, honor, and *obey* her spouse. Even the structure of our language serves to reinforce the belief in male dominance. Conflict theorists hold that the position of women in most societies today is similar to that of a subordinate ethnic minority, such as African Americans in the United States.

There are many indications, however, that the traditional male advantages are declining in importance. The superior strength of the male means little in a highly mechanized society. The real barriers to women's liberation are now the institutions and attitudes that were established in the days of unquestioned male dominance. An increasing number of women are coming to realize this fact, and they are organizing themselves to break these barriers. According to the conflict perspective, the feminist movement is thus both a reflection and a cause of the growing strength of women in industrial societies. Conflict theorists advise women to continue publicizing their grievances, to bring all women and sympathetic men together in a unified movement, and to solicit the support of other dissatisfied social groups as well. For the conflict theorist, social action is the road to social change and a just society.

The Feminist Perspective

Most feminists would agree with the conflict analysis of gender inequality given in the previous two paragraphs. In fact, conflict-oriented feminists were responsible for creating it, so there is no point in repeating it here. But although most feminists accept such a theoretical analysis, as in other social movements, there are significant differences between feminists about what to do now. The liberal feminists are the largest group in the movement, and their approach is the predominant one in groups such as the National Organization for Women (NOW). Drawing on the values of freedom and individual liberty that are central to the liberal tradition, these feminists call for a vigorous government attack on all forms of prejudice and discrimination: tougher legislation punishing gender discrimination in hiring and promotion, new initiatives against sexual harassment, and longer sentences for rapists and other sex offenders. Liberal feminists also call for changes in the family, the schools, and the mass media so that people will no longer be socialized into rigid gender roles but will be allowed the freedom to follow their own unique individual paths. The liberal feminists nonetheless have their critics both inside and outside the movement. Socialist feminists find common ground with many of the liberals in advocating a more generous and humane welfare system, but they also argue that the exploitation of women arises from the capitalist system and that only fundamental changes in our economic institutions can liberate women. Thus socialist feminists argue that it is necessary to do more than attack sexism. The racism and economic exploitation that lie at the root of the capitalist system must also be ended if women are to be truly free. Radical feminists, on the other hand, focus more on the social arena than the others, and they call for a "woman-centered" culture to replace the current pattern of patriarchal (male-dominated) society. To achieve this end, each woman must recognize her own value and strength and must band together with other women to reject the patriarchal system and create an alternative woman-based society.[61]

The Interactionist Perspective

Interactionists see gender roles, and the sense of identity we derive from them, as critical components of human personality. They are convinced that sexual identity develops in the early years of childhood in interaction with parents, peers, teachers, and the mass media. Once formed, these ideas and concepts are quite durable. Interactionists note that prejudice and discrimination against women arise from differences in socialization. Females are conditioned to be passive and dependent and are therefore less dominant than males, who are encouraged to be more aggressive and independent. Thus, both sexes are often taught to see females as inferiors.

Interactionists are convinced that gender roles and the inequality they promote can be changed if the process of socialization is changed. These theorists argue that girls should be encouraged to be more aggressive and that boys be urged to accept the passive, dependent side of their nature. Because parents have been socialized into traditional gender roles, persuading them to teach their children to behave differently is extremely difficult; but perhaps schools, which are an increasingly important influence in socialization, can be changed more easily. Feminists are already pressing to remove gender role stereotypes from schoolbooks and lectures and to promote higher educational and occupational aspirations for girls. The media have made some progress, but there is much more they could do to promote these changes. Showing more women as powerful, assertive figures and allowing men who do not live up to the code of male dominance to be heroes equal to the "he-men" idealized in so many adventure films would do much to foster equality between the sexes. Interactionists also hold that greater tolerance of human differences is desperately needed. No matter what characteristics a culture attributes to the ideal woman or the ideal man, many people of both genders will not live up to those standards. The nonconformist must often pay an enormous personal price for being a little different. There is no reason, aside from prejudice and bigotry, that society cannot recognize the full range of human diversity as a normal and healthy phenomenon.

Quick Review

What are the differences in the ways a functionalist and a conflict theorist see the problems of gender?

What solutions do feminists recommend for the problems of gender inequality?

What is the interactionist perspective on the origins of gender inequality?

Summary

Gender roles (sets of expectations about the proper behavior for each sex) are basic components of individual personalities as well as of the larger social system. The male role has traditionally been centered on work and providing for the family. The male is expected to be more aggressive than the female and to have tighter control over his emotions. The female role has centered on child rearing and the family. Females are expected to be emotionally expressive, dependent, and passive. Gender roles show a wide range of variation among cultures, and in our culture, as in others, the behavior of many men and women does not fit the expected patterns.

Two important factors have influenced the development of gender roles: biology and culture. The fact that females bear and nurse children has had an obvious influence on the definition of gender roles, as has the fact that males tend to be larger and stronger than females. But gender roles are nonetheless cultural constants that vary greatly from one society to another. Some cultures assign what we consider "feminine" traits to both sexes, while others assign "masculine" traits to both.

In early foraging societies, relationships between men and women were generally egalitarian. With the coming of agriculture, the power of women declined because their contribution to food production was reduced. The economic and social conditions accompanying industrialization then neutralized many male advantages. Mechanization made physical size and strength less important, and the sharp drop in infant mortality and the spread of birth control reduced women's child-rearing burdens.

Gender socialization is the process by which children learn the behaviors and attitudes expected of their sex. The family plays a critical role in this process. Parents begin treating boys and girls differently almost from the moment of birth. Schools reinforce the traditional gender roles learned at home. Teachers encourage high aspirations in boys and discourage them in girls. Radio, television, popular music, and motion pictures also convey sexual stereotypes.

The roles we assign to each sex clearly promote gender inequality, and the same inequality is reflected in our social institutions. Men are given the dominant position, and a variety of evidence reveals a clear pattern of discrimination against women in education, employment, politics, and social life.

The feminist movement emerged when women organized to protest against discrimination and to work actively for their economic, political, and social rights. It has won some remarkable successes, but much remains to be done. The small but growing men's movement points out that our current system of stereotyped gender roles has many negative consequences for men as well as for women.

Functionalists see the problems of present-day gender roles as stemming from economic changes that upset the traditional cultural pattern. They advocate a reduction in the gap between expectations and actual conditions. Conflict theorists are convinced that these problems arise from domination and exploitation of the weak by the strong. They advise women to organize and to use political power to gain equality. Liberal feminists advocate a vigorous attack on all forms of discrimination against women; socialist feminists call for a fundamental restructuring of capitalist society; and radical feminists call for the creation of a more "woman-centered" social order. Interactionists are convinced that gender roles and sexual identity are learned in the process of socialization and that sexual inequality can be reduced by changing gender roles.

Questions for Critical Thinking

The question of what relationship the genders should have is a controversial one that often stirs deep emotions. Some people see traditional gender roles as preordained by God or biology, while others see them as repressive and unjust. Examine the traditional and the egalitarian pattern of gender relationships from a general sociological perspective. What are the overall advantages and disadvantages of each? Now, put those patterns into the context of an agricultural society and an industrial society. Why have gender roles grown more egalitarian as societies have industrialized? What directions do you see for the future?

Key Terms

androgynous   homophobia
double standard   sexism
gender inequality   sexual harassment
gender roles   sexual stereotyping
gender socialization

Further Readings

Phyllis Burke, *Gender Shock: Exploding the Myths of Male and Female* (New York: Anchor, 1996). A persuasive attack on some of the common myths about the differences between females and males.
Alison M. Jaggar and Paula S. Rothenberg, *Feminist Frameworks*, 3rd ed. (New York: McGraw-Hill, 1993). A comprehensive collection of articles analyzing the relations between women and men from a feminist perspective.

Sam Keen, *Fire in the Belly: On Being a Man* (New York: Bantam Books, 1991). One of the most thoughtful of the recent books about being male in contemporary society.

Marie Richmond-Abbott, *Women, Men, and Society,* 3rd ed. (Boston: Allyn & Bacon, 1995). A good general text examining a wide range of gender issues.

Gloria Steinem, *Moving Beyond Words* (New York: Simon & Schuster, 1994). A recent collection of articles by one of today's best-known feminists.

Notes

1. See, for example, Ann Ferguson, "Androgyny as an Ideal for Human Development," in Paula S. Rothenberg, ed., *Racism and Sexism: An Integrated Study* (New York: St. Martin's Press, 1988), pp. 362–371.

2. Sandra L. Bem, "Androgyny and Gender Schema Theory," in T. B. Sonderegger, ed., *Nebraska Symposium on Motivation: Psychology of Gender* (Lincoln: University of Nebraska Press, 1985).

3. Jane B. Lancaster and Chet S. Lancaster, "The Watershed: Changes in Parental Investment and Family Formation Strategies in the Course of Human Evolution," in Jane B. Lancaster et al., eds., *Parenting Across the Lifespan* (New York: Aldine de Gruyter, 1988), p. 191.

4. See Hilary M. Lips, *Sex and Gender* (Mountain View, CA: Mayfield, 1988), pp. 1–26.

5. Ibid., pp. 105–109.

6. Christine de Lacoste-Utamsing and Ralph L. Holloway, "Sexual Dimorphism in the Human Corpus Callosum," *Science* 216 (1982): 1431–1432.

7. Bruce Svare and Craig H. Kinsley, "Hormones and Sex-Related Behavior," in Kathryn Kelley, ed., *Females, Males and Sexuality: Theories and Research* (Albany: State University of New York Press, 1987), pp. 13–58.

8. Laurel Richardson, *The Dynamics of Sex and Gender: A Sociological Perspective* (New York: HarperCollins, 1988), p. 145.

9. Richard Borsay Lee, *The !Kung San: Men, Women and Work in a Foraging Society* (Cambridge: Cambridge University Press, 1979); Margaret Mead, *Sex and Temperament in Three Primitive Societies* (New York: Mentor, 1935); James A. Doyle, *The Male Experience* (Dubuque, IA: Brown, 1983), pp. 82–85.

10. Margaret L. Anderson, *Thinking About Women: Sociological Perspectives on Sex and Gender,* 2nd ed. (New York: Macmillan, 1988), pp. 49–52; John Money and A. A. Ehrhardt, *Man, Woman, Boy and Girl: The Differentiation and Dimorphism of Gender Identity from Conception to Maturity* (Baltimore: Johns Hopkins University Press, 1972).

11. Ernestine Friedl, *Women and Men: An Anthropologist's View* (New York: Holt, Rinehart & Winston, 1975).

12. See, for example, Eleanor Leacock, "Women's Status in Egalitarian Society: Implications for Social Evolution," *Current Anthropology* 19 (June 1978): 247–255.

13. Richardson, *The Dynamics of Sex and Gender,* pp. 155–156.

14. Anderson, *Thinking About Women,* pp. 82–83.

15. See Richardson, *The Dynamics of Sex and Gender,* pp. 16–34; Simone de Beauvoir, *The Second Sex* (New York: Knopf, 1957).

16. Ruth E. Hartley, "Sex-Role Pressures and the Socialization of the Male Child," in Deborah S. David and Robert Brannon, eds., *The Forty-nine Percent Majority: The Male Sex Role* (Reading, MA: Addison Wesley, 1976), p. 236.

17. Leslie Brody, "Gender Difference in Emotional Development: A Review of Theory and Research," *Journal of Personality* 53 (1985): 102–149.

18. Richardson, *The Dynamics of Sex and Gender,* pp. 56–59.

19. Myra Sadker, David Sadker, and Susan S. Klein, "Abolishing Misconceptions About Sex Equity in Education," *Theory into Practice* 25 (Autumn 1986): 220.

20. Beverly A. Stitt, *Building Gender Fairness in Schools* (Carbondale: Southern Illinois University Press, 1988), pp. 29–32.

21. Myra Sadker and David Sadker, *Failing at Fairness* (New York: Scribner, 1994); American Association of University Women, *How Schools Shortchange Girls* (Washington, DC: AAUW Educational Foundation, 1992); C. S. Dweck, W. Davidson, S. Nelson, and B. Enna, "Sex Differences in Learned Helplessness," *Developmental Psychology* 14 (1978): 268–276.

22. P. Purcell and L. Stewart, "Dick and Jane in 1989," *Sex Roles* 22 (1990): 177–185.

23. J. H. Feldstein and S. Feldstein, "Sex Differences on Televised Toy Commercials," *Sex Roles* 8 (1982): 581–587.

24. F. E. Barcus, *Commercial Children's Television on Weekends and Weekday Afternoons* (Newtonville, MA: Action for Children's Television, 1982).

25. N. S. Feldman and E. Brown, "Male Versus Female Differences in Control Strategies: What Children Learn from Saturday Morning Television." Paper presented at the annual meeting of the Eastern Psychological Association, Baltimore, April 1984.

26. See G. Metzger, "T.V. Is a Blonde, Blonde World," *American Demographics* (November 1992): 51; A. E. Courtney and T. W. Whipple, *Sex Stereotyping in Advertising* (Lexington, MA: Lexington, 1983); Richardson, *The Dynamics of Sex and Gender,* pp. 69–82; Claire M. Renzetti and Daniel J. Curran, *Women, Men and Society,* 3rd ed. (Boston: Allyn & Bacon, 1995), pp. 172–175.

27. G. Berbner, *Women and Minorities on Television: A Study in Casting and Fate,* Report to the Screen Actors Guild and the American Federation of Radio and Television Artists, Annenberg School of Communications, University of Pennsylvania, 1993.

28. F. J. Fejes, "Masculinity as Fact," in S. Craig, ed., *Men, Masculinity and Media* (Newbury Park, CA: Sage, 1992), pp. 9–22.

29. Metzger, "T.V. Is a Blonde, Blonde World"; I. J. Silverstein, L. Perdue, B. Petterson, and E. Kelly, "The Role of the Mass Media in Promoting a Thin Standard of Bodily Attractiveness for Women," *Sex Roles* 12 (1986): 519–532.

30. B. L. Sherman and J. R. Dominick, "Violence and Sex in Music Videos: TV and Rock n' Roll," *Journal of Communication* 7 (1986): 94–106; also see J. D. Brown and K. Cambel, "Race and Gender in Music Videos: The Same Beat but a Different Drummer," *Journal of Communication* 36 (1986).

31. See S. McClary, *Feminine Endings: Music, Gender, and Sexuality* (Minneapolis: University of Minnesota Press, 1991), pp. 94–106.

32. U.S. Bureau of the Census, *Statistical Abstract of the United States, 1996* (Washington, DC: U.S. Government Printing Office, 1996), p. 191.

33. Ann P. Parelius, "Mathematics and Science Majors: Gender Differences in Selection and Persistence," in Laura Kramer, ed., *The Sociology of Gender* (New York: St. Martin's Press, 1991), pp. 140–160.

34. U.S. Bureau of the Census, *Statistical Abstract, 1996,* p. 395.

35. United Nations Development Programme, *Human Development Report, 1997* (New York: Oxford University Press, 1997), p. 209.

36. U.S. Bureau of the Census, *Statistical Abstract, 1996,* p. 426.

37. Lawrence Mishel, Jared Bernstein, and John Schmitt, *The State of Working America, 1996–97* (New York: Sharpe, 1997), pp. 147–148.

38. U.S. Bureau of the Census, *Statistical Abstract, 1996,* p. 428.

39. Monica Roman, "Women Beware: An MBA Doesn't Mean Equal Pay," *Business Week,* October 29, 1990, p. 57.

40. "Women: The Road Ahead," *Time,* Special Issue, Fall 1990, p. 26.

41. Nancy Gibbs, "The Dreams of Youth," in "Women: The Road Ahead," pp. 10–14.

42. U.S. Bureau of the Census, *Statistical Abstract, 1996,* pp. 405–407.

43. Karen Nussbaum, "Removing Barriers for Working Women," *Christian Science Monitor,* March 24, 1994.

44. Nancy Rivera Brooks, "Gender Pay Gap Found at Highest Corporate Levels," *Los Angeles Times,* June 30, 1993, pp. A1, A20.

45. Donna K. H. Walters, "Barriers Still Persist, Women Lawyers Say," *Los Angeles Times*, March 10, 1994, pp. D1, D4.
46. U.S. Bureau of the Census, *Statistical Abstract, 1996*, p. 405.
47. B. Drummond Ayers, Jr., "Women in Washington Statehouse Lead U.S. Tide," *New York Times*, April 14, 1997, pp. A1, A12; United Nations Development Programme, *Human Development Report, 1997*.
48. Ibid.
49. S. McConnell-Ginet, "The Sexual (Re) Production of Meaning: A Discourse-Based Theory," in F. W. Frank and P. A. Treichler, eds., *Language, Gender and Professional Writing* (New York: Modern Language Association of America, 1989); C. Edelsky, "Who's Got the Floor?" *Language and Society* 10 (1981): 383–421.
50. Deborah Tannen, *You Just Don't Understand* (New York: Morrow, 1990).
51. N. Henley, M. Hamilton, and B. Thorne, "Womanspeak and Manspeak: Sex Differences and Sexism in Communication," in A. G. Sargent, ed., *Beyond Sex Role* (New York: West, 1985), pp. 168–185.
52. Theodore Caplow, *American Social Trends* (San Diego: Harcourt Brace Jovanovich, 1991), pp. 153–154.
53. Carol McGraw, "Employers, Workers Act to Fight Job Harassment," *Los Angeles Times*, October 21, 1990, pp. A1, A30.
54. Brooks, "Gender Pay Gap Found at Highest Corporate Levels."
55. Lloyd D. Elgart and Lillian Schanfield, "Sexual Harassment of Students," *Thought & Action* 7 (Spring 1991): 21–42.
56. Gibbs, "The Dreams of Youth."
57. Mishel, Bernstein, and Schmitt, *The State of Working America, 1996–97*, pp. 148.
58. U.S. Bureau of the Census, *Statistical Abstract, 1996*, p. 95.
59. Andrew Kimbrell, "A Time for Men to Pull Together," *Utne Reader*, May–June 1991, pp. 66–74.
60. Warren Farrell, "Men as Success Objects," *Utne Reader*, May–June 1991, pp. 81–84.
61. See Josephine Donovan, *Feminist Theory* (New York: Ungar, 1985); Anderson, *Thinking About Women*, pp. 287–361.

Conformity and Deviance

All societies have strong expectations about how their members are supposed to behave. Until the 1960s, most sociologists simply accepted the dominant norms of their society and sought the causes of social problems in **deviant behavior**—that is, behavior that violates society's rules. While deviant behavior is unquestionably a major source of social problems, this approach has proved far too simplistic. Contemporary societies no longer have a single set of norms that almost everyone agrees with. Instead, we are confronted by a mosaic of fragmented subcultures and communities, each with its own unique standards and expectations. Conflict theorists have shown us another problem with the old approach: it automatically assumes that our laws reflect the best interests of society as a whole and ignores the fact that raw political power also plays a critical role in shaping our legal system. Finally, the horrors of World War II and the blind allegiance so many have shown to totalitarian dictators in this century have proved that conformity can be as much a social problem as deviance. The chapters in this section therefore examine the problems of sexual behavior, drug use, crime, and violence in light of this new, more complex understanding of the relationship between social norms and social problems.

Sexual Behavior

Was there really a sexual revolution?

How has our sexual behavior changed?

What are the origins of our sexual orientation?

What kinds of discrimination do gays and lesbians confront?

Why do so many unmarried teenagers become pregnant?

Should prostitution and pornography be considered social problems?

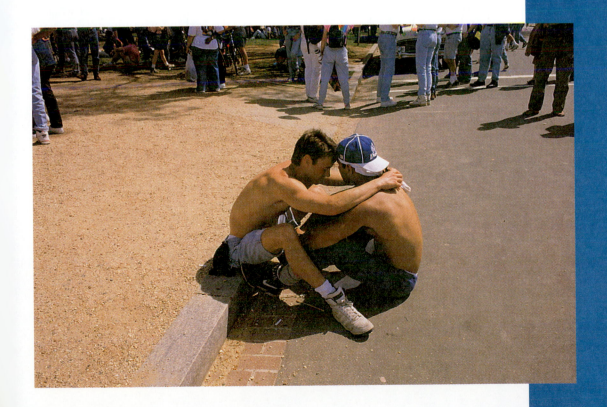

When Jamie Nabozny was in middle school, he was verbally harassed and pushed around, and he was even the subject of a mock rape. Why? Because he was gay and didn't hide his sexual orientation from the other students. By the time he was in high school, his classmates had beaten him up and urinated on him at school. He went to the school administrators to complain again and again, but they never intervened to stop the abuse. It became so bad that Jamie attempted suicide three times; ultimately he dropped out of high school when he was in the eleventh grade. His story does have a happier ending, however, for when he was 21 a jury awarded him almost $1 million in damages in his suit against the school district.

Few things seem more private than our sexual behavior, yet it is shaped by the same social forces as any other human activity. Society defines what is attractive and what is ugly. Our social groups tell us when sex is acceptable, when it is forbidden, and when it is required. Popular culture creates powerful expectations about our sex lives, and people who fail to live up to those expectations are often left feeling frustrated or shameful or are even subjected to the kind of outright physical abuse that tormented Jamie Nabozny.

In the past, Western culture held some of the most negative attitudes toward sex found anywhere in the world. The Puritans, who played such an important role in the colonization of North America, condemned all sexual activity outside marriage and even disapproved of sexual relations between husbands and wives except as a means to have children. Not surprisingly, society's main problem with sexual behavior was how to restrict it within those narrow limits. Tremendous changes in values and attitudes have taken place since Puritan times. The old consensus about what is right and wrong has broken down, but no new standard has won universal acceptance. Many of the old laws nonetheless remain on the books, and people continue to be harassed, even jailed, for private sexual activities that are perfectly acceptable to large segments of society. Discrimination based on **sexual orientation** is widespread and openly practiced.

To make matters worse, many businesses take advantage of our sexual interests and fears for a quick profit. Images of bathing beauties and muscular young men are used to sell everything from automobiles to soap. Television shows, books, and movies routinely depict a kind of fantasy sex devoid of real-life consequences, while promoting a virtual cult of glamour and sex appeal. Advertisers play on the insecurities these attitudes create, telling us that such products as deodorants, mouthwash, and cosmetics are essential if we are to attract the right sexual partner. In this environment, many young people become involved in sexual activities before they are emotionally prepared for them, perhaps ending up with an unwanted pregnancy; and people of all ages may feel inadequate when they are unable to match the impossible sexual ideals promoted by the mass media.

sexual orientation
The primary direction of one's sexual desires, either heterosexual, homosexual, or bisexual.

Human Sexuality

Although many people believe that the kinds of sexual practices that are acceptable in our society are the only natural ones and that the rest are violations of "human nature," anthropological studies have revealed a wide range of sexual customs and behavior in cultures around the world. Indeed, almost every form of sexual behavior is considered normal somewhere under some circumstances. Historically, Western culture has been sexually conservative. In their classic study, Clellan S. Ford and Frank A. Beach found that only 10 of the 190 societies they analyzed shared our traditional disapproval of both premarital and extramarital sex.[1] The Polynesian peoples of the central Pacific, for example, have long been noted for their free sexual attitudes. Before the growth of Christian influence, Tahitians worshiped physical beauty. Young people of both sexes were encouraged to engage in masturbation and premarital intercourse, and both activities were openly discussed and practiced.[2]

Although North Americans are shocked by the thought of sexual activity among children, it is encouraged in some places. In some cultures intercourse is believed to be necessary if preadolescents are to mature sexually. The Trukese of the Caroline Islands build small huts especially for this purpose. Among the Alorese of Indonesia, mothers routinely masturbate their children in order to relax them.[3]

Yet such liberalism is far from universal. The men of Yap Island believe that intercourse causes physical weakness and reduces resistance to disease. At one time Yap attitudes toward sex were so negative that the Yap people almost became extinct. The Manus of New Guinea consider intercourse a degrading and disgusting act that a woman must endure in order to produce children. People of the neighboring Dani tribe do not have sexual relations until two years after marriage, and women refrain from sex for five years following the birth of each child. Closer to home, the Shakers, a Protestant sect founded in New England, banned all sexual activities, acquiring children only by adoption. Rural Ireland is also notable for its repression of sexuality. Men and women are segregated in public places, and there is a strong taboo against the discussion of sexual matters. Women's capacity to experience orgasm is denied by some and considered deviant by others.[4]

The kinds of sexual behavior that are considered deviant also vary widely from culture to culture. The use of force to obtain sexual favors is strictly forbidden in our culture and in most of the rest of the world, but among a tribe living in southwestern Kenya, normal intercourse is a kind of ritualized rape.[5] Women are encouraged to frustrate men with sexual taunts, and the men overcome women's resistance with force, often inflicting pain and humiliation in the process. Attitudes toward homosexuality also show enormous variation. Heterosexuality is preferred over homosexuality in most societies, in part because of its essential role in reproduction, yet there are at least two societies in New Guinea in which homosexuality is more highly valued. The Marind-anim people are so strongly homosexual that they kidnap children from other tribes to maintain their population.[6] At the opposite extreme are such peoples as the Rwala Bedouin, who consider homosexuality so base that it is punishable by death. Even the **incest taboo** (the prohibition of sexual relations between parents and their children or between the children themselves), which is the most common restriction on sexual behavior, is not universal.

There is clearly nothing innate in human beings that makes certain types of sexual behavior normal and other types abnormal. The distinction between "normal" and "deviant" sex comes from society, not biology. We are all born with a sex drive and certain sexual tendencies, but they can be satisfied in a great variety of ways. We learn to channel our sexual energy into one type of behavior and not another the same way we learn to satisfy our hunger with socially acceptable foods and not with dog meat or human flesh.

incest taboo
The prohibition of sexual relations between family members—usually between parents and their children and between the children themselves.

Quick Review

Why is some sexual behavior considered deviant and other behavior considered normal?

Contemporary Sexual Behavior

The study of sexual behavior is a difficult and confusing task. Social scientists have repeatedly found that many people are unwilling to describe their sexual behavior even to the most discreet investigators. As a result, it is impossible to say exactly how common various forms of sexual behavior actually are. Researchers even find it hard to describe public attitudes about sex, because so many people are confused about this controversial issue. This uncertainty has put sex researchers in the uncomfortable position of influencing as well as describing contemporary sexual standards. Some people evaluate their own sexual behavior by comparing it with the findings of the sex surveys, apparently assuming that unusual sexual behavior is wrong but that "if everyone else is doing it, it must be all right."

Sex surveys, such as the pioneering studies conducted by Alfred Kinsey and his associates in the 1940s and 1950s, are the best sources of data we have on sexual behavior, but they have serious methodological weaknesses.[7] Kinsey interviewed volunteers, including people in social clubs and prisons, and it is doubtful that his subjects were representative of the overall population. Magazine surveys are even worse, since they usually rely on responses from whoever happens to answer their published questionnaires. More recent scientific research has avoided some of the problems of Kinsey's work, but all the studies have shortcomings of their own. Studies of sexual behavior seldom have strong financial backing, and they therefore tend to use small local samples of high school or college students and neglect the rest of the population. The most notable exception was the 1992 survey conducted by a team of researchers working with the National Opinion Research Corporation. This survey, known as the National Health and Social Life Survey (NHSL), used a national sample of 3432 persons.[8] But even broad surveys that use good sampling techniques still find that many people refuse to cooperate. Despite a vigorous effort by the researchers, more than one in every five persons approached by the NHSL refused to answer their questions. There are probably important differences between people who respond to sex surveys and those who do not. Moreover, because of the sensitive nature of the subject, many respondents are undoubtedly less than honest in their replies. Most of the survey takers in the NHSL study, for example, were conservatively dressed middle-aged white women, and many respondents may have been reluctant to report extramarital affairs or homosexual activity to women who reminded them of their mothers.[9] Despite the methodological drawbacks, however, conclusions based on these studies are vastly superior to the unsupported opinions and generalizations voiced by so many people. It should be kept in mind, however, that the percentages given in this chapter are just rough estimates that may be very wide of their mark.

A major source of confusion about contemporary sexual behavior is the tendency of many people to see sexual orientation in absolute terms. Most people assume that individuals are sexually attracted either to members of the opposite sex (and thus are heterosexual) or to members of the same sex (and thus are homosexual). In reality, most people have both homosexual and heterosexual urges at one time or another. The differences among **homosexuals, bisexuals,** and **heterosexuals** are a matter of degree. Many heterosexuals briefly engage in homosexual activities during their adolescent years, and surveys show that a large majority of those who identify themselves as homosexual have had some sexual relations with members of the opposite sex.[10] The next section focuses on heterosexual behavior and the following one on homosexuality, but there is no hard-and-fast dividing line between the groups of people who engage in such behavior.

Heterosexual Behavior

A Historical Sketch After the fall of the Roman Empire with its liberal sexual attitudes, Western society adopted a very restrictive sexual morality. In general, sexual relations were approved only between a husband and wife, often only for the purpose of reproduction. The origins of these attitudes are to be found in the Judeo-Christian religious tradition, particularly the New Testament teachings of St. Paul and the lectures of early Christian leaders such as St. Augustine. These leaders held sexual abstinence to be the ideal but allowed that "it is better to marry than to burn." Sex was seen as something evil and degrading, to be avoided as much as possible. Although such standards continued to be supported by religious and secular leaders for centuries, it is doubtful that more than a small percentage of the population actually adhered to them.

The Puritans of the seventeenth century reemphasized the strict moral code of the early Christians and demanded an almost complete repression of sexuality. Puritan immigrants in North America helped establish this rigid code as a dominant force on the new continent. The Victorian era in the nineteenth century was also noted for its repression of sexuality. Victorians avoided discussion of anything that could be considered even remotely sexual. Legs became limbs, sweat became perspiration, and underwear became "unmentionables." Masturbation was believed to cause everything from mental disorders to blindness. The double standard was so strong that female sexuality was almost entirely denied. The surgeon general of the United States reflected the prevailing opinions of the time when he said that "nine-tenths of the time decent women feel not the slightest pleasure in intercourse."[11] The Victorian era was, however, noted for its hypocrisy as well as its sexual repression. Prostitution and pornography flourished, and there appears to have been a wide gap between what people said and what they did.

A Sexual Revolution? There is no doubt that sexual attitudes and practices have become much more liberal since the time of the Victorians, but as we have seen, such changes are difficult to measure precisely. One obvious development is that the media now make far more use of sexual material than ever before. Not only has there been explosive growth in "X-rated" videotapes and "cyberporn," but even mainstream magazines, movies, and television programs are now far more sexually explicit, while our newspapers and billboards are full of sexually oriented advertising.

Changes in the media do not necessary reflect changes in actual behavior, however. So despite their methodological problems, the sex surveys still provide our most reliable source of information about the ways our sexual behavior is changing. When Kinsey's report on male sexual behavior was first published in 1948, it

homosexuals
People who are sexually attracted to members of the same sex.

bisexuals
Those who are sexually attracted to members of both sexes.

heterosexuals
People who are sexually attracted to members of the opposite sex.

premarital intercourse
Sexual relations before
marriage.

shocked the nation, and his later study on female behavior had much the same effect. Kinsey concluded that 85 percent of all American men had experienced **premarital intercourse,** 70 percent had visited a prostitute, and over one-third had participated in at least one homosexual act. Kinsey's data suggest that the first wave of sexual liberation in the United States occurred much earlier than is usually believed, probably in the generation that came of age after World War I. His study found that only 8 percent of white women born before 1900 had premarital intercourse by age 20, but that among those born between 1910 and 1929, the figure was 22 percent. Later surveys indicate that a second wave of liberalization occurred in the 1960s and 1970s.[12]

double standard
A set of norms requiring
different behavior for men and
women, especially in regard to
sexual behavior.

An important part of these changes was the decay of the **double standard** (discussed in Chapter 10). Traditionally, both sexes were supposed to refrain from "sinful" sexual activities, but violating this taboo was considered a greater sin for women than for men. To be a "loose woman" or an unfaithful wife was a social disgrace, but young men were expected to gain some sexual experience before marriage, and a husband's carousing was often ignored. A century ago the "good" woman was not supposed to enjoy sex; she was merely to tolerate it for her husband's sake.

Although the double standard has not disappeared, it has certainly weakened. There has been some increase in the amount of premarital sexual experience reported by males since the 1940s, but the change has been much more dramatic for females. Only one-third of all the women in Kinsey's original sample reported having engaged in premarital intercourse by age 25; but according to the Centers for Disease Control, in 1970 about 40 percent of 18-year-old females had experienced premarital sex, and more current data indicate that figure has risen to about 70 percent. (The Kinsey Institute, founded by the pioneering sex researcher, now estimates that the average American becomes sexually active around age 16 or 17.)[13]

Kinsey's research indicated that, contrary to popular belief, the first wave of sexual liberation occurred in the generation that came of age in the "Roaring Twenties."

One should not conclude, however, that because women are enjoying more of the freedoms formerly reserved for men, the double standard no longer exists. It is still with us. A 1993 poll found that 60 percent of mothers tell their daughters they should not have intercourse until they are married, but fewer than half say the same thing to their sons.[14] Moreover, most surveys show that females are less likely than males to engage in premarital and extramarital sex. For example, while the current estimates of the frequency of extramarital affairs by the Kinsey Institute and the National Opinion Research Corporation are widely divergent, they both find that **extramarital sex** is more common among husbands than wives. The Kinsey Institute estimates that 29 percent of wives and 37 percent of husbands have had at least one other partner during their marriages, while the NHSL survey puts those figures at 15 percent for wives and 25 percent for husbands.[15]

extramarital affair
A sexual relationship between a married person and someone other than his or her spouse.

The surveys indicate that sexual activity is increasing within marriage as well as outside it. Particularly striking is the growth in oral-genital sex. The original Kinsey survey found that only 40 percent of the married males surveyed had ever engaged in oral sex with their wives; current surveys put that figure around 90 percent.[16] There is also evidence that married couples have intercourse more often than they did in the past and that masturbation is more common among both married and single people.[17] However, not all forms of sexual behavior have become more common. There is no evidence that male or female homosexuality has increased,[18] and several studies indicate that as women have become more sexually active, **prostitution** has actually declined.[19] Surprisingly, the NHSL survey found that about one-third of Americans ages 18 to 59 had sex only a few times a year or not at all.[20]

prostitution
The act of engaging in sexual relations for money.

The increasing sexual freedom described in these surveys is one result of the sweeping cultural changes of the twentieth century. The weakening influence of traditional religious morality lowered the barriers that once prevented many kinds of sexual activity. As women have gained economic and political power, they gained greater sexual freedom as well. Growing emphasis on individual freedom and self-determination in all aspects of our lives has made many people more willing to challenge traditional sexual restraints. The use of erotic materials to entertain and to sell products has also exerted an influence in many subtle ways. Another very important factor was technological: the development of more effective birth control techniques reduced the fear of unwanted pregnancy. Finally, sexuality itself seems to be undergoing a basic redefinition. Although sinful and degrading to Victorians, sexual activity is increasingly seen as a normal part of daily life.

Homosexual Behavior

Of all types of sexual behavior, homosexuality is one of the most misunderstood. Popular stereotypes hold that male homosexuals all put on a flashy display of femininity and that female homosexuals all lift weights and dress like men. In fact, most **gays** (male homosexuals) and **lesbians** (female homosexuals) look and act like everyone else. The few who fit the popular stereotype are just more noticeable. Another common myth is that homosexuals and heterosexuals have different personality characteristics. An experiment by Evelyn Hooker, however, showed that even experienced clinical psychologists were unable to identify the sexual orientation of a mixed group of subjects by examining their responses to a battery of psychological tests. Nor were any differences found in personal adjustment.[21] Some people believe that homosexuals endanger children, but there is no evidence to indicate that

gays
Male homosexuals. The term is sometimes also used to refer to all homosexuals.

lesbians
Female homosexuals.

homosexuals are more likely to be child molesters than heterosexuals. Finally, many people are not aware that many homosexuals form stable, long-term relationships, just as heterosexuals do.

Origins There are many theories about the causes of our sexual orientation (whether we are attracted to members of our own sex, the opposite sex, or both), but as yet, there is no conclusive proof for any of them. Since most people are heterosexual, researchers have tended to focus on the question of why homosexuals differ from the majority. Some evidence indicates that there may be a biological predisposition to homosexuality. One source of support for this contention comes from studies of twins. Several investigations have found that identical (one-egg) twins are more likely to show the same sexual preference than fraternal (two-egg) twins.[22] However, the problem with such studies is that identical twins are more likely to be treated alike by family and friends; thus, their similarities may be the result of environment, not heredity. A study published in 1993 found that gay men had a disproportionately large number of gay relatives on their mothers' side of their family, but not their fathers'—a pattern typical of hereditary characteristics such as color-blindness that are carried on the X (female) chromosome. In fact, those researchers believe they have found the general area on the X chromosome (but not the specific gene) that carries the predisposition for homosexuality.[23] Other support for the biological theory comes from Simon LeVay, who conducted autopsies on a small number of men and found some differences in brain structure between those who were homosexual and those who were not.[24] Despite such new evidence, however, there is little to suggest that homosexuality is entirely determined by biological factors. Biological theories have great difficulty, for example, explaining the significant differences in the extent of homosexuality in various cultures and in various time periods, or the reasons some people are homosexual during one period of their life and heterosexual during others.[25]

Classical psychoanalytic theory views homosexuality in males as the result of an excessively close relationship with the mother and a poor one with a distant and rejecting father. Several empirical studies have found that homosexual males are indeed more likely to experience paternal rejection than heterosexual males. Surveys also show that lesbians report much more fear and hostility toward their fathers than heterosexual women.[26] However, this parental rejection may be the result of the sexual orientation of the children rather than the cause. In one of the few long-term studies of the same group of subjects, psychiatrist Richard Green found that a homosexual orientation begins long before adolescence and so might easily contribute to early parental rejection. Three-fourths of the "feminine" boys he studied went on to homosexual lives as adults, while only one of the "masculine" boys became involved in homosexual activity.[27]

Sociologically, homosexuality is explained by examining the conditions in which it is learned. Given the enormous range of sexual behavior in the cultures of the world, it would actually be much harder to explain the absence of homosexuality in diverse societies such as those of the United States and Canada than to explain its presence. Although there is a strong social condemnation of homosexuality, it is actually encouraged in many other ways. For instance, when adolescents first begin to feel strong sexual urges, society forbids them to engage in heterosexual intercourse. Young males and females are not permitted to sleep or shower together, but these activities are acceptable for members of the same sex. The encouragement of marked gender differences, combined with the pressures of mate selection, may make association with the same sex less painful and embarrassing than association with the opposite sex. Some adolescents can carry on homosexual activities without arousing the suspicion of their parents, when heterosexual activities would be out of the question. Further, the widespread belief that one is either homosexual or heterosexual often causes individuals who engage in exploratory homosexual behavior to define themselves as homosexuals. Once such a self-concept takes hold, it is likely to persist, perhaps for a lifetime.[28]

The Gay and Lesbian Community There is considerable disagreement about how common homosexuality actually is. The original Kinsey study found that about 10 percent of American men were mainly homosexual, and that figure has often been cited through the years. However, it is highly doubtful that Kinsey's figures are accurate, since he used prisons as a source of subjects, and inmates are obviously more likely to engage in homosexual behavior than men who are allowed normal contact with women. It seems more likely that somewhere between 1 and 4 percent of American men are primarily or exclusively homosexual. For example, a federally funded study by the Guttmacher Institute released in 1993 found that 2.3 percent of men had engaged in homosexual activity in the last 10 years, and 1.3 percent said that they were exclusively homosexual. The NHSL survey found that 2.7 percent of its male respondents and 1.3 percent of its female respondents reported a homosexual experience in the last year.[29] Almost all the surveys are consistent in showing less homosexuality among women. Most estimates indicate that women are only about half as likely as men to engage in homosexual acts.[30]

Unlike many other minorities, homosexuals can conceal their differences from the public if they choose to do so. There is even a common slang term—the "closet queen"—for gay men who disguise their sexual preference and pass as heterosexuals. Such deception creates great emotional stress, however, and discovery and possible blackmail are a constant danger. In the last two decades, there has been a growing trend among homosexuals to "come out of the closet" and openly participate in the homosexual community. **Coming out** means more than just publicly admitting one's homosexuality, however; it also means admitting it to oneself, and the powerful stereotypes condemning homosexuals in our society can make that extremely difficult.

coming out
Publicly recognizing one's homosexual orientation.

In the past, the gay and lesbian communities were largely hidden from public view, but they are now an acknowledged part of urban life throughout North America. Like many ethnic communities, the gay and lesbian communities provide a variety of services for their members. Perhaps most important is the supportive social environment that allows gay and lesbians to be themselves without fear of condemnation by the outside world. Clubs, restaurants, and bars that cater to homosexuals are important to life in the gay community. They are places for socializing and relaxing, and they serve as a place to meet people with the same sexual orientation. Some cities even have gay and lesbian "yellow pages" that help homosexuals patronize businesspeople and professionals from their own community.

Although there is a common stereotype that homosexuals are more likely to be affluent and well educated than the general population, few reliable data support such claims. It is generally agreed, however, that gays and lesbians are more likely

In the past, most homosexuals were forced to conceal their sexual preference, but an increasing number of gays and lesbians are now "coming out" and openly declaring their sexual orientation.

than others to live in big cities where it is easier to escape the prejudice against them. Homosexuals also tend to be more liberal politically, since many conservatives are openly hostile to the gay community. An exit poll of voters in the 1992 presidential election found that two-thirds of those who identified themselves as homosexuals said they were Democrats, a much higher proportion than in the overall population.[31]

Gays and lesbians share many common problems created by the prejudice against them, but their sexual attitudes reflect some of the same differences that exist between heterosexual men and women. Many studies show that gay men are more likely to have numerous sexual partners, while lesbians are more likely to form sexually exclusive couples. One thing gay and lesbian couples do share is a greater tendency toward egalitarianism, perhaps because both partners have undergone a similar pattern of gender socialization.[32]

Starting in the 1960s, homosexuals began making steady progress against the hatred and prejudice so often directed against them. The AIDS epidemic among gay men has, however, dealt a severe blow to efforts to liberate the homosexual community from the centuries of bigotry it has faced. Irrational fears that one might catch that fatal disease from casual contact with homosexuals led to a new wave of hostility and even violence toward gays. At the same time, gays themselves have come to live with the fear that any new sexual contact might be a fatal experience—or the even more frightening thought that they may already have an undetected case of the disease. Not surprisingly, the AIDS epidemic has produced major changes in behavior among male homosexuals. Many "bathhouses," which served as sex clubs, have been closed, and there has been a sharp decline in casual sexual contact. The frightening toll of the AIDS epidemic also helped galvanize the gay community into a new sense of awareness and solidarity. Even though the rate of infection is quite low among female homosexuals, the lesbian community has rallied to the support of AIDS sufferers. As a result, the gay and lesbian communities have shown considerably more solidarity in recent years than they did in the past.

Quick Review

How do social scientists measure sexual behavior?

What are the problems with those measurements?

How have our sexual attitudes and behavior changed?

What are the main theories about the origins of our sexual orientation?

What is the gay and lesbian community?

Sexual Behavior and Social Problems

Considering society's deep uncertainty about sexuality, it is hardly surprising that there is a great deal of confusion about the problems of sexual behavior and what to do about them. There is a consensus that those who victimize others—for example, through rape or child molestation—deserve stiff punishment. But what about prostitution and pornography, in which those involved are usually willing participants? Everyone would like to reduce unwanted pregnancies and sexually transmitted diseases, but there are bitter ideological conflicts whenever it comes to putting specific programs into action. Even efforts to end discrimination against gays and lesbians have raised a storm of controversy.

Discrimination Against Gays and Lesbians

No other minority group is subject to such open and blatant discrimination as gays and lesbians. One obvious reason for this is to be found in our legal system. Not only does the law fail to protect the basic civil rights of homosexual citizens in most states, but in many of them, homosexual activity between consenting adults is actually a crime. Historically, the Judeo-Christian tradition has condemned homosexuality as a vile sin, and lawmakers in Western nations have acted accordingly. During the Middle Ages, homosexuals were commonly tortured to death. In Britain, until 1956, homosexual activities were punishable by life imprisonment.[33] The recent trend in the industrialized nations has, however, been toward greater tolerance. Britain repealed its most repressive laws in 1965, and most other European nations followed suit. Canada passed a law similar to Britain's in 1969, but some official harassment of homosexuals has persisted. The United States has lagged behind most other industrialized nations. The majority of the states have legalized homosexual

sodomy

A legal term applying to what are called "unnatural" sex acts, usually some form of homosexual behavior.

acts between consenting adults, but 23 states continue to have **sodomy** laws (which forbid oral or anal sex) aimed at homosexuals.[34] Some states continue to threaten homosexuals with long terms of imprisonment. However, in states where homosexuality remains a crime, the laws are not vigorously enforced. Only a few unlucky or unwise individuals are arrested, prosecuted, or punished. Moreover, the enforcement efforts are directed almost exclusively against gay men. Lesbian activities are usually ignored.

Even where criminal penalties have been reduced or abolished, homosexuals nonetheless suffer from open legal discrimination. In some places the professions of law, medicine, and teaching are closed to homosexuals. The federal government of the United States openly discriminates against homosexuals in military service. After a major national controversy in the early 1990s, the U.S. military adopted the "Don't ask, don't tell" standard, which its supporters claimed was a major improvement for gays and lesbians in the military. In reality, the military continues its open discrimination against gays and lesbians under this new policy and has merely agreed not to fire homosexuals who keep their sexual orientation secret.

Another source of discrimination is the failure of the law to recognize same-sex marriages. This policy not only denies committed gay and lesbian couples the emotional satisfaction of having their bond officially recognized; more importantly, it denies them the right to tax breaks and health insurance benefits that are enjoyed by legally married couples. In December 1996, a Hawaiian Circuit Court judge ruled that the state's law banning same-sex marriages was unconstitutional. But his ruling stirred bitter attacks from religious fundamentalists and may well be overturned by an amendment to the state constitution before it goes into effect. (The judge suspended the implementation of his ruling until it could be reviewed by the state supreme court.)[35] Underlying all these problems is the lack of legal protection for the basic civil rights of gay citizens, which allows employers and public organizations to discriminate against them openly.

Like many ethnic minorities, homosexuals have been organizing and demanding an end to such discrimination. After a sustained debate, gay activists persuaded the American Psychiatric Association to drop homosexuality from its list of mental disorders; television networks have been pressured to cancel programs that cast homosexuals in an unfavorable light; and boycotts have been launched against communities that have enacted antigay legislation. Activists have been successful in winning passage of legislation protecting gay rights in eight states and the District of Columbia and in a number of cities, including Los Angeles, Minneapolis, and Seattle. Hawaii recently passed a sweeping bill allowing the partners in same-sex couples the same benefits as married couples in such areas as inheritance, worker's compensation, and health insurance. However, the movement has had its failures as well. The Hawaiian legislation just mentioned, for example, was passed along with a bill that would put a constitutional amendment before the state's voters to ban same-sex marriages. The U.S. Supreme Court has refused to forbid the prosecution and imprisonment of people for homosexual activities, even if those activities are conducted in private between consenting adults. Moreover, the gains of homosexual activists have often stirred counterattacks by religious fundamentalists, who have sponsored bills and constitutional amendments in several states that would prohibit any legislation to protect gay people against discrimination. (See

Personal Perspectives A Homosexual Student

Despite considerable improvements over the years, gays and lesbians still often face a wall of hostility and prejudice. The following description comes from a student in her thirties.

> Being gay in America is not easy. The hardest thing for me is finding ways to feel good about myself. I get so many negative messages about what I am and who I am. Looking back, I was about 15 when I realized I was gay, and I didn't acknowledge it to myself until I was 20. It was a hard thing to do. I remember my mother's reaction when I told her. She burst into tears. It just broke her heart that I wasn't going to have a nice Barbie/Ken wedding and fill the societal expectations of getting married and having kids. I think she would have preferred it if I were a heroin addict instead. There would at least have been some hope that I could be rehabilitated.
>
> I haven't had as many negative consequences for being gay as a lot of people that I know. I am fairly mainstream and relatively discreet. Still, though, I've had a Bible shaken at me, and I've been told to get down on my knees and repent. I've had people avoid sitting at my lunch table because they didn't want to associate with "the lesbian." It really hurts. It's hard not to take it personally.
>
> I'm working toward the day when gay people will have the same rights as heterosexuals. When you can't be fired or passed over for a promotion for being gay. When my partner and I can be on the same car insurance policy or get the same tax breaks that married couples get. As it stands now, we pay higher taxes. That sort of discrimination just isn't right.

the Personal Perspectives box above for a firsthand account of the problems faced by one lesbian student.)

Adolescent Sex and Unwanted Pregnancy

There have been numerous surveys of adolescent sexual behavior, but their results have been inconsistent. In eight studies reported by Gerald R. Adams and Thomas Gullotta in 1983, the percentage of females from ages 16 to 19 who reported having had intercourse ranged from 18 to 57 percent, and for males the range was 21 to 72 percent.[36] More recently, two studies of 15- to 19-year-olds put that figure at 51 percent for females and 56 percent for males,[37] and another found that 55 percent of all 16- and 17-year-olds have had intercourse.[38] There is, however, general agreement about one point: young people are having sex at an earlier age than they did in the past. Although this change is just one part of an overall trend toward more liberal sexual attitudes and behaviors, it poses some special problems. In the erotically charged atmosphere of today's society, young people are often confused about how to deal with their own sexuality. They see the overwhelming importance given sexual attractiveness in the media—one study estimated that the average teenager has witnessed nearly 14,000 sexual encounters on television[39]—yet they also hear their parents and religious advisers telling them that sex is wrong. As a result, many young people begin having sex without really intending to and without taking precautions against pregnancy.

As we saw in Chapter 2, the birthrate among unmarried American teens skyrocketed in the last two decades (see Figure 11.1). Teenagers in other industrialized nations, however, have far lower pregnancy rates. Some of this difference can be attributed to the high pregnancy rates of African American teenagers, but white

Figure 11.1

Birthrates

The birthrate among single teenagers has risen significantly over the years.

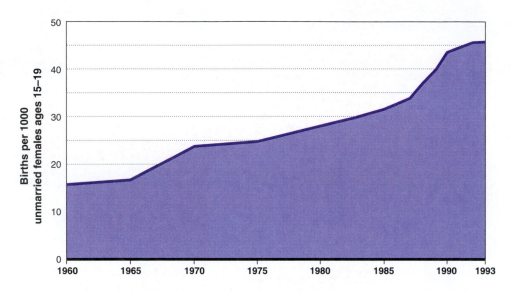

Source: U.S. Bureau of the Census, *Statistical Abstract of the United States, 1988* (Washington, DC: U.S. Government Printing Office, 1988), p. 62; *Statistical Abstract of the United States, 1993* (Washington, DC: U.S. Government Printing Office, 1993), p. 78; *Statistical Abstract, 1996,* p. 29.

American teens are still twice as likely to become pregnant as British or French teenagers and six times as likely as Dutch teenagers. The cause of this difference is clear. Although studies show that American teenagers are no more sexually active than their European counterparts, they are far less likely to use contraceptives.[40]

Why don't more sexually active teenagers use contraceptives? In some cases they actually want to have a child, but many teenage pregnancies are accidental. Many teenagers are simply ignorant about sexual matters and believe such myths as "You can't get pregnant the first time" or "You won't get pregnant if you only have sex once in a while." Teenagers are also influenced by parents and religious leaders who tell them to abstain not only from having sex but from using birth control as well. While birth control requires planning and forethought, it is easy to be swept into an unplanned sexual encounter in the heat of passion. Moreover, some teenagers feel that planning a sexual encounter is immoral but that if they are caught up in the heat of the moment and unable to stop, they can't be blamed for their actions. Finally, teenagers often do not know how to get birth control devices or are afraid that their parents will get angry if they do.

AIDS

Sexually transmitted diseases (STD) are an old problem. Descriptions of such diseases have been found in records dating back thousands of years. The first sexu-

sexually transmitted disease (STD)

A disease passed from one person to another during sexual activity.

Unmarried American teenagers are far more likely to become pregnant than are their counterparts in Europe or Japan.

ally transmitted diseases to be widely recognized were syphilis and gonorrhea—both caused by bacteria. More recent medical research has added numerous others to the list, including chlamydia and such viral diseases as genital warts and herpes. Some cervical cancer may also be caused by a sexually transmitted virus. A study by the Guttmacher Institute concluded that more than one in every four Americans will contract a sexually transmitted disease during their lifetimes.[41]

The problems caused by these diseases nonetheless pale in comparison with the devastating effects of acquired immune deficiency syndrome. The AIDS epidemic was apparently caused by an entirely new virus; since the first reported case did not occur until 1981. (See Figure 11.2.) Fortunately, the HIV virus that causes AIDS is not as easily transmitted as most diseases—some direct exchange of body fluids is usually necessary. Although it is often hard to determine the specific source of infection, about one-third of AIDS cases in the industrialized nations are probably caused by needle-sharing among intravenous drug users, so in a substantial number of cases, AIDS is actually not a sexually transmitted disease. Worldwide, heterosexual intercourse is the most common way AIDS is transmitted, but in the industrialized nations, about two-thirds of AIDS victims are gay men and heterosexual transmission is far less common. Although AIDS is not very easily transmitted to a

Figure 11.2

AIDS

For the first time since the beginning of the AIDS epidemic, the number of new cases reported declined in 1996.

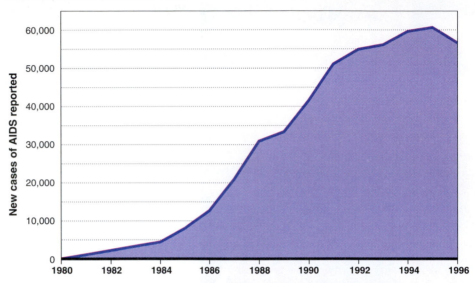

Source: U.S. Bureau of the Census, *Statistical Abstract of the United States, 1996* (Washington, DC: U.S. Government Printing Office, 1996), p. 142; Sheryl Gay Strolberg, "U.S. Says AIDS Cases Fell in '96, Ending 16-Year Rise," *New York Times,* September 19, 1997.

healthy partner by heterosexual intercourse, infection is much more likely if the partner has another sexually transmitted disease or is in poor overall health—and both conditions are more common among Third World people.[42]

The difficulty in diagnosing the disease, and the enormous fear that makes many people reluctant to be tested for the human immunodeficiency virus (known as HIV) that causes AIDS, make any estimate of the size of the epidemic a difficult task. The most widely quoted figure is that about 1 million persons are infected with HIV in the United States, but the first study based on blood tests of a random sample of the American population concluded that about 550,000 were infected.[43] Data from the Centers for Disease Control indicate that number of reported new cases of AIDS peaked in 1993 and has declined since then and that the number of deaths from AIDS peaked the following year.[44]

What is generally accepted is that there has been a significant shift in the kinds of people who are getting AIDS. Originally, the AIDS epidemic was heavily concentrated among male homosexuals, but there is evidence that the epidemic among gays has peaked and is now declining. At the same time, AIDS has been increasing rapidly among intravenous drug users. Heterosexual transmission is also increasing, especially among women whose partners are intravenous drug users (AIDS is more easily transmitted sexually from men to women than the other way around). Although the number of new cases is declining among older gay men, there is a growing fear young gays are failing to take the same precautions as their older peers and that there may be a second wave of infection among gays in the near future.

This new epidemic has touched off a near panic among some people. Unfounded fears that one can get AIDS from casual contact with an infected person are common. Yet at the same time, many people are failing to take reasonable precautions to protect themselves. Reports indicate that the biggest behavioral changes have been among gay men, who, of course, have borne the brunt of the epidemic. In contrast, one survey found that only one-third of sexually active single women had changed their behavior to lower the risks of getting AIDS.[45] The use of a condom—especially if it is lubricated with a spermicidal gel such as nonoxynol-9, which also kills HIV—can greatly reduce the chance of contracting AIDS. But too many people still fail to take this simple precaution. (See Chapter 6 for more on the AIDS epidemic.)

Child Molestation

Few kinds of deviant behavior are more repugnant to the general public or more frightening to parents than the sexual molestation of a child. But the image most people have of the child molester as a demented stranger who seizes a child and forces her to have intercourse with him is highly inaccurate; it is generally estimated that 50 to 80 percent of child molestations are committed by family friends, relatives, or acquaintances.[46] Most cases of **child molestation** do not involve actual intercourse but such things as exposure, fondling, and masturbation. A. C. Jaffe found that only 11 percent of victims were physically penetrated by the offender,[47] and Charles H. McCaghy concluded that physical violence is used in no more than about 3 percent of molestation cases.[48] The only accurate part of the popular stereotype is that most offenders are male and most victims are female, but even that is not always the case.

child molestation
The sexual abuse of a child by an adult.

Accurate measurement is even more difficult for child molestation and incest (sex between persons with a close biological relationship, such as a father and daughter) than for other types of sexual behavior. In a survey in the 1980s, 1 in 10 Boston couples reported that their child had been the victim of sexual abuse or attempted sexual abuse, and 15 percent of the mothers and 6 percent of the fathers said that they themselves had been abused as children.[49] A nationwide study published in 1991 that went to unusual lengths to assure the anonymity of the respondents concluded that 1 in 7 Americans had been sexually abused as children.[50] Although some claim that there has been a big increase in child molestation in recent times, there is no convincing evidence to support this assertion. The estimates produced in the original Kinsey studies, for example, were within the same range as the later research. One thing that has increased is the willingness to acknowledge the problem and talk about it, and as a result, the number of cases of child molestation reported to the police has gone up in the last few years.

Child molestation stems from complex social and psychological causes, and no single theory explains them all. Most psychologists depict child molesters as insecure and sexually inadequate people who turn away from adult sexual relationships to seek out children, who are less threatening and more easily controlled.[51] However, some child molesters are married people with adult sexual relationships, and most people with feelings of sexual inadequacy never become child molesters. There is mounting evidence that child molesters often learned their behavior in their own childhood, when they themselves were the victims of sexual abuse. Other evidence indicates that father-daughter incest most often occurs in disturbed families. Often there is no sexual relationship between the parents, and the father forces his daughter to assume that part of his wife's role.[52]

Prostitution

Prostitution—selling sex for money or something else of value—is sometimes called the world's oldest profession. Although that old saying underlines the fact that people have probably always used sex to get things they want, an act of prostitution must be more than that. In the modern context, at least, it has to be some kind of commercial transaction carried on in an impersonal way—otherwise anyone who married someone they didn't love or even went on a date with a person they didn't like might be considered a prostitute.

Although the evidence is far from conclusive, it appears that prostitution has declined dramatically during this century. Kinsey's data suggested that prostitution had already begun to decline in the 1940s when he did his research. Morton Hunt's survey in the 1970s found that prostitution had decreased by over 50 percent since the time of the Kinsey report, and more recent studies show the same trend.[53] It appears that the demand for prostitution has decreased as sexual freedom has increased, and the growing fear of AIDS in the last decade and a half has probably accelerated this trend. Nevertheless, it is unlikely that prostitution will disappear by itself, and repeated efforts to stamp it out have been remarkably unsuccessful.

The Social World of Prostitution Prostitutes are condemned by "respectable" people, but within their own world they have a status hierarchy similar to those of other professions. **Call girls** are the aristocrats of female prostitutes. They are the most sophisticated, the best paid, the best dressed, and the most attractive. They are highly selective about their customers, charge high fees that begin at several hundred dollars a night, and see the same clients again and again. Their clients usually come from personal referrals and phone contacts, and because they seldom accept unknown customers, call girls' chances of arrest are low. A notch below call girls are the successful female "hustlers" who work out of bars and nightclubs. They tend to wear expensive clothes and jewelry as a way of distinguishing themselves from less successful prostitutes who charge lower prices. The women who work in a house of prostitution are on the next step in the status hierarchy. The "house girl" does not have to cruise the bars and street corners in search of customers, so she has a higher degree of personal safety than some other kinds of prostitutes, but neither can she screen her clients. She must service a large number of men each night and split her fees with the **madam** who runs the house. **Streetwalkers** on the bottom rung of the status ladder prowl the streets in search of clients. Streetwalkers often rob their customers and are themselves highly vulnerable to assault, robbery, and arrest. Most streetwalkers work for a **pimp,** who usually takes most of their income. In return, the pimp pays for the prostitute's apartment, buys her clothes, arranges legal services, provides protection, and often gives her emotional support and affection.

Many people think that all prostitutes are women, but male prostitution is also common. Male prostitutes sometimes have female clients, but most of their business comes from other men. In his interviews with male prostitutes in Chicago, David F. Luckenbill found that they too had a clear-cut occupational hierarchy. At

call girl
A prostitute who accepts customers only from personal references and phone contacts.

madam
Someone who runs a house of prostitution.

streetwalker
A prostitute who gets clients on the streets and in other public places.

pimp
Someone who solicits customers or performs other services for a prostitute in exchange for a share of the profits.

Streetwalkers, both female and male, are the lowest-status prostitutes. Those who work in a house of prostitution are somewhat better off, while the call girl (or call boy) has the highest status and the best working conditions.

the bottom are the *street hustlers*, similar to female streetwalkers except that they do not work for a pimp. Next are the *bar hustlers,* who find their customers in bars, and at the top of the hierarchy are the prostitutes who work for an "escort service."[54] A few brothels also have male prostitutes who work alongside the women.

Becoming a Prostitute Even in this age of sexual liberation, there is still an enormous stigma to being a prostitute, and the work is often degrading and highly dangerous. So why do so many women and men ignore the stigma and risk physical abuse or contracting AIDS to become prostitutes? The short answer is, of course, for money. A person from a poor home who has few skills can make far more in prostitution than in any legitimate profession—especially if he or she is reasonably young and attractive.

The desire for money is, however, only part of the story, for most people, no matter how impoverished, never turn to prostitution. Williams and Kornblum found that young women who live in poor neighborhoods where the presence of prostitution is highly visible are the most likely to become prostitutes themselves.[55] James and Meyerding found that well over half the prostitutes they studied had been raped as children and that they were also far more likely to have been the victims of incest and other sexual abuse than other women.[56] Studies based on interviews with streetwalkers and other prostitutes have found that they often had very difficult family situations and poor self-images before turning to "the life" (prostitution). Most of the prostitutes in these studies report that their families were dysfunctional, that they were alienated from their parents, and that they were often labeled as "troublemakers" in school.[57] Finally, studies show that many prostitutes are also drug addicts,[58] and the incessant demand for money to buy drugs is another important push toward prostitution.

After interviewing 30 prostitutes in a women's prison, Nanette Davis concluded that the road to prostitution typically has three stages. Before entering "the profession," these women often engaged in a wide variety of sexual encounters and were labeled as "bad" by parents and school authorities. Next, they entered a transitional stage in which they learned the necessary skills and turned an occasional "trick" while still keeping their jobs and other ties to the "straight" world. In the final stage, they turned to prostitution as a full-time career, accepted the definition of themselves as prostitutes, and rejected the "respectable" people who reject them.[59]

Prostitution and the Law   In the ancient Middle East, the sex act was sometimes carried on as part of religious rituals, and "temple prostitution" was a thriving business in some places. During the Middle Ages, Europeans saw prostitution as a kind of necessary evil, and it was rarely illegal. But with the coming of the Protestant Reformation and a growing concern about the spread of syphilis, prostitution came to be defined as criminal behavior, and it has remained illegal in most Western countries ever since.

A hundred years ago, prostitution was widespread in North America. It was illegal, but it was carefully ignored by most police departments. At that time, most prostitutes worked in **brothels** concentrated in the "red-light" districts of larger cities. Madams paid the police to leave their "girls" alone, and they were not usually disturbed as long as they did not venture out of the district. In the early part of the twentieth century, this cozy arrangement was upset by a wave of vice crusades. The American Society of Sanitary and Moral Prophylaxis, the American Purity Alliance, the YMCA, and other organizations mounted a powerful offensive against prostitution. One by one the red-light districts were closed down, and increasing numbers of prostitutes became streetwalkers instead.

The laws that were intended to solve the problems of prostitution have in many ways made them worse. Closing houses of prostitution increased the number of streetwalkers, who pose a more serious problem than house girls because they solicit men who are not interested in their services, ply their trade in areas in which they are not welcome, and are often involved in criminal activities such as robbery and narcotics dealing. The prohibition of prostitution also encourages organized crime to enter the business because of the enormous potential for tax-free profits. Although the coming of the AIDS epidemic has encouraged more prostitutes and their clients to use condoms, the brothels are also in a better position to require their customers to practice safe sex.

Pornography

Like many other issues of sexual behavior, the debate about **pornography** centers around deep conflicts of values. Even attempts to define pornography clearly have ended in failure and confusion. The same book or movie that is beautiful and exciting to one person is pornographic to another. For example, some hold that any material intended to be sexually arousing is obscene and, thus, pornographic. By this definition, however, a large percentage of all advertising, books, and movies would be pornography. On the other side are those who argue that an interest in the erotic is normal and healthy and that the whole concept of pornography is a relic from Victorian times.

brothel
A house of prostitution.

pornography
A form of expression judged to be obscene.

The U.S. Supreme Court, while upholding the legality of banning "obscene" materials, has created a fairly strict definition of obscenity. According to the Court, sexually explicit materials are not obscene unless they (1) appeal to "prurient" (lewd, lustful, indecent) interests, (2) are contrary to community standards, and (3) lack all "redeeming social value."[60] Although these criteria appear to be clear and precise, they are impossible to apply objectively. Any book, magazine, or film can be said to have some social value. In fact, the President's Commission on Obscenity and Pornography found that 60 percent of all Americans believed that exposure to erotic materials provides entertainment and information about sex, both of which appear to be of "redeeming social value." A more recent survey by *Newsweek* magazine found that only one out of five Americans favored a ban on magazines that show nudity, and fewer than one out of three favored a ban on rentals of X-rated films.[61]

Critics of sexually explicit materials charge that they lead to immorality and social decay. However, standards of sexual morality differ so widely that it is difficult for sociologists even to determine what is or is not considered immoral, much less to decide whether or not pornography encourages it. There is, moreover, considerable evidence to support the argument that looking at "dirty" books and pictures does not lead the viewer to rape, child molestation, or other sex crimes. W. Cody Wilson found that his sample of sex offenders had less exposure to pornographic materials than the average citizen, and this finding has been confirmed by other researchers.[62] Even more telling evidence comes from Denmark, the first European nation to repeal its pornography laws. Studies revealed a substantial reduction in exhibitionism (58 percent), peeping (80 percent), and child molesting (69 percent) as erotic materials became more easily available. Examinations of criminal statistics show no relationship between the amount of pornography available in a state and its rate of forcible rape.[63]

Critics of such studies, however, point out that they often fail to consider important differences between the types of materials that are labeled as pornography. A nude photograph or an explicit love scene is a far cry from a graphic videotape showing a woman being raped and murdered. There is, moreover, good reason to believe that violent pornography contributes to violent sex crime. For one thing, laboratory studies have found a correlation between exposure to violent pornography and favorable attitudes toward rape[64] and a greater willingness to inflict suffering (electric shocks) on other experimental subjects.[65] Moreover, the much more extensive body of research on television violence clearly indicates that it encourages violence in real life (see Chapter 13), and TV violence is usually far less graphic than violent pornography. After a thorough review of the available literature, Edward Donnerstein, Daniel Linz, and Steven Penrod concluded that scientific evidence generally supports the idea that violent pornography promotes sexual violence. On the other hand, they found only weak and inconclusive evidence that materials showing "degrading" sex (for example, a film showing a woman having sex with numerous men in a short period of time) promote violence or other criminal behavior, and they concluded that depictions of "nondegrading" sex and simple nudity do not promote illegal activities.[66]

These findings are consistent with the attitudes of the general public. Polls show that most Americans believe that violent pornography and so-called kiddie porn (sexually oriented materials involving children) should be banned, but that other kinds of erotic material should not be prohibited. Seventy-four percent of the subjects in the *Newsweek* poll mentioned earlier favored a total ban on magazines that show sexual violence, and 68 percent favored a ban on movies that depict sexual violence.[67] Research shows, however, that most hard-core X-rated movies actually contain very little violence. It is the R-rated "slasher" movies that are the worst offenders.[68]

When thinking about such issues, it is also important to keep in mind that any type of restriction on the freedom of expression creates its own problems. Censorship has a chilling effect on personal freedom as well as on artistic expression. Works ranging from Shakespeare's plays to *Alice's Adventures in Wonderland* have been banned at one time or another. If censors are given broad powers to prohibit "pornography," many works of art will be affected as well. Pornography is so difficult to define that there is also a real danger that the decision to ban a particular book or picture would be based on political considerations and that authors who threaten powerful special interests would be more likely to have their works censored.

Today's hottest controversy concerns "cyberporn"—graphic sexual material available over the Internet and on CD-ROMs. Virtually unknown two decades ago, there is now a flourishing business in sexually oriented entertainment over the Internet which includes such Web sites as "Cyber Erotica," "Pleasuregirls," and "IEG's Love Club." In 1997, the latter had about 54,000 subscribers who paid a $10 subscription fee and a by-the-minute charge when they are on line.[69] Since children are often the most computer-literate members of their families, many parents have become concerned that their kids may pay unauthorized visits to such Web sites. In 1996 Congress passed the Communications Decency Act, which prohibited sending "indecent" material over the Internet that could be accessed by minors. But the following

"Cyberporn"—sexually explicit materials easily available over the Internet—has become an increasing concern to parents.

year the law was struck down in a lopsided decision of the Supreme Court, which saw such restrictions as a direct threat to the freedom of speech and expression.[70]

Quick Review

How big a problem is discrimination against gays and lesbians?

Why do so many teenagers have an unwanted pregnancy?

How is AIDS usually transmitted, and how can it be prevented?

What are the common myths about child molestation?

What are the causes of child molestation?

What are the most common types of prostitution?

What effects has the effort to eliminate prostitution had?

What is pornography, and what kinds of social effects does it have?

Solving the Problems of Sexual Behavior

The many diverse issues concerning sexual behavior obviously require some very different responses. Most proposals for dealing with them can be put into three categories: those that focus on education and the media, those that advocate changes in the laws and the criminal justice system, and those that seek some more basic social changes.

Education and the Media

The first set of proposals in this category aims to correct the irresponsibility of the broadcast media. As we have seen, the average teenager has seen thousands of erotic encounters and titillating references to sex on television, but references to birth control, unwanted pregnancy, and AIDS are relatively rare. For years the three major television networks not only refused to run public service announcements to inform sexually active teenagers about the importance of birth control but also would not even accept paid advertising from the manufacturers of birth control products.[71] Growing pressure from AIDS activists and other concerned groups have begun to win changes in such policies, and a few public service announcements are now made to encourage the use of condoms, but much more needs to be done to change the implication that sexual titillation is fine but birth control is somehow dirty. A law requiring television stations to run public service announcements for birth control and AIDS prevention would be a major step in the right direction and might help reduce both the problem of unwanted pregnancy and the spread of AIDS. Unfortunately, such proposals are opposed by powerful groups that confuse the advocacy of birth control and safe sex with the advocacy of promiscuity.

Another issue involving the media is the concern that many parents have that their children may be exposed to sexually explicit material on television and over the Internet. Although some propose a total ban on such materials, that would be an infringement on the freedom of adult citizens. A much more popular approach is to utilize new technology that enables parents to electronically block their children's access to objectionable material. New television sets sold in the United States are now required to have "V-chips" that allow parents to block television programs with a particular content rating, and this same technology could someday be applied to the Internet. At the time of this writing, there is a vigorous debate about exactly what kinds of ratings the government will require. The television industry prefers only a broad, general rating system such as the one currently applied to movies, but parent groups want separate ratings for sex, violence, and objectionable language. New technology should go a long way toward reducing parents' concerns about the television shows their children watch, assuming that the rating system that is finally put into effect gives parents sufficient accurate information.

One of the most promising approaches to reducing teenage pregnancy is to create more effective programs in the schools. Sex education, for example, has been growing increasingly common in recent years. In 1980, only 3 states required sex education in their schools; today, 47 states recommend or require it. However, most secondary students take only 6 to 20 hours of sex education a year, and the curriculum is often watered down because of strong opposition from conservative parents.[72] Moreover, research by Douglas Kirby shows that it is much more effective to create clinics on school campuses to distribute contraceptives to students than it is to expand educational programs.[73] Several such clinics are now operating in the United States, and in some cases they have reduced the number of pregnancies in their schools by over 50 percent—a record unmatched by any other type of program. Unfortunately, proposals to distribute contraceptives in the schools run into even more vehement opposition than sex education. Studies nonetheless indicate that despite the fears of some parents, such programs do not encourage teenage sex. In fact, girls in schools that provide birth control services apparently begin sexual intercourse at a somewhat later age than girls in schools without such programs.[74] (See the Debate "Should the Schools Provide Free Birth Control to Teenagers?")

The Legal System

The legal system's role in regulating our sexual behavior has been criticized from two different directions. The most common complaint about crimes in which there is a clear-cut victim—such as incest, child molestation, and rape—is that the criminal justice system is not enforcing the law strictly enough. (See Chapter 13 for a discussion of ways to improve the efficiency of the criminal justice system.) When it comes to sex crimes without victims, however, many critics take the opposite approach, arguing that the criminal justice system has no business interfering in private sexual acts between consenting adults. The most universal prohibition of this kind is on prostitution, but homosexuality, adultery (sex with someone other than one's spouse), fornication (sex between unmarried people), and cohabitation (living with someone of the opposite sex to whom one is not married) are still crimes in many states. Of course, most of these laws are seldom enforced, but that very fact can create its own problems. When unenforced laws stay on the books, they can still be dusted off and used to attack some person or group that is politically unpopular. Moreover, the prohibition on homosexual acts serves to stigmatize gays and lesbians and to encourage occupational and social discrimination against them. The laws against prostitution are more commonly enforced than the others, and critics charge that the result is not only the creation of a thriving deviant subculture among prostitutes but the prevention of any effective regulation and control of the prosti-

Debate   Should Schools Provide Free Birth Control to Teenagers?

Yes

The time has come to face facts. We may not want teenagers to have sex, but they are having it. We continue to pretend that "good girls" don't have sex or use birth control, and the result is that our unmarried teenagers have a higher birthrate than any other industrialized nation. These young mothers often drop out of school and into years of welfare dependence. Many of their children are raised in poverty by a single parent unready for the burdens of motherhood. Too often the ultimate result is a negligent and abusive parent and a disturbed child who grows into a troubled adult.

Fortunately, there is an effective and inexpensive way to deal with this problem: realistic sex education and free birth control provided directly in the schools. This kind of program has already been tried and proved effective in numerous schools, and if applied nationwide, it could slash the birthrate among single teenagers. Critics say that such programs encourage teenagers to have sex, but there isn't a shred of evidence to support such a claim. Surveys show that adolescents in European countries that provide access to birth control are no more sexually active than those in the United States. Studies of the U.S. schools that already have these programs show no increase in sexual activity among the students. The real reason that there is such vehement opposition to effective birth control programs is that self-righteous moralists want to make these girls suffer for their "sins." What these young mothers really suffer from is our shortsighted birth control policies, and it is time for a change.

No

The proposal that schools should give out condoms and birth control pills like popcorn in the movies is offensive and wrong. The way to deal with the shocking increase in illegitimate births among teenagers is to return to the traditional values that have made our society strong. We can stop illegitimate births by convincing teenagers to wait until they are married to have sex, not by helping them violate one of the most sacred commandments of the Judeo-Christian tradition.

A program to allow schools to give out birth control information and devices would be a highly unwelcome intrusion of government power into the private lives of millions of families. If parents don't want their children to use birth control, what right does the government have to go ahead and give it to them anyway? One of the most important of all parental duties is to teach children how to tell right from wrong, but what chance do parents have to instill a strong sense of sexual morality when the government steps in and helps teenagers behave in an immoral way?

The problem of unmarried mothers is indeed a serious one, but pursuing a policy that will encourage sexual promiscuity is not the way to deal with it. Classroom discussion of sex and easily available contraceptives would encourage many students to become sexually active and might well result in more, not less, illegitimacy. Even if it prevents a few illegitimate births, the moral damage such a program would cause is far too high a price to pay.

tution industry. Many criminologists therefore believe that the legalization of all private sexual acts between consenting adults not only would remove an unnecessary burden from the criminal justice system but also would help reduce rampant discrimination against homosexuals and allow government regulation of prostitution in order to reduce the spread of sexually transmitted diseases.

Another much needed legal reform is the enactment of national legislation to protect the civil rights of gays and lesbians. Although some states and cities have already enacted such laws, most have not. (See the Signs of Hope box "Gays and Lesbians Are Gaining More Civil Rights.") We do not allow arbitrary discrimination against people because of the color of their skin, their ethnic group, or their gender, and it makes no sense to allow it because of their sexual orientation either.

Tolerating Diversity

Sexuality is a deep, powerful, and often unpredictable force in human life. As we have seen, different societies attempt to manage this fundamental drive in radically different ways, but whatever approach they use, sexuality always poses a social problem in one way or another. When sexuality is repressed, the result is often hypocrisy and rebellion. When it is given free rein, it may bring instability and confusion with it. From a sociological standpoint, there is simply no perfect way to manage our sexuality. The easy going !Kung people of the Kalahari desert openly accept sexual interest and sexual activity. When they were still living as foragers, they were peaceful and cooperative, and seldom engaged in any form of violence—*except* when it came to the often bitter conflicts over sexual partners.[75] Europeans of the Victorian era attempted to banish sexuality from respectable society, only to give rise to a flourishing trade in prostitution and pornography as well as many neurotic psychological problems.

Contemporary culture contains a bewildering mishmash of contradictory attitudes, beliefs, and values about our sexuality. Some people feel that almost any kind of sexual pleasure is sinful; others feel that virtually anything that feels good is O.K.; and practically every other kind of attitude exists in between. It is unlikely that such

Signs of Hope   Gays and Lesbians Are Gaining More Civil Rights

Although the struggle has been a long and difficult one, gays and lesbians are slowly making progress toward winning their civil rights. Many nations around the world have repealed their laws against homosexual activity, and although the United States lags behind the other industrialized nations, homosexuality is no longer illegal in the majority of American states. Moreover, eight states and the District of Columbia now have legislation prohibiting discrimination based on sexual orientation. In Europe, Denmark has enacted a law granting gay partners the same economic and social rights as married couples (except in the adoption of children). In the United States, about 150 different cities and municipalities now give medical and other benefits to the gay partners of city employees, and many private corporations, such as Apple Computer, are doing the same.*

*Jane Gross, "After a Ruling, Hawaii Weighs Gay Marriages," New York Times, April 25, 1994, pp. A1, C12.

a heterogeneous society will ever arrive at a new consensus comparable to the one that existed in the past, and it is even less likely that we can find some problem-free way to handle our sexuality. What we can do, however, is to recognize our diversity of attitudes and accept the fact that in a democratic society we have to be tolerant of those who do not share even our most strongly held opinions and behavioral norms. When we make an effort to encourage communication among groups with different attitudes and standards, we often find that there are more areas of agreement for common action than we realized.

Quick Review

What are the best ways to deal with the problems of sexual behavior?

Sociological Perspectives on Problems of Sexual Behavior

Because sexual behavior is deeply rooted in human biology, many people lose sight of the fact that it is socially controlled and directed. Instead, they often believe that the sexual standards of their group are a part of human nature and that other behaviors are abnormal or unnatural. Such ethnocentric attitudes have made it far more difficult to deal with the complex issues concerning sexual behavior and how to regulate it. Each of the major sociological perspectives therefore has a great deal to contribute to our understanding of these issues.

The Functionalist Perspective

Kingsley Davis's early analysis of prostitution set the pattern for most of the functionalist work on this subject.[76] Following Davis's lead, most functionalists hold that prostitution is inevitable. As long as there are sexual restrictions in a society, the argument goes, sex will be for sale. Functionalists also note that prostitution benefits society by creating jobs for people with few skills, by providing a sexual outlet for people who would otherwise be without one, and by reducing the risk that frustrated, hostile men might use violence to satisfy their sexual desires. Consequently, many functionalists, including Davis, advocate the legalization of prostitution.

At the same time, however, other restrictions on sexual expression are often considered functional. Thus, the prohibition of premarital and extramarital sex is seen as a device to keep society's kinship system intact, ensuring a clear knowledge of a child's paternity and facilitating the transmission of money and power from parents to children. Sexual restrictions in general are considered to be functional because they direct individuals' energy away from pleasure seeking and into more socially beneficial activities. Pornography is held to be dysfunctional because it encourages extramarital affairs and therefore threatens an essential social institution: the family. Similarly, many functionalists believe that homosexuality should be banned because this sexual outlet does not contribute to society's need for new members. In other words, homosexuality is dysfunctional because it does not contribute to reproduction. Considering the current overpopulation of the world, however, it can now be argued that some amount of homosexuality has actually become functional.

The Conflict Perspective

It is obvious that many of the problems of sexual behavior stem from conflicting ideas about sexual morality. Although there are many diverse standards of sexual behavior, supporters of traditional norms have most of the power and have been able to write their convictions into law. Those whose sexual morality and behavior differ from that of the dominant group are made into criminals and threatened with imprisonment. Conflict theorists see such actions as part of a larger effort by traditional groups to maintain their cultural dominance by controlling the criminal law. The same power struggle leads to the imprisonment of marijuana smokers, bigamists, political radicals, and others who challenge established beliefs and customs.

Conflict theorists see attempts to stamp out prostitution and homosexuality as the oppression of "sexual minorities," similar to the oppression of ethnic minorities by segregation laws. Aside from noting the obvious injustice of such policies, conflict theorists point out that repression causes secondary problems such as the creation of a black market for forbidden goods and services and a burning hostility to the current social order among "deviant" groups.

Conflict theorists recommend that homosexuals, prostitutes, and other so-called sexual deviants organize and agitate for social change, as some have already begun to do. In addition, conflict theorists encourage them to form alliances with other oppressed groups, such as drug users and religious and ethnic minorities. The "problem" of sexual behavior would be far less severe, according to conflict theorists, if we repealed laws prohibiting sexual acts between consenting adults and instead passed laws banning discrimination against homosexuals and others who engage in unpopular sexual activities.

The Feminist Perspective

Feminists generally agree with the conflict theorists' contention that we should pass legislation legalizing all sexual behavior between consenting adults and protecting the civil rights of our gay and lesbian citizens. Their principal area of disagreement concerns pornography. Although feminists are by no means unanimous in their condemnation of pornography, many have been its outspoken critics. Feminists see the violence of men against women as one of the principal causes of women's oppression, and they tend to take a strong stand against violent pornography because it desensitizes us to the enormous suffering such behavior causes and sometimes even provides justifications and encouragement to potential offenders. Some feminists take that position much farther and argue that even nonviolent pornography should be banned. In the view of these feminists, pornography is inherently degrading and demeaning to women. Moreover, it encourages men to look at women not as human beings with a full range of emotions and needs but merely as objects of sexual desire to be used and then ignored. They also point out that men, too, suffer negative effects; they are less likely to be able to enjoy normal sexual relationships with real women if pornography has led them to believe that their sexual fantasies are attainable in real life.

The Interactionist Perspective

Many interactionists have become concerned about the effects of the constant use of sex to sell consumer goods and to boost television ratings, motion picture receipts, and magazine sales. This erotic bombardment creates a worldview that has became a serious problem for many people who cannot live up to the demands for sexual attractiveness and instant fulfillment generated by the media. Although such difficulties are common among people of all ages, they are particularly prevalent among the young, who have little sexual experience and are more likely to uncritically accept the expectations fostered by the media. The mystique of sexuality used to sell products and attract audiences has also contributed to the extremely high rate of pregnancy among teenagers. In response to this problem, interactionists recommend more effective sex education in the schools, therapy and counseling for those with sexual problems, easier availability of contraception, and greater social responsibility on the part of advertisers and the media. The resolution of these problems seems unlikely in the short run, but many interactionists are optimistic that a healthier, more matter-of-fact definition of sexual behavior will eventually replace the current state of confusion.

Other Perspectives

Biosocial theorists also have a great deal to say about sexual behavior. They point out that humans are the most sexually active animals on earth. The human female is unique because she is sexually receptive throughout her menstrual cycle, whereas the females of other species are receptive only around their periods of fertility. Nonetheless, men are more likely than women to desire a large number of sexual partners and to force others to have sex with them. Biosocial theorists often attribute these differences between the sexes to the process of evolution. According to one widely accepted theory, men have a higher sex drive and are naturally more promiscuous because sexual contact with a large number of women increases a man's chances of passing his genes on to the next generation (which, according to the theory of evolution, is the goal of all organisms). The more women a man has sex with, the more children he is likely to father, and the more descendants he is likely to leave. However, a woman's reproductive success is enhanced not by having sex with numerous men but by attaching herself to one man who will protect the children she bears, and women therefore tend to be more monogamous and less interested in forcing sexual relations on an unwilling partner.[77] Critics of this theory point out that even monkeys must be properly socialized or they will be unable to have sex or reproduce, and humans have a far greater capacity for learning than monkeys. Moreover, the critics charge that the rigid programming of sexual behavior hypothesized by some evolutionary theorists would actually be maladaptive for a species whose survival is dependent on effective cultural adaptation to a changing environment.

Quick Review

How do the functionalists see the problems of sexual behavior?

How is the approach of the feminists and conflict theorists similar, and where do they often disagree?

What responses to the problems of sexual behavior do interactionists recommend?

What do biosocial theorists say about the differences in the sexual behavior of males and females?

Summary

In view of the enormous range of sexual customs and beliefs found in different cultures, it is clear that all sexual behavior is not biologically determined. It derives from a biological drive, but a drive that is channeled, directed, and controlled by social forces.

Traditionally, Western culture has been sexually conservative: intercourse was permissible only between a husband and wife, and then only for reproduction. But these attitudes and values have changed. Comparisons of surveys taken over the past six decades show that there has been a substantial increase in many types of sexual activity. The double standard has weakened but has not disappeared; premarital and extramarital sex have increased significantly, as has sexual activity within marriage. The same surveys show no change in the incidence of homosexuality and a decrease in prostitution. A number of forces have contributed to the rise in sexual activity, including changing attitudes about sex, a weakening of the power of families to control the sexual behavior of their children, and improvement in birth control techniques.

Homosexuality is an often misunderstood form of sexual behavior. Contrary to popular belief, the differences among homosexuals, bisexuals, and heterosexuals are not absolute but are a matter of degree. Biosocial theorists feel that homosexuality is hereditary. Psychologists often argue that homosexuality is learned in the early years of childhood, and sociologists point out that strong prohibitions against adolescent heterosexual activity also encourage homosexual experimentation. In the past, most homosexuals concealed their sexual preference, but now many are "coming out" and publicly acknowledging their sexual preference, and there are flourishing gay and lesbian communities in the big cities of North America. Most European countries, Canada, and 27 American states have repealed their antihomosexual legislation, but homosexuality remains a crime in many places. Moreover, gays and lesbians are still subject to some of the most blatant occupational and social discrimination directed at any group in North America.

Unmarried teenage girls in the United States have sex about as often as those in other industrialized nations do, but because they are less likely to use birth control, U.S. teenagers are more likely to get pregnant. Another unintended complication of sexual activity may be exposure to sexually transmitted diseases; the worst of these is, of course, acquired immune deficiency syndrome (AIDS).

Child molestation is in a different category of sexual problems: the intentional sexual victimization of one person by another. Contrary to popular opinion, most cases of child molestation involve sexual behaviors that stop short of intercourse, and the offenders are not usually strangers but family members or friends. Psychologists argue that child molesters are sexually inadequate people who turn to children because they cannot handle adult sexual relations. Sociologists point out that many child molesters learned that behavior when they themselves were victimized as children.

Prostitution has declined in this century, but it is unlikely that it will ever disappear. Prostitutes have a hierarchy of occupational prestige from the call girl at the top to the streetwalker at the bottom. Although most prostitutes are females, there are a substantial number of men in the profession as well. Legal efforts to restrict prostitution have often aggravated the situation. Closing houses of prostitution created more streetwalkers, who are a far greater social problem than the "house girls" they replaced.

There are deep value conflicts concerning the issue of pornography, and there is no consensus about what the term means or whether it should be used at all. Many believe that all sexually explicit materials promote sex crimes, but the scientific evidence suggests that most is harmless. There is, however, reason for concern about explicit materials that contain violence or use children as sexual objects.

Several different responses to the social problems created by sexual behavior are commonly suggested, including (1) an effort to balance the unrealistic image of sexuality presented in the media with public service announcements promoting birth control and the use of condoms to prevent the spread of sexually transmitted disease; (2) the use of electronic technology to allow parents to block their children's access to sexually explicit material in the media; (3) more sex education in the schools and easier access to contraceptives for teenagers; (4) better enforcement of laws protecting children and other victims of sexual aggression; (5) legalization of all sexual behavior between consenting adults in private; (6) national legislation to protect the civil rights of gays and lesbians; and (7) encouraging greater social tolerance and understanding.

Many functionalists feel that prostitution is functional for society and should be legalized, but many also feel that other restrictions on sexual expression should be maintained in an effort to help protect the family. Conflict theorists say that problems of sexual behavior stem from value conflicts and from efforts by powerful groups to force their morality on others. Feminists argue that pornography degrades women and may encourage sexual violence. Interactionists are concerned about the harmful effects of the media's exploitation of sex to maximize their profits. Biosocial theorists argue that a great deal of our sexual behavior has been biologically predetermined by the process of evolution.

Questions for Critical Thinking

Sexual behavior is one of the areas in which we have deep disagreements about basic values and attitudes. Take a minute and look at yourself. What are your beliefs and values about sexuality and sexual behavior? How have those beliefs shaped your opinions about the way society should handle such issues as prostitution, pornography, teenage pregnancy, and protecting the civil liberties of gays and lesbians? Can you think of any social policies concerning these issues that you might be able to agree upon with someone who has different values than your own?

Key Terms

bisexuals
brothel
call girl
child molestation
coming out
double standard
extramarital sex
gays
heterosexuals
homosexuals
incest taboo

lesbians
madam
pimp
pornography
premarital intercourse
prostitution
sexual orientation
sexually transmitted disease (STD)
sodomy
streetwalker

Further Readings

Edward Donnerstein, Daniel Linz, and Steven Penrod, *The Question of Pornography: Research Findings and Policy Implications* (New York: Free Press, 1987). A comprehensive examination of the pornography issue. Contains an excellent review of the research on the effects of pornography.

Barbara Ehrenreich, Elizabeth Hess, and Gloria Jacobs, *Re-Making Love: The Feminization of Sex* (New York: Anchor/Doubleday, 1988). An interesting feminist analysis of the changes in our sexual attitudes and behaviors.

John H. Gagnon, Edward O. Laumann, Robert T. Michael, and Gina Kolata, *Sex in America: A Definitive Survey* (Boston: Little, Brown, 1994). The more popularly written of the two excellent books based on the 1992 National Health and Social Life Survey of sexual behavior.

Kristin Luker, *Dubious Conceptions: The Politics of Teenage Pregnancy* (Cambridge: Harvard University Press, 1996). An examination of Americans' misconceptions about teenage pregnancy and the impact they have had on social policy.

William Masters, Virginia Johnson, and Robert Kolodny, *Heterosexuality* (New York: HarperCollins, 1994). A comprehensive but easily readable examination of heterosexual behavior by the Masters and Johnson team that pioneered the scientific study of human sexual response.

Stephen O. Muray, *American Gay* (Chicago: University of Chicago Press, 1996). A look at the history of gays and lesbians in the United States.

Notes

1. Clellan S. Ford and Frank A. Beach, *Patterns of Sexual Behavior* (New York: Ace, 1951), p. 14.
2. William H. Davenport, "Sex in Cross-Cultural Perspective," in Frank A. Beach, ed., *Human Sexuality in Four Perspectives* (Baltimore: Johns Hopkins University Press, 1977), p. 124.
3. Ian Robertson, *Sociology,* 3rd ed. (New York: Worth, 1987), pp. 227–229.
4. Davenport, "Sex in Cross-Cultural Perspective," pp. 122–124.
5. Ibid., p. 125.
6. Conrad Kottak, *Cultural Anthropology,* 4th ed. (New York: Random House, 1987), pp. 152–153. For a more detailed description of the homosexual tribes of New Guinea, see V. van Baal, *Dema: Description and Analysis of Marid-Anim Culture* (The Hague: Nijhoff, 1966).

7. Alfred C. Kinsey, Wardell B. Pomeroy, and Clyde E. Martin, *Sexual Behavior in the Human Male* (Philadelphia: Saunders, 1948); Alfred C. Kinsey, Wardell B. Pomeroy, Clyde E. Martin, and Paul H. Gebhard, *Sexual Behavior in the Human Female* (Philadelphia: Saunders, 1953).

8. John H. Gagnon, Edward O. Laumann, Robert T. Michael, and Stuart Michaels, *The Social Organization of Sexuality* (Chicago: University of Chicago Press, 1994).

9. John H. Gagnon, Edward O. Laumann, Robert T. Michael, and Gina Kolata, *Sex in America: A Definitive Survey* (Boston: Little, Brown, 1994), p. 32.

10. June Reinisch, *The Kinsey Institute New Report on Sex* (New York: St. Martin's Press, 1990), pp. 139–141.

11. Robertson, *Sociology,* pp. 227–230.

12. Gagnon, Laumann, Michael, and Kolata, *Sex in America,* pp. 88–92; Morton Hunt, *Sexual Behavior in the 1970s* (New York: Dell, 1974), pp. 147–149.

13. Reinisch, *The Kinsey Institute New Report on Sex,* p. 6.

14. Nancy Gibbs, "How Should We Teach Our Children About Sex?" *Time,* May 25, 1993, pp. 60–66.

15. Reinisch, *The Kinsey Institute New Report on Sex,* p. 7; Gagnon, Laumann, Michael, and Kolata, *Sex in America,* pp. 88–110.

16. Reinisch, *The Kinsey Institute New Report on Sex,* p. 132.

17. Gagnon, Laumann, Michael, and Kolata, *Sex in America;* James Leslie McCary and Stephen P. McCary, *McCary's Human Sexuality* (Belmont, CA: Wadsworth, 1982), pp. 367–369, 382–389.

18. Gagnon, Laumann, Michael, and Kolata, *Sex in America,* pp. 169–183; Kinsey, Pomeroy, and Martin, *Sexual Behavior in the Human Male* and *Sexual Behavior in the Human Female.*

19. Gagnon, Laumann, Michael, and Kolata, *Sex in America,* p. 95; McCary and McCary, *McCary's Human Sexuality,* p. 431.

20. Gagnon, Laumann, Michael, and Kolata, *Sex in America,* p. 116.

21. Evelyn Hooker, "The Adjustment of the Male Overt Homosexual," *Journal of Projective Techniques* 21 (1957): 18–31; "Male Homosexuality and the Rorschach," *Journal of Projective Techniques* 22 (1958): 33–54.

22. See Philip Feldman, "The Homosexual Preference," in Kevin Howells, ed., *The Psychology of Sexual Diversity* (Oxford: Blackwell, 1984), pp. 20–22.

23. Sharon Begley, "Does DNA Make Some Men Gay?" *Newsweek,* July 26, 1993, p. 59; Natalie Angier, "Report Suggests Homosexuality Is Linked to Genes," *New York Times,* July 16, 1993, pp. A1, C18.

24. Simon LeVay, "A Difference in Hypothalamic Structure Between Heterosexual and Homosexual Men," *Science* 253 (1991): 1034–1037.

25. Hilary M. Lips, *Sex and Gender* (Mountain View, CA: Mayfield, 1988), pp. 114–115; Feldman, "The Homosexual Preference," pp. 22–24.

26. Ibid., pp. 24–28; A. P. Bell, M. S. Weinberg, and S. K. Hammersmith, *Sexual Preference* (Bloomington: Indiana University Press, 1981).

27. Richard Green, *The "Sissy Boy Syndrome" and the Development of Homosexuality* (New Haven, CT: Yale University Press, 1987).

28. See Ronald L. Akers, *Deviant Behavior: A Social Learning Approach,* 3rd ed. (Belmont, CA: Wadsworth, 1985), pp. 192–203.

29. Gagnon, Laumann, Michael, and Kolata, *Sex in America,* pp. 169–183; Boyce Rensberger, "2.3% of U.S. Men in Survey Report Homosexual Acts," *Los Angeles Times,* April 15, 1993, pp. A1, A17; Associated Press, "New Study Charts Men's Sex Habits," *San Luis Obispo Telegram-Tribune,* April 15, 1993, pp. A1, A12.

30. Gagnon, Laumann, Michael, and Kolata, *Sex in America,* pp. 169–183; McCary and McCary, *McCary's Human Sexuality,* pp. 446–450; Reinisch, *The Kinsey Institute New Report on Sex,* pp. 139–140; Thomas H. Maugh II, "Sex American Style: Trend to the Traditional," *Los Angeles Times,* February 19, 1990, pp. A1, A22; Scripps News Service, "Sexual Revolution: Most of America Missed It," *San Luis Obispo Telegram-Tribune,* February 19, 1990, p. A1.

31. Bettian Boxall, "Statistics on Gays Called Unreliable," *Los Angeles Times,* May 1, 1994, pp. A1, A24–A25.

32. Joseph Harry, "Gay and Lesbian Relationships," in Eleanor D. Macaklin and Roger H. Rubin, eds., *Contemporary Families and Alternative Lifestyles* (Beverly Hills, CA: Sage, 1983), pp. 216–234.

33. Marshall B. Clinard, *The Sociology of Deviant Behavior*, 4th ed. (New York: Holt, Rinehart & Winston, 1974), pp. 545–546.

34. Jane Gross, "After a Ruling Hawaii Weighs Gay Marriages," *New York Times*, April 25, 1994, pp. A1, C12.

35. Susan Essoyan, "Hawaii Approves Benefits Package for Gay Couples," *Los Angeles Times*, April 30, 1997, pp. A3, A14; Susan Essoyan and Bettina Boxall, "Hawaii Ruling Lifts Ban on Marriage of Same-Sex Couples," *Los Angeles Times*, December 4, 1996, p. A1, A 19.

36. Gerald R. Adams and Thomas Gullotta, *Adolescent Life Experiences* (Monterey, CA: Brooks/Cole, 1983), pp. 330–335.

37. Cimons, "Study Says More Young Women Have Sex"; Maugh, "Sex American Style"; Scripps News Service, "Sexual Revolution."

38. Gibbs, "How Should We Teach Our Children About Sex?"

39. Ibid.

40. Alan Guttmacher Institute, "Sex and America's Teenagers, 1994"; Claudia Wallis, "Children Having Children," *Time*, December 9, 1985, pp. 78–90.

41. Felicity Barringer, "Report Finds 1 in 5 Infected by Viruses Spread Sexually," *New York Times*, April 1, 1993, p. A1, A11.

42. William A. Rushing, *The AIDS Epidemic: Social Dimensions of an Infectious Disease* (Boulder, CO: Westview, 1995), p. 18.

43. Lawrence K. Altman, "Obstacle-Strewn Road to Rethinking the Numbers on AIDS," *New York Times*, March 1, 1994, p. B8; Daniel Q. Haney, "Survey Cuts Estimate of Americans with AIDS," *Boulder Daily Camera*, December 14, 1993, p. 1A.

44. U.S. Bureau of the Census, *Statistical Abstract of the United States, 1996*, (Washington DC: U.S. Government Printing Office, 1996), pp. 99, 142.

45. Steven Findlay, "AIDS: The Second Decade," *U.S. News & World Report*, June 17, 1991, pp. 20–23.

46. McCary and McCary, *McCary's Human Sexuality*, p. 413.

47. A. C. Jaffe, "Child Molestation," *Medical Aspects of Human Sexuality* (April 1976): 73, 93.

48. Charles H. McCaghy, "Child Molesting," *Sexual Behavior* (August 1971): 16–24.

49. Sue Titus Reid, *Crime and Criminology*, 4th ed. (New York: Holt, Rinehart & Winston, 1985), p. 260.

50. James Patterson and Peter Kim, *The Day America Told the Truth* (New York: Prentice Hall, 1991), p. 7.

51. Alex Thio, *Deviant Behavior*, 3rd ed. (New York: HarperCollins, 1988), pp. 157–160; McCary and McCary, *McCary's Human Sexuality*, pp. 412–414.

52. See Reid, *Crime and Criminology*, pp. 261–263.

53. Hunt, *Sexual Behavior in the 1970s*, p. 145; McCary and McCary, *McCary's Human Sexuality*, p. 431.

54. David F. Luckenbill, "Deviant Career Mobility: The Case of Male Prostitutes," *Social Problems* 33 (April 1986): 283–296.

55. T. M. Williams and William Kornblum, *Growing Up Poor* (Boston: Heath, 1985).

56. Jennifer James and Jane Meyerding, "Early Sexual Experience as a Factor in Prostitution," *Archives of Sexual Behavior* 7 (1977): 31–42.

57. Nanette Davis, "The Prostitute: Developing a Deviant Subculture," in J. H. Henslin, ed., *Studies in the Sociology of Sex* (Englewood Cliffs, NJ: Prentice Hall, 1987); K. N. Ginzberg, "The 'Meat-Rack': A Study of the Male Homosexual Prostitute," in C. D. Bryant, ed., *Sexual Deviancy in Social Context* (New York: New Viewpoints, 1977); N. R. Jackman, R. O'Toole, and Gilbert Geis, "The Self-Image of the Prostitute," *Sociological Quarterly* 4 (1963): 150–161.

58. N. Marshall and J. Hendtlass, "Drugs and Prostitution," *Journal of Social Issues* 16 (Spring 1986): 237–248.

59. Davis, "The Prostitute."

60. *Report of the President's Commission on Obscenity and Pornography* (New York: Bantam, 1970), p. 49.

61. Aric Press, "The War Against Pornography," *Newsweek,* March 18, 1985, pp. 58–66.

62. W. Cody Wilson, "Facts Versus Fears: Why Should We Worry About Pornography?" *Annals of the American Academy of Political Science* 397 (1971): 105–117.

63. Ibid., p. 113; Clinard, *Sociology of Deviant Behavior,* p. 534; David G. Savage, "Violence Against Women," *Los Angeles Times,* June 1, 1985, sec. 2, pp. 1, 6; Press, "The War Against Pornography."

64. See Frank E. Hagan, *Introduction to Criminology* (Chicago: Nelson-Hall, 1986), p. 247.

65. Edward Donnerstein and L. Berkowitz, "Victim Reactions in Aggressive Erotic Films as a Factor in Violence Against Women," *Journal of Personality and Social Psychology* 41 (1981): 710–724.

66. Edward Donnerstein, Daniel Linz, and Steven Penrod, *The Question of Pornography: Research Findings and Policy Implications* (New York: Free Press, 1987), pp. 172–179.

67. Press, "The War Against Pornography."

68. Savage, "Violence Against Women."

69. Michelle V. Rafter, "Urls! Urls! Urls!" *Los Angeles Times,* March 17, 1997, pp. D1, D6.

70. Jube Shiver, Jr., David G. Savage, and Elizabeth Shogren, "Law Curbing Indecency on Internet Overturned," *Los Angeles Times,* June 27, 1997, pp. A1, A 13.

71. Sharon Bernstein, "Condoms: Television's Dirty Little Secret," *Los Angeles Times,* October 19, 1990, pp. F1, F24–25.

72. Gibbs, "How Should We Teach Our Children About Sex?"

73. Tom Gorman, "Sex Classes: A Changing Direction," *Los Angeles Times,* July 19, 1985, pp. 1, 19; Wallis, "Children Having Children."

74. Ibid.

75. See Marjorie Shostack, *Nisa: The Life and Words of a !Kung Woman* (New York: Vintage, 1983).

76. Kingsley Davis, "The Sociology of Prostitution," *American Sociological Review* 2 (1937): 744–755.

77. Donald Symons, *The Evolution of Human Sexuality* (New York: Oxford University Press, 1979).

Is drug use increasing or decreasing?

Which drugs create the most serious problems?

Why do people use drugs?

How has legal repression affected drug use?

How can we deal with the drug problem?

Scott Krueger graduated near the top of his high school class in upstate New York and moved to Boston to attend the Massachusetts Institute of Technology. As an engineering major and a member of the crew team, he had a lot of demands on his time, but he still decided to pledge the Phi Gamma Delta fraternity. During Greek Week of his freshman year, Scott went to a fraternity party and apparently downed the equivalent of 16 shots of alcohol in a single hour. After he passed out, his friends carried him down to the basement of their rambling frat house, and then they discovered that he wasn't breathing well. He was rushed to the hospital, where he was kept on life support systems for a few days until he died. Blood tests showed that Scott's alcohol level was 0.41—more than four times the legal driving limit of .08. The doctors said that he died either from an alcohol-induced thickening of the blood, which prevented oxygen from reaching his brain, or from choking on his own vomit.[1]

Few other social problems are surrounded by more myths and misinformation than drug use. The confusion starts with the very meaning of the term. Many people mistakenly believe that only illegal substances, such as heroin, cocaine, or marijuana, are drugs; but, as Scott Krueger's death shows, alcohol can be just as dangerous as the illicit drugs, and so can tobacco. Nor is drug use confined to a few ragged deviants on the margins of society. Drugs are big business: Americans spend billions of dollars a year for coffee, tea, chocolate (which contains the stimulants caffeine and theobromine), tobacco, and alcohol, and the manufacturers of these products have a respected place among the corporate giants of today's economy.

One of the most widespread myths is that we are in the midst of an exploding "drug epidemic," but the truth is much more complex than that. The use of most drugs increased rapidly in the 1960s and 1970s, but drug use declined sharply after its peak in 1979 and continued to drop until the early 1990s and has more or less leveled off since then. Between 1980 and 1994, the amount of beer and wine consumed by the average American dropped over 12 percent, and the consumption of distilled liquors such as whiskey and vodka declined by over one-third.[2] The decrease in tobacco smoking began even earlier. In 1965, over 40 percent of adult Americans smoked; today, only about 25 percent do.[3] The use of illegal drugs is much less common than the use of legal ones, and there has been a steep decline in drug consumption. Among young adults age 18 to 25, marijuana use was almost three times more common in 1979 than it is today, and the use of cocaine was nine times more common. Although illicit drugs have never been as popular among older adults, marijuana use was still twice as common among Americans age 26 and over in 1979 as it is today, and cocaine use was about half again as common.[4] Although overall levels of drug use haven't changed much in the last few years, surveys show a marked increase in teenage drug use—especially marijuana and tobacco—since 1992. Marijuana use, for example, has more than doubled among adolescents aged 12 to 17.[5]

One common belief that is certainly not a myth is that the drug problem is widespread and extremely costly. According to the National Safety Council, about 60 percent of all drivers killed in automobile accidents had drunk enough alcohol to impair their driving skills. Alcohol abuse is estimated to cost $43 billion to $120 billion each year in lost workdays, medical expenses, and accidents.[6] Some of the most tragic problems occur among adolescents who turn to drugs to escape the intense

Figure 12.1

Drugs

Legal drugs are far more commonly used than illegal ones.

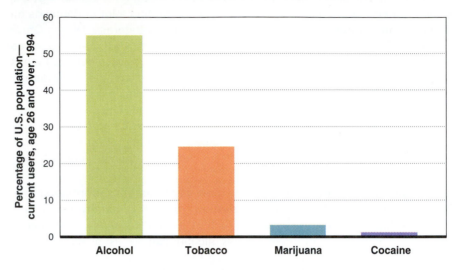

Source: U.S. Bureau of the Census, *Statistical Abstract of the United States, 1996* (Washington, DC: U.S. Government Printing Office, 1996), p. 144.

emotional problems they face. According to government surveys, about 16 percent of U.S. adolescents use alcohol at least once a month; 10 percent smoke tobacco, 7 percent use marijuana, and 0.4 percent use cocaine.[7] (See Figure 12.1.)

Drugs and Drug Addiction

Addiction is a technical term that is difficult to define precisely. In the broadest sense, addiction refers to an intense craving for a particular substance, but this definition can be applied to almost any desire or craving, whether it is for ice cream, potato chips, or heroin. To avoid this confusion, drug addiction is sometimes erroneously defined as the physiological dependence that a person develops after heavy use of a particular drug. Most addicts, however, experience periods when they "kick" their physical dependence, yet their psychological craving continues undiminished and they soon return to drugs. It is therefore more useful to define **addiction** as the intense craving for a drug that develops after a period of physical dependence.

Two essential characteristics of an addictive drug are tolerance and withdrawal discomfort. **Tolerance** is another name for the immunity to the effects of a drug that builds up after heavy use. For instance, if someone takes the same amount of heroin every day for a month, the last dose will have much less effect than the first. If the user wants the same psychological effect at the end of the month, the dosage must be increased. **Withdrawal** is the name given to the sickness that habitual users experience when they stop taking drugs. Addictive drugs produce both toler-

addiction
The intense craving for a drug that develops after a period of physical dependence.

tolerance
The immunity to the effects of a drug that builds up after repeated use.

withdrawal
The sickness that habitual users experience when they stop taking drugs.

ance and withdrawal distress. Drugs that produce tolerance but no withdrawal discomfort, such as LSD, are not addictive.

Drug addiction is not solely a physiological matter, however. Psychological craving supplements biological dependence. Moreover, the behavior of those who use specific drugs is influenced by cultural expectations that are quite independent of the drug's physiological effects. For example, anyone who drinks a large quantity of alcohol will pass out—a physiological reaction; but behavior of people who are drunk (but not dead drunk) varies greatly from culture to culture and even from group to group within a culture. For example, in some cultures people become more violent and aggressive when they drink, but in other cultures such a reaction is rare.[8]

By examining such things as the percentage of users who become dependent on a particular drug, the difficulty of stopping use, and the relapse rate, researchers are able to rate how addictive different drugs are. When measured by such criteria, nicotine (a drug found in tobacco) is the most addictive, followed by heroin, cocaine, and alcohol. Second from the bottom is caffeine, and the least addictive of the commonly used drugs is marijuana.[9]

Alcohol

The use of alcohol is an accepted part of our culture. Businesspeople make deals over a bottle of expensive wine, college students escape the pressures of final exams with a keg of beer, restaurants offer champagne brunches and boast vast wine cellars, and neighborhood bars serve as social centers for many local residents. The fact that alcohol is so widely accepted and so widely used means that it creates more problems than other drugs.

Alcohol, like most other drugs, is rather harmless when used in moderation (except in the case of pregnant women), but it is extremely dangerous when used to excess. Alcohol is called a **depressant** drug because it depresses the activity of the central nervous system and thereby impedes coordination, reaction time, and reasoning ability. Large doses of alcohol produce disorientation, loss of consciousness, and even death. The psychological reaction to alcohol varies from person to person, but the physiological effects of alcohol clearly increase as the level of alcohol in the blood rises. The effects first become apparent when the concentration of alcohol in the blood reaches about 0.05 percent, and most states hold 0.08 to 0.10 percent to be the point of legal intoxication. Extreme intoxication occurs between 0.20 and 0.30 percent. A user with over 0.4 percent blood alcohol is likely to pass out, and concentrations over 0.6 percent are usually fatal.[10]

depressant
A drug that slows the responses of the central nervous system, reduces coordination, and decreases mental alertness.

Prolonged heavy drinking may generate a number of health problems. Alcoholic beverages are high in calories but have little other food value; for this reason, heavy drinkers often lose their appetites and suffer from malnutrition. The harmful effects of excessive drinking on the liver are well known: the end result may be cirrhosis, a condition in which liver cells are destroyed by alcohol and replaced by scar tissue. Heavy drinkers are more likely than others to have heart problems, and there is evidence that they suffer from a higher rate of cancer as well. Drinkers may also be a problem to their children. Studies show that the children of alcoholic mothers have lower birthweights, slower language development, lower IQs, and more birth defects than other children.[11]

Alcohol will produce addiction if used in sufficient amounts over a long period. The so-called DTs (short for *delirium tremens*) are actually symptoms of alcohol withdrawal. These symptoms commonly include nausea, vomiting, and convulsions; sometimes they involve hallucinations and coma as well. Death from heart failure or severe convulsions occurs in about 10 percent of victims of the DTs. A much more common cause of death is the use of alcohol in combination with other depressant drugs. Many people have unintentionally killed themselves by taking sleeping pills after an evening of heavy drinking. Death occurs because two depressant drugs taken together have a *synergistic* effect; that is, the effect of the two drugs is much greater than that of either drug taken alone.

When asked by survey takers, most Americans agree that heavy drinking is a serious problem in the United States, and one out of five persons questioned told the Gallup poll that drinking had been a source of distress in their own families.[12] It is doubtful that all the people who cause such problems should be considered alcoholics, but the term is often used so loosely that anyone who takes more than an occasional drink might be included. For the purposes of this book, we will define an **alcoholic** as a person whose persistent drinking problem disrupts his or her life, interfering with the ability to hold a job, complete household tasks, or participate in family and social affairs. Statistics suggest that alcoholics can expect to die 10 to 12 years sooner than other people and are more likely to suffer from a variety of serious health conditions. Estimates of the number of alcoholics in the United States range from 8 to 25 million—more than the total number of users of most illicit drugs.[13]

One of the most serious problems associated with the use of alcohol is drunk driving. There are many different estimates about how many traffic fatalities are caused by drunk drivers every year, but it is a substantial number. What we do know

alcoholic
A person whose work or family and social life are disrupted by drinking.

Drunk driving continues to be a major social problem. This photo shows the car in which Diana, the former Princess of Wales, died. Her driver is believed to have been under the influence of alcohol at the time of the accident.

Figure 12.2

Drinking

Males drink more alcohol than females, and whites are more likely to drink than blacks or Latinos.

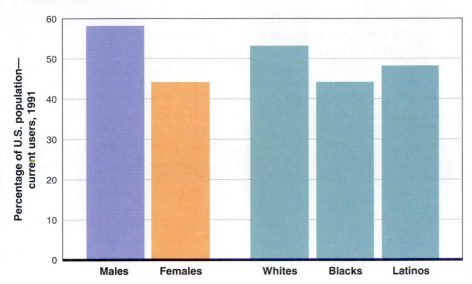

Source: U.S. Bureau of the Census, *Statistical Abstract of the United States, 1993* (Washington, DC: U.S. Government Printing Office, 1993), p. 137.

is that in 1993, 22 percent of the drivers in fatal crashes were drunk—a substantial decline from 1982, when that figure was about 30 percent.[14] In recent years, the victims of drunk drivers have banded together with other concerned citizens in such organizations as MADD (Mothers Against Drunk Driving) and SADD (Students Against Drunk Driving) to increase awareness of the problem and push for stiffer punishments. Public attitudes have grown less tolerant of those who drink and drive, and the laws have grown increasingly tough as well. Forty-four states now have mandatory jail sentences for second-time offenders, and many have also lowered the level of alcohol in the blood that defines legal drunkenness.

In the most current surveys, a little more than half of all Americans say they have had at least one drink in the last month,[15] but as we have seen, the use of alcohol has been decreasing in the last two decades. The prevalence of drinking also varies widely among different social and ethnic groups. Most studies indicate that more men than women drink, but the differences have narrowed as women have gained more freedoms and taken on more financial burdens.[16] Whites drink more frequently than African Americans, and the prevalence of drinking is greatest among the college-educated and those with higher incomes. (See Figure 12.2.)

Drinking is a particular problem among college students. One survey found that 42 percent of college students had had a drinking binge (five or more drinks in a row) within the last two weeks. The stereotypes about drunken fraternity parties apparently have some basis in fact as well: alcohol consumption is three times higher among students who live in fraternity or sorority houses than among others.

Although female students still drink less than males, the biggest increase in recent years has been among women.[17]

Tobacco

About one in every four Americans over the age of 17 smokes cigarettes, and about one in every eight between ages 12 and 17 does. Men smoke more than women, but the use of tobacco has been declining more rapidly among men.[18] About 70 percent of all smokers have more than 15 cigarettes a day, making tobacco one of the few drugs that addicts use nearly every waking hour of every day. Sales of tobacco, like those of alcohol, have been falling in recent years. Since 1965, the percent of adult Americans who smoke has dropped 40 percent.[19]

The principal drug in tobacco is nicotine, which is clearly addictive. The average smoker takes in about 25 milligrams of nicotine a day and will begin to experience withdrawal when intake drops below 5 milligrams.[20] Symptoms include drowsiness, nervousness, anxiety, headaches, and loss of energy. Nicotine is a stimulant that raises blood pressure, speeds up the heartbeat, and gives the user a sense of alertness. However, nicotine also seems to have the contradictory effect of producing a feeling of relaxation and calm in some people. Some claim that this relaxation is due to the ritual of smoking and not to the drug itself, but the issue remains unclear.[21]

In 1964 the surgeon general's Advisory Committee on Smoking and Health issued its famous report concluding that smoking is hazardous to health, and since then the annual report issued by the federal government has painted an ever bleaker picture. Commenting on the particularly detailed 1979 report, the secretary of the Department of Health, Education and Welfare said that it "reveals with dramatic clarity that cigarette smoking is even more dangerous—indeed, far more dangerous—than was supposed in 1964."[22] In issuing the 1988 report, the surgeon general took another major step by forcefully acknowledging the addictive properties of nicotine and its similarity in that regard to heroin and other illegal drugs.[23] A study published in the *Journal of the American Medical Association* in 1993 concluded that tobacco smoking is implicated in almost one in every five deaths in the United States, making it America's *number one* cause of death.[24] The most common estimate is that tobacco smoking kills about 400,000 Americans every year.[25]

Cigarette smoking has been linked to cancer of the larynx, mouth, and esophagus as well as to lung cancer. Other diseases linked to smoking include bronchitis, emphysema, ulcers, and heart and circulatory disorders. The babies of women who smoke weigh less than other babies and have slower rates of physical and mental growth.[26] Even nonsmokers are at risk if they live or work in a smoke-filled environment. A 1991 report by the Environmental Protection Agency, which some of its own officials tried to cover up, estimated that 53,000 Americans a year die from **passive smoking.** In 1993 the EPA declared secondhand smoke a "group A" carcinogen.[27] A 1997 study by a team of Harvard researchers concluded that exposure to secondhand smoke nearly doubles the risk of heart disease.[28]

If smoking is so dangerous, why do so many people smoke? One reason is that cigarette smoking is addictive and most smokers find it difficult to stop. But what about the substantial number of young people who begin smoking every year despite medical warnings? Youthful rebelliousness is certainly part of the reason. Another factor is the tobacco industry's success in establishing an association in the public mind between smoking and maturity, sophistication, and sexual attractive-

passive smoking
Exposure to "secondhand" tobacco smoke from other people's cigars and cigarettes.

ness. Cigarette manufacturers spend about $4 billion a year advertising their products, and the smokers in those ads are invariably young and good-looking. The surgeon general's 1994 report on smoking concluded that the money the tobacco industry spends on advertising and publicity is contributing to an increase in smoking among the young.[29] As overall sales of cigarettes have decreased in recent years, the tobacco industry has responded with ever more sophisticated marketing campaigns targeted at specific groups. The popularity of smoking among women reflects the special efforts the tobacco companies have made to encourage them to smoke, and similar campaigns have been directed at African Americans and Latinos. Not surprisingly, rates of lung cancer and other respiratory diseases have shown an alarming increase among these groups in recent years.[30]

Marijuana

Marijuana is the most widely used illegal drug. More than 1 in 3 Americans acknowledges having tried marijuana, but only about 1 in 20 is classified as a current user (that is, reported using the drug at least once within the previous month).[31] Marijuana use is most frequent among those between 18 and 25 years of age and drops off sharply after age 35. Marijuana use increased greatly during the 1960s and 1970s, but as with most other drugs, marijuana smoking has decreased significantly since then.

The health hazards of marijuana are still the subject of an emotional debate that has often had more to do with politics than with scientific research. Numerous claims made about the damage caused by marijuana have later proved to be false. The current evidence indicates that the main health hazard in marijuana use is the risk of cancer and other lung problems caused by inhaling the smoke. Studies show that the way marijuana is usually smoked (deep inhalations that are held for a long time) makes it more damaging than tobacco, puff for puff.[32] However, this effect is offset by the greater number of cigarettes smoked by tobacco users. Two or three "joints" a day is heavy marijuana use (and because marijuana is usually shared among a group of people, each user smokes less), whereas many heavy tobacco users smoke more than fifty cigarettes a day. There is also evidence that marijuana may harm a user's unborn baby, and pregnant women should not use the drug. Thus, those who claim that marijuana is harmless are wrong: there are clearly significant health hazards involved in the excessive use of marijuana. However, on the whole, marijuana is probably less dangerous than most other widely used recreational drugs, including alcohol. Marijuana has also proved to be a useful treatment for several medical conditions—for example, increasing appetite among AIDS patients suffering from "wasting syndrome"—and there is a growing movement to legalize the medical use of marijuana. In 1997, California voters approved an initiative to do just that; however, federal drug enforcement officials are struggling to prevent the medical use of marijuana in that state.

The psychological effects of smoking marijuana are strongly influenced by the social environment and the expectations of the users. Howard S. Becker found that users must learn from their peers how to identify the effects of the drug before they actually get "high."[33] Descriptions of the drug's psychological effects vary considerably from one person to another. Typical effects include relaxation, increased sensitivity, and hunger. Studies show that a marijuana "high" impairs reaction time and coordination and therefore makes driving or operating other machinery more dangerous.[34]

Debate   Should Smoking Be Outlawed?

Yes

The evidence is clear. Tobacco is a deadly killer. Tobacco kills more people than alcohol, heroin, marijuana, cocaine, amphetamines, and barbiturates combined. Deaths from guns and even from automobiles don't even come close. In fact, it is the *number one* cause of death in this country.

Numerous programs and policies have been tried to stem its deadly tide. Minors were forbidden to buy it. A health warning was placed on every pack. Television and radio ads were banned. The government issued endless reports warning of its dangers. Smoking was forbidden in many offices and public buildings. Yet after all this, one in every four adults still smokes. The fact is that this drug is highly addictive, and once people start smoking, many of them can't stop. The only cure for this deadly plague is the total prohibition of all smoking. That way addicts will be forced to quit and young people will no longer be tempted to start the deadly habit.

The opponents of prohibition claim that it will not stop smoking but will simply create the same kind of black market for tobacco that there is for other illegal drugs. Such arguments overlook one critical difference between tobacco and most other drugs: most tobacco addicts smoke virtually all day long. Once tobacco is prohibited and people are arrested for smoking in public, they simply would not be able to keep up that kind of consumption unless they stayed home all day. Tobacco is an addictive drug that is turning billions of dollars in profits for the corporations that produce it, while killing hundreds of thousands of people every year. If not for the political influence that money has brought the tobacco corporations, this drug would have been prohibited years ago. We must act to end this legalized murder. We must ban tobacco now.

Opiates

The opiates are a group of natural (opium, codeine, morphine, and heroin) and synthetic (meperidine, methadone) depressants, all of which are highly addictive. Users rapidly develop a tolerance and must continually increase their dosage to get the same effects. Although the intensity of opiate withdrawal varies with the amount taken and with the individual involved, withdrawal seldom causes the screaming agony depicted in so many books and movies. Withdrawal distress usually resembles a bad case of the flu accompanied by a feeling of extreme depression. In some cases, however, it can be much more severe.

Opiate addiction has serious consequences for the health of the addict. Ironically, most of these problems come not from the drug itself but from the way in which it is used. (See the Personal Perspectives box for the story of a college student who was also a heroin addict.) The opiate addict's life-style, as well as impure drugs and infected needles, produces most of the severe health problems. Addicts often share the same needles without proper sterilization, and this practice spreads disease. Until recently, hepatitis, a dangerous liver infection, was the most serious

No

Although a small number of alarmists are trying to whip the public into a frenzy, the fact is that millions of Americans enjoy smoking and have no desire to quit. A democratic government simply has no right to tell its citizens how to live their lives.

Look at the historical record. Prohibition didn't work for alcohol, and it won't work for tobacco either. After alcohol was prohibited, a huge black market sprang up and made millionaires out of organized criminals. There was an unprecedented wave of gang violence as bands of organized thugs fought to control that vast new illegal market. Moreover, prohibition did not even stop people from drinking. The same thing would happen today if tobacco were banned. Gangs and organized criminals would get rich, and the battle for control of the multibillion-dollar tobacco market would touch off a wave of violence and bloodshed the likes of which this nation has never seen. Millions of average Americans would be turned into criminals overnight, and before long a new deviant subculture would spring up to meet the needs of tobacco smokers. As selling and transporting tobacco products became increasingly difficult, producers would be certain to develop more and more potent products that bring a higher price and are easier to conceal. Just as opiate prohibition eventually spawned the heroin market, so new "supertobaccos" would soon be on the market, and they would make our current problems with cocaine look like kid stuff.

Tobacco prohibition would be a national disaster. It would turn millions of upstanding citizens into criminals, put billions of dollars into the pockets of the real criminals, and violate our most basic civil liberties, and on top of it all, it wouldn't even do much to stop the use of tobacco. How can anyone seriously suggest such a utterly misguided policy?

risk, but intravenous (IV) drug users are now stalked by a much more deadly disease: AIDS. About one-third of all new cases of AIDS are now among IV drug users, and a majority of the addicts in some cities are believed to be infected with the virus.[35] Overdose is another threat to the addict's survival and is a major cause of death among young males in many American cities. In many cases, however, death can more properly be attributed to the combination of opiates with other depressant drugs, such as alcohol.

Despite all the publicity, opiate use is actually quite rare. Only 1 of every 1000 respondents in a recent federal survey acknowledged having used heroin in the last month.[36] However, the Colombian drug cartels that dominate the cocaine market have recently been moving into heroin sales, and there has been a significant decrease in the cost and an increase in the purity of street heroin. As recently as 1985, the average purity of street heroin was about 5 percent; today, it averages as much as 37 percent.[37] As heroin use increases, some observers are becoming concerned about a new heroin epidemic, particularly if the price remains low enough to allow recreational users to smoke or sniff the drug rather than inject it.

Personal Perspectives   A College Heroin User

Most people know someone who has used marijuana or cocaine, but heroin is often seen as the kind of drug confined to the slums and ghettos. The following account from a middle-class college student shows us a different side of the heroin problem.

I knew there were people using it, and I knew it was very addictive. I knew it was dangerous, but I had this drive to try it one time. There was this intrigue involved with being a heroin addict. In the drug culture it was the top of the ladder—or the bottom of the hole. Or rather both at the same time. You had just graduated to the hard core if you were using heroin. It was not looked upon favorably among the people that I went around with, but it was still sort of held in awe. So when I got the chance I jumped at it.

My friends first thought I was crazy. But they weren't that aware of the dangers of how one can break down and degenerate. It started out almost as being a joke. . . . By the time it was six months later and I was still shooting dope, people were getting worried and upset. They tried to talk sense into me but I didn't listen. Gradually people began to shy away from me. I started to shy away too. . . .

I hated heroin and I loved it. I was totally under its grip, I had no will of my own. I loved to be loaded and nodded back, but at the same time I sensed that if I kept doing it I could kill myself. . . . I got into having no interest in sex at all. It was just something that was replaced by heroin. It was something I didn't need anymore.

I am convinced that the normal state of affairs is going through cycles of being disturbed about things and then being happy about things. Heroin interrupts this process. . . . After addiction sets in there is a middle ground of this gray area where nothing is terribly depressing while again nothing is terribly exciting. The definition of what's good and what's bad, what's happy and what's sad all melts into one thing, and as long as you have dope it's cool, you can maintain life. . . . Aside from the rush and the high, the state of just not caring at all was very attractive to me at the time. That was the way I wanted to live my life at the time.

Well over half of all heroin addicts in the United States live in its three largest cities, with the heaviest concentration in New York City. Addiction is an urban phenomenon in Canada as well, with its major center in Vancouver. Despite some increase in heroin use among the middle class, most addicts are young males from the poorest segments of society. However, not all opiate users fit this stereotype: there are more addicts in the medical profession than in any other occupation.[38]

Psychedelics

The physical effects of the most popular psychedelic drugs, such as LSD (lysergic acid diethylamide), mescaline, and MDMA (methylenedioxymethamphetamine), are generally minor. However, taken in large doses, they produce some of the most sweeping psychological effects of any drugs, including profound changes in emotion, perception, and thought. The psychedelics rank only third in popularity among the illicit drugs, but after years of decline, their use has been increasing.

Mescaline was probably among the first psychedelic drugs used in North America. The consumption of the peyote cactus (which contains mescaline) was apparently an important element in some Native American religions long before Europeans came to the continent. At the other extreme is MDMA, which is one of the newest arrivals on the drug scene. Sometimes known as "ecstasy" when sold on the streets, the drug is the center of controversy between some psychiatrists, who believe that it is a useful therapeutic tool, and drug enforcement officials, who have succeeded in banning its use.

LSD is probably the best known of the psychedelic drugs. A tiny dose of the colorless and tasteless drug produces a tremendous psychological effect that is highly unpredictable. Some users report an intensely beautiful experience, whereas others find it the most frightening experience of their lives, and still others swing from one extreme to the other on the same "acid trip." Aside from such profound emotional changes, LSD also produces hallucinations and perceptual distortions. Colors and smells often appear more intense under the influence of these drugs. Although some have charged that LSD produces brain damage and birth defects, there is little evidence to support this claim.[39]

The greatest dangers of psychedelic drugs are psychological rather than physical. The "bad trip"—a terrifying experience that often throws the user into a panicky state—is always a possibility, especially among inexperienced users. Such bad trips have apparently brought on serious mental disorders in some susceptible persons. The average dose of LSD used today is only one-fourth to one-half of what it was during the drug's first wave of popularity in the 1960s, and as a result, the intensity of the psychological effects and the likelihood of a bad trip are both reduced.[40] Because the environment is so important in determining whether a psychedelic experience is wonderful or terrifying, many users take the drug with a "guide" who understands the effects of the drug and can help point them in the right direction.

Sedative-Hypnotics

Sedative-hypnotics, such as barbiturates and tranquilizers, depress the central nervous system. In moderate doses, these drugs slow down breathing and normal reflexes, interfere with coordination, and relieve anxiety and tension. Speech becomes slurred, the mind clouded. In larger doses, they produce drowsiness and sleep. Medically, these drugs are used to produce two effects: relaxation (sedation) and sleep (hypnosis). The psychological effects of many of these drugs are similar to those of alcohol. Indeed, the state of intoxication produced by barbiturates (the sedative-hypnotic most commonly used by recreational drug users) is often indistinguishable from alcoholic drunkenness. Like alcohol, these drugs are addictive; repeated doses produce a growing tolerance, and heavy use can create severe withdrawal distress. In fact, abrupt barbiturate withdrawal is fatal for about 1 in every 20 persons. As already mentioned, another serious danger with the sedative-hypnotics is the risk of overdose if they are combined with each other or with alcohol.[41]

Amphetamines

The amphetamines are a group of synthetic **stimulants** that includes Benzedrine, Dexedrine, and methedrine. These drugs were once widely marketed as "diet pills," although physicians are now much more likely to use other methods to help patients

stimulant
A drug that arouses the central nervous system, increases the metabolic rate, and reduces drowsiness.

lose weight. Amphetamines reduce the appetite, increase blood pressure, and step up the rate of breathing. In moderate doses they generate heightened alertness, even excitement. Continuous heavy doses of an amphetamine produce a psychosis-like state that is often indistinguishable from schizophrenia. Fear and suspicion are common symptoms, and fits of violent aggression may occur. Hallucinations, delusions, and general confusion are also common. Repeated use of amphetamines leads to tolerance; withdrawal symptoms, mainly severe depression, also occur.

Most amphetamine users take the drug in pill form, but some inject it directly into the bloodstream, producing a brief but extremely intense high or "rush." Such heavy use takes a tremendous toll on the health of the user; so-called speed freaks often go on "runs" lasting several days, during which they often do not eat properly or sleep at all. Long-term users lose their hair, their teeth, and a large portion of their normal body weight, and amphetamine-induced psychosis becomes increasingly severe.[42] There is evidence that the crackdown on the cocaine trade has caused some users to switch to amphetamines—lower-priced drugs that are relatively easy for black-market chemists to produce.[43]

Cocaine

Cocaine is a natural stimulant derived from the leaves of the coca plant, which Peruvians have chewed for at least 1500 years. Until 1906 it was a major ingredient of Coca-Cola and a number of patent medicines. The effects of cocaine are similar to those of amphetamines, but there are two differences: first, cocaine is a powerful local anesthetic, and second, the effects of cocaine do not last as long. Cocaine users often repeat their doses every hour or so as the effects wear off. Heavy cocaine users may experience the same personality changes and psychotic episodes as heavy amphetamine users, but the most frequent psychological effect is irritability and depression that occur after the drug wears off. The easiest way to avoid those discomforts is, of course, to take more cocaine, and compulsive use of the drug is a widespread problem. Many wealthy cocaine users report having spent hundreds of thousands of dollars on their drug habit.

Most users sniff cocaine powder into their nose through a tube or straw. Heavy users who "snort" cocaine in this way often suffer damage to the nasal passages and have a constantly runny nose. Smoking cocaine has become popular because it produces an intense and immediate high, but it also has the potential to cause severe lung damage as well as a host of other serious health conditions. Street cocaine cannot, however, be smoked unless it is chemically treated in a process known as *freebasing*. In response to the rising popularity of freebasing, dealers introduced "crack": a special form of cocaine that comes in a small "rock" that can be smoked immediately without further chemical treatment. The enormous success this new product found among hard-core users created a crisis in many inner-city neighborhoods as gang wars broke out between groups trying to control the lucrative trade in crack.[44]

In the early part of this century, cocaine use was concentrated mainly among poor African Americans, but the demographics of cocaine use have changed dramatically. In the 1970s and early 1980s, cocaine became known as a "rich man's drug" because of its high cost and its popularity among some middle-class professionals. However, the popularity of crack in the underclass, as well as more negative attitudes about cocaine in the middle class, reshaped the demographics of cocaine use once again. Surveys indicate that cocaine use has plummeted in the last few years.[45] However, such studies generally miss large segments of the underclass, and it is quite possible that their behavior is not following the national trend.

Steroids

The anabolic steroids are synthetic drugs similar in structure to the male hormone testosterone. They are unique among the drugs discussed here because they are taken not for their immediate psychological effects but for building muscle and increasing athletic performance. (Steroids also have legitimate medical uses, but it is their use as a performance booster that makes them a social problem.) Although there is no evidence that simply taking the drug produces athletic benefits, it does heighten the effectiveness of training programs designed to enhance muscularity and strength. Such benefits carry a heavy price, however, which may include elevated cholesterol levels, high blood pressure, heart problems, irritability, liver damage, and sterility. In males, heavy steroid use may cause atrophy of the testicles, and in females, heavy use may cause development of some male characteristics such as a deeper voice and more body hair. Steroid use by adolescents may also disrupt normal growth patterns. Thus, young steroid users who seek to build muscle may also be stunting the growth of their skeletal systems.[46]

Although steroids are banned by virtually all reputable athletic organizations, including the International Olympic Committee, their use is still extremely common. In the ultracompetitive atmosphere of today's sports, many athletes feel they need every advantage possible. There are numerous reports that coaches as far down as the high school level have ignored the rules and encouraged their athletes to take these drugs. In some cases, coaches even act as drug dealers by providing steroids to their athletes. There is also disturbing evidence of increasing steroid use among teenage boys—both for improved athletic performance and for muscle-building. A 1990 survey by the Department of Health and Human Services estimated that about 3 percent of the boys in grades 7 through 12 have taken steroids.[47]

Quick Review

What are the definitions of *addiction, tolerance,* and *withdrawal?*

What are health dangers associated with each of the most commonly used drugs?

How do the physical effects of those drugs differ?

Why Use Drugs?

Researchers seem to be fascinated with the question of why we use drugs. Tremendous effort has gone into the investigation of this topic, much of it on the assumption that if we can find out why people take drugs, we can find ways of preventing them from doing so. Most of this research has been on the social psychological level, but we will also examine some structural theories in the section on theoretical perspectives at the end of this chapter.

Biological Theories

Many observers believe that drug problems are caused by the nature of the drugs themselves: once someone takes too much of a drug, he or she becomes addicted and is simply unable to stop. Although such theories are probably most popular with the general public, biological explanations of drug problems have also won increasing attention from scientists over the last two decades. For example, a Danish study found that 65 percent of people whose identical twin was an alcoholic became alcoholics themselves, compared with only 25 percent of nonidentical twins. Although much of this difference may stem from the fact that identical twins are treated more similarly than are fraternal twins, some studies indicate that alcoholism in adopted children correlates more closely with the alcoholism of biological parents than with the alcoholism of adoptive parents.[48] In one of the best-known biological theories of alcoholism, E. M. Jellinek argued that it is not voluntary behavior but a disease with a consistent pattern of symptoms.[49] Some studies have attempted to find the exact biochemical reason that one person is more susceptible to alcoholism than another. The evidence shows that alcoholics have higher levels of a chemical known as acetaldehyde that is produced by the metabolic breakdown of alcohol in the body. However, some researchers hold that these high levels of acetaldehyde are the result, not the cause, of alcoholism. Others argue that persons who are better able to metabolize alcohol are more likely to become alcoholics. Because they have a higher tolerance to the effects of alcohol, such persons drink more heavily, and their metabolism in turn produces more of the chemicals that create the physical addiction to alcohol.[50]

We must nonetheless be careful not to let the impressive findings of biological research lead us to unwarranted conclusions. Although there apparently is a genetic predisposition toward particular drug problems in some individuals, drug use is still a learned behavior, created and controlled by society. There are no alcoholics or heroin addicts in cultures where the use of those drugs is unknown or is practiced only in tightly restricted ritual situations. Drug problems are much more severe than they were two centuries ago because of the wrenching changes brought on by industrialization, not because there has been a genetic change in our population. Although biological theories cannot explain the historical changes in drug consumption or the reasons drug problems are so much worse in big cities than in traditional small towns, they do help us understand why one person develops a drug problem while another person with similar experiences and background does not.

Behavioral Theory

Psychologists have done extensive studies of the effects of drug use on animals, and they have found that animals can be trained to use drugs and that some become habituated. Behaviorists argue that such experiments show that drug use is learned through a process of conditioning. Taking a drug often provides a reward (positive reinforcement), and when experimental animals or humans use a drug and find it pleasurable, they are likely to use it again.

Alfred Lindesmith, on the other hand, turned this behavioral theory on its head.[51] Rather than being attracted to an enjoyable experience, he said, the addict is

trying to escape the unpleasant experience of withdrawal distress (negative reinforcement). According to Lindesmith, addicts so frequently use drugs to relieve
withdrawal discomfort that they begin to associate the drug with the relief it brings.
They continue to use drugs even when there is no physiological dependence because they associate drug use with the elimination of discomfort and pain.

Critics complain that the basic idea behind behavioral theory—that people use
drugs because they find them pleasurable and continue to use them because doing
so prevents withdrawal distress—is nothing new. But whether the concept is old or
new, there is little doubt about the importance of this kind of reinforcement in developing a drug habit.

Personality Theories

Many psychologists have tried to explain drug problems by investigating users' personalities. However, there is no general agreement among psychologists about the
personality characteristics of addicts and drug abusers. Drug addicts have been classified as narcissists, psychopaths, sociopaths, dependent personalities, immature, schizophrenic, neurotic, and character-disordered, to list only a few of the labels used.

The most common theory is that alcoholics and drug addicts have weak personalities and low self-esteem and therefore turn to drugs to try to escape their problems. G. E. Barnes, for example, argues that there is an "alcoholic personality" that
displays such characteristics as "neuroticism, weak ego, stimulus augmenting [a hy-
persensitivity to the environment that results in fear and anxiety], and field dependency [a passive-dependent orientation to life]."[52] Because these traits may be a response to alcoholism rather than its cause, psychologists also talk about a
"prealcoholic personality." The characteristics that are believed to lead to alcoholism include impulsivity, gregariousness, and nonconformity.[53] Isador Chein and
his associates reached similar conclusions about their sample of heroin addicts.[54]
They found that heroin addicts have major personality disorders originating in the
addicts' early family histories. The mother was usually the most important parental
figure to the child, and the father was usually cold or even hostile. Children from
these homes were found to be overindulged or frustrated and were uncertain of the
standards expected of them. These conditions were said to produce such personality traits as passivity, defensiveness, and low self-esteem.

Critics of these studies charge that they are little more than a reflection of the
popular stereotypes that condemn people who suffer from drug problems. They argue that heavy drug users have as many diverse personality characteristics as any
other group of people and that the findings of these psychologists are based on their
own prejudices and the fact that addicts with inadequate personalities are more
likely to seek psychological treatment. Support for this position comes from an unusually comprehensive 40-year longitudinal study of 660 young men drawn both
from Harvard University and from an inner-city slum. Although the study found a
strong correlation between alcoholism in parents and children, no personality differences were found between those who became alcoholics and those who did
not.[55]

Despite the weaknesses in these theories, there is no question that personality
plays an important role in an individual's decision to use a drug. After all, there are
wide differences in drug use among people in the same environment, even when
they have similar risk factors in their family backgrounds. It is too simplistic, however, to assume that there is a single type of personality that leads to drug problems.

Rather, a great number of learned behavior patterns and personality traits interact in a given environment either to promote or to discourage drug use.

Interactionist Theory

Most social psychologists see drug use simply as one more behavior pattern that is learned from interaction with others in our culture. They observe, for example, that most people in our society who drink alcohol do so not because they have some personality defect or a biological urge to drink but because drinking is a widely accepted cultural pattern. Most children see adults drink, and they learn attitudes, beliefs, and definitions that are favorable to alcohol use. When such children reach adulthood, they are likely to use alcohol just as their parents did.

Interactionists hold that the use of illegal drugs is also culturally learned, although in a slightly different way. Because the dominant culture encourages negative attitudes toward illegal drugs, some contact with a drug subculture is necessary before most people start using such drugs. The longer and more intense a person's contact with a drug subculture, the greater the likelihood that he or she will accept attitudes and definitions that are favorable to drug use. A person who actually begins to use an illicit drug is likely to grow closer to other drug users and to become more deeply committed to the values of the drug subculture. In fact, some people use drugs for the companionship of other drug users as much as for the effects of the drugs themselves.

Drugs are used in many social settings. According to interactionist theory, people use drugs because of the attitudes and values they learn in their daily contacts with other people.

The key point in interactionist theory is that drug use is determined by individuals' attitudes toward drugs, the meaning drug use has for them, their overall worldview, and their system of values—all of which are learned from interaction with people in a certain culture or subculture. Drug users, according to interactionist theory, quit only when their attitudes and values change and the drugs involved are redefined in negative terms.[56] Labeling theorists point out that such changes are much more difficult when a drug user has been publicly labeled as an "addict," "alcoholic," or "junkie." Those who have been branded in this way often find that they are excluded from contact with groups and individuals who might support their attempts to reform.

Quick Review

Compare and contrast the biological, behavioral, personality, and interactionist theories about the causes of drug use.

Drug Control in North America

The European colonists who came to North America brought their drinking customs with them. Before 1700 most drinking was moderate and socially accepted. The most common beverages were beer and wine. Strong religious and family controls limited drunkenness and disorderly conduct. However, as the westward expansion continued, drinking patterns changed. The traditional restraints of family and religion were less effective among rugged pioneers, and heavy consumption of distilled spirits became commonplace. This type of drinking, often accompanied by violent, destructive behavior, was the first alcohol problem to gain widespread social attention. At the same time, total abstinence was becoming more popular among farmers and people in more established rural areas.

By the nineteenth century there were two different drinking patterns among Americans: rural middle-class people were largely abstainers, while settlers on the frontier and the thousands of immigrants in the big cities tended to be alcohol users. Three waves of state prohibition laws swept the United States as people from small towns tried to impose their customs on urban drinkers. The last wave resulted in the passage of the Eighteenth Amendment to the Constitution in 1919, which prohibited the manufacture, sale, and transportation of intoxicating liquors. This amendment was repealed in 1933 by the Twenty-first Amendment.

Just as the drive against alcohol intensified in the nineteenth century, so did the drive against the use of other drugs, particularly the opiates. At that time, opium was sold legally in over-the-counter patent medicines as a cure for everything from diarrhea to whooping cough, and most habitual users were middle-aged, middle-class women who were no more involved in crime or deviant behavior than anyone else.

By the turn of the century, however, the wave of negative publicity had changed the public's attitude, and the opiates came to be seen as "dope," not medicine. All nonprescription use of the drugs was prohibited in Canada in 1908 and in the United States in 1914.[57] This prohibition produced a sharp drop in the number of opiate users. However, users who were unwilling or unable to quit were placed in a very difficult position. They found themselves labeled "dope fiends" and were virtually forced to associate with smugglers and other criminals to obtain supplies of the drug. This small group of opiate users was the beginning of the subculture of opiate addiction that was to become such a problem in the years ahead. As the price of illicit opiates steadily rose, so did users' need for money. The method of consumption changed from drinking opiated medicines to injecting morphine and finally heroin. Within a few decades after opium prohibition, the modern junkie emerged: predominantly young, predominantly male, and often deeply involved in crime.[58]

Although shorter-lived, alcohol prohibition had similar consequences for American society. The Volstead Act, which amended the U.S. Constitution to prohibit the manufacture or sale of "intoxicating liquors," went into effect in January 1920 and was finally repealed in December 1933. While the prohibition law was in effect, Americans witnessed an unprecedented wave of crime and gangsterism. The drinking public was not willing to give up alcohol, no matter what the law said. They turned to illegal sources of supply, thus creating a huge illicit market for alcohol. Members of organized crime and many independent operators jumped into the alcohol business, and speakeasies (illegal bars) sprang up in every city.[59]

Marijuana was the last major drug to be prohibited during this "era of temperance." As late as 1930, only 16 states had laws prohibiting marijuana use, and these laws were not vigorously enforced. A single government agency, the Federal Bureau of Narcotics, played the key role in bringing about the prohibition of marijuana in the United States. This agency was set up to enforce opium prohibition in 1930, and its director became convinced that marijuana use was a form of wrongdoing that should be under his jurisdiction. Accordingly, the bureau began an intensive program of lobbying for the prohibition of marijuana. It also circulated a number of phony horror stories about the effects of marijuana, but virtually no one challenged the bureau's distortions and outright lies. In 1937, Congress passed the Marijuana Tax Act, which was designed to stamp out use of the drug, and every state eventually passed an outright prohibition of its own.

Most of the new drugs that have become popular among recreational users in the twentieth century were created by the pharmaceutical corporations, and many were initially promoted with erroneous claims that they were less addictive than their predecessors. Heroin was synthesized in 1874 and first placed on the market by Bayer Laboratories in 1898. It was widely promoted as a safe substitute for codeine and a cure for morphine addiction. The first barbiturate was clinically tested in 1903, and by the 1930s barbiturates were in common use. Although references to barbiturate intoxication and withdrawal convulsions were made as early as 1905, it was not until 1950 that a controlled study was done to prove their addictive properties. As the barbiturates were coming to be recognized as a major drug problem, methaqualone (often known by the brand name Quaalude) was falsely advertised as a safe substitute. LSD was first created in 1938. Although it was never promoted as a prescription drug, the Sandoz Laboratories did give LSD samples to scientists from 1953 to 1966 in hopes of finding some commercial use. Moreover, it has now come to light that the Central Intelligence Agency and the U.S. Army conducted secret experiments with LSD during this period that included dosing unsuspecting citizens with the drug to test its effectiveness as a combat weapon.[60]

Of course, the pharmaceutical companies never sold these drugs directly to recreational users on the black market. Drugs legally produced for the prescription market are often diverted into the black market, however, and once a particular drug gains popularity with recreational users, illegal laboratories soon spring up to meet the demand.

During the second half of the 1980s, American society began to focus on the problem of drug abuse more intensely than ever before. Drug use became a powerful public symbol for a host of social ills from the decline of the work ethic to the decay of the traditional family structure. In the frenzy that followed, politicians from all sides of the political spectrum seemed to be competing to outdo each other with their condemnations of drug users, and the federal government launched what was probably the biggest antidrug campaign ever. This so-called war on drugs involved many programs, but its principal focus was tougher enforcement. Unprecedented media attention and billions of dollars were devoted to the antidrug campaign, and prisons were soon overflowing with drug offenders (see Chapter 13). Supporters of this enforcement effort have claimed that it was responsible for the decline in drug use during the last decade. This seems unlikely, however, for as we have seen, drug use was going down well before the big increases in funding for drug enforcement, and the use of tobacco and alcohol (obviously not affected by the crackdown) declined along with the use of the illicit drugs. Rather, most sociologists would attribute these changes to the aging of the population and to a predictable counterreaction to the excesses of the 1960s and 1970s.

Quick Review

Summarize the history of the efforts at drug control in North America.

The main focus of the "war on drugs" was increased law enforcement, as shown in this photo of a narcotics arrest in Miami.

Solving the Drug Problem

Where do We Stand?

During the last two decades, the United States has been experiencing what sociologists sometimes term a "moral panic" about the use of illicit drugs. Before we judge the best ways to respond to drug abuse, we need to take a calm look at the overall problem. Many Americans see the spread of illicit drugs as a new plague the reflects the moral decay of modern times. If we look at the problem in historical perspective, however, we see that it is really nothing new and that we have already gone through several cycles of rapidly growing drug use followed by eras of "temperance" and declining use. For example, Daniel Patrick Moynihan points out that "distilled spirits in early America appeared as a font of national unity, easy money, manly strength, and all-round good cheer. . . . It became routine to drink whiskey at breakfast and to go on drinking all day."[61] In 1830, the average American drank five gallons of distilled liquor a year—almost five times more than we do today. But by 1840, a vigorous temperance movement had brought consumption down to two gallons a person.[62]

Americans disagree on just how serious our current drug problems are. What we can say is that we currently appear to have just completed another cycle, with big increases in the 1960s and 1970s and declining usage since then. The recent upswing in drug use among teenagers may signal the beginning of another upward cycle, but it may not. Much will depend on the wisdom of the policies we pursue in the coming years.

Prevention

Most people agree that the best way to deal with drug problems is to discourage young people from using drugs before they start—but how do we do that? One common approach is to try to frighten them by presenting horror stories in "drug education" classes. However, such attempts seriously underestimate the awareness and intelligence of our youth. Sooner or later they discover that they have not been told the whole truth, and they may come to doubt even the accurate information

Signs of Hope   An Effective Antismoking Program

In 1988, California voters approved a state initiative that added an additional $0.25 tax on each pack of cigarettes. About 15 percent of the $3.1 billion the tax has collected since its enactment has been spent on various antismoking programs. The most controversial, and probably the most effective, of those programs was a hard-hitting advertising campaign that often depicted tobacco executives as cynical purveyors of death who would do anything for a profit. How effective has the program been? It is always difficult to evaluate such efforts, but research shows that smoking has been declining faster in California than in any other state. Per capita cigarette consumption has been declining at roughly three times the national rate since the new law went into effect.*

*Paul Jacobs, "Smoke, Fire and Funding," *Los Angeles Times,* June 26, 1994, pp. A1, A12.

they have been given about drug problems. A more reasonable approach is to present the best factual information available, regardless of whether it is likely to discourage students from using drugs. Critics of educational programs argue that so much talk about drugs in the classroom excites some teenagers' interest in trying them. Education programs need not, however, be administered exclusively by the schools. Another approach that has been widely used is to run public service advertising about the problems caused by drugs, and a further step would be to prohibit all advertising for drugs such as alcohol and tobacco. (See the Signs of Hope box for a description of one effective antismoking program.)

Others believe that prevention programs are doomed to failure because such programs pursue an unrealistic goal. These critics think that a certain amount of drug use is inevitable in our complex and insecure society and that the goal therefore should be to encourage moderation, not total abstinence. Most research indicates that moderate drug use does not usually cause serious psychological or physical problems. For example, a University of California study that tracked 739 young people from junior high until young adulthood concluded that the harm caused by drugs depends largely on the level of use. No measurable harm was found from moderate drug use, but as use increased, so did its damage.[63]

Many people therefore advocate more balanced educational programs that allow students to make a rational choice based on all the available information. In this view, the best way to prevent drug problems is to accept a certain level of use but encourage the creation of clear social standards about how much is too much. Researchers have found, for example, that the rate of alcoholism is low among Italians (and Italian Americans) even though their per capita alcohol consumption is significantly higher than in most countries. Italian culture does not condemn drinking but contains clearly defined norms that limit alcohol consumption to mealtimes and other social occasions. On the other hand, alcohol use was not part of the traditional culture of Native Americans, and their high rate of alcoholism today is often attributed to the weakness of the norms regulating alcohol use.[64]

Treatment

The treatment approach, like prevention, tries to discourage drug use. The difference is that treatment programs attempt to help people stop using drugs after they have already developed a problem. A variety of treatment programs have been tried, but no single program works for everyone. Many drug users go through several programs before kicking the habit.

Individual psychotherapy has proved to be one of the least successful approaches to drug problems.[65] Drug use is a social phenomenon, and no matter how much psychiatric care drug users receive, strong social support is usually needed to help them to give up the drug habit.

Aversive therapy, a treatment based on the principles of behavioral psychology, is designed to discourage drug use by teaching the patient to associate the effects of the drug with some unpleasant sensation such as an electric shock or nausea. Aversive techniques are widely used to discourage smoking, but they have been less successful with other drugs, such as alcohol and heroin.

The most successful treatment programs involve group support. Alcoholics Anonymous (AA) is one of the oldest such groups and is now a worldwide organization. Treatment takes the form of meetings at which members describe their troubles with alcohol and the help they have found in Alcoholics Anonymous. Members

individual psychotherapy
Psychological therapy with a single patient and therapist.

aversive therapy
A therapeutic approach that attempts to discourage drug use by teaching the patient to associate it with some unpleasant sensation.

Many social scientists believe that treatment programs—such as the one shown in this photo—are the most effective way to deal with the problems created by the abuse of alcohol and other drugs.

are encouraged to call on one another for help when they feel a desire to start drinking again. The AA program is religiously oriented, but its success seems to derive primarily from its system of encouraging each member to try to reform others, thus reinforcing the reformer's own nondrinking behavior. There are also successful nonreligious programs, such as Rational Recovery (RR) and the Secular Organization for Sobriety (SOS), which follow the same principles but emphasize individual responsibility instead of reliance on a "higher power" as AA does.[66]

therapeutic community
A live-in community for drug treatment.

More intensive than AA-style programs are the **therapeutic communities,** in which patients live together in a special house or dormitory for long periods of time. The first of these communities was Synanon, founded in Santa Monica, California, in 1958. Synanon members were ex-users who maintained strict discipline, prohibited all drug use, and helped each other avoid drugs. Frequent group sessions were held in which members discussed their problems and criticized individuals who failed to live up to the expectations of the group.[67] Although Synanon has changed drastically in recent years, other therapeutic communities, such as Phoenix House, which now has about 15 percent of all the beds in the nation's therapeutic communities, still follow its original principles.[68]

Most therapeutic communities claim high rates of success, but few researchers have conducted rigorous studies to support those claims. One major drawback is that these programs appeal only to drug users who can accept their ideology and discipline. It has been estimated that only 10 to 25 percent of drug users who join these communities finish their program but that most of those who do so remain drug free.[69] Another problem with some therapeutic communities is that those who complete the program successfully may have difficulty leaving. Many become "professional ex-addicts" working in halfway houses or other drug programs.

Legal Repression

When the use of a particular drug comes to be seen as a problem, the most common response is a legal one—prohibiting the manufacture and sale of the drug and punishing the users. This approach has been tried with almost all psychoactive drugs used in North America except caffeine and nicotine. The assumption is that people will not use drugs if there are simply none available or they are threatened with jail, but it is difficult to evaluate the success of this approach. For example, opiate use declined sharply after it was declared illegal, but marijuana use has increased enormously since its prohibition. Supporters of this approach argue that its failures are due to a lack of tough laws and enough money to enforce them.

While it seems fair to conclude that the prohibition approach usually does reduce (but not eliminate) the use of the condemned drug, the matter is a good deal more complex than that. For one thing, the cost of effectively repressing a popular drug may be far more than society can afford. As the drug becomes more scarce, the price is driven up, and drug dealers have more money to offer in bribes and corruption (a key reason for the frequent failure of this approach). Political factors also obstruct the enforcement effort. For example, evidence has emerged showing not only that the Central Intelligence Agency has been involved with drug-dealing schemes to help finance its secret operations but also that several presidential administrations have intentionally ignored drug-running activities by their allies in volatile Third World countries. Even if the enforcement effort could somehow dry up the supply of illicit drugs, this approach would still have unintended side effects. A policy that completely removed all popular drugs from the black market, while continuing to allow almost unrestricted over-the-counter sales of alcohol and tobacco, seems likely to achieve little more than the substitution of one dangerous substance for another.

In the real world, of course, a black market would almost certainly remain, and that situation fosters the growth of organized crime. When a drug is prohibited by law, legitimate businesses are forced out of the market. The demand for the drug is still there, however, and criminals organize to meet it. Because such criminals have no competition from legitimate enterprise, legal prohibition guarantees them huge profits. The classic example of this process was the prohibition of alcohol in the United States during the 1920s and early 1930s. As many Americans sought new sources of alcoholic beverages, gangs of criminals began to supply them. The result was widespread gangsterism and disrespect for the law. Gang bosses such as Al Capone, who built his illegal empire by bootlegging alcohol, virtually controlled some American cities. Today, it is estimated that illegal drug dealers take in between $50 and $60 billion a year in the United States alone.[70]

In addition to organized crime, drug prohibition encourages the growth of deviant subcultures among users who band together to share their experiences and defeat government efforts to cut off supplies of their drug. Many marijuana users report that they originally were more attracted to the camaraderie and friendship of other drug users than to the effects of the drug itself. Finally, the enforcement effort poses a serious threat to civil liberties. Drug offenses seldom have victims who call the police. Law enforcement agencies must therefore resort to such questionable techniques as the use of wiretaps, undercover agents, and spies to flush out violations. A final problem with prohibition programs is their cost. As a result of the antidrug campaigns of the last decade, there are now over 330,000 Americans in prison for drug offenses, and the total cost of the enforcement effort runs about $20 billion a year.[71]

Of course, these criticisms do not necessarily mean that the enforcement approach should be abandoned, for the results may be judged to be worth the price. They do suggest, however, that it is far more preferable to reduce the demand for drugs through education and treatment.

Increased Social Tolerance

An alternative approach to the drug problem is to increase social tolerance. This approach includes a variety of proposals, ranging from reductions in penalties for some types of drug offenses to full legalization of all drugs. Advocates of such proposals claim that a less punitive reaction to drug use would reduce the negative side effects stemming from legal repression and, in the long run, reduce the need for treatment. If drugs could be obtained legally, it is argued, their attractiveness as "forbidden fruit" would decrease. Further, legalization would take the profit out of drug distribution, thus taking drugs off the street. Even if this approach failed to reduce drug use, its advocates assert that it would still reduce the drug problem by reducing organized crime, destigmatizing drug users, undermining drug subcultures, and eliminating the need for addicts to commit crimes to pay for high-priced illegal drugs.

Legalization   Proponents of legalization believe that attempts at legal repression of drug use have been so disastrous that the problem can be solved only by taking the government out of the business of enforcing drug laws. In practice, regulation by government agencies would undoubtedly continue, as it does in the case of alcohol. Minors would be prohibited from purchasing drugs, and taxation and standards for potency and quality could be expected.

Most proponents of legalization do not advocate over-the-counter sales for all drugs. In fact, marijuana is the only drug for which full legalization has widespread support. Those who do advocate the legalization of all drugs often base their arguments on philosophical opposition to government interference in individuals' lives. The psychiatrist Thomas Szasz, for instance, feels that the decision to use a drug is entirely an individual matter in which the government has no legitimate concern.[72]

decriminalization
Repeal of the penalties for possession and use of a drug while sales remain illegal.

Decriminalization   A step halfway between prohibition and full legalization is **decriminalization.** Its advocates argue that penalties for possession and use of a given drug should be dropped but that the sale of the drug should continue to be illegal. The aim is to stop punishing those who use drugs, since they are not hurting anyone else, and instead discourage use indirectly by forbidding sales. Critics of this policy point to the contradiction between allowing legal possession but penalizing sale or purchase. Its advocates fear that legalization would encourage a new wave of drug use, yet they want to reduce the repression of users, so they propose decriminalization as a compromise.

Decriminalization of marijuana use, or a reduction in the penalties for possession and use of marijuana, has at various times been endorsed by American and Canadian commissions on drug use, the American Medical Association, and the American Bar Association. Eleven states decriminalized possession of small amounts of marijuana during the 1970s. The new wave of concern about drug abuse has reversed this trend, however, and the legal repression of marijuana use has grown more intense in recent years. Well over 300,000 people a year are arrested for marijuana offenses in the United States; and there are now about 15,000 persons in federal prisons for such offenses and perhaps twice that number in state and local jails.[73] However, some observers believe that the 1997 passage of a California voter initiative legalizing the medical use of marijuana in that state may mark another turning point in the public's view of marijuana use.

Maintenance Through **drug maintenance** programs, addicts or habitual users can be supplied with a drug while it is still prohibited among the public at large. The only legal maintenance program in the United States involves the distribution of methadone (a synthetic opiate) to heroin addicts, and there are now about 125,000 persons in such programs.[74] Although methadone maintenance is often called treatment, it has little in common with real treatment programs. In essence, these programs simply provide a restricted legal supply of an opiate to people who otherwise would obtain opiates illegally. Supporters of methadone maintenance programs point to research showing a very substantial drop in criminal activities among addicts who participate.[75] They also argue that methadone has several advantages over heroin: its effects last longer, it can be given orally, and it does not generate the intense high that is produced by heroin. However, many heroin addicts refuse to participate in methadone programs because they prefer heroin, and for that reason, some researchers argue that heroin should be used in maintenance programs as well. Critics of maintenance programs, including some ex-addicts, argue that methadone is just another narcotic and that dispensing it to heroin users does nothing to solve their addiction problem.

> **drug maintenance**
> A program that provides addicts with a legal drug supply.

The Dutch Approach Some advocates of a new approach to the drug problem point to the Netherlands as a possible model. Dutch drug policy is an interesting combination of four elements. The first is the official tolerance of "soft drugs" (marijuana and hashish—a condensed form of marijuana). Although sale is technically illegal, many cafés openly sell marijuana without fear of arrests or fines. The second is a tough enforcement effort aimed at the dealers of hard drugs, such as heroin and cocaine, that are often smuggled into Rotterdam, the world's largest port. The third element of Dutch policy is the decriminalization of all users. No one is jailed for merely using or possessing small amounts of any drug. Finally, the Dutch have made treatment and maintenance programs easily available to all addicts.

Since this program was begun, Holland has seen both a sharp decline in the number of heroin addicts and an increase in their average age (indicating that fewer young people are starting the habit). Equally impressive is the fact that the Netherlands never experienced the cocaine epidemic that created such a crisis in North America. Despite these successes, however, the critics of increased tolerance for drug users remain unconvinced. They argue that the Dutch experience is not applicable to the United States because the Netherlands has no large ethnic ghettos and has a much more generous welfare system that makes poverty far less severe. As the barriers to free movement among European countries have come down, the Dutch are also being faced with a problem known as "drug tourism" as an increasing number of people from countries with more restrictive laws are coming to Holland to buy marijuana.[76]

Quick Review

Summarize the different possible responses to the drug problem. Which one seems the best to you? Why?

Sociological Perspectives on Drug Use

The Functionalist Perspective

Functionalist theory does not attempt to explain the specific reasons why individuals use or do not use drugs. It concerns itself with the social conditions that have caused the tremendous increase in drug use in industrial society. Many functionalists assume that drug use is a means of escaping from difficult and unpleasant social circumstances. Consequently, drug abuse is seen as a response to other social problems, such as poverty, worker alienation, and racism. To these functionalists, the way to reduce substance abuse is to deal with its underlying causes. This is obviously no simple matter, but functionalists have numerous proposals for improvements, many of which are described in the other chapters in this book.

Other functionalists, however, look at the causes of drug use in a different way. They feel that the use of drugs is inherently pleasurable and that, despite the serious consequences, people will take them unless prevented from doing so. The steep increase in drug consumption in the twentieth century is seen as the result of the weakening of the family and religious institutions that formerly kept antisocial behavior in check. The most direct way to deal with the drug problem is therefore to strengthen these institutions. Many functionalists feel, however, that the historical changes that have occurred are irreversible and that industrial societies must rely on formal mechanisms of social control—that is, the criminal justice system. These functionalists often criticize the disorganization of our system of justice. They argue that the inefficiency, inadequate funding, and payoffs and corruption that plague so many of our criminal justice agencies must be halted if we are to solve the drug problem.

The Conflict Perspective

Some conflict theorists also assume that drug users are escapists and agree that drug use is caused by other social problems. However, they hold that these social problems, such as unemployment and poverty, stem from exploitation and injustice rather than from social disorganization. Like their counterparts among the functionalists, these conflict theorists advocate a direct attack on the primary problem—exploitation—rather than on drug use, which they view as a symptom of the problem. They argue that drug use will decrease only after a just society, free from racism, poverty, and oppression, is created.

Other conflict theorists strongly disagree, asserting that drug use itself is neither escapist nor a social problem. Rather, it is normal behavior that occurs in all societies around the world. According to these theorists, drug use becomes a problem only when groups who oppose drugs use the power of the state to force their morality on everyone else. The inevitable result of such actions is social conflict, violent repression of drug users, and a booming black market.

Most conflict theorists argue that people should not be jailed for using drugs if their behavior causes no danger to others. Conflict theorists also say that the attempt to repress drug use creates secondary social problems, such as organized crime and a seething discontent with the legal system. Those who hold this viewpoint advocate a simple solution to the drug problem: legalize the prohibited drugs and stop jailing people who have done nothing worse than refuse to accept the dominant society's idea of what is good for them. If drug users victimize others to support their habit, they should be sent to prison; otherwise, they should be left alone.

The Feminist Perspective

Feminists point out the strong link between gender role expectations and our drug problems. Drinking and smoking have traditionally been more acceptable among men than women, and women continue to have lower rates of drug use than men. As a result, women who are heavy drug users often go to great lengths to conceal their behavior, and in general the drug problem among women tends to be more hidden. Interestingly, the one group of drugs that are used significantly more often by women are psychoactive prescription drugs, such as tranquilizers. Part of the cause of this difference may be the stereotypes among some physicians that women are more likely to be emotionally unstable and thus more in need of drug therapy. But the use of such prescription "medicines" also allows women to avoid the definition of their behavior as drug use. Men, on the other hand, are likely to feel a stronger stigma in seeking help from a physician for their emotional problems than in heavy drinking. Thus, feminists advise that people trying to do something about the drug problem must be sensitive to the important differences between the genders if they are to maximize their chances for success.

The Interactionist Perspective

Interactionists have devoted a great deal of attention to drug use, and we have already examined their theory that it is learned in social interaction like any other behavior. Another major contribution of interactionist theory is its emphasis on the critical importance of the way society defines drugs and drug use. In their view, our definitions shape the way we respond to our social problems and even determine whether or not we consider something to be a social problem. In the nineteenth century, for example, opiates were defined primarily as medicine, and although their use was widespread, it was not considered a social problem. As sensationalistic press reports began to associate opium smoking with the unpopular Chinese minority, attitudes changed. Once the opiates came to be seen as dope, not medicine, they were soon prohibited, and we saw the growth of what might be termed the "junkie subculture." Interactionists point out that similar changes now appear to be happening in the definition of tobacco smoking. What used to be considered chic and sexy is increasingly being defined as dependence on an addictive drug. As more restrictions are placed on tobacco smoking, interactionists urge antismoking activists to learn from the mistakes of the past and avoid the prohibitionist policies that proved to be so disastrous for alcohol and the opiates.

Quick Review

What are the differences between the recommendations of conflict theorists and those of functionalists for dealing with the drug problem?

What are the differences in the drug problems of men and women?

What do interactionists say that the way society defines drug use is important?

Summary

Many people have mistaken ideas about drug use. For example, it is widely believed that because alcohol and tobacco are legal, they are not drugs, but there is actually little difference between these drugs and the illegal ones. Another misconception is that drug use is a new epidemic that is sweeping through our society. Surveys and sales figures indicate that total drug use has actually gone down in the last twenty years, although there has been a significant increase in drug use among teenagers since the early 1990s.

Physical dependence occurs when a user takes enough of a drug to produce a tolerance and will become sick when it is withdrawn. Addiction is the strong craving that often develops after a period of physical dependence.

Alcohol is the most popular recreational drug, and it also creates the most problems for society. It is a depressant and is addictive if used in excess. Tobacco is another widely used legal drug. Cigarette smoking has been shown to be highly dangerous, yet large numbers of people start smoking every year. Although its popularity has declined in recent years, marijuana is still the most widely used illegal drug. The opiates are all highly addictive, and their use is associated with an extremely dangerous life-style. Mescaline and LSD are two of the most popular psychedelic drugs, and both produce powerful psychological changes. The psychedelics produce few health problems but may create serious emotional disturbances in some users. The sedative-hypnotics have effects similar to those of alcohol. They are frequently prescribed by physicians, but there is also a flourishing black market for many of these drugs. The amphetamines are stimulants, and excessive use can produce a psychotic state as well as considerable physical damage. Cocaine is a natural stimulant with effects similar to those of the amphetamines.

Biological theories hold that some people have an inherited predisposition toward alcoholism or drug addiction. Behavioral theory sees drug use and addiction as products of conditioning: people use drugs because they find the experience to be rewarding, and addicts continue to take drugs because they want to avoid painful withdrawal. Personality theorists argue that individuals who use drugs have inadequate or impulsive personalities. According to interactionist theory, drug use stems from attitudes, values, and definitions favorable to such behavior, often learned in drug subcultures.

The original colonists had relatively few problems with drugs. Later, heavy drinking patterns developed among single men on the frontier, while farm families began to give up drinking. Several prohibitionist movements swept North America in the early twentieth century and resulted in the banning of alcohol, opiates, and marijuana. Prohibition of these drugs fostered drug subcultures among some users, who were branded as criminals.

Proposals for dealing with the drug problem fall into four main categories. The first consists of prevention programs designed to stop people from getting involved with drugs or using them to excess. The second approach is to treat drug users to help them stop using drugs. The most successful treatment programs use some form of group support. A third strategy calls for increasing legal repression of drug use. This approach discourages drug use but has damaging side effects, including the growth of organized crime and drug subcultures. A fourth alternative is increased social tolerance of drug use. Included in this category are legalization, decriminalization, and maintenance programs.

Most functionalists assume that drug use is a means of escaping from unpleasant social conditions that have arisen as society has become disorganized. Some conflict theorists also assume that drug users are escapists, but they are convinced that the tensions drug users seek to avoid stem from exploitation rather than from social disorganization. Other conflict theorists consider drug use to be normal behavior and argue that the problem lies in the state's attempts to repress it. Feminists point out the significant differences in the drug problem between women and men, and interactionists emphasize the critical importance of the way society defines the use of a particular drug.

Questions for Critical Thinking

In the last decade or so, the public has often seen drug use as America's number one social problem, but many critics have argued that the problem has been blown far out of proportion to its real importance. How would you evaluate the importance of the drug problem compared with other difficult issues, such as poverty, warfare, violence, and racism? Why has the issue of illicit drug use been so popular among politicians? What effect have the media had on our perception of the drug problem?

Key Terms

addiction
alcoholic
aversion therapy
decriminalization
depressant
drug maintenance

individual psychotherapy
passive smoking
stimulant
therapeutic community
tolerance
withdrawal

Further Readings

Joseph Gusfield, *Symbolic Crusade: Status Politics and the American Temperance Movement* (Urbana: University of Illinois Press, 1963). A classic work on the historical origins of the drive to prohibit alcohol use in the United States.

James A. Inciardi, *The War on Drugs II: The Continuing Epic of Heroin, Cocaine, Crack, Crime, AIDS, and Public Policy* (Mountain View, CA: Mayfield, 1992). A sociological examination of the drug problem and what to do about it.

Edmundo Morales, *White Gold* (Tucson: University of Arizona Press, 1988). A Peruvian sociologist examines the impact of the cocaine trade on the villagers of the Andes Mountains.

Richard G. Schlaadt and Peter T. Shannon, *Drugs,* 3rd ed. (Englewood Cliffs, NJ: Prentice Hall, 1991). A good text covering a broad range of drugs and drug problems.

Peter Stafford, *Psychedelics Encyclopedia,* 3rd ed. (Berkeley, CA: Ronin, 1992). A comprehensive examination of the use of psychedelic drugs and its social context.

George Vaillant, *The Natural History of Alcoholism* (Cambridge, MA: Harvard University Press, 1996). An updated version of a classic book on alcoholism.

Notes

1. Debra Rosenberg and Matt Bai, "Drinking and Dying," *Newsweek,* October 13, 1997, p. 69.
2. U.S. Bureau of the Census, *Statistical Abstract of the United States, 1996* (Washington, DC: U.S. Government Printing Office, 1996), p. 148.
3. Ibid., p. 138.
4. U.S. Bureau of the Census, *Statistical Abstract of the United States, 1996,* p. 144.
5. Marlene Cimos, "Marijuana, Tobacco Use on Rise Among U.S. Teens," *Los Angeles Times,* December 20, 1996, p. A20; Carey Goldberg, "Survey Reports More Drug Use by Teen-Agers," *New York Times,* August 21, 1996, p. A12; Barnaby J. Feder, "Increase in Teen-Age Smoking Sharpest Among Black Males," *New York Times,* May 24, 1996, p. A9.
6. Richard G. Schlaadt and Peter T. Shannon, *Drugs,* 3rd ed. (Englewood Cliffs, NJ: Prentice Hall, 1990), p. 45.
7. U.S. Bureau of the Census, *Statistical Abstract, 1996,* p. 144.
8. See Craig MacAndrew and Robert B. Edgerton, *Drunken Comportment: A Social Explanation* (Chicago: Aldine-Atherton, 1966).
9. Philip J. Hilts, "Is Nicotine Addictive? It Depends on Whose Criteria You Use," *New York Times,* August 21, 1994, p. B6.
10. Schlaadt and Shannon, *Drugs,* p. 175.
11. Jack H. Mendelson and Nancy K. Mello, *Alcohol Use and Abuse in America* (Boston: Little, Brown, 1985), p. 225.
12. Timothy J. Flanagan and Kathleen Maguire, eds., *Sourcebook of Criminal Justice Statistics, 1989,* U.S. Department of Justice, Bureau of Justice Statistics (Washington, DC: U.S. Government Printing Office, 1990).
13. Schlaadt and Shannon, *Drugs,* p. 185.
14. B. Drummond Ayres, Jr., "Big Drop in Drunken Driving," *San Francisco Sunday Examiner and Chronicle,* May 22, 1994, p. A7.
15. U.S. Bureau of the Census, *Statistical Abstract, 1996,* p. 144.
16. Ibid., p. 146.
17. Associated Press, "College Boozing an Epidemic—Panel," *San Luis Obispo Telegram-Tribune,* June 7, 1994, pp. A1, A12.
18. U.S. Bureau of the Census, *Statistical Abstract, 1996,* p. 145.

19. U.S. Bureau of the Census, *Statistical Abstract, 1996*, p. 145; Schlaadt and Shannon, *Drugs,* p. 117.

20. Philip J. Hilts, "Visions of Nationwide Withdrawal," *New York Times,* April 27, 1994, p. B7.

21. Oakley Ray and Charles Ksir, *Drugs, Society, and Human Behavior* (St. Louis: Mosby), pp. 199–202.

22. Quoted in Matt Clark, "Slow-Motion Suicide," *Newsweek,* January 22, 1979, pp. 83–84; see also U.S. Department of Health and Human Services, *Smoking and Health: A Report of the Surgeon General* (Washington, DC: U.S. Government Printing Office, 1979).

23. Associated Press, "Koop: Tobacco Like Heroin, Cocaine," *San Luis Obispo Telegram-Tribune,* May 16, 1988, p. A1.

24. Sheryl Stolberg, "Mortality Study Finds Tobacco Is No. 1 Culprit," *Los Angeles Times,* November 10, 1993, pp. A1, A33.

25. See James William Coleman, *The Criminal Elite: Understanding White Collar Crime* (New York: St. Martin's Press, 1998), pp. 79–80.

26. Schlaadt and Shannon, *Drugs,* pp. 116–150.

27. Sheryl Stolberg, "Science Stokes the Tobacco Debate," *Los Angeles Times,* May 26, 1994, pp. A1, A22, A23; Associated Press, "EPA Official Tries to Bury Smoking Report," *San Luis Obispo Telegram-Tribune,* May 30, 1991, p. B8.

28. Denise Grady, "Study Finds Secondhand Smoke Doubles Risk of Heart Disease," *New York Times,* May 20, 1997, pp. A1, A10.

29. Marlene Cimons, "Teen-Agers Face Special Smoking Risk, Report Warns," *Los Angeles Times,* February 25, 1994, p. A19.

30. Barnaby J. Feder, "Increase in Teen-Age Smoking Sharpest Among Black Males," *New York Times,* May 24, 1996, p. A9; Jeff Bingaman, "Tobacco Has Dead Aim on Latinos," *Los Angeles Times,* February 11, 1990, p. M5; Donna K. H. Walters, "Cigarettes: Makers Aim at Special Niches to Boost Sales," *Los Angeles Times,* September 15, 1985, sec. 5, p. A3; Associated Press, "EPA Official Tries to Bury Smoking Report."

31. U.S. Bureau of the Census, *Statistical Abstract, 1996*, p. 144.

32. Eric Schlosser, "Reefer Madness," *Atlantic Monthly,* August 1994, pp. 45–63; Janny Scott, "Pot Takes a Hit in New Study of Health Dangers," *Los Angeles Times,* February 11, 1988, sec. 1, pp. 3, 36.

33. Howard S. Becker, *Outsiders* (New York: Free Press, 1963), pp. 41–58.

34. Schlaadt and Shannon, *Drugs,* pp. 258–259.

35. See William A. Rushing, *The AIDS Epidemic: Social Dimensions of an Infectious Disease* (Boulder, CO: Westview, 1995); Lawrence K. Altman, "Obstacle-Strewn Road to Rethinking the Numbers on AIDS," *New York Times,* March 1, 1994, p. B8; Schlaadt and Shannon, *Drugs,* p. 215.

36. U.S. Bureau of the Census, *Statistical Abstract, 1993*, p. 136.

37. Juanita Darling, "Colombians Up Quality, Lower Price of Heroin," *Los Angeles Times,* February 24, 1997, pp. A1, A6, A7; Joseph B. Treaster, "With Supply and Purity Up, Heroin Use Expands," *New York Times,* August 1, 1993, p. 1; Robert Sabbag, "The Cartels Would Like a Second Chance," *Rolling Stone,* May 5, 1994, pp. 35–37, 43.

38. Ray and Ksir, *Drugs, Society, and Human Behavior,* pp. 342–359; James William Coleman, "The Myth of Addiction," *Journal of Drug Issues* 6 (1976): 135–141.

39. See Schlaadt and Shannon, *Drugs,* pp. 238–243; Ray and Ksir, *Drugs, Society, and Human Behavior,* pp. 336–337.

40. Peter Wilkinson, "The Young and the Reckless," *Rolling Stone,* May 5, 1994, pp. 29–32; Harry Nelson, "LSD Still on Some Minds," *Los Angeles Times,* March 25, 1991, p. B3; Schlaadt and Shannon, *Drugs,* p. 240.

41. Ray and Ksir, *Drugs, Society, and Human Behavior,* pp. 314–319.

42. Schlaadt and Shannon, *Drugs,* pp. 82–87.

43. See Anthony R. Lovett, "Wired in California," *Rolling Stone,* May 5, 1994, pp. 39–40.

44. Schlaadt and Shannon, *Drugs,* pp. 91–100.

45. U.S. Bureau of the Census, *Statistical Abstract, 1996*, p. 144.

46. Schlaadt and Shannon, *Drugs,* pp. 39–44.
47. Marlene Cimons, "Youth Steroid Use Believed Rising," *Los Angeles Times,* September 8, 1990, p. A2.
48. Sidney Cohen, *The Alcoholism Problems: Selected Issues* (New York: Haworth, 1983), p. 86; D. W. Goodwin, "Genetics of Alcoholism," in R. W. Pickens and L. L. Heston, eds., *Psychiatric Factors in Drug Abuse* (New York: Grune & Stratton, 1979).
49. E. M. Jellinek, *The Disease of Alcoholism* (Highland Park, NJ: Hillhouse, 1960).
50. Kathleen Whalen Fitzgerald, *Alcoholism: The Genetic Inheritance* (New York: Doubleday, 1985), pp. 1–21.
51. Alfred R. Lindesmith, *Addiction and Opiates* (Chicago: Aldine-Atherton, 1968), pp. 64–67.
52. G. E. Barnes, "The Alcoholic Personality: A Reanalysis of the Literature," *Journal of Studies on Alcohol* 40 (1979): 622.
53. Ray and Ksir, *Drugs, Society and Human Behavior,* p. 160.
54. Isador Chein, Donald Gerard, Robert Lee, and Eva Rosenfeld, *The Road to H* (New York: Basic Books, 1964).
55. George Vaillant, *The Natural History of Alcoholism* (Cambridge, MA: Harvard University Press, 1983).
56. James William Coleman, "The Dynamics of Narcotic Abstinence: An Interactionist Theory," *Sociological Quarterly* 19 (1978): 555–564; Coleman, "The Myth of Addiction."
57. D. F. Musto, "The History of Legislative Control over Opium, Cocaine, and Their Derivatives," in Ronald Hamowy, ed., *Dealing with Drugs: Consequences of Government Control* (San Francisco: Pacific Research Institutes for Public Policy, 1987), pp. 37–71.
58. Coleman, "The Myth of Addiction."
59. See Randy E. Marnett, "Curing the Drug-Law Addiction: The Harmful Side Effects of Legal Prohibition," in Hamowy, *Dealing with Drugs,* pp. 73–102.
60. Ray and Ksir, *Drugs, Society, and Human Behavior,* pp. 314–319, 334–335, 377–380.
61. Daniel Patrick Moynihan, "Iatrogenic Government," *American Scholar* 62 (Summer 1993): 354.
62. Seymour Martin Lipset, *American Exceptionalism: A Double-Edged Sword* (New York: Norton, 1996), pp. 271–272.
63. Janny Scott, "Debate Resurrected over Risks of Casual Drug Use," *Los Angeles Times,* August 10, 1988, sec. 1, pp. 1, 20.
64. See Marshall B. Clinard, *The Sociology of Deviant Behavior,* 4th ed. (New York: Holt, Rinehart & Winston, 1974), pp. 412–419; Erich Goode, *Drugs and American Society* (New York: Knopf, 1972), pp. 147–148.
65. Roger Meyer, *Guide to Drug Rehabilitation* (Boston: Beacon Press, 1972), pp. 61–63.
66. David Gelman, "Clean and Sober—and Agnostic," *Newsweek,* July 8, 1991, pp. 62–63.
67. See Rita Vokman and Donald R. Cressey, "Differential Association and the Rehabilitation of Drug Addicts," *American Journal of Sociology* 69 (1963): 129–142.
68. Norman Atkins, "The Cost of Living Clean," *Rolling Stone,* May 5, 1994, pp. 41–42.
69. Ibid.; Meyer, *Guide to Drug Rehabilitation,* p. 72; Ray and Ksir, *Drugs, Society, and Human Behavior,* pp. 360–362.
70. Ethan Nadelmann and Jann S. Wenner, "Toward a Sane National Drug Policy," *Rolling Stone,* May 5, 1994, pp. 24–26.
71. Ibid.
72. Thomas Szasz, *Ceremonial Chemistry: The Ritual Persecution of Drugs, Addicts, and Pushers,* rev. ed. (Holmes Beach, FL: Learning Publications, 1985).
73. Schlosser, "Reefer Madness."
74. Atkins, "The Cost of Living Clean."
75. Ibid.
76. Marlise Simons, "Dutch Swamped by Flood of Drugs," *New York Times,* April 20, 1994, p. A7; Rone Tempest, "Drugs: Dutch Gain with a Tolerant Tack," *Los Angeles Times,* September 22, 1989, pp. A1, A10–11.

Crime and Violence

What are the most serious types of crime and violence?

What do the statistics tell us about the crime problem?

What are the causes of crime?

How does society deal with crime?

What can be done to reduce crime and violence?

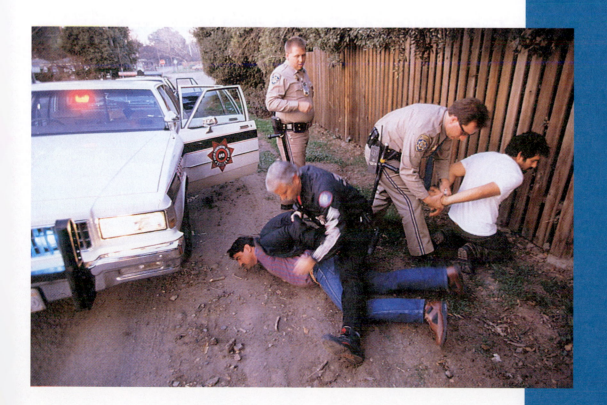

"I got over it a little bit, but I still think about it. James was my best friend. . . . He was lying there, shaking." Fourteen-year-old Alburto Dorner will never forget the afternoon he was walking with his best friend and a group of kids pulled up and started shooting. James was shot 22 times before he died. He had been in a fight with one of his assailants earlier in the day, and, as often happens in tough neighborhoods, the loser came back for vengeance with his older brother and some friends. The result was a cold-blooded murder.[1]

Every night the news is full of stories like this one—murders, rapes, and assaults— and people are afraid. Home security has become a billion-dollar industry, and the polls show that most women and a good number of men are afraid to walk outdoors at night even in their own neighborhoods.[2] The statistics say that one in every four American households is touched by crime every year, and the losses they total are staggering.[3] Yet despite enormous public concern, the average citizen is poorly informed about the real nature of the crime problem. The public is often misled by sensationalistic reporting looking to sell newspapers or win TV ratings and by the claims of opportunistic politicians who inflame popular fears for their own political benefit. To understand the crime problem more clearly, we will begin by examining the nature of crime and violence. Next we will take a hard look at what the scientific evidence shows us about the trends and distribution of crime, and then we will examine the various theories about the causes of crime and violence.

The Nature of Crime and Violence

violence
Behavior intended to cause pain, injury, or death to another.

Violence can be defined as any act that is intended to cause physical pain, injury, or death to another. When most people talk about violence, however, they are usually thinking only about the acts they dislike. When a criminal knocks an elderly woman down, we call it violence, but when a police officer knocks down the criminal, we call it necessary force. This chapter will focus on criminal violence, but it is important to remember that there are many other types of violence as well.

crime
Violation of a criminal law.

Crime is usually defined as a violation of the criminal law. Thus, no matter how indecent or immoral an act may be, it is not a crime unless the criminal law has listed it as such and provided a punishment for it. In practice, of course, it is not always easy to tell whether a specific act is or is not a crime. The famous legal scholar Roscoe Pound once pointed out that there is a great difference between "law on the books" and "law in action." In other words, what the criminal law says and what police and the courts actually do are often quite different. For example, some old laws—such as those outlawing certain sex acts—remain legally valid but are almost never enforced, and other laws, such as those making it a crime to go nude on a beach, are sometimes enforced and sometimes ignored. Even the most widely accepted laws are still enforced selectively. This means, for example, that an act might be called burglary if it is committed by a poor person—especially one with a criminal record—but might be ignored if committed by the mayor's son.

Because of the confusing hodgepodge of different behaviors that are considered crimes, much effort has gone into the attempt to classify them in some orderly way. Legally, the most serious offenses are classified as **felonies** and the less important ones as **misdemeanors.** Generally speaking, the more serious the crime, the less frequently it occurs, and misdemeanors are certainly far more common than felonies. For example, the police are about 130 times more likely to make an arrest for drunkenness, disorderly conduct, or driving under the influence of alcohol than for murder.[4] For statistical purposes, crimes are usually classified as offenses against persons **(violent crime),** crimes against property **(property crime),** and crimes against public decency and order **(victimless crime).** This approach is useful for sociologists because it groups similar types of offenses together, and we will begin by briefly examining the most important crimes in each category. But as valuable as this classification is, it is sometimes more useful to focus on the differences in the criminals and the way they behave, and we will end this section with a look at three broad types of offenses that are directed against both persons and property—juvenile delinquency, syndicated crime, and white-collar crime.

Violent Crime

Murder and Assault Murder is not the same as homicide. **Homicide** is the killing of any human being; **murder** is an illegal homicide committed with what lawyers call "malice"—the intention of doing a wrongful act. Thus, the killing of enemies in wartime, killing in self-defense, and killing in lawful execution of a judicial sentence are all homicides but not murders, because they are neither malicious nor unlawful. **Manslaughter** is the unlawful killing of another person without malice. For example, if you intentionally run over and kill someone with your car, you have probably committed a murder; but if you kill someone while driving drunk or speeding, you would more likely be judged to have committed manslaughter, because there was no malice (intent to cause harm). Finally, if you accidentally killed someone but were observing all the appropriate driving laws, you would not have committed any crime at all.

An **assault** occurs when one person attacks another with the intention of hurting or killing the victim. There is little difference between some murders and some assaults. The fact that one victim of an attack got to a hospital in time to save her life and another did not may spell the difference between an assault and a murder. Most assaults do not involve deadly force, however. A punch in the belly is an assault; so is a slap in the face. The essence of assault is the intention to do harm. If your professor raises his fist at you in a menacing manner, you have been assaulted. You are also assaulted by anyone who takes a swing at you and misses. However, most states have laws that recognize a difference between "simple assaults" that produce relatively minor injuries and "aggravated assaults," which involve more serious harm to the victim.

Newspaper and television reports focus on dramatic crimes such as mass murders, "gang wars," and particularly brutal and vicious attacks, but such media coverage is seriously misleading. The fact is that few people are attacked or killed by demented strangers. We are actually far more likely to be killed by a relative, friend, or acquaintance. Indeed, the closeness of the relationship may add to the violence of the attack when someone feels betrayed or insulted.

Marvin E. Wolfgang's classic study of murder in Philadelphia found that only 15 percent of the 550 murders he analyzed occurred between strangers; almost 60 percent occurred between relatives or close friends.[5] More recent data show much the same picture. Fewer than one in four murders from 1976 to 1994 were committed

felony
A serious offense, usually punishable by death or a prison term of a year or longer.

misdemeanor
A minor offense, usually punishable by a short term in jail or by payment of a fine.

violent crime
A crime directed against a person.

property crime
A theft or other crime against property.

victimless crime
A crime with no obvious victim, such as gambling or prostitution.

homicide
The killing of a human being.

murder
The unlawful killing of a human being with malice.

manslaughter
The unlawful killing of another person without malice.

assault
An attack on a person with the intention of hurting or killing the victim.

Personal Perspectives   Young Murderers

There has been an epidemic of murder among teenagers in the last decade. The following story describes a murder carried out by a 14-year-old boy and his 11-year-old accomplice.

As Elizabeth Alvarez, a pregnant mother with three children, was walking away from an automatic teller machine, she was stopped by 11-year-old Jacob. Jacob's partner, Damien, approached her with a gun and demanded her money. When she refused, he shot her in the head. As she fell to the ground, they scooped up the money and ran off to divide it up. They had killed a mother of three for $80. After they were caught, they both denied they had intended to kill her. However, Jacob later recalled that his partner had "sharpened the bullet so it would go in real good. It was real pointy."

What kind of boy could kill someone at age 14? Damien was abandoned by his father when he was a child, and he was repeatedly beaten by his mother—when he wasn't totally ignored. He more or less raised himself on the streets. After a long history of trouble, he dropped out of the seventh grade. He went to live for a time with his older brother, who was a drug dealer, and Damien soon picked up the trade. Shortly before the robbery, Damien decided he wanted to quit dealing, but he was $430 in debt to his suppliers. So he talked Jacob into what he thought would be an easy scheme to make some money.

Jacob came from the same kind of background. His mother was raped in the seventh grade, and she had seven children. Court records show that she drank heavily, smoked crack cocaine, and once even sold her children's clothes for drug money. Jacob, the youngest of her children, began smoking marijuana at age 9, and he grew up on the streets, where his heroes were drug dealers and gangsters. His mother never showed up for Jacob's first court hearing. When she finally did testify, Jacob's lawyer said it was obvious that she was drunk.*

*Isabel Wilkerson, "Two Boys, a Debt, a Gun, a Victim: The Face of Violence," *New York Times*, May 16, 1994, pp. A1, C10, C11.

by strangers.[6] Studies show that assault victims are less likely to know their attackers but are still acquainted in almost half of the cases.[7] One's chances of being assaulted or killed, therefore, depend more on one's relationship with relatives and friends than on the whim of some predatory stranger.

Alcohol is frequently an important contributing factor in murders and assaults, as it is for violent crime in general. Slightly over half of inmates in prison for violent crimes report they were under the influence of alcohol or other drugs at the time of their offense.[8] Gender also plays a major role—both assault and murder are much more common among men than women. Not only are the large majority of the offenders men, but so are most of their victims. Men are more than twice as likely as women to be the victims of aggravated assault, and men are three times more likely to be murdered. However, a woman is almost eight times more likely to be killed by someone she is romantically involved with than a man would be, and more than one-fourth of the women who are murdered in the United States are killed by their husbands or boyfriends.[9]

Rape Although the laws differ from place to place, **forcible rape** is usually defined as sexual intercourse forced on a person without consent. So-called **statutory rape** is not a violent crime; it is sexual intercourse between an adult and someone below

forcible rape
Sexual intercourse forced on someone against his or her will.

statutory rape
Sexual intercourse with someone below the legally defined age of consent (usually 16 or 18).

the legally defined age of consent, which is usually 16 to 18 years old. Many jurisdictions now use the more appropriate term *illegal intercourse* for this offense.

Studies show that there are two distinct patterns of forcible rape. In the first type, the rape arises from social interaction between friends or acquaintances, often on a spur-of-the-moment basis. This type of sexual assault is sometimes known as date rape; however, that term is misleading because this kind of offense occurs in many other circumstances as well. The other pattern of rape usually involves strangers. The rapist, often a repeat offender, actively seeks out a victim with the prior intention of raping her. The rapist may wait on a dark street for a lone woman to walk by, search for an unsuspecting hitchhiker, or break into a woman's home. Because the first type of rape is less likely to be reported to the police, it is difficult to determine which pattern is more common. Only about one of five women who told the National Crime Victimization Survey that they had been raped or sexually assaulted said that their attacker was a stranger, but other research has not provided consistent support for this or any other conclusion.[10] According to the NCVS, about one-fourth of all rapes occur in the home of the victim and one in five in the home of a friend or relative. The rest occur in a variety of more public places.[11]

It is extremely difficult to measure the incidence of rape accurately. The NCVS puts the annual rate of victimization at about one rape or sexual assault for every 500 persons over the age of 12, but other research, using different methodology and different definitions of rape, has put the figure far higher.[12] Studies of college women, for example, have found that somewhere between 11 and 25 percent report having been forced to have sexual intercourse at some time in their life by a date or a boyfriend, and studies of high school students also show a high incidence of reported rape.[13] Whatever the exact number, the fear of rape has a profound effect on the way most women live their lives, forcing them either to severely restrict their freedom of action or to run the constant risk of victimization. As one woman put it: "I know what I can't do and I've completely internalized what I can't do. I've built a viable life that basically involves never leaving my apartment at night unless I'm directly going someplace to meet somebody. It's unconsciously built into what it occurs to women to do."[14]

Unlike the victims of other violent crimes, most rape victims are female. For every male who reported being the victim of a rape in the crime survey, there were 10 females.[15] The attackers, on the other hand, are overwhelmingly males. Fewer than 1 in 20 victims said that their attacker was female.[16] Thus, even most male victims are raped by other men. However, these figures greatly underestimate the number of men who are raped because they exclude the group with the highest rate of victimization: prison inmates. Although no one knows for sure, Stephen Donaldson, the head of a national organization dedicated to reducing prison rapes, estimates that 290,000 male prisoners are raped every year.[17]

Young women have the greatest risk of being raped, and the rate of victimization drops off sharply after age 34. The victim is under 19 years old in almost half of all reported rapes.[18] The poor are also far more likely to be victimized than the wealthy. In 1994, those with family incomes under $7,500 a year were more than eight times more likely to report being raped than those with family incomes above $50,000.[19] Data from the National Crime Victimization surveys indicate that those who physically resist their attackers are often successful in preventing the completion of the rape. The attacker completes the rape in only 32 percent of the cases in which the victim resists, but in 56 percent of the cases where she does not. However, resistance by the victim is also related to an increase in the probability of such injuries as black eyes and cuts.[20] Nonetheless, about 55 percent of rape victims who resisted their attacker said they believed it improved their situation, while only about 10 percent said it made things worse.[21]

robbery
Taking another person's property by force or threat of force.

Robbery Although **robbery**—theft by force—is officially classified as a violent crime, in many ways it has more similarities with the property crimes since it is actually a type of theft. Unlike most other violent crimes, robbery is seldom a crime of passion but is usually based on some measure of rational calculation. Perhaps for that reason, the offenders and their victims are unlikely to know each other; most robbers would not select a victim who could easily identify them. Although the law doesn't require that a criminal actually use violence in order for a robbery to occur (threatening to use it is enough), robbery often results in the same kind of human carnage as other violent crime. In the last two decades, there has been a disturbing increase in the number of persons killed in robbery attempts, probably because robbers are better armed than they were in the past. About 40 percent of all robberies in the United States are now committed with firearms.[22]

Property Crime

Although most people are much more worried about being the victim of violence than of a property crime, the latter is nearly ten times more frequent. (As the Signs of Hope box shows, however, there has been a steep decline in property crime in the last two decades.) **Theft**—taking the property of another—is by far the most common property crime. (Legally, this crime is called *larceny* in many jurisdictions.) Many thefts are related in one way or another to the automobile. According to FBI figures, stealing something from an automobile (or truck) is the most widespread type of theft reported to the police. Taking the whole vehicle is the second most common, and the theft of motor vehicle accessories such as stereos or wheels is third. Motor vehicle crimes are followed by thefts from buildings (such as homes or factories), shoplifting, and bicycle theft.[23]

theft
Taking the property of another; stealing.

Burglary is the unlawful entry into a structure with the intent to commit a felony. In most cases, the crime the burglar intends to commit is a theft, but it might also be a rape or assault. A burglary may also turn into a robbery if the burglar confronts the occupants and uses force to subdue them or take their property. (Remember that one action may break several laws at the same time—for example, burglary and theft are a common combination.) The most common targets of burglary are private homes and commercial businesses such as stores or offices. Although most residential burglaries are committed by strangers, a study by the Department of Justice found that in about 40 percent of the cases, the victims knew the offenders well enough to be able to identify them by sight.[24]

burglary
Unlawful entry into a structure with the intent to commit a felony.

fraud
Acquiring money or property through the use of deception or false pretenses.

A **fraud** involves trickery and deception rather than just walking off with someone's property. Fraud is common in the business world, and offenses of this sort will be discussed in the section on white-collar crime. Off the job, the most common forms of fraud involve checks and credit cards. Contrary to popular belief, it is a crime to write a check when you know that you do not have sufficient funds to cover

Signs of Hope A Steep Decline in Property Crime

Although many people are growing more and more fearful of falling victim to crime, the evidence shows that crime is actually declining and that the steepest drop has been in the property crimes (which have always been far more common than violent crimes). Criminologists agree that our most reliable source of data about the trends in crime comes from the National Crime Victimization Survey. Although our population has been growing rapidly, the NCVS shows that the total number of property crimes committed every year is actually lower now than it was in 1973, when the first survey was done. More importantly, the *rate* of property crime has shown a steady and steep decline since 1973. The percentage of Americans who reported that they had something stolen from them dropped 43 percent from 1973 to 1995. And the burglary rate showed an even steeper decline—about 50 percent.*

*Bureau of Justice Statistics, *Criminal Victimization, 1973–95* (Washington, DC: U.S. Government Printing Office, 1997), p. 4.

it. Finally, **arson** is the intentional burning of a structure or other property and is often part of some kind of insurance fraud. It is estimated that 30 percent of all losses from fires are caused by arson.[25]

arson
The illegal burning of a structure or other property.

The key to understanding these crimes is to recognize the diversity in the offenders' motivations and techniques. On one end of the spectrum are the "occasional criminals" who steal something only when they are short of money or happen to stumble on an especially attractive opportunity—a woman's purse sitting on the seat of an unlocked car or a store left untended while the clerk runs out to get some coffee. The occasional criminal is not usually very skilled and lacks a wide range of criminal contacts. At the other extreme are the highly skilled professional criminals, such as safecrackers and counterfeiters, who know the "fences" who pay the best prices for stolen merchandise, the lawyers who might be able to "fix" a case, and the latest anticrime technology. Amateur criminals usually commit crimes with a relatively small take—often stealing things for their own personal use or, in the case of juveniles, just to prove they have the guts to do it. The professional thief looks for the highest possible cash return and is far less likely to deterred by such things as deadbolt locks or burglar alarms. The skills of professional criminals make it far less likely that they will be caught for any one crime, but because they repeat their offenses so often, the odds are that their luck will eventually run out.

Victimless Crimes

In addition to crimes against persons and crimes against property, there is another category of crimes without a clear victim. These victimless crimes include such things as gambling, prostitution, and the use of illicit drugs, and many of them have already been covered in Chapters 11 and 12. While some claim that marijuana smokers, gamblers, and the buyers of illicit sex are actually victimizing themselves, most of the people involved don't see it that way, and for that reason these offenses are sometimes called crimes against public order and morality. With the exception of the use of illicit drugs, the public is generally far less concerned about the victimless crimes than any of the other crimes we are discussing here. Perhaps as a result, the laws prohibiting such activities contain many puzzling contradictions. For example, in most states, it is a crime to place a bet on a horse race with a bookie, but it is perfectly legal to bet at the racetrack. It is a crime to pay someone to have sex with you, but it is perfectly legal to have sex with someone and then give the person cash, a mink coat, or a new car. It is illegal to smoke marijuana, but it is perfectly legal to drink alcohol, which in most respects is a far stronger drug. These crimes also present some unique problems for the criminal justice system. Since there are no victims to complain to the police, law enforcement agencies must rely on an elaborate network of undercover agents and informers if they are to uncover violations. Moreover, syndicated criminals build huge criminal empires supplying the goods and services that the law forbids legitimate businesses to provide, and the enormous profits from such operations are often used to corrupt law enforcement officials.

Syndicated Crime

syndicated crime

A crime committed by an organized group of professional criminals working together over a long period of time.

From the *yakuza* of Japan to the South American cocaine cartels, **syndicated crime** is a worldwide problem. In North America, the most famous criminal syndicate is the Italian-Sicilian organization sometimes known as the Cosa Nostra or Mafia, but this old-time criminal organization is being strongly challenged by new African American, Hispanic, Russian, and Asian groups. Although such criminal syndicates are more frequently referred to as *organized crime,* that term is misleading, since many other types of crime are also highly organized.[26] What sets syndicated criminals apart from other criminals is that they work together in large groups. As a result, they have far more power to threaten their enemies and to buy protection from law enforcement agencies. In fact, it is often said that large-scale syndicated crime would be impossible without the widespread corruption it creates.[27] In testimony before the U.S. Senate, representatives of the Central Intelligence Agency estimated that as much as half the money many criminal syndicates earn goes to pay off various officials.[28]

Criminal syndicates are, in many ways, very much like legitimate businesses (and as we will see, some legitimate businesses also have their similarities to the criminal syndicates). Like most businesses, they earn most of their income by selling goods and services to the public. The main difference is that the criminal syndicates sell illegal goods such as drugs and offer forbidden services such as gambling, loan sharking (providing loans at illegally high rates), and prostitution. In the beginning, a new criminal syndicate is usually run by violent young toughs who operate only in a small area. If the group grows and prospers, it is likely to come into greater contact with the legitimate world, seeking to corrupt law enforcement, curry favor with politicians, and hide its profits in legitimate investments. Eventually, such syndicates may come to operate a number of legitimate businesses along with their criminal ones.

The latest concern of law enforcement officials is the growing links among criminal syndicates operating in different parts of the world. The drug cartels of Colombia, the traditional Chinese triads, the Italian Mafia, and new gangs in such places as Russia and Nigeria have begun to cooperate with their American counterparts to facilitate the sales of drugs, weapons, and other contraband. Many experts are afraid that these groups will forge closer ties in the years ahead. Even more disturbing are the efforts of syndicated criminals in Russia and other parts of the former Soviet Union to sell the material to make nuclear weapons on the black market. We do not know if any such deals have already gone through, but German police arrested a Russian smuggler in 1994 with a sample of weapons-grade plutonium that was allegedly from a large cache being offered for sale.[29]

White-Collar Crime

There are white-collar criminals in every occupation, from accounting to zoology, and in every type of organization, from the corner grocery store to huge government bureaucracies. Unlike the victims of most other crimes, many of the victims of white-collar criminals do not even know that they have been victimized, and therefore they do not complain to the police or anyone else. As a result, the public is often unaware of how serious the problem of white-collar crime really is.

Edwin H. Sutherland originally coined the term to call attention to weaknesses in theories that say crime is due to personal pathologies or poverty (such theories obviously cannot account for most criminal activities among the upper classes). He defined **white-collar crime** as any "crime committed by a person of respectability and high social status in the course of his occupation."[30] There are two basic types of white-collar crime: **organizational crimes** are committed by people who are acting on behalf of the organization for which they work; **occupational crimes** are committed solely to advance the personal interests of the criminal. For example, when employees embezzle money from a bank, the crime is occupational because the employees are obviously not working for the interests of their employer; but when an executive of a pharmaceutical company covers up negative findings from its research lab and claims that a potentially dangerous new drug is perfectly safe, it is an organizational crime because the offense was committed to benefit the company.

White-collar crimes cost more money and more lives than all other types of crimes put together. Although accurate tallies of the financial burden of white-collar crime are hard to come by, a conservative estimate places the yearly losses from 20 to 30 times higher than the losses from street crime. For example, the Department of Justice estimates that losses from conventional crimes cost the public $13 to $14 billion a year. Although that is a lot of money, it is dwarfed by the sums involved in white-collar crime. The yearly losses from antitrust violation alone are estimated to be about $250 billion, and that is only one of hundreds of different types of white-collar crime.[31]

Most people do not think of white-collar offenses as violent crime, and it is true that these criminals seldom intend to injure or kill anyone. Nonetheless, the yearly death toll from unsafe products, worker safety violations, illegal dumping of toxic wastes, and other corporate crimes is far higher than that from murder. The cover-up of the deadly hazards of asbestos by its manufacturers will probably cost as many lives as all the murders in the United States for an entire decade. In addition to our lives and our money, white-collar criminals threaten something else as well: political freedom. Assassination of foreign political leaders, illegal surveillance and harassment of groups opposed to government policy, election fraud, and the political dirty tricks like the ones involved in the Watergate scandal are all white-collar crimes.[32]

Numerous studies have also shown that those charged with white-collar crimes are less likely to be prosecuted and convicted than those charged with comparable "street crimes," and when the defendants in white-collar cases are convicted, they receive lighter sentences.[33] Big corporations are the recipients of the greatest le-

white-collar crime
Crime committed by someone of respectability and high social status in the course of his or her occupation.

organizational crime
Crime committed by someone acting on behalf of a larger organization, often his or her employer.

occupational crime
Crime committed in the course of the offender's occupation but without the support or encouragement of his or her employer.

White-collar crime costs the public far more than any other type of offense. The man shown here, Nicholas Leeson, is believed to have made fraudulent trades that resulted in $1.3 billion in losses.

niency. Take the case of the tobacco industry. It is estimated that in the United States alone, cigarette smoking kills about 400,000 people a year, and there is mounting evidence that the tobacco industry orchestrated an intentional effort to lie about its products and conceal their dangers from the public. Yet not a single tobacco executive has ever been charged with fraud or any of the other crimes the companies were apparently involved in.[34]

There are several reasons why white-collar criminals receive such lenient treatment. For one thing, their status and respectability make many people—including law enforcement officials—reluctant to believe the defendants are criminals; and, of course, if they are charged with a crime, they can afford the best defense available. In the case of corporate crimes, the defendants can actually overwhelm many enforcement agencies, which are often underfunded and understaffed. Their enormous economic and political power also enables many corporate criminals to bring almost irresistible outside pressures to bear on enforcement agents. Even the laws themselves are often written to reflect the interests of the corporate offenders and not the general public. Finally, the tens of thousands of victims of white-collar crimes such as false advertising and price-fixing lose only a few dollars each, so there is less public resentment than when a criminal strikes more heavily at a few individual victims. Indeed, many of the victims of white-collar crimes never know they have been victimized at all.

Juvenile Delinquency

Adults who violate criminal laws are called criminals, while juveniles who do the same things are called delinquents. The difference between a criminal and a **juvenile delinquent** is not simply a matter of age, however. A substantial number of juvenile delinquents have never been accused of doing anything that would be against the law if they were adults. Runaways, truants, and violators of curfew laws, for example, are delinquents only because they have broken laws pertaining to the behavior of juveniles.

Anthony Platt has shown that the concept of delinquency was created in the latter part of the nineteenth century by middle-class reformers he calls the "child savers."[35] Despite their good intentions, Platt argues, the child savers' efforts to create a special juvenile justice system to deal with delinquency introduced government controls over juveniles who did nothing more than violate middle-class standards of propriety. In the 1960s, civil libertarians began voicing strong objections to the practices of the juvenile courts. In theory, the juvenile courts were allowed to operate with fewer legal safeguards because they were intended to help, not punish, young people. Civil libertarians argued that the juvenile courts were actually just as punitive as the adult courts. They eventually persuaded the Supreme Court to go along with changes, and the juvenile courts are now run more like their adult counterparts. For instance, many states no longer define running away, incorrigibility, and other **status offenses** (juvenile offenses that do not violate adult criminal law) as delinquency. More recently, pressure from conservatives has led to increasing emphasis on punishment rather than rehabilitation for juveniles. The laws in many states have been rewritten to allow more young offenders to be tried as adults; the average sentence of those tried as juveniles has greatly increased; and the authorities are pressing charges against many juvenile offenders who, in the past, would have been released after a warning and a parent conference. Public opinion polls show that over 85 percent of Americans now believe that juveniles who commit serious crime should be tried as adults.[36]

Juvenile delinquency has probably been studied more carefully than any other category of crime. The principal explanations of crime were developed from the study of delinquency as well as adult criminality and are used to understand delinquency as well as crime. Nevertheless, juveniles have special problems and should not be considered merely young criminals. For one thing, the influence of the family on the lives of juvenile delinquents is certainly much greater. A number of studies show that children are much more likely to become delinquent if a parent is a criminal. Self-report studies show that children from all economic backgrounds commit minor acts of delinquency at about the same rate but that children from poor homes are much more likely to commit serious criminal acts.[37] Delinquency also occurs more often among children in single-parent families. After a careful review of 50 different studies on this subject, L. Edward Wells and Joseph H. Rankin concluded that the prevalence of delinquency was 10 to 15 percent higher among children from broken homes. However, it seems to make no difference whether the family is disrupted by a divorce or by the death of a parent.[38] Another unique problem of juvenile offenders is youth itself (see Chapter 9). In traditional cultures, everyone goes directly from being a child to being an adult, but in industrialized nations there is an extended in-between period of adolescence in which difficult demands are placed on young people. Adolescents are not considered old enough for marriage

juvenile delinquent
A minor (usually defined as an individual below the age of 18) who violates the criminal law or the special legal standards set for juveniles.

status offense
A juvenile offense that is not in violation of the criminal law.

and family responsibilities of their own, yet they are too old to remain totally dependent on their parents. In a sense they are between two worlds and part of neither.

Finally, there is the problem of juvenile gangs. Adolescents all over the world form groups based on friendship and mutual interests. When these groups meet social approval, we call them clubs or organizations; but when the community condemns them, we call them gangs. Juvenile gangs of streetwise young toughs roam the streets of most urban slums and ghettos. The primary motivation of the "fighting gang" is to control their "turf" (territory) and defend their honor, sometimes by fighting to the death. The graffiti that cover so many urban neighborhoods are symbols to gang members—marking their territory and oftentimes issuing a challenge to rival gangs. Some of these gangs have long histories going back thirty or forty years, and gang fights and killings have been a fact of life in some urban neighborhoods for generations. Some juvenile gangs, however, are more concerned with making an illicit profit than fighting gang wars, and they are more likely to resort to violence to protect their financial interests than their reputation in the neighborhood.

There is considerable disagreement among criminologists about how well-organized juvenile gangs are. Michael Gottfredson and Travis Hirschi argue that juvenile gangs have very little formal structure and are really just loose aggregations of friends and associates.[39] Martin Sanchez Jankowski, on the other hand, holds that gangs are highly organized, with clear leadership, many distinct roles, and sets of rules that are enforced by the members.[40] Whichever form is most common, it is clear that juvenile gangs run the gamut: some are so loosely structured that they soon fall apart, while others run well-organized illicit businesses, such as drug dealing or extortion rackets, operating very much the way adult criminal syndicates do.

Quick Review

Explain the ways criminologists classify different types of crimes.

Define each of the four major types of violent crime.

How do victim-offender relationships differ among the different violent crimes?

Define each of the most common property crimes.

What is the difference between occasional criminals and professional criminals?

What are the most common victimless crimes?

How does syndicated crime differ from the crimes committed by single individuals?

What is the difference between organizational and occupational crime?

Why do white-collar criminals get off easier than other criminals?

What is the difference between a delinquent and an adult criminal?

Why do kids join juvenile gangs?

Measuring Crime and Violence

If we are to understand crime, we must measure it accurately, but that is much harder than it sounds. Criminals are often unwilling to talk about their activities, and the general public's knowledge about their own victimization is frequently inaccurate. For example, a homeowner who develops cancer may not know that the cause was toxic waste illegally dumped on a nearby lot, or a man who loses his wallet may mistakenly believe it was stolen.

Criminologists use four principal means of measuring crime, each with its own strengths and weaknesses. The first statistics available to criminologists were based on the crimes reported to the police. Since the 1930s, the FBI has published a summary of all the crimes reported to police agencies in the United States, and other industrialized nations now have similar publications. These FBI statistics, known as the **Uniform Crime Reports** or UCR, were virtually the only source of nationwide data on crime until the 1970s, when the federal government began conducting a yearly crime survey. This **National Crime Victimization Survey (NCVS)** asks a random sample of Americans to report information about any crimes in which they were the victim in the last year. Of the two, the NCVS is generally considered the more accurate because many victims are either afraid to report their problem to the police or simply do not want to take the time. The National Crime Victimization Survey's reports show about twice as much crime as the UCR.

Neither the victimization surveys nor the tallies of the crimes reported to the police contain very much direct information about who commits those crimes. For that, criminologists often use arrest statistics. Such figures give us a variety of information about the characteristics of people who are arrested (sex, age, ethnic group, etc.), but they have one major flaw. Everyone who commits a crime does not have an equal chance of being arrested, and therefore these statistics may not paint an accurate picture of the typical criminal. To try to solve this problem, some criminologists conduct what are called **self-report studies.** That is, they ask a sample of people to report anonymously on the crimes they themselves have committed. The obvious drawback to this approach is that despite the assurance of anonymity, many people are still afraid to describe their criminal activities honestly, especially their more serious offenses.

Uniform Crime Reports
A national summary of all the crimes reported to the police.

National Crime Victimization Survey (NCVS)
A yearly survey of Americans, which attempts to determine how many have been victimized by crime.

self-report study
A survey that asks its respondents to report crimes they have committed.

Is There a Crime Wave?

Many people throughout the industrialized world are convinced that we are in the midst of a massive crime wave that is threatening our property and personal safety. In the United States, the main support for this belief comes from the Uniform Crime Reports. UCR data showed a steady increase in crime from the end of World War II until 1980. Crime declined from 1980 to 1984, then rose until 1991, and has declined slightly since then.[41] However, there are serious questions about how accurate those data are. Greater confidence in the police, quicker and easier ways of reporting crime, improved record keeping, and the growing popularity of theft insurance (which requires victims to report a crime in order to collect) have all tended to artificially increase the number of crimes that are reported. Moreover, many criminologists believe that some police departments intentionally exaggerate the increases in crime in order to justify their requests for more money and more personnel. On the other hand, data from the National Crime Victimization Survey show a decline in crime. The property crimes measured by the NCVS have shown a steady decline from 1974 to 1995. Overall, the crime rate declined by about one-fourth during that period. The rates of violence were less stable, increasing in some years and declining in others, but overall there was about an 8 percent decrease during that period.[42] (See Figure 13.1.) Given the weakness of the Uniform Crime Reports, the most likely conclusion is that crime has been going down, not up, over the last two decades. There are, moreover, good reasons for believing that the crime

Figure 13.1

Crime

While the rate of crimes reported to the police has gone up since 1973, victimization surveys indicate that crime has been going down.

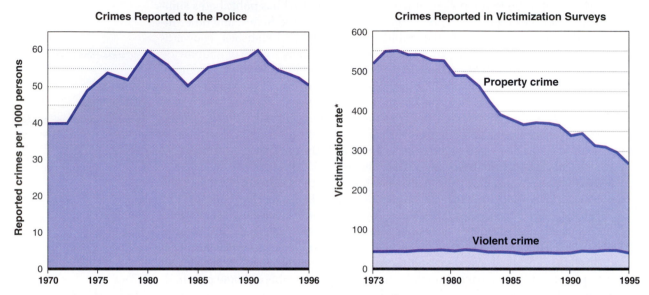

Crimes Reported to the Police

Crimes Reported in Victimization Surveys

Source: Federal Bureau of Investigation, *Uniform Crime Reports, 1996* (Washington, DC: U.S. Department of Justice, 1997), p. 63; Bureau of Justice Statistics, *Criminal Victimization, 1973–1995* (Washington, DC: U.S. Department of Justice, 1997).

*Property crimes per 1000 households; violent crimes per 1000 persons age 12 or older.

rate should be declining. The average age of our population has been rising, and, as we will see in the next section, older people commit fewer crimes.

Who Commits Crime?

Criminologists agree that three variables—age, gender, and geographic area—all have an important influence on the incidence of crime. In the United States, 4 times as many men as women are arrested, and there are about 16 times more men than women in prison.[43] In many nations, such as the Islamic countries of the Middle East, the gender differences are far greater. Of course, some of these differences may stem from the fact that the criminal justice system expects more men to be criminals and therefore watches them more closely. When the respondents in the crime survey are asked about the gender of the criminals who victimized them, however, their responses are generally consistent with the gender ratios in the arrest reports.[44] The crime rate for women has, however, been growing faster than the rate for men. The biggest increases have been in the nonviolent property crimes, such as larceny (theft), fraud, and embezzlement, for which 30 to 40 percent of the arrestees are now female. The rise in violent crime among women, on the other hand, has not been very significant. And even for the nonviolent property crimes, there are still some important differences in the kinds of offenses committed by women and by men. The value of the take from women's crimes is generally much lower than from men's crimes, and women are more likely to act as single individuals rather than as part of an organized group.[45] (See Chapter 10 for an examination of the reasons men's and women's behavior often differs so sharply.)

Records of arrests and convictions show that teenagers and young adults have the highest crime rates. In the United States, the likelihood of arrest peaks in the 19- to 21-year-old age group and slowly declines after that. Contrary to the popular image of the violent teenage hoodlum, however, minors commit fewer violent crimes than young adults do. Thirty-five percent of people arrested for property crimes are under age 18, but minors make up only nineteen percent of people arrested for violent crime.[46]

Both victimization surveys and police reports also show that the highest crime rates are found in inner-city slums and that crime rates decrease as one moves out from the central city to the wealthier residential areas. Crime is lower in the suburbs than in the cities and lower still in the rural areas (see Chapter 14).

Most criminologists also believe that social class and ethnic group have a powerful effect on crime rates, but there is more controversy about this point. Arrest statistics show some significant differences among ethnic groups in the United States. Jews and Japanese have lower-than-average arrest rates, while African Americans, Latinos, and Native Americans have higher-than-average rates. Although African Americans make up about 12 percent of the population of the

There has been a big increase in the crime rate for women, but mostly for nonviolent offenses.

United States, they account for about 30 percent of all those arrested. The difference is even more pronounced for violent crime. In 1994, 56 percent of those arrested for murder, 42 percent of those arrested for rape, and 60 percent of those arrested for robbery were African Americans.[47] Official statistics also show that poor people are more likely to be arrested and sent to prison than those from middle- or upper-class backgrounds. Over two-thirds of the men and nine-tenths of the women in prison are from the poverty class or the working class. However, there is good reason to doubt that arrest and incarceration statistics are an accurate measure of the extent of crime among those groups, because poor people and members of ethnic minorities are probably more likely to be arrested and sent to prison for their crimes than others are. For one thing, money and influence often serve to protect someone from being arrested or incarcerated, and ethnic stereotypes may lead the police to watch minorities more closely than members of other groups.

Most of the other data, nonetheless, point to the same conclusion as the arrest statistics. At one time, some criminologists claimed that the self-report studies did not indicate any consistent relationship between crime and social class,[48] but subsequent analyses have shown that to be true only for very minor offenses. Self-report studies that include serious offenses do reveal higher crime rates among the poor and minorities.[49] The victimization surveys also provide support for this conclusion. They show that the rates of victimization are highest in poor and minority areas, and the most probable explanation is that the crime rates are higher in those neighborhoods because more criminals live there.[50] According to studies of murder victims, African Americans are about seven times more likely to be murdered than other Americans, and we know from other studies that murderers and their victims are usually from the same ethnic group. Further, when the NCVS asked respondents to identify the race of the criminals who victimized them, African Americans were selected in roughly the same proportion as we would predict from the arrest statistics.[51] There is still one serious weakness in our data, however. We have no good measures of the true incidence of most white-collar crimes because many of the victims of those crimes do not know they have been victimized. Since white-collar offenses are mainly committed by affluent individuals who are not from minority groups, it is impossible to be certain who has the highest overall crime rate. We can say that poor people and ethnic minorities commit more "street" crimes, such as murder, burglary and theft, but that is all.

America: Land of the Violent?

The question of which nations have the highest crime rates and how we can explain the differences among nations is an extremely important one. Unfortunately, the data we have are not very good. Most nations do not conduct victimization surveys comparable to the NCVS, and variations in the laws and in the way police departments handle their record keeping make comparisons of the statistics on reported crime virtually meaningless. There is, however, one exception to this rule, and that is for the crime of murder. Murder is illegal in virtually all nations, and the seriousness of the offense and the existence of a dead body as evidence mean that most murders are in fact reported to the police.

Although a few less developed countries such as Thailand and the Philippines report higher murder rates, the United States has by far the highest rate of any in-

Figure 13.2

Rape and Murder

The United States has far higher rates of rape and murder than other industrialized nations.

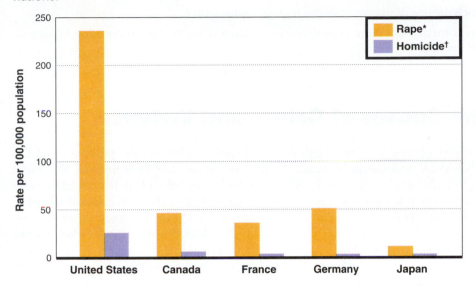

Source: United Nations Human Development Programme, *Human Development Report, 1997* (New York: Oxford University Press, 1997), p. 213.

*Average rate of reported rapes from 1987 to 1989.
†Average rate of homicides committed by males from 1985 to 1990.

dustrialized nation (see Figure 13.2). According to the World Health Organization, the murder rate is 5 times higher in the United States than in Canada and 7.5 times higher than in Europe. Data from the International Police Organization (Interpol) indicate that murder is 3 times more common in the United States than it is in Canada and 5 times more frequent than in Europe.[52] Although the statistics on rape and robbery are less reliable, there seems little reason to doubt that those crimes are also much more common in the United States.

The high level of violence in America is often seen as a holdover from the rowdy days of frontier expansion. According to this view, violence became a way of life as an unending stream of settlers fought among themselves and with native peoples for land and profit. However, Canada and Australia were also settled by rough pioneers, and the citizens of those countries have apparently not passed down a violent frontier tradition. The United States was unique, however, in its extensive use of slave labor, and slavery's legacy of racism and resentment is a major contributor to the persuasiveness of violence in this country. Furthermore, the United States is an extremely wealthy nation, but, compared with other Western countries, it has a bigger gap between the rich and the poor and inferior welfare and social programs (see Chapter 7). Thus, those at the bottom of the social hierarchy tend to be more frustrated and desperate and more resentful of those who possess the wealth they are denied.

What are the different ways criminologists measure crime?

What does the evidence tell us about whether crime is going up or down?

Which groups of people have the highest crime rates?

Why is there more criminal violence in the United States than in the other industrialized nations?

The Causes of Crime and Violence

The birth of modern criminology can be traced to 1764 and the publication of the Italian nobleman Cesare Beccaria's book *On Crimes and Punishments*. The great English philosopher Jeremy Bentham applied Beccaria's ideas to legislation, and these two men became the leaders of what came to be called the classical school of criminology. They thought that all people were guided by a rational desire to seek pleasure and avoid pain. According to the **classical theory,** people who commit crimes choose to do so. They weigh all the options and find that a crime will give them the most pleasure for the least amount of pain. This idea was regarded as a complete explanation of crime, and these early theorists saw no need for research on the economic, psychological, political, or social conditions associated with crime. The classical school has been heavily criticized for its view of human beings as something like rational calculating machines. Nonetheless, these ideas remain popular today. Like its classical predecessor, **rational choice theory** sees lawbreaking as the result of a rational choice by the criminal, but it uses a much more sophisticated analysis of the social structures that provide the context in which that choice is made.

classical theory
A theory holding that people commit crimes because it offers them more pleasure and less pain than their other possible options.

rational choice theory
A theory that holds crime to be the result of the rational choice of the offender.

Biological Theories

The first real challenge to the classical school was mounted by an Italian physician, Cesare Lombroso, and his supporters in the last quarter of the nineteenth century. The **positive school** of criminology rejected classical theory's assumption that crime was based on free choice. Proponents felt that most criminals were biologically different from "normal" people and had easily identifiable physical traits such as sloping foreheads, small brains, overdeveloped jaws, and other apelike characteristics. Indeed, Lombroso believed that criminals were actually evolutionary throwbacks to our "savage" ancestors.

positive school
A theoretical school in criminology that rejected the classical theory's assumption that crime was based on free choice.

Although Lombrosian ideas about the physical characteristics of criminals have been discredited by the scientific community, other kinds of evolutionary theories are still used to explain violent behavior. Martin Daly and Margo Wilson, for example, argue that the basic motives and structure of the human psyche evolved to serve one evolutionary goal: the survival of our genes. Utilizing admittedly incomplete data, they argue that within the family we are most likely to kill those with whom we do not share common genes (for example, spouses and adopted children) and least likely to kill those who carry our genes (biological children). They see violence between strangers as rooted in the conflicts between males over access to the reproductive powers of females and the right to father as many children as possible. This

"Darwinian psychology" raises some interesting new issues, but is still unable to account for the known patterns of violent behavior. For example, we are actually more likely to kill ourselves than to commit a murder, and suicide obviously is an act that will greatly diminish our chances of passing our genes on to the next generation.[53]

Most of the current research in this area is concerned not with evolution but with the overall importance of biological factors as a cause of criminal behavior. The usual approach is to try to determine whether people who have a close biological relationship to a known criminal are themselves more likely to be involved in crime. One technique is to compare the criminal records of identical twins (whose genetic makeup is presumed to be identical) to see if such records are more similar than those of fraternal twins. Although most of these studies have found that to be the case, the interpretation of that fact is unclear because parents and friends tend to treat identical twins more similarly than fraternal twins.

A better methodological approach is found in studies that compare the crime rates of adopted children with those of their biological parents. Once again, most of these studies have found higher crime rates among adopted children whose biological parents were criminals than among those whose biological parents were not. Barry Hutchings and Sarnoff A. Mednick's study of 1145 boys adopted in Copenhagen, for example, found that having a biological parent as a criminal significantly increased a boy's chances of growing up to be a criminal and that the highest crime rates were among those boys whose adoptive *and* biological parents were criminals.[54] Adoption studies have serious weaknesses, however. For one thing, adoption agencies do not randomly assign babies to adoptive parents, as scientists would like. Rather, they match up parents and children with similar characteristics, and the social environment of the adopted children may therefore be far more similar to that of their biological parents than the researchers assume. Another problem comes from the fact that adoption agencies screen out those they consider undesirable parents. Since people in homes with conditions that are likely to encourage criminality are not allowed to adopt children, adoption studies are bound to underestimate the impact of the home environment on criminal behavior.[55]

A general problem with the biological theories is that they have yet to determine exactly what inherited characteristics contribute to criminal behavior. James Q. Wilson and Richard Herrnstein speculate that low intelligence or an impulsive personality might be involved, but there is little conclusive evidence on the matter.[56] Criminality obviously cannot be directly inherited because crime is defined by legislators and politicians, and the definition of what is criminal and what is not is continually changing. It seems likely that inherited traits are often related to criminal behavior only by virtue of the fact that people have learned to react to them in a certain way. For example, a student with high intelligence will be more likely to do well in school and thus receive praise and support from teachers, whereas a student with lesser abilities is far more likely to feel rejected and to rebel against school authorities.

Personality Theories

There is a widely held belief that many criminals, especially violent ones, are mentally disturbed. After a particularly gruesome murder has occurred, we often hear the comment, "A person would have to be crazy to do something like that." Although such statements express understandable shock and disbelief, they do not really tell us much about the causes of crime. Psychiatric examinations of convicted criminals show that only a small percentage are psychotic, and official records indicate that most psychotics are not criminals and have not attacked or harmed other people.[57]

Many psychologists and psychiatrists who examine convicted criminals have nonetheless concluded that criminals often have a **sociopathic personality.** This term is somewhat vague, but it refers to an inability to form close social relationships, combined with a lack of moral feelings or concern for others. Some psychiatrists think that this personality type is hereditary, but the most common explanation is that it develops in early childhood. The method of diagnosing a sociopathic personality is not at all standardized. For this reason, the labels "sociopathic" and "sociopath" can be applied to almost anyone. It appears that the idea of causation is often circular. People are labeled sociopathic because they have broken the law, and then it is claimed that people break the law because they are sociopaths.

Standardized personality tests and rating scales have also been used to compare criminals and noncriminals. Although researchers have constructed scales that have been fairly successful at predicting criminal behavior, it isn't entirely clear what personality characteristics, if any, those scales are actually measuring. Three comprehensive reviews of studies of the most widely used personality test, the Minnesota Multiphasic Personality Inventory (MMPI), have all concluded that little evidence supports the claim that criminals have distinctive personality characteristics.[58] Recent research by Avshalon Caspi and his associates, on the other hand, found significantly higher rates of delinquency among juveniles who had a high tendency to feel negative emotions such as anger and frustration and had weak impulse control (a tendency to act impulsively).[59]

Sociological Theories

There are dozens of sociological theories of crime and violence. In general, however, either they focus on the reasons an individual commits criminal acts or they examine the larger social forces that determine the overall rates of crime and violence.

The most common answer that sociologists give to the question of why someone becomes a criminal is that he or she has learned to act that way from others. One of the earliest and most influential of these learning theories is known as **differential association.**[60] This theory, developed by Edwin H. Sutherland, says that people become criminals because they are exposed to more people with attitudes and definitions that are favorable to a certain type of crime than are opposed to it. However, all associations and personal contacts do not have the same influence. The longer, the more frequent, the more intense, and the more important an association is to a person, the stronger its effect. Most criminal behavior, like most noncriminal behavior, is therefore learned in intimate personal groups and not from impersonal sources such as movies and television.

Numerous studies of violent behavior have shown that it is often learned from other family members. Murray A. Straus, Richard J. Gelles, and Suzanne K. Steinmetz found that men who grew up in families in which violence was prevalent were 10 times more likely to beat their wives than men from nonviolent families.[61] A number of studies show that individuals who were abused as children are at greater risk than others to become child abusers when they grow up.[62] Two studies have found that even the physical punishment of children increases the probability that they will commit a violent crime as an adult,[63] and a recent long-term study found

sociopathic personality
An antisocial person with a complex of personality characteristics including impulsiveness, immaturity, and a lack of concern for other people.

differential association theory
A theory holding that people commit crimes because they have more and stronger associations with those who favor a certain criminal behavior than with those who oppose it.

Sociologists argue that criminal behavior is often learned from participation in a deviant subculture.

higher rates of arrest among people who were abused or neglected as children than among a control group matched for gender, race, and income.[64] Socialization into violence is especially pronounced for boys, who are expected to be tough, strong, and aggressive. Straus, Gelles, and Steinmetz summarized the literature on violence well when they wrote that "over and over again, the statistics . . . suggest the same conclusion. Each generation learns to be violent by participating in a violent family."[65]

Crime and violence are also learned from contact with **deviant subcultures**—that is, groups that have developed perspectives, attitudes, and values that support criminality. The more someone is involved with the members of such a subculture, the more likely he or she is to join in its criminal activities. Many sociologists consider the culture of poverty to be a deviant subculture, since many of its attitudes and values seem to encourage criminal behavior (see Chapter 6). The drug subculture and the subculture of juvenile gang members are also distinctive perspectives on the world, and both reject at least parts of the conventional morality embodied in the criminal law. For a girl or boy from the underclass who is a drug user and a member of a juvenile gang, committing a crime of one kind or another is almost automatic.

Labeling theory has added to our understanding of the way crime is learned by exploring the process by which people are branded as criminals and the effects such labeling has on them. Contrary to popular opinion, labeling theorists hold that branding someone as a deviant usually encourages further criminal behavior. For example, take the case of an adolescent boy whose "play" includes breaking windows and stealing hubcaps. He might consider such activities as akin to the fun of Halloween, but to most adults his behavior is delinquent, and they soon demand

deviant subculture
A social group with perspectives, attitudes, and values that encourage crime or other deviant activity.

labeling theory
A theory that holds that branding someone with a deviant label (junkie, juvenile delinquent, insane, etc.) encourages further deviant behavior.

that he stop it. If he continues, there is a shift away from the definition of the acts as delinquent to the definition of the boy as delinquent. The boy, realizing he is being branded as "bad," draws closer to others with the same problem. The community responds with punishment, then counseling, and finally with commitment to an institution. The boy acquires a police record and eventually comes to define himself as he is defined: as a delinquent—by this time an incorrigible one committed to a long-term criminal career.

There is little doubt that many types of criminal behavior are learned, but critics claim that theories based on learning have some serious weaknesses. For one thing, they are incomplete. Where do the behavior patterns that criminals learn come from in the first place? Differential association and labeling theory provide no answer. A second common criticism is that these theories are so vague and general that they can be used to explain almost anything but are difficult to prove or disprove scientifically.

Another group of sociologists who take a different approach to criminology see crime as normal and natural. If all people are born with an "aggressive instinct" or automatically commit crimes for some other reasons, it is not very useful to ask why they commit crimes. It is more reasonable, according to this way of thinking, to ask why people do *not* commit crimes. **Control theory** answers this question by saying that noncriminals are constrained by society and thus are prevented from breaking the law. Some control theorists emphasize the importance of the internal reins that society builds up in the individual through the process of socialization. They say it is a strong conscience and a sense of personal morality that stops most people from breaking the law. In this sense, Freud's psychoanalytic theory can be seen as a control theory. Other control theorists, such as Travis Hirschi, believe that what stops crime is the bond that individuals form to conventional social institutions. Still other control theorists have returned to the rationalistic assumptions of the classical school, arguing that most of us do not commit crimes because we are deterred by the criminal justice system and the fear of legal punishment. These different versions of control theory are not mutually exclusive; in fact, the most convincing form of control theory sees all three types of controls working simultaneously.[66]

Critics point out that control theory, like the learning theories, is extremely broad and virtually impossible to prove or disprove. The critics have passed particularly harsh judgment on control theory's assumption that people "naturally" commit crimes. Like the religious idea that human beings are evil by nature, it is an assumption that is almost impossible to study scientifically.

To understand the rates and distribution of crime, sociologists must link these individual explanations of crime to the larger social forces that shape contemporary society. For example, sociologists have been trying for generations to explain why there apparently is more crime among the poor than among the other social classes. Probably the most influential of these is Robert K. Merton, who developed what is often called **strain theory**.[67] Crime, according to this concept, is produced by the strain in societies that (1) tell people that wealth is available to all but also (2) restrict some people's access to the means for achieving wealth. Because lower-class people in such societies cannot legally obtain the things they are taught to desire, they may try to reach their goals by breaking the law.

Learning theorists, on the other hand, tend to emphasize the cultural characteristics of the lower classes that encourage crime. For example, Walter B. Miller

control theory

A theory that holds that people commit crimes because of the failure of social controls on criminal behavior.

strain theory

A theory holding that crime is caused by the strain produced when society tells people that wealth is available to all but nevertheless restricts access to the means for achieving wealth.

argues that although the subculture of poverty may have originated from a process similar to the one described by Merton, strain and frustration are not the causes of the high crime rate in the lower class. Rather, the cause is the distinctive attitudes and values found among the poor.[68] Another explanation comes from control theorists, who feel that the punishments that keep most people from getting involved in crime are less effective on the poor because they usually have a weaker bond to conventional social institutions and have much less to lose in terms of material possessions and social prestige if they are caught breaking the law.

Of course, crime is not limited to the lower class. Another crucial sociological question concerns the reasons our society as a whole has such a high level of crime. To answer this question, many sociologists turn to the pioneering work of Emile Durkheim, who saw the roots of the problem in what he termed **anomie** or normlessness. According to Durkheim and his contemporary followers, modern industrial society has become so diverse and impersonal that consensus about what is right and wrong has broken down, and many people no longer belong to strong supportive groups that regulate their behavior. As a result, there is not only more crime but more frustration and suicide as well.[69] On the other hand, supporters of **critical theory** argue that it is the capitalist economic system that is the root cause of our crime problem. According to this school of thought, capitalism fosters crime by encouraging, and even requiring, the exploitation of one group by another and by promoting the selfish quest for personal gain as if it were the inevitable goal of all human behavior.[70]

anomie
A condition in which social norms have broken down and no longer regulate individual behavior.

critical theory
A theory holding that the capitalist economic system is the root cause of the crime problem in modern industrial societies.

Quick Review

What role does biology play in criminal behavior?

What do psychologists say about the causes of crime?

Discuss and critically evaluate the most important sociological theories of crime.

Criminal Justice

The criminal justice process reflects a conflict between two very different social goals. On the one hand, there is the need to stop crime and rid society of troublemakers. On the other hand, there is the need to protect, preserve, and nourish the rights and liberties of individuals. All societies pit these two needs against each other. Some are police states, in which the methods of crime control bulldoze citizens into submission. At the other extreme is chaos, in which individuals run wild. Democratic societies take a middle ground, tempering the need to repress crime with concern for the rights of their citizens. Even in democratic societies, few people agree on what the proper balance should be. Some North Americans favor what Herbert L. Packer called the **crime control model** of criminal justice, a program for the speedy arrest and punishment of all who commit crimes. Others advocate a **due process model** that tempers the rush to punishment with concern for human rights and dignity.[71] Speaking generally, those who fear the official abuse of power

crime control model
A model of criminal justice that favors speedy arrest and punishment of anyone who commits a crime.

due process model
A model of criminal justice that places more emphasis on protecting human rights and dignity than on punishing criminals.

favor the due process model, while those who fear crime more advocate the crime control model.

The Police

Police officers are on the front line of the criminal justice process. They are much more visible than other criminal justice personnel, and they have more contacts with the citizenry. They have become the symbols of the whole system of justice. In addition to their symbolic importance, police officers are the gatekeepers for the other criminal justice agencies. They cannot possibly arrest all suspected lawbreakers. There aren't enough police, and even if there were, there wouldn't be enough courts to try the accused or enough jails to hold them. Equally important, it is not in the interest of justice to arrest everyone who has violated the law regardless of the circumstances. Thus, police officers must use a great deal of discretion in deciding how to carry out their duties, and those decisions, in turn, determine how much business there will be for the criminal justice agencies down the line.

Contrary to popular opinion, only a small part of all the work done by a police department is directly concerned with fighting crime. For example, only 10 to 20 percent of the calls to most police departments require officers to perform law enforcement duties, and most of the incidents an officer handles on any given day are not criminal matters.[72] Outsiders who have observed police activities confirm the idea that they function more as *peace officers* than *law enforcement officers*.

Although most police work is routine, even boring, there is always an element of danger for the officer on the street. At least partially for that reason, police officers form tightly knit groups that stick together. The effort to protect fellow officers is vital on the streets but is a serious barrier to controlling police misconduct. Time and again, efforts to investigate charges of racism, corruption, and brutality run into a "wall of silence." As a result, no one can say how widespread this problem actually is, but there have been enough substantiated cases to know that **police brutality** is indeed serious.

police brutality
The use of excessive and unnecessary force by police officers in the performance of their duties.

The Courts

After an arrest, police officers must take the suspect promptly before a lower-court magistrate (judge), who will decide whether the suspect must come back to the lower court for further proceedings and will set the conditions under which temporary release on **bail** can be granted. Under the American bail system, accused persons put up a sum of money to be forfeited if they do not show up for trial. In most courts, the accused with good credit or collateral can pay a relatively small fee to a bail bonder, who then provides the financial security (called a bail bond) necessary for release. The bail system clearly discriminates against the poor. The amount of money required is usually determined by the charge against the suspect, with little consideration for the defendant's personal finances. Poor people who cannot raise enough money stay in jail awaiting trial, sometimes for months, while the more affluent post their bail and go free.

Most people think that the defendant's fate is decided in a public trial, in which the prosecutor and defense attorney battle to prove their case. Actually, the trial

bail
A sum of money put up as security to be forfeited if a person accused of committing a crime does not appear for trial.

plays a small part in the criminal justice process. Most defendants make a deal with the prosecutor by agreeing to plead guilty in exchange for a reduction in the charges or some other consideration. This process, called **plea bargaining,** is much faster and cheaper than taking each case to trial. The state saves money, and the defendants receive more lenient punishment than they would have if they had gone to trial and been convicted. Critics from both the left and the right have nonetheless passed disparaging judgments on the process of plea bargaining. Civil libertarians complain that it takes the process of justice behind closed doors, where violations of defendants' rights are hidden from the public view, and that innocent people are coerced into pleading guilty because they know that if they demand a trial and are convicted, they will receive much harsher punishment. Conservatives, on the other hand, complain that plea bargaining lets the guilty off with lighter sentences than they deserve.

After the defendants have pleaded guilty or have been found guilty, they are called back into court for sentencing. Until fairly recently, judges were given wide discretion in deciding how severe a sentence to hand down, but complaints about what were perceived to be excessively lenient sentences have led to much greater restrictions on judges' powers. In most cases, the judge must still decide whether to give the defendant probation or sentence him or her to prison for the term prescribed by law, but even that power has been restricted by various laws requiring mandatory sentences for some offenses or for defendants with long criminal histories.

Corrections

Originally, prisons were nothing but places to hold criminals until society could decide how to punish them (for example, by fines, whipping, or execution). Prisons for the long-term confinement of inmates were originally established in order to achieve three goals, and they are still central objectives of today's prison system. The first is to get even (**retribution**). The public wants to make criminals suffer by depriving them of their liberty. The second is to scare potential criminals so much that they will be afraid to violate the law (**deterrence**). The third is to protect the public from dangerous individuals by locking them up (**incapacitation**). In the 1940s and 1950s, an innovative new goal was added: to reform prisoners through such programs as job training and psychotherapy (**rehabilitation**). Unfortunately, this new objective often clashed with the prison's other goals. In most cases, prison officials adopted the language of rehabilitation (for example, penitentiaries became "correctional institutions"), but they continued to give the goal of reforming prisoners a low priority. As a result, few rehabilitation programs were effective, and many of them have been dismantled in recent years. However, the prisons have proved no more effective at deterring crime than they have been at reforming criminals. Although it is a matter of some dispute, the most commonly cited figure is that about two-thirds of those released from prison commit another serious crime within four or five years.[73]

Despite such evidence of failure, America's prison population is growing at an alarming rate. The number of Americans behind bars has almost tripled since 1980 (see Figure 13.3). The United States now has a higher percentage of its population

plea bargaining
A process by which a defense attorney and a prosecutor agree to let a defendant plead guilty in return for a reduction in the charge or other considerations.

retribution
The idea that criminals should be punished because they deserve it.

deterrence
The idea that criminals should be punished in order to discourage criminal behavior.

incapacitation
The idea that criminals should be locked up (or executed) so that they cannot commit other crimes.

rehabilitation
The idea that criminals should be helped to change their ways.

Figure 13.3

Prison

There has been a huge increase in the number of people in American prisons since 1970.

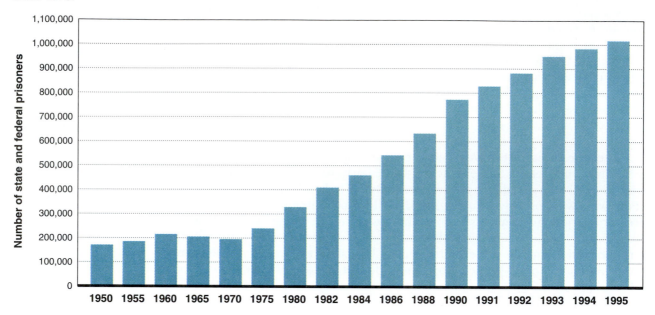

Source: U.S. Bureau of Justice Statistics, *Prisoners in 1993* (Washington, DC: U.S. Department of Justice, 1994); Bureau of Justice Statistics, *Sourcebook of Criminal Justice Statistics 1996* (Washington, DC: U.S. Department of Justice, 1997), p. 502.

probation

Suspension of the sentences of persons who have been convicted but not yet imprisoned, on the condition that they live up to the terms set by the court.

in jail than any other country in the world. Even more disturbing is the fact that one in every three young African American men in the United States is either in prison or on probation or parole.[74] Prisons are becoming increasingly overcrowded, and living conditions have gone from bad to worse. Murder, assault, and homosexual rape are everyday events in our prisons, and mere survival has become the primary goal of many inmates.

Probation, which allows convicted criminals to remain in the community under government supervision, is the principal alternative to incarceration. In theory, probation officers work to help offenders stay on the right track, while keeping close tabs on them to make sure they do not return to crime. In practice, probation is seldom very effective in achieving either goal, primarily because probation officers are given such a huge number of cases to handle. A Rand Corporation study of 1600 probationers found that the majority are eventually arrested again for another offense; however, other research shows that people placed on probation are less likely to commit new crimes than are those who are sent to prison.[75] The most hardened and dangerous criminals are not given probation; therefore, it is unclear whether current probation programs are really any more effective than incarceration at stopping crime.

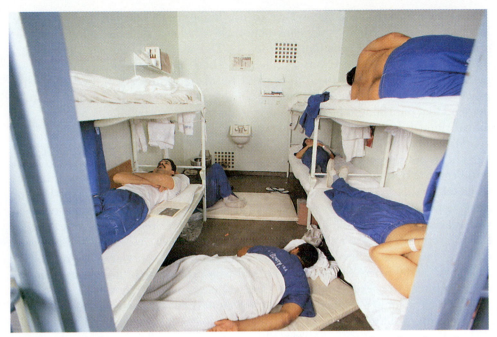

The prison population in the United States has exploded in the last decade and a half, and as a result, prisons are becoming more and more overcrowded.

Quick Review

What is the difference between the crime control and the due process models of criminal justice?

Describe the role the police play in the process of criminal justice.

What is plea bargaining, and why do so many people criticize it?

What are the four general goals of the correctional system?

Solving the Problems of Crime and Violence

Everyone seems to have an idea about how to stop crime. Politicians, police officers, criminologists, sociologists, and ordinary citizens propose one solution or another almost every day. Many of these proposals are contradictory, but it would seem possible to combine the best features of each in one comprehensive program. The following are a few of the most frequently suggested alternatives.

Increasing Punishment

The United States punishes its criminals more severely than any other democratic nation. American criminals receive longer prison terms than criminals in other industrialized countries, and, as we have seen, a higher percentage of the U.S. population is in prison. Many Americans nonetheless believe that the solution to the crime problem is to get even tougher. (See the Debate "Would Putting More Police on the Streets Solve the Crime Problem?") These proposals generally have two parts. First, they demand that punishment be made more certain, even if such a practice reduces legal protection against abuse of government power. Second, they demand that punishment be more severe, that prison terms be lengthened, and that more criminals be executed.

Such ideas are popular with the general public, and both kinds of proposals have been put into effect in the last decade. Not only have prison sentences been significantly lengthened, but recent Supreme Court decisions have cut back on the legal safeguards granted by earlier, more liberal courts. Perhaps the harshest of these new policies are the so-called three strikes laws that mandate a life sentence without possibility of parole for a third conviction for a serious crime. Critics charge that it simply isn't fair to lock up a young man in his early twenties until he dies of old age, just because he was convicted three times for burglaries or robberies. Moreover, many worry that our prisons will have to devote an increasing share of their resources to geriatric care since they will never be able to release any of this new class of prisoners, no matter how little danger they pose to society.

Supporters of the "get-tough" policies that have been enacted in the last decade and a half claim that they are responsible for the drop in the crime rate; however, critics point out that most of the decline is the natural result of an aging population. While most criminologists will grant that get-tough policies can produce some short-term reductions in crime, many argue that in the long run they will do little to stop crime and may even increase it. Sooner or later almost all prisoners are released, and these criminologists argue that their experience in jail is likely to leave them bitter and hardened in their criminal ways. As Joan Petersilia, the author of a Rand Corporation report on California's get-tough policies, concluded: "The analysis suggests that the much higher imprisonment rates in California had no appreciable effect on violent crime and only slight effects on property crime."[76] Even more troubling is the threat such programs pose to civil liberties in a democratic society; and their enormous costs are growing so large that many states are sacrificing other vital programs to help pay the bills for prisons. The critics pass particularly harsh judgment on the "war on drugs" that has sent huge numbers of nonviolent drug users into our prisons, where they are cut off from their families, their communities, and virtually all the other positive influences on their lives. We now send substantially more people to prison for drug offenses than for all violent crimes combined.[77]

Focusing on Violence

An alternative approach to criminal justice reform would focus the most severe punishment on the violent criminals, who virtually everyone agrees are the greatest threat to the public. Prison sentences would be significantly lengthened for such offenders as murderers, rapists, and business executives who knowingly endanger public safety. At the same time, prison terms for nonviolent property offenders could be reduced and greater reliance placed on restitution programs that force offenders to work to repay their victims. The primary response to drug users would be shifted from punishment to treatment and therapy.

Another reasonable response to the problem of violence is to enact stronger gun control laws. Some opponents of this idea claim that criminals would simply use other weapons if guns were not available, but even if that were so, the evidence shows that guns are far more lethal than other weapons. A study of violence in St. Louis, for example, found that a person attacked with a small-caliber gun was almost twice as likely to die than one attacked with a knife, and gunshot victims were three times more likely to die if attacked with a larger-caliber weapon. Others claim that even tough gun control laws would not get most guns off the street. However, international comparisons indicate that the nations with the toughest gun control laws have the lowest level of gun ownership and the lowest percentage of criminals who use guns. For example, about 60 percent of all murders in the United States are committed with firearms, but in Canada, which has stricter gun control laws, that figure is only 31 percent.[78] There are currently about 200 million privately owned firearms in the United States, including 60 million handguns, and they kill almost 40,000 people a year in homicides, accidents, and suicides.[79]

Although the regulation of firearms in the United States is extremely loose and ineffective, public opinion polls starting as far back as 1959 have repeatedly shown that Americans favor more gun control. Currently about 62 percent of all Americans say they want stricter gun control laws, and only about 5 percent want to loosen them. Large majorities favor universal gun registration and an outright ban on assault weapons and plastic guns (which cannot be discovered by metal detectors).[80] Why, then, aren't tougher laws passed? The major opposition comes from several powerful organizations—known collectively as the gun lobby—that are funded by sports enthusiasts and firearms manufacturers. Public opinion is apparently less influential than a well-financed and highly organized special-interest group such as the National Rifle Association.

Another controversial issue concerns the pervasive use of violence in the media. After conducting an extremely large number of studies using a variety of different methodologies, scientists have reached a consensus that media violence encourages real-life violence.[81] As Jeffrey H. Goldstein puts it, "After nearly three decades of research social scientists are now almost unanimous in their agreement that portrayed violence increases aggressive behavior."[82] However, it is also widely accepted that government censorship of the media poses a fundamental threat to democratic institutions. Some way therefore needs to be found to get the media corporations to be more responsible and reduce the huge amounts of graphic violence in the movies and on television without creating a new government bureaucracy to do the job. To date, public pressure has been to little avail. Nonetheless, organized minority groups have been successful in sharply reducing the racist stereotypes that were once common in the media, and if the public were concerned enough, there is no reason similar improvements couldn't be made in reducing gratuitous violence.

Combating White-Collar Crime

As we have seen, white-collar crime costs more money and more lives than all other types of crime put together, yet it receives a relatively low percentage of the resources that go to law enforcement. An effective program to solve the crime problem must therefore allocate far more time and more money to deal with white-collar crime. In theory, it should actually be easier to deter white-collar crime than

Yes

The crime problem has reached crisis proportions, and something must be done. Changing the underlying sociological causes of crime is a good idea, but that would be an extraordinarily slow and difficult process. Proposals to imprison more criminals also make sense, but that approach is not only becoming prohibitively expensive—it also runs the risk that long prison terms will turn inmates into more hardened and bitter criminals. A more realistic solution is to substantially increase funding for local police departments that agree to put more police officers on the street. While such a program would probably lead to an increase in arrests in the short run, the primary goal would be to prevent crimes before they occur. It is simply common sense that if there are more police officers on patrol, our streets and our property will be safer. It is especially important to have more officers walking a beat in the inner cities in order to bring residents some relief from the reign of lawlessness and terror so common in ghetto neighborhoods.

In addition to reducing crime, an increase in the number of police will produce other benefits. Neighborhood police officers on patrol would provide a positive role model for children in slum neighborhoods, who too often see drug dealers and gang lords as the only local success stories. The new jobs created would help reduce our nagging unemployment problem. New officers could provide other important services, including better traffic control and faster response to emergency situations. Perhaps most important, a more visible presence by the police will make our citizens feel safer and help end our paralyzing fear of crime. We need more police on the streets—now.

common street crimes, because the typical offenders, especially when they are big corporations, are acting not out of irrational passion but from rational self-interest. If we increased the certainty and severity of punishment, it is likely that white-collar crime would show a significant decline. Because white-collar crimes are hard to detect and expensive to prosecute, there is a crying need for more investigators and more prosecutors. Tougher laws with mandatory penalties would also be a big help.

The greatest problem in combating white-collar crime is not that we don't know what to do, but that we lack the political will to do what needs to be done. Many corporate criminals have enormous wealth and power, and time and again they have been able to cripple the effort to bring them to justice. Individual white-collar offenders seldom have as much political influence as the huge corporations, but they are still far less attractive targets for prosecution than the impoverished street criminals who have few social connections and lack the assets to put on a strong defense. An effective drive against white-collar crime will therefore require that the public put far greater pressure on the government to force it into action against these powerful offenders. The first step may well have to be an effort to reform the whole po-

No

Everyone realizes that the crime problem is a serious one, but are we really willing to turn the United States into a police state in order to solve it? We already have a larger proportion of our population in prison than any other nation in the world, and an increase in the number of police would only make the political climate more authoritarian and oppressive. If the current trends continue, the majority of our adult population could end up either in prison or working for the military or the criminal justice system. What kind of society would that be? What would remain of the individual freedoms we have fought so long to maintain? Who would dare to be different in a society with a police officer on every street corner and a prison in every neighborhood? Many people in ghettos already regard the police as an occupying army, and this kind of program would only make things worse.

The reason proposals to put more police officers on the streets are so politically attractive is that they offer a quick fix for the crime problem. Unfortunately, there aren't any quick fixes for problems as complex and deeply rooted as the phenomenon of crime in modern society. To solve this problem, we must attack its roots: unemployment, racism, poverty, despair, and erosion of the family. If we solve these problems, the crime rate will come down of its own accord. If we don't solve these problems, all the police in the world won't do us any good. Turning America into a police state is not the way to solve the crime problem.

litical system in order to reduce the dominating influence wielded by those with great wealth and positions of institutional power (see Chapter 5).

Attacking the Roots of Crime

Proposals for punishing criminals, increasing our defenses against criminal activities, and employing social intervention are all concerned with preventing crime. Crime is prevented when perpetrators are afraid to commit new crimes. It is also prevented when criminals are killed or kept behind bars and when citizens lock up their valuables and themselves, thus frustrating people who would behave criminally. Finally, crime is prevented when the personal and social situations of criminals are improved or when the economic, political, and social order that generates high crime rates is modified so that it no longer does so.

Of these three approaches, social intervention has the greatest potential for producing a safer society. We have seen that crime is rooted in the economic, political, and social order. Most social scientists realize that it is foolish to leave this situation the way it is and then try to reduce crime by punishing criminals or defending against them. Such an approach is something like trying to cool down a burning house by turning on the air conditioner. Relying on punishment and defense are, however, easier than carrying out the sweeping social changes that have been proposed—reducing poverty, unemployment, and discrimination, for example, and attacking the whole complex of problems that has made life in the urban underclass more hopeless and more violent with every successive year. It is certainly no easy task to make such changes or to reshape the attitudes that glorify violence and define the "real man" as aggressive and domineering. In the long run, however, genuine crime prevention—changing the conditions that cause crime—is both the cheapest and most effective way to fight the crime problem.

Quick Review

Critically evaluate the most common proposals for dealing with the crime problem.

Sociological Perspectives on Crime and Delinquency

The Functionalist Perspective

Functionalists study crime rates rather than individual criminal behavior. They hold, generally, that a certain amount of crime is inevitable in any society because crime makes a contribution to social order. For instance, crime is said to promote the solidarity of the group, just as war does, by providing "common enemies" (in this case criminals). It is also argued that crime is functional because it provides an "escape valve" for the pressures arising from unjust laws or excessive conformity. Although some crime is natural and even healthy, too much crime is highly dysfunctional. Today most functionalists, like the general public, feel that current levels of crime pose a major social problem.

Functionalists argue that the high crime rates in the industrialized nations have been caused by the hectic pace of social change in the twentieth century and the social disorganization it created. Old traditions have been shattered, but a new consensus has not developed to take their place. The weakening of such institutions as the family and the community has disrupted the socialization process and left many children without proper supervision and guidance. Increasing numbers of people find themselves socially isolated, and the bonds that are supposed to regulate and control our behavior are eroding. As a result, many people feel alienated from society and frustrated by the conditions of their lives. Some lash out in bursts of violence; others simply drift into criminal activity because society is too disorganized to prevent it.

To deal with these problems, functionalists often call for greater social integration and a return to the traditional values of the past. Many functionalists believe that crime and violence would be reduced if people were encouraged to commit themselves to primary groups such as the family, religious organizations, social clubs, and political groups. Functionalists also recommend a thorough reorganization of the criminal justice system so that criminals can be dealt with more quickly and efficiently, as well as a greater effort by the schools to deal with the problems that promote delinquency among their students. Much more difficult to carry out are their calls for a return to a more stable family system and the traditional values on which it was based.

The Conflict Perspective

Conflict theorists emphasize that both crime and the laws defining it are products of a struggle for power. They argue that a few powerful groups control the legislative process and that these groups outlaw behavior that threatens their interests. For example, laws prohibiting vagrancy, trespassing, and theft are said to be designed to protect the interests of the wealthy from attacks by the poor. Although laws against such things as murder and rape are not so clearly in the interests of a single social class, the poor and powerless are much more likely than the wealthy to be arrested if they commit such crimes.

Conflict theorists also see class and ethnic exploitation as a basic cause of many different kinds of crime. Much of the high crime rate among the poor is attributable to a lack of legitimate opportunities for improving their economic condition. Exploitation of the poor and ethnic minorities creates a sense of hopelessness, frustration, and hostility. Such feelings often boil over into acts of violence that are aimed not only at the system that oppresses the underprivileged but also at their friends, relatives, and neighbors. More generally, conflict theorists hold that the greed and competitiveness bred by our capitalist consumer culture encourage crime among all social groups. Every day we are given countless subtle and not-so-subtle messages that wealth is the key to happiness and the measure of a successful woman or man. Thus, it is hardly surprising that even our richest citizens are often willing to break the law to enhance their fortunes and outdo their competition.

Conflict theorists believe that crime will disappear only if inequality and exploitation are also eliminated. Because that is obviously a distant goal, they advocate more limited responses to the crime problem as well. They ask, for example, that the police and the courts treat different classes and ethnic groups more equally. Thus, they want to see more attention given to white-collar crime, they support bail reform and programs to provide better defense lawyers for the poor, and they call for the elimination of class and ethnic discrimination in law enforcement. The repeal of laws that enforce one group's cultural dominance over another is also supported by many conflict theorists. Thus they often support repealing laws prohibiting the use of marijuana, private sexual acts between consenting adults, and such activities as gambling.

The Feminist Perspective

Feminists have long been concerned with the role that violence plays in the exploitation of women, and their general conclusion is that violence has always been a principal means of establishing and enforcing male dominance. Although modern industrial societies have a legal prohibition against most forms of violence, feminists point out that the enforcement effort is often weak and ineffective. Some feminists feel that as industrialization and technological advances have eroded the underpinnings of male privilege, violence has become an increasingly important tool in keeping women "in their place." But whether or not violence against women has become more common, there is no doubt that some men use rape and physical brutality to degrade women who challenge their sense of superiority and to express their rage against women in general. As a result, the fear of violence forces women to change their ways of living, acting, and dressing and thus deprives them of many basic freedoms.

Of course, women are not only the victims of crime; they are its perpetrators as well. Although the overall crime rate of women is still well below that of men, it has been increasing much more rapidly. As women have gained more power and taken on more financial responsibility, their crime rates have gone up. Since the attack on gender inequality advocated by most feminists might accelerate this trend, feminists generally support many of the proposals made by conflict theorists to reduce the crime rate among all sectors of our society. They also call for the criminal justice system to crack down on spouse abuse and the other kinds of violence men perpetrate against women, so that society can create truly equal relations between the genders.

The Interactionist Perspective

Interactionists have probably been more focused on the causes of crime than the proponents of any of the other theoretical perspectives, and many of the theories we have already examined, such as differential association and labeling theory, have their roots in interactionism. Their general conclusion is that crime and deviance are not special or unique phenomena. Rather, they are learned in interaction with other people like any other behavior. People commit crimes because they learn attitudes and motivations that are favorable to crime. A boy who associates with other boys who believe that stealing is exciting is likely to adopt that attitude and start to steal. A woman who sees her co-workers getting rich by embezzling from their employer is more likely to do it herself.

If crime is learned, it follows that it can be unlearned, and interactionists advocate a host of proposals to modify criminal behavior. For one thing, the media have become a powerful cultural influence in contemporary society. One way or the other, the media should be made to promote the ideals of cooperation and nonviolence and stop the glorification of mayhem and destruction so common in today's films, books, and television programs. Interactionists also urge those who are struggling to deal with the crime problem to be sensitive to the critical role social learning plays in criminal behavior. For example, care should be taken to avoid the contagion of youngsters by confirmed criminals as sometimes happens in juvenile halls and prisons, and programs intended to help offenders should seek to integrate them into primary groups that strongly discourage criminal behavior.

Quick Review

How do functionalists explain the high crime rates in the industrialized countries, and what do they propose to do about them?

Critically evaluate the conflict theory about the causes of crime.

What is the sociological importance of male violence against women?

What proposals do interactionists make to deal with the crime problem?

Summary

A crime is a violation of the criminal law. Violence includes any behavior intended to cause physical harm to a person. Murder is the unlawful killing of a human being with malice. Research shows that the victims and attackers in most murders are friends or relatives. An assault occurs when one person physically attacks another; it differs from a murder in that the victim does not die. Sexual intercourse forced on someone without consent is known as forcible rape. There are two types of forcible rape. The first kind occurs on a date or in the course of some other social contact, the second when the rapist simply selects a victim and attacks her (or him). Property crime includes a wide variety of offenses such as theft, burglary, arson, and fraud. Although robbery (theft by force) is officially classified as a violent crime, for sociological purposes it too is best considered a property offense. Offenses such as the use of illegal drugs, gambling, and prostitution are known as victimless crimes because in most cases no one is forced to participate in those activities against their will. Offenses committed by highly organized groups of professional criminals are known as syndicated crime. White-collar crime is defined as a crime committed by a person of high status in the course of his or her occupation. Such crimes probably cost more than all other crimes put together. Juvenile delinquency includes a broad range of deviant behaviors committed by young people, some of which would also be against the law if committed by adults and some of which would not.

Although the rate of reported crime has increased substantially in the last two decades, most criminologists have more confidence in the victimization surveys, which indicate that the crime rate has actually decreased. The data show that crime is most common among males, young adults, and those who live in cities. For most types of crime, the poor and minorities are also the most likely to be the offenders; however, that is not true of white-collar crimes. International comparisons show that the United States has the highest rate of violent crime of any industrialized nation.

The classical school holds that criminals choose to violate the law because that is the easiest way to get what they want. Biological theorists see crime as rooted in human nature and often look to the process of evolution to explain it. Psychologists and psychiatrists argue that crime is caused by the personality of the criminals. Some sociologists hold that crime is learned from social interaction (differential association), while others see it as a result of society's failure to prevent it (control theory). Still other sociologists feel that our high crime rates are a result of the social and economic structure of contemporary society.

The police are the first to respond to most individual crimes, and how well they do their jobs has an enormous impact on the effectiveness of the rest of the criminal justice system. If the police make an arrest, the suspects are usually held in jail until they can raise bail. If their case is not dropped, most defendants participate in a process called plea bargaining, under which they agree to plead guilty in exchange for some form of leniency from the prosecutor. In most cases, the judge sentences offenders either to prison or to a period of probation, during which they are allowed to remain free under official supervision. The huge increase in the inmate population of the United States has created serious overcrowding and deteriorating prison conditions.

There are many different proposals for dealing with the crime problem. Although the United States already has the highest percentage of its population in prison of any country in the world, some say we should get tougher still. Others propose focusing on violent criminals by lengthening their prison sentences but relying on other alternatives such as restitution and drug treatment for nonviolent offenders. Probably the most popular approach among criminologists is to attack the underlying causes of crime, such as poverty, unemployment, racism, and a deteriorating family structure.

Functionalists argue that the growing crime rate is but one symptom of increasing social disorganization. Conflict theorists emphasize the role of exploitation and inequality in promoting crime. Feminists see male violence against women as a major source of gender inequality. Interactionists argue that crime is learned like any other behavior.

Questions for Critical Thinking

All democratic societies face a fundamental dilemma in dealing with the crime problem. On the one hand, there is a need to maintain order and repress dangerous or antisocial behavior. But on the other, there is also a need to protect individual freedom from the untrammeled power of the government. Every democratic government has to strike a balance between the need to repress crime and the need to protect civil liberties. How good a job are we doing of reconciling these two conflicting demands? Is our society more likely to dissolve into a sea of crime and violence or to evolve into a repressive police state? Is there some way to have more civil liberties and still reduce the crime problem?

Key Terms

anomie
arson
assault
bail
burglary
classical theory
control theory
crime
crime control model
critical theory
deterrence
deviant subculture
differential association theory
due process model
felony
forcible rape
fraud
homicide

incapacitation
juvenile delinquent
labeling theory
manslaughter
misdemeanor
murder
National Crime Victimization Survey (NCVS)
occupational crime
organizational crime
plea bargaining
police brutality
positive school
probation
property crime
rational choice theory
rehabilitation
retribution

robbery
self-report study
sociopathic personality
status offense
statutory rape
strain theory
syndicated crime

theft
Uniform Crime Reports
victimless crime
violence
violent crime
white-collar crime

Further Readings

James William Coleman, *The Criminal Elite: Understanding White Collar Crime,* 4th ed. (New York: St. Martin's Press, 1998). An examination of the problem of white-collar crime by the author of this text.

David T. Courtwright, *Violent Land* (Cambridge, MA: Harvard University Press, 1996). Explores the history of violence in America and the role single men have played in it.

Liz Kelly, *Surviving Sexual Violence* (Minneapolis: University of Minnesota Press, 1989). An exploration of the causes of violence against women and the best strategies to cope with it.

Herbert L. Packer, *The Limits of Criminal Sanction* (Palo Alto, CA: Stanford University Press, 1968). A law professor's classic case against the legislation of morality.

Dean G. Rojeck and Gary F. Jensen, eds., *Exploring Delinquency: Causes and Control* (Los Angeles: Roxbury, 1996). A collection of articles that provides a comprehensive look at the problem of delinquency.

Joseph F. Sheley, *Criminology: A Contemporary Handbook,* 2nd ed. (Belmont, CA: Wadsworth, 1995). A useful collection of essays on a number of key issues in criminology by specialists in each field.

Notes

1. Jimmie Briggs, "Childhood's End," *Village Voice,* February 18, 1997, p. 50.
2. Kathleen Maguire and Ann L. Pastore, eds., *Sourcebook of Criminal Justice Statistics 1995* (Washington, DC: U.S. Government Printing Office, 1996), p. 152.
3. Bureau of Justice Statistics, *Highlights from 20 Years of Surveying Crime Victims* (Washington, DC: U.S. Government Printing Office, October 1993).
4. Maguire and Pastore, *Sourcebook of Criminal Justice Statistics 1995,* p. 410.
5. Marvin E. Wolfgang, *Patterns in Criminal Homicide* (Philadelphia: University of Pennsylvania Press, 1958).
6. Maguire and Pastore, *Sourcebook of Criminal Justice Statistics 1995,* p. 361.
7. Bureau of Justice Statisitics, *Criminal Victimization 1994* (Washington, DC: U.S. Government Printing Office, 1996), p. 7.
8. Timothy J. Flanagan and Kathleen Maguire, eds., *Sourcebook of Criminal Justice Statistics 1990,* (Washington, DC: U.S. Government Printing Office, 1991), p. 618.
9. Bureau of Justice Statistics, *Violence Against Women: Estimates from the Redesigned Survey* (Washington, DC: U.S. Government Printing Office, 1995), p. 4.
10. Ibid., p. 5.
11. Ibid., p. 252.
12. Bureau of Justice Statistics, *Criminal Victimization 1994* (Washington, DC: U.S. Government Printing Office, 1996), p. 1.

13. Elizabeth Shogren, "Survey of Top Students Reveals Sex Assaults, Suicide Attempts," *Los Angeles Times,* October 29, 1993, p. A22; McClatchy News Service, "Study of Sexual Abuse, Rape," *San Luis Obispo Telegram-Tribune,* November 29, 1993, p. A2; Sue Titus Reid, *Crime and Criminology,* 5th ed. (New York: Holt, Rinehart & Winston, 1988), pp. 234–235.

14. Quoted in Timothy Beneke, "Male Rape: Four Men Talk About Rape," *Mother Jones,* July 1983, pp. 13–22.

15. Bureau of Justice Statistics, *Violence Against Women: Estimates from the Redesigned Survey* (Washington, DC: U.S. Government Printing Office, 1995), p. 2.

16. Kathleen Maguire, Ann L. Pastore, and Timothy J. Flanagan, eds., *Sourcebook of Criminal Justice Statistics 1992* (Washington, DC: U.S. Government Printing Office, 1993), pp. 287, 290.

17. Stephen Donaldson, "The Rape Crisis Behind Bars," *New York Times,* December 29, 1993, p. A13.

18. Bureau of Justice Statisitics, *Criminal Victimization 1994* (Washington, DC: U.S. Government Printing Office, 1996), p. 4.

19. Ibid.

20. Flanagan and Maguire, *Sourcebook of Criminal Justice Statistics 1990,* p. 269.

21. Maguire and Pastore, *Sourcebook of Criminal Justice Statistics 1995,* p. 240.

22. Ibid., p. 338.

23. Calculated from data in Robert J. Bursik, "The Dynamics and Distribution of Property Crime," in Joseph F. Sheley, *Criminology: A Contemporary Handbook* (Belmont, CA: Wadsworth, 1995), pp. 186–199, and Piers Beirne and James Messerschmidt, *Criminology* (San Diego: Harcourt Brace Jovanovich, 1991), pp. 97, 106.

24. See John E. Conklin, *Criminology,* 5th ed. (Boston: Allyn & Bacon, 1995), p. 73.

25. Beirne and Messerschmidt, *Criminology,* p. 116.

26. Ibid., pp. 204–238.

27. See Donald R. Cressey, *Theft of the Nation: The Structure and Operations of Organized Crime in America* (New York: HarperCollins, 1969).

28. John Dillin, "U.S. Probes Crime's Global Reach," *Christian Science Monitor,* April 22, 1994, pp. 1, 16.

29. Craig R. Whitney, "Germans Suspect Russian Military in Plutonium Sale," *New York Times,* August 16, 1994, pp. A1, A6.

30. Edwin H. Sutherland, *White Collar Crime* (New York: Dryden, 1949), p. 9.

31. James William Coleman, *The Criminal Elite: Understanding White Collar Crime,* 4th ed. (New York: St. Martin's Press, 1998), pp. 8–11.

32. Ibid., pp. 1, 9–10, 55–65.

33. Ibid., pp. 123–175.

34. See ibid., pp. 79–80.

35. Anthony M. Platt, *The Child Savers: The Invention of Delinquency* (Chicago: University of Chicago Press, 1969).

36. Maguire and Pastore, *Sourcebook of Criminal Justice Statistics 1995,* p. 178.

37. Anthony R. Harris and Lisa R. Meidlinger, "Criminal Behavior: Race and Class," in Sheley, *Criminology,* pp. 115–144.

38. L. Edward Wells and Joseph H. Rankin, "Families and Delinquency: A Meta-analysis of the Impact of Broken Homes," *Social Problems* 38 (February 1991): 71–93.

39. Michael R. Gottfredson and Travis Hirschi, *A General Theory of Crime* (Stanford, CA: Stanford University Press, 1990).

40. Martin Sanchez Jankowski, *Islands in the Street: Gangs and American Urban Society* (Berkeley: University of California Press, 1991).

41. Maguire and Pastore, *Sourcebook of Criminal Justice Statistics 1995,* p. 324.

42. Bureau of Justice Statistics, *Criminal Victimization, 1973–95,* pp. 1, 4.

43. Maguire and Pastore, *Sourcebook of Criminal Justice Statistics 1995,* pp. 406, 554–555.

44. Darrell Steffensmeier and Emilie Allan, "Criminal Behavior: Gender and Age," in Sheley, *Criminology,* pp. 82–111.

45. Ibid.

46. Maguire and Pastore, *Sourcebook of Criminal Justice Statistics 1995*, p. 404.

47. Ibid., p. 410.

48. Charles R. Tittle, Wayne J. Villemez, and Douglas A. Smith, "The Myth of Social Class and Criminality," *American Sociological Review* 43 (1978): 643–656.

49. Delbert Elliott and Suzanne Ageton, "Reconciling Race and Class Differences in Self-Reported and Official Estimates of Delinquency," *American Sociological Review* 45 (1980): 95–110; Delbert Elliott and David Huizinga, "Social Class and Delinquent Behavior in a National Youth Panel: 1976–1980," *Criminology* 21 (1983): 149–177.

50. Bureau of Justice Statistics, *Highlights from 20 Years of Surveying Crime Victims.*

51. Harris and Meidlinger, "Criminal Behavior: Race and Class."

52. U.S. Bureau of Justice Statistics, *International Crime Rates* (Washington, DC: U.S. Government Printing Office, May 1988); United Nations Development Programme, *Human Development Report 1997* (New York: Oxford University Press, 1997), p. 213.

53. Martin Daly and Margo Wilson, *Homicide* (New York: Aldine de Gruyter, 1988).

54. Barry Hutchings and Sarnoff A. Mednick, "Criminality in Adoptees and Their Adoptive and Biological Parents: A Pilot Study," in S. A. Mednick and K. O. Christiansen, eds., *Biosocial Bases of Criminal Behavior* (New York: Gardner, 1977); for a follow-up study with a different population, see Sarnoff A. Mednick, William Gabrielli, and Barry Hutchings, "Genetic Influences in Criminal Behavior: Evidence from an Adoption Cohort," in Katherine S. Van Dusen and Sarnoff Mednick, eds., *Prospective Studies of Crime and Delinquency* (Boston: Kluver-Nijhoff, 1983), pp. 39–57.

55. Janet Katz and William J. Chambliss, "Biology and Crime," in Sheley, *Criminology*, pp. 275–303.

56. James Q. Wilson and Richard Herrnstein, *Crime and Human Behavior* (New York: Simon & Schuster, 1985).

57. Edwin H. Sutherland and Donald R. Cressey, *Criminology*, 10th ed. (New York: Lippincott, 1978), pp. 158–191.

58. Karl Schuessler and Donald R. Cressey, "Personality Characteristics of Criminals," *American Journal of Sociology* 55 (1950): 476–484; Gordon Waldo and Simon Dinitz, "Personality Attributes of the Criminal: An Analysis of Research Studies 1950-1965," *Journal of Research in Crime and Delinquency* 4 (1967): 185–201; David Tennenbaum, "Research Studies of Personality and Criminality," *Journal of Criminal Justice* 5 (1977): 1–19.

59. Avshalon Caspi, Terrie E. Morritt, Phil A. Silva, Magda Stouthamer-Loeber, Robert F. Krueger, and Pamela S. Schmutte, "Are Some People Crime-Prone? Replications of the Personality-Crime Relationships Across Countries, Genders, Races and Methods," *Criminology* 32 (1994):163–191.

60. Sutherland and Cressey, *Criminology*, pp. 77–98.

61. Murray A. Straus, Richard J. Gelles, and Suzanne K. Steinmetz, *Behind Closed Doors: Violence in the American Family* (New York: Doubleday, 1981), p. 101.

62. See, for example, Reid, *Crime and Criminology*, pp. 240–246; and David G. Gil, *Violence Against Children: Physical Child Abuse in the United States* (Cambridge, MA: Harvard University Press, 1970), pp. 113–114.

63. Murray A. Straus, "Discipline and Deviance: Physical Punishment of Children and Violence and Other Crimes in Adulthood," *Social Problems* 38 (May 1991): 133–152; Joan McCord, "Parental Aggressiveness and Physical Punishment in Long-Term Perspective," in Gerald T. Hotaling, David Finkelhor, John T. Kirkpatrick, and Murray A. Straus, eds., *Family Abuse and Its Consequences* (Newbury Park, CA: Sage, 1988), pp. 91–98.

64. National Institute of Justice, *The Cycle of Violence Revisited* (Washington, DC: U.S. Government Printing Office, February 1996).

65. Straus, Gelles, and Steinmetz, *Behind Closed Doors,* p. 121.

66. See Walter Reckless, "A New Theory of Delinquency and Crime," *Federal Probation* 25 (1961): 42–46; Travis Hirschi, *Causes of Delinquency* (Berkeley: University of California Press, 1969); James Q. Wilson, *Thinking About Crime* (New York: Random House, 1975); and Marvin Krohn, "Control and Deterrence Theories," in Sheley, *Criminology*, pp. 294–313.

67. Robert K. Merton, "Social Structure and Anomie," *American Sociological Review* 3 (1938): 672–682.

68. Walter B. Miller, "Lower Class Culture as a Generating Milieu of Gang Delinquency," *Journal of Social Issues* 14 (1958): 5–19.

69. Emile Durkheim, *Suicide* (New York: Free Press, 1966).

70. See Gary Cavender, "Alternative Approaches: Labeling and Critical Perspectives," in Sheley, *Criminology,* pp. 339–367.

71. Herbert L. Packer, *The Limits of Criminal Sanction* (Palo Alto, CA: Stanford University Press, 1968).

72. Bureau of Justice Statistics, *Report to the Nation on Crime and Justice: The Data* (Washington, DC: U.S. Government Printing Office, 1983), p. 47; Eric J. Scott, *Calls for Service: Citizen Demand and Initial Police Response, National Institute of Justice* (Washington, DC: U.S. Government Printing Office, July 1981), p. 26.

73. See, for example, Allen J. Beck, *Recidivism of Prisoners Released in 1983,* U.S. Bureau of Justice Statistics (Washington, DC: U.S. Government Printing Office, April 1989); and John Wallerstedt, *Returning to Prison,* U.S. Bureau of Justice Statistics (Washington, DC: U.S. Government Printing Office, 1984).

74. Bureau of Justice Statistics, *Correctional Populations in the United States* (Washington, DC: U.S. Government Printing Office, 1995); Fox Butterfield, "More Blacks in Their 20s Have Trouble with the Law," *New York Times,* October 5, 1995, p. A8.

75. Joan Petersilia, Probation and Felony Offenders, *National Institute of Justice* (Washington, DC: U.S. Government Printing Office, 1985).

76. Quoted in David S. Broder, "Population Explosion" *Washington Post,* national ed., April 25–May 1, 1994, p. 4.

77. Maguire and Pastore, *Sourcebook of Criminal Justice Statistics 1995,* p. 567.

78. U.S. Department of Justice, *Violent Crime in the United States,* p. 11; Chris Wood, "Violent Land," *Maclean's,* June 10, 1991, pp. 12–13.

79. Wendy Kaminer, "Crime and Community," *Atlantic Monthly,* May 1994, pp. 111–120; Bob Herbert, "Deadly Data On Handguns," *New York Times,* March 2, 1994, p. A15; "Guns Gaining on Cars as Bigger Killer in U.S.," *New York Times,* January 28, 1994, p. A8.

80. Maguire and Ann L. Pastore, eds., *Sourcebook of Criminal Justice Statistics 1995,* pp. 181, 191, 192.

81. National Institute of Mental Health, *Television and Behavior,* vol. 1., *Summary Report* (Washington, DC: U.S. Government Printing Office, 1982); Surgeon General's Scientific Advisory Committee on Television and Social Behavior, *Television and Growing Up: The Impact of Televised Violence* (Washington, DC: U.S. Government Printing Office, 1972); George A. Comstock and Eli Rubenstein, eds., *Television and Social Behavior,* vols. 1–5 (Washington, DC: U.S. Government Printing Office, 1972).

82. Jeffrey H. Goldstein, *Aggression and Crimes of Violence,* 2nd ed. (New York: Oxford University Press, 1986), p. 39.

Problems of a Changing World

None of the problems discussed in this book can be understood by looking at only a single nation, even one as large and important as the United States. Not only does a cross-cultural approach help put our own difficulties in perspective, but today's economic, social, and political problems are interlinked in ways that transcend national boundaries. The difference between the chapters in this section and those in the rest of the book is one of focus. In the earlier chapters, the focus was close to home, and international material was used primarily to help us understand our own problems and to point out some other alternatives for dealing with them. The focus of the chapters in this section is more global, and the problems of the United States and Canada are treated as one case among many. In the chapters that follow, center stage is taken by the crisis of the less developed nations and by the global problems with the world's environment and political economy.

Urbanization

CHAPTER 14

How does life differ in a rural area, a suburb, and a big city?

What are the most serious problems created by the process of urbanization?

How do the problems in the cities of the less developed countries differ from those in the industrialized nations?

What are the best ways to deal with the problems of urbanization?

Rush hour was just beginning in Austin, Texas, and traffic was building up around the intersection of Fifth Street and Congress Avenue in the middle of the central business district. Half a dozen young men from one of East Austin's toughest gangs—the Este Grande Varrios or EGV—crossed the street and began taunting the dozen or so youths on the opposite side. As the EGVs approached, one of the boys from the other gang, known as the Latin Kings, grabbed a bottle from a trash can and threw it at his rivals. One of the EGVs pulled out a 9-mm Smith & Wesson pistol and began shooting. Three people were hit—two 16-year-olds (a girl and a boy from the Latin Kings) and a 61-year-old man who tried in vain to stop the fight.[1]

urbanization

The movement of people from rural areas to cities.

Scenes like this have become commonplace in cities across North America, but the sweeping impact **urbanization** has had on our everyday life goes far beyond the occasional incidents of violence and chaos that grab our attention. Indeed, no other social change in the last two hundred years has had a more far-reaching impact than the transition from rural to urban living. In 1790, only 1 in every 20 Americans lived in an urban area; today, 15 in every 20 do. The same process has occurred in the other industrialized nations as well. Canada and Japan are slightly more urbanized than the United States (about 77 percent), while 85 percent of Germany's people live in its cities.[2] Most poor nations have only begun their urban explosion, but their cities are now growing much faster than those in the industrialized countries. Almost two-thirds of the people in the less developed countries still live in rural areas today, but it is expected that in a few decades the majority will live in cities.[3]

The origins of the city can be found at the very beginning of recorded history, but the cities in agricultural societies were only small islands in a sea of rural farmlands. It was not until the industrial revolution sent waves of immigrants to the cities in search of new jobs and new opportunities that the first urban societies emerged. Existing cities grew to an unprecedented size, and small satellite communities sprang up around their borders. The land between some cities has been completely filled in, creating what is known as a **megalopolis**—a large area in which cities fuse together to form one vast urban network. The largest megalopolis in North America is the nearly unbroken stretch of cities and suburbs along the East Coast of the United States from Boston to Virginia. Another sprawling urban area is growing in California from San Diego to San Francisco, and a third runs from Milwaukee through Chicago to northern Indiana. In Canada, 60 percent of the population lives in a 600-mile strip from Quebec City to Windsor, Ontario. However, because these huge areas often have little overall political or economic integration, the U.S. Bureau of the Census uses a slightly narrower concept, the **metropolitan statistical area (MSA),** which includes a central population center and the surrounding communities that are dependent on it.

megalopolis

An area in which several large cities are fused together forming a single urban region.

metropolitan statistical area (MSA)

The U.S. Bureau of the Census term for a central city and the surrounding suburbs that depend on it.

Although the nations of the Third World have yet to experience a complete industrial revolution, they are nonetheless undergoing a massive wave of urbanization. The principal motivation of urban migrants in the less developed countries is not so much the attractions of the city but the fact that rapid population growth and the spread of large export-oriented farming businesses have made it impossible for them to continue making a living on the land. The cities in the less developed nations are now growing almost twice as fast as those in the industrialized countries, and 12 of the world's 15 largest cities are in the Third World.[4] Yet the poor nations have little money for new housing, roads, water, sanitation, or electricity.

Quick Review

What is the process of urbanization?

Understanding Human Communities

The Cities Civilizations have always been centered in cities. Despite the flight to the suburbs, cities are still a dominant force in our social life. Huge corporations and government bureaucracies spread their influence outward from a few major cities. The large newspapers and broadcasting companies, which set our tastes and define our world, are based in cities and reflect their realities. The cities spawn and attract actors, artists, writers, and other intellectual innovators who set the cultural style of our age. There is a particularly big gap between the sophisticated Western-influenced cultural life found in the major cities of the less developed countries and the life of the tradition-bound villagers. Foreign visitors and immigrants stop in the great cities, rarely in country villages. In North America, new immigrants usually first settle in run-down sections of the inner cities, then move to more affluent areas as they become acculturated. This process has left the cities dotted with fragments of many different cultures—Irish, Italian, French, Chinese, Mexican, German, Russian, and more—thus adding to the diversity of city life.

Along with the attractions go a host of urban problems that include everything from traffic congestion to street crime, and public opinion polls show that most people in cities say they would rather live somewhere else.[5] Moreover, people in rural areas are almost 2.5 times more likely to say that they are "completely satisfied" with their community than those in big cities.[6]

One of the most fascinating questions confronting urban sociologists concerns the nature of life in cities. Do urban people have a unique way of thinking, a special outlook on life? One of the first people to answer this question was the German sociologist Georg Simmel. In a classic essay published in 1903, Simmel noted that city dwellers are bombarded by a tremendous amount of "nervous stimulation."[7] Noise, traffic, crowds, the rapid pace of life, and dozens of other stimuli overload the urban resident. City dwellers simply cannot pay attention to everything that goes on around them, and as a result they become indifferent to their surroundings. Because urbanites deal with so many strangers, their relationships tend to be directed toward external goals rather than personal satisfaction. On the whole, the city offers its people greater freedom, but it also increases the danger that they will be isolated and alone.

The most famous essay in urban sociology is Louis Wirth's "Urbanism as a Way of Life."[8] Published in 1938, this article summarized much of the thought of the "Chicago school" of urban sociology, which developed at the University of Chicago in the early twentieth century. Wirth painted with a broader brush than Simmel, but he reached similar conclusions about the psychological impact of urban life. To Wirth, the diversity of social life is the most important of the city's characteristics.

One of the things that makes most modern cities so interesting is their rich diversity of people, life-styles, and architectures.

According to this sociologist, urban dwellers are specialized in the work they do and in their relationships with other people. Being highly specialized, they know one another only in superficial and impersonal ways. One person will be recognized as a bank teller, another as a co-worker, and a third as a bus driver, but they are seldom known in an intimate way. Financial interests dominate this impersonal urban world. The city becomes a complex mass of people living close together but without deep emotional ties. The city dweller often feels lonely and isolated even in the midst of vast crowds. Urbanites learn to tolerate the attitudes and customs of other people, but they also come to accept insecurity and instability as the normal state of the world. These characteristics work together to increase the incidence of what Wirth called "pathological conditions," including "personal disorganization, mental breakdown, suicide, delinquency, crime, corruption, and disorder."

Few contemporary sociologists agree that city life is as dismal as Wirth pictured it. Some argue that Wirth's ideas merely reflect small-town America's dislike of cities and their rapid growth. For example, Herbert J. Gans noted that Wirth overlooked the many city dwellers who have a strong sense of community, such as the affluent, well-educated people who choose to live in the city because of its cultural life or the "ethnic villagers" who live in tightly knit ethnic neighborhoods.[9] Gans concluded that social class and age have a greater effect on urban life-styles than does city living itself. He also argued that the problems described by Wirth exist principally among deprived groups, such as the poor and the ethnic minorities and residents who are financially trapped in urban neighborhoods that have begun to decay.

The Suburbs

More Americans now live in **suburbs**—the parts of an urban area that lie outside the central city—than in cities or rural areas. The first suburbs can be traced back at least as far as the 1760s, and by the end of the nineteenth century, most American cities had suburbs where the wealthy could live away from the congestion of the city. The fastest suburban growth took place in the two decades after World War II, when millions of Americans poured into newly built housing tracts. In one sense, the big city, with its congestion, crime, pollution, and decay, pushed them out; in another sense, the suburbs pulled them in—offering space for growing families, good schools, personal safety, and a pleasant environment at a price that the expanding middle class could afford.[10]

The suburbs did not, however, simply spring into being because people wanted to live there. Their growth required three things: automobiles, highways, and private homes. When the suburban explosion was just beginning, the **highway lobby,** composed of such diverse interests as oil companies, automobile manufacturers, and truckers' unions, pushed through a massive program of freeway construction that laid the foundation for continued suburban growth. The government also spent billions of dollars subsidizing private homes for middle- and upper-class Americans. The biggest subsidy is the full tax deduction for interest paid on home mortgages. The government also worked to keep interest rates down on home mortgages and even directly underwrote home loans through the Federal Housing Authority and the Veterans Administration.

North Americans have a kind of love-hate relationship with the suburbs, seeing them as both a cause of social blight and its solution. The proponents of suburban living picture it as a refuge from the troubles of the big city. In this view, the neatly trimmed lawns and the close-knit families of the suburbs stand in sharp contrast to the crime and confusion of city life; but critics picture the situation differently. They see the suburbs as an endless expanse of cracker-box houses that are so alike that it is difficult to tell one from the other. They say that because suburbanites are mostly from the white middle class, they lack individuality and diversity and are bland and dull.

Both these views are faulty, however, for they are based on an image of the suburb as a "bedroom community" for the affluent that is decades out of date. Although they started as residential areas for the wealthy, the suburbs are now heterogeneous and diversified. As people first moved to the suburbs, they were quickly followed by small shops and stores and eventually by huge shopping malls. Suburban retailers have grown steadily more prosperous while sales in the central city have stagnated. Along with new jobs in retail has come a tremendous influx of manufacturing, wholesaling, and warehousing businesses that used to be found only in the central cities. Even the administrative offices of many major corporations have moved to the suburbs. There are now more corporate headquarters in the suburbs surrounding New York City than in the city itself. Overall, more than 70 percent of those who live in the suburbs of large metropolitan areas work in them too.[11]

As the suburbs have diversified economically, they have diversified socially as well. Many older suburban neighborhoods have become less desirable, and developers have put up more apartment buildings, allowing less affluent people to move in. The poor and minorities are now the fastest-growing segment of the suburban population. From 1980 to 1990, the African American population of the suburbs

suburb
The part of an urban area that lies outside the central city.

highway lobby
The powerful lobby supporting construction of new roads and highways.

grew by one-third and the Latino population by two-thirds, and the Asian population more than doubled.[12] However, this trend has not led to a new era of integration but rather to the reproduction of the patterns of segregation found in the cities.[13] Many large suburbs are now a checkerboard of European American, Latino, African American, and Asian neighborhoods.

This growing diversity does not, however, mean growing equality. As John R. Logan and Harvey L. Molotch point out, "In the suburban milieu, as in the larger world system, the advantages adhere to the places of the rich and the disadvantages to the places of the poor."[14] The rich neighborhoods have the best sanitation, fire, and police services, the best shopping, and the least pollution and crime. Because the process of suburbanization has fragmented the political control of metropolitan areas, the wealthy often live in their own towns and cities, well apart from the deprivation of the poor. One result is that local taxes paid by the wealthiest families no longer go to help those who need it most.

Small Towns and Rural Areas

villages
Small, traditional communities in rural areas.

Until the industrial revolution, most of the world's people lived in rural **villages.** Even today, the majority of the people in the less developed countries live in rural settlements, which tend to be traditional in their cultural outlook and skeptical of new ideas and attitudes. These villagers are not only isolated from world affairs and concerns; they generally have weak ties to their own nations. Illiteracy is still the rule, and televisions, radios, and other means of electronic communications are luxuries. The villagers' main concern is therefore with local events. Villages are very homogeneous places. Not only do villagers share the same set of values, but they have spent their whole lives together and know the intimate details of each others' pasts—both the good and the bad. Although most villagers are content to continue with their traditional life-style, population growth and changing economic conditions are making it harder and harder to do so.

In the industrialized nations, traditional village life is largely a thing of the past. Of course, many people still live on farms and in small towns, but their numbers have decreased sharply over the last two centuries. Moreover, the character of rural life has changed. People who live in open country and small towns are no longer as isolated as they once were. Universal education instills a similar cultural outlook in people regardless of where they live and brings rural residents into the cultural mainstream by giving them the ability to read books and newspapers. The spread of telephones, radio, television, computers, and modern transportation has also increased the integration of rural areas into a unified national fabric. Farm families no longer raise their own vegetables, butcher their own hogs, milk their own cows, or cut their own wood for lumber and fuel. They buy their beans, pork, and milk at the supermarket and order building materials and fuel oil from local distributors. Gone are the days when spare time meant sitting around the stove telling tales, mending clothes, or repairing tools. Today's rural families watch television or go to the movies, just as families in the cities and suburbs do.

Another major factor in the transformation of rural life is the sharp decline of farming as an occupation (see Figure 14.1). Traditionally, the vast majority of people who lived in the country were farmers, but as nations industrialize, agricultural technology improves and fewer and fewer people are needed on the farm. People

Figure 14.1

Farmers

The percentage of the population who make their living as farmers has been declining for decades.

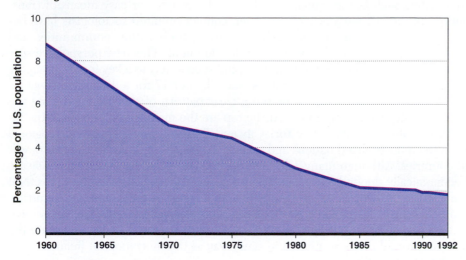

Source: U.S. Bureau of the Census, *Statistical Abstract of the United States, 1988* (Washington, DC: U.S. Government Printing Office, 1988), p. 607; U.S. Bureau of the Census, *Statistical Abstract of the United States, 1993*, p. 652; *Statistical Abstract of the United States, 1996*, p. 661.

born in rural areas are therefore continuing to migrate to cities in search of opportunity, as they have for centuries. But in recent times, the number of people migrating from the cities to smaller towns has greatly increased. In fact, between 1990 and 1995, 1.6 million more Americans moved to rural areas from the cities and suburbs than the other way around.[15] The reasons people are moving to smaller towns are probably much the same as the reasons they move to the suburbs: the lure of cheaper land, a slower pace, and the desire to escape from urban problems.

Despite all these changes, life on a farm or in a small town retains many special features. People know one another as people rather than as role players. The background of residents of rural communities tends to be more homogeneous than that of city dwellers, giving them a stronger feeling of group identity and a clearer sense of where they fit in as individuals. Deviant behavior is less common in rural areas than in urban ones; and though crime rates have been increasing faster in rural than in urban areas, they are still comparatively low. Living in a small town has its drawbacks, however. There is less deviance because everyone knows everyone else's business. The absence of anonymity reduces opportunities for many types of crime, but it also affects personal freedom, innovation, and individuality. Because people can't get lost in the crowd, their neighbors often know the details of their personal lives, and small-town gossip can be malicious and spiteful. Rural communities lack much of the spice of city life because they are so small and homogeneous. Still, as we have seen, people in rural areas report being far more satisfied with their communities than do those in the cities.[16]

Growth, Competition, and Dominance

Traditionally, urban sociologists have looked at the process of community growth and decay as the result of the interaction of technological changes with environmental factors such as the availability of natural resources or easy means of transportation. In the last few decades, however, conflict-oriented sociologists have begun emphasizing the importance of competition, both within communities and between them, in shaping the patterns of development. This new perspective sees the world system and the demands of its capitalist economy as a key force in shaping urban, suburban, and rural communities (see Chapter 17 for a discussion of world system theory). For one thing, they see a clear pattern of dominance among the world's many diverse communities. At the top are the major metropolises of the industrialized nations, such as New York City and Tokyo. Below them are the regional cities in the industrialized nations and a network of satellite cities in the less developed countries. Although many Third World satellite cities are enormous, they are still economically dependent on the major cities of the industrialized nations. Not only are the multinational corporations headquartered in the industrial countries, but so is the world financial system that has such a powerful influence on the economic fate of the less developed countries. The lesser cities in turn dominate the rural areas around them, in much the same way as the metropolitan financial centers dominate the cities.

This pattern of unequal global exchange has done much to enrich the elites and the upper middle class in the industrialized nations; but the increasing globalization of capital and technology has been eating away at the economic foundations of the working class and much of the rest of the middle class. As well-paying manufacturing jobs have moved to low-wage countries, the major metropolitan centers have been left with an economy increasingly polarized between the affluent and the poor.

The struggle for domination is not, however, limited to the global arena. Individual communities within the same nation also compete with each other for private investment and government favors, and corporations looking to locate a new plant or facility have become extremely skillful in playing one community off against another. The community that fails to offer a hefty package of incentives, such as tax breaks and free land, has little chance of landing such new ventures. The game is played a little differently in the competition for government dollars. Here the key factor is political clout, but the goal is largely the same. For example, Joe Feagin argues that the amazing growth of Houston, Texas, from a sparsely populated swampland to one of America's largest cities was the result of the ability of local economic elites to pull together and win the support of local, state, and national governments.[17]

These same struggles also go on within individual communities. Logan and Molotch argue that pressure from land developers, large property owners, and local businesses push cities to become virtual "urban growth machines," doing everything in their power to encourage development projects. But while rapid urban growth benefits those elites, it is often harmful to the general population, which must put up with clogged highways, higher school taxes, and a deteriorating environment.[18]

Quick Review

How did sociologists like Worth and Simmel describe urban life?

What do their contemporary critics say about their theories?

What made the growth of the suburbs possible?

How do the suburbs differ from the cities?

What are the unique characteristics of rural life, and how has modern technology changed them?

What role does regional and international competition play in determining the patterns of urban development?

Problems of Urbanization

As the process of urbanization has transformed the way we live, it has brought a new range of problems. Many farms and rural areas were left to decay as people rushed to the cities; then the growth of the suburbs led to the decline of many inner-city neighborhoods. Because of population pressures, housing costs in desirable areas have skyrocketed, and there is an ever increasing demand on the transportation system.

Crisis on the Farm

No one has been harder hit by the process of urbanization than the farmers. The percentage of farmers in the population has been declining for generations, as has the number of farms. In 1920, there were around 6.4 million farms in the United States. By 1950, the number had fallen to 5.4 million, and today there are only about 2 million left.[19] This crisis did not hit all farmers equally, however. Big corporate farms have flourished, while hundreds of thousands of family farms have ended up in bankruptcy and foreclosure. One result of this trend has been the "graying" of the American farmer as children born on the farm seek more promising careers in other lines of work.

There are several reasons for the crisis of the family farmer. Agriculture has always been a volatile business. Nature's unpredictability makes the price of farm goods bounce up and down more than virtually any other product. In the past, hard times meant that family farmers had to cut back and live off the food they produced themselves. Today, agriculture is run like any other business, and in good times or bad, loans must be paid back. Big corporate farms have the financial resources to weather the storms, but many family farmers do not. As a result, well-financed corporate farms have been able to buy up prime land at bargain prices. About 5 percent of the farms now hold over half of all agricultural land; and although the government's farm subsidy programs were originally intended to help the family farmer, powerful agribusiness enterprises actually receive most of the money. The fact is that the family farm, which once was the backbone of American life, is hopelessly outmatched by the wealth and power of its huge corporate competitors. Although most rural people no longer work on farms, the plight of the family farmer has sent economic shock waves through many rural areas. Migration to the cities and suburbs and the narrow economic base of many rural communities have left their residents with lower average income, poorer health care, and less education than their urban counterparts. Some rural towns have been flooded with new immigrants from the cities, while others have seen their population dwindle away. Although an influx of new residents requires many difficult adjustments, towns with declining populations suffer the most. For one thing, a smaller population means higher taxes because the cost of maintaining essential services must be carried by

The relentless growth of big corporate farms has driven more and more family farmers out of business.

fewer people. Stores and businesses that depend on local trade go bankrupt, further reducing the tax base. As job opportunities dry up and education, health care, and other community services decline, even more people move out, and a community may enter a downward spiral. Since it is usually the young adults who migrate to the cities, they leave a disproportionately large population of children and elderly people, who must be supported by the productive workers who remain.

The Decline of the Central City

The big cities used to be a dominant political and economic force in North America, but year by year the flight to the suburbs has eroded their power. Congestion, rising costs, crime, and pollution have driven out large segments of the middle class, leaving the inner cities with a disproportionate share of the poor, the minorities, and the new immigrants. Although our cities are still major centers of corporate and government activity, an increasing number of businesses have followed the middle class to the suburbs. The result has been a more or less permanent crisis in many big-city governments as they struggle to repair their crumbling **infrastructure** (roads, sewers, water systems, and other basic necessities) and meet the growing needs of their poor and minority populations with a shrinking tax base. In the past, the big cities could always turn to the state or federal government to get them through hard times, but the loss of the middle class has also meant the loss of political power. The federal government has slashed the funds that used to go to the cities, and big-city mayors searching for financial aid face increasingly skeptical and unsympathetic state legislatures.

infrastructure
Roads, sewers, water systems, and other basic physical necessities of modern societies.

Some urban neighborhoods have managed to flourish despite these difficulties, but others have deteriorated into the kinds of festering slums seldom seen in the cities of Europe or Japan. The general decline in the demand for unskilled labor has combined with the economic disintegration of the inner city to produce pockets of intense poverty. Since 1976, the percentage of poor African Americans who live in extreme poverty has increased by about 50 percent.[20] Studies show that the people who live in poverty-stricken urban ghettos are trapped by formidable economic barriers. For example, welfare mothers who are assigned subsidized housing in the inner cities are less likely to find a job or to earn a decent wage than those assigned to housing in suburban areas (see Chapter 7).[21]

Almost inevitably, many residents of these poverty zones—especially the young men—turn to the illicit economy to find the opportunities otherwise denied them. Prostitution, gambling, and extortion all flourish, but in recent times the drug business has been the most profitable. Big cities from coast to coast now have what police term "dead zones," ruled by street criminals and gang violence, where people from all over the region come to buy drugs on the streets and in the crack houses (fortified houses that are used to sell cocaine and other drugs). Life in these lawless neighborhoods can be a nightmare for many of the residents, but such communities often include low-income housing projects and some of the least expensive private apartments, and many people simply cannot afford to move out. (For a personal perspective on what it is like to live in such a community, see the box below.)

Personal Perspectives   A Former Member of a Los Angeles Gang

Gangs are a continual problem in many urban communities. The following account comes from a former gang member who is now working in a juvenile detention camp.

What do you think happened when that kid there first began to seek out his masculinity? What happened when he first tried to assert himself? If he lived in any other community but Watts there would be legitimate ways to express those feelings. Little League. Pop Warner. But if you're a black kid living in Watts those options have been removed. You're not going to go play Pop Warner. Not in Watts. Maybe if you live in Bellflower, maybe if you live in Agoura, but not in Watts—it's just not there, there's no funding for it. But you're at that prepubescent age, and you have all those aggressive tendencies and no legitimate way to get rid of them. And that's when the gang comes along, and the gang offers everything those legitimate organizations do. The gang serves emotional needs. You feel wanted. You feel welcome. You feel important. And there is discipline and there are rules. . . .

The very fact that a kid is in a gang means that something is missing. So many of them are functioning illiterates. So many of them come from abusing backgrounds. The hardest cases were probably sexually molested or they were routinely beaten—probably both. Depends on what kind of father influence was around the house. If any. You find a gang member who comes from a complete nuclear family, a kid who has never been exposed to any kind of abuse, I'd like to meet him. Not a wannabe who's a Crip or a Blood because that's the thing to be . . . , I mean a *real* gangbanger who comes from a happy, balanced home, who's got a good opinion of himself. I don't think that kid exists.*

*Leon Bing, *Do or Die* (New York: HarperCollins, 1991), pp. 12, 14.

Local Government

The rapid growth of the suburbs has, as we have seen, created an intractable financial bind for many city governments. As large segments of the middle class have moved out, cities are left with a high percentage of poor people who need many services but are unable to pay for them. Taxes are higher in the cities than in the suburbs, but the cities still cannot raise tax rates enough to meet their needs, for that would only accelerate the exodus of people and businesses. Moreover, such problems are not limited to the big cities. As the suburbs have grown larger and more diverse, these same problems have begun to crop up there. While taxes are low and the services generous in wealthy suburbs, the poor ones are little better off than the central cities.[22]

Caught between the inescapable demands of the marketplace and an increasingly apathetic public, the power of local political institutions has steadily declined. Today, many town and city governments have surprisingly little control over their own affairs. For one thing, states often place tight legal restrictions on their freedom to act, particularly with respect to the types and amounts of taxes that can be levied. Local governments also rely on federal grants that specify how the money is to be spent. The economies of many cities are heavily dependent on a few large corporate employers. When these firms make demands on local government, elected officials often have little choice but to comply or face the financial devastation that would result from a corporate decision to move to another area. Even when local officials do oppose corporate plans, businesses are often able to use their influence on the state or federal level to overpower local opposition.

Local governments are also beset by a variety of other problems ranging from graft and corruption to the wasteful duplication of services. Zoning changes, for example, have repeatedly been the focus of corruption scandals. Millions of dollars are often involved in an agency's decision to change the zoning of a piece of land. Developers and land speculators looking for a fast profit go to great lengths to convince officials to make the "right" decision. Officials are sometimes bribed with cash payments or a percentage of a developer's profits. The result is likely to be a new suburban community that turns its real estate operators into millionaires but fails to meet the needs of local residents.[23] Another product of haphazard urbanization is the creation of a confusing network of fragmented local governments and overlapping service districts. Metropolitan areas often have dozens of police chiefs, fire chiefs, and department heads when only a few are really needed; such duplication of services is expensive and inefficient.

Housing

The stunning increase in the cost of buying a private home has been a major contributor to the growing division between the haves and the have-nots in our society. Those who already own a home have received windfall profits, but first-time home buyers are often shut out of the market. Even though the pace of real estate inflation has slowed, the cost of an average home more than doubled in the last two decades. As a result, the average buyer is now older, and families are more likely to need two incomes to make the payments.[24]

These problems, however, pale in comparison with the critical shortage of low-cost housing for those without comfortable middle-class incomes. Since 1978 more than 2 million units of low-cost housing have been abandoned or converted into more expensive housing. Thus, while the number of poor people has been growing, the supply of affordable housing has been shrinking. Rents for the least expensive apartments are rising much faster than the income of their tenants.[25] The average poor family now spends about 65 percent of its income on housing—more than double the maximum amount the Department of Housing and Urban Development says they should have to spend.[26] An increasing number of people are being forced to move in with relatives and friends or are living in converted garages, in old cars and vans, or on the streets. Estimates of the number of homeless people in the United States vary widely (see Chapter 7), but virtually everyone agrees that their numbers have soared in the last decade.

What happened to the supply of low-cost housing? One problem is **gentrification,** the refurbishing of old, low-cost neighborhoods to accommodate more wealthy people. One good example of this is the area known as Capitol Hill in Washington, D.C. In the 1960s it was occupied by poor and working-class African Americans, but because of its close proximity to downtown employment centers, artists, architects, and middle class people seeking a first home began purchasing homes in the neighborhood and fixing them up. These first immigrants were soon followed by upper-income professionals and government workers. Over 90 percent of the newcomers were whites, and over 90 percent had college educations. As the newcomers bought up the existing housing, many less affluent residents had to leave their old neighborhood and search for other accommodations from the city's shrinking supply of affordable housing.[27]

A second cause of this shortage can be laid directly at the government's doorstep. For one thing, the efforts of community redevelopment agencies have tended to have much the same impact as private gentrification: old neighborhoods are renovated, and the poor are moved out to make way for the affluent. Perhaps more important, the federal government has also turned its back on the housing needs of the poor. During the last two decades, federal appropriations for subsidized housing were slashed, and the tax breaks designed to encourage private investment in rental properties were ended.

gentrification
The renovation of older low-cost neighborhoods to accommodate wealthier residents.

Inefficient Transportation

It is often said that Americans have a love affair with the car and that even kings in their carriages did not know the speed, comfort, or convenience of the automobile that an average wage earner can now afford. But this romantic picture hardly fits the realities of American life, where pollution fouls the air and almost 42,000 people die in traffic accidents every year.[28] Traffic congestion is growing so bad in some urban areas that it often approaches **gridlock,** a situation in which traffic simply stops moving and no one gets anywhere. Local, state, and national governments spend billions of dollars a year in a losing battle to build roads faster than new cars clog them. One study found that since 1982 traffic has gotten better in only 3 major American cities, while it has gotten worse in 47 of them.[29] Still, the 1990 census found that only 1 in 20 Americans relied on public transportation to get to work and only 3 in 20 carpooled.[30] Our dependence on the automobile often imposes a severe hardship on the 1 in every 7 American households that does not own a car,[31] making it difficult for many of the poor and the elderly to get around.

gridlock
Extreme congestion in which all traffic comes to a stop.

The automobile provides one of the fastest and most convenient forms of transportation ever created, but we have too much of a good thing. In urban areas around the world, traffic clogs city streets, exhaust pollutes the air, and engines consume huge amounts of fuel.

Why do we depend on such an inefficient system of transportation? Part of the answer is simply that we like cars. But there is another reason as well: the automobile, tire, and petroleum industries decided that there was more money to be made from the automobile, and they intentionally set out to impede the growth of public transportation. In Los Angeles, for example, General Motors and Standard Oil organized a corporation that acquired a controlling interest in the Pacific Electric Railway, which operated what was then the world's largest system of electric trolleys. The quiet and efficient trolleys were then replaced by polluting diesel-powered buses. The new owners gave up the special rights-of-way enjoyed by the trolleys and pulled up the tracks. After these "improvements," passenger mileage on the buses plummeted, and Los Angeles became one of the most automobile-dependent big cities in the world.[32]

Ethnic Segregation

Most large cities have a number of "ethnic villages": areas populated mostly by members of a particular ethnic group. Whether such a residential pattern is desirable or not is open to debate. As noted in Chapter 8, pluralists hold that such communities provide support for new immigrants and a place where their children and grandchildren can go to renew ties with their cultural roots. New immigrants often find jobs working for other members of their own group, and access to this supply of cheap labor provides an opportunity for other immigrants to move up the social lad-

Signs of Hope Safer Transportation

Our heavy dependence on private automobiles for daily transportation creates a host of difficult problems for our society, but at least automobile transportation has grown significantly safer over the years. The average number of accidents per driver has declined sharply, and so have traffic fatalities. Since 1970, the death rate from motor vehicle accidents has dropped by over one-third, yet the percentage of people who drive and their average mileage both increased.* There are many explanations for this improvement. The law now requires newly built automobiles to have a host of safety equipment from seat belts and air bags to special bracing to protect against side-impact crashes. Speed limits have been lowered in many places, and that gives drivers more time to react in a crisis situation. It also seems likely that tougher enforcement of drunk driving laws has played an important role, as has better driver education.

*U.S. Bureau of the Census, *Statistical Abstract of the United States, 1996* (Washington, DC: U.S. Government Printing Office, 1996), pp. 91, 101.

der.[33] The advocates of integration argue that the isolation of immigrants and minorities in ethnic communities actually cuts them off from many economic opportunities and makes them easy victims of exploitation, by members either of their own group or of another. They point out that such segregated communities encourage the separate ethnic identities that divide us against each other and have created so much hatred and conflict through the years.

Whatever they may think about the value of separate ethnic neighborhoods, both pluralists and integrationists agree that no one should be forced to live in them. Yet that is exactly the position in which many African Americans and other nonwhite minorities find themselves. The laws explicitly requiring racial segregation have all been overturned, but racial minorities are still excluded from many neighborhoods by the hostility and prejudice of their residents and by landlords and rental agents who cater to it. Although sociologists use different ways of measuring segregation, it appears that about three out of four African Americans in American cities live in segregated neighborhoods.[34] Analysis of data collected by Karl Taeuber and Alma Taeuber shows a slow decrease in the level of segregation in American cities over the years.[35] Logan and Molotch, on the other hand, found that segregation has been increasing in the suburbs,[36] but other research indicates that they are still less segregated than the cities.[37] If this pattern of forced segregation is to be broken, the federal government will have to take much more vigorous action than it has in the past.

Urban Problems in the Less Developed Countries

If you look around the downtown area of a major Third World city, it is easy to think that it is simply a poorer version of the cities in the wealthy countries. But the pattern of community development has a very different character in the Third World than it does in the industrialized nations. For one thing, the urban population of most poor nations is much higher than would be expected from their overall level of industrialization. Many urban sociologists refer to them as "overurbanized" because

Figure 14.2

Urbanization

The cities of the less developed countries have been growing at a staggering pace.

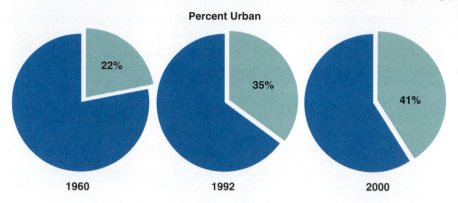

Percent Urban

22%   35%   41%

1960   1992   2000

Source: United Nations Human Development Programme, *Human Development Report, 1997* (New York: Oxford University Press, 1997), p. 193.

more people live in the cities than they can reasonably be expected to support. Another characteristic of most of the less developed countries is that the population is skewed toward a single huge city that dominates the entire nation: for example, Bangkok is over 30 times larger than Thailand's second-largest city.[38] The average age of the population is much lower in the less developed countries than in the industrialized nations, and that is especially true in the cities, where usually almost half the residents are under 18.[39]

Because the less developed countries have more than double the population growth rate of the industrialized nations and only a fraction of their wealth, urban problems often take on staggering proportions. Moreover, the process of urbanization is occurring much faster in the less developed countries than it ever did in the West. The impact of this runaway urbanization can be most easily seen by comparing individual cities. In 1950, the population of Mexico City was less than one-fourth of the New York City area's 12 million people. In the next 25 years, Mexico City's growth rate was five times New York's, though New York still had around 6 million more people. In the next 20 years, however, Mexico City grew to almost 24 million people—making it the world's second-largest city—while New York's population grew to less than 15 million.[40] Mexico City's frantic growth is typical of many other large Third World cities as well. For example, in the next 20 years, Bombay, India, is expected to almost double the 15 million residents it currently has, and Jakarta, Indonesia, is projected to grow even faster.[41] (See Figure 14.2.)

But can such impoverished cities build enough new housing to accommodate all these people? Sadly, the answer is that they probably cannot. Most of the people will either squeeze into existing housing (much of it already crowded and dilapidated) or become urban squatters, finding an empty piece of land and building a small shack from whatever materials they can beg, borrow, or steal. There are now over 4 million squatters in Mexico City and over 2 million in Calcutta, India, and the shantytowns of the Third World are doubling in size every six years.[42] These shantytowns are more than just overcrowded: they lack the basic services necessary for a decent life. The streets are unpaved, there is little fire or police protection, clean water is scarce, and proper sewage facilities are often nonexistent. As a result, health conditions are deplorable, death rates are high, and disease runs rampant. Urban squatters have no legal rights to the land they live on, and they are in constant danger of losing their homes. If the government decides it needs the land or that the squatters are an eyesore or a source of political unrest, they can simply be moved out. In one sense, however, the residents of these shantytowns are the lucky ones, for most cities in the less developed countries have a substantial number of "pavement people" who sleep in the streets without any permanent home. In Calcutta, one of the world's most troubled cities, there are between 500,000 and 1 million of these homeless people.[43]

Of course, all the residents of Third World cities do not live in such deplorable conditions. The Westernized elite typically live in conditions of luxury that would make most middle-class Americans envious. Even the common people often find the city a far more rewarding place to live than rural villages. One survey of migrants who had been living in Mexico City for four years found that 80 percent of those interviewed were satisfied with their decision to move.[44] After all, millions of people wouldn't migrate to the cities every year if they didn't think that their life would be better there. The urban problems of less developed countries must therefore be seen in the context of the crowding, unemployment, and hunger of the rural areas (see Chapter 17).

Shantytowns like this one are common in the poor nations.

What is the "crisis on the farm"?

What are the causes of the decline in our inner cities?

What problems are faced by our local governments?

Why is there such a shortage of low-cost housing?

What's wrong with our system of urban transportation?

Why are so many urban neighborhoods still segregated?

Why are urban problems so much worse in the Third World than in the industrialized nations?

Solving the Problems of Urbanization

Despite the complexity of today's community problems, there is no shortage of proposals for solving them. Some are wildly utopian and others too narrow to be worthwhile. But they all have one thing in common: their successful implementation will require two scarce commodities—money and the political will to get the job done.

Creating Community

community

(1) A place where people live. (2) The bonds and feelings of belonging that develop among people who live in the same place.

Community has two different meanings. In one sense, it is simply a place where people live, but it also refers to the feelings of solidarity and togetherness that people who live near each other often develop. If there is one thing that urban sociologists agree is lacking in contemporary cities and suburbs, it is this sense of community and belonging. The hard question is what we can do about it.

Architects and urban planners have found that the way we design our homes and parks can play an important role in developing community. The traditional suburb, with its isolated family houses each surrounded by its own lawn, almost seems designed to discourage a sense of togetherness. New designs facilitate friendly contacts when families share common walls, recreational facilities, and green areas. Similarly, urban apartments can encourage community building by creating common areas for recreation and relaxing. A new style of living called "co-housing" goes a step further by including shared child care and kitchen facilities and intentionally seeking out residents who want to live in a tight-knit community. Criminologists have even found that if such new housing patterns are properly designed, they reduce the crime rate because neighbors look out for each other's safety and property.

Another approach advocated by some urban sociologists is to give local communities more political autonomy. The idea is that if we let local neighborhoods run their own schools, direct their own police officers, and decide how highway, park, and maintenance money is to be spent, people will be bound to get more politically involved with their neighbors. Such proposals for **political decentralization** certainly do not win universal support, but it is clear that the voter turnout for local elections is dismally low, and something must be done to restore people's faith in

political decentralization

Transferring power from centralized government to local communities and agencies.

government and get them more involved in local issues. With an active, involved citizenry, none of the problems we have discussed is beyond solution; without it, the chances for effective reforms are slight.

Urban Renewal

The first **urban renewal** programs in the United States were begun during the Great Depression to improve housing and provide employment for construction workers. To this day urban renewal usually means housing renewal, although a renewal of business and other economic activities is also desperately needed in many urban neighborhoods. From the beginning, urban renewal projects were plagued with problems. The original idea was simple: government agencies were to buy up decaying central-city areas, demolish the buildings, and sell the land to private developers, who would build apartments for people with low and moderate incomes. But the developers were seldom required to build inexpensive housing; therefore, most built office buildings, factories, and luxury apartments, which bring in higher profits. The poor were forced to move from substandard homes in one area to substandard homes in another area.

At various times, the federal government has also backed a smorgasbord of other programs, including building its own low-income housing, guaranteeing mortgages so that some low-income people could afford to buy homes, and providing subsidized loans for developers to build or rehabilitate rental units for qualified low-income tenants. More recently, the federal government has been moving away from such specific programs to deal with housing problems and relying instead on general "block grants" and "revenue sharing" to be spent as the community sees fit. The idea that local leaders know more about the needs of their own community makes a great deal of sense, but such programs ignored the political reality that poor people have little influence on the decisions of their local governments. According to research by Kenneth K. Wong and Paul E. Peterson, block grants generally result in a smaller—not a larger—proportion of federal money actually going to help the poor.[45] Moreover, funding for such programs has never been sufficient to meet the need for low-income housing.

The history of government programs to improve housing in the United States has been one of misplaced priorities. Most federal assistance has gone to the wealthy and the middle class in the form of low-interest home loans and tax exemptions for home mortgage payments, while programs to help the poor have consistently been shortchanged. To deal with the growing need for low-income housing, these priorities must be reversed. For example, if some or all of the tax exemption for home mortgages were repealed, billions of dollars could be freed to provide housing for the poor.

The proposals for reducing poverty discussed in Chapter 7 could obviously go a long way toward improving poor inner-city communities as well. Another idea, popular among conservatives, is to make such communities into **enterprise zones** that offer special tax breaks and other incentives to encourage businesses to locate there. Although several states have already created such enterprise zones, their effectiveness is still a matter of controversy. Critics charge that they simply move businesses from one part of the city to another and do little to cure the underlying economic

urban renewal
A program intended to upgrade decaying city neighborhoods.

enterprise zone
A low-income area that is given special tax breaks and other incentives to encourage business.

problems. Although the creation of enterprise zones may well provide some assistance to desperate inner-city communities, a long-term solution to their problems will require a much broader approach, including a direct assault on society's deep-seated economic problems, a better system of public education and training, better crime control, and welfare reforms.

Controlling Urban Growth

The destruction of the natural environment, endless urban sprawl, traffic congestion, air pollution, and a feeling that our overall quality of life is declining have led an increasing number of people to question the old assumption that more growth means more prosperity and a better society. As a result, many people are calling for tighter government controls to regulate growth and ensure that we protect the environment, expand public transportation, and conserve our natural resources. (See the Debate "Should We Limit Suburban Growth?") The logical approach is to redirect urban development away from the sprawling automobile-based suburbs and increase the population density of existing cities and towns. This high-density strategy has many advantages over current policies that allow the seemly endless proliferation of new suburban housing tracts. Not only does it protect virgin land from the developers' bulldozers, but higher-density housing is less expensive to build, more energy-efficient, and much more compatible with effective public transportation. Another important way to save energy and alleviate transportation headaches is to zone cities and suburbs so that residential areas are near the offices and factories where most people work.

The primary obstacle to the implementation of such proposals is economic. Developers stand to make far more money building whole new housing tracts on empty land than they would remodeling existing buildings, tearing down and replacing dilapidated structures, and building on small vacant lots in existing urban areas. Pitched battles between developers and local homeowners who want to restrict growth have already broken out in small towns and suburbs across North America. Money buys influence, and studies show that developers usually win in the end.[46] A successful effort to redirect urban growth therefore will probably require federal assistance. One approach, for example, would be to provide tax breaks for higher-density structures near existing urban services, paid for by increased taxes on low-density suburban developments.

Improving the Cities of the Less Developed Countries

As serious as they are, the plight of the cities in the industrialized nations looks almost trivial when compared with the urban problems of the less developed countries. It is easy to make a list of the steps that must be taken to improve the cities of the Third World: millions of new dwellings must be constructed, transportation must be improved, vast networks of sewage and water lines must be built, makeshift buildings and shacks need to be improved or replaced, and, of course, jobs must be created for an exploding population. It is far more difficult to list realistic ways to

Many people see the relentless expansion of the suburbs as a serious threat to the environment.

achieve these goals, but in one way or another they all depend on improving the economic foundation of less developed countries and controlling the population explosion. (See Chapter 17 for a discussion of the different proposals for promoting economic development in the poor countries.)

Another obvious response is to slow down the unprecedented speed of Third World urbanization to allow time for the needed improvements to be made. Some propose strict government controls that directly limit the size of the cities. The government of the People's Republic of China, for example, requires that all persons register their place of residence and legally restricts the rights of its people to move to the cities. Most urban experts recommend a more positive approach that discourages migration to the cities by making rural areas more attractive. Effective programs to bring electricity, running water, modern sanitation, and health care facilities to the rural villages of the less developed countries not only could help them but would alleviate some of the pressure on the cities as well. Another essential requirement is for economic development programs to create jobs in rural areas so that fewer villagers will have to move to the cities to search for work.

Even if all these measures were put into effect, however, they would be unlikely to succeed without another critical step—bringing the population explosion under control. Lowering birthrates will obviously slow down both urban and rural growth, and, equally important, it will allow impoverished countries to get off the treadmill that requires their economy to grow 2 or 3 percent a year just to stay even with population growth. (See Chapter 15 for a discussion of population control programs.)

Debate   Should We Limit Suburban Growth?

Yes

Greedy developers have ruined one scenic area after another, replacing trees and grass with asphalt and tract houses. The destruction of animal habitat has already led to the extinction of numerous species, and more are soon to follow. The ever growing number of automobiles required by the suburban explosion is choking our skies with smog, burning up our reserves of petroleum, and maiming or killing hundreds of thousands of people in traffic accidents every year. If we don't change our course, we will soon face a crisis that will threaten the very survival of our society.

Those who spread this suburban blight claim that any new restrictions would be a violation of their civil rights, but all that has to be done is shift the costs of suburban developments from the public to the entrepreneurs who get rich from them. Runaway suburban growth would no longer be a problem if developers were forced to pay all the costs of the roads, schools, hospitals, police stations, and other facilities needed to serve these new communities and were required to pay for pollution reduction systems to offset the smog created by the additional automobile traffic.

Developers always claim that anything that cuts their income will cause an economic disaster, but new homes will still be needed to accommodate a growing population; they will simply be built in existing urban areas where developers have a harder time making such exorbitant profits. Despite what the real estate investors say, increasing the density of existing urban areas is clearly the best way to meet our housing needs because it costs less, saves transportation and energy costs, and protects our fragile environment. If we stop the subsidies for the developers and make them pay for the damage they do, the problem of suburban sprawl will take care of itself.

Quick Review

What are some of the ways we can respond to the problems created by the process of urbanization?

Sociological Perspectives on Problems of Urbanization

The Functionalist Perspective

Most functionalists believe that the rapid urbanization of North America has disrupted family life as well as economic, educational, political, and religious institu-

No

The growth of the suburbs was not the result of some plot between the developers and the politicians. The suburbs have grown because people want to live there. Numerous public opinion polls have shown that people who live in the suburbs are far happier with their communities than those who live in big cities. Proposals to restrict suburban growth violate civil liberties because they trap people in crowded cities and prevent them from living where they choose.

Aside from that, the half-baked plans to cut off suburban growth would have a devastating economic impact. For one thing, such drastic restrictions would probably cost hundreds of thousands of well-paying jobs in the construction industry and produce a chain reaction with devastating economic consequences. Retail stores and service workers who depend on customers who work in the construction industry would go broke, and local governments would be forced to increase taxes to make up for the decline in their revenues. As usual, the effects of this antigrowth policy would hit average workers far more severely than the wealthy and powerful. As the supply of new suburban housing ran out, prices in the suburbs would go through the ceiling, and eventually no one but the wealthy would be able to afford the private homes that are so much a part of the American dream. Supporters of such limits on growth suffer from a "drawbridge" mentality: they move to pleasant suburbs and want to pull up the drawbridge so that no one else can follow them.

There is no denying that some suburbs have serious problems with traffic congestion and air pollution. The best solution to such difficulties, however, is a concerted effort to build more mass transit, cars that pollute less, and more superhighways, not some radical program to strangle suburban growth.

tions. The fact that bonds of affection have weakened and people have become more isolated is taken to be a symptom of more general social disorganization. When masses of people left rural villages to settle in cities, the villages became disorganized and unable to meet the needs of those who remained. Likewise, the cities were not prepared to assimilate the migrants and to provide them with a sense of mutual identity that would encourage loyalty and contentment. The old cultural patterns that were functional for village living were abandoned, but new integrating patterns did not arise. As a consequence, rates of crime, suicide, and mental illness grew, as did other symptoms of social disorganization. Before a new balance could be established, another shift in population—the flight to the suburbs—threw the social system back into chaos.

Functionalists see similar problems developing in the poor nations, even though the process of urbanization there has taken a somewhat different course. In Western countries, industrialization and urbanization developed at the same time, but in the less developed countries, the cities started growing before there had been much industrialization. Some functionalists have therefore concluded that the less developed countries are "overurbanized" because the population of the cities has grown too large for the economic system to support. The difficulty with such claims is that there is even less economic opportunity in the countryside than there is in the cities. Thus, the urban disorganization must be seen in the context of the economic disorganization that affects all aspects of life in less developed countries.

Functionalists argue that we must slow the pace of social change and allow metropolitan areas to adjust to these new conditions. Of particular importance is the need to reduce the rapid rate of urbanization in the less developed countries before the cities collapse under their crushing burdens. This goal can be achieved either by placing restrictions on immigration to the cities or by launching large-scale development programs that create new economic opportunities in rural areas. For the developed countries, functionalists tend to favor the creation of larger, more centralized metropolitan governments to replace the hodgepodge of fragmented governmental units that now exist in many urban areas. Functionalists also favor programs that seek to build a greater sense of community and mutual cooperation in urban neighborhoods—for example, neighborhood watch programs that get people together to protect themselves against crime and administrative reforms that return the control of local schools to citizen councils elected from the neighborhoods they serve.

The Conflict Perspective

From the conflict perspective, the problems of urbanization are seen as the result of the struggles between competing interest groups. When rural landowners were a dominant political force in North America, they did all they could to maintain their power, using it to obtain special economic benefits. For example, in the 1930s they persuaded the federal government to build farm-to-market roads, provide rural electricity, and pay farmers more than the free-market price for their crops. When urbanization shifted power to the cities, industrialists took advantage of cheap labor provided by those who could no longer make a living on the farm. Because these powerful groups placed profits ahead of social welfare, our rural communities began to deteriorate. These small towns were exploited and then abandoned the way people abandon worn-out cars.

As wealthy and influential people moved from the cities to the suburbs, another change in the balance of power took place. The cities were filled with ever increasing numbers of the poor, the weak, and the powerless. Meanwhile, well-to-do suburbanites began to dominate the political scene, using their power to gain advantages for themselves. The federal government responded by favoring suburbs with freeways and expressways, low-interest loans for single-family houses, and other benefits that diverted funds away from projects to help the inner-city residents who were left behind.

The struggle for power takes a different form in the poor nations, but its effects are just as profound. Conflict theorists point out that the ruling class in most Third World nations (especially in those countries with large investments by foreigners) are much more Western and more urban in their outlook than the masses of the poor. The pattern of community development in such countries is dominated by the elite's drive to make the money necessary to buy foreign luxury goods and maintain a Western standard of living. Peasants are often driven from their land to make room for large corporate farms, whose products are then sold on the world market. Government tax policies frequently place a heavy burden on rural villagers in order to pay for grandiose industrialization programs, and the prices paid to peasants for their crops are often kept artificially low in order to prevent political unrest among the urban masses. The few well-paying jobs that are created by the new industries spur unrealistic dreams of urban affluence among poor villagers. The effect of all this has been a staggering wave of immigration to the cities, which most poor nations have found impossible to handle. Further, as we will see in Chapter 17, conflict theorists hold that the Third World as a whole is subject to the economic exploitation of the developed countries, which in turn is the root cause of many of their community problems.

Conflict theorists are convinced that the solution to community problems lies in political organization and action. People in city slums and poor rural areas must band together and demand fairer treatment. Such a movement should not be directed at isolated problems such as poor housing or crime but rather should attack inequality in every social sphere. This kind of movement is particularly important in the Third World, where conflict theorists often see the overthrow of the old ruling elites and the expulsion of the foreign multinationals that support them as the only hope for real improvement.

The Feminist Perspective

When viewed from a feminist perspective, the process of urbanization that has unfolded in the last two centuries has had contradictory results. On the one hand, women in traditional rural communities were usually forced to live as second-class citizens. Their husbands and fathers made the decisions that guided their lives, and their opportunities to take independent action were severely limited. Migration to the cities broke up many of the traditional cultural patterns and gave many women new opportunities they would never have enjoyed back on the farm. On the other hand, the breakdown of the constraints of traditional community life also led to huge increases in the crime and violence directed against women and often made child rearing a more difficult and uncertain task. Many feminists therefore call for a new effort to build community and sense of mutual responsibility in our urban neighborhoods, but unlike the situation in traditional rural cultures, this new sense of community must be built upon the assumption of full equality between women and men.

The Interactionist Perspective

Centuries ago Thomas Jefferson warned that city life could corrupt the virtue and undermine the political liberty of the American people. As we have already seen, the original urban sociologists expressed similar attitudes around the turn of this century. To Simmel and Wirth, there was no question that the impersonality and the hectic pace of urban life were harmful to most city dwellers. The next generation of sociologists, who were more likely to have been raised in the urban areas themselves, often rejected such conclusions as the mere product of small-town bias.

Yet despite the claims made in defense of urban life, it is hard to avoid the conclusion that small-town living, with its sense of community and identity, has some important psychological advantages over the cold impersonality of the city. Interactionist theory has shown that we build our sense of who we are out of the expectations and reactions of other people, and when our lives become too fragmented we are likely to be confused and unsatisfied. Many interactionists therefore support efforts to bring a stronger sense of community back to urban neighborhoods, recreating the supportive and coherent social environment characteristic of rural life at its best. How this might be done, however, is very much an open question. One possibility would be to decentralize the city into smaller units, each with its own government and commercial and recreational centers, so that genuine neighborhoods would have a better chance to develop. The breakdown of community is probably worst in the inner-city slums, which not coincidentally have the highest rates of alcoholism, mental disorder, and drug addiction. Many interactionists therefore advocate special programs aimed specifically at those neighborhoods that seek to bring people together to attack their common problems.

Quick Review

Compare and contract the functionalist and conflict explanations of the causes of our urban problems.

Would most interactionists and feminists agree or disagree about the ways to respond to problems caused by urbanization?

Summary

The shift from rural to urban living has profoundly altered the lives of millions of people. Traditionally, most families lived on farms in rural areas, but industrialization spurred the rapid growth of cities. In the past few decades there has been a new shift of population, this time toward the suburbs.

Pioneering sociologists such as Georg Simmel and Louis Wirth argued that city life encourages impersonal social relationships, a blasé attitude toward life, a materialistic outlook, and a feeling of indifference toward others. Later urban sociologists argued that this picture exaggerates the negative aspects of city life and is true only for some types of city dwellers.

The availability of government-backed loans, a growing system of highways, and the prosperity following World War II made it possible for many people to move to the suburbs. Although the stereotype of suburbia pictures miles of well-kept houses populated by young, middle-class, white professionals on the way up, there is actually a great deal of diversity in the suburbs. Many suburbs are business and industrial centers as well as "bedroom communities." As suburbs have aged, they have come to resemble the cities near them. They are no longer islands in a sea of urban problems, and the suburban way of life is coming to resemble the urban way of life.

Rural towns and villages have been deeply affected by urbanization and the decline in their population. With the growth of mass transportation and communication, rural life itself has become increasingly "urban." Yet life on a farm or in a small town retains its distinctive characteristics, including closer personal relationships, a sense of identity and belonging, a homogeneous culture, and intolerance of deviant behavior.

In the last two decades, conflict-oriented sociologists have begun emphasizing the importance of the competitive struggle for profit in shaping patterns of community development. On a global level, metropolitan centers in rich nations dominate a network of huge urban centers in the Third World, while they in turn exploit the less powerful regions of their own nations. The communities within a nation struggle among themselves for private investment and government benefits, just as the classes within each community struggle to determine its pattern of growth and who will benefit from it.

The process of urbanization has contributed to a crisis on the farm that is making it increasingly difficult for family farmers to survive. The economic and political decline of many big cities in North America has left them with growing inner-city slums that have high rates of poverty and crime. The growth of the suburbs resulted in an inefficient and environmentally destructive system of transportation and has created a financial predicament for many local governments. The lack of low-cost housing is a growing national problem that is aggravated by segregation and housing discrimination against African Americans and other minorities. As bad as all these problems are, however, conditions are far worse in the poverty-stricken and rapidly expanding cities of the less developed countries.

There are many proposals for dealing with the problems created by urbanization. Some urban planners recommend that local governments be reorganized into larger and more efficient units, while others call for a new spirit of public involvement in community politics and development. So far, urban renewal programs have not been successful in producing adequate housing for the poor, and much greater efforts are needed to create low-cost housing and improve economic conditions in our inner cities. Environmentalists recommend tighter controls on suburban growth and policies that encourage greater urban density rather than suburban sprawl. Perhaps most important, programs of economic development and population control are needed to help Third World cities with their heavy burdens.

According to functionalists, rapid urbanization has disrupted our basic social institutions. The rates of crime, suicide, and mental illness have grown as the disorganization brought about by rapid urbanization has increased. Conflict theorists see the problems of urbanization as a result of competition between interest groups. Each group exercises power for its own benefit and not for the general welfare. Feminists point out that urbanization has had contradictory effects on women, loosening some of the traditional restraints that held them back but also reducing community support and protection. Interactionists are concerned with the psychological impact of city life, and they support efforts to build genuine communities in urban neighborhoods.

Questions for Critical Thinking

If you read this chapter carefully, you should have a pretty good idea about the kinds of problems that trouble modern communities. But what about where you live? Take some time to examine your community and its problems. How much crime is there? How easy is it to get around from one place to another? Is it safe? Are there areas of poverty and urban decay? How involved are its citizens in local government? Do people pitch in and help their neighbors when they need it? What about pollution and public sanitation? After you've looked at all these questions, try to think of some ways to make things better in your community.

Key Terms

community
enterprise zones
gentrification
gridlock
highway lobby
infrastructure
megalopolis

metropolitan statistical area (MSA)
political decentralization
suburb
urbanization
urban renewal
villages

Further Readings

Mark Gottdiener, *The New Urban Sociology* (New York: McGraw-Hill, 1994). A comprehensive look at urban problems from a critical perspective.

John R. Logan and Harvey L. Molotch, *Urban Fortunes: The Political Economy of Place* (Berkeley: University of California Press, 1987). A highly influential analysis of the growth of cities and suburbs from a conflict perspective.

Terry Williams and William Kornblum, *The Kids Uptown: Struggle and Hope in the Projects* (New York: Putnam, 1994). A look at what it is like to grow up in public housing.

William Julius Wilson, "Studying Inner-City Social Dislocations: The Challenge of Public Agenda Research," *American Sociological Review* 56 (February 1991): 1–14. An insightful look at the causes of the problems of the inner city.

World Resources 1996–97: The Urban Environment (New York: Oxford University Press, 1996). A comprehensive look at global urban problems, sponsored by the United Nations, the World Resources Institute, and the World Bank.

Louis Wirth, "Urbanism as a Way of Life," *American Journal of Sociology* 44 (1938): 1–14. Perhaps the single most influential essay on the nature of urban life.

Notes

1. Ellen Painter and Deborah Lamm Weisel, "Crafting Local Responses to Gang Problems," *Public Management,* July 1997, p. 4.
2. Population Reference Bureau, *World Population Data Sheet, 1997* (Washington, DC: Population Reference Bureau, 1997).
3. Ibid.
4. *Information Please Almanac, Atlas, and Yearbook, 1997* (Boston: Houghton Mifflin, 1997), p. 132.

5. See Claude S. Fischer, *The Urban Experience,* 2nd ed. (New York: Harcourt Brace Jovanovich, 1984).

6. Harvey M. Choldin, *Cities and Suburbs: An Introduction to Urban Sociology* (New York: McGraw-Hill, 1985), pp. 303–304.

7. Georg Simmel, "The Metropolis and Mental Life," in Kurt Wolf, ed. and trans., *The Sociology of Georg Simmel* (New York: Free Press, 1950). This article was originally published in 1903.

8. Louis Wirth, "Urbanism as a Way of Life," *American Journal of Sociology* 44 (1938): 1–14.

9. Herbert J. Gans, "Urbanism and Suburbanism: Ways of Life," in Arnold M. Rose, ed., *Human Behavior and Social Processes: An Interactionist Approach* (Boston: Houghton Mifflin, 1962), pp. 625–648.

10. Ivan Light, *Cities in World Perspective* (New York: Macmillan, 1983), pp. 214–215; Fischer, *The Urban Experience,* p. 209.

11. Choldin, *Cities and Suburbs,* pp. 363–367.

12. Karen De Witt, "Wave of Suburban Growth Is Being Fed by Minorities," *New York Times,* August 15, 1994, pp. A1, A12.

13. John R. Logan and Harvey L. Molotch, *Urban Fortunes: The Political Economy of Place* (Berkeley: University of California Press, 1987), p. 194.

14. Ibid., p. 198.

15. Drik Johnson, "Influx of Newcomer Part of a Rural Upturn," *New York Times,* September 23, 1996, pp. A1, A10.

16. Choldin, *Cities and Suburbs,* pp. 303–304.

17. Joe Feagin, *The Free Enterprise City* (New Brunswick, NJ: Rutgers University Press, 1988).

18. Logan and Molotch, *Urban Fortunes.*

19. U.S. Bureau of the Census, *Statistical Abstract, 1997,* p. 661; U.S. Bureau of the Census, *Statistical Abstract, 1993,* p. 655.

20. Lawrence Mishel, Jared Bernstein, and John Schmitt, *The State of Working America, 1996–97* (Armonk, NY: Sharpe, 1997), p. 307.

21. James E. Rosenbaum and Susan J. Popkin, "Employment and Earnings of Low-Income Blacks Who Move to Middle-Class Suburbs," in Christopher Jencks and Paul E. Peterson, eds., *The Urban Underclass* (Washington, DC: Brookings Institution, 1991), pp. 342–356.

22. See Mark Gottdiener, *The New Urban Sociology* (New York: McGraw-Hill, 1994), pp. 227–247.

23. See Logan and Molotch, *Urban Fortunes,* pp. 195–199.

24. Theodore Caplow, *American Social Trends* (San Diego: Harcourt Brace Jovanovich, 1991), p. 134.

25. Marta Elliott and Lauren J. Krivo, "Structural Determinants of Homelessness in the United States," *Social Problems* 38 (February 1991): 113–131.

26. Sam Fulwood III and Stanley Meisler, "Poor Feeling the Pinch as Low-Rent Housing Shrinks," *Los Angeles Times,* July 16, 1990, pp. A1, A16–A17.

27. Choldin, *Cities and Suburbs,* pp. 333–334.

28. U.S. Bureau of the Census, *Statistical Abstract, 1997,* p. 101.

29. Sam Walker, "Heavy Traffic Strains Roads and Manners in America," *Christian Science Monitor,* April 25, 1994, pp. 11–13.

30. Ibid.

31. U.S. Bureau of the Census, *Statistical Abstract, 1993,* p. 476.

32. Bradford Curie Snell, "American Ground Transport," in Jerome H. Skolnick and Elliott Currie, eds., *Crisis in American Institutions,* 8th ed. (New York: HarperCollins, 1991), pp. 327–341; Light, *Cities in World Perspective,* pp. 210–211.

33. Logan and Molotch, *Urban Fortunes,* pp. 124–126.

34. Calculated by Richard A. Shaffer from data in Choldin, *Cities and Suburbs,* pp. 247–249.

35. Choldin, *Cities and Suburbs,* p. 246.

36. Logan and Molotch, *Urban Fortunes,* p. 194.

37. Douglas S. Massey and Nancy A. Denton, "Suburbanization and Segregation in U.S. Metropolitan Areas," *American Journal of Sociology* 94 (November 1988): 592–626.

38. J. John Palen, *The Urban World,* 4th ed. (New York: McGraw-Hill, 1992), p. 371.

39. Ibid., p. 368.

40. *Information Please Almanac, Atlas, and Yearbook, 1997* (Boston: Houghton Mifflin, 1997), p. 132.

41. *The World Almanac and Book of Facts, 1997* (Mahwah, NY: World Almanac, 1996), p. 838.

42. Palen, *The Urban World,* pp. 369–370.

43. Ibid., p. 382.

44. Choldin, *Cities and Suburbs,* p. 485.

45. Kenneth K. Wong and Paul E. Peterson, "Urban Response to Federal Program Flexibility: Politics of Community Development Block Grants," *Urban Affairs Quarterly* 21 (March 1986): 293–309.

46. Logan and Molotch, *Urban Fortunes,* pp. 159–162.

Population

CHAPTER 15

What is the cause of the population explosion?

How does runaway population growth affect our way of life?

What kinds of problems does migration create?

Can food production keep up with population growth?

How can population growth be controlled?

Amanda Blanco is a slim, dark-eyed woman in her early forties. She lives behind her husband's tiny store in El Naranjo, Guatemala. On the clapboard wall of her home hang several pictures of the youngest of her nine children, Edwin, who died from diarrhea when he was just 4 months old. When asked whether she will have any more children, she simply says, "If God wishes." It's been almost three years since Edwin was born, and after a moment she asks: "I would be pregnant again by this time, right, if I were going to be pregnant at all?" Having so many children, she says, "may have hurt my health, and I think that is why I am always tired." But when asked about which birth control methods are available in her town, she only giggles and says, "My husband won't allow it. He thinks it will make me go with other men."[1]

population explosion
The rapid increase in the human population of the world.

The attitudes expressed by Amanda Blanco are typical of many poor people around the world, and they are still shared by some people in the middle and upper classes as well. The number of men, women, and children on this planet is now over 5.8 billion—twice as many as there were only a few decades ago. If the current rate of growth continues, the world's population will double again in less than fifty years.[2]

Many scientists wonder how long the earth can support such growth. To understand the problems caused by this **population explosion,** it is helpful to look at the history of world population in units of 1 billion people. It took all of human history until 1800 for the world's population to reach 1 billion, but the next unit of 1 billion was added in only 130 years (1800–1930), the unit after that in 30 years (1930–1960), and the next in 15 years (1960–1975). The last billion people were added in only 12 years (1975–1987).[3] (See Figure 15.1.) If this trend continues, the world will soon be adding 1 billion people every year and eventually every month. Obviously we will not be able to sustain such enormous population growth indefinitely. Experts now expect the world's population to stabilize sometime in the next two centuries, but estimates vary widely as to when that will be and at what size. The crucial task facing the human race is to ensure that the population explosion is curbed by a rational program of population control and not by massive famines or devastating wars.

The long-range forecasts are ominous, but the population crisis is not a thing of the future. It is here now. Next year the world must house, clothe, and feed about 90 million more people. To make matters worse, the 250,000 who will be added in the next 24 hours will not be evenly distributed throughout the world.[4] Most will be born in the underdeveloped nations of Africa, Latin America, and Asia—countries that are too poor to provide for the populations they already have (see Figure 15.2).

Although these nations may seem alike to Western eyes, there are important differences in their population problems. The most immediate crisis is in the overcrowded nations of Asia (including Bangladesh, India, Pakistan, Indonesia, and China), which already contain over half the world's people. The current growth rate (excluding immigration) in Asia is 1.6 percent per year, much higher than the rates of the industrialized nations of Europe (−0.1 percent) and North America (0.6 percent), but generally lower than those of poor nations in other parts of the world. Although current population densities are lower in Africa and Latin America than in Asia, their growth rates are higher: 2.6 percent in Africa and 1.8 percent in Latin

Figure 15.1

Population

In the last three centuries, the world's population has been growing faster than at any other time in human history. There are now almost 6 billion people on this planet.

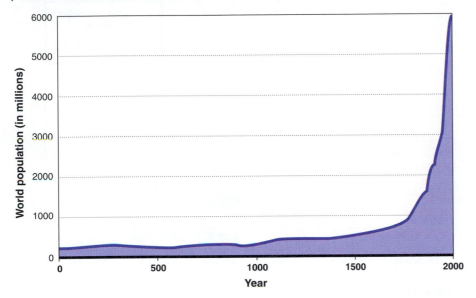

Source: Population Reference Bureau, *World Population Data Sheet, 1997* (Washington, DC: Population Reference Bureau, 1997).

America.[5] These continent-wide generalizations cover up many important differences among nations. The Philippines, for example, has a growth rate of 2.3 percent a year, which is much higher than the average in Asia as a whole. At that rate, its population of 62 million will double in only 30 years. In 60 years, if its growth rate does not go down, the Philippines will have a population as large as the United States today, but with less than one-thirtieth the land area.[6]

Quick Review

What is the population explosion?

Why the Explosive Growth?

If the population explosion is to be brought under control, it must be understood. That task falls largely to the scientific discipline known as **demography,** which studies the causes and effects of changes in human population. Demographers must be mathematicians as well, for they study such things as the rates of births and deaths, the flow of migration, and the age and sex distribution of a population.

demography
The scientific discipline that studies human population.

Figure 15.2

Growth

The population of the poor countries is growing much faster than the population of the rich ones.

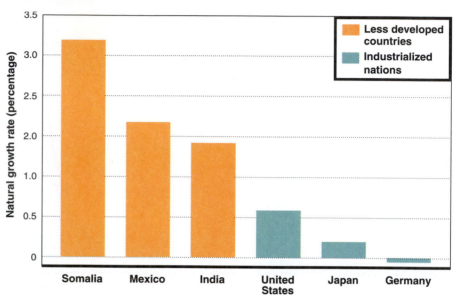

Source: Population Reference Bureau, *World Population Data Sheet, 1997* (Washington, DC: Population Reference Bureau, 1997).

Growth Rates

migration
The movement of people from one geographic area to another.

birthrate
The number of babies born in a year divided by the total population.

death rate
The number of people who die in a year divided by the total population.

growth rate
The birthrate minus the death rate.

A nation's rate of population growth is obviously affected by the number of people who move into or out of the country. The world's population is not affected by **migration,** however: it is determined by **birthrates** and **death rates** alone. The birthrate is the number of babies born in a year divided by the total population. The death rate is the number of people who die. For convenience, the figures refer to 1,000 members of the population rather than to the total. For example, in 1996 the population of the United States was about 264 million. In that year there were 3,921,000 births and 2,329,000 deaths. Dividing by the size of the total population, we get a birthrate of 14.9 per 1,000 and a death rate of 8.8 per 1,000. The **growth rate** is determined by subtracting the death rate from the birthrate and then adjusting the figures to account for migration. Thus, for every 1,000 Americans in 1996, there were 6 more births than deaths; immigration added another 3 people, making the total growth rate approximately 9 per 1,000, or 0.9 percent.[7]

However, these are only crude rates. They are called "crude" by demographers because they do not take the sex and age composition of the population into account. National populations usually consist roughly of half men and half women (although there are some important exceptions, as we will see), but age composition varies from time to time. Therefore, the age composition of a population must be examined to determine whether its growth rate is unusually high or low. The percentage of the population below age 15 is much higher in poor countries (36 percent) than in industrialized ones (21 percent). Because the girls in this age group are normally too young to have children, the crude birthrate actually underestimates the differences in fertility between women in the rich and poor countries. To measure this more accurately, demographers calculate the **total fertility rate,** which is an estimate of the number of children a woman is likely to have in her lifetime. The average woman in an industrialized country is now projected to have about 1.6 children, whereas a woman in a poor country can be expected to have 3.4 children.[8] The **replacement rate**—the number of children each woman must have to keep the population from growing or shrinking—is between 2.1 and 2.5, depending on the death rate. Therefore, if the total fertility rate does not change, the population in the industrialized countries could be expected to decline slowly, while the population of the poor countries continues its rapid growth. Migration from the poor countries is likely to keep the population of most industrialized nations from actually shrinking, however.

Many people believe that increasing birthrates are the cause of the population explosion, but overall birthrates have actually declined. The real cause is the decrease in death rates resulting from the rise in the average life span. Throughout most of human history, average life expectancy seldom exceeded 30 years. Under such conditions, a woman must have four children for two to survive to adulthood and have children of their own. That is just about how many children women in the less developed countries are having today (if we exclude China from those calculations), but the life expectancy in these countries is now about 61 years, and the result is an exploding population.[9]

The origins of the population crisis are thus to be found in the remarkable decline in death rates that began in western Europe in the second half of the eighteenth century and later spread throughout most of the world. In the early years of the population explosion, the European nations led the world in population growth. However, birthrates began decreasing in most of the industrialized nations in the latter part of the nineteenth century, reducing their rates of population growth. In the poor agricultural nations, birthrates did not begin to decrease until much more recently, and they have not gone down nearly as rapidly as death rates in those countries. As a result, the patterns of world population growth have been reversed, and the poor nations are now growing much faster than the rich ones. In 1997, the growth rate in the less developed countries (excluding migration) was more than 18 times higher than in the industrialized nations.[10]

The Demographic Transition

Explaining these trends in world population has been one of the central tasks of modern demography. The most popular explanation is known as the theory of **demographic transition,** which attempts to put these changes in a long-term historical perspective. According to this theory, there are three distinct stages of population growth. In the first stage, which is characteristic of all traditional societies, both birthrates and death rates are high and population growth is moderate. In the second stage, the process of industrialization begins, and technological improvements bring a sharp decline in death rates. However, birthrates decline more slowly, and there is a population explosion. Finally, in the last stage, birthrates drop far enough to balance death rates, and population stabilizes.

total fertility rate
The average number of children a woman is likely to have in her lifetime.

replacement rate
The average number of children each woman must have to keep the population from growing or shrinking.

demographic transition
The changes in the birthrates and death rates that occur during the process of industrialization.

Why does industrialization bring down death rates? For one thing, industrial technology increases the food supply, thereby reducing the number of deaths from starvation. Industrialization also prolongs life by giving people safer water and better diets, clothing, housing, and sanitation. Insecticides prevent epidemics spread by insects and thus increase life spans even more. As we noted in Chapter 6, improvements in medical technology also contribute to declining death rates. Vaccinations have brought numerous contagious diseases under control, and the discovery of antibiotics produced a cure for such killers as syphilis and pneumonia.

Although it takes longer, the economic changes industrialization creates eventually bring down birthrates as well. Children in agricultural societies make an important contribution to farm labor and usually support their parents when they grow old. In contrast, children in industrial societies are economic liabilities rather than assets. They make little economic contribution to the family, and they consume considerably more resources than their counterparts in agricultural societies. Thus, the economic rewards no longer go to those with big families, but to those with small families. Changes in traditional gender roles are another factor in the lowering of birthrates. In industrial societies women have a far wider range of economic opportunities, and bearing and rearing children is no longer seen as their main social responsibility.

More efficient methods of birth control, such as the contraceptive pill and the IUD (intrauterine device), and improvements in abortion and sterilization techniques have also helped bring down birthrates. Although modern technology has made it easier for couples to have the number of children they want and no more, we should not overestimate its impact. As Charles F. Westoff has pointed out, some of

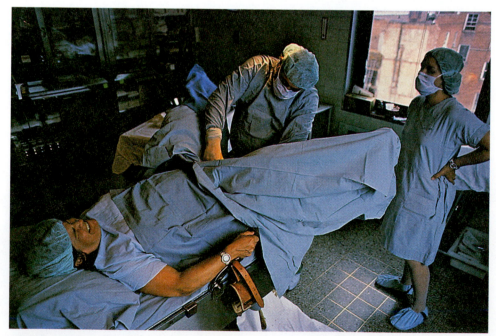

On the average, women in industrialized nations have only about half as many children as those in Third World nations, but infant mortality is much lower in industrialized countries.

the lowest birthrates in many European countries occurred during the Great Depression of the 1930s, before the invention of the pill and the IUD, and before the legalization of abortion.[11] Thus, it appears that social change was a more important factor in bringing down birthrates than the mere availability of contraceptive technology.

The theory of demographic transition has clear implications for the future of world population. According to the theory, the less developed countries with rapidly growing populations are in the second phase of the demographic transition. Once these countries become industrialized, their birthrates will come down and their population problems will be over. Critics point out, however, that this theory was based on population changes that occurred during the industrialization of the Western countries and that the situation in the less developed countries is quite different than the theory implies. There is little doubt that industrialization was the direct cause of the decrease in the birthrates and death rates in the Western nations (and in Japan as well). The decline of death rates in the less developed countries has not been caused by industrialization but by the spread of foreign technology and know-how. Since the population explosion in the Third World started before the process of industrialization, it will probably take much longer for industrialization to progress far enough to bring the birthrates and death rates back into balance naturally (if indeed that ever happens).[12]

Quick Review

How do demographers calculate a nation's growth rate?

Explain the theory of the demographic transition and what its critics say about it.

The Impact of Population Growth

As we have seen, environmental limitations will make it impossible for the human population to keep growing at its present pace forever. The question is not whether the growth rate will decrease but, rather, how it will decrease. There are only two possibilities: either birthrates will drop or death rates will rise.

One of the first people to recognize the dangers of unrestricted population growth was an English minister, Thomas Malthus. His famous *Essay on the Principle of Population* raised a storm of controversy when it was published in 1798.[13] Malthus argued that the human population naturally increases much more rapidly than its food supply. Food supplies increase arithmetically (1, 2, 3, 4, 5, etc.), but uncontrolled populations increase geometrically (1, 2, 4, 8, 16, etc.). This doubling effect occurs because two parents can produce four children; each of the four children can marry and produce four more children; and so on. Eventually, Malthus said, a population that keeps doubling in this way is doomed to outrun its food supply. He believed that only death-dealing disasters—famine, pestilence, and war—kept the human population within its environmental limits.

This gloomy theory was not popular in Malthus's time, when most Europeans believed in the inevitability of progress and saw a bright future for the human race. Although Malthus clearly underestimated the world's capacity to produce food for its people, many demographers fear that he will be proved right in the long run. Today's farming techniques require much more energy than before, and as the world's supply of fossil fuel is used up, food production may fall short of the need.

The Less Developed Countries

Runaway population growth contributes to a host of Third World problems, from mass poverty to environmental degradation; but none of these is more overwhelming than the lack of food. Of course, famines were a common event long before the population explosion. Modern technology has enabled the industrialized nations with slow growth rates to banish this ancient scourge, but millions still starve in the overpopulated nations of the Third World.

Since the end of World War II, the world's food supplies have grown faster than its population. Between 1950 and 1985, new technology helped world food production increase faster than it ever had before. Despite record population growth, the amount of food produced per person increased by almost 30 percent.[14] Since then, however, the increases have slowed down, and food production has fallen behind population growth.[15] Nonetheless, the overall increases since 1950 made some significant improvements possible in the diet of the world's people. Although per capita food consumption went up in the less developed countries as a whole, most of the increase occurred in the industrialized nations that were already well fed, and there are significant regional differences within the Third World as well. Since 1980, the Asian nations have made great improvements and Latin America has made more modest gains, but per capita food production has actually dropped 3 percent in sub-Saharan Africa.[16]

Rapid population growth contributes to hunger and overcrowding in the Third World.

Even though most people are able to get enough food to survive, 10 to 25 percent of the world's population suffers from chronic hunger or malnutrition.[17] A poor diet during the childhood years delays physical maturity, produces dwarfism, impairs brain development, and reduces intelligence, even if the children affected later receive an adequate diet. The undernourished adult is apathetic, listless, and unable to work as long or as hard as the well-fed adult. Diseases caused directly by dietary deficiency, such as beriberi, rickets, and marasmus, are common in poor nations. Malnutrition also lowers resistance to disease, so the undernourished are likely to have a number of other health problems. The danger of epidemics is always high in overpopulated and underfed areas.[18] Moreover, research shows that the damage of malnutrition is passed on from one generation to the next. Babies born to malnourished mothers are weaker and in poorer health than the babies of well-fed mothers.[19]

The lack of adequate nutrition is, unfortunately, only one of a host of problems explosive population growth creates for less developed countries. One of the most difficult is the pressure it places on traditional village life-styles. The tiny plots of family land typical of the Third World can support only a limited number of people. Many young men and women are forced to migrate to the cities, adding to the flood of unskilled and uneducated immigrants that is creating a crushing burden on the urban centers of the less developed countries. A substantial percentage of people in the major cities of the poor nations already live in slums or in shantytowns built by squatters on land they do not own. These homes often lack running water, sewers, and electricity, and the rapid urbanization projected for the next decade can only make matters worse (see Chapter 14 for more details).

Poverty is another problem intensified by the population explosion. Because the population of the poor nations is growing so much faster than the population of the rich ones, the percentage of the world's people who live in poverty is increasing every year. Moreover, rapid population growth in the less developed countries makes it far more difficult to improve the living conditions of the average person. More people inevitably mean more congestion, more crowding, and more damage to the environment. At the present rate of population growth, the economies of most poor nations must grow around 2 percent a year just to keep their standard of living from falling.

Societies with rapid growth rates also have a disproportionate number of children in their population. In many less developed countries, there are so many children that working-age adults make up a bare majority of the total population. For example, Africa is growing much faster than North America, and as a result only 53 percent of all Africans are in their most productive years (15 to 64), compared with 65 percent of all North Americans.[20] Because a smaller percentage of working-age adults actually have jobs in Africa, each African worker must support almost twice as many people as each North American worker. These problems, moreover, are just the beginning: as today's children grow up, they must find jobs, and about 45 percent of the workers in the less developed countries are already unemployed or underemployed.[21]

The Industrialized Nations

Population growth creates similar problems for agricultural and industrialized nations. The difference is in scale. The growth rates of industrialized countries are lower, but some nations still face serious problems. At the present time the total population of Europe is actually declining, but if you include the effects of immigration, the United States is expected to double its population in just 75 years.[22] That means that if the current growth rate were to continue, two centuries from now the United States would have almost 2 billion people. Most demographers expect these growth rates to decrease, but until a stable population is achieved, population growth will continue to have profound effects on the quality of life in industrialized countries.

Although the industrialized nations clearly have enough money to provide food, shelter, and clothing for an expanding population, many fear that those nations will not actually do so. One of the main stumbling blocks is that birthrates are highest among the poorest people, who are not only the least able to support their children but also the least able to win more help from the government. The other principal source of population growth—immigration from the underdeveloped countries—also tends to swell the ranks of the poor. The current pattern of population growth in the industrial nations therefore aggravates the problem of poverty and increases the level of social inequality. The kinds of antipoverty programs discussed in Chapter 7 could go a long way toward resolving these conditions, but it remains to be seen if the political will can be found to carry out such projects.

Another important issue concerns the serious shortages of energy and essential raw materials expected in the near future. This question will be discussed in Chapter 16. Here we merely note that the growing population of industrialized nations is

The population of the industrialized nations is rapidly aging, and many economists are concerned about how society will shoulder the burden of their care.

a major contributor to the problem. One American baby will use more resources in its lifetime than thirty Asian babies. Thus, even the relatively slow population growth of the industrialized nations places great burdens on the environment and on available natural resources. If the population of the industrialized nations continues to grow and demand for consumer goods is not curtailed, there may be no energy or raw materials left for some poor nations when they try to industrialize.

The effects of population growth on the overall quality of life in the industrialized nations are more difficult to measure. No dollar value can be placed on the loss of a beautiful lake or forest; yet the cost of disrupting nature so that more humans may live in comfort is certainly very high, and it is a cost that must be borne by all the generations to come. When the habitats of birds, mammals, and reptiles are destroyed and they are driven to extinction, we are all poorer. Destruction of this kind is nothing new, but population growth has greatly accelerated the process. Scientists estimate that 500,000 to 1 million species will soon face extinction at the hands of the ever growing numbers of humans on this planet.[23] As the population of the industrialized nations increases, there are other effects as well—the cities grow larger, the traffic gets worse, and the amount of noise, air pollution, and toxic waste inevitably increases.

Quick Review

Why did the future look so gloomy to Thomas Malthus?

Compare and contrast the effects of population growth on the poor and the rich countries.

Migration

Next to its exploding size, the most significant development in world population is the waves of migration that have affected every country on earth in one way or another. We have already discussed one of the most important of these human tides: the steady flow of people from overpopulated rural villages to the urban slums of the Third World. While such migrants often face enormous hardships, their problems pale in comparison to those of people caught up in the forced migrations that follow the disasters, such as floods, famines, and wars, that so often strike the less developed countries. Such crises can send millions of refugees running for safety. Sometimes they are able to escape to a neighboring country, but more often they are turned back at the borders and must find a new place to live in their own nation. Most of these desperate people end up in refugee camps that are crowded, dirty, and dangerous. All the basic necessities—food, water, sanitation, shelter—are likely to be in short supply, and deaths from malnutrition, epidemic disease, and violence are common. The United Nations estimates that there are now about 18 million refugees in foreign lands throughout the world and another 24 million people who have been displaced within their own nations.[24]

Leaving the Third World

A second tide of human population runs from the Third World to the industrialized nations. About 9 million immigrants were granted permanent residence in the

*Many of the world's growing number of refugees end up in camps such as the one
shown in this photo.*

United States from 1982 to 1992, and there were believed to be anywhere from 3 to
10 million more illegal immigrants. Western Europe accepted around 15 million immigrants in a similar period of time.[25] Although not all these migrants were from the
poor nations, the vast majority were. Given the desperate poverty and rapidly growing population in so many countries, most experts expect the current tide of immigration to grow even stronger in the years ahead. (For an account of the problems
faced by one refugee, see the Personal Perspectives box, "A Political Refugee.")

The millions of immigrants who come to the industrialized nations every year
face a host of daunting problems, starting with all the psychological ramifications of
leaving friends, family, and native country. Some try the legal route—filling out applications and going through lengthy waiting periods in hopes that they will ultimately be given permission to come. But most people have little chance of success
unless they have a lot of money, special skills, or close relatives in an industrialized
nation. For most people who want to immigrate, the only realistic option is to come
illegally. Sometimes they hire what Latin Americans call a "coyote"—a professional
who smuggles them into a country like the United States for a big fee. Other immigrants buy forged papers, stow away on a boat, climb a fence, swim a river, or do
anything else they can think of to get across on their own. However it is done, an il-

Personal Perspectives   A Political Refugee

There is a constant flow of world population from the less developed countries to the wealthier and more politically stable nations. This story comes from a woman who fled from political persecution in Afghanistan.

I left Afghanistan in 1979, after the Russian invasion. My main reason for leaving was not because of the economic opportunities in the United States, but that Afghanistan had become unsafe for me. I was from a wealthy family and my boss warned me that the communists had my name on a list and I would be arrested. I wasn't able to take any of my things . . . nothing. I just had to go to the airport and get on the first plane I could.

I became an American citizen in 1989, and that was one of the saddest days of my life. I felt as if I had betrayed my country and my past. I did feel like I was losing part of my identity. My passport meant something to me, part of my personal life, and when I was asked to give it up, it was giving a part of my life away.

My children don't mention it, but they do suffer to live in a family where a mother has a very thick accent. For example, I used to make them sandwiches, so-called Afghan sandwiches, and when the other kids would smell the hamburger and spices I used, they would say, "Yuk." My children said, "Mama, we want peanut butter, just to be like everybody else." They feel threatened, they do feel powerless, and they do want to be accepted by the dominant culture. During the Gulf War my son was so upset because someone called him a "camel jockey."

Sometimes I think America gives the illusion that it is everybody's land and is a land of immigrants. There seems to be much more negativism toward immigrants in the nineties than there was before. When I lived in Europe they made it very clear you were not wanted, whereas in America the kind of discrimination you confront is very covert—they say there is no discrimination, but in fact there is discrimination.

legal border crossing is a dangerous affair, and illegal immigrants are the targets of both government officials and a host of unscrupulous criminals.

If Third World migrants have relatives or close friends in their new country, their immediate adjustment is likely to be easier. But most immigrants face daunting problems. They have to find a job, learn a new language, and adjust to a whole new culture. While their new country may be far richer than their old one, they are likely to find that it is also a dangerous and extremely competitive place. If they came illegally, the new migrants must live with the constant danger of being caught and deported, and they are likely to find that without official documents, all but the most marginal jobs are closed to them. To make matters worse, both legal and illegal immigrants are often the targets of racism, cultural prejudice, and bitter resentment from members of the native population who feel threatened by the new arrivals.

Although tearing up their roots and moving to a foreign land is usually a traumatic affair for the immigrants themselves, this migration has two beneficial effects for the less developed countries. First, the flow of immigrants (who tend to be young males) acts as a pressure valve to help reduce their huge problems of overpopulation and unemployment. Second, these immigrants send more than $20 billion a year to their relatives back home. For many countries—Turkey, India, and Morocco, for example—those remittances total more than all the foreign aid they receive.[26] On the other hand, however, many poor nations are experiencing a "brain drain" because of this migration—that is, they are losing many of their best-trained and most highly skilled people because they cannot compete with the wages paid in the industrialized nations.

The Impact on the Industrialized Nations

The impact of immigration from the Third World on the industrialized nations is an emotional and hotly debated issue. In the past, immigrants provided a valuable pool of cheap labor for the industrialized nations; but as automation has made unskilled jobs increasingly scarce, public opinion in the industrialized nations has turned against immigration. Nonetheless, the new immigrants are probably an economic asset overall. Some bring desperately needed talents and special skills, and as a whole immigrants tend to be more ambitious and harder working than most other people. They do the jobs nobody else wants to do for less money than anyone else would be willing to do them for. Another benefit is demographic. As we saw in Chapter 9, the native population of all the industrialized nations is rapidly aging. Most immigrants, on the other hand, are young people in their prime earning years, and as time goes by they are likely to be an essential link in the support network for the growing number of retirees.

The benefits derived from immigrant labor are not, however, evenly distributed throughout society, and some segments tend to gain while others lose. The biggest winners are, of course, businesspeople and corporate stockholders, who benefit from the productivity and low cost of immigrant labor. The biggest losers are the low-skilled workers who are competing with the new immigrants for jobs. Not only do immigrants take some jobs away from native-born citizens, but they may also hold down the overall wages paid for low-skilled work. Among the losers are the big cities where most of the immigrants end up living. In the United States, for example, new immigrants tend to gravitate to Los Angeles, New York, Miami, and Chicago, and those cities and their surrounding communities shoulder a disproportionate share of the costs of the social needs of immigrant populations, such as health care, education, and police services.

Quick Review

What are the different patterns of migration we see in today's world?

What problems do immigrants from the poor countries face?

Describe the different impact immigration has on the rich and the poor countries.

Solving the Population Problem

Some observers argue that there is no population crisis at all and that dire warnings about the future are just the cries of a few alarmists. However, most demographers, politicians, and informed citizens have come to agree that the world indeed faces a grave population emergency. Perhaps the best proof of this new global consensus was the recent United Nations Population Conference, which produced an aggressive plan to limit world population growth. The plan was approved by 180 nations.

Developing this kind of awareness is itself a response to the problem. It is the first step toward an effective solution. The next two steps before us are clear: we need to work to feed the hungry people already on the planet, and we need to take stronger action to reduce population growth.

Feeding the Hungry

Scientists in laboratories around the world are working hard to invent new methods for growing more food. The greatest single advance in recent decades was the creation of new strains of wheat and rice that yield much more food per acre. A **green revolution** occurred in places where these "miracle" seeds were planted. This new technique has been one of the main reasons that world food production has kept ahead of population growth in the last fifty years.[27] The green revolution is not a cure-all for the problem of world hunger, however. The new strains of wheat and rice require more fertilizer, insecticides, and irrigation if they are to produce higher yields, and many poor farmers simply cannot afford such things. Moreover, all three depend on petroleum, which was in short supply several times in the last two decades. Research also shows that increasing inputs of water, fertilizer, and pesticides produce diminishing returns: in the first few years, the new crops produce dramatically improved yields, but as time goes on, productivity levels off. Finally, the green revolution has encouraged the trend toward larger farms, and that has often had devastating effects on peasants who have been forced off their traditional lands. While the average yields from wheat crops have more than doubled since the early 1970s and rice yields have increased by 160 percent, the yield from crops like millet, sorghum, and cassava, which are most often grown by poor people on marginal land, have barely increased.[28]

Despite the problems with the green revolution, some experts believe that the new techniques of biological engineering, which allow scientists to manipulate the genetic structure of plant and animals, offer the best hope of keeping food production up with the population explosion. Critics of this technology take a very different view, however. They fear that releasing a host of new synthetic organisms into the environment runs an enormous risk of disrupting existing ecosystems and causing a drop instead of an increase in world food production.[29]

The American way of improving agricultural production relies heavily on mechanization, but this approach is not appropriate for most poor countries with severe population problems. Few of the world's farmers can afford even the least expensive tractors. When the price of such machines is subsidized by the government or some other agency, they still cannot be operated economically on the small plots of land owned by most peasant farmers. It is sometimes suggested that small farms be consolidated so they can be worked with such laborsaving equipment, but even if a program of this sort were politically feasible, it would create a staggering unemployment problem. It is, moreover, hard to imagine anything that makes less sense for Third World countries with runaway population growth than spending their precious reserves on laborsaving machinery. Furthermore, a greater dependence on sophisticated mechanized equipment will only exhaust the planet's supply of petroleum that much faster and make the poor nations that much more dependent on the rich ones.

The late English economist E. F. Schumacher advocated an ingenious compromise. He proposed that poor nations use **intermediate technology:** machines that are less sophisticated than the gas-guzzling marvels of the industrialized nations but

green revolution
The increase in agricultural production created by the use of new strains of wheat and rice.

intermediate technology
Technology that is less complicated and less expensive than that typically used in the industrialized nations but more efficient than animal power and other traditional technologies.

more effective than the traditional reliance on human and animal power.[30] What the world needs, Schumacher said, is simple machines that can be manufactured in poor nations at low cost and are suitable for small-scale farming. Schumacher himself helped design a small gasoline-powered plowing machine that is more efficient than a horse or an ox but much less costly than a tractor.

Another way to get farmers to grow more food is to reorganize the agricultural economy. One program that has proved effective is **land reform:** taking land away from rich landlords and redistributing it among the peasants who actually do the work. Land reform programs in Mexico and Taiwan have shown that people work harder and produce more when they own their own land and receive the benefits of their own labor. A different version of this approach has also proved effective in the communist and formerly communist nations. Agricultural production is far higher when farmers are allowed to sell their own crops and keep the profits; the communist-style collective farms provided few incentives for individual farmers to increase production.

A serious problem in some poor nations, especially in Africa, is that their governments intentionally hold down the price of agricultural products to keep the cost of food for urban workers low. While that is a worthwhile objective, the result is that farmers often lose money on their crops and production decreases. A better approach is to encourage farm prices to rise and subsidize the food budgets of the urban poor by taxing the local elite.

Some propose feeding the world's hungry by merely cultivating more land, but almost all the good land is already in use. The remainder would require large amounts of oil and other energy to produce even low yields. Some arid soil could be put into production with new irrigation projects, and perhaps new hydroelectric power would come as a bonus. However, such projects are extremely expensive, and unless carefully thought out, they often do more harm than good. The proposal that tropical jungles be cleared for farming is even less realistic. Jungle land is not farmland. Brazil's attempts to farm the Amazon valley have shown that rain forest land has few plant nutrients and that tropical rains quickly wash away artificial fertilizers.[31]

As open land ran out, humanity turned to the sea. Fish and other seafoods now make up almost one-fourth of all the animal protein consumed by humans.[32] Like agricultural production, the world's catch of fish increased rapidly after World War II. It more than quadrupled between 1950 and 1989. Since then, however, the world's total catch has leveled off, and because the human population has kept growing, that means there is less fish to eat.[33] The lakes and oceans can support only a limited number of fish, and some species are already near extinction. Nevertheless, experts believe that the total catch of fish could be expanded by concentrating on smaller and less appetizing species of fish and through more careful management and control of the fishing industry. Several Asian countries, including China, South Korea, and Japan, raise fish specifically for human consumption, and "fish farming" is bound to increase as the human population grows. Future efforts to get more food from the sea will, however, have to focus on plants as well as animals. Various forms of edible algae and seaweed are already being harvested in Asia, but if marine plants are to make a major contribution to the human food supply, they too will have to be farmed. Several experimental sea farms are now in operation, but it will be some time before this technology is economically feasible for large-scale use.

Finally, a different way to get more food for the hungry is to waste less. It has been estimated that people in the wealthy nations throw away one pound of food

land reform

The redistribution of land from wealthy landlords to peasant farmers.

for every three that are eaten.[34] Poor nations also waste a great deal of food, but for different reasons: insects and rats eat up food in storage, and slow and inefficient methods of distribution allow more food to rot before it can be eaten. Another way to increase food supplies without increasing food production is to get more people to eat a vegetarian diet. Eight to ten kilograms of grain must be fed to a cow to produce one kilogram of meat, and it is far more efficient, and often more healthful, simply to eat the grain and other vegetable products ourselves.[35]

Controlling Population Growth

Gaining control over the world's explosive population growth is the most urgent task before the human race today. If we fail, we will surely have to face our ancient enemies—famine, pestilence, and war—on a new and unprecedented scale. At present the industrialized nations are much closer than their less developed neighbors to achieving population control. The population of the industrialized nations is growing at about 0.1 percent a year, which is only about one-twentieth the rate for poor nations. The following discussion will therefore focus on the less developed countries; however, the proposals and programs designed for the poor nations can be modified to fit the industrialized nations if the need arises.

Some political leaders see a large population as a national asset and have used government programs to encourage growth. As far back as the thirteenth century, a number of European nations established tax benefits for parents. Hitler's Germany enacted a variety of measures aimed at increasing its population, as have several

Voluntary family planning programs are common all over the world, but such programs have little chance of success unless traditional attitudes about the value of a large family are changed.

communist countries. Romania's communist dictator Nicolae Ceausescu created a program designed to increase his country's population by one-third. He forbade abortion and birth control and created so-called baby police to give monthly tests to female workers to guard against any illegal termination of pregnancy. In late 1990, shortly after Ceausescu's overthrow, there were 200,000 abandoned children in state care in Romania's orphanages.[36] Fortunately, such efforts are the exception, not the rule. The harsh realities of unchecked population growth are forcing most poor nations to adopt population control programs.

Social Change Many political leaders who are interested in controlling population focus their efforts on industrialization, believing that attitudes toward the family and reproduction will change as the economy develops. As we have already shown, industrialization does bring about a demographic transition—a change in birthrates and death rates that ultimately results in slower overall growth. Many leaders insist that the population problem will take care of itself if we wait for this "natural" process to occur in the agricultural nations. Such expectations are, unfortunately, ill-founded. The fact that industrialization has occurred in a few poor countries hardly means that it will occur in all of them. Moreover, even if all the poor nations of the world were somehow to industrialize, the demographic transition could not possibly occur quickly enough to limit the world's population to a manageable size.

Industrialization is not, however, the only economic influence on population control. The key variable may be the maintenance of a minimum standard of living for the poor. As Jon Bennett put it: "High birth rates are primarily related to economic uncertainty. In nearly every country where malnutrition has been reduced and child death rates have decreased, birth rates have also dropped dramatically."[37]

As the United Nations Population Conference of 1994 forcefully pointed out, one of the most effective ways to help stabilize population growth is to improve the status of women. In less developed countries, women often live a very restricted life under the domination and control of their husbands and other relatives. They have few roads to status or social rewards other than bearing and rearing a large family. One of the best ways to reduce this pressure is, as John R. Weeks put it, to change "the sex roles taught to boys and girls, giving equal treatment to the sexes in the educational and occupational spheres. If a woman's adulthood and femininity are expressed in other ways besides childbearing, then the pressures lessen to bear children as a means of forcing social recognition."[38] The power of women's labor can also provide a big boost to industrialization, thus making an indirect contribution to lower birthrates as well. Equal opportunities and equal status for women are revolutionary ideas in many Third World countries (see Chapter 17), but the success of that revolution would go a long way toward solving the problems of poverty and overpopulation.

family planning
A program that seeks to control population by helping families to have only the number of children they desire.

Birth Control Most population control programs try to encourage people to use birth control and limit the size of their families voluntarily. The assumption is that the birthrate will drop if couples have only the number of children they desire. To help achieve that goal, information and birth control devices are usually given to the poor without charge. Such programs are called **family planning,** but the real objective is to cut the birthrate. Some countries support their family planning programs with publicity stressing the desirability of small families and the dangers of overpopulation. In India, for example, the symbol of population control—a red triangle with the smiling faces of two parents and two children—can be seen in every village.

Such programs help reduce the number of unwanted children, but by themselves they are unlikely to achieve the kind of reduction in birthrates that the world needs to stabilize its population at a manageable size. For one thing, many family planning programs in the less developed countries have been poorly organized and underfunded. There is a more basic problem, however. Publicity campaigns and speeches simply cannot change deeply rooted attitudes favoring large families. The most successful family planning programs have therefore been in countries such as South Korea and Taiwan, which have also been undergoing rapid industrialization.

The traditional attitude in most cultures is that having more children means a stronger family. In the past, big families have been essential to the prosperity of the peasants, and often to their very survival. The belief in the value of having many children is often reinforced by religious and political doctrines as well. Of all the world's major religions, Roman Catholicism is the most strongly opposed to birth control. In 1968, Pope Paul VI reaffirmed church doctrine by ruling that all forms of artificial contraception block the normal "transmission of life" in marriages and thereby violate the "creative intention of God." According to Catholic doctrine, only two methods of birth control are permitted: total abstinence from sexual relations or periodic abstinence during a woman's most fertile period (that is, the rhythm method). However, both methods have proved unreliable since they demand a higher level of self-control than most people appear to possess.

The weaknesses in family planning programs have led some nations to provide additional incentives for parents to limit the size of their families: bonuses for couples with few children and penalties for those with many children. Some countries have even proposed mandatory restrictions, which require all families to limit the number of children they have. (See the Debate "Are Mandatory Limits on Family Size Needed to Control the Population Explosion?")

Of all the large Third World nations, the People's Republic of China has made the greatest progress in reducing its birthrate (see the Signs of Hope box in this chapter). China's powerful central government has put intense pressure on its people to abstain from premarital sex, to delay marriage and childbearing, and to use birth control and abortion. China also has a strong incentive program designed to encourage each family to have no more than one child. Couples who agree to this limit are given a "single-child certificate," which entitles them to such benefits as priority in housing, better wages, a special pension, and preference in school admissions. Couples who have too many children are often fined and required to pay for all the maternity, medical, and educational costs their children may incur. As a result of this program, China's birthrate has shown a significant decline. Although an increase in the number of women in their prime childbearing years (due to a "baby boom" in the 1960s) has kept up the total number of babies born each year, China's current growth rate is only about 1 percent a year—an extremely low figure for a poor agricultural nation.[39] It is clear that China is now firmly committed to an all-out effort to stabilize the size of its population. Not only is that good news for the future of China, it is good news for the entire world, for one of every five people now lives in China.

These gains have not been made without considerable social cost, however. The government pressure for population control in China's highly centralized society has been so intense that the one-child limitation has become virtually mandatory for some Chinese. This policy has placed a particularly great strain on rural villagers. Chinese peasants have traditionally put a high value on having sons, who live with the extended family throughout their lives. Daughters, on the other hand, are expected to move in with their husbands' families and are therefore considered more of a burden than an asset. The Chinese have always taken better care of male than female children, and the new population limitation measures seem to have encouraged more female infanticide and selective abortion as well. The result has been a growing gender imbalance in the population: today, there are nearly three men for every two women in China. Although this tendency poses some obvious problems for unmarried Chinese men, some experts believe that the growing scarcity of women will help improve their status in Chinese society.[40] There is little doubt that this imbalance in the sex ratio will also help to further slow the growth of the Chinese population, since demographers have found that it is the number of women that determines the overall birthrate, not the number of men. (This is because one man can father a very large number of children, but a woman is more limited in the number of children she can bear).

Quick Review

Describe and critically evaluate the proposals to feed the world's hungry.

Critically evaluate the different approaches to controlling population growth.

Sociological Perspectives on Population

Only a few centuries ago, the main population problem was not how to reduce population growth but how to encourage it. Plagues and disasters sometimes brought sharp declines in population, and at times people must have thought the very survival of humanity to be in doubt. As we have seen, improvements in technology and changes in social organization sent death rates plummeting and created a new problem: overpopulation. Most people were slow to recognize this fundamental change and continued in their old ways. Social scientists, including sociologists, were the first to recognize these new realities and to urge government leaders to take action. Although there is now a specialized discipline devoted to the study of population, a great many demographers are trained as sociologists as well, and the major sociological perspectives provide important insights into the population problem.

The Functionalist Perspective

Functionalists argue that population growth can perform several important functions: because greater size often means greater strength, a large population offers more security during natural disasters and a stronger defense against foreign aggressors. Many economists believe that economic growth is essential to the prosperity of an industrial society and that an increasing population promotes economic growth by providing labor and creating new markets for consumer goods.

Debate Are Mandatory Limits on Family Size Needed to Control the Population Explosion?

Family planning programs are now common around the world, and several nations also offer various incentives to encourage families to have fewer children. Some people feel such efforts do not go far enough, however, and they call on the governments of the poor, overpopulated nations to set strict legal limits on the number of children a family is allowed to have.

Yes

The population explosion is the greatest problem facing humanity today. If forceful and effective action is not taken to reduce growth rates, it soon will be too late to head off international disaster. Near-starvation diets are already common in some countries, and unchecked population growth will lead to massive international famine, disrupting the political and economic balance of the entire planet. Battles among the hungry nations for control of scarce food reserves would be likely, and it is doubtful that the industrialized world could avoid the spreading conflict. Because some of the poorest nations already have nuclear weapons and others are developing the capacity to build them, it is conceivable that the population explosion could lead to a nuclear holocaust.

In the face of such dreadful prospects, it is clear that population growth must be controlled. Mandatory limits on family size are repugnant, but there may be no other choice. Most voluntary programs have failed, and unless a new approach is found, strict limits may be the only solution to this menacing problem. Legal restrictions on family size would violate some of our traditional rights, but it is far better to give up a little freedom than to face the international disaster that otherwise seems certain.

No

The world's population problem is not as serious as the alarmists claim. Many overpopulated nations are already reducing their growth rates. The claim that population growth will result in international disaster is wild speculation without scientific support. It would be foolish to invoke measures as drastic as mandatory population controls because of such fears. The world's food supply has always kept up with population growth, and it will continue to do so.

Limits on the number of children that people can legally conceive violate the basic human freedoms. How could we send a person to prison for becoming a parent? Government has neither the right nor the wisdom to tell us how many children we may have. Trampling on individual rights may occasionally solve a problem, but democratic solutions are best in the long run.

If overpopulation became as serious as the doomsayers predict, parents would limit the size of their families voluntarily. Indeed, voluntary programs are already proving effective in a number of nations. Mandatory controls are therefore an unnecessary violation of our basic rights and should never be used by any nation, no matter what population problems they think they have.

Signs of Hope   A Successful Birth Control Program

Because of its enormous size and importance, China certainly provides one of the world's most striking examples of a successful population control program, but it has used some extremely harsh tactics to attain its goals. Although not quite as successful as its huge neighbor, Indonesia has had considerable success with a much less coercive approach. When Indonesia's population control program was first launched in the 1960s, it focused its efforts on a publicity campaign to make the people, and the country's conservative religious leaders, more aware of the problem of overpopulation and the advantages of smaller families. Then the effort shifted to making contraceptives available to everyone who wanted them, while still being careful to respect the conservative sexual attitudes of most Indonesians. (Condoms, for example, are not commonly used by married couples because many Indonesians associate them with prostitution.) The government now also offers some positive inducements for the long-term use of contraception, including valuable agricultural products, subsidies for government employees, and even free trips to Mecca—the holiest site of the Islamic religion. As a result of such efforts, and some rapid economic growth, Indonesia's birthrate has declined by about 45 percent in the last 20 years. Although its population has not yet stabilized, its current annual growth rate is around 1.7 percent— significantly lower than that of most other countries with a similar level of development.*

*Charles P. Wallace, *"Popular Population Control,"* Los Angeles Times, September 7, 1993, pp. A1, A14; Population Reference Bureau, *World Population Data Sheet, 1997* (Washington, DC: Population Reference Bureau, 1997).

Population growth may also be dysfunctional, however. Although all the services an expanding population requires—such as the construction of more houses, the cultivation of more land, and the manufacture of more clothing—may stimulate the economy, these activities may also produce serious environmental damage and a shortage of natural resources. Moreover, young adults face intense competition for jobs, and unemployment fosters alienation and even despair. Overcrowding contributes to urban decay, the spread of disease, and a general decline in the standard of living.

When the world's population was low and there was no shortage of natural resources, the functions of population growth far outweighed its dysfunctions. Now the same social forces that promoted population growth in the past, when it was desirable, produce hunger, poverty, and social instability. For this reason, functionalists say, the population problem will be solved only when dysfunctional attitudes, values, and institutions that promote excessive birthrates are changed. Given time, the social system will reach a new balance. The critical question is whether this balance will come about as a result of famine, wars, or other disasters or because of well-organized programs to change traditional attitudes toward childbearing.

The Conflict Perspective

The conflict perspective sees the population crisis in the Third World as a direct result of European colonialism and the growth of a world economy that is divided between rich industrialized nations and poor agricultural ones. In the nineteenth century, when technological advances were producing a sharp decline in death rates in western Europe, the process of industrialization was creating economic incentives that were eventually to bring the birthrate down as well. Conflict theorists note that these same technological developments also began lowering the death rate in the Third World, but the European nations prevented their colonies from industrializing. As a result, the economic system continued to reward those with large families, and the population of the Third World exploded. Daniel Chirot cites the role of the British in India as a classic example of this process:

> Along with maintaining a colonial class structure, the British also prevented the imposition of protective tariffs which would have helped Indian industry compete against the more advanced British industries. . . . By the time India had escaped from British colonial rule, . . . the country's overpopulation problem was quite severe, and world technology still more advanced and capital intensive than in the early 1900s [thus making it still harder for India to industrialize].[41]

Conflict theory also provides important insights into the forces that oppose population control. Official opposition to contraception and abortion is viewed as a reflection of a conflict between the interests of the masses and those of leaders and ruling elites. Overpopulation is harmful to most people, but an expanding population is an economic and political asset to the ruling class. A large national population means greater international power. Population growth among a society's lower classes also helps the elite by keeping wages down and providing a large pool of labor. Unionization and strikes are less likely when jobs are scarce and there are many unemployed workers waiting to replace those who protest poor working conditions. In the long run, religious groups that prevent their followers from practicing birth control are likely to have more members than those that allow contraception.

Perhaps the most significant contribution of the conflict perspective is its analysis of the causes of malnutrition and hunger. Conflict theorists point out that the current "food shortage" is really a problem of distribution, not production. The world currently produces more than enough food to provide an adequate diet for all people. Starvation and malnutrition result from the unequal distribution of the food that is produced. The rich industrialized countries have less than one-fourth of the world's people, but they consume more than half of its food.[42] Every year millions of people starve to death in the poor countries, while in the wealthy nations many others die from heart conditions caused by overeating. Moreover, the same system of unequal distribution is found within nations. The ruling elite of even the poorest countries eat well while poor people in rich countries such as the United States and Canada are often malnourished.

The obvious solution to this problem is to redistribute the world's food so that everyone is adequately fed, but there are enormous political and economic barriers to such a project. Most of the surplus food is in the wealthy industrialized nations, and most of the hungry are too poor to pay for it. Even in the unlikely event that the wealthy nations could be persuaded to give away a substantial proportion of their surplus food, redistribution might drive many marginal Third World farmers out of business and create even more poverty and deprivation. On a national level, however, the outlook for an effective program of redistribution is brighter. Such countries as Sweden and Norway already guarantee a good diet to their poor by means of welfare programs, and some Third World governments ration food supplies during hard times to ensure that most people get enough to eat.

The Feminist Perspective

Traditionally, most demographers have seen economic and technological causes at the root of the population explosion: technological advances linked to the process of industrialization brought down death rates faster than cultural changes brought down birthrates. In recent years, however, feminists have proved that social restrictions placed on women also play a critical role in the population problem. The cultures with the highest birthrates are those that deny women equal access to education and jobs. When women are restricted to their family roles as mothers and as subordinates of their husbands, their whole social status derives from their ability to bear and raise children. The feminist response to the population crisis is therefore obvious: Give the women of the developing nations more rights and more freedoms. Following the urgings of the feminists, development workers have found that the most successful family planning programs are indeed those that focus on women—not just to provide birth control technology, but to provide the economic assistance and emotional support necessary to help women create a more powerful independent role for themselves. Not surprisingly, such programs have often proved highly controversial in traditional patriarchal cultures. The obstacles have not, however, proved insurmountable, because husbands also benefit from the extra income their wives are able to earn and from overall advantages of family planning.

The Interactionist Perspective

Interactionists see the problem of overpopulation as the result of the way traditional cultures define the world, including their attitudes and beliefs about childrearing and family life. Peasant farmers in traditional societies have a fatalistic attitude toward life. The idea of planning a family, let alone a world population, is alien to them. Fertility continues to be seen as a sign of virility and competence. The "real man" is one who has fathered many sons, and the "real woman" is one who has borne and reared them. Even in the industrialized nations childless couples are sometimes pitied, and the inability to bear children may be reason enough for a husband to divorce his wife.

From the interactionist perspective, it is obvious that such learned attitudes and beliefs must change before birth control measures can be effective. But such attitudinal changes do not occur in a vacuum; rather, they interact with shifting economic, social, and political conditions. Mere propaganda and personal appeals are not enough; they must be accompanied by concrete economic and social improvements. For example, a sound social security plan can do much to convince people that a large family is not necessary for support in their old age. Similarly, like the feminists, many interactionists argue that women who are provided with alternatives to the roles of wife and mother will soon learn that caring for a large family is not the only important activity in life, and their birthrates will drop.

What are the functions and dysfunctions of population growth?

What role does exploitation play in the population problem?

How do feminists say we should respond to the population problem?

How do interactionists explain the causes of the population explosion?

Summary

The world's population is growing at a rapid rate. Demographers agree that the reason for the population explosion is the dramatic reduction in death rates. According to the theory of demographic transition, this process is caused by industrialization. Industrialization raises the average life span by increasing food production and improving public health conditions. In the early stages of industrialization, birthrates remain high and there is a population explosion. Eventually, economic changes make children more of a financial liability than an asset, and birthrates come down. Thus, this theory implies that industrialization will soon lower the birthrates in the less developed countries, where population growth is now the highest. Critics, however, point out that this theory was based on Western societies and does not describe conditions in the less developed countries very accurately.

Thomas Malthus was among the first to point out the dangers of unrestricted population growth. He argued that the human population naturally multiplies much faster than its food supply. So far, Malthus has been wrong because food supplies have kept up with or exceeded population growth, but many demographers feel that there is a limit to the number of people the world can support and that Malthus will eventually be proved right.

The runaway population growth of recent years has caused problems throughout the world. Poor agricultural nations with high growth rates are exhausting their land and other natural resources. Millions of people starve to death every year, and many of the world's people are underfed. Industrialized nations must spend enormous sums to provide for their increasing populations, thus aggravating the world's shortage of essential raw materials and further damaging the environment. Increasing numbers of people in the less developed countries are migrating to cities, where unemployment is high and social integration is low. There are also a growing number of refugees seeking to avoid the social and environmental disasters so common in the Third World, and a growing tide of migration flows from the poor to the rich countries.

There are two general ways to deal with the population explosion: increasing the amount of food and lowering birthrates. Proposals for expanding the world's food supply include enhancing the productivity of agriculture, increasing the sea's food production, and wasting less of the food that we do produce. In order to lower birthrates, the governments of many countries have established family planning programs. Such programs encourage the use of birth control, on the assumption that the birthrate will decline if couples have only the number of children that they desire. Some nations have also introduced incentive programs that give rewards to families with few children and penalize those with many. Another approach is to provide more economic and social opportunities for women so that they will have a real alternative to the role of mother and child rearer.

Sociologists of all theoretical persuasions agree that the population explosion has become a real global crisis. Functionalists note that as death rates have dropped, attitudes encouraging fertility have become dysfunctional. Conflict theorists point out that the food shortage is caused by a distribution system that gives too much food to the wealthy and too little to the poor. Feminists see elimination of restrictions placed on the lives of women as the key to solving the population problem. Interactionists have shown that high birthrates are created by the attitudes and beliefs found in traditional cultures.

Questions for Critical Thinking

Many scientists feel that the population explosion is the most serious problem facing the human race today, but others feel that those who sound such warnings are just alarmists and that we will have no trouble feeding and housing our growing population. After reading this chapter, which side do you think is right? At the current rate of population growth, the world's population will more than double by 2050 from just under 6 billion people to over 12 billion. How different would a world with 12 billion people be from the one we know today?

Key Terms

birthrate
death rate
demographic transition
demography
family planning
green revolution
growth rate

intermediate technology
land reform
migration
population explosion
replacement rate
total fertility rate

Further Readings

Jon Bennett, *The Hunger Machine: The Politics of Food* (Cambridge, MA: Polity Press, 1987). A dramatic account of the way the modern world economy produces hunger in the poor countries.
Leon F. Bouvier, *Peaceful Invasions: Immigration and Changing America* (Lanham, MD: University Press of America, 1992). A comprehensive look at immigration in the United States.
Paul Kennedy, *Preparing for the Twenty-first Century* (New York: Vintage Books, 1993). A comprehensive look at the state of the world, with good coverage of population and food problems.

Thomas Malthus, *An Essay on the Principle of Population* (New York: Oxford University Press, 1993). The classic essay, first published in 1798, that started the modern study of demography.

Charles B. Nam, *Understanding Population Change* (Itasca, IL: Peacock, 1994). A good general text covering population problems.

E. F. Schumacher, *Small Is Beautiful: Economics as if People Mattered* (New York: HarperCollins, 1974). A brilliant critique of the human and environmental irrationality of the current economic system.

Notes

1. Mary Jo McConahay, "Seven Children . . . Four Alive," *Sierra*, November–December 1993, pp. 62–73.
2. Population Reference Bureau, *World Population Data Sheet, 1997* (Washington, DC: Population Reference Bureau, 1997).
3. Population Reference Bureau, *World Population Data Sheet, 1994;* John Balzar, "Doomsayers of Overpopulation Sound a New Jeremiad," *Los Angeles Times,* June 7, 1994, p. A5.
4. Calculated from Population Reference Bureau, *World Population Data Sheet, 1997.*
5. Ibid.
6. Ibid.
7. U.S. Bureau of the Census, *Statistical Abstract of the United States, 1997* (Washington, DC: U.S. Government Printing Office, 1997), p. 9.
8. Population Reference Bureau, *World Population Data Sheet, 1997.*
9. Ibid.; John R. Weeks, *Population: An Introduction to Concepts and Issues,* 3rd ed. (Belmont, CA: Wadsworth, 1986), p. 55.
10. Population Reference Bureau, *World Population Data Sheet, 1997.*
11. Charles F. Westoff, "Populations of the Developed Countries," *Scientific American* 231 (1974): 114.
12. For an analysis of the theory of demographic transition, see Weeks, *Population,* pp. 39–48.
13. Thomas Robert Malthus, *Essay on the Principle of Population* (New York: Oxford University Press, 1993).
14. Calculated from John Bennett, *The Hunger Machine: The Politics of Food* (Cambridge, MA: Polity Press, 1987), p. 32; U.S. Bureau of the Census, *Statistical Abstract, 1993,* p. 867; also see Paul Kennedy, *Preparing for the Twenty-first Century* (New York: Vintage, 1993), pp. 65–70.
15. U.S. Bureau of the Census, *Statistical Abstract, 1997,* p. 849; U.S. Bureau of the Census, *Statistical Abstract, 1993,* p. 867.
16. United Nations Development Programme, *Human Development Report, 1997* (New York: Oxford University Press, 1997), p. 179.
17. David Norse, "A New Strategy for Feeding a Crowded Planet," in Robert M. Jackson, ed., *Global Issues 94/95* (Guilford, CT: Dushkin, 1994), pp. 95–105; Brad Knickerbocker, "Sustainability—Before It's Too Late," *Christian Science Monitor*, February 28, 1994, p. 13; Bennett, *The Hunger Machine,* p. 12.
18. See Tyler Miller, *Living in the Environment,* 5th ed. (Belmont, CA: Wadsworth, 1988), pp. 242–245.
19. See Robert N. Ross, "The Hidden Malice of Malnutrition," in Jackson, ed., *Global Issues 88/89,* pp. 98–101.
20. Population Reference Bureau, *World Population Data Sheet, 1997.*
21. Norman Myers, ed., *GAIA: An Atlas of Planet Management,* rev. ed. (Garden City, NY: Anchor, 1993), pp. 178–181.
22. Population Reference Bureau, *World Population Data Sheet, 1997;* U.S. Bureau of the Census, *Statistical Abstract, 1996,* p. 9.

23. Miller, *Living in the Environment,* pp. 295–296.

24. Robin Wright, "Millions Adrift in Their Own Lands," *Los Angeles Times,* March 8, 1994, pp. H1, H4.

25. Peter Skerry, "Has Immigration Collided with the Welfare State?" *Los Angeles Times,* May 1, 1994, pp. M1, M6; Stanley Meisler, "Migration Viewed as 'Human Crisis,'" *Los Angeles Times,* July 7, 1993, p. A4.

26. United Nations Development Programme, *Human Development Report, 1994* (New York: Oxford University Press, 1994), p. 62.

27. Miller, *Living in the Environment,* p. 247.

28. United Nations, *Human Development Report, 1997,* p. 70; Miller, *Living in the Environment,* pp. 247–249; Bennett, *The Hunger Machine,* pp. 23–27.

29. See Kennedy, *Preparing for the Twenty-first Century,* pp. 65–81.

30. E. F. Schumacher, *Small Is Beautiful: Economics as if People Mattered* (New York: HarperCollins, 1974), pp. 171–190.

31. Weeks, *Population,* pp. 381–383.

32. Miller, *Living in the Environment,* pp. 253–254.

33. Associated Press, "World's Oceans Nearly Fished Out, Institute's Report Warns," *Los Angeles Times,* July 24, 1994, p. A22; Melissa Healy, "Servings at World Table Get Smaller," *Los Angeles Times,* August 19, 1993, p. A5; Lester R. Brown, "Natural Limits," *Los Angeles Times,* July 29, 1993, p. A11.

34. Weeks, *Population,* pp. 385–386.

35. Bennett, *The Hunger Machine,* p. 37.

36. Carol Williams, "The Unwanted Children: Casualties Left by a Tyrant," *Los Angeles Times,* December 10, 1990, pp. A1, A16–A17.

37. Bennett, *The Hunger Machine,* p. 22.

38. Ibid., p. 423.

39. Population Reference Bureau, *World Population Data Sheet, 1997.*

40. See Philip Shenon, "China's Mania for Baby Boys Creates Surplus of Bachelors," *New York Times,* August 16, 1994, pp. A1, A4.

41. Daniel Chirot, *Social Change in the Modern Era* (San Diego: Harcourt Brace Jovanovich, 1986), p. 177.

42. Bennett, *The Hunger Machine,* p. 34.

The Environment

CHAPTER 16

How have we damaged our environment?

Are we running out of natural resources?

What are the causes of the environmental crisis?

How can we clean up the environment and conserve our resources?

The observation platform on the Telecoms Tower in Kuala Lumpur, Malaysia, usually provides a panoramic view of the city, but at the end of 1997 there was little to see except a brownish fog. All of Southeast Asia was in the grip of one of the world's first multinational air pollution crises. Brush and forest fires blanketed over 1 million of acres of land in Borneo and Sumatra and spread a dangerous, choking haze for thousands of miles. The death rate from respiratory illness skyrocketed; people were advised to wear surgical masks when walking outside; and visibility became so bad it is believed to have contributed to the crash of an Airbus jetliner that killed 234 people and to the collision of two huge ships at sea. Although it would be easy to pass off these events as natural disasters beyond human control, it turns out that the fires were intentionally started by wealthy property owners seeking to clear their land for plantations to produce palm oil, paper, and pulp.[1]

For centuries we have seen our environment as a boundless storehouse of wealth. Nature was to be conquered, tamed, and used in any way we saw fit. Until recently only a few people realized how fragile and limited our world really is. Now a seemingly endless series of environmental disasters such as the air pollution crisis in Southeast Asia are forcing this realization on us all. One by one the natural resources we have come to depend on are dwindling away, and as they are used up, their by-products are fouling our land, air, and water, disrupting the delicate web of life on which our very existence depends.

Ecology

Western culture views us as special creatures, separate and apart from our environment. Humans are seen not as animals but as superior beings destined to rule over the planet and its lesser creatures. There is, however, no scientific evidence to support such beliefs. The science of **ecology**—the study of the interrelations among plants, animals, and their environment—shows us that humans are but one part of a complex network of living things. No human could live more than a few seconds if separated from the sheltered terrestrial environment with just the right proportions of water, oxygen, heat, and the other essential components that support human life. Nor could we live more than a few days without the food supplied by the plants and animals of the earth. We cannot even digest our food properly without microorganisms that live inside our bodies.

Life on this planet exists in only a thin surface layer of soil and water and the air immediately surrounding it. This life zone, known as the **biosphere,** is a mere 14 kilometers (9 miles) thick. Within the biosphere there are many **ecosystems:** self-sufficient communities of organisms living in an interdependent relationship with one another and with their environment. Each ecosystem has its own natural balance, both internally and with other self-sufficient ecosystems, and human interference may set off a chain reaction with deadly consequences.

All ecosystems require energy, and virtually all energy comes from the sun. Green plants convert solar energy into food through a process known as **photosynthesis.** In addition, photosynthesis produces the oxygen required for respiration in both plants and animals. Respiration, in turn, produces carbon dioxide, which is

ecology
The study of the interrelationships among plants, animals, and their environment.

biosphere
The life-containing region of the earth extending from about 200 feet below sea level to about 10,000 feet above it.

ecosystem
A self-sufficient community of organisms living in an interdependent relationship with each other and their environment.

photosynthesis
The process by which green plants convert solar energy to food.

used in photosynthesis. Thus, like other aspects of an ecosystem, photosynthesis is part of a cycle that continually reuses the same basic elements. All that is needed from outside is the energy that comes from the sun.

Animals cannot make direct use of the sun's energy for food production; therefore, all our food must ultimately come from plants. The food produced by green plants usually goes through many transformations in what is known as a **food chain** before it decomposes enough for natural recycling. For example, a simple food chain may start with the grass and other green foliage eaten by a deer. The deer is then eaten by a wolf, and when the wolf dies, its decomposed body provides nutrients so that more grass can grow. Of course, most food chains are much more complex than this, involving many intricate relationships between plants and animals.

food chain
The set of transformations beginning with production of food by green plants and ending with decomposition of the bodies of animals.

Quick Review

Briefly define *ecology, biosphere, ecosystem,* and *food chain.*

The Human Impact

Early hunting and gathering people interfered very little with the ecosystems in which they lived. They used only a few simple tools, and muscle power was the main source of energy. As technology became more sophisticated and new sources of energy were tapped, the human impact on the environment grew ever larger. With the invention of agriculture, we attempted to replace the delicate complexity of the natural environment with a narrow range of plants and animals that were best suited to supporting human life. The surplus food produced by agriculture made the development of cities possible, and with the cities came a host of new threats to the earth's ecological balance. Forests were cut down, rivers rechanneled, and tons of human waste dumped into the water and plowed into the soil. Some organisms were exterminated; others multiplied more rapidly than ever before. Humans soon became the single greatest force in changing the ecological balance of the planet. The process did not stop there, however. Industrialization with its countless new machines and technologies once again intensified the human role in shaping the course of environmental change. More forests were leveled, and huge cities were built and connected with a complex web of highways and railroads. Newly developed industries consumed energy and raw materials at an ever increasing rate and in the process poured out an unending stream of **pollution.** Time and again the human impact on the environment has produced unexpected, unpleasant, and even dangerous consequences, and environmental deterioration has become a social problem of major proportions.

pollution
The release of harmful substances into the environment.

Air Pollution

Few of us give a second thought to the invisible and seemingly inexhaustible ocean of air in which we live. But consider the fact that a person can live for weeks without food and for days without water but can survive for only a few minutes without air. We have been able to take our atmosphere for granted because rain and other processes naturally cleanse and renew it, but we are now dumping more pollutants into the air than can be removed by these natural processes. Air pollution is worst in the big cities, but because the ocean of air connects all parts of our planet, pollution has become a menacing global problem. On a local level, the air pollution in the rapidly growing cities of the Third World has grown worse and worse while the air in many cities of the industrialized nations has actually improved. The average level of carbon monoxide in the air in the United States has declined about 14 percent since 1985, and ozone levels have dropped about 12 percent.[2]

The single greatest source of air pollution in North America is transportation. Coal, oil, and natural gas used for heating and for generating electricity are also major contributors. Additional tons of pollutants are spewed into the air by paper mills, steel mills, oil refineries, smelters, and chemical plants. Even trash burning is a substantial cause of air pollution.[3]

The amount and kinds of pollutants in the air vary greatly from one area to another. The most common pollutants are carbon monoxide, hydrocarbons, oxides of sulfur, oxides of nitrogen, ozone, and tiny particles of soot, ashes, and other industrial by-products. The amounts of these pollutants vary in different industrial regions. Thus, areas that depend on oil for power have different pollution problems from those that use coal.

No matter which chemicals are involved, valleys and closed air basins are more likely to have air pollution than plains and mountains, where the air can circulate freely. Air quality can become especially bad when a layer of warmer air moves over a layer of cooler air and seals in pollutants that would ordinarily rise into the upper atmosphere. This condition, known as a **temperature inversion,** is temporary, but while it lasts, it may create an intense bout of air pollution. Local winds also affect the distribution of pollutants, carrying them from one area to another. Finally, climate has an important effect on the kinds of pollutants that are present in different areas. For instance, sunlight acts on oxygen, hydrocarbons, and nitrogen oxides to produce new compounds collectively known as **photochemical smog.**

Air pollution is not merely a minor irritant that burns our eyes and clouds the skies: it is a major health hazard, contributing to many chronic diseases and killing a substantial number of people each year. Air pollution is believed to contribute to the deaths of at least 50,000 Americans every year, and it has been linked to such serious respiratory diseases as bronchitis, emphysema, and lung cancer. It is also a known contributor to several other types of cancer and to heart disease as well.[4] The effects of pollutants on an individual's health are, however, difficult to determine. For one thing, the various chemicals we release into the air combine to produce many entirely new substances. Further, all people living in a particular area are not necessarily exposed to the same amount of pollution. An executive who drives an air-conditioned car from her home to an air-conditioned office is exposed to less air pollution than a traffic officer who breathes smog all day long.

The damaging effects of air pollution are not limited to humans. Although there has been little research in this area, it appears that domesticated animals living in polluted areas suffer as well. It has also been shown that air pollution has harmful effects on trees, shrubs, and flowers. The orange groves of California and the vegetable farms of New Jersey, for instance, both suffer from smog damage.

In many areas, chemicals from coal-burning power plants and other industrial sources combine with water in the atmosphere to produce **acid rain.** Not only do these rains harm plant life and eat away exposed metal surfaces and buildings made of limestone and marble, but they decrease the fertility of some soils and destroy the life in streams and rivers. Acid rain has killed the fish in hundreds of lakes in the United States, Canada, and northern Europe. Many scientists also believe that acid

temperature inversion
A condition in which a layer of warm air moves over a layer of cool air, sealing in pollutants that would otherwise rise into the upper atmosphere.

photochemical smog
A group of noxious compounds produced by the action of sunlight on oxygen, hydrocarbons, and nitrogen oxides.

acid rain
Rain with usually high acidity produced by atmospheric pollution.

Photochemical smog has made the air in many cities unhealthy, while the breakdown of the ozone layer in the upper atmosphere is increasing the risks of contracting skin cancer from exposure to the sun.

rain is one of the major causes of the decline in forest lands in industrialized nations. The control of acid rain poses a difficult international dilemma because pollution created in one country often rains down on another. For example, more than half the air pollution that causes acid rain in Canada comes from the United States.[5]

Air pollution is also creating some disturbing changes in the upper atmosphere and especially in the thin ozone layer that protects us from the harmful ultraviolet rays of the sun. Scientists have known for years that a group of chemicals—the chlorofluorocarbons (CFCs) used in air conditioners, refrigerators, Styrofoam containers, and many other applications—decomposes ozone. Many refused to take the threat to the upper atmosphere seriously, however, until a giant hole in the ozone layer, which opens up a few months every year, was discovered over Antarctica. As scientists began to investigate conditions in the upper atmosphere more closely, they were shocked to discover how rapidly the ozone layer has been thinning over the rest of the world as well. Between 4 and 5 percent of the ozone layer over North America, for example, has apparently been lost just since 1978. In many places, especially in the north, the losses have been even more severe. Canadian scientists have found that the amount of ultraviolet light reaching the ground in Toronto during the winter has been increasing by about 5 percent a year. In the United States, the Environmental Protection Agency now predicts an additional 200,000 deaths from skin cancer over the next 50 years as a result of the increased ultraviolet radiation caused by **ozone depletion.** In addition to causing skin cancer, increased ultraviolet radiation also causes cataracts and other eye problems, suppression of the immune system, harm to animals, and a decrease in crop yields.[6]

ozone depletion
The reduction in the protective layer of ozone in the upper atmosphere.

The first international response to this crisis occurred in Montreal in 1987, when 24 major nations met and agreed to cut their CFC production in half by the turn of the century. As the full scope of the threat became apparent, a larger group of nations met in Copenhagen in 1992 and set up a timetable to eliminate all production of CFCs, added other substances to the list of ozone-destroying chemicals, and set up a fund to help the poorer nations stop their use of CFCs.[7] Although progress has been made in reducing CFC emissions since the Copenhagen meetings, there has also been strong resistance to the effort to protect our ozone layer. It is estimated that between 10,000 and 20,000 tons of CFCs are sold on the black market every year.[8]

Of all the hazards of air pollution, perhaps the greatest potential threat comes from what is known as the **greenhouse effect.** The buildup of gases from the burning of various fuels and other human activities is changing the composition of the atmosphere. These gases are holding in more of the energy that comes to earth from the sun and are thereby raising the air temperature like the greenhouse of an orchid grower. The biggest problem is carbon dioxide, but methane and other gases also play a role. Worldwide, the air we breathe now contains about 25 percent more carbon dioxide than it did just a century ago, and the United States is by far the biggest polluter—contributing 22 percent of the world's total emissions of carbon dioxide (see Figure 16.1).[9]

greenhouse effect
The trapping of heat in the atmosphere by gases produced by human activities.

Although there is a great deal of controversy about the subject, most experts expect the greenhouse effect to raise the average temperature of the earth from 2 to 8 degrees Fahrenheit over the next century. Although that may not seem like much of a difference, the consequences could be devastating. For one thing, the increases will not be spread evenly over the planet: some areas will have much greater increases, while a few places may actually experience cooler weather. More important, the changing temperatures will also change the pattern of rainfall, which could turn some major agricultural areas into a dust bowl. Although some northern areas might see improved crop yield, the overall impact will be a decrease in food production, especially in the poor nations in the southern part of the globe. Moreover, as the temperature rises, the water in the oceans will expand and the polar icecaps will begin to melt. The result will be a higher sea level and the flooding of many low-

Figure 16.1

Greenhouse Gases

The atmospheric gases that produce global warming are expected to increase rapidly in the years ahead.

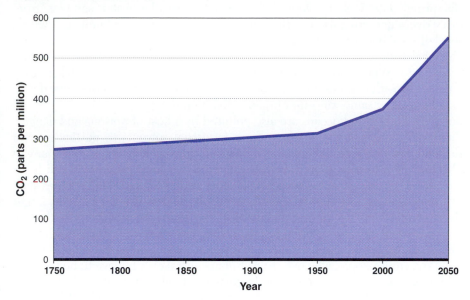

Source: New York Times, December 1, 1997, p. D1.

lying coastal areas. In sharp contrast to the response to ozone depletion, the world community has done little about the dangers of global warming. Although the developed countries said at the Earth Summit in Rio de Janeiro in 1992 that they would reduce their emissions of greenhouse gases, the Berlin Climate Summit, which followed in 1995, ended without any agreement to binding limits on these emissions. The fact is that it is far easier to ban CFCs than to reduce our dependence on petroleum, coal, and the other fossil fuels that create so much of the global warming problem.[10]

Water Pollution

Over two-thirds of the world's surface is covered by water. It is continually evaporating, forming clouds, and raining back to the earth in a cycle that provides a seemingly endless supply of clean water. Perhaps it is blind faith in the enormous reserves of water and the natural purification system that has led people to dump so much garbage into lakes, rivers, and oceans. For a time the earth's water resources could tolerate such an onslaught, but with the population explosion and the increased dumping of industrial wastes, marine animals and plants began to die in large numbers.

Organic wastes are important water pollutants. In small quantities, they are quickly broken down by waterborne bacteria, but if too much organic material is

organic waste
Waste products with a biological origin.

dumped into the water, the bacteria use up all the available oxygen as they decompose the waste. Fish and other complex organisms suffocate, and a barren body of water is left. Human waste is a major contributor to the problem, but so are the wastes from animal feedlots, oil refining, food processing, and textile and paper manufacturing. The U.S. Geological Survey takes regular water samples from America's rivers and streams, and the percentage of samples contaminated with a high level of fecal bacteria increased 13 percent from 1985 to 1995.[11]

Chemical fertilizers have much the same effect as organic wastes and cause similar damage. When rains wash nitrogen fertilizers into rivers and lakes, they stimulate the growth of huge "blooms" of algae. When these blooms die, they decay, using up oxygen the same way other organic pollution does.[12]

Our rivers, lakes, and oceans are also polluted by a host of poisons and dangerous chemicals that include everything from industrial solvents to pesticides. Not only do these substances kill wildlife and threaten our drinking water, but many of them become more concentrated as they move up the food chain. When fish eat plants exposed to toxic substances such as arsenic and mercury and pesticides such as DDT, the pollutants build up in their tissues. When these fish are eaten by larger fish, the toxins become still more concentrated, and so on. Because most of the fish we eat come from the top of the food chain, they are likely to have high levels of contamination. Moreover, no part of the world, however remote, is immune to the problem. The Inuit people, who live in what many mistakenly believe to be the pristine wilderness of northern Canada, eat large amounts of seal meat, fish, and other local game. Their diet exceeds the Canadian government's maximum limit for PCBs (a family of dangerous organic chemicals) 10 to 20 percent of the time, and the milk of Inuit mothers contains five times more PCBs than the milk of mothers who live in southern Canada.[13]

A study by the Environmental Protection Agency concluded that one out of every three American rivers was not in good condition,[14] and the situation in our coastal waters is even worse. About one-fourth of the coastal waters in the continental United States are closed to shellfishing, and the catch of other seafood has plummeted in many areas. Nonetheless, recent studies of chemical pollution in mussels and oysters found a small but steady decline since 1983.[15] Studies indicate that as many as 2 million seabirds and 100,000 marine mammals such as whales, dolphins, and seals die every year when they eat or become entangled in trash dumped into the ocean.[16] There are also periodic oil spill crises, usually caused by the wreck of an oil tanker. The *Exxon Valdez,* for example, dumped 11 million gallons of crude oil when it broke up off the Alaska coast.[17] As dramatic as such events are, at least an equal amount of oil reaches the oceans from land runoff and the intentional dumping of waste oil.[18]

To many people, the most important water is that coming out of the tap in their homes. Drinking water once commonly carried such dread diseases as cholera and typhoid, but modern water treatment has eliminated that risk. Now our drinking water is being threatened in another way: by chemical contamination. Dangerous industrial chemicals are seeping into the water supplies of many towns and cities, and the underground water in many agricultural areas now contains a host of different pesticides. A study released by the Natural Resources Defense Council in 1994 concluded that 20 percent of America's drinking water is not adequately treated for toxic chemicals, bacteria, parasites, and other pollutants and that 14 percent of the

Even the world's great oceans are vulnerable to human pollution. This seabird is covered with oil from a ruptured petroleum tanker.

American population drinks from water systems that have been caught violating federal water standards within the previous three years.[19]

The Deteriorating Land

Third World countries, faced with overpopulation and shortages of food and housing, once looked at the environment as a problem that only the rich can afford to worry about. In recent years, however, many of these poor nations have begun to realize that they are caught in the grip of an even greater environmental crisis than the one their industrialized neighbors face. The world's forests are shrinking at an alarming rate while the desert wastelands grow, and most of these changes are occurring in the less developed countries. More than half the world's tropical rain forests have been cut down just since 1945.[20] Every year, the world loses 17 million hectares of tropical forest—an area about the size of Wisconsin.[21] The problem is particularly severe in the great Amazon rain forest, which is by far the largest of tropical forest remaining in the world today. Although the rate of **deforestation** is lower than it was two decades ago, it has actually increased since the early 1990s.[22] At this rate there will be virtually no tropical forests left in thirty to forty years, and

deforestation
The destruction of the forests.

if the rain forests are destroyed, millions of unique species of plants and animals will die with them.

Desertification—the transformation of productive land into desert—is a slower process. It is estimated that 20 percent of the earth's land surface is threatened by desertification; this threatened land is home to more than 80 million people.[23] Natural forces such as the periodic droughts that have recurred throughout history are an important part of this problem, but a great deal of the damage is being done by human beings. Desertification results from overgrazing by livestock, poor irrigation techniques that poison the soil with salts and alkalis, and desperate attempts to farm land that is not suited for agriculture.[24]

Deforestation is caused almost entirely by humans who log trees to get lumber and fuel and intentionally destroy the forests to make room for the farms and cities demanded by a growing population. Although conditions are worse in the less developed countries, the industrialized nations have serious problems of their own. Reforestation has allowed the industrialized nations to slow down the loss of their temperate forests and in some cases reverse it. An estimated 7 million hectares of land are now planted with trees every year, but that is less than the area that is logged. Moreover, enormous damage has already been done. At one time, more than 80 percent of Europe was covered by forests, but as far back as 1800, only 14 percent of the land in Europe was still forested.[25]

The heavily mechanized techniques used by agribusiness do long-term damage to the soil, and North America is now facing a serious erosion problem. The impact of years of environmentally damaging plowing methods is adding up, and windbreaks, terraces, and antierosion ditches built during the 1930s are being torn out to make it easier to operate today's huge farming machines. The United States is now losing its productive soil seven times faster than natural processes can replace it. The problem is at its worst in the heavily farmed lands of the Midwest. Iowa, for example, is believed to have lost about half its topsoil.[26]

Another heavy burden on our beleaguered land is the huge quantity of solid waste produced by industry (see Figure 16.2). Each year the United States generates about 1 ton of trash and garbage for every man, woman, and child in the country.[27] Some of this refuse is burned, thus adding to air pollution, but most of it is buried in landfills and dumps. This creates two problems. One is that an increasing number of ravines, gullies, valleys, and sloughs are being covered as the trash mounts up. Another comes from the disposal of plastic and other synthetic materials, which, unlike organic material, never decompose. Americans dump about 100 million tires and 38 billion bottles and jars each year.

As if these problems were not enough, new threats to the land are looming on the horizon. The population explosion demands that more and more land be used for cities and for agriculture, and the shortage of energy and raw materials is leading us to use ever more environmentally destructive methods to obtain them. For instance, there are enormous reserves of coal in North America, and much of the fuel lies close to the surface. This makes it cheaper to extract, but the **strip-mining** technique that is normally used creates severe environmental damage. Strip mines are long, shallow valleys gouged out of the earth. After the coal has been removed, the dislocated earth is dumped back into the hole. Unless the topsoil is carefully replaced (an expensive and time-consuming process), the land will not be fertile again for centuries, if ever.[28] Perhaps the world's worst example of the hazards of strip mining come from the small island of Nauru,

desertification
The transformation of productive land into desert.

strip mining
A mining technique in which long strips of soil are dug up and processed.

Figure 16.2

Garbage

Citizens of the United States produce more trash per person than those of any other country.

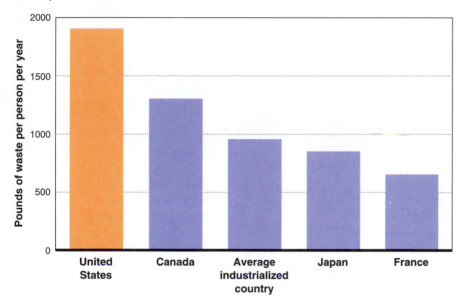

Source: Andrew L. Shapiro, *We're Number One* (New York: Vintage, 1992), p. 151.

which used to be something of a Pacific paradise. After ninety years of strip-mining phosphate deposits, four-fifths of the island is now a barren moonscape of gray limestone pinnacles. Despite a considerable income from the mining industry, conditions on the island have grown so bad that the few remaining residents may have to move away.[29]

The growth of cities poses yet another threat to the ecological balance of our land. Great portions of the landmass of our planet are being covered by expanding cities and suburbs. These vast metropolitan areas are beginning to threaten the existence of the wilderness that harbors so many different species of plants and animals. Many ecosystems have already been destroyed by urban sprawl, and the outlook for the future is not bright. If population growth continues at its present rate, only the most remote mountains and deserts will remain unspoiled.

Chemicals and Radiation

The human race is dosing itself with thousands of chemicals. The air we breathe and practically everything we eat or drink contains synthetic substances. Although many of these chemicals seem harmless enough, the fact is that we know almost nothing about most of their long-term effects. Recent history is full of examples of supposedly harmless food additives, drugs, and industrial wastes that were found to be serious health hazards. Only about 10 percent of the 70,000 chemicals in commercial use have been adequately tested, and about 1,000 new chemicals are introduced into the marketplace every year.[30]

The safe disposal of toxic wastes is a daunting problem. Estimates are that the United States alone produces 128 to 509 million tons of toxic wastes a year.[31] Although everyone agrees that the United States is the largest producer of toxic waste, the improper disposal of toxic wastes is a worldwide problem that is probably at its worst in what were once the communist nations. Industrialized nations usually see a small yearly increase in the life expectancy of their population, but in Russia life expectancy has plummeted in recent years, and the blame is often placed on pervasive chemical and radiation pollution. In 1990, the life expectancy for Russian men was about 64 years, but today it is only 58 years.[32]

The United States has exerted far more effort to deal with its toxic waste problems, but by and large its response has been inadequate. In 1980, Congress created a billion-dollar "superfund" to help clean up dangerous waste dumps. Though tens of thousands of sites are in need of immediate action, only a handful have been cleaned up. Even worse is the fact that over *three-fourths* of the superfund money has been spent on legal fees and administrative costs.[33] Critics have charged, moreover, that what little work was done was not done well. The EPA's approach to cleaning up most unsafe dumps is simply to move the dangerous chemicals to a different dump, which in some cases is no safer than the original site. The government has repeatedly been accused of dragging its feet on toxic-waste cleanups and, more generally, of supporting the interests of industrial polluters instead of the interests of the American public.

Even more frightening than toxic waste is radiation pollution, probably because we know so little about it. Small doses of radiation have no immediate effects. Moderate doses cause vomiting, fatigue, loss of appetite, and diarrhea. Death is practically certain for people exposed to high doses. However, no one knows much about the long-term effects of low and moderate doses of radiation. Studies of the survivors of the nuclear bombings of Hiroshima and Nagasaki show a high incidence of leukemia and other cancers, but it is not known exactly how much exposure is needed to produce cancer. There is ample proof that radiation causes genetic mutations, but again there is little information about how dangerous specific doses of radiation actually are.

The ultimate environmental disaster—nuclear war—will be discussed in Chapter 18. But there is also growing alarm about the dangers of radiation from other sources, such as nuclear power plants and the factories that produce nuclear weapons. At present, such sources contribute little to the overall levels of radiation in the world, but environmentalists fear that nuclear pollution will increase as the world's nuclear plants continue to age. One major concern is the danger of a nuclear accident. There is little chance of a reactor erupting in a nuclear explosion, but if the cooling system of such a plant should fail, the tremendous heat of the nuclear reaction would melt the concrete and steel surrounding it, thus releasing enough radiation to wipe out an entire city. Nuclear power plants have elaborate safeguards against such **meltdowns,** and advocates of nuclear power argue that the probability of such an accident occurring is very low. The 1979 accident at the Three Mile Island reactor in Pennsylvania and the 1986 disaster at the Chernobyl reactor in the former Soviet Union have, however, convinced many people that serious accidents are far more likely than the public has been led to believe. Although the official

meltdown
An accident in which the cooling system of a nuclear power plant fails, allowing the heat of the nuclear reaction to melt the reactor's core, thus releasing large amounts of radiation.

death toll from the Chernobyl accident was originally only 32 people, it is now clear that figure was part of a sweeping effort by the government to cover up the real extent of the damage. In 1995, the health minister of Ukraine estimated that 125,000 people had died from the radiation released by the Chernobyl reactor, and the long-term effects of the massive radiation exposure are not expected to peak for another decade. The rate of leukemia in Kiev, the nearest large city, is four times higher than normal, and the overall death rate in northern Ukraine near the reactor has increased 16 percent. Moreover, the economic losses have been staggering—an estimated $358 billion—because of expenses such as the permanent relocation of 200,000 people (leaving another 4 million people still living on contaminated ground) and the destruction of 20 percent of the farmland of the republic of Byelorussia. It would be no exaggeration to say that the Chernobyl disaster was the worst accident of the twentieth century.[34]

Even in the unlikely event that no other major accidents ever occur, the radioactive wastes generated by nuclear plants are deadly pollutants, and we have no effective way to handle them. The main problem is that these wastes remain dangerous for so long that scientists cannot agree on a safe disposal technique. For example, the EPA requires that spent fuel rods from nuclear plants be stored safely for 10,000 years—a staggering amount of time. The United States itself is only a little over two hundred years old. Currently almost 50,000 of these old fuel rods are stored temporarily at U.S. nuclear plants because the federal government has yet to open a permanent disposal site. Even the temporary storage of nuclear wastes has proved to be inadequate: hundreds of thousands of gallons of highly radioactive liquids have already leaked out of U.S. nuclear weapons plants, and it is becoming clear that the cloak of national security has been used to cover up horrible safety conditions that would never have been allowed at civilian facilities. Moreover, old nuclear power plants, whether civilian or military, are also a radiation hazard. Whatever techniques are ultimately developed to decommission such plants, the process is bound to be slow and costly, perhaps running as much as $1 to $3 billion for each plant.[35]

Another serious hazard in the use of nuclear energy is crime. Security is tight in most nuclear power plants, but this is a chaotic and uncertain world. The more this energy source is used, the more shipments of radioactive materials there will be, and the easier it will be for a terrorist group to steal them. Although it is difficult to turn low-grade nuclear fuels into atomic bombs, there is still great danger. The explosion of a conventional bomb placed next to some radioactive materials could spread a deadly radioactive cloud big enough to poison a large area. Moreover, some civilian nuclear plants use weapons-grade nuclear materials. **Breeder reactors** that turn uranium 235, into plutonium pose an especially serious problem. Unlike other nuclear fuels, the plutonium produced by breeder reactors can be made into bombs. Moreover, the chance that terrorists and the nations that support them might seize some plutonium and hold entire cities for ransom is growing greater every year. In 1994, German police arrested a Russian smuggler with over 300 grams of plutonium in his baggage; it turned out to be a sample from 4 kilograms of plutonium that were being offered for sale for $250 million.[36] After analyzing the sample, Western experts concluded that its source was probably Russia's civilian, not its military, nuclear program.[37] It is estimated that Russia has 170 tons of military and civilian plutonium and 1000 tons of highly enriched uranium that could be used in nuclear weapons.[38]

breeder reactor
A type of nuclear reactor that produces plutonium, a fuel that can be used in nuclear weapons.

Biological Diversity

One of the most serious consequences of our assault on the air, water, and land of this planet has been a sharp reduction in **biodiversity**—the number of plant and animal species living together in the ecosystems of the world. Although no one knows exactly how many species of plants and animals there are on earth or how many species humans have driven to extinction, it is clear that the pace of extinction has been increasing at an alarming rate. Just twenty years ago, in the mid-1970s, only a few hundred species a year were believed to have become extinct. Today, the number of extinctions is estimated to be between 10,000 and 50,000 a year and increasing rapidly. During the twentieth century, humans have killed off some 1 million species of plants and animals.[39]

The biggest threat to our wildlife is the loss of their habitat as we cut down trees, plow up the land, and put up buildings, dams, and highways. Two-thirds of the original wildlife habitat in tropical Africa has been destroyed or severely degraded, and the picture is much the same in the rest the world. One-third of the forests in the United States have been destroyed, as have half of the wetlands and most of the tall-grass prairies.[40] Commercial hunting and fishing have had a devastating impact on the populations of the most sought-after species, and, of course, the pollution problems we have just examined often have an even greater impact on wildlife than on our own species.

As disturbing as the statistics are, some people argue that the extinction of plant and animal species is a natural part of the process of evolution and that extinctions are nothing we need to worry about. It is true that the history of life on earth shows several other periods like our own in which a huge number of species met their end, but such arguments overlook the tremendous benefits biological diversity brings us. For example, a study by David Tilman and John Downing found that diverse ecosystems with many different kinds of plants and animals recovered from natural stress (such as severe drought) much more quickly than simpler ecosystems.[41] Scientists are also coming to look at the many diverse species that currently live on this planet as a kind of storehouse of potentially useful biological material. Today, most of the world's food comes from domesticated versions of plants originally found in the tropics, and about half of all medicinal drugs have active ingredients extracted from wild plants.[42] The destruction of the rich biodiversity of the tropical rain forests might also destroy species that could provide the next "green revolution" in food production (see Chapter 15) or the cure for countless dread diseases. Beyond all this, there is an intangible benefit derived from the rich parade of life on our planet. It might not hurt our food production or medical skills if there were no more elephants or sperm whales, but the world would surely be a poorer place for it.

biodiversity
The number of plant and animal species living together in an ecosystem or on the planet as a whole.

Quick Review

What causes smog?

What are the causes and consequences of ozone depletion?

What is the greenhouse effect, and what effects is it likely to have?

What are the major sources of water pollution?

How are we harming our land?

What are deforestation and desertification?

How effective have we been at disposing of our toxic wastes?

Evaluate the environmental consequences of using nuclear reactors to generate electricity.

Why has the world's biodiversity been declining so rapidly?

Dwindling Resources

Photographs of the earth taken from space have done much to further the cause of conservation. One look at a picture of that tiny blue-green globe hanging in the vast emptiness of space shows us how limited our world and its resources really are. Through most of human history, we have been acting as though the world were a rich mine to be exploited. We are just beginning to realize that there are only limited amounts of oil, coal, and uranium. When the supply is used up, there will be no more.

The United States, with less than 5 percent of the world's people, uses 25 percent of all the energy consumed each year.[43] All the industrialized nations combined hold only 25 percent of the world's people, but they use 80 to 90 percent of its resources. There is a growing feeling in less developed countries that the industrialized countries are using up the world's resources so rapidly that there will soon be nothing left. There is much talk about industrializing the poor nations so that they can stabilize their population growth and bring their standard of living up to those of the more fortunate nations. With current technology, however, the world's supply of oil and minerals cannot possibly support all the world's people in the style to which those in the wealthy nations have become accustomed.

Our world contains only a limited amount of the resources on which our lives depend.

Energy

Modern industrial society would be impossible without massive supplies of energy. If enough energy is available, most raw materials—iron, copper, aluminum—can be recycled; but most of our energy currently comes from sources that are not renewable: once the supply is used up, it is gone forever. The fossil fuels (oil, coal, and natural gas) are nonrenewable: they took millions of years to form from organic materials deposited in the earth and cannot be replaced. Fortunately, we also have many sources of **renewable** energy: we can grow more wood and organic materials to burn in our fireplaces, and the supply of solar energy constantly renews itself, whether we use it or not.

Worldwide consumption of **nonrenewable** energy has grown at a staggering pace. As recently as the nineteenth century, the vast majority of the world's energy came from renewable sources. Particularly important were human and animal labor and the burning of wood and dung, but the industrialized world's appetite for energy grew so rapidly that it could not be satisfied by these renewable sources. By the beginning of the twentieth century, coal was the world's principal source of energy, and oil was just coming into use. Now the world gets over half its energy from oil and natural gas, about one-fourth comes from coal, and renewable sources provide only about one-fifth.[44] North Americans are particularly heavy users of fossil fuels and consume more total energy than people in other nations (see Figure 16.3).

Until 1973, oil was plentiful and cheap. The price had been steadily declining for years, and few people gave any thought to the possibility that we would ever run out of petroleum. Then, in 1973, the modern world was shaken by its first great energy crisis. War broke out in the Middle East, and the Arab oil producers tried to stop all shipments to nations that they believed to be supporters of their enemy, Israel. At the same time, the oil-producing countries quadrupled the price of oil. Although the oil boycott was soon ended, oil prices continued to rise, and the economic shock set the industrialized world spiraling into a severe recession. Energy consumption in the industrialized world fell the following year but soon started to rise again. A second major petroleum shortage occurred in 1979, after the Iranian revolution disrupted that country's oil production. A "panic" soon followed, causing long lines of frustrated customers at gas pumps around the world. Many people came to see that the energy supplies so essential to the industrialized nations are dependent on a fragile international network of political and economic relations. But as the price of petroleum products has dropped over the following years, that important lesson seems to be fading from memory. After controlling for inflation, the average cost of crude oil is only about 60 percent as high as it was in 1980, and energy conservation has fallen far down on the list of national priorities.[45] For example, for many years the federal laws that required manufacturers to meet increasing fuel efficiency standards for their cars or face financial penalties produced a steady increase in the average miles per gallon new cars would get. But the growing popularity of trucks and huge "sport utility vehicles" (which are covered by weaker standards) means that the average economy of new *vehicles* is now actually declining.[46]

No one knows how much longer the world's supply of oil will last. Experts disagree widely about how much oil remains to be discovered and the rate at which we are likely to consume it. If we continue to use petroleum at the present rate and no new reserves are discovered, the world's usable supply will last only about forty years. Even if we eventually find substantial new reserves—and many experts be-

renewable resource
A resource that is replenished through natural processes.

nonrenewable resource
A resource with a fixed supply that cannot be replenished.

Figure 16.3

Energy
The people of the wealthy nations use far more energy than the people of the poor nations.

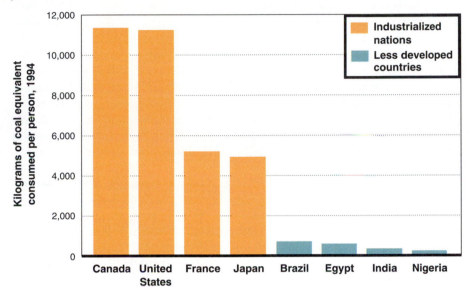

Source: U.S. Bureau of the Census, *Statistical Abstract of the United States, 1996* (Washington, DC: U.S. Government Printing Office, 1996), p. 842.

lieve this to be possible—most of the world's supply of oil will still be exhausted in seventy to eighty years.[47] Moreover, the world's population is now growing at about 1.5 percent a year, and many poor nations are starting to industrialize, so a considerable effort will be needed to keep consumption from increasing and depleting our petroleum reserves even faster.[48] Heavy oils from tar sands and oil shale could provide some additional reserves, but they will be costly and environmentally damaging to develop. No matter what steps we take, however, it is clear that we are quickly approaching the day when there will be no more oil at affordable prices.

The world's reserves of coal are much greater than its reserves of oil and natural gas. Most experts believe that there is enough coal in the ground to meet the world's energy needs for about two hundred years.[49] As with petroleum, however, the actual amount of coal available for human consumption is a matter of economics. The size of the world's usable coal reserves depends on the cost of mining them and the amount of energy we must use to dig them up. Finally, we should remember that coal, like oil, is fossilized organic matter. No matter how much we pay for it, no matter how much energy we use to mine it, and no matter how much land we destroy in the process, someday the supply will be exhausted.

Some people believe that nuclear power plants will be able to supply more of the world's energy as oil and coal are burned up. Nevertheless, it is highly unlikely that nuclear reactors, at least in their present form, can replace the energy now obtained from fossil fuels. For one thing, it takes enormous amounts of energy and labor to build a nuclear power plant, so a substantial portion of the energy produced by the plant merely replaces the energy consumed by its construction. With staggering increases in the cost of building new nuclear plants and doubts about their safety in the wake of the Chernobyl disaster, nuclear power seems to have reached a dead end in the United States. No new plants have been ordered since 1978, and numerous plants have been abandoned in various stages of planning and construction. Nuclear plants have a limited operational life, and many of the nuclear plants now operating in the United States will have to be shut down in the next decade.

For the poorest one-third of the human population, the real energy crisis is the shortage of wood to burn. Over 3 billion people in the world still rely on wood as their primary source of energy for cooking and heating, and more than 1 billion of them do not have access to enough wood to supply their basic energy needs. Moreover, the supply of wood is dwindling every year. For many poor families, it now costs as much to heat their supper bowl as to fill it. About half of all the wood cut every year is used for fuel, and that has been a major contributor to the acute problem of global deforestation.[50]

hydroelectric power
Electric power generated by the movement of water.

There are, fortunately, other sources of renewable energy. **Hydroelectric power,** generated by turbines turned by flowing water, is clean and efficient. New hydroelectric power stations are built every year, but the cost of transporting electricity limits their use. Currently, about 30 percent of North America's electricity bill pays for the production of power; the other 70 percent is for transporting the power from the generators to the consumers. However, breakthroughs in superconductivity may someday allow us to slash these costs by sharply reducing the amount of electricity lost from the wires during transmission. **Geothermal energy**—the heat of the earth's inner core—can be used to generate electricity and steam and is thus a possible substitute for fossil fuels. At present, however, this energy can be harnessed only in places with very special geological conditions. **Solar energy** is just beginning to make a major contribution to our energy supplies. The sun bathes the earth with an enormous amount of energy every day, and if that energy can be used efficiently, a clean substitute for coal, oil, and wood will be at hand.

geothermal energy
Energy derived from the heat of the earth's inner core.

solar energy
The energy supplied by the sun.

Minerals and Raw Materials

Although humans were using the earth's mineral wealth long before they used petroleum, it does not appear that there will be a mineral crisis any time in the near future. Modern industry depends on about 80 basic minerals. About three-fourths of them are either abundant enough to meet all our needs or can be easily replaced. There are about 18 minerals that present more of a challenge. The known reserves of tin, zinc, and lead, for example, will last only twenty to thirty years at the current rate of consumption.[51] Although the known reserves are likely to increase, no one can say by how much. It is clear, however, that as high-grade deposits of these materials are used up, we will be forced to turn to deposits of ever lower quality, which are difficult to collect and refine.

The seas and oceans contain many minerals both in the water and on the bottom. If it were economically feasible to mine these resources, they would greatly boost the world's supplies of raw materials. Currently, it costs more to mine many of these minerals than they are worth, but technological advances are rapidly reducing the cost. As a result, there have been bitter political battles over the control of undersea mineral resources between the less developed countries with extensive coastal territory and the wealthy industrialized nations with the technology required to exploit it.[52]

Unlike energy, most minerals can be recycled. A significant portion of the copper, lead, gold, silver, and aluminum being used today has been recycled at least once. Recycling of most other raw materials is not profitable at present prices. As world stores are emptied, however, prices will rise, and recycling will look better and better because it both conserves mineral resources and saves energy. An added benefit is that recycling can also reduce the production of solid wastes that are now choking our dumps and landfills. One problem, however, is that some industrial metals stay in use so long that only small amounts are available for recycling.

Quick Review

What is the difference between renewable and nonrenewable sources of energy?

What are the world's main sources of energy today? Are any of them in danger of running out?

What are our most promising sources of renewable energy?

Is there a shortage of minerals?

What are the benefits of recycling?

Origins of the Environmental Crisis

Many ecologists and demographers predict that an ecological disaster is on the way, most likely in the form of a devastating famine in the Third World. (See the Debate "Are We Headed for an Environmental Disaster?") Although not everyone is so pessimistic, there is no disagreement about the fact that we have been destroying the very ecosystems that sustain us. Such irrational behavior is not easy to explain. Its complex causes have roots stretching far back into history. Ironically, the same characteristics that have made humans such a successful species—high intelligence and an enormous ability to manipulate the environment—have also contributed to the development of the technology and cultural orientation that are threatening many forms of life on earth.

Exploitative Technology

More and more people are coming to realize that the magnificent technological advances that have made life so much more comfortable have a dark side as well. As we have seen, agricultural technology has brought havoc to the biosphere; industrial technology is polluting the environment; and military technology has for the first time in history given humanity the means to destroy itself. And even if we do not destroy ourselves directly with nuclear bombs, we may do so indirectly by disrupting ecosystems, food chains, and the whole life-supporting system.

Condemning technology as though it were separate from the humans who use it is both pointless and misleading. Every group of humans, from prehistoric times to the present, has used some form of technology to meet its needs for food, clothing, and shelter. Only a few of those technologies, however, have caused serious damage to the environment. The real culprit is **exploitative technology,** designed to produce the greatest immediate rewards without regard to the long-term consequences to the environment or the quality of human life.

exploitative technology
Technology designed to produce immediate rewards without regard to long-term consequences.

Debate   Are We Headed for an Environmental Disaster?

Throughout history we have faced environmental challenges, but the unprecedented size of today's population and the ever growing power of our technology have led some observers to predict an environmental crisis in the years ahead that will have devastating effects around the world.

Yes

Predicting the future is always a risky business, but there are so many signs warning of an environmental crisis that the only question is when, not if, it will occur. Never before in the history of this planet has a single species had such a devastating impact on so many other organisms. Humankind is driving thousands of species of plants and animals into extinction every year. We are replacing complex and diversified ecosystems with simple, artificial systems such as farms and urban neighborhoods; and it is a basic ecological law that the narrower the ecosystem, the more fragile it will be.

There are two main forces driving us toward disaster—overpopulation and pollution. The world is now choking with almost 6 billion people, but at the current rate of growth, there will be over 1 trillion people on earth in just three centuries. Of course, the world can't support that many human beings, and one of two things has to happen. Either we reduce our birthrates or increase our death rates. Despite all the talk and all the birth control programs, we have failed to stop runaway population growth. Without a truly effective program of population control, only devastating plagues and famines can keep population growth in check.

As if the staggering increases in the size of the human population weren't bad enough, the average person is producing more and more pollution every year. Toxic chemicals and radioactive wastes are piling up in hundreds of thousands of sites around the world. Our rivers, lakes, and oceans are becoming toxic cesspools, and the fish they once supported are dying or taking in so many pollutants that they are dangerous to eat. The ozone layer is breaking down, and the smoke from all the fuels we burn is clouding the air, poisoning our bodies, and transforming the weather in unpredictable ways. Year by year, the lush forests are shrinking while the deserts grow. How much more evidence do we need? Unless we voluntarily make a radical transformation in our attitudes and in our way of life, a devastating environmental crisis will soon force us to do it.

This problem is nothing new. Although the earliest foraging peoples did little damage to their environment, the human race has been using exploitative technologies for thousands of years. Historians now believe that an environmental crisis caused by unsound farming techniques contributed to the collapse of many of the agricultural societies of the past; but the overall environmental damage done by industrial societies is far worse. For one thing, their technology is much more powerful and sophisticated, and, for another, they support many more people. Industrialization also brings about a qualitative change in the kind of technology we use.

No

Environmental problems are nothing new. Compared with the overwhelming difficulties our ancestors faced, we are actually far better off. Human history is a record of plagues, droughts, floods, and famines, which were all caused, in one way or another, by environmental forces. Life was precarious, and the slightest environmental disturbance could prove fatal. In contrast, today's environmental concerns are more a matter of aesthetics than survival. Certainly trash dumps are unsightly, and unspoiled woodlands are more attractive than housing tracts, but such eyesores aren't much of a price to pay for our current standard of living.

Of course, some of the damage to the environment does create health hazards, but they are minor compared with the problems of the past. Otherwise, why would the average life span be going up year after year? In fact, the steady increase in human population that worries the environmentalists so much is actually proof that the human race is prospering. If things were really as bad as some scientists claim, the population should be declining, as it did in many other historical eras.

The alarmists who predict some kind of environmental disaster are basing their conclusions on emotion, not logic. They find a problem that is getting worse and then make wild predictions based on the assumption that it will never improve. Actually, most environmental problems are self-limiting. If a particular kind of pollution starts to cause a real threat, that very fact motivates people to do something about it. The more serious an environmental problem becomes, the harder we work to fix it. It is true that we face serious environmental issues today, but our difficulties can and will be resolved. In fact, the amazing technological progress of the last century has given us more power to shape our environment and tackle its problems than ever before. Far from an environmental collapse, the future holds the promise of unprecedented prosperity.

From nuclear radiation to the destruction of the ozone layer in the upper atmosphere, the cornucopia of modern science has produced problems undreamed of by our ancestors.

Unregulated Growth

The average person in the industrialized nations has a higher standard of living and is using more nonrenewable resources than ever before in human history. At the same time, the people of the less developed countries are struggling to feed millions of new mouths every year. The environmental effects of such growth are obvious. The more people there are and the more resources each of them uses, the faster they will pollute the environment and deplete the world's reserves of raw materials.

The damage caused by reckless growth is easily seen, but our traditional belief in economic expansion and progress has blinded many people to the problem. Governments around the world pursue policies concerned more with the quantity of possessions than with the quality of life, and not a single nation officially opposes economic growth. Fifty years ago the same thing could have been said about population growth. In the past quarter century, however, the harsh realities of the population explosion have forced numerous political leaders to change their minds and introduce population control measures. The same realities are now starting to eat away at the cherished belief in the value of economic growth at any cost.

Over the years, numerous scientists have come to accept the idea that the world is headed for an ecological disaster unless we change our attitudes and behavior. As a group they are known as **neo-Malthusians,** after the famous demographer Thomas Robert Malthus (see Chapter 15). Businesspeople and industrialists, as well as average workers, are usually skeptical about such gloomy predictions and reluctant to abandon the ideal of growth that has been profitable for so long. The scientists who hold this perspective are known as **cornucopians,** and they argue that by the time our resources are gone, we will have found new resources and new technologies to keep the economy growing.[53] It is impossible to prove or disprove either set of claims, but it appears extremely unwise to continue using up our resources at the present rate, thus gambling our future on possible technological advances that may never occur.

Culture

Rapid population growth and increasing use of exploitative technologies are the direct causes of the environmental crisis. Underlying them both are culturally based attitudes toward nature and humanity's place in it. As was already noted, one fundamental characteristic of Western culture is the idea that humans are superior to the natural world they inhabit. According to the Book of Genesis, humans were made in the image of God, who told them, "Be fruitful, and multiply, and replenish the earth and subdue it; and have dominion over the fish of the sea, and over the birds of the sky, and over every living thing that moves upon the earth." Western culture tends to see nature as a wilderness to be conquered and subdued by human effort. The art, literature, and folktales of the West repeatedly show people in a heroic struggle against the forces of nature.

The attitudes of most tribal peoples are quite different. In tribal cultures human beings are seen as part of nature. They are expected to live in harmony with their environment, not to subdue or conquer it. Native Americans, Australian aborigines, and many other traditional peoples see all of nature as sacred: the rocks, the trees, the mountains, the animals. To them, the Europeans' assault on the environment is not merely unwise, it is sacrilege: the desecration of a holy place.

The attitude that nature is something to be subdued and exploited has been overlaid with newer beliefs in progress and materialism. The people of many ancient civilizations believed that the past contained some lost utopia, and they looked to the past for guidance in making important decisions. A radically different idea

neo-Malthusian
Someone who believes we are heading for a crisis resulting from overpopulation, resource depletion, and environmental destruction.

cornucopian
Someone who believes that scientific progress will allow continued economic expansion and prosperity despite population growth and the depletion of natural resources.

took hold in seventeenth-century Europe. In this new perspective the golden era lies in the future, when scientific progress will banish poverty, ignorance, disease, and perhaps even death itself. Thus, the faster technological development and economic growth take place, the sooner the new utopia will appear. Such optimism about the future has, however, been hard to sustain in a century that has seen the two most devastating wars in human history, the development and use of nuclear weapons, and the extermination of countless species of plants and animals. Many people, nevertheless, see little choice but to continue down the perilous path of "progress."

Although our faith in progress may be shaken, our materialism seems stronger than ever. Day after day we are bombarded with advertising that tells us that we are what we own: a woman is judged by her clothes and jewelry, a man by the car he drives. A society that sees the road to happiness in wealth and the accumulation of material possessions is hardly likely to value the environment over the economic rewards its destruction may bring.

It is easy to see how these attitudes have led to our current crisis. We have mastered some living things but destroyed others. We have transformed the natural world in our quest for wealth and progress, but we have not conquered it. Sooner or later we will inevitably pay the price for abusing the web of life on which we all depend.

Quick Review

Discuss the causes of our environmental crisis.

What are the differences between the neo-Malthusians and the cornucopians?

Solving Our Environmental Problems

Pollution, energy consumption, and economic growth are interdependent problems. Effective programs for dealing with one of them often aggravate the others. For example, devices that clean automobile exhaust and reduce air pollution also decrease fuel economy, thereby using up our limited oil reserves more rapidly. Exploiting new reserves of fossil fuel worsens environmental pollution as land, animals, and scenery are sacrificed for strip mines and oil wells, and the wastes produced by the fuel pour into the environment. On the other hand, ignoring the need for more energy retards the economy, thereby contributing to unemployment and possibly reducing food production. There is a way out of this trap, however. In a word, it is sacrifice. The fact is that there is no way to clean up the environment and conserve natural resources without changing the life-style of people in the industrialized nations. The challenge is to motivate people to make the necessary changes now, before a worldwide disaster forces much more difficult adjustments upon us. (For the views of three noted environmentalists, see the Personal Perspectives in this chapter.)

Political Action

Despite the growing social activism of the 1960s, the environment can hardly be said to have been a political issue in North America during that decade. More than

Personal Perspectives   Environmentalists Speak Out

In this excerpt from their book *Beyond the Limits,* three well-known environmentalists speak out about what they think needs to be done to create a more environmentally sustainable society.

There are many things to do to bring about a sustainable world. New farming methods have to be worked out. New kinds of businesses have to be started and old ones have to be redesigned to reduce throughputs. Land has to be restored, parks protected, energy systems transformed, international agreements reached. Laws have to be passed, and others repealed. Children have to be taught and so do adults. Films have to be made, music played, books published, people counseled, groups led.

Each person will find his or her own best role in all this doing. We wouldn't presume to prescribe that role for anyone but ourselves. But we would make one suggestion about how to do whatever you do. Do it humbly. Do it not as a declaration of policy but as an experiment. Use your action, whatever it is, to learn.

The depths of human ignorance are much more profound than most humans are willing to admit. Especially at a time when the global society is coming together as a more integrated whole than it has ever been before, when that society is pressing against the dynamic limits of a wondrously complex planet, and when wholly new ways of thinking are called for, no one really knows enough. No leader, no matter how authoritative he or she pretends to be, understands the situation. No policy can be declared as The Policy to be imposed on the world.

Learning means the willingness to go slow, to try things out, and to collect information about the effects of actions, including the crucial but not always welcome information that an action or policy is not working. One can't learn without making mistakes, telling the truth about them, and moving on. Learning means exploring a new path with vigor and courage, being open to other peoples' explorations of other paths, and being willing to switch paths if new evidence suggests that another one leads more efficiently or directly to the goal.*

*Donella H. Meadows, Dennis L. Meadows, and Jorgen Randers, *Beyond the Limits: Global Collapse or a Sustainable Future* (Post Mills, VT: Chelsea Green, 1992), p. 231.

anything else, it was the observance of Earth Day on April 22, 1970, that first brought the environmental crisis to public attention. As a result of the unprecedented media attention this event received, membership in environmental organizations skyrocketed. The pressure from these groups and the publicity created by a seemingly endless string of environmental disasters helped win the passage of new legislation aimed at protecting North America's air, land, and water. As the environmentalists organized themselves and became a more effective political force, however, so did their opposition. From the smallest decisions over local land use to overriding global concerns about the greenhouse effect and the depletion of the ozone layer, environmentalists face powerful foes that reap huge profits from their environmentally destructive activities. Those profits in turn provide the opponents of environmental protection with enormous financial resources to make campaign contributions, hire lobbyists, fund scientific research, purchase advertising, and pay for hundreds of other things that the defenders of the environment simply cannot afford. Moreover, environmentally destructive patterns of behavior are already deeply ingrained in modern society and will require a great effort to change.

There are, however, grounds for optimism in the fact that the world's people are becoming increasingly aware of the current crisis and the ways in which their prosperity and even their survival depend on the protection of our environment. As American pollster Louis Harris put it: "Poll after poll has come up with similar results. Whenever the public is asked about environmental issues, the returns point almost always nearly unanimously in one direction: deep worry, and concern about the ecological state of the country."[54] This same environmental concern has also been growing in the other industrialized countries and even in the less developed countries. A poll by the Gallup International Institute found that the majority of people in 16 of the 22 nations studied (including such poor countries as Mexico, Brazil, and India) said they would be willing to pay higher prices for what they buy in order to protect the environment.[55]

If we are to preserve the natural environment for ourselves and the generations to come, two important steps must be taken. First, a stronger effort must be made to educate people about our current crisis and to spread environmental awareness. Second, people from around the world must join more closely together and get involved in the political and social actions necessary to bring about meaningful change.

Conserving Resources

There is no doubt that our existing resources can be used far more efficiently. Just as the necessities of life are used by one organism after another in various ecological cycles, so human society could reuse many of its essential raw materials over and over (see Figure 16.4). To take a simple example, garbage could be used as fuel to

Figure 16.4

Who Recycles Most?

The United States is not one of the leaders in the movement to recycle our waste.

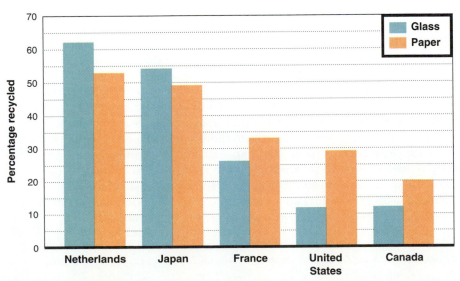

Source: Andrew L. Shapiro, *We're Number One* (New York: Vintage, 1992), p. 153.

run mills to make recycled paper, and mill wastes could also be burned as fuel. Similarly, it is possible that community water districts will someday become closed systems, meaning that the water would be used again and again, never being discharged into an ocean or river. Some factories already have such closed systems. It is possible to envision larger closed systems designed so that no industrial material would ever be discarded as either waste or pollution.

Energy conservation can also stretch our natural resources. North Americans waste so much energy that significant amounts of oil, gas, and coal could be saved without lowering our standard of living. Sweden, for example, has a higher standard of living than Canada but only uses about half as much energy per person.[56] Insulating homes; driving smaller cars at slower speeds; using more trains, buses, and bicycles; recycling the heat used in factories; and restricting the manufacture of energy-wasting gadgets are obvious ways of eliminating waste. Although some advances will require developing new, more efficient technologies, we must also find ways of persuading people to use the conservation measures that are already available.

Better Technology

fusion
Merging of atoms to produce energy, as in the sun.

fission
Splitting of atoms to produce energy, as in a nuclear reactor.

Conservation can stretch our energy supplies, but new sources of energy will eventually be needed. We have already mentioned proposals for more nuclear, hydroelectric, and geothermal power stations. Some scientists are now proposing the development of power plants equipped with nuclear reactors using **fusion** (the merging of atoms) rather than **fission** (the splitting of atoms). However, nuclear fusion generates temperatures comparable to those of the sun, and no one knows whether it is possible to control such a powerful force or how safe such a source of power would be.

A growing number of scientists and concerned citizens are coming to see solar power as the best answer to the world's energy problems. Solar power units use the

Signs of Hope   Less Smog and More Recycling

More than two decades of environmental activism have produced many tangible benefits for our society. The numerous environmental laws activists helped pass have forced many polluters to clean up their emissions, and a new awareness of environmental problems has encouraged many people to change their behavior. One obvious result of those new laws has been the decline in air pollution. Our total emissions of carbon monoxide were about 25 percent higher in 1970 than they are today, and emission of sulfur oxides has declined by one-third—despite that fact that we now have far more cars, more industries, and more people. The new environmental awareness has also contributed to the growing recycling movement. Today, we recycle almost 35 percent of our paper products, compared to only 17 percent in 1970, and there have been even bigger increases in the recycling of glass, aluminum, and ferrous metals.*

*U.S. Bureau of the Census, *Statistical Abstract of the United States, 1997* (Washington, DC: U.S. Government Printing Office, 1997), pp. 234, 237.

Solar energy, which is clean and virtually limitless, is one of the brightest prospects to help meet our future needs.

endless supply of energy from the sun, produce little pollution, and pose no threat of radiation or explosion. Solar energy is already being used on a small scale to heat water, homes, and offices. Most experts are confident that more efficient technologies for storing and using the sun's energy can be developed. Considerable effort is being made to find cheap methods of turning sunlight directly into electricity through the use of **photovoltaic cells.** Other promising approaches use specially prepared ponds of water to trap solar energy or mirrors to concentrate it on a single location where it can be used to generate electrical power. There are also many indirect forms of solar energy that can be tapped for human purposes: power generated by wind, ocean tides, rivers, and dams all depend on the sun, and they all offer environmentally sound alternatives to our current dependence on burning fossil fuels. Such technology is an imitation of nature, since nearly all the energy in natural ecosystems ultimately comes from the sun.

photovoltaic cells
Solar energy batteries.

Limiting Growth

Technological solutions are attractive, but it is doubtful that they alone can resolve the environmental crisis. Any effective response to the environmental crisis must include some form of population control. If the world's population keeps on doubling every forty or fifty years, there is bound to be more pollution and an ever increasing drain on natural resources. Restrictions on unplanned economic growth will be needed as well. It seems inescapable that the wrong kind of economic growth means faster depletion of resources and more pollution.

It is often argued that industrial growth is necessary to create new jobs for a growing population, but those who make this argument tend to ignore many other possible solutions. These include creating service jobs or shortening the work week in order to distribute existing jobs among more people. Advocates of a decentralized solar technology point out that installing and maintaining solar collectors in millions of homes and offices would create far more jobs than the highly centralized technology based on burning fossil fuels that we now use. The argument that economic growth is necessary to eliminate poverty and create a more egalitarian society is also misleading. Despite decades of rapid economic growth, the industrialized nations continue to show enormous inequalities of wealth and power. The most egalitarian societies are those that depend on simple foraging technologies. This does not mean that the answer to the environmental crisis is for everyone to return to hunting and gathering—the world's current population is far too large even to consider such an idea. It does seem likely, however, that the world would be more peaceful and more secure if the people of the industrialized nations learned to accept a more leisurely life-style and a lower standard of living, while encouraging economic growth in the less developed countries.

Changing Our Lives

As is true for most important social problems, solving our environmental crisis will require both individual and collective changes. As individuals we may not be able to discover a new source of clean energy or solve the population problem, but we can commit ourselves to leading more environmentally sustainable lives. There is a long, long list of things we can do. A few quick examples include living as close to work or school as we can, walking or taking a bike when we don't need to drive, recycling our waste, boycotting products whose manufacturers show wanton disregard for the environment, and on a more fundamental level, dedicating ourselves to living a simpler life and taking no more of the world's resources then we really need. Of course, nothing we do as single individuals is likely to have a very large impact on this enormous problem, but such small individual changes add up and gain an kind of momentum of their own. If enough people start making these changes, the environment will improve.

Quick Review

Critically evaluate the different proposals for solving the environmental crisis.

Sociological Perspectives on the Environment

Pollution of the air and water, degradation of the land, and wasteful use of oil and other natural resources seem to be topics for engineers, biologists, and geologists to ponder; but environmental issues are also sociological issues. Sociologists take the broad view, repeatedly pointing out that social institutions are organized systems similar to the ecosystems of nature; that one must understand interacting physical, biological, economic, political, and psychological conditions if one is to understand collective human behavior; and that purposive human actions have unanticipated consequences. In short, sociologists try to teach people to understand that few human problems are as simple as they seem. The origins of the environmental crisis are not to be found in a few polluting industries but in the basic social organization and cultural outlook of the modern world.

The Functionalist Perspective

Functionalists see today's environmental problems as latent dysfunctions of industrialization. Most of the technological advances that help society perform its basic functions easily and efficiently have had negative effects as well. The manufacturing, distributing, and consuming processes that make increases in our standard of living possible also produce undesirable by-products: pollution and resource depletion. Thus, the economic changes that helped create modern industrial society also threw the environment out of balance and created our current problems.

To many functionalists, the answer to our environmental problems is simple: the dysfunctions of the industrial economy must be reduced through more efficient pollution control and through new technological improvements that will produce more energy and use new raw materials. Thus, the environmental crisis is best solved by refining and improving our present way of doing things, not by making basic changes in our social and economic system. Most functionalists are therefore cornucopians: they believe that the solution to the problems of modern technology is more and better technology.

Other functionalists disagree, however, arguing that the present industrial economy is inherently unstable because it depends on steady growth to maintain economic prosperity, yet it is using up the resources that are necessary for that growth. To this way of thinking, minor reforms cannot solve our environmental problems. Basic changes must be made because many of the central values of our social system have become dysfunctional. At one time, ideas about conquering nature and the importance of constantly increasing our personal wealth inspired the effort necessary for survival. Now, such attitudes threaten human existence because they ignore the long-term effects of the relentless pursuit of wealth by billions of people. The economic system is thus dysfunctional because it wastes resources and pollutes the environment in order to produce more than is necessary for the health and well-being of the people. To these functionalists, a solution to the environmental crisis will require major changes in our system of values and a reorganization of society.

The Conflict Perspective

Conflict theorists see exploitation of the environment as just one more result of social exploitation. More specifically, conflict theorists hold that the economic structure of capitalist nations depends not only on the exploitation of the poor by the rich but also on an ever increasing exploitation of the natural environment. Private businesses must win the competitive struggle for profits if they are to survive, and that places enormous pressure on them to use exploitative technologies to gain quick profits regardless of the environmental costs. Conflict theorists argue that if a firm carried out more responsible policies, it would be driven out of business by its less ethical competitors. One solution is obviously for the government to make firms pay for the environmental damage they cause. Conflict theorists argue, however, that the giant corporate polluters are so powerful that they have been able to block effective environmental programs that are clearly in the interests of the vast majority of the people.

This same pattern of exploitation occurs internationally as well. According to conflict theorists, the wealthy industrialized nations are using their power to loot the poor nations of their irreplaceable natural resources, thus making the rich nations richer and the poor nations poorer. Now that the less developed countries are finally trying to industrialize, they find that the cheap energy and raw materials that helped develop the wealthy nations are gone. To make matters worse, the industrialized world is now exporting its pollution to the poor nations, either by using them as dumping grounds for toxic wastes or by moving their most dangerous and polluting factories there.

Conflict theorists insist that to solve the environmental crisis, we must create a new kind of world system based on equality and respect for the dignity of all people. To stop the exploitation and destruction of our natural environment, we must reverse our priorities and put the welfare of humanity first and profits second. The competitive materialistic orientation that has produced such stunning economic achievements has also degraded us by making material possessions the measure of a person's worth. Conflict theorists argue that as long as this orientation and the economic system that fostered it continue, we will continue to brutalize both the environment and ourselves.

The Feminist Perspective

To the "eco-feminists," the roots of our environmental crisis are to be found in the same patriarchal culture that has oppressed women for so many centuries. These feminists see a basic contradiction between the values of cooperation, nurturance, and mutual support that often predominate among women and the more competitive ideals of power and achievement often found among men. Because patriarchal culture places a one-sided emphasis on those masculine values, it has developed an exploitative relationship with the very environmental systems that keep us alive. Irreplaceable natural resources are wasted and huge amounts of toxic pollutants are dumped into the environment with little concern for the impact those actions will have on generations to come. To the eco-feminists, the solution to our environment crisis is obvious. There must be a fundamental shift in the values and perspectives of our culture. The cooperative nurturant values so central to most women's lives must now be given the same importance in our culture as a whole, while the cultural traditions that value aggressive, domineering behavior must be changed. Feminists therefore urge women and sympathetic men to band together to make fundamental changes in our culture and the economic system that supports it.

The Interactionist Perspective

Sociologists from all theoretical perspectives agree with the interactionists that learned attitudes and values are at the root of the environmental crisis. The belief in progress, in materialism, and in our superiority to the natural world are all important parts of the problem. Some interactionists hold that even more fundamental parts of our definition of ourselves and the world around us are also involved. Most of us see things in individualistic terms, doing whatever seems most likely to satisfy our personal needs. Such an approach works fine in many situations, but when a large group of people all follow the individualistic road to happiness at the same time, the result is likely to be chaos and confusion. Environmental resources are often held in common for use by many people, but it is in the individualistic interest of each to use as much of these resources as possible before someone else does. In a phenomenon often known as the **tragedy of the commons,** this individualistic pursuit of self-interest leads to the complete destruction of the resource and long-term harm to everyone.[57]

tragedy of the commons
The destruction of common resources in the pursuit of individual benefits.

Such attitudes are learned, and interactionists tell us that if we are to deal effectively with our environmental problems, these attitudes must be unlearned by an entire generation. As they are unlearned, new, more appropriate attitudes will have to take their place. Citizens of the twenty-first century must learn what tribal people have always known: that our survival as individuals depends on our concern for the interests of the community, that nature is to be regarded with respect and reverence, and that a life-style that attempts to achieve harmony with nature is more satisfying than one that attempts to conquer it.

Quick Review

Compare and contrast the functionalist and conflict perspectives on the environment.

What do the eco-feminists say about our environmental problems?

What is the "tragedy of the commons"?

Summary

As the use of exploitative technologies has grown, the by-products of industrialization have fouled the land, air, and water, thus disrupting the delicate web of life on which human existence depends. The science of ecology—the study of the interrelationships among plants, animals, and their environment—has shown that we are but one part of this complex network of living things.

Humans have had a tremendous impact on natural ecosystems and are now the principal source of change in the biosphere. Our activities have produced numerous unintended effects that are harmful to ourselves and many of the other forms of life on this planet. Air pollution, for example, is a severe health hazard and is causing harmful changes in the world's weather and atmospheric conditions. Despite the world's enormous reserves of water, water pollution both above and below ground is becoming a serious concern. Organic wastes from human sewage and industry are water pollutants, as are the chemical fertilizers and pesticides used extensively in modern farming. Poisonous chemicals such as mercury and arsenic build up in the tissues of one marine animal after another, eventually reaching the humans at the top of the food chain. Overgrazing, logging, urban sprawl, faulty irrigation, strip mining, and poor farming techniques have combined to deface huge expanses of land. Over the years, forests have steadily shrunk as deserts, wastelands, and cities have grown. Moreover, the chemicals used in business and industry are being dumped on the land, in the water, and in the air, and there is growing concern about radioactive wastes. One result of all these problems has been the extinction of many species of plants and animals and a sharp reduction in the biological diversity of our world.

The modern industrial economy is rapidly using up the world's irreplaceable natural resources. Many scientists believe that the world's supply of oil and natural gas will be depleted in less than a century. Coal is more abundant, but even those reserves can supply the world's energy needs for only a limited period of time. Many key minerals and raw materials are also in increasingly short supply; however, given enough energy, most of them can be effectively recycled.

The complex causes of the environmental crisis have roots stretching far back in human history. Technology has become highly exploitative, using huge amounts of energy and natural resources and producing a large volume of pollution in the process. The growth of the total human population and economic growth in the industrialized nations severely aggravate the problem. Underlying these conditions are three basic cultural attitudes: the belief in progress, the belief in materialism, and the idea that nature is something for humans to subdue and exploit.

The current concern about environmental problems first developed in the 1970s. The environmental movement met with some success, but government programs have often been stymied by powerful special interests, and stiffer laws and more rigorous enforcement are needed. Many programs for using existing resources more efficiently have also been proposed; among them are recycling and environmental education. Although conservation will stretch energy supplies, new sources of energy will eventually be needed. Many scientists believe that solar energy offers the brightest hope for the future. Proposals for dealing with other aspects of the environmental crisis call for a greater effort to control the population explosion and for a slower pace of economic growth.

Because social institutions resemble the ecosystems of nature, it is logical that sociologists should show concern for the interaction between human systems and environmental systems. Functionalists see environmental problems as latent dysfunctions of the industrial revolution because the attitudes that inspired the explosion of economic growth are no longer functional. Conflict theorists see exploitation of the environment as part of a continuing struggle between the rich and the poor. They note that profits have been given a higher priority than human welfare, and they call for a reversal of these priorities. Feminists call for a return to the traditional female values of cooperation and mutual support and for an end to the aggressive, competitive orientation that encourages exploitation of the environment. Interactionists argue that the attitudes, values, and definitions that cause the environmental crisis are learned and that if we are to deal effectively with our environmental problems, an entire generation of citizens must unlearn these beliefs.

Questions for Critical Thinking

Many sociologists believe that our abuse of the environment will be the Achilles' heel of modern industrial capitalism. We keep using up more and more of our natural resources and pumping out more and more dangerous pollutants, and in their view we are inevitably headed for an environmental catastrophe. The optimists, on the other hand, feel that newer and better technology will solve our environmental problems and allow us to continue on our present course without radical change. Considering what you have read in this chapter, what do you think our environmental future will be like? Do you think one of these two sides will be proved right, or are we likely to follow a middle course?

Key Terms

acid rain	hydroelectric power
biodiversity	meltdown
biosphere	neo-Malthusian
breeder reactor	nonrenewable resource
cornucopian	organic waste
deforestation	ozone depletion
desertification	photochemical smog
ecology	photosynthesis
ecosystem	photovoltaic cells
exploitative technology	pollution
fission	renewable resource
food chain	solar energy
fusion	strip mining
geothermal energy	temperature inversion
greenhouse effect	tragedy of the commons

Further Readings

Lester R. Brown, ed., *The State of the World* (New York: Norton, published yearly). An excellent collection of articles examining current environmental issues from the World Watch Institute. Revised yearly.

Michael R. Edelstein, *Contaminated Communities: The Social and Psychological Impact of Residential Toxic Exposure* (Boulder, CO: Westview, 1988). An examination of the human impact of the exposure to toxic chemicals.

John Elkington, Julia Hailes, and Joel Makower, *The Green Consumer* (New York: Viking Penguin, 1990). A detailed look at what we as consumers can do to benefit the environment.

Murry Feshbach and Alfred Friendly, *Ecocide in the USSR: Health and Nature Under Siege* (New York: Basic Books, 1992). The disturbing story of the damage wreaked by the communist government and its environmentally exploitative economy before the collapse of the Soviet Union.

Nick Middleton, *The Global Casino: An Introduction to Environmental Issues* (London: Arnold, 1995). A general overview of today's environmental problems.

Norman Myers, *Gaia: An Atlas of Planet Management* (New York: Anchor, 1993). A fascinating presentation of the world's environmental problems; full of maps and visual aids.

Notes

1. "An Asian Pea-Souper," *The Economist,* September 27, 1997, p. 40.
2. U.S. Bureau of the Census, *Statistical Abstract of the United States, 1997* (Washington, DC: U.S. Government Printing Office, 1997), p. 234.

3. Ibid.

4. G. Tyler Miller, *Living in the Environment: An Introduction to Environmental Science*, 6th ed. (Belmont, CA: Wadsworth, 1990), p. 498.

5. Nick Middleton, *The Global Casino: An Introduction to Environmental Issues* (London: Arnold, 1995), pp. 114–126; Karen Arms, *Environmental Science*, 2nd ed. (Fort Worth: Harcourt Brace, 1994), pp. 451–452.

6. Mark Dowie, "A Sky Full of Holes: Why the Ozone Layer Is Torn Worse Than Ever," pp. 230–233 in John L. Allen, ed., *Environment 97/98* (Guilford, CT: Dushkin/McGraw-Hill, 1997); Marla Cone, "Ozone Hole Blamed for Frog Decline," *Los Angeles Times,* March 1, 1994, pp. A1, A20; Miller, *Living in the Environment,* pp. 501–503.

7. Arms, *Environmental Science,* p. 444.

8. Mark Dowie, "A Sky Full of Holes."

9. World Resources Institute, *World Resources 1996–97* (New York: Oxford University Press, 1996), p. 316; Miller, *Living in the Environment,* p. 503.

10. World Resources Institute, *World Resources 1996–97,* pp. 313–325; Arms, *Environmental Science,* pp. 444–448; Miller, *Living in the Environment,* pp. 503–507; David E. Pitt, "Computer Vision of Global Warming: Hardest on Have-Nots," *New York Times,* January 18, 1994, p. B7.

11. U.S. Bureau of the Census, *Statistical Abstract of the United States, 1996,* p. 233.

12. Middleton, *The Global Casino,* pp. 155–170; Miller, *Living in the Environment,* pp. 519.

13. Andrew Goudie, *The Human Impact on the Natural Environment,* 3rd ed. (Cambridge, MA: MIT Press, 1990), pp. 154–201; Mary Williams Walsh, "In Arctic, a Toxic Surprise," *Los Angeles Times,* June 18, 1991, pp. A1, A9.

14. Brad Knickerbocker, "New 'Endangered' List Targets Many U.S. Rivers," *Christian Science Monitor,* April 21, 1994, pp. 1, 4.

15. William J. Broad, "Survey of 100 U.S. Coastal Sites Shows Pollution Is Declining," *New York Times,* January 21, 1997, p. B10.

16. Miller, *Living in the Environment,* pp. 529–535.

17. Agis Salpukas, "A New Slant on Exxon Valdez Spill," *New York Times,* December 1, 1993, pp. C1, C7.

18. Miller, *Living in the Environment,* p. 533.

19. Frank Clifford, "Study Finds Peril in Water Supply," *Los Angeles Times,* July 28, 1994, pp. A4, A26; Associated Press, "20% Drinking Inadequately Treated Water," *San Luis Obispo Telegram-Tribune,* July 27, 1994, p. A10.

20. Arms, *Environmental Science,* p. 375.

21. Alan Thomas, *Third World Atlas,* 2nd ed. (Washington, DC: Taylor & Francis, 1994), p. 62.

22. Diana Jean Schemo, "Burning of Amazon Picks Up Pace, with Vast Areas Lost," *New York Times,* September 12, 1996, p. A3.

23. Arms, *Environmental Science,* pp. 304–305.

24. Ibid.; Middleton, *The Global Casino,* pp. 43–55.

25. Middleton, *The Global Casino,* pp. 28–42; Arms, *Environmental Science,* pp. 379, 382–383.

26. Middleton, *The Global Casino,* pp. 71–84; Miller, *Living in the Environment,* p. 225; Goudie, *Human Impact on the Natural Environment,* pp. 138–140.

27. U.S. Bureau of the Census, *Statistical Abstract, 1993,* p. 227.

28. See Branley Allan Branson, "Is There Life After Strip Mining?" *Natural History* 95 (August 1986): 30–36.

29. Philip Shenon, "Pacific Island Nation Is Stripped of Everything," *New York Times,* December 10, 1995, p. A3.

30. Miller, *Living in the Environment,* pp. 453–454.

31. Ibid., pp. 473–475; World Resources Institute, *World Resources 1996–97,* p. 292.

32. Population Reference Bureau, *World Population Data Sheet, 1997* (Washington, DC: Population Reference Bureau, 1997); Michael Specter, "Plunging Life Expectancy Puzzles Russia," *New York Times,* August 2, 1995, pp. A1, A 4.

33. Arms, *Environmental Science,* p. 404.

34. Nicholas Lenssen and Christopher Flavin, "Meltdown," pp. 119–126 in Allen, *Environment 97/98;* Carol J. Williams, "9 Years Later, Chernobyl Disaster Looks Worse," *New York Times,* April 27, 1995, p. A4; "Ukraine to Keep Chernobyl in Operation," *New York Times,* October 22, 1993, p. A6; Scripps News Service, "Tragedy of Chernobyl Keeps on Building in Byelorussia," *San Luis Obispo Telegram-Tribune,* March 27, 1991, p. D1; Associated Press, "Mystery Ailments Plague Chernobyl," *San Luis Obispo Telegram-Tribune,* April 22, 1991, pp. A1, A12; Michael Parks, "Chernobyl," *Los Angeles Times,* April 23, 1991, pp. H1, H6; Scripps News Service, "Chernobyl Worse Than Earlier Feared," *San Luis Obispo Telegram-Tribune,* April 28, 1991, p. A1.

35. Lenssen and Flavin, "Meltdown"; Miller, *Living in the Environment,* pp. 399–402.

36. Craig R. Whitney, "Germans Suspect Russian Military in Plutonium Sale," *New York Times,* August 16, 1994, pp. A1, A6.

37. William J. Broad, "Experts in U.S. Call Plutonium Not Arms-Level," *New York Times,* August 17, 1994, pp. A1, A4.

38. Michael R. Gordon, "Russian Controls on Bomb Material Are Leaky," *New York Times,* August 18, 1994, pp. A1, A8.

39. Peter Raven, "A Time of Catastrophic Extinction: What We Must Do," pp. 175–178 in Allen, *Environment 97/98;* Patrick Huyghe, "New-Species Fever," pp. 253–257 in Allen, *Environment 94/95;* Miller, *Living in the Environment,* pp. 320–321; Arms, *Environmental Science,* p. 62.

40. Miller, *Living in the Environment,* p. 322.

41. William K. Stevens, "Study Bolsters Value of Species Diversity," *New York Times,* February 1, 1994, p. B7.

42. Miller, *Living in the Environment,* p. 318.

43. U.S. Bureau of the Census, *Statistical Abstract, 1997,* p. 585.

44. Norman Myers, ed., *Gaia: An Atlas of Planet Management,* rev. ed. (New York: Anchor Books, 1993), p. 97; Miller, *Living in the Environment,* p. 57.

45. U.S. Bureau of the Census, *Statistical Abstract, 1997,* p. 585.

46. See Agis Salpukas, "What's Next, Tail Fins?" *New York Times,* February 15, 1996, pp. C1, C5.

47. Myers, ed., *Gaia,* p. 107.

48. Population Reference Bureau, *World Population Data Sheet, 1997* (Washington, DC: Population Reference Bureau, 1997).

49. Myers, ed., *Gaia,* p. 99.

50. Arms, *Environmental Science,* pp. 208–209.

51. Ibid., pp. 286–287.

52. See Miller, *Living in the Environment,* pp. 357–358.

53. For a discussion of the differences between the neo-Malthusians and the cornucopians, see Miller, *Living in the Environment,* pp. 22–25.

54. Louis Harris, *Inside America* (New York: Vintage, 1987), p. 245.

55. Associated Press, "Most Would Pay Higher Prices to Save Environment, Poll Finds," *Los Angeles Times,* June 8, 1992, p. A11.

56. U.S. Bureau of the Census, *Statistical Abstract, 1997,* p. 847.

57. See Garrett Hardin, "The Tragedy of the Commons," *Science* 162 (1968): 1243–1248.

What are the economic differences between the industrialized and
the less developed countries?

What is it like to live in a poor country?

How do sociologists explain the huge gap between the rich and the
poor countries?

What can be done to make life better for all the world's people?

Yeshi Alamayu is around 45, and she lives in Addis Ababa, Ethiopia. She supports herself, her eight children, and her aging mother by gathering wood in the government's plantation forests. When she was a girl, she used to gather wood from the eucalyptus groves on the edge of town. But in the last three decades, the population of Addis Ababa doubled and then doubled again, and the residents of the tiny tin-roofed shacks and the plastic hovels clinging to downtown sidewalks stripped nearby areas naked of trees in an unending search for fuel. So Alamayu now has to get up every morning at dawn for the five-mile walk to the government forest. When she arrives, she scours the ground for leaves, twigs, and spindly branches, binds them with rope, and heaves them onto her back. Finally, she hauls her heavy burden to the doorstep of a local trader, who gives her the equivalent of about 80 cents. After subtracting the daily bribe she must pay to enter the forest, she is left with about 70 cents for a long day's work.[1]

The images of global poverty are becoming more familiar every day: the tiny famine victim with stick legs and bulging eyes, the desperate young mother begging for food, a crowd of refugees fenced off in a pen like cattle. Bit by bit, media coverage is helping the people of the rich countries to realize how fortunate they are. But the media cover only the most dramatic and desperate problems, so many people have a distorted concept of what life in the rest of the world is really like, and only a few know about the causes of global poverty or what to do about them.

The question of why the countries of the world are so sharply divided into an affluent minority and a poor majority is one of the most controversial in all social science. This chapter will examine the most common explanations for this global divide and the kinds of solutions they each imply. Before we attempt to explain this problem, however, we must describe it.

Global Inequality

Each of the more than 170 nations on this planet has its own unique economic, political, and social institutions, yet at the same time, all these countries are growing increasingly interdependent. Some are fabulously wealthy, while others are mired in seemingly hopeless poverty. A few exercise awesome global power, but others are hardly noticed on the world stage. One of the best ways to make sense of this bewildering complexity is to think of the nations of the world as making up a kind of international class system, similar in many ways to the classes found within individual countries (see Chapter 1). A century ago, the industrialized world, which makes up the "upper class," included only the United States and a few western European nations, but today it encompasses countries as far away as Japan and Australia. The countries in the "lower class," collectively known as the **less developed countries (LDCs)** or the **Third World,** are concentrated in the southern two-thirds of the planet, in Latin America, Africa, and much of Asia. Although they have some manufacturing industries, they are more likely to depend on agriculture and the sale of raw materials to get by.

less developed countries (LDCs), Third World
Two terms for the poor nations of the world.

Between these two extremes is a smaller group of nations, including South Korea, Taiwan, and Mexico, that have characteristics of both kinds of societies. They are more industrialized and have higher standards of living than the poorest nations, but they are still a long way from the affluence enjoyed by the established industrialized powers. More often than not, these "middle-class" nations are counted as part of the Third World, but several more narrow terms are also used, including "moderately developed" or "newly industrialized nations." In addition, there are the numerous independent nations that emerged from the collapse of the communist empire in eastern Europe and the Soviet Union. Many of these nations have a well-educated population and a lot of heavy industry, but their standard of living is far below that of the developed capitalist countries in the global upper class and even many of the newly industrialized nations of East Asia. It is therefore important to remember that the world is a complex place and that there is a broad spectrum of nations on both sides of the global divide.

Just as individuals occasionally move up or down in the class system of their nation, so the status of the nations changes. Some of the countries in the world's "middle class" seem likely to become full-scale industrial powers; others do not. Several nations have been knocked out of the elite club of industrial powers by wars or internal chaos but later rejoined it. Still other countries appear to be permanently stuck at the bottom of the heap.[2]

Wealth and Poverty

Many people look at the differences between the industrialized nations and the Third World as simply a matter of money. When seen in these terms, the gap is certainly enormous. In 1997, the average industrialized nation produced about $19,310 in goods and services for each of its citizens, while the less developed countries produced only $1,120 per citizen—a difference of more than 17 to 1 (see Figure 17.1). There are also major differences among the less developed countries. The per capita income in the world's poorest region, **sub-Saharan Africa,** is less than one-fourth as large as it is in Latin America or in most parts of Asia.[3] But as we will see, the differences go far beyond money. Moreover, dollars, marks, and yen are not necessarily the best way to measure wealth. The cost of living varies greatly between one country and another; so, for example, a dollar's worth of rupees may buy two or three times more goods in India than a dollar's worth of lire does in Italy. To complicate matters further, many people in the poor nations depend more heavily on the barter system—trading one thing directly for something else they want—and goods that are informally traded seldom show up in official statistics.

Another way to compare different nations is to look at how much wealth they have accumulated. Some of this wealth is kept in dollars or pounds, but more important are the physical assets of a nation—its roads and bridges, its power plants, its sewers and canals, its supply of housing, and its factories. The simplest way to make this comparison is just to look around. The industrialized nations are crisscrossed with telephone and electric lines and with highways full of cars and trucks. Their buildings are modern and are equipped with running water and indoor plumbing. Almost everyone has shoes to wear, and during the cold months most people have warm clothing. In the less developed countries, such comforts are far less common, and only a privileged few enjoy the affluent life-style taken for

sub-Saharan Africa
Africa south of the Sahara desert.

Figure 17.1

The Privileged and the Deprived

There is a huge gap between the income of the average person in industrialized nations and less developed nations.

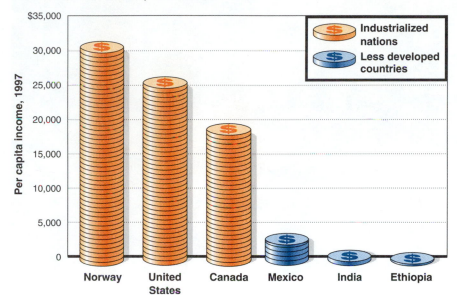

Source: Population Reference Bureau, *World Population Data Sheet, 1997* (Washington, DC: Population Reference Bureau, 1997).

granted by so many North Americans. The less developed countries have paved roads connecting their major cities, but the roads are likely to be much smaller than those in the industrialized nations and in a poor state of repair. Access to smaller towns is often only by footpaths or dirt roads that become very hard going when it rains. Most rural areas are further isolated by a lack of telephones and the electricity necessary to run radio transmitters. Even on major highways, the traveler will see far fewer private cars, and the trucks and buses are often dilapidated, noisy, and polluting. These motor vehicles must also share the road with a host of oxcarts, horses, bicycles, and pedestrians.

Sanitation is often primitive, with open fields or shallow outhouses serving as the only toilets. In the cities and crowded villages, human waste may flow down the sides of streets in open sewers. Underground plumbing is now more common, but untreated sewage is usually dumped directly into rivers and lakes, which can create serious health problems. The quality of housing varies enormously. The wealthy live in sumptuous mansions with servants and all the latest conveniences, while in most big cities hundreds of thousands of people live on the streets with no permanent shelter, and huge shantytowns of squatters have grown up on whatever vacant land is available. Since these squatters have neither the legal rights to the land they occupy nor the money to build homes, their structures are primitive affairs. Often lacking electricity and plumbing, these shacks provide poor protection against the elements (see Chapter 14). In rural areas, most villagers at least have the legal right

The standard of living is far lower in the Third World than in the industrialized nations, and transportation and communication are much slower.

to live where they do, but construction techniques are still primitive—buildings often have walls of mud bricks and thatched or corrugated iron roofs—and the basic amenities are lacking.

One of the most fundamental problems in the poor nations is the absence of economic opportunities for their young people. Rapid population growth (see Chapter 15) and a weak educational system mean there is almost always a large surplus of unskilled labor. In the past, these young people would have just gone to work on the family farm, but because so many more children now reach adulthood, there is often not enough land to support them all. To make matters worse, birthrates are the highest in the poorest countries and among the poorest people within each country. Young people from throughout the Third World are therefore migrating to the cities in search of work, but only the lucky find permanent jobs. Most become part of what is sometimes called the **urban subsistence economy.** They work a few temporary jobs, trade their labor for the help of other poor people, receive an occasional handout from the government or a relief agency, and in some cases turn to begging or crime to make ends meet. (See this chapter's Personal Perspectives for an account of what it was like growing up as a Guatemalan peasant.)

urban subsistence economy
The way of life of the city dwellers in poor countries who make just enough to get by.

Health and Nutrition

There is nothing more fundamental to the quality of life than good health, and the health statistics show the same global divide as the economic statistics. A baby born in a less developed country is at least five times more likely to die in its first year of life than a baby born in a wealthy nation (see Figure 17.2). Overall, demographers say that the people of the industrialized world can expect to live 12 years longer than their counterparts in the poor nations.[4]

Many of the causes of these staggering differences can be traced to the economic conditions we have already discussed, especially poor sanitation and lack of clean drinking water. On the average, almost one in three people in the poor nations does not have access to safe drinking water, and in sub-Saharan Africa it is one in two.[5] Waterborne diseases such as typhoid and cholera, almost unknown in the wealthy nations, sweep through the less developed countries in epidemic after epidemic, taking millions of lives every year. Another of the most lethal diseases, malaria, is transmitted by insects and not water. But poverty is a major contributor to the malaria problem as well because many poor nations cannot afford the expensive mosquito eradication programs that are the best way to deal with the disease.

When people in the poor countries do get sick, they are often unable to find a doctor to help. There is only 1 doctor for every 5833 people who live in the less developed countries, but in the industrialized nations there is 1 doctor for every 341 people.[6] Even those lucky enough to find a doctor who will see them are likely to

Personal Perspectives   Growing Up as a Guatemalan Peasant

Rigoberta Menchu is a Quiche Indian who grew up in a poverty-stricken Guatemalan village. Her father and brother were murdered by the Guatemalan military, and her struggle for justice in her country won her the 1992 Nobel Peace Prize. The following is an account of some of her memories of growing up.

I worked from when I was very small, but I didn't earn anything. I was really helping my mother because she always had to carry a baby, my little brother, on her back as she picked coffee. It made me very sad to see my mother's face covered in sweat as she tried to finish her work load, and I wanted to help her. But my work wasn't paid, it just contributed to my mother's work. I either picked coffee with her or looked after my little brother, so she could work faster. My brother was two at the time. Indian women prefer to breastfeed their babies rather than give them food because, when the child eats and the mother eats, that's duplicating the food needed. So my brother was still feeding at the breast and my mother had to spend time feeding him and everything.

I was five when she was doing this work and I looked after my little brother. I wasn't earning yet. I used to watch my mother, who often had the food ready at three o'clock in the morning for the workers who started work early, and at eleven she had the food for the midday meal ready. At seven in the evening she had to run around again making food for her group. In between times, she worked picking coffee to supplement what she earned. Watching her made me feel useless and weak because I couldn't do anything to help her except look after my brother. That's when my consciousness was born. It's true. My mother didn't like the idea of me working, of earning my own money, but I did. I wanted to work, more than anything to help her, both economically and physically. The thing was that my mother was very brave and stood up to everything well, but there were times when one of my brothers or sisters was ill—if it wasn't one of them it was another—and everything she earned went on medicine for them. This made me very sad as well. It was at that time, I remember, that when we went back to the Altiplano after five months in the finca [a large farm] I was ill and it looked as if I'd die. I was six and my mother was distressed because I nearly died. The change of climate was too abrupt for me. After that, though, I made a big effort not to get ill again and, although my head ached a lot, I didn't say so.*

*Rigoberta Menchu, *I Rigoberta Menchu: An Indian Woman in Guatemala* (New York: Verso, 1984), p. 33.

Figure 17.2

Life Expectancy

People in the rich countries live longer than people in the poor ones.

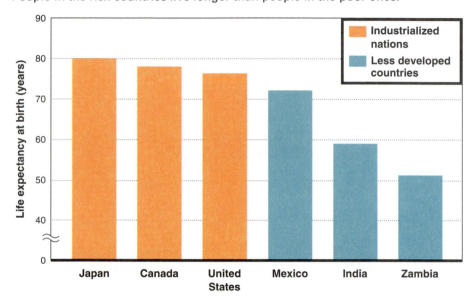

Source: Population Reference Bureau, *World Population Data Sheet, 1997* (Washington, DC: Population Reference Bureau, 1997).

have their treatment hampered by shortages of everything but the least expensive medicines and equipment. The lack of medical care is particularly acute in the rural areas of most poor countries, where traditional healers often provide the only medical help available.

Food is, of course, another basic factor in determining our health. Lack of refrigeration and poor sanitation mean that food itself is often a cause of illness in the poor countries, but the biggest problem with food is simply the lack of it. According to United Nations figures, the average person in an industrialized country consumes about one-fourth more calories and two-thirds more protein a day than someone in a less developed country. Of course, those are just averages, and many people in the rich nations eat more than is good for them. The fact remains, however, that people in the less developed countries who fall below the norm may be in for serious trouble. In sub-Saharan Africa, the *average* person consumes almost 10 percent fewer calories than needed for good health.[7] It is estimated that 10 to 20 percent of the world's people suffer from chronic malnutrition and that millions die of starvation every year.[8]

Education

Another major economic advantage of the industrialized nations is their high level of education. In most industrialized nations, less than 1 percent of the population is completely illiterate. But one in three people in the less developed countries cannot

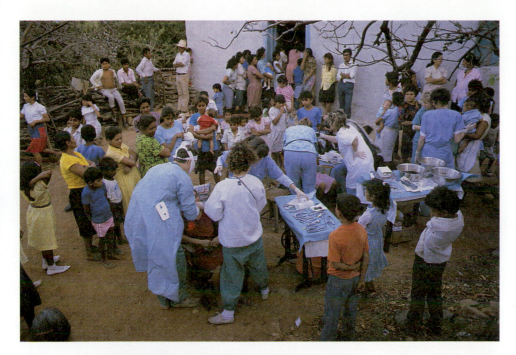

Good health care can be hard to come by in the less developed countries, and educational facilities, where they are available, are often primitive affairs. The photo on the top is from an American-sponsored medical clinic in rural Honduras, and the other photo shows students in Sudan.

read and write, and the majority of people are illiterate in the 45 countries the United Nations ranks at the bottom of its human development index.[9] Workers in the industrialized countries are far more likely to have specialized skills—for example, in word processing or automobile mechanics. Their labor force also contains large numbers of physicians, engineers, scientists, and other highly trained specialists. Moreover, many of the skilled professionals the poor nations do produce migrate to the industrialized countries, where wages are far higher.

The system of universal education in the rich nations also serves as a kind of social cement to help hold their people together. Children of widely different backgrounds acquire similar values and attitudes as they learn the history of their nation and read its literature. Mass communication contributes to the sense of national unity because people who read the same newspapers and watch the same television programs tend to develop a similar perspective on the world. In contrast, the perspective of most people in the poor countries is much more local. They often know little of the history or politics of their country; many can't read the newspaper; and televisions are few and far between (see Figure 17.3). To complicate matters, ethnic and linguistic differences are often far more pronounced in less developed countries. Thus, these nations must deal with traditional ethnic animosities and suspicions without the benefit of the strong mass institutions that help hold the wealthy nations together.

Women and Children

Women suffer from prejudice and discrimination in every nation, but the problem is far more severe in the less developed countries. As we saw in Chapter 10, traditional agricultural societies have a high degree of gender inequality. Although all poor nations have undergone some degree of economic development, the traditional attitude that sees women as second-class citizens remains strong. Female infanticide, inadequate care for childbearing women, and the preference often given to male children when resources become scarce mean that there are considerably more males than females in the poorer nations of the world. (In industrialized nations, women normally live longer than men and thus outnumber them.) In the industrialized countries there are no overall gender differences in the literacy rate, but in the less developed countries women are twice as likely to be unable to read and write as men. According to United Nations figures, 44 percent of the administrators and managers are women in the industrialized nations, but only 12 percent are women in the less developed nations.[10]

The industrialized nations have made great progress toward the goal of giving women and men equal treatment under the law. In many parts of the world, however, equal treatment is not even recognized as a social goal, and women are commonly given second-class legal status similar to that of a dependent child. Property often passes from fathers to sons, and daughters do not receive an equal share of the inheritance. Husbands are commonly given the legal right to control the household property, and women find it difficult or impossible to get credit or establish financial independence. Women are expected to follow the orders of their husbands, and the legal authorities seldom intervene to prevent a husband from beating a wife who disobeys him. In most Islamic nations, men are allowed up to four wives, but a

Figure 17.3

Communications

Communication is much faster and easier in the rich countries than in the poor ones.

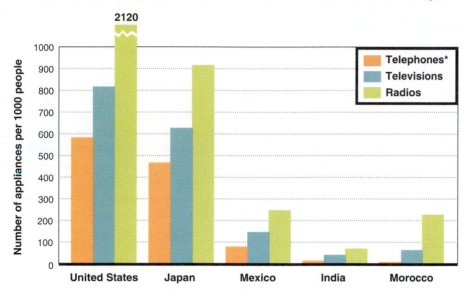

Source: U.S. Bureau of the Census, *Statistical Abstract of the United States, 1996* (Washington, DC: U.S. Government Printing Office, 1996), p. 839.

*Indicates telephone lines, not individual telephones.

wife is permitted only a single husband. In many places around the world, it is also far easier for a husband to win a divorce than for a wife.

The children of the less developed countries also face a host of special problems. As in all societies, they are the most vulnerable to famines and plagues, and young children have far higher death rate than any other age group. The mortality rate among infants is about seven times higher in the less developed countries than in the industrialized ones.[11]

In agricultural societies, children were traditionally seen as a source of farm labor. When people in poor countries move to urban areas, they often send their children off to find jobs. There is a world of difference, however, between having children work on the family farm under the supervision of their parents and having children work for strangers in a factory or shop. It is estimated that more than 200 million children work daily jobs and that they may make up about 15 percent of the total labor force in the less developed countries.[12]

Such problems as poverty, warfare, and just too many mouths to feed have combined to force a growing number of children out of their homes to fend for themselves in the streets of the big cities. The United Nations Children's Fund estimates that there are about 30 million such "street children" in the less developed countries,[13] but others have placed that figure much higher.[14] Life is hard for these children. They usually live in desperate poverty—begging, stealing, selling sex, or doing whatever work they can find. To make matters worse, they are often viewed with suspicion and hostility by the adult population. In Brazil, where such attitudes seem to be at their most extreme, thousands of these children have been murdered by police and vigilante organizations in the last decade.

Social Structure

Underlying the disparities in the quality of life are fundamental differences in the social structures of rich and poor societies. The class system, political institutions, and economic structures are all markedly different in the less developed countries. For example, farming is only one of dozens of industries in the wealthy nations, but it is still the most common way people make their living in Africa, Latin America, and most parts of Asia. Despite the rapid urbanization of recent years (see Chapter 14), almost two-thirds of the people in the less developed countries still lived in rural areas in 1997.[15] Many of these nations depend heavily on the exploitation of natural resources such as petroleum, timber, copper, and uranium—if they are lucky enough to have them. A third major source of employment is low-wage jobs in industries that require large amounts of relatively unskilled labor. Sometimes the factories are owned by local businesspeople or governments, but more often they are branches of huge multinational corporations run from headquarters in one of the industrialized nations. As was already mentioned, rapid population growth and weak overall economies mean that there is a very large group of workers without steady jobs. The United Nations estimates that currently around 700 million people in the poor nations are unemployed or underemployed.[16]

Another important difference between the rich and poor nations is their class systems. Both types of societies have a relatively small upper class that commands a disproportionate share of wealth and power. The industrialized nations also have a large middle class that has the skills necessary to keep the technological economy going. In less developed countries, the middle class is much smaller and weaker, and the gap between the rich and the poor is far larger. For example, the income of the richest one-fifth of the Canadian population is about 9 times that of the poorest one-fifth, and in the United States that ratio is about 12 to 1.[17] In Ethiopia, the richest one-fifth makes 21 times the poorest fifth, and in Brazil the ratio is over 32 to 1.[18] As in the wealthy countries, the disparities in wealth tend to be even greater than the disparities in income. In Mexico, for example, just 37 families control half the wealth, while over 35 million people live in severe poverty.[19]

The nations on the two sides of the global divide also have significant differences in their political institutions. The most obvious is that the rich industrialized nations have stable democratic governments, while less developed countries are much more likely to have some type of dictator or a small group of bureaucratic rulers who are not elected by the public. (Of course, many of these nations hold elections, but the results are rigged against the government's opponents.) Although there has been a trend toward more democracy in the less developed countries, such governments are usually fragile affairs. Elected leaders often face a constant threat of a military coup or a disruptive outbreak of social violence if they make the wrong move.

Whether dictatorships or democracies, governments in the less developed countries tend to be weaker and more unstable than their counterparts in the wealthy nations. For one thing, sharp ethnic and class differences and the lack of strong unifying institutions produce a high level of conflict in many poor nations.

Popular discontent often leads to a succession of new governments that seem unable to get at the roots of the nation's problems or to an entrenched dictatorship that ignores public opinion. Significant parts of some countries are not actually controlled by their central government at all but by bands of organized rebels, as in the Tamil areas of Sri Lanka and the opium-producing regions of Burma. Even relatively stable governments are hopelessly outmatched by the military and economic power of the industrialized nations. No matter how independence-minded Third World leaders may be, they often find that their destiny is determined by decisions made in Washington, Tokyo, or Berlin.

Quick Review

What is the "global class system"?

Describe the differences between life in the industrialized countries and life in the Third World in terms of economic conditions, education, and health.

What are the special problems faced by women and children in the Third World?

What are the differences in social structure between the rich and poor countries?

Explaining the Global Divide

In the distant past, when all human societies were based on hunting and gathering, inequalities among the peoples of the world were fairly small. The transition to an agricultural economy greatly increased social inequality, but the beginnings of today's global divide can be found in the **industrial revolution** and the capitalist economic system that made it possible (see Chapter 4).[20] This new kind of society was

industrial revolution
The change from an agricultural to an industrial society.

Signs of Hope   The Quality of Life Improves

It is extremely difficult to measure something as intangible as the "quality of life" in the different countries of the world. The United Nations attempts to do this with what it calls the Human Development Index. This index is based on the combination of the scores for three variables that most people would agree reflect the quality of life in a particular country (at least to some degree). Those three factors are the *standard of living*, which is measured by the average income per person adjusted to take account of the local cost of living; *education*, as measured by adult literacy and the average years of schooling; and *longevity*, measured by life expectancy at birth. When you look at the way the Human Development Index has changed over the years, you get an optimistic picture. In 1960, almost three-fourths of the world's people lived in countries classified as having a low level of human development; today, only about one-third of all people do. The proportion of people living in countries with a high level of human development increased by about one-third, from 16 to 23 percent of the world's population, and the percentage living in countries with medium human development more than tripled, from 11 to 45 percent. Canada is now rated as having the world's highest level of human development and Sierra Leone the lowest.*

*United Nations Human Development Programme, *Human Development Report, 1997* (New York: Oxford University Press, 1997), pp. 43–47.

based not on farming but on trade, commerce, and manufacturing, and as it took shape in western Europe, it stimulated one technological advance after another at an ever quickening pace. The European countries used their technological superiority for political gains as well. They built up a huge network of colonies (foreign territories under their political control) throughout the world. Even areas that managed to stay outside these colonial empires were often dominated by the economic and military power of the European nations. From the beginning of the colonial period (around the end of the fifteenth century), the standard of living of the European nations grew at an unprecedented rate as wealth and resources poured in from their colonial empires. Most of the rest of the world, however, remained mired in poverty. Although European **colonialism** lasted well into the twentieth century, its days are now over. Nonetheless, the economic inequality between the rich and poor nations is still growing larger year by year.[21]

Today's global inequalities clearly stem from the fact that some nations have undergone a full process of industrialization while others have not. The key question is why. In the early days of their colonial expansion, most Europeans simply assumed that their technological advantage was the result of the biological and religious inferiority of other peoples. Although such **ethnocentrism** is certainly still around, few social scientists take that attitude seriously. The effort to explain these differences scientifically has been a long and difficult process. Many of our greatest sociologists and historians have struggled with this crucial question, and even today, opinions remain sharply divided along political lines. In this chapter, we will examine two broad theories—modernization theory and world system theory—that both seek to explain this global divide. The aim of this section is to present each approach in a clear and coherent form, but it is important to keep in mind that there are many disagreements among those who support the same theory and that many social scientists freely combine insights from both approaches.

Modernization Theory

This theory, which borrows heavily from the classic sociological work of Max Weber (1864–1920), was developed in the 1950s and 1960s by a group of functionalists who saw industrialization as part of a process of social evolution they called **modernization.**[22] According to this perspective, modernization is the result of the buildup of numerous improvements in the structure and function of social institutions. The most obvious are the technological innovations that have been made throughout the course of human history, but modernization also involves what economists call **capital accumulation**—that is, the buildup of wealth. The important thing is not so much amassing money, which is only a symbol of wealth, but increases in real assets (such as roads, buildings, and power plants) and improvements in the education and skill of the work force. There are also important changes in the organization of society as its institutions become more specialized and more efficient. For example, in most agricultural societies, the extended family serves as the school, the employer, the welfare agency, and the punisher of deviant behavior—all rolled into one. As part of the process of modernization, a great deal of the responsibility for these functions is transferred to more specialized social institutions such as the schools and the criminal justice system.

Although modernization takes place as a result of the buildup of one improvement on another, this process does not necessarily occur at a steady pace. In fact, economist Walter W. Rostow has shown that industrialization in the Western na-

colonialism
A system in which one nation extends its political and economic control over other nations or peoples and treats them as dependent colonies.

ethnocentrism
The tendency to view the norms and values of one's own culture as absolute and to use them as a standard against which to measure other cultures.

modernization
The process by which a nation moves from a traditional agricultural society to an industrialized state.

capital accumulation
The buildup of wealth in a nation—including not only money but also the skills of its labor force and its infrastructure.

tions took place in distinct stages, and he argues that all the less developed countries will eventually follow this same road.[23] According to Rostow, all nations begin at the traditional stage, in which people cling to their old ways and are very reluctant to accept sweeping changes. As a nation enters the "takeoff stage," there is a slow but steady accumulation of wealth, assets, and skills until the nation reaches a kind of critical mass. Once it reaches this third stage, which Rostow terms the "drive for technological maturity," society undergoes a rapid process of industrialization and social change. A more stable balance returns in the fourth and final stage, when the society emerges as a mature industrial power. This process of transition is a tumultuous one, and Rostow maintains that the instability it causes may leave the developing nation vulnerable to communism or some other totalitarian system.

Why are some nations so much further ahead in the process of modernization than others? Max Weber pointed out several unique conditions in western Europe that helped make the industrial revolution possible. Weber argued that the spread of Puritan religions, which placed an enormous value on hard work and frugality, stimulated the accumulation of wealth necessary for industrialization. He also felt that the political disunity of Europe and the independence of its cities and towns prevented its feudal rulers from repressing the development of capitalism as they did, for example, in China.[24] Contemporary modernization theorists tend to put the blame on the "traditionalism" of less developed countries, which has made them resist the kind of changes necessary to create a modern industrial society. Rostow, for example, argues that less developed countries tend to have a religious, rather than a scientific, cultural orientation, which makes it more difficult to develop and utilize modern technology. According to this view, people in less developed countries often cling to their traditional ways of doing things and resist the innovations that inevitably go with the process of modernization. Rostow and other modernization theorists also cite the centralization of wealth and power in the hands of a small elite, the numerous restrictions on competitive markets, and the low overall level of education as other important barriers to modernization.[25]

World System Theory

The perspective known as world system theory is one of the newest and fastest-growing theoretical schools in contemporary sociology. While modernization theory has its source in the functionalist perspective, world system theory is a conflict theory that can trace its roots back to Karl Marx. The immediate origins of this theory are often credited to Andre Gunder Frank's studies of Latin America,[26] but it was Immanuel Wallerstein who actually created world system theory.[27] Much of the inspiration for this approach came from a critique of modernization theory and what the world system theorists saw as its ethnocentrism and its hidden bias in favor of the status quo. Some world system theorists nonetheless accept many of the points made by modernization theory, and many have also been heavily influenced by the works of Max Weber. Virtually all world system theorists agree, however, that modernization theory leaves out the most fundamental cause of Third World poverty—exploitation by the rich industrialized powers.

The most fundamental insight of this new perspective is that industrialization does not take place in isolated individual nations, as modernization theory assumes, but within a complex web of international economic and political relationships known as the **world system.** In its beginnings, the modern world system was a rather small affair limited to a part of northern Europe, but it eventually grew into

world system
The network of economic and political relationships that links the world together.

core

The wealthy industrialized nations that dominate the world system.

periphery

The poor nations of the world, which are subject to the economic and political domination of the core nations.

semiperiphery

The partially industrialized nations that have characteristics of both the core and the periphery.

hegemonic power

The strongest of the industrialized powers, which assumes leadership of the world system.

the global financial and political network that now dominates the planet. At the center of the world system are the rich and powerful industrialized nations, known as the **core.** These core nations are surrounded by a much larger number of poor nations, called the **periphery.** The core nations exploit the periphery for its natural resources and cheap labor while using their military and economic power to prevent peripheral nations from growing strong enough to challenge the interests of the core. Between these two extremes is the **semiperiphery.** Countries in this category are more industrialized than the peripheral nations but are far behind the core. Although they are still subject to the economic and political domination of the core, the semiperipheral nations are themselves able to exploit their poorer neighbors.

World system theorists disagree about how to classify the remaining communist nations. The most common view is that communism represented an effort by exploited nations to pull out of the world system and industrialize on their own, without foreign interference. The collapse of European communism is seen as evidence of how powerful the capitalist world system is and how difficult it is for any nation to challenge it. World system theorists argue that the former communist countries, such as Russia and the eastern European nations, are now back in the capitalist world system and once again in a subordinate role.

The historical record shows that the core is often led by a single **hegemonic power**—a dominant nation that is far stronger economically, militarily, and politically than the other core states. The first hegemonic power was Holland, followed by Great Britain and then the United States. However, the military and economic costs of protecting the world system impose a heavy burden on the hegemonic power, and many world system theorists argue that the United States is already slipping from its position of dominance, as Holland and Britain did before it.

According to world system theory, the fundamental cause of poverty in the peripheral nations is not that they are too traditional but that the core nations have forced them into a position of economic and political dependence. While modernization theory sees poor nations as simply places where economic development has yet to take place, world system theorists point out that the peripheral nations have in fact undergone enormous social and economic changes. However, those changes have not been dictated by their own needs but by those of the core nations. Many poor countries have great natural resources, but it is the needs of the core nations that determine which minerals are to be produced and the price that such things as timber and petroleum will bring. Many poor nations have lush plantations, but their agricultural bounty is consumed by the people of the rich nations. Many poor nations have beautiful beaches and resorts, but they are full of wealthy tourists from the industrialized countries. Underlying all these inequities is the fact that many of the most productive assets in the poor nations are owned and operated by multinational corporations from the core nations.

Critics of world system theory complain that it is too ideological and that its supporters see only the bad side of capitalism. Such critics point out that both life expectancy and the standard of living in the Third World are actually much higher now than they were in the past. They argue that far from exploiting the less developed countries, the industrialized countries are in fact helping them. The critics claim that if industrial capitalism had never developed in western Europe, the Third World would still be suffering from the extreme poverty and class exploitation typical of most agricultural societies. Defenders of world system theory respond that the standard of living as calculated by the economists is not a very good measure of actual conditions in the Third World. World system theorists argue that while monetary income may have gone up, the quality of life has declined as the traditional life-style of Third World people has been destroyed, and they say that conditions certainly would have been much better in the periphery without foreign interference.[28] (See the Debate "Are the Rich Nations Exploiting the Poor Ones?")

Evaluation

It may seem frustrating to students that the enormous amount of time and effort social scientists have spent analyzing global inequality hasn't produced more agreement about its causes. But behind the academic and political rivalry between these two theoretical camps, there are actually considerable areas of agreement. The naive version of world system theory would blame all the world's problems on the capitalist core nations, while naive modernization theorists see the "traditionalism" of the Third World as the cause of all its difficulties. More sophisticated members of both camps recognize that no single factor can explain the complexities of the modern world. Traditional values, the lack of capital, low educational levels, weak government, and the other factors cited by the modernization theorists have certainly played a major role in creating today's global divide, but so has the exploitation of the poor nations by the rich ones. To understand our current problems, we must look at both the internal conditions within individual nations that impede development and the world system of economic and political relationships in which those nations are embedded.

Quick Review

What impact did the industrial revolution have on global inequality?

Compare and contrast the ways the modernization theory and world system theory explain inequality between groups of nations.

What are the strengths and weaknesses of the modernization and world system theories?

Solving the Problems of Global Inequality

As we have seen, the less developed countries are faced with daunting and complex problems. Many social scientists and political leaders have a pet proposal they see as a solution to our global crisis; but just as there is no one cause of the global divide, there is no single solution. This section will examine some of the most common suggestions, but there are still strong disagreements about the wisdom and the possible effectiveness of all these proposals. We will begin by exploring some ideas about what the industrialized world can do to help the less developed countries, and then we will look at what those nations can do themselves.

The Industrialized Nations

Although there are a number of ways the industrialized nations could help the less developed countries, there is a real question about whether they will make a serious

Debate   Are the Rich Nations Exploiting the Poor Ones?

Yes

All you have to do is look around any Third World country. The evidence of victim-ization is everywhere. The children are sickly and malnourished while their parents are often tired and hopeless. Those who live in mud huts and crowded tenements are actually the lucky ones, for whole families often sleep in the streets. Most Third World cities are jammed with legions of unemployed young men and women who have little real chance of ever finding a steady job. Yet this poverty and deprivation occur in the shadow of the incredible abundance of the industrialized nations. The per capita income in the world today is far higher than it has ever been before, but most of that wealth stays in the hands of a privileged few.

Exactly how do the rich nations take advantage of the poor countries? First, Third World people are exploited for their labor. The Third World is now dotted with factories producing consumer goods for the rich nations. The wages paid by the multinational corporations that own most of these factories are pitifully low—often less than $1 a day. Not only are the hours long and the pay low, but the factories are hot, polluted, and dangerous. Hundreds of thousands of workers die every year be-cause of working conditions that would never be tolerated in the wealthy nations. Second, Third World nations are exploited for their natural resources. Their forests are stripped, their petroleum reserves pumped out, and their mineral deposits de-pleted in order to satisfy the core nations' voracious appetite for raw materials. Al-though the peripheral countries receive some money for these commodities, the economic monopoly of the industrialized nations enables them to keep the price of raw materials far below their real value. Third, the poor nations are forced to follow political and economic policies dictated by the rich ones. Through the careful use of bribes, covert operations, and outright military force, the core keeps the poor na-tions from mounting an effective challenge to the world order that exploits them. In addition, a new form of exploitation is developing as the southern part of the planet becomes the dumping ground for toxic wastes and unsafe products manufactured in the core.

The next time someone tells you how much good our corporations and our governments are doing in the Third World, stop and think for a moment. Picture Europeans and North Americans dying from the clogged arteries that come from overeating while millions of people starve to death in the Third World. Or picture a Third World dictator slaughtering his people with the guns, tanks, and aircraft supplied by his supporters in the core nations. The truth will soon become obvious.

effort to do so. Of course, virtually all the governments of the core nations say they want to assist the poor countries, but those fine words are seldom translated into ef-fective programs. Many influential people in the industrialized nations simply don't care what happens in the far-off countries of the Third World, while others may fear that the industrialization of those countries would mean more economic and politi-cal competition for their own nations. Thus, the first step is to educate the people of

No

It's human nature to try to find someone to blame for our problems. When we compare the poverty of the Third World with the affluence of the industrialized nations, it is natural to blame one on the other. When we place these problems in historical perspective, however, it is apparent that the industrialized nations have actually helped to improve the standard of living in the Third World. The most useful comparison is not between the rich and poor nations of today's world but between the Third World today and the way most countries in Africa, Asia, and Latin America were before they were influenced by the industrialized powers. When seen in these terms, there is simply no question that the people of the Third World are far better off as the result of their contacts with the industrialized nations. Their average income and standard of living are much higher than they used to be. Even though most people in the Third World do not have all the latest technological innovations, they still have electric lights, radios, bicycles, and other inventions created in the industrialized nations. Health conditions have vastly improved—infant mortality has plummeted, and the average life expectancy in the Third World is probably double what it was five centuries ago. Although there are a lot of complaints about "political meddling" in the Third World, the industrialized nations have actually been a vital force, encouraging democracy and fighting communism and other totalitarian systems. Five hundred years ago, there wasn't a single democracy in the entire world; today, democracy is flowering in even the poorest nations.

The charges that the industrialized nations are exploiting the Third World are just ideological rhetoric intended for political purposes. When revolutionary leaders come to power and cut their nations off from "foreign influence," the people's standard of living goes down, not up. It is easy to complain about the low wages of the workers in the Third World. The economic fact is that these workers are less educated and less productive than workers in the industrialized nations. If their wages were raised too much, Third World factories would no longer be competitive with those in the industrialized nations. Besides, the Third World workers employed by foreign multinationals are actually the lucky ones because they earn far more than they could in almost any of the other jobs available to them. Of course, none of this means that the multinationals or the governments of the industrialized nations never take advantage of the people in the poor nations; the real world is not that simple. It is clear, however, that the industrialized nations have done far more to help than to hurt the Third World.

the industrialized countries about the acute problems of the less developed countries and the international dangers posed by their poverty and political instability.

Dropping Trade Barriers Most wealthy nations use a complex system of import taxes, quotas, and other restrictions to protect their own industries and limit the flow of goods from the low-wage countries of Africa, Latin America, and Asia. When

This photograph shows American troops in Bosnia. World system theorists argue that the rich nations are able to dominate most Third World countries through economic means, but when that fails, they resort to military power.

leaders of the less developed countries discuss the problems of economic development with their counterparts in the core nations, one of their most frequent requests is that those trade barriers be dropped and their goods be allowed to compete freely on the open market. The United Nations estimates that if the developed nations dropped all their trade barriers, the less developed countries could nearly double their exports of textiles and clothing and could earn an additional $22 billion a year in agricultural exports.[29] The North American Free Trade Agreement (NAFTA) takes this approach and has allowed Mexico far greater access to the North American market. Of course, this agreement does nothing to help the vast majority of the people in the poorer nations and may actually hurt some countries whose export markets in North America are taken over by Mexican firms.

Although the representatives of industries threatened by foreign competition often make dire predictions about what will happen if trade barriers are removed, the impact on the core nations is likely to be relatively minor. A few industries that use simple technology and a lot of labor would be hurt, but poor countries lack the technology and skills to produce most of the high-quality products demanded by the industrialized nations.

Forgiving Debt One of the most serious problems facing the less developed countries is what has come to be known as the debt crisis. The roots of this problem can be traced to the oil crisis of the early 1970s. When sharp increases in the price of petroleum sent hundreds of billions of dollars in new income to the Middle Eastern oil producers, Western banks were flooded with huge new deposits. At the same time, however, the oil crisis also created a severe recession in the world economy, so there were few attractive investment opportunities in the industrialized nations. The bankers' response was to make massive new loans to various less developed countries. Unfortunately, most of this money simply went to pay for higher oil bills or was wasted through corruption and inefficiency.

Today, many of the less developed countries are saddled with debts so large that they cannot even pay the interest, much less the principal, and as a result they are falling farther and farther behind (see Figure 17.4). In 1970, the external debt of all the less developed countries was about $100 billion; today, it is more than $1400 billion. On the average, Third World nations now pay over 2.5 times more in interest on their debt than they receive in foreign aid.[30] Most poor nations have turned to the World Bank and the International Monetary Fund as their only possible sources of capital to meet their debt payments. In exchange for their money, international development agencies typically demand that national governments take harsh austerity measures to balance their budgets and reduce imports. The effects of these

The most effective foreign aid is often targeted to the specific needs of the recipient. This photograph shows an American relief worker in Somalia.

Figure 17.4

Debt

There has been a staggering increase in the debt poor nations owe to foreign lenders.

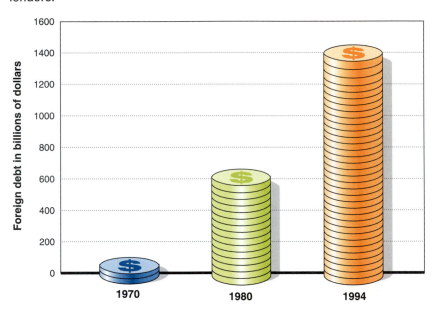

Source: United Nations Human Development Programme, *Human Development Report, 1994* (New York: Oxford University Press, 1994), p. 63; *Human Development Reprint, 1997,* p. 191.

government cutbacks fall hardest on the poor—whatever meager government assistance they receive is reduced or eliminated while new economic policies drive their countries into recession.

The effects of the debt crisis are easily seen in Latin America. In earlier times, Latin America was often one of the world's fastest-growing regions, but during the 1980s its per capita income declined by 10 percent—a catastrophe most economists blame on debt problems. In the 1990s, economic activity began picking up in Latin America, and its major nations have signed various agreements to restructure their loans. Their overall debts are still huge, however, and they continue to be a major drag on the economies of nations throughout Latin America. While things are looking a little brighter in Latin America,[31] sub-Saharan Africa has continued to sink deeper into debt.[32] The banks are obviously reluctant to write off these loans as bad debts, but sooner or later it must be done. Many of these nations simply have no way to pay back the money, and the human costs of the continuing demand for payment are enormous.

Foreign Aid Many Americans think that their government spends huge sums in foreign aid to help the developing nations. Actually, the United States spends only one-tenth of 1 percent of its national income on foreign economic assistance. Although the American economy is twice as large as Japan's, the Japanese actually give twice as much foreign aid. In fact, when viewed in terms of the percentage of their total economy that nations give in foreign aid, the United States is far down on the list. Norway gives about nine times more, Canada almost four times more.[33] Moreover, most American aid is not targeted to help the world's poorest people. The politically sensitive Middle East gets more American money than Latin America, Africa, and the Far East put together, although it has only a tiny fraction of their population. Unfortunately, the United States is not alone in this politicized approach to foreign aid. Otherwise, it would be hard to explain why the richest Third World nations receive twice as much aid per person as the poorest ones.[34]

It seems clear that a serious effort on the part of the United States and the other industrialized nations to help alleviate the poverty of the less developed countries should include a significant increase in the total amount of foreign aid and a change in the way it is allocated so that the assistance goes to the people who need it most. Nonetheless, foreign aid is no cure-all for the problems of the peripheral nations. For one thing, the governments of some countries are so corrupt that foreign aid only enriches the local elites and does nothing for the poor. Another problem is that handouts can inadvertently create a vicious cycle of dependency. For example, food from the core nations given to help feed the hungry often drives down the prices paid local farmers, resulting in lower agricultural production and an even greater need for foreign aid the next year. Wherever possible, foreign aid should therefore be carefully targeted toward training, education, birth control, and other specific development projects.

Being Good Neighbors Traditionally, most nations haven't been very concerned with anything outside their borders that didn't have a direct impact on them. If neighbors were weak, they were looked on as possible prey; if strong, they were viewed as possible aggressors; otherwise, they were usually ignored. Modern technology and the growth of the world system have made all the world's nations neighbors, but most nations still see the world in terms of narrow self-interest. Even after the end of European colonialism, the rich industrialized nations continued to advance their own interests by meddling in the internal affairs of the poor countries. Since World War II, the United States has fought three full-scale wars in the Third World (in Korea, Vietnam, and Iraq); invaded the Dominican Republic, Grenada, and Panama; organized and funded independent armies in such places as Nicaragua and Cambodia; made assassination attempts against Third World leaders; supported and even arranged numerous coups and revolutions, such as the one that brought the Shah of Iran to power and the one that killed Salvador Allende, the leftist president of Chile; and given huge amounts of secret financial assistance to help some political causes and hurt others.[35]

Defenders of these actions claim they actually benefited the countries involved, but the foreign policy of the United States is, after all, designed to advance America's own interests and those of its upper class—not those of the less developed countries.[36] The justification for most of these policies was America's overriding concern with defeating the communist challenge. With the end of the **Cold War** and the collapse of Soviet communism, much of the rationale for such measures is also gone, and this would seem to be an ideal time for a fundamental reorientation of foreign policy. Most countries would still like to see the United States and the other industrialized nations take action to help out during acute international crises. But it is critical that such actions be supported by international law and a consensus of the international community, not based simply on naked self-interest. The

Cold War
The struggle for world domination between the capitalist and communist nations after World War II.

United States and the other core powers will undoubtedly continue to be politically involved in the Third World in one way or another, and it is essential that they act like good neighbors and not the local bullies.

The Less Developed Countries

Economic development is obviously a much more vital issue in the poor nations than in the industrialized ones, but that does not mean that peripheral nations do not have their own powerful vested interests that oppose significant change. Elite groups that reap the benefits of the current system obviously have little desire for reform. Nonetheless, a growing number of Third World leaders realize that it is not a question of whether their societies will change but how they will change.

Those governments committed to major reforms face many perplexing issues. Some Third World leaders feel that the best path is simply to copy the nations that are already industrialized. But others, although attracted by the wealth and power of Japan and the Western nations, are also deeply disturbed by the threat industrialization poses to their traditional moral standards and way of life. In the Middle East, for example, many leaders advocate some kind of distinctive "Islamic" approach to development, but it is not clear exactly what that might be or what chances such an approach would have for success. A related question concerns the role of the core powers. Should the leaders of the less developed countries encourage foreign investment and accept the risk of domination it brings, or should they try to go it alone without much outside money? No matter which course they take, funds are likely to be in short supply, and Third World governments will have to make difficult choices among competing options.

Population Control By itself, population control will not solve the problems of the less developed countries, but neither can those problems be solved without it. The current rate of population growth in Latin America and Asia (excluding China) is around 1.6 percent a year, which means that there must be at least 1.6 percent economic growth every year just to keep the standard of living from falling. The situation is far worse in sub-Saharan Africa, where the population growth rate is 2.7 percent, and in the Middle East, where it is about 2.2 percent.[37] It is not just an issue of making the economy grow faster than the population, however. There are concrete environmental limits on how many people can comfortably live in a given area. Even if the average income grows, the quality of life declines as overcrowding and pollution make conditions more and more difficult. An increasing number of governments are coming to see excessive population growth as a serious national problem and are starting to take measures to control it.[38] But it remains to be seen how effective these programs will be (see Chapter 15 for a discussion of these efforts).

economic development
Economic growth in the poor nations.

Economic Development Practically all Third World leaders say they are committed to **economic development,** but that phrase has different meanings to different people. One of the biggest issues concerns priorities and goals. Those who want to emulate the industrialized nations tend to focus on large-scale development projects in urban areas. Typically, local governments use loans, foreign investments, or their own funds to build modern factories like those in the core nations. Critics charge that expensive factories with laborsaving equipment make little sense in nations that are short on money but have vast resources of unused labor. They advocate simpler, "low-tech" industries that utilize inexpensive technology and local labor to turn out low-cost products. Others claim that the whole emphasis on industrialization is misguided and that the number one priority of the governments in the poor nations should be rural development. They argue that since the majority of the people live in rural areas, an effort to increase farm production and prevent runaway urban growth will create the greatest benefits for the most people (see Chapter 14).

Most leaders in the poor nations nonetheless want to see their countries grow powerful enough to compete on equal terms with the core nations, and that means industrialization. How is that to be achieved? One key ingredient is capital—that is, the money to build the schools, roads, and factories necessary to an industrial economy. Unless a country is blessed with unusually rich natural resources, there are only two ways to get capital—raise it locally or rely on foreign investment. The latter is often a far more attractive alternative to the leaders of the less developed countries because foreign investors can provide huge sums of money immediately, without the sacrifices and political tensions necessary to raise significant amounts of local capital. However, a great deal of research indicates that although investment by foreign multinational corporations provides a short-term boost to a local economy, in the long run, self-reliance is the most effective approach.[39] Investments by multinational corporations represent a quick infusion of cash, but once the factories are built, the flow of capital is reversed as the firms take their profits back home. Moreover, the more multinational investment a country allows, the greater the percentage of its economy that will be under foreign control. Time and again, the vast financial resources of the multinationals have enabled them to corrupt local officials and win economic concessions that benefit the corporations at the cost of the host economy.

These generalizations do not mean that multinational investment cannot be beneficial in some circumstances. For example, nations so poor and disorganized that they have few sources of local capital may have no choice but to rely on foreign investors. At the other extreme, the most prosperous and well-organized of the less developed countries may be able to accept significant amounts of multinational investment and still maintain strict enough controls to ensure that it provides real benefits to their own economies.

Political Reform All the nations that have undergone a successful process of industrialization, such as the United States, Germany, and Japan, have had strong, unified governments.[40] The process of industrialization is a grueling one that creates enormous social pressures that cannot be effectively managed in a weak, divided country. Of course, it is easy to tell the people of less developed countries that they need to pull together and support a unified government, but how are they to do it? Some nations, such as Japan, had a long tradition of powerful government and obedience to authority that gave them a significant advantage from the beginning of their drive for industrialization. As we have seen, however, governments in the peripheral nations are likely to be weak and deeply divided along class and ethnic lines. In some cases, democratic reforms can be extremely helpful; they bring a much wider spectrum of people into the process of government and help create more popular support for the regime. Social movements based on religious or economic ideologies have sometimes served to bring a new sense of organization and purpose to floundering governments as well. At other times, violent revolutionary change is required before an unstable government can be replaced by a strong one. Revolution was necessary in the United States, Russia, and even Japan before those nations could launch an effective drive for industrialization. Even the current trend toward fragmentation of large countries into smaller nations with more ethnic homogeneity may be beneficial if the end result is the creation of more unified nations with stronger governments. It is clear, however, that no single factor—including a unified and well-run government—can guarantee economic success. The emperors of classical China used the authority of their government to prevent the merchant class from becoming prosperous enough to threaten the power of the feudal landlords, and they thereby also prevented the growth of a modern economy. The powerful communist state in the Soviet Union was extremely effective in carrying out a crash program of industrialization, but the militarism and the rigid bureaucratic mentality of that regime eventually choked off its own economic growth.

Quick Review

What can we in the industrialized nations do to help the poor nations of the world? What are the poor nations' best options for improving themselves?

Sociological Perspectives on the Global Divide

Most sociologists are convinced that in order to deal with social problems effectively, we must first understand their causes and then formulate our response based on that understanding. As we have seen, functionalism (by shaping modernization theory) and conflict theory (through its influence on world system theory) have played a major role in explaining the deep divisions in today's world, and each approach implies a different program of action. Feminists and interactionists have also given their attention to these problems and have made their own important contributions to our understanding of global inequality.

The Functionalist Perspective

Wherever functionalists look among the less developed countries, they see the problems of social disorganization. Under pressure from rapid economic change, the extended family is breaking down and its traditional power is slowly ebbing away. There is a growing cultural lag as people cling to traditional attitudes that were useful in the past but have now become a serious drawback. For example, most people in the less developed countries still place a high importance on having a large family, even though today's population explosion makes that an extremely dysfunctional attitude. Traditional religious beliefs are being challenged by secular ideas from the West and a rising tide of materialism. The educational institutions that foster the scientific worldview are often so weak that they do not even reach large segments of the population. As we have noted, governments are ineffective and deeply divided. Perhaps most serious of all, economic institutions have not made a smooth transition from an agricultural to an industrial system and often flounder somewhere between the two. A flood of immigrant villagers pours into cities that lack enough jobs, sanitation, and housing to support them. Thus, functionalists see the less developed countries to be in a difficult state of transition from one kind of social and cultural system to another.

Since functionalists generally assume that the less developed countries will ultimately end up as Western-style industrial nations, they feel that the best way to help is to speed up the process of transition so these societies can regain their balance as quickly as possible. Functionalists therefore recommend a much stronger emphasis on education in less developed countries in order to teach people the skills necessary in an industrial economy. They advocate a strong program of family planning to help change dysfunctional attitudes favoring large families. Urban development programs must be launched to create enough housing for the expanding urban population. Since functionalists are not very concerned about the issue of economic exploitation, they often advocate more foreign investment by multinational corporations as a good way to spread modern attitudes and economic structures. Finally, the governments of the less developed countries need to be made more democratic so that they can gain the support of their population for the difficult reforms that must be made.

The Conflict Perspective

Where the functionalists see disorganization, the conflict theorists see the results of international exploitation. In the past, the exploitation was obvious. When the Europeans first colonized a new area, they would loot whatever gold and jewels they could find and then take over direct political control of the native peoples. Today the exploitation is more subtle, but conflict theorists are convinced that it is just as real. The peripheral nations now have their own governments, but conflict theorists feel that the armies and the secret agents of the industrial powers are always waiting to punish any Third World leader who gets out of line. The people of the peripheral nations are no longer forced to work as slaves in the mines and plantations, but they work for wages so low that they are barely better off than slaves. Foreigners no longer simply steal the wealth of the peripheral countries—they buy up their precious natural resources at a fraction of their real value.

To the conflict theorists, the answer to the problems of the Third World is a simple one—end the economic exploitation that has victimized so much of the earth's population. Exactly how that is to be done is a more difficult matter. Despite the failure of the communist government of the Soviet Union, many conflict theorists are still strong supporters of Third World revolutionary movements that seek to overthrow their local governments. They urge the revolutionaries to create new regimes, free from foreign influence, that represent the interests of all their people and not just a small elite. Conflict theorists also encourage Third World nations to band together in the struggle against the industrialized nations. They point to the success the Organization of Petroleum Exporting Countries (OPEC) had in increasing the price of oil, and they call for the creation of similar cartels for other raw materials. Many conflict theorists feel that the key to liberating the Third World lies in the core nations. They argue that because the multinational corporations are exploiting workers in the industrialized nations in much the same way they exploit the workers in the Third World, the two groups must join together to demand the creation of a more just world order that will benefit them all.

The Feminist Perspective

From the feminist perspective, the poor women of the Third World are the most exploited of the most exploited. Not only are their countries exploited by foreigners, but the poor people within a country are exploited by the rich, and the poor women are exploited by their husbands and their other male family members. As we have seen in this chapter, the women of the Third World are denied the most basic human rights to control their own lives and are often treated as little more than domestic servants by their family members.

Aside from its obvious injustice, this system also wastes the talents and leadership abilities of the Third World's women. Feminists therefore advocate the kind of female-oriented development projects that have proved not only to be able to improve the status of women but to be one of the most effective techniques to stimulate economic development. One of the best examples is the Grameen Bank, which was started in Bangladesh but now has over a thousand branches around the world. The Grameen Bank specializes in making small loans to poor women in order to help them do such things as set up businesses or improve their farms. The bank prefers female clients because they have found that money loaned to women was more likely to be used to benefit the whole family and that women were more likely to repay their loans than men. The results of these modest loans have often proved to be revolutionary—not only improving the local economy but liberating women from the domination of their husbands.[41]

The Interactionist Perspective

Interactionists' primary contribution to the study of global inequality has been through their efforts to understand the psychological consequences of modernization. Agricultural societies are characterized by mass poverty and a huge gap between the elite and the common people. Nonetheless, these tradition-bound societies provide their members with a sense of security and belonging seldom found in the industrialized world. Most people are born, live, and die in the same close-knit villages. The important transitions in life are all marked by religious rituals, and everyone holds similar definitions of the world and of each other. Since poverty is the rule, not the exception, it holds no shame. The difficulty of social mobility and the absence of a profit-oriented economy minimize competition and the tensions it causes.

Sooner or later, the process of modernization shatters this traditional perspective, and people must grope for a new way to define the world. Many leave their familiar villages and move into urban environments where few of the old rules seem to apply. Even if they can maintain strong family ties in this new world, the old sense of belonging is gone. The pressures of overpopulation and a changing economy create an intensely competitive environment in which those who fail may literally starve to death. Even those who remain in the villages are likely to find their lives changing in disturbing ways. Increasing levels of education and exposure to the media slowly undermine the old perspectives and spread the new commercial orientation. At the same time, economic dislocation and environmental deterioration make it harder and harder to make a living off the land.

Solutions to these problems must come from the kinds of proposals advanced by the macro theories, but interactionists make two additional recommendations. First, they urge the governments of the less developed countries to focus their efforts on improving the rural economy so that people can stay in their villages and avoid the wrenching psychological changes that accompany urban migration. Second, they advise the leaders of these nations to learn from the mistakes of the West and do their best to maintain strong family and community institutions.

Quick Review

Compare and contrast the functionalist and conflict approaches to global inequality.

What solutions do feminists offer for the problems of global inequality?

What has the psychological impact of modernization been?

Summary

The nations of the world make up a kind of international class system with the rich industrialized nations at the top and a much larger group of what are often called less developed countries below them. The most obvious difference between these two groups of nations is their wealth—in terms of both money and accumulated assets such as buildings, roads, and factories. Because of runaway population growth and rapid urbanization, most cities in the less developed countries have a large number of homeless people and huge shantytowns. Inadequate nutrition and contagious disease make the life expectancy far below that in the industrialized nations. Women are commonly denied the most basic rights men enjoy, and children face serious health and economic problems. Literacy rates are low, and because there is only a small middle class, the gap between the rich and the poor is usually a large one. The less developed countries are also more likely to have deep ethnic divisions and ineffective governments.

The enormous difference between the wealthy nations and the poor nations developed in the modern era as some countries underwent a rapid process of industrialization while others did not. Modernization theorists see industrialization as a universal process that has simply taken place more quickly in some parts of the world than in others. The less developed countries have made slower progress because they have clung to traditional attitudes and values that impede industrialization. World system theory, on the other hand, sees industrialization as a global process, not a national one. All nations are seen to be part of a single world system dominated by the industrialized nations (the core), which exploit the poor nations (the periphery).

The rich countries can help the less developed ones by opening up their markets, forgiving the debts owed by the poor nations, increasing foreign aid, and ending their political interference in the internal affairs of the poor nations. The less developed countries themselves are faced with many difficult choices. Do they emphasize industrialization or rural development? Do they encourage investment by multinational corporations or depend on their own resources? How are their limited development funds best spent? There are no simple answers to these questions, but it does seem clear that most less developed countries need better population control programs, a greater effort at economic development, and stronger governments.

Functionalists see today's global divide as the product of social disorganization in the less developed countries, and they recommend programs to speed up the transition to full industrialization in order to bring more stability to these societies. Conflict theorists see most of today's global problems as the direct result of European colonialism and the exploitative economic system that developed from it. They recommend an international effort by poor and working-class people around the world to create a more just international order. Feminists call for more female-oriented development programs both to improve the status of women and to promote general economic improvements. Interactionists point out that the destruction of the traditional worldview and way of life in agricultural societies has also meant a great deal more insecurity and anxiety for the average person. They urge the leaders of the less developed countries to work to keep their family and community institutions strong.

Questions for Critical Thinking

When most Americans think about improving conditions in the Third World, they think of making those countries more like us, but is that really a good idea? What problems has our process of industrialization created for us? Is there some way the developing countries can avoid repeating our mistakes? Would it even be possible for the whole world to consume as many resources and produce as much pollution as we do?

Key Terms

capital accumulation
Cold War
colonialism
core
economic development
ethnocentrism
hegemonic power
industrial revolution

less developed countries (LDCs),
    Third World
modernization
periphery
semiperiphery
sub-Saharan Africa
urban subsistence economy
world system

Further Readings

York W. Bradshaw and Michael Wallace, *Global Inequalities* (Thousand Oaks: Pine Forge, 1996). A readable review of the current state of the world, showing the huge inequalities between the rich and poor nations.

Daniel Chirot, *How Societies Change* (Thousand Oaks: Pine Forge, 1996). A highly respected sociologist's concise study of the sweeping historical changes that produced the modern world.

Gerald Epstein, Julie Graham, and Jessica Nembhard, *Creating a New World Economy* (Philadelphia: Temple University Press, 1993). If you are interested in what can be done to improve conditions in the less developed countries, this collection of articles is a good place to start.

Thomas Richard Shannon, *An Introduction to the World-System Perspective,* 2nd ed. (Boulder, CO: Westview, 1996). A clearly written summary of world system theory, with a useful analysis of its strengths and weaknesses.

L. S. Stavrianos, *Global Rift: The Third World Comes of Age* (New York: Morrow, 1981). A compelling history of the development of the Third World.

Notes

1. Vivienne Walt, "Women's Work," *Mother Jones,* September–October 1995, p. 34.
2. See Harold R. Kerbo, *Social Stratification and Inequality,* 3rd ed. (New York: McGraw-Hill, 1996), pp. 397–433.
3. Population Reference Bureau, *World Population Data Sheet, 1997* (Washington, DC: Population Reference Bureau, 1997).
4. Ibid.
5. United Nations Development Programme, *Human Development Report, 1997* (New York: Oxford University Press, 1997), p. 165.
6. Ibid., pp. 177, 204.
7. See Ibid., pp. 164–167, 169.
8. Bruce Stutz, "The Landscape of Hunger," in Robert M. Jackson, ed., *Global Issues 94/95* (Guilford, CT: Dushkin, 1994), pp. 89–94; G. Tyler Miller, *Living in the Environment,* 5th ed. (Belmont, CA: Wadsworth, 1988), p. 245; Jon Bennett, *The Hunger Machine: The Politics of Food* (Cambridge: Polity Press, 1987), p. 12.
9. United Nations Development Programme, *Human Development Report, 1997,* pp. 146–148.
10. Ibid., pp. 149–151, 172–173.
11. Population Reference Bureau, *World Population Data Sheet, 1997.*
12. Editors of the Christian Science Monitor, "Aiming at Child Labor," *Christian Science Monitor,* March 19, 1994, p. 18.
13. Robert M. Press, "More African Kids Take to the Streets," *Christian Science Monitor,* February 7, 1994, pp. 11–13.
14. Germaine W. Shames, "The World's Throw-Away Children," in Jackson, ed., *Global Issues 94/95,* pp. 229–232.
15. Population Reference Bureau, *World Population Data Sheet, 1997.*
16. Jeremy Brecher, "Global Unemployment at 700 Million," in Jackson, ed., *Global Issues 94/95,* pp. 32–35.
17. Kerbo, *Social Stratification and Inequality,* p. 29.
18. United Nations Development Programme, *Human Development Report, 1994,* pp. 164–165, 185.
19. Mark Fineman, "Anxious Mexicans Await Day of the Vote," *Los Angeles Times,* August 21, 1994, pp. A1, A10.
20. See Gerhard Lenski, *Power and Privilege* (New York: McGraw-Hill, 1966).
21. See United Nations Development Programme, *Human Development Report, 1997,* pp. 142–143, for some comparative statistics; and see L. S. Stavrianos, *Global Rift: The Third World Comes of Age* (New York: Morrow, 1981) for a comprehensive history of the development of the Third World.
22. See, for example, Talcott Parsons, *Societies: Evolutionary and Comparative Perspectives* (Englewood Cliffs, NJ: Prentice-Hall, 1966), and Wilbert Moore, *Social Change,* 2nd ed. (Englewood Cliffs, NJ: Prentice-Hall, 1974).

23. Walter W. Rostow, *The Stages of Economic Growth* (New York: Cambridge University Press, 1960).

24. For a contemporary discussion of these issues from a Weberian perspective, see Daniel Chirot, "The Rise of the West," *American Sociological Review* 50 (1985): 181–195.

25. See Walter W. Rostow, *The World Economy: History and Prospect* (Austin: University of Texas Press, 1980).

26. Andre Gunder Frank, *Capitalism and Underdevelopment in Latin America* (New York: Monthly Review Press, 1967).

27. See, for example, Immanuel Wallerstein's three-volume historical work, *The Modern World-System* (New York: Academic Press, 1974, 1980, 1988).

28. For an excellent summary of world system theory and an analysis of its strengths and weaknesses, see Thomas Richard Shannon, *An Introduction to the World-System Perspective,* 2nd ed. (Boulder, CO: Westview, 1996).

29. United Nations Development Programme, *Human Development Report, 1994,* pp. 66–67.

30. Ibid., p. 63; United Nations Development Programme, *Human Development Report, 1997,* p. 191.

31. William R. Rhodes, "Third-World Debt: The Disaster That Didn't Happen," in Jackson, ed., *Global Issues 94/95,* pp. 135–137.

32. United Nations Development Programme, *Human Development Report, 1997,* p. 191.

33. Ibid., p. 214.

34. United Nations Development Programme, *Human Development Report, 1994,* pp. 69–77.

35. See James William Coleman, *The Criminal Elite: Understanding White Collar Crime* (New York: St. Martin's Press, 1998), pp. 61–66.

36. On the control of foreign policy by elite groups, see G. William Domhoff, *The Power Elite and the State* (New York: Aldine de Gruyter, 1990).

37. Population Reference Bureau, *World Population Data Sheet, 1997.*

38. See ibid., for a description of each nation's official view of its current rate of population growth.

39. See Volker Bornschier and Christopher Chase-Dunn, *Transnational Corporations and Underdevelopment* (New York: Praeger, 1985).

40. See Daniel Chirot, *Social Change in the Modern Era* (San Diego: Harcourt Brace Jovanovich, 1986).

41. Muhammad Yunus, "Helping the Poor to Help Themselves," *Los Angeles Times,* February 17, 1997, p. B5; Robin Wright, "Women as Engines Out of Poverty," *Los Angeles Times,* May 27, 1997, pp. A1, A6.

Warfare: Revolutionary, Ethnic, and International Conflict

18

What are the differences between international wars and revolutions?

What are the consequences of war?

What are the causes of war?

How does terrorism differ from conventional warfare?

What are the prospects for world peace?

How can international conflict be prevented?

The daughter of a country judge from the small New England town of Putney, Vermont, Jody Williams is a political crusader. She began her career as an activist working against U.S. policy in Central America in the early 1980s and eventually became director of the Los Angeles–based relief organization Medical Aid to El Salvador. In 1991, she began working with the Vietnam Veterans of America Foundation to form a coalition to push for an international ban on land mines. Unlike other weapons, land mines—small explosive devices that are usually buried in the ground—continue to wreak their havoc long after a war is over. They currently kill or brutally maim some 26,000 people a year. Although Williams started the campaign with only three people, she was a tireless and effective organizer, and she soon put together an alliance of 1000 groups working against land mines, which came to be known as the International Campaign to Ban Landmines. In only six years, they succeeded in getting nearly 100 countries to support a treaty to end the production, sale, and stockpiling of land mines and to clean up existing minefields around the world. Ironically, her own country has been the only major power to refuse to cooperate. Despite that disappointment, in 1997 she received the crowning award of her career—the Noble Peace Prize.

The twentieth century has seen the two most devastating wars in human history and hundreds of other regional conflicts, revolutions, and uprisings. But as we head into the twenty-first century, most Americans don't seem very worried about the great issues of war and peace. Perhaps that's because the Cold War between the Soviet Union and the United States is finally over, and there don't seem to be any other serious challenges to American power. But whatever its causes, such apathy is deeply misguided. None of the rich industrialized nations may be at each other's throats, but much of the world is still a simmering cauldron of conflict and hatred. In this interdependent world, even the smallest conflicts can have wide-ranging effects that go far beyond the immediate human carnage. And as more and more countries develop nuclear bombs and other **weapons of mass destruction,** the chances of another massive international holocaust steadily grow. People like Jody Williams prove that even a single individual who cares can make a difference. But before we can have any hope of taking effective action, our first task is to understand the problem of warfare.

weapons of mass destruction
Military weapons that indiscriminately kill large numbers of people, for example, nuclear or biological weapons.

The Nature of War

Although warfare goes back to the earliest recorded history, it is difficult to define precisely. Part of the problem is that the difference between war and peace is a matter of degree. Everyone will agree that World War II deserves to be called a war and that a typical murder does not, but what about an ethnic riot in which two groups throw rocks and insults at each other? What if they throw hand grenades and firebombs? To qualify as a war, such incidents must be organized and violent and must last over a reasonably long period of time. Thus, **war** may be defined as a protracted military conflict between two or more organized groups. This definition still does not tell us, however, exactly how long or how violent these conflicts must be to qualify as a war. Wars are classified in many different ways, but for sociological under-

war
A protracted military conflict between two or more organized groups.

standing, a simple division between **international wars** and **revolutionary wars** is most useful. The former are armed conflicts between the governments of two or more sovereign nations; the latter are armed conflicts between an official government and one or more groups of national rebels.

international war
Protracted armed conflict between two or more nations.

revolutionary wars
Armed conflicts between an official government and one or more groups of rebels.

The Escalation of Military Violence

Throughout human history, periods of conflict have been the rule and peace the exception. Melvin Small and J. David Singer's study of warfare from 1816 to 1980 found only 20 years in which there were no international wars in progress.[1] This century alone has seen two "world" wars and countless lesser conflicts. Even in the most peaceful times, the next war is seldom far away. There are so many international and national tensions, and the traditions of warfare are so deeply entrenched, that the world is likely to show this pattern for years to come.

Although history records a seemingly endless series of wars, the nature of those conflicts has changed significantly over the years. Traditionally, wars were limited. They usually aimed to achieve fairly narrow objectives, such as seizing part of a neighboring ruler's territory. A small group of military men, who were ordinarily from wealthy and privileged backgrounds, did most of the fighting. In fact, these professional soldiers actually had far more in common with the enemies they fought than with the average men and women who watched from the sidelines. The behavior of soldiers in battle was often regulated by a code of gallantry, and those who did not conform ran the risk of losing honor in the eyes of their comrades.

Modern warfare, starting with Napoleon (emperor of France 1804–1815), has been marked by a steady escalation of violence. Modern warfare is often **total war**—an all-out national effort to kill or subdue enemy civilians and soldiers alike. Today's wars are no longer fought mainly by professional soldiers and privileged elites; most of the soldiers are average citizens, often drafted against their will. Civilians now have a key role in the military effort: manufacturing trucks and airplanes, producing oil, growing food. In modern warfare, the victorious nations are usually those with the greatest productive capacity. It follows that civilians contributing to such production are prime military targets. Moreover, the tremendous range and destructiveness of modern weapons has expanded the combat zone to include most civilians.

total war
A war whose goal is the unconditional surrender of an enemy nation and in which both military personnel and ordinary citizens are targeted for attack.

Over the years, we have invented more and more efficient ways of killing our enemies at longer distances. The spear was replaced by the bow and arrow, which became the crossbow. The musket developed into the cannon, the rifle, and the machine gun. In World War I (1914–1918) the cannon and rifle were fused into the long rifle, a huge gun that enabled the Germans to shell Paris from a distance of 75 miles. The hand grenade of World War I became the bomb of World War II, dropped from high-flying airplanes 1000 miles from their base. The TNT bomb gave way to the atom bomb, and the bomber was replaced with the guided missile. Now, a modern military force can wreak destruction virtually anywhere in the world at any time.[2]

Some people consider this tremendous destructive power an instrument of peace. At a minimum, it makes total war less appealing, since even the victors are likely to suffer terrible devastation. Although modern nations are organized for total

nuclear war
A war in which the combatants use nuclear weapons.

nuclear proliferation
The spread of nuclear weapons to an ever larger number of countries.

war, the wars that have occurred since the development of nuclear weapons have been confined to limited areas, as in Korea, Southeast Asia, and the Middle East. It appears that fear of a **nuclear war** has helped to head off full-scale global conflict. Nevertheless, the possibility remains that such limitations will someday be broken, and all-out nuclear war remains a real threat to human survival.

One of the main reasons that this threat remains so strong is **nuclear proliferation:** the spread of nuclear weapons to more and more nations around the world. At the dawn of the nuclear age, only the United States had these frightening weapons. Soon the Soviet Union, Britain, and France developed their own atomic bombs. For a few years, nuclear weapons were exclusively in the hands of the major industrial powers, but in the 1960s, China developed an atomic bomb, and it was soon followed by its neighbor to the south, India. Western experts believe that like China, India now has a considerable nuclear arsenal, some of which may be mounted on intermediate-range ballistic missiles. The next link in this chain was India's archenemy, Pakistan. When India resumed its nuclear testing in 1998, Pakistan set off its own series of atomic blasts in a new nuclear arms race in south Asia. It also seems certain that Israel has a large stockpile of nuclear bombs, although it refuses to admit that it posseses such weapons. In addition to Russia itself, the breakup of the Soviet Union produced three new nuclear powers—Belarus, Kazakhstan, and Ukraine, which have, however, pledged to remove or dismantle their nuclear weapons. There is also considerable concern that some of the more than 30,000 nuclear weapons the Soviet Union possessed at the time of its collapse or part of its huge stockpiles of weapons-grade nuclear material might fall into the wrong hands. Moreover, several of the world's most belligerent and unpredictable governments, including Libya and Iran, are apparently working to develop their own nuclear capability. It is becoming increasingly clear that the "peaceful" nuclear power plants and technical know-how that the United States, Canada, and other industrialized powers have sold to nations around the world have made it far easier for these nations to make nuclear bombs. As more nations develop their own nuclear weapons, it seems almost inevitable that someone, somewhere, will use them.[3]

The Consequences of War

Human history is filled with the carnage of war. Small and Singer concluded that there have been an average of 7.9 international and 6.4 revolutionary wars every decade for the last 165 years.[4] These wars have reaped a staggering toll in human lives—in the last two centuries, wars have killed over 150 million people.[5] The battles of World War II alone are believed to have cost about 15 million lives, and when civilian casualties are added in, the total comes to almost 48 million deaths.[6] Although many Americans think that the world has been relatively peaceful in recent times, there have actually been another 40 million war-related deaths since the end of World War II.[7] The dead are not the only victims, however. Every war leaves a human legacy of the maimed and crippled, widows and widowers, grieving parents, and orphans. Even the soldiers who escape physically unharmed often suffer psychological wounds that stay with them for the rest of their lives.

Economically, the price tag for even a small war is astronomical. Property worth hundreds of millions of dollars has often been destroyed in a single day. Military technology has made it possible to transform a thriving community into a pile of rubble in a matter of seconds. Even if there were no loss of property, the costs of war are still enormous: businesses fail; production of consumer goods slows down or stops; fields go unplanted and crops unharvested for want of labor. Many nations have plunged from affluence to starvation during a single war.

Even in times of peace, we pay a price for war. Almost 23 million people are currently employed by the world's armed forces, and in 1997, the nations of the world spent about $823 billion on their military (see Figure 18.1). Of this amount, over one-fifth was spent by the less developed countries, which, of course, often have trouble just feeding their people.[8] These figures are so large that they are difficult to grasp. There are a number of ways to put them in perspective. We could, for example, build 12,000 high schools for the cost of a single aircraft carrier. The cost of developing a new bomber would pay the yearly salaries of a 250,000 teachers to staff those schools. Yet as huge as these military costs seem to us, they are an even heavier burden to the poor countries, where money spent on human needs goes much further. The cost of one tank, a relatively low-priced piece of military hardware in the industrialized world, could build 1,000 classrooms in a poor nation. Some experts believe that we could eradicate malaria with the money the world spends on the military in just 12 hours.[9]

There are economists who argue that such enormous military outlays are beneficial because they create jobs and stimulate the economy. This might be true, but if it is, it also follows that much greater benefits would be reaped if the money were spent on goods and services that are economically useful. For example, a nation is no better off economically with 1,000 nuclear missiles than it is with 1, but a nation

Figure 18.1

Guns Versus Butter

In comparison with other industrialized nations, the United States tends to spend more on the military and less on education.

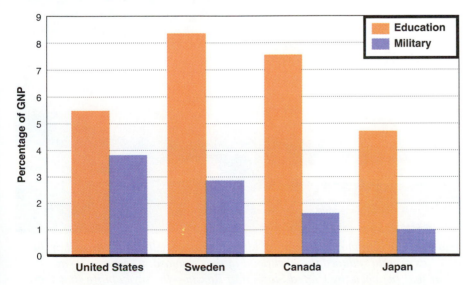

Source: United Nations Human Development Programme, *Human Development Report, 1997* (New York: Oxford University Press, 1997), pp. 208, 215.

is much better off with 1,000 hydroelectric power plants than with only 1. Two of the nations that are often considered the world's economic powerhouses, Germany and Japan, both have small armed forces and low military budgets.[10]

As heavy as all these military costs are, they are minuscule compared with those of a full-scale nuclear war. Such a war has never occurred, so it is impossible to be sure what would actually happen, but scientists have been able to make some educated guesses. The best source of data is the only two atomic explosions that ever occurred in populated areas: the U.S. attacks on Hiroshima and Nagasaki. Those two bombs killed 110,000 people in the first seconds after the blast, and another 100,000 people died within a year. Tens of thousands more were severely injured, and people are still dying from the long-term effects of radiation poisoning. Despite this horrible toll, the bombs dropped on those two cities were small and primitive by today's standards. There are tens of thousands of nuclear warheads in the hands of the world's governments today, and some of them are over *4,000 times* more powerful than the bombs dropped on Japan. Scientists estimate that a nuclear exchange involving only about one-third of those weapons would kill over 1 billion people in the first few hours. As clouds of radiation spread throughout the globe, entire species of plants and animals would die, along with 50 to 75 percent of the world's human population.[11]

Grim as this scenario is, many scientists believe that it may be too optimistic. Studies first published a decade ago and since subjected to intense scientific

Nuclear war is the ultimate nightmare of human conflict. Although the end of the Cold War has greatly reduced the likelihood of the "doomsday scenario"—an all-out nuclear war between the United States and Russia—the probability that there will someday be a more limited nuclear conflict somewhere in the Third World seems to be increasing.

scrutiny indicate that an all-out nuclear exchange would create a huge cloud of dust and smoke that would cover the globe. Estimates based on studies of much smaller clouds released by volcanic eruptions suggest that some 96 percent of the sunlight normally reaching the northern hemisphere would be blocked out. The result would be a **nuclear winter** in which the average temperature, even in warm areas, would drop below freezing for several months. The lack of sunlight and plummeting temperatures would have a devastating effect on the plants and animals that produce our food, perhaps changing the ecological system of the earth in an irreversible way.[12]

nuclear winter
The sharp decline in average temperatures caused by dense clouds that would cover the earth after a major nuclear war.

The threat of an all-out nuclear war is a nightmare that has haunted humanity for half a century. Many nonetheless feel that more limited military conflicts can still have beneficial effects. The most obvious is the overthrow of oppressive and unjust governments. For example, both Germany and Japan developed stable democratic states after their totalitarian regimes were destroyed in World War II. Although some argue that even the most ruthless dictatorship can be changed by nonviolent resistance, most people doubt that such tactics would have been successful against the bloodthirsty tyrants that fill the pages of the history books. Warfare can also promote the solidarity of a nation or some of the groups within it, and it has often been a stimulant to scientific and technological progress.[13]

There are, nonetheless, many other ways of acquiring the benefits of war without paying its staggering costs. Technology has, as we have seen, brought great increases in the costs of war and reduced its benefits. Since it is quite possible that no human beings would survive an all-out nuclear conflict, the ancient practice of warfare can only be seen as a menacing social problem of the greatest magnitude for the modern world.

Quick Review

What are the differences between revolutionary warfare and international warfare?

What is nuclear proliferation, and why is it such an important issue?

Discuss the costs of warfare.

Terrorism

Although politicians and journalists talk with great authority about the problem of **terrorism,** the concept is usually vaguely defined and its application charged with political bias. Even social scientists have had little success in agreeing on a definition. One review of the literature found over 100 different definitions, often with substantial differences in the kinds of acts they included.[14] Most students of terrorism would agree that it must involve violence used for political ends, but as it stands, such a definition is far too broad, for it would include everything from total war to everyday police work. Numerous attempts have been made to narrow the definition, but there is no agreement about the best way to do it. Many definitions include the additional qualification that the political violence must be aimed against a nonmilitary population. It is, however, doubtful that there has ever been a war in which civilians were not the target of some military violence, so the distinction between terrorism and warfare remains a vague one. Perhaps the problem is that terrorism is used primarily as an emotional label to brand political acts we dislike, so

terrorism
The attempt to utilize the terror created by violence against a civilian population to achieve some political ends.

scientific definitions are largely beside the point. Groups we support are "freedom fighters," and those we oppose are "terrorists." From a sociological perspective, it would probably be better to dispose of the concept of terrorism altogether and simply consider such acts as one more form of political violence, but the term seems to have become too popular in the media and the political arena to ignore.

Despite the vagueness of its definition, it is possible to distinguish two general types of terrorism. The best known is **revolutionary terrorism.** It is used by groups trying to bring about major political changes in a particular country. Such groups believe that random terrorist attacks will create such chaos that the government they oppose will fall or at least will meet their demands. Terrorists often try to goad a government into taking extreme measures to combat them so that it will lose popular support. Underground groups also hope that their acts of violence will make the public more aware of their cause, enabling them to recruit more members and build stronger popular support. Some of today's more sophisticated terrorists openly cultivate reporters and other representatives of the media by granting special interviews, releasing prepared statements for the press, and holding open press conferences. Some terrorists even time their attacks to avoid other newsworthy events that might compete for media attention. Revolutionary terrorists often secretly receive the help of established governments that support their goals and objectives.[15]

Repressive terrorism is the opposite of revolutionary terrorism, in that its goal is to protect an existing political order. Although revolutionary terrorists receive most of the publicity, repressive terrorism is probably a far greater threat. Governments all over the world—from Haiti to the People's Republic of China—use violence to terrorize their political opponents and maintain their grip on power. Time after time, the opponents of Third World leaders mysteriously disappear and are never seen again. Torture and imprisonment without just cause are also common tools of repressive terrorists. One of the most extreme examples since the end of World War II occurred in the small country of Cambodia (now known as Kampuchea), where about 2 million of its citizens were killed in less than four years.[16] Although the scale of the violence in Cambodia was unusual, repressive terrorism is a fact of political life in many nations around the world. (For one woman's experience as a victim of repressive terrorism, see the Personal Perspectives box in this chapter.)

Some experts fear that revolutionary terrorists might someday build or steal nuclear weapons. No one has ever carried out such nuclear terrorism, but it remains a disturbing possibility. For a group that has a supply of the right fuel, such as enriched plutonium, a nuclear bomb is relatively simple to build. With such a weapon, a band of revolutionary terrorists could gain enormous power. Even if they could only get less highly refined atomic material, a terrorist group could still wreak enormous damage by simply blowing it up with conventional explosives and sending a huge cloud of poisonous radioactive material into the air. Nuclear weapons are less suited to repressive terrorism; still, a government controlled by a small, unpopular minority might conceivably use such weapons against its own population. In the modern world, nuclear weapons are the ultimate source of terror.

revolutionary terrorism
Acts of violence against civilians, intended to bring about political changes in a nation.

repressive terrorism
Acts of violence against civilians, intended to protect the existing political order of a nation.

Quick Review

Compare and contrast revolutionary and repressive terrorism.

Acts of revolutionary terrorism, such as the bombing of the federal building in Oklahoma City, are the focus of intense media attention. Repressive terrorism, on the other hand, is much more likely to be hidden from public view.

The Causes of Warfare

Many people believe that warfare is part of human nature. The same aggressive instinct that is said to make us violent is also said to lead inevitably to war. However, there is a great deal of evidence that this is not the case. Most important is the fact

Personal Perspectives   A Victim of Repressive Terrorism

Repressive terrorism is a common phenomenon around the world. The following account comes from a Tibetan woman who was tortured because of her attempts to free her country from China, which seized control of Tibet in the early 1950s.

> I was part of a demonstration against the Chinese. We shouted "Free Tibet" and "Human rights for Tibetans." As the crowd built up, the Chinese started shooting. The shots came from everywhere, and we were trapped in the middle. Many people died. I was arrested and taken to prison. They stripped off my clothes, stood me up, and kicked me in the breasts and groin. They hit me in the head again and again. Later they forced open my mouth and pushed an electric cattle prod in. They attached wires to my fingers and when they turned on the electric current it was unbearable. I was sitting when they turned on the power and my whole body flew across the room and I was shaking and screaming. They tortured me for day after day. Then they gave me my sentence—only two years in prison—because I was just 16 years old.

that the people of some cultures never go to war. As Marvin Harris, a noted anthropologist, put it: "Although humans may have aggressive tendencies, there is no reason that such tendencies cannot be suppressed, controlled or expressed in ways other than by armed combat. . . . There is no instinct for war. War is fought only to the extent that it is advantageous for some of the combatants."[17] The point is that warfare and violence are not the same thing. Humans may well have some kind of innate tendency to behave violently in certain circumstances, but that does not mean that we have an innate tendency to engage in organized warfare.

Another common approach seeks to find the causes of a particular war in the specific acts that set it off and the leaders who made the key decisions. It may be argued, for example, that if Hitler had not been born, World War II would never have happened. Since it is impossible to rerun history, there is no way of proving or disproving such claims. It does appear, however, that individual decisions have made the difference between war and peace in some cases. During the Cuban missile crisis of 1962, for example, the world seemed to be teetering on the brink of a nuclear war. The leaders of the United States and the Soviet Union made decisions that averted war, but one leader could well have plunged the world into a holocaust. Even so, this approach explains only the superficial causes of warfare. Certain social conditions must be present before war is possible. If the United States and the Soviet Union had not had enormous military machines and the willingness to fight, no conflict could have taken place, no matter what the decisions of their leaders.

In order to deepen our understanding of modern warfare, we need to understand the major theories about its causes. It will, however, be necessary to examine revolutionary and international wars separately, since they often spring from quite different roots.

Revolutionary Warfare

Revolutions are romantic. They have given us some of the most dramatic episodes in human history. The revolutionary theme—a small group of freedom-loving patriots fighting against overwhelming odds—has captured the imagination of countless writers and artists. Even American cowboy stories show plain and simple folk in heroic struggles against land barons and railroad tycoons. Several theories help make sense of revolutions—but these theories are far from perfect. All the conditions that are said to cause revolutions are sometimes present in societies in which no revolutionary conflict takes place, and revolutions sometimes take place in societies that lack the important characteristics mentioned by the theorists. The unique cultural traditions of individual societies play an important part in revolutionary struggles, as does the influence of individual leaders.

Exploitation and Oppression One of the earliest and most influential theories of revolution was formulated by Karl Marx and Friedrich Engels.[18] They believed that the injustices they saw in the capitalism of their time would produce a worldwide revolution. As the workers in capitalist nations sank deeper and deeper into poverty and personal alienation, they would eventually come to realize that they were being exploited by the owners of the factories in which they worked. The workers would then band together, overthrow their oppressors in a violent revolution, and create a classless utopia with liberty and justice for all.

The Marxist theory of revolution is almost a century and a half old, and the revolutionary movement it predicted has not occurred. The revolutions fought in the name of Marxism in China, Russia, Cuba, and elsewhere did not happen the way Marx's theory predicted and did not produce anything like the communist utopia he described. Nevertheless, many Marxists and non-Marxists alike still believe that exploitation and oppression of the lower classes may eventually produce a revolutionary uprising. Far less accepted is Marx's idea that such a revolution will necessarily destroy capitalism and create a new, utopian economic system. Moreover, contemporary sociologists are likely to see a broader range of groups as the victims of exploitation and oppression. For example, in recent times it seems that ethnic oppression has been at least as common a cause of revolutions as pure **class conflict.** Nonetheless, virtually all sociologists who have studied the subject agree that class conflict precedes many revolutions. Before a revolution, the various social classes come to view one another as hostile economic competitors. The English and French revolutions, for example, were fueled by the revolt of the merchants and traders against the feudal aristocracy.

class conflict
The political and economic struggle between different social classes.

Relative Deprivation Considerable research since Marx's time suggests that it is relative poverty, not absolute poverty, that is most likely to spark a violent class conflict. According to **relative deprivation theory,** revolutions are caused by differences between what people have and what they think they should have.

James C. Davies, one of the leading exponents of this theory, presented some interesting data on several of history's most famous revolutions.[19] He concluded that "revolutions are most likely to occur when a prolonged period of objective economic and social development is followed by a short period of sharp reversal."[20] In other words, the people were actually better off at the start of the revolutions he studied than they had been in previous decades. Apparently, improvement in social conditions creates an expectation of even greater progress. If a sharp downturn occurs and the people are unwilling to reduce either their standard of living or their expectations, they rise up against the government.

relative deprivation theory
A theory holding that revolutions are caused by differences between what people have and what they think they should have.

Institutions and Resources Psychologically oriented approaches such as relative deprivation theory hold, in effect, that misery breeds revolt. More recent theorists have argued that to understand why people rise up against their government, we also need to look at the imbalances in the social institutions of their society. Samuel P. Huntington, for example, asserts that the changes created as a country modernizes its economy throw its institutions out of equilibrium. As people become more educated, their desire to become involved in politics increases faster than traditional political institutions can accommodate, and the result may be a revolution.[21]

Charles Tilly responded to Huntington's theory by pointing out that the discontent caused by such institutional imbalances is unlikely to lead to a revolt as long as the discontented remain disorganized and lacking in resources. Arguing that conflict is a normal part of politics, Tilly felt that political violence is likely to occur only when dissatisfied groups are able to mobilize enough resources to mount a significant challenge to the existing government.[22]

Failure of the Government Studies of the world's great revolutions show that the people who ran the governments that were overthrown had been doing a very poor job of it. Crane Brinton's classic study of the American, British, French, and Russian revolutions concluded, for example, that the old ruling class in all these societies was "divided and inept."[23] The authorities seemed to make the wrong decisions and then overreact or underreact to the beginnings of revolutionary ferment. Brinton also showed that these prerevolutionary governments were teetering on the verge of bankruptcy, although the economies of their societies were reasonably sound.[24]

Theda Skocpol, among other theorists, emphasizes the fact that governments do not always reflect the interests of the social elite of their society.[25] Often, the government and its top officials have special interests of their own that conflict with those of elite groups. For example, governments often become enmeshed in the game of international power politics, but the cost of war may threaten the welfare of substantial segments of the elite. When this occurs, the likelihood of an armed revolt is greatly increased, especially when elite groups have sufficient resources to mount a credible challenge to government forces.

Ethnic and Regional Conflicts The collapse of the Soviet Union and the cooling of the great ideological conflicts that fueled the Cold War seem to have marked a turning point in the patterns of contemporary warfare. Ethnic hostility has become the leading cause of revolutionary violence, whether it is the Serbs, Croatians, and Muslims in the Balkans; the Hutus and Tusis in East Africa; the Kurds and the Turks and Iraqis in western Asia; or any one of dozens of other regional conflicts.

Of course, ethnic conflict often led to violence in the past as well. History is full of examples of revolts by an ethnic group in one part of a nation against its central government, but the ideal of ethnic pride and autonomy seems to have taken on new force in recent times. Another major source of revolutionary conflict involves regional differences, which more often than not have an ethnic element as well. Regional differences were, for example, a major factor in the American Civil War.

When a rebellious ethnic or regional group wins control of one part of a country, these conflicts may be transformed into something more similar to an international war. Generally, if the rebels are successful, the nation is divided into two or more new countries, and future conflicts (which are extremely common in such cases) are then waged between sovereign nations. Sometimes, however, the rebellious group takes over the entire nation and reverses its relationship with the old dominant group, forcing it into a subordinate position.

International Warfare

The causes of revolutionary and international wars are usually quite different, but in some cases the internal conditions conducive to a revolutionary uprising may also contribute to an international war. For example, political leaders who are having trouble at home sometimes stir up an international conflict in an attempt to divert the people's attention from their domestic problems. It is said that "nothing makes friends like a common enemy," and such a strategy sometimes reunites a nation, but in the long run the internal problems reemerge, often aggravated by the strains of the international conflict.

militarism

(1) The glorification of war and combat. (2) An economic system that is organized around military spending.

Militarism There are two faces of **militarism** that both contribute to international wars. The first is glorification of war. International warfare is obviously more likely when a society sees it as a heroic show of strength or when young people see it as a path to personal fame and fortune. Although such attitudes are still common in the nuclear age, they seem to be on the decline in the wealthy industrialized nations.

The growth of complex military technology has taken the glory out of person-to-person combat, and the fear of nuclear annihilation has quieted the cheers of civilians.

The second face of militarism is institutional. Many countries around the world, both rich and poor, devote a major portion of their wealth to military purposes, and their military institutions have become a powerful force in shaping national attitudes and priorities. Even when one of these nations has no aggressive plans, its military leaders demand huge "defensive" forces. In fact, as social support for war for its own sake has declined, there seems to have been an increasing concern with warding off foreign aggressors. Such desires are reflected in enormous military budgets and constant preparation for war. Nations that devote major parts of their economies to military purposes now claim that they are doing so merely for defensive purposes. The idea that the strength and integrity of a nation depend on military superiority over its competitors often leads a country to a frantic effort to build up its military forces faster than its enemies. Such arms races usually increase rather than decrease a nation's sense of insecurity and have often led to major international conflicts.[26]

Nationalism and Ideology Like patriotism, **nationalism** is a sense of identification with and devotion to one's nation. In the past, growing nationalism discouraged local wars by unifying petty feudal kingdoms into larger and more stable national units. In the modern world, however, nationalism all too often produces the opposite result.[27] Many wars have started over some petty incident that was interpreted as an affront to "national honor." Rational settlements based on fair compromise are difficult when nationalistic feelings are involved. After all, what wise politician would dare compromise his or her nation's honor? Nationalism is also a critical part of the motivation for **imperialism,** the creation or expansion of an empire. As Quincy Wright pointed out in his classic study of war, some wars arise "because of the tendency of a people affected by nationalism . . . to acquire an attitude of superiority to some or all other peoples, to seek to extend its cultural characteristics throughout the world, and to ignore the claims of other states and of the world community."[28]

Nationalism is not, however, the only kind of ideology that can stimulate violent confrontations. Sometimes the conflict between secular political ideologies such as Marxism and capitalism has led to full-scale war, but religion has more often played this role. From the European Crusades to the conflicts in the Middle East in our time, the belief that one must protect and expand one's faith by force of arms has sent millions of people off to war.

Economic and Political Gain Most wars are fought to achieve some kind of gain. One nation may attack another in an attempt to capture valuable natural resources, desirable land, cheap labor, or political control over a larger population. Sometimes an entire nation reaps advantages from its conquests, but more often only a small segment of a society benefits from a war. Some people—for example, high-ranking military officers and those who supply the arms and materials necessary to keep a war going—stand to gain from an outbreak of almost any sort of war. Other interest groups may profit from a war if it helps secure beneficial resources; exporters profit from the conquest of a new seaport, while farmers gain by winning access to valuable land or water. Although its political leaders gave various justifications, it is clear that Iraq's invasion of Kuwait in 1990 was prompted by the desire to gain a better port on the Persian Gulf and to seize Kuwait's rich oil fields. Similarly, the American-led invasion that freed Kuwait was justified on idealistic grounds, but it was motivated

nationalism
A sense of identification with and devotion to one's nation.

imperialism
The creation or expansion of an empire.

Nationalism has been an important part of the motivation for countless wars over the centuries, including Nazi Germany's attempt to conquer Europe in World War II.

primarily by the desire to protect the industrialized world's supply of low-cost petroleum.

The enormous destructive power of modern warfare has nonetheless made it difficult for any nation to profit from an international war. As Kurt Finsterbusch and H. C. Greisman put it:

> Not only have the costs of wars increased greatly because of the vastly improved technology of devastation and the practice of total warfare, the benefits have also declined decidedly. Wars no longer gain booty, spoils or tribute; and they infrequently gain economic concessions.[29]

International Political Organization In many ways, the most basic cause of international war is the way in which the world is politically organized. Our planet is divided into almost 200 sovereign states, most of which have their own military forces and a belief in their right to use them to protect or advance their national interests. With so many different governments and so many different armies, it is no surprise that international wars are frequent. Indeed, the threat of war is often just one more chip in the poker game of political bargaining between nations. In the famous phrase of the nineteenth-century military strategist Karl von Clausewitz, "War is nothing but a continuation of political intercourse, with a mixture of other means."[30]

Despite appearances to the contrary, the nations of the world do not act like a pack of gunslingers in the Old West. There is a delicate and long-standing balance of power among the nations in the world system. Although it is often claimed that peace is most likely when there is a **balance of power,** A. F. K. Organski and Jacek Kugler found just the opposite to be true.[31] According to their research, peace is most likely when one power is clearly dominant and the others are afraid to challenge it, as was the case when Britain dominated the world system in the nineteenth century. Major wars break out only when new nations feel strong enough to challenge the old leader.

balance of power
A rough equality of power between competing nations or groups of nations.

Quick Review

Critically evaluate the main theories about the causes of international warfare.
Critically evaluate the main theories about the causes of revolutionary warfare.

Solving the Problems of Warfare and International Conflict

People have long dreamed of creating a world without war. Like other idealistic visions, this one may never come true. It may be that war cannot be altogether eliminated, but it is not too idealistic to believe that international conflict can be reduced in both frequency and scope. Ironically, this optimism is partially justified by the awesome destructive power of modern military technology. Pacifists who would have been dismissed as head-in-the-clouds dreamers in the past are now given serious attention. Nearly every educated person in the world recognizes the incredible destruction that a nuclear war would produce, and political leaders all over the world are trying to ensure that it will never happen.

Deterrence

Most military and political leaders assert that the best way to prevent another devastating world war is through **deterrence.** The idea is that our side (whichever one that is) must be so strong that its adversaries will be afraid to attack it. Thus, it is argued that building up a vast military machine actually promotes peace because it improves a nation's capacity to deter potential enemies. In the nuclear age this strategy has become known by a very appropriate acronym: MAD, short for **mutual assured destruction.** To guarantee mutual assured destruction, both sides not only must be able to deliver enough nuclear weapons to devastate their opponent but must be able to do so even after their opponent has launched a successful surprise attack.

As a strategy to prevent war, deterrence has serious weaknesses. It assumes that important political decisions are made in a cool, rational way. In fact, nationalistic or religious fervor has often whipped nations into an emotional frenzy and led to an unrealistic belief in their invulnerability to the attacks of foreign enemies. Technology is also a destabilizing factor in the system of deterrence. Innovations in defensive techniques threaten to weaken one side's deterrent threat and touch off a new

deterrence
The attempt by a nation to prevent war by maintaining such a strong military force that other states will be afraid to attack it.

mutual assured destruction (MAD)
A political standoff in which two or more enemy nations realize that each has the power to destroy the other.

conflict. Moreover, the massive military forces both sides must keep in constant readiness greatly increase the chances of an accidental war. Even if armed conflict never breaks out, the constant preparations for war required by the deterrence strategy are extremely expensive. All things considered, it seems obvious that a system of mutual deterrence cannot be counted on to maintain international peace. It is a desperate arrangement among enemies, based on fear, not cooperation. Yet trying to maintain a strong deterrent threat seems to be the only thing that many world governments are doing to keep the peace.

Arms Control and Disarmament

disarmament

The reduction or elimination of military armaments.

The advocates of arms control argue that attempting to achieve peace by building up the means to make war is ridiculous. They recommend a balanced reduction in weapons or, ideally, total **disarmament** and the elimination of all means for making war. Even proposals for relatively minor arms reductions are nonetheless likely to meet strong opposition. The most obvious obstacle is the lack of trust between the competing nations of the world; many fear that someone else will cheat and hide a secret cache of weapons. There is also an underlying economic and political issue that diplomats seldom openly admit: the opposition of what career army officer and U.S. President Dwight D. Eisenhower called the military-industrial complex—the armed forces and the civilian industries that supply their needs (see Chapter 5). This complex wields vast economic influence that comes from the hundreds of billions of dollars it spends every year, and its most basic financial interests are threatened by those who advocate arms control and disarmament.

Arms control agreements are most likely to be reached when the actual threat of war is lowest. In the decades following the end of World War II, when the Cold War between the United States and the Soviet Union was at its peak and there was a serious danger of nuclear conflict, only a few minor treaties were signed. As the communists fell from power and the Soviet Union broke apart, several major agreements were finally reached. Thus, arms control treaties may not head off an impending conflict between enemy states, but they can play an important role in helping nations to stop seeing each other as enemies.

There is, however, another kind of arms control that does not require as high a degree of trust between avowed enemies: control of the international trade in military equipment. The industrialized nations now spend an average of about 2.7 percent of their national income on "defense," but the developing nations, which are far less able to afford it, spend over 3 percent, and virtually all their sophisticated weaponry is imported from the developed countries. In 1995, the industrialized nations exported about $22 billion worth of armaments. Although that was a substantial decrease from the high point of nearly $65 billion in 1985, the reduction is not as significant as it appears. The end of the Cold War led to a significant drop in the military expenditures of the industrialized nations (especially the former Soviet Union), but it also created a cut-rate arms bonanza for many Third World countries as the industrialized nations sold or gave away some of their surplus armaments and fierce competition led many arms manufacturers to slash their prices (see Figure 18.2).[32]

The United States has a particular obligation to try to work to limit the international arms trade. It is not only the world's leading military power but accounts for almost 57 percent of all arms sales to less developed countries. Critics point out that if the United States refused to make such sales, many nations would simply buy

Figure 18.2

Arms Sales

The United States is the world's number one exporter of military weapons.

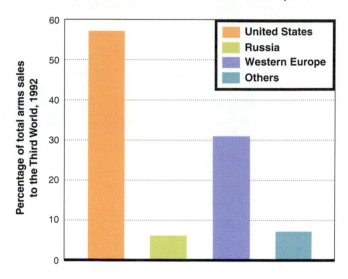

Source: Robin Wright, "Shifting Battle Lines In Arms Race," *Los Angeles Times,* August 17, 1993, pp. H1, H5.

their arms from someone else. There is, however, a way out of this dilemma: an international agreement to limit arms sales. The Code of Conduct on Arms Transfers advocated by arms control groups around the world is designed to do exactly that. Under the terms of this proposed agreement, signatories would be required to limit their arms sales to democratic governments that respect human rights and have civilian control of their military. Such an international agreement would have several important benefits. The cost of high-tech weaponry is a major financial drain on many poor countries, and a ban on its sale would free them from the fear that they need to buy such weapons before their neighbors do. Although such an export ban is unlikely to stop new wars from breaking out, it could reduce their scope and intensity and keep the latest weaponry out of the hands of the regimes most likely to put it to use. However, the Code of Conduct does not go far enough in limiting the sale of equipment necessary to produce weapons of mass destruction (that is, chemical, biological, and, most importantly, nuclear weapons). After the end of the Persian Gulf War in early 1991, the Western powers discovered that Saddam Hussein's totalitarian regime in Iraq was much closer to producing its own nuclear weapons than anyone had previously believed. If the international community does not ban the sale of nuclear technology and equipment, the next time the world may not be as lucky as it was with Iraq.[33]

Social Justice

As we saw in the previous section, feelings of resentment among exploited groups are a major factor in uprisings, rebellions, and revolutions. Although it is sometimes possible to reduce such resentment without major social reforms, the best way to prevent revolutionary violence is to change the conditions of inequality that cause this resentment.

This seems to be a rather obvious principle, but it is seldom followed, largely because most elites—whether national or international—are either unable or unwilling to do it. Some are unaware that their special status is unjust; others simply do not care. Entrenched elites are often indifferent to the need for compromise until it is too late. A stable government depends on its **legitimacy:** the consent of the governed, based on their belief that their leaders have a right to their position and are acting in an appropriate way. The more quickly a government moves to rectify just grievances, the greater the legitimacy it will have in the eyes of its people, and the more peaceful and secure it will be.

As the world develops into a more tightly knit economic and political community, the causes of international war will increasingly come to resemble the causes of revolutionary wars. Vast inequalities in wealth between the north and south are creating a festering sense of resentment and hostility in the Third World. Citizens of the industrialized countries are beginning to realize that something must be done to improve the standard of living of the world's impoverished masses if we are to have a more peaceful world in the years ahead. Handouts of food and other essential supplies can help stave off immediate disasters, but they are obviously not a long-term solution. Chapter 17 discusses some proposals to help promote economic growth in the poor countries. Whichever approach is used, it is clear that the hunger and desperation so common in the world today fuel a political instability that is as much a threat to the wealthy nations as to the poor ones.

Encouraging Global Cooperation

In addition to improving the poverty-stricken economies of the Third World, many other steps must be taken to build the foundations for a peaceful world. Cultural exchanges and direct networks of international communication help promote global understanding. Programs designed to encourage economic cooperation among nations could also build stronger bonds of mutual support and understanding.

Another necessary ingredient in the formula for world peace is international guidance and control. Just as national governments use their power and authority to settle disputes among their citizens, so a world organization could limit conflicts among nations. (See this chapter's Debate, "Is World Government the Way to Eliminate International Warfare?") Two components are needed in any serious effort to create international controls to prevent war. First is the formulation and acceptance of a body of international law. Like criminal law, international statutes must state what kinds of actions constitute international aggression or domestic crimes against humanity and must specify punishments for each. The second requirement is an international organization to enforce the law. There must be an arrangement whereby an international body (a "court") decides whether an accused nation has broken the law and punishes the violator.

A framework for international law already exists. The United Nations—and the League of Nations before it—have already created a considerable body of legal codes. The **Universal Declaration of Human Rights,** for example, is an international equivalent of the Bill of Rights in the Constitution of the United States, and it clearly prohibits the repressive terrorism practiced by so many countries around the world. International law also explicitly forbids aggression by one country against an-

legitimacy
The consent of the governed based on a belief that those who govern have the right to do so.

Universal Declaration of Human Rights
A United Nations declaration that sets forth a list of basic human rights.

other. Although some of these statutes are vague, they are no less specific than the statutes outlawing murder or manslaughter. As in criminal law, international legal principles and traditions will develop only with experience.[34]

A more fundamental stumbling block to international control over warfare and violence is the difficulty of establishing an organization to enforce international law. Again, the basics are already in place. The problem is to obtain the consent of the governed. Most nations refuse to give up any of their authority to a global organization because they do not believe in international law. The United Nations has been effective only when its most powerful members are able to agree on a course of action. When they disagree, it becomes obvious that the United Nations has no power of its own; and, unfortunately, there are many good reasons for such disagreements. The resolution of international grievances is such a delicate process that there are bound to be injustices.

Despite these problems, there are signs of hope. The development of advanced technology and changes in the world economy have made nations more dependent on one another than ever before. No modern society can survive entirely on its own resources, and international trade and commerce can help build bonds between nations. For example, William K. Domke found that the more deeply involved a country is in foreign trade, the less likely it is to go to war.[35] As the nations of the world become more and more interdependent, the demand for greater international law and order has steadily grown. The cost of international peacekeeping efforts has risen steadily in recent years, and world leaders are beginning to recognize the need to find better ways of deciding when such force should be used and how it should be organized and directed.

Quick Review

Critically evaluate the various proposals for encouraging world peace.

The Prospects for the Future

Almost everyone seems to have an idea about how to solve the world's political problems, but what are the prospects that our planet really will be a more peaceful place in the years ahead? To explore this difficult question, we must understand the background of the current world order and the fundamental transformation it is undergoing. Until relatively recently, there was no common world system because the traditional methods of transportation and communication were simply too slow and inefficient. People from one part of the globe often did not even know of the existence of other civilizations, and most conflicts were local affairs. The coming of the industrial revolution changed all that, and in the nineteenth century, Great Britain became history's first real global power. Britain not only had a far-flung network of colonies that it ruled directly; it also exercised unequaled financial and political influence around the world. As Britain's power waned, the twentieth century saw a struggle for domination among the industrial powers that produced the two bloodiest conflicts in human history.

After these great world wars, the two major challengers to the old order, Germany and Japan, were in ruins, and the United States assumed Britain's position as the world's dominant power and protector of the capitalist world economy. America

Debate   Is World Government the Way to Eliminate International Warfare?

The United Nations has been an active participant in world politics since it was created at the end of World War II, but it can take action only when it wins consent of all the most influential nations. Some observers therefore advocate the creation of a world government with the independent power to stop international aggression and keep the peace.

Yes

As long as sovereign nations control their own military forces, there will be wars. World government is the only solution to this ancient problem. Such a government could curb international wars by limiting each nation's military strength and forcing nations to settle their differences in accordance with international law.

Although it would certainly be difficult to create a world government, critics who say that it cannot be done are wrong. The United Nations has already laid the foundation for world unification. World government would be weak and ineffective at first, but if it were well managed, its strength and unity would grow. There is no basis for the fear that such a government would violate national sovereignty and subject small countries to the domination of large ones. The new government would be a federation of independent states very much like the United States or Canada. Each nation would be permitted to keep some armed forces and to control its domestic affairs. The international government would concern itself only with the economic and political relations between countries in order to promote the common good of all people. Just as the unification of the small feudal states of Europe provided great economic and social benefits for their people, world government would provide similar benefits for the entire human race.

was generous in its economic assistance to Germany and Japan, and they soon rebuilt their economies and became peaceful members of the elite club of wealthy capitalist nations. But these nations still faced bitter opposition from another quarter: the Soviet Union and the other communist countries. For the next four decades, the communist and capitalist nations were locked in a bitter nuclear standoff. During this Cold War, the two sides struggled for control of the Third World nations that were finally throwing off the colonial domination of the European powers. The two superpowers nonetheless managed to avoid the direct military confrontation they knew would destroy them both. (See Chapter 17 for more details on colonialism.)

With the collapse of the Soviet Union and the end of the Cold War, many people thought that the world was headed for a new era of international peace and cooperation, but instead, those momentous changes were followed by a new wave of ethnic violence and bloodshed in the less developed countries. To the optimists, those problems are merely temporary adjustments to the rapid changes in the world's balance of power—especially the withdrawal of foreign support from un-

No

Dreamers and idealists have talked about the need for a world government for centuries, but such an idea is as unrealistic today as it was a hundred years ago. History shows that governments rarely surrender their sovereignty voluntarily. Only the gun and the sword can meld small states into larger ones. The idea that this quarreling planet could be unified peacefully without an international holocaust is hopelessly naive. Can you imagine trying to get Iranians, Chinese, and Americans to agree on a common government? Getting the whole world to go along would be even harder.

Even if world government were possible, it would be a mistake. No matter how decentralized and limited such a government might be in the beginning, it would inevitably grow larger and more powerful. The people of the democratic nations are vastly outnumbered by those who have been raised under totalitarian regimes; therefore, a world government would eventually reflect the political traditions of the totalitarian majority. The dictatorial superstate that could be expected to emerge would be vastly more powerful than today's totalitarian regimes, for it would not be hampered by pressure from other, hostile states. Its overwhelming power would leave its opponents no place to hide. Clearly, world government is both an impractical and a dangerous idea.

popular governments that used to be propped up by the American or the Soviet camp.

While there is a good deal of truth to such claims, there are also convincing reasons to believe that a fundamental shift in patterns of military conflict is taking place. The chances of an all-out war between the major world powers, as occurred during the two great world wars, seems greatly diminished, but regional and ethnic conflicts in the Third World appear likely to continue at much higher levels than in the past. One cause of this new global reality is the weakening power of the traditional nation-state. The communications revolution has made it far more difficult for totalitarian leaders to hide unpleasant truths from their citizens, and it facilitates contacts and cooperation among the members of repressed ethnic groups scattered in different geographic areas. This dramatic improvement in communications has also created a revolution of rising expectations as people in the impoverished nations learn about the prosperity of other lands and demand that their governments find a solution for their economic problems. At the same time, the growing importance of the global economy is reducing national leaders' ability to control their own

Although the foundations of international law have already been laid, it is seldom actually enforced. The United Nations can take action only when it receives the support, or at least the acquiescence, of all the world's major powers.

economic policies. For example, nations that try to tax corporate profits to meet the needs of their poor find that the multinationals simply pick up and move somewhere else. Organizations such as the International Monetary Fund and the World Bank commonly dictate the economic policies a poor nation must follow if it is to get desperately needed development funds.

A second problem is environmental. As we saw in Chapter 15, runaway population growth is placing relentless economic pressure on the less developed countries. Essential resources such as good farmland and pure water are becoming increasingly scarce, and many experts expect more and more military confrontations over their control. The population explosion has created growing legions of young adults whose future appears to hold nothing more than unemployment or marginal jobs, and the young will continue to be a major source of political instability. An entirely different kind of problem is likely to arise if the greenhouse effect does indeed create the global warming most experts expect (see Chapter 16). Sea levels will rise, and shifting patterns of rainfall and climate will create numerous local crises that are likely to lead to mass migrations and violent conflicts over the resources that remain.

Signs of Hope   The World's Military Spending Declines

The collapse of the Soviet Union and the sudden end of the Cold War fundamentally changed the world's political climate. Although military spending has not dropped as much as many had hoped, it has gone down. According to United Nations data, the world's total military spending declined a little over 3 percent from 1985 to 1995. While that isn't much of a drop, the percentage of the total world economy that is spent for military purposes declined almost 40 percent. Even more encouraging is the fact that the biggest decline was among the developing countries, which saw the share of their economy devoted to military purposes drop from around 7 percent to around 3 percent. Military spending nonetheless remains at an extremely high level. It is currently almost *$800 billion* a year—an amount that nearly equals the total national income of India and China put together.*

*United Nations Development Programme, *Human Development Report, 1997* (New York: Oxford University Press, 1997), pp. 189, 200, 201.

It is, however, far from certain that these depressing predictions will actually come true. Much will depend on the response of the wealthy industrialized nations. In this ever more interdependent world, it is clearly in the long-term interest of the rich nations to promote the economic and social development of the poor countries, if for no other reason than to head off the tidal wave of desperate migrants who otherwise will head for their shores. With a concerted effort, there is every reason to believe that the problems of the poor countries can be effectively managed; but if the wealthy nations turn their backs on the plight of the Third World, the twenty-first century is likely to be filled with even more violence than the twentieth.

Quick Review

How is warfare likely to be different in the twenty-first century than it was in the twentieth?

Sociological Perspectives on Warfare and International Conflict

Political scientists have devoted a great deal of time and attention to the study of warfare, but sociologists and social scientists in general have not. Research on war and military matters is a minor specialty within the sociological discipline. For this reason, the three principal sociological perspectives are not as sharply defined with reference to warfare as they are in regard to such problems as crime or poverty. In recent years, however, a great deal of attention has been paid to the economic development of the Third World and to other problems of the world system, and warfare itself is gaining increasing sociological attention.

The Functionalist Perspective

Functionalist theory sees warfare and international conflict as an inevitable result of the world's political disorganization. From time immemorial, humanity has been creating political structures that are conducive to warfare. When there are so many large and small countries with so many conflicting interests, disagreements are bound to occur. The international organizations set up to handle these disputes simply cannot do the job.

This high degree of international disorganization actually makes war functional: it is the only effective method for settling major international disputes. Warfare also provides short-term psychological and political benefits to individual nations, and it may function to keep a weak, divided society together for a time. For these reasons, we denounce warfare but nevertheless organize ourselves to retain it. It follows that the best solutions to the problem of international war are those that try to reorganize the world's political system. The primary need is for a program to replace our patchwork of international relations with a genuine world order.

To functionalists, revolutionary warfare arises from a different kind of disorganization. When national systems do not work smoothly and become increasingly dysfunctional, revolution is one possible result. For example, a society might exclude capable people from positions of power and distribute its wealth so unequally that citizens become bitter and resentful. Political organization also becomes dysfunctional when it champions established ways of doing things while the citizens' attitudes, values, and opinions are changing. Such rigidity is sometimes softened by revolution. Functionalists therefore believe that the best way to head off revolutionary conflict is to implement the kinds of gradual reforms already described in the chapters on economics, government, poverty, and ethnic minorities.

The Conflict Perspective

political economy
The economic and political system of a community, nation, or group of nations.

Conflict theorists do not ordinarily separate economics and politics. Instead, they speak of **political economy.** To them, the world system is not disorganized—it is organized for economic and political exploitation. The powerful capitalist nations buy cheap raw materials and labor from the Third World and in return sell high-cost services and manufactured goods. The result is a steady flow of wealth from the Third World to the industrialized countries and ever deepening poverty and desperation among the disadvantaged of the world. In this view, revolutionary wars usually result from the effort of the downtrodden people of a Third World country to throw off the yoke of the rich nations and to topple the local elites who are in league with them.

On the international level, conflict theorists see a vicious struggle for worldwide dominance and the economic rewards it brings. As long as one power or group of allied powers is strong enough to intimidate the rest of the world, we enjoy relative peace. Sooner or later, however, challengers will arise to question the existing international order. Sometimes they can be accommodated peacefully, but bloody conflicts, such as the ones in World Wars I and II, are the more common result.

According to the conflict perspective, the best way to eliminate warfare and international conflict is to eliminate oppression, both international and national. Some conflict theorists advocate a system of deterrence, but one in which economic goods and the military power to protect them are distributed equally. Others call for radical economic changes that would make all government unnecessary; in such a utopian state, both governments and the wars they fight would vanish. Conflict theorists are not necessarily against all wars, however. Their position is that conflict is basic to all human societies, and some recommend that collective violence be used to undo economic injustices that are maintained by military power. Nonetheless, the ultimate aim of conflict theorists and functionalists alike is a peaceful world with full equality among all peoples.

The Feminist Perspective

Feminists generally see the problem of warfare from a very different perspective than most other theorists. Since wars are organized and carried on primarily by men, many feminists focus on the question of why men are so much more warlike than women. Although some see biological roots to these behavioral differences, most feminists lay the blame on male gender role socialization. Young boys around the world are encouraged to "stand up for themselves" and not to be "sissies." In many cultures, the very definition of manhood involves the ability to successfully wield violent force. The aggressive, domineering male is the ideal, while the "wimp" is not a "real man." This process of socialization naturally leads men in positions of political power to resort to violence far sooner than they should, and the result is our ongoing epidemic of warfare and political violence.

Feminists propose two general responses to the problem of political violence. Public opinion polls show that women look far less favorably on military spending and an aggressive foreign policy than men. So one thing feminists propose is for women to band together and use their collective power to change the priorities and attitudes of the world's governments. A second tactic is to change the socialization practices that encourage warlike male attitudes. Once again, women are the key, since they are the ones who usually have primary responsibility for child rearing. But their efforts must be supported by sweeping changes in our schools and in our media if they are to bear significant fruit.

The Interactionist Perspective

Interactionists see the roots of war in the process of socialization and the way we are taught to see ourselves and the world around us. As we are growing up, we are taught to identify with a particular ethnic group and a particular nation, and we learn to respond with hatred and aggression when someone seems to threaten the interests of those groups. War allows us to identify enemies as evil and then to win honor, glory, and a sense of righteousness by defeating them. Political leaders who stand to profit from encouraging conflict quickly learn how to manipulate the powerful emotions these identifications create; fiery rhetoric and common symbols such as flags and patriotic music are used to whip up fervor for war. The obvious solution to this problem is to encourage people to identify with the human race as a whole rather than just some small part of it. The less we divide ourselves along ethnic, racial, or national lines, the more peaceful world we are likely to have.

Interactionists have also identified other learned attitudes that contribute to the climate of violence. People growing up in cultures that place great importance on honor and pride are likely to encourage warlike national policies, as are people growing up in cultures that emphasize competition and individual aggressiveness.

Thus, interactionists say that to reduce warfare we must emphasize cultural characteristics that favor the peaceful resolution of differences. Rather than glorifying victory over evil, it would be more sensible to applaud the rational compromise that heads off deadly conflict. Rather than applauding the "hero" who kills a dozen people to save the victim of a kidnapping, it makes more sense to glorify the negotiator who talks the criminals into peacefully releasing their captive. The ideals of nonviolence must be substituted for the glorification of violence that is so common in the mass media and in our everyday lives.

Quick Review

Compare and contrast the functionalist and conflict explanations of the causes of warfare.

What proposals do feminists make to discourage warfare and international conflict?

What do the interactionists see as the root causes of warfare?

Summary

War can be defined as protracted military conflict among two or more organized groups. Wars can be classified on the basis of the groups involved as international (between independent nations) or revolutionary (between groups within a nation).

Throughout history, periods of warfare have been more the rule than the exception. The cost of such warfare has been enormous. Hundreds of millions of people have been killed or injured in wars. Economically, the cost of any war is staggering, but the greatest potential threat is the unprecedented devastation that would come from a large-scale nuclear war.

Since the nineteenth century, there has been a steady escalation of the scale of violence in revolutionary and international conflicts. Although some claim that wars produce economic benefits by increasing the demand for armaments and other products, in the vast majority of cases, modern wars have had devastating economic and social consequences. In fact, some scientists even doubt the ability of the human race to survive an all-out nuclear war.

Terrorism involves attacks on civilians to gain political ends and is often used in situations that stop just short of full-scale war. The two main types are revolutionary terrorism, which aims to change an existing government, and repressive terrorism, aimed to protect it.

The causes of revolutionary and international wars overlap but are nevertheless distinct. There are many theories about the causes of revolutionary wars. One says that they stem from exploitation and the oppression of subordinate groups by a society's ruling elite. Another asserts that relative deprivation stimulates the discontent essential to a revolution. Other theories hold that revolutions occur when an imbalance exists in the institutions of a society, when dissatisfied groups are able to mobilize sufficient resources to challenge the existing government, or when a government weakens and loses its political support. A final theory notes that ethnic conflicts and geographic divisions are major contributors to revolutionary conflict.

Militarism and the buildup of armaments are major causes of international war. Ethnocentrism, when expressed in nationalism or dogmatic religious ideologies, may also encourage the conquest of other people. Plain greed cannot be ignored either: some wars are fought more for profit than for anything else. Underlying all international wars is the nature of the world's political organization. The large number of heavily armed independent states, each determined to advance its own interests, makes warfare almost inevitable.

Despite its obvious weaknesses, the most common proposal for preventing war is to urge nations to become so strong that they can deter any possible aggression by their neighbors. A second approach advocates some form of arms control or total disarmament. A third set of proposals calls for social justice and the economic development of the poor nations. If inequality were greatly reduced, the chief motivation for revolution would disappear and international tensions would relax. Finally, many leaders propose that military aggression be eliminated by the development of world government, including world law, world courts, and world law enforcement.

The end of the Cold War has greatly reduced the chances of a full-scale military conflict among the major powers, but ethnic and regional conflicts in the less developed countries seem to be on the increase. There appear to be several causes of this escalation of violence, including the political instability caused by the end of the Cold War, the weakening power of the traditional nation-state, and growing environmental pressures.

Functionalists see warfare and international conflict as the inevitable result of the way the world is politically organized into large numbers of competing nations. National systems do not function smoothly either, and revolution is evidence of this fact. Conflict theorists hold that the world system is far from disorganized: it is organized for economic exploitation of the weak by the strong. Conflict theorists favor a system in which economic goods and the military power to protect them are distributed equally. Feminists see the roots of warfare in the process of male socialization, and interactionist see them in the way we are taught to identify with particular ethnic or national groups. Both would agree that to prevent wars we need to emphasize nonviolent cultural traits that favor the peaceful resolution of differences.

Questions for Critical Thinking

Since the end of the Cold War, Americans seem to show little concern about the dangers of new military conflicts, and perhaps as a result, public opinion polls show a sharp decline in interest in international affairs in general. Is this change in attitude justified? How likely do you think it is that the United States will become involved in a major military conflict in your lifetime? What are the chances that there will be a war somewhere in the world that uses nuclear or biological weapons? What effect would a major war between Third World countries be likely to have here?

Key Terms

balance of power
class conflict
deterrence
disarmament
imperialism

international war
legitimacy
militarism
mutual assured destruction (MAD)
nationalism

nuclear proliferation
nuclear war
nuclear winter
political economy
relative deprivation theory
repressive terrorism
revolutionary terrorism

revolutionary wars
terrorism
total war
Universal Declaration of
    Human Rights
war
weapons of mass destruction

Further Readings

Seyom Brown, *The Causes and Prevention of War* (New York: St. Martin's Press, 1994). A comprehensive look at the ways to maintain peace as well as at the wars that disrupt it.

Jack A. Goldstone, ed., *Revolutions: Theoretical, Comparative, and Historical Studies* (San Diego: Harcourt Brace Jovanovich, 1986). A fine collection of articles about revolutions that provides useful historical and sociological perspectives.

Martin van Creveld, *The Transformation of War* (New York: Free Press, 1991). A controversial military thinker some call the new Clausewitz, van Creveld argues that the old style of large-scale warfare between organized states is being replaced by lower-intensity conflicts among a shifting array of competing regional and ethnic interests.

Karl von Clausewitz, *On War,* trans. O. J. Matthkijs Jolles (Washington, DC: Infantry Journal Press, 1950). The classic work on warfare, written by a Prussian general.

Jonathan R. White, *Terrorism: An Introduction* (Pacific Grove, CA: Brooks/Cole, 1991). One of the numerous textbooks on the subject of terrorism.

Notes

1. Melvin Small and J. David Singer, *Resort to Arms: International and Civil Wars, 1816–1980* (Beverly Hills, CA: Sage, 1982), p. 293.

2. See Rudi Volti, *Society and Technological Change* (New York: St. Martin's Press, 1988), pp. 171–201.

3. Doyle McManus, "The New, Dangerous Dominoes," *Los Angeles Times,* May 8, 1994, pp. A1, A14; Bruce W. Nelan, "Fighting Off Doomsday," *Time,* June 21, 1993, pp. 36–38; David P. Barash, *Introduction to Peace Studies* (Belmont, CA: Wadsworth, 1991), pp. 126–127.

4. Small and Singer, *Resort to Arms,* pp. 293–294.

5. James F. Dunnigan and William Martel, *How to Stop a War: The Lessons of Two Hundred Years of War and Peace* (New York: Doubleday, 1987), p. 81.

6. Ibid., p. 239; Small and Singer, *Resort to Arms,* p. 91.

7. Mark Hatfield, "US Needs Code of Conduct for Conventional-Arms Trade," *Christian Science Monitor,* April 15, 1994, p. 18.

8. United Nations Development Programme, *Human Development Report, 1997* (New York: Oxford University Press, 1997), pp. 215.

9. Rex de Silva, "Developing the Third World," *World Press Review,* May 1980, p. 48.

10. U.S. Bureau of the Census, *Statistical Abstract of the United States, 1993* (Washington, DC: U.S. Government Printing Office, 1993), p. 875.

11. G. Tyler Miller, *Living in the Environment: An Introduction to Environmental Science,* 5th ed. (Belmont, CA: Wadsworth, 1988), p. 128.

12. Ibid., p. 129; Barash, *Introduction to Peace Studies,* pp. 107–113.

13. See Quincy Wright, *A Study of War,* abridged by L. L. Wright (Chicago: University of Chicago Press, 1964), p. 85.
14. Peter C. Sederberg, *Terrorist Myths: Illusion, Rhetoric, and Reality* (Englewood Cliffs, NJ: Prentice Hall, 1989), pp. 22–43.
15. See Harold J. Vetter and Gary R. Perlstein, *Perspectives on Terrorism* (Pacific Grove, CA: Brooks/Cole, 1991), pp. 87–104.
16. Dunnigan and Martel, *How to Stop a War,* p. 247.
17. Marvin Harris, *Culture, People, Nature,* 6th ed. (New York: HarperCollins, 1993), p. 301.
18. Karl Marx and Friedrich Engels, *The Communist Manifesto* (Englewood Cliffs, NJ: Prentice Hall, 1955). This pamphlet was originally published in 1848.
19. James C. Davies, "Toward a Theory of Revolution," *American Sociological Review* 27 (1962): 5–19; James C. Davies, "The J-Curve of Rising and Declining Satisfactions as a Cause of Some Great Revolutions and a Contained Rebellion," in Hugh Davis Graham and Ted Robert Gurr, eds., *Violence in America: Histories and Comparative Perspectives* (New York: Holt, Rinehart & Winston, 1958), pp. 547–576.
20. Davies, "Toward a Theory of Revolution," p. 5.
21. Samuel P. Huntington, *Political Order in Changing Societies* (New Haven, CT: Yale University Press, 1968).
22. Charles Tilly, *From Mobilization to Revolution* (Reading, MA: Addison Wesley Longman, 1978).
23. Crane Brinton, *The Anatomy of Revolution* (New York: Random House, 1965), p. 51.
24. Ibid., pp. 28–39.
25. Theda Skocpol, *States and Social Revolution* (Cambridge: Cambridge University Press, 1978).
26. See Ronald J. Glossop, *Confronting War* (Jefferson, NC: MacFarland, 1987), pp. 66–68.
27. Ibid., pp. 58–65.
28. Wright, *A Study of War,* pp. 213–214.
29. Kurt Finsterbusch and H. C. Greisman, "The Unprofitability of Warfare in the Twentieth Century," *Social Problems* 22 (February 1975): 451.
30. Karl von Clausewitz, *On War,* trans. O. J. Matthkijs Jolles (Washington, DC: Infantry Journal Press, 1950), p. 16.
31. A. F. K. Organski and Jacek Kugler, *The War Ledger* (Chicago: University of Chicago Press, 1980).
32. United Nations, *Human Development Report, 1997,* pp. 188–189, 215.
33. Hatfield, "Code of Conduct."
34. See Raymond J. Michalowski and Ronald Kramer, "The Space Between the Laws: The Problem of Corporate Crime in a Transnational Context," *Social Problems* 34 (February 1987): 34–53.
35. William K. Domke, *War and the Changing Global System* (New Haven, CT: Yale University Press, 1988).

Social Problems in the Twenty-first Century: Looking Forward and Looking Back

It isn't unusual for students getting their first introduction to the study of social problems to become depressed about the whole state of the world. After a glance through the pages of this book, it would be easy to conclude that our problems are overwhelming and to see the future with nothing but a deep pessimism. But as usual, the reality of our situation is far more complex than it appears at first glance. We are facing many grave problems, but as we have repeatedly pointed out, there are numerous signs of hope as well. Some of our problems are indeed getting worse year by year, but others are getting better, while still others cycle up and down in a more or less regular pattern.

The study of social problems must inevitably focus more on what is wrong than what is right. The vignettes that opened each chapter showed us many stories of typical people who have suffered from such things as racism, violence, and economic disaster. But that is only part of the story. Time and again, average people show an amazing ability to bounce back from personal crisis and even to profit from their experience. Of course, all this doesn't mean that a naive optimism is any better way to face the future than a hopeless pessimism. Even the best sociological analysis can't give us a crystal ball to see what lies ahead, but a careful analysis of the trends can allow us to make some reasonable predictions that avoid emotional extremes, and it is to that task that we now turn.

Three Critical Issues: Justice, Cohesion, and Survival

Everybody has an opinion about whether things will be getting better or getting worse in the years ahead, but what do we really mean when we make such sweeping statements about the future of society? There are many different answers to the question of what a good society should be, but there are at least three critical areas of concern for most sociologists. First, a good society must be just—it must treat people fairly whether they are rich or poor; black, brown or white; male or female; gay or straight. Second, a good society must be cohesive. Society has to hold itself together and provide the support and continuity its members need. Third, and perhaps most obvious, a good society must be able to survive. For one thing, it needs to have a sustainable relationship to the environment. Any society that uses up its natural or its human resources faster than they can be replenished is headed for disaster. Societies may also face external threats to their survival from international conflicts and competition. These three issues are, of course, closely interrelated. A more just society is likely to have fewer hostile, alienated citizens and therefore to be more cohesive; a more cohesive society has a far greater chance of survival in the face of external threats; and so forth. Each of these issues nonetheless deserves a bit of individual attention. So how just, how cohesive, and how sustainable is our society, and where do the trends seem to be headed?

Justice

Look down the long list of social problems covered in this book, and you will see how critical this question of social justice is. Virtually all the problems we discussed in Part II—racism, sexism, discrimination against the young and old—turn on issues of social justice. Even poverty, which in some societies might be seen as the result of failure of the economic system to produce enough wealth, is really a problem of social justice, since there is more than enough wealth to go around in contemporary industrial societies. Although the world is just starting to see itself as one common community, the problem of global inequality is very much like our domestic problem of poverty except on a far larger scale.

If we look back in history, it is easy to see many ways in which society has become more just over the years. In the United States, slavery was widely practiced as recently as the nineteeth century, and it was followed by many long years of segregation that systematically denied African Americans their most basic civil rights. Not only were women refused the right to vote; the law relegated them to the status of perpetual children living under the authority of their husbands, and the most prestigious social, political, and economic institutions simply shut them out. Gays and lesbians suffered such universal condemnation that they were forced to hide their sexual orientation or face vicious physical attacks and long periods of incarceration. We are, of course, a long way from a truly just society here or in the rest of the world. The problems of women, ethnic minorities, and gays and lesbians continue to be grave ones. The historical trends do, however, give us grounds for some reasonable optimism.

The issue of poverty and international inequality is more complex. In an absolute sense, poverty has declined as the overall level of affluence has grown. But at the same time, the gap between the rich and the poor, both domestically and internationally, has been increasing. Moreover, there are many who believe that the *quality* of life for many of the world's poor has declined, even if their standard of living has increased. Population growth has produced more crowding and congestion, environmental quality has declined, and hundreds of millions of poor people have been forced out of their familiar villages and into a stressful and uncertain life in the cities of the Third World. And whether or not we see an improvement in the problem of poverty, the world's political inequalities remain as great as ever. The rich industrialized nations, with the United States at their head, continue to be dominant, while the poor countries that have the vast majority of the world's people have far less weight on the international stage.

Cohesion

In addition to social justice, the other great concern of the industrial world in the twentieth century has been social cohesion and the nagging fear that despite all our

Although their status has improved in the twentieth century, American women are still fighting for equal rights. The plight of black women in America is even more dire. In October 1997, 700,000 black women joined in the Million Woman March in Philadelphia to focus on "repentance, resurrection, and restoration."

affluence and success, society is somehow falling apart. The historical record reveals some obvious reasons for concern. The twentieth century saw huge increases in crime as people poured into the cities and gave up the ways of the farm for the competitive world of industrial capitalism. The second half of the century also saw explosive growth in the use of illicit drugs, and perhaps most unsettling of all were the enormous changes in the family. The divorce rate skyrocketed, and many more women had children without ever being married at all.

The pessimists see the seeds of doom in these trends, but once again there is reason to doubt such extreme conclusions. For one thing, such problems as crime and drug use seem to follow natural cycles as the balance swings between the desire for individual freedom and the desire for social order and cohesion. When people are fearful of crime and disorder, the government responds by increasing its repression of "deviant" activities it considers threatening. But such repression is not without its own social costs, and from time to time the pendulum swings back toward more individual freedom and greater tolerance of deviance. It should also be borne in mind that despite large overall increases in the twentieth century, crime has actually been on the decline in recent decades.

The changes in the family present a somewhat different picture. The divorce rate and the birthrate among single women do seem to have stopped increasing. At the present time, at least, it doesn't seem likely that we will have the same long-term reductions we have seen in the crime rates, but neither does some new crisis appear to be looming on the horizon. As we saw in Chapter 2, the enormous changes in the family are the result of the shift to a new urban life-style in an industrialized society. That change is more or less complete now, so it seems far more likely that the family system will continue with the same structure it has today than that we will see generations of ever growing chaos and decay or a return to the family patterns of the past.

Survival

Survival has always been a central social concern, and the pages of history are full of the stories of societies that no long exist. But this critical issue gained profound new importance in the twentieth century, when our ever growing technological prowess came to pose a threat not just to a single society but to the survival of the entire human race. With the development of atomic weapons at the end of World War II and the nuclear arms race that followed, we humans gained the ability to exterminate ourselves and a good deal of the other life on this planet as well. The end of the Cold War greatly diminished the chances of the "doomsday scenario" of a massive exchange of nuclear-tipped intercontinental ballistic missiles. But as we saw in Chapter 18, the likelihood of a more limited nuclear conflict seems to be growing by the year as an increasing number of nations develop their own nuclear capabilities. A nuclear war between, for example, India and Pakistan, might not produce the doomsday that an all-out war between the United States and the Soviet Union would have produced, but it would be an immense human tragedy with unpredictable consequences for the global environment.

The greatest threat to our survival may no longer come from nuclear war but from the damage we are wreaking to our environment. As we saw in Chapter 15, the human population is growing at a staggering pace, and more people and more industrial development have meant that we are using up our resources faster and spewing out an ever increasing amount of pollution. No one can know for certain how much our environment can take before we are struck by some global crisis, but there are ominous signs that the quality of our water, our land, and especially our air is deteriorating. The signs, however, are not all bad. Scientists have learned a great deal about our environmental problems, and the industrialized nations have made significant strides in reducing some kinds of pollution (see Chapter 16). Even the growth rate of the world's population has begun to slow. Nonetheless, we seem to be in a deadly race between an exploding population and runaway industrial growth, and the scientific efforts to control the damage they produce.

Although the growth rate of the world population has begun to slow, the human race is still increasing at a staggering pace. In China, which continues to experience rapid population growth, the government actively promotes one-child families.

Looking to the Twenty-first Century: Three Scenarios for the Future

No one from Karl Marx to Jules Verne (the great French science fiction writer) has proved very good at predicting the future of human society. About the best modern sociology allows us to do is to make some educated guesses about the road we are likely to travel. Not surprisingly, there are enormous differences of opinion about the direction we are headed, and perhaps the best way to summarize these views is to present three hypothetical scenarios for the future—one optimistic, one pessimistic, and one in the middle.

Many pessimists feel that the self-centered greed fostered by the competitive capitalistic system that has swept across the world will ultimately tear human society apart. These pessimists see an ever growing gap between the educated and well-connected haves and the increasingly desperate have-nots. Conditions in the poor nations will deteriorate as more and more people leave the farms and crowd into urban slums. As low-skilled jobs in rich countries are shifted to the poverty zones of the Third World, the economic usefulness of the have-nots in the industrialized nations will decline and governments will become less and less interested in really helping them with their problems. The crime rate among the poor and minorities will steadily increase, and prisons will overflow as the state grows progressively more repressive. And just as the global economic system will drive the poor and minorities into ever greater desperation, so it will continue wreaking its relentless environment havoc—the forests will be cut down, the oceans polluted, and the skies filled with choking gases. The pessimists see the inevitable outcome as a social and economic crisis—perhaps touched off by massive rebellion among the poor and dispossessed, by a devastating war between the rich and poor nations, or by some new environmental disaster.

The optimists look at the same world as the pessimists, but they draw very different conclusions about its future. The optimists are greatly encouraged by the enormous increase in the education and sophistication of the world's people and by the great improvements modern technology has made in our ability to communicate with each other. One group of optimists sees the solution to our problems in more and better technology that will clean up our environment, create bountiful sources of new wealth that even the poorest people can enjoy, and knit our planet together into a single global community. Another group of optimists sees the solutions to our pressing problem as coming from the inside, not the outside. We will ultimately see through the greed and materialism that drives us on an endless, destructive quest for more and more wealth. In this scenario, a progressive disillusionment with consumerism, as well as the horrible damage it is causing to our society and our planet, will lead us to adapt a more leisurely style of life and a more sustainable relationship to our environment.

The third scenario might be called "just muddling through." Its advocates do not see an insurmountable crisis lying in the road ahead, but neither do they see some rosy utopia. Rather, they believe things will continue along pretty much as they are. Some problems will get better and perhaps even disappear, but other ones will come along to take their place. They also believe that some problems might get

Most attempts to predict the future, whether by scientists or by artists and writers, have not proved very successful. This photo shows a vision of the future from the 1968 film 2001: A Space Odyssey.

much worse, perhaps even resulting in some kind of social disaster. But human history is full of one disaster after another, and none of them have proved insurmountable. Indeed, we often seem to require some kind of crisis before we take the painful steps necessary to really deal with our most pressing problems.

Of course, all these scenarios are just educated guesses, and there are many possible "wild cards" that could make them all seem hopelessly off the mark. What would happen, for example, if some of the science fiction writers' technological fantasies—such as an endless source of cheap energy, speedy interplanetary travel, or a real elixir of immortality—actually came true? History shows that nature often has surprises of its own, and a devastating new epidemic or some unexpected environmental crisis is always a possibility. Then there is the social dimension. The twenty-first century might well see the rise of some threatening new state comparable to Hitler's Germany, but it could also be the era that finally produces some kind of "human nationalism" that sees us shift our allegiance from individual nations to the whole human community. The one thing that is sure is that the future is in our hands, and the kind of world that unfolds will depend on the actions we take and the ideals we follow today.

Glossary

absolute approach Defining poverty by dividing the poor from the nonpoor on the basis of an objective standard (e.g., income).

absolute deprivation Lack of one or more of the necessities of life.

acid rain Rain with unusually high acidity produced by atmospheric pollution.

acquired immune deficiency syndrome (AIDS) A fatal disease that attacks the body's defenses against illness.

activity theory A theory of aging that holds that older people are happiest when they continue to be actively involved in social life.

addiction The intense craving for a drug that develops after a period of physical dependence stemming from heavy use.

adolescence The age grade of persons who have reached puberty but have not been given full status as adults.

adulthood The age grade of persons who are considered to have reached full social and physical maturity.

affirmative action program A program designed to make up for past discrimination by giving special assistance to members of the groups that were discriminated against.

age composition The percentage of a population in each age category.

age grade People of similar age, such as children, adolescents, and adults.

aging A set of biological and social changes that develop in all people throughout life, but at different rates.

Aid to Families with Dependent Children (AFDC) A welfare program providing direct financial aid to poor mothers.

alcoholic A person whose work or social life is disrupted by drinking.

alienation (1) A feeling of estrangement from society and social groups. (2) A feeling of the loss of control of one's activities, especially one's labor.

Alzheimer's disease A disease that causes mental deterioration in older people.

androgynous Having the characteristics traditionally ascribed to both males and females.

anomie A condition in which social norms have broken down and no longer regulate individual behavior.

antitrust laws Laws designed to protect free competition in the marketplace.

anxiety disorder A mental disorder involving severe and prolonged anxiety, irrational fears, panic attacks, obsessive thoughts and rituals, or the dehabilitating consequences of some traumatic event.

arson The illegal burning of a structure or other property.

assault An attack on a person with the intention of hurting or killing the victim.

assimilation A process by which a person takes on a new culture.

authoritarian personality The personality of someone who is rigid and inflexible, has a very low tolerance for uncertainty, and readily accepts orders from above.

authoritarianism A extreme belief in the importance of authority and the individual responsibility to submit to it.

aversive therapy A form of behavioral therapy that uses punishment to discourage a particular behavior.

baby boom generation The large generation of Americans born after World War II.

bail A sum of money put up as security to be forfeited if a person accused of committing a crime does not appear for trial.

balance of power The condition in which the military strength of the world's strongest nations or groups of nations is roughly equal.

behavioral therapy Modification of the specific behavior that is causing a patient's problems.

behaviorism A theory explaining human actions only in terms of observable behavior.

biodiversity The range of plant and animal species living together in an ecosystem or on the planet as a whole.

biosocial theory A theory that explains social behavior by reference to biological traits.

biosphere The life-containing region of the earth extending from about 200 feet below sea level to about 10,000 feet above it.

bipolar disorder A mental disorder characterized by extreme swings in mood.

birthrate The number of babies born in a year divided by the total population.

bisexual A person willing to have sexual relations with individuals of either sex.

blacklisting The practice of denying employment and economic opportunities to people because of their political views.

blended family A family to which at least one of the marital partners brings children from a previous relationship.

blue-collar worker Someone employed in a job requiring manual labor.

bourgeoisie The class of people who, according to Marx, own capital and capital-producing property.

breeder reactor A type of nuclear reactor that produces plutonium, a fuel that can be used in nuclear weapons.

bribery Giving money or some other reward in order to influence the way an official carries out his or her duties.

brothel A house of prostitution.

budget deficit The amount of money the government spends in excess of the amount it receives in taxes and other revenue.

bureaucracy A form of social organization characterized by division of labor, a hierarchy of authority, a set of formal rules, impersonal enforcement of rules, and job security.

burglary Unlawful entry into a structure with the intent to commit a felony.

business cycle The ups and downs that characterize the economies of all capitalist nations.

call girl A prostitute who accepts customers only from personal references and phone contacts.

capital accumulation The buildup of wealth in a nation—including not only money but also its infrastructure and the skills of its labor force.

capitalism An economic system characterized by private property, the exchange of commodities and capital, and a free market for goods and labor.

case study A detailed examination of specific individuals, groups, or situations.

chief executive officer (CEO) The head of a corporation.

childhood The earliest age grade, lasting from birth to the onset of puberty.

civil rights movement The social movement in the United States that brought an end to the segregation system.

class conflict The struggle for wealth, power, and prestige among the social classes.

class consciousness A feeling of unity among people of a particular class.

classical theory A theory that sees criminal behavior as the result of the rational choice of the criminal.

child molestation The sexual abuse of a child by an adult.

Cold War The struggle for world domination between the capitalist and communist nations after World War II.

colonialism A system in which one nation extends its political and economic control over other nations or peoples and treats them as dependent colonies.

coming out Openly admitting one's homosexuality for the first time.

communism An economic system in which the government owns and controls all the major economic institutions.

communitarian capitalism A capitalistic economic system that emphasizes the importance of the group or community over the individual.

community (1) A place where people live. (2) The bonds and feelings of belonging that develop among people who live in the same place.

compensatory education program A special program whose goal is to help disadvantaged students reach educational levels comparable to those achieved by more privileged students.

conflict of interest The ethical dilemma that occurs when an officeholder's official duty and his or her personal interests would lead to different actions.

conflict perspective A sociological approach that sees society in terms of conflicts and tensions between different social groups.

contagious disease A disease spread from one person to another.

contrast conceptions The strong stereotypes ethnic groups often develop about each other.

control theory A criminological thesis holding that people commit crimes when social norms and other social forces no longer control them.

conventional war A war in which two or more armies meet directly without guerrilla tactics or nuclear weapons.

core The wealthy industrialized nations that dominate the world system.

cornucopian Someone who believes that scientific progress will allow continued economic growth and prosperity despite population growth and the depletion of natural resources.

covert operations Secret operations carried out by government agencies such as the CIA.

crime Violation of a criminal law.

crime control model A model of criminal justice that favors speedy arrest and punishment of anyone who commits a crime.

critical theory A theory holding that the capitalist economic system is the root cause of the crime problem in modern industrial societies.

culture The way of life of the people in a certain geographic area, particularly their ideas, beliefs, values, patterns of thought, and symbols.

culture of poverty A self-perpetuating subculture among some (but not all) poor people that traps them in poverty.

cyclical unemployment Unemployment resulting from changes in the business cycle, which in turn cause changes in the demand for labor.

death rate The number of people who die in a year divided by the total population.

decriminalization The proposal that penalties for possession and use of a drug be abolished even if sales of the drug remain illegal.

de facto segregation Segregation of minority groups that results from existing social conditions (such as housing patterns) but is not legally required.

defense conversion Changing corporations and workers from military to civilian work.

definition of the situation The meaning the actors give to a social situation in which they are involved.

deforestation The destruction of the forests.

deinstitutionalization The movement to reduce the number of patients treated in mental hospitals.

de jure segregation Segregation of minority groups that is required by law.

demographic transition Changes in birthrates and death rates occurring during the process of industrialization.

demography A scientific discipline dealing with the distribution, density, and vital statistics of populations.

depressant A drug that slows the responses of the central nervous system, reduces coordination, and decreases mental alertness.

deregulation Dropping government control over economic activities.

desegregation Mixing of people of different races who were formerly kept apart by law or custom.

desertification The transformation of productive land into desert.

deterrence The strategy of preventing war by maintaining so strong a military force that other nations will be afraid to attack.

deviant (1) An individual who violates a social norm. (2) An individual who is labeled as a deviant by others.

deviant behavior (1) Behavior that violates a social norm. (2) Behavior that is labeled as deviant by others.

deviant subculture A set of perspectives, attitudes, and values that support criminal or other norm-violating activity.

differential association theory A theory holding that people become criminals because they are exposed to more behavior patterns that are favorable to a certain kind of crime than are opposed to it.

disarmament Elimination of armed forces and weaponry, usually by means of a treaty.

discouraged workers People who have given up looking for work; not counted in unemployment statistics.

discrimination The practice of treating some people as second-class citizens because of their minority status.

disengagement theory A theory of aging that holds that older people are best off when they slowly disengage from social activities as they age.

domination A social system in which one ethnic group holds power and uses it to keep other groups in a subordinate position.

double bind A situation in which a parent gives a child two conflicting messages at the same time.

double standard A code of behavior that gives men greater sexual freedom than women.

dual-earner family A family in which both wife and husband are employed.

due process model A model of criminal justice that places more emphasis on protecting human rights and dignity than on punishing criminals.

drug maintenance A program providing drugs to addicts or habitual users.

dysfunction The way a social phenomenon interferes with the maintenance of a balanced social order.

ecology The study of the interrelationships among plants, animals, and their environments.

economic democracy The control of economic institutions by the people who are involved in them.

economic development Economic growth in the poor nations.

economic planning The active involvement of the government in attempting to plan a healthy economy.

ecosystem A self-sufficient community of organisms living in an interdependent relationship with each other and their environment.

elder abuse The physical or psychological mistreatment of the elderly.

elitist One who believes that nations are ruled by a small elite class.

enterprise zone A low-income area that is given special tax breaks and other incentives to encourage business.

erosion of childhood The deterioration of the specially protected status accorded our children.

ethnic group A group whose members share a sense of togetherness and the conviction that they form a distinct group or "people."

ethnic minority An ethnic group that suffers prejudice and discrimination at the hands of a larger dominant group.

ethnic stereotype The portrayal of all the members of a particular ethnic group as having similar fixed, usually unfavorable, traits.

ethnocentrism The tendency to view the norms and values of one's own culture as absolute and to use them as a standard against which to measure other cultures.

Eurocentric A view of the world or an educational curriculum that takes an exclusively European perspective.

experiment A research method in which the behavior of individuals or groups is studied under controlled conditions, usually in a laboratory setting.

exploitative technology Technology designed to produce immediate profits without regard to long-term consequences.

extended family Members of two or more related nuclear families living together in the same place.

extramarital sex A sexual relationship of a married person with someone other than his or her spouse.

extreme poverty Conditions of poverty among people who have less than half the poverty-level income.

family A group of people related by marriage, ancestry, or adoption who live together in a common household.

family allowance A welfare program that provides a small government allowance for every family with children.

family planning A population control program whose objective is voluntary reduction of the birthrate.

fee-for-service compensation A form of payment in which a physician is paid a fixed fee for each service rendered.

felony A serious offense, usually punishable by death or by confinement in a central prison.

feminist theory An approach to understanding society and social behavior that focuses on the importance of gender and the inequalities based on it.

fission Splitting of atoms to produce energy, as in a nuclear reactor.

food chain The set of transformations beginning with production of food by green plants and ending with decomposition of the bodies of animals.

food stamp program A government program that provides vouchers that can be exchanged for food.

forcible rape Sexual intercourse forced on someone against his or her will.

fraud The acquisition of money or property through the use of deception or false pretenses.

function The contribution of each part of society to the maintenance of a balanced order.

functionalist perspective A sociological theory viewing society as a delicate balance of parts and holding that social problems arise when societies become disorganized.

functionally illiterate Someone whose skills in reading and writing are so poor that he or she cannot perform many of the basic tasks necessary to daily life in an industrial society.

fusion Merging of atoms to produce energy, as in the sun.

gays Usually refers to male homosexuals, but sometimes to all homosexuals in general.

gender inequality The differences in the economic, social, and political conditions of females and males.

gender role A social role assigned on the basis of biological sex.

gender socialization The process by which a person learns the behaviors and attitudes that are expected of the female or male gender.

gentrification The renovation of older low-cost neighborhoods in the central cities to accommodate wealthier residents.

geothermal energy Energy derived from the heat of the earth's inner core.

goal displacement The substitution of a new goal or goals for the official stated objectives of an organization.

grade inflation The assignment of higher student grades than were formerly given for the same quality of work.

greenhouse effect The trapping of heat in the atmosphere by gases produced by human activities.

green revolution The increase in agricultural production created by the use of new strains of wheat and rice.

gridlock Extreme traffic congestion that virtually stops all traffic in an area.

growth rate The birthrate minus the death rate.

health A state of physical and mental well-being.

health maintenance organization An organization in which a group of medical personnel offer a range of medical services to subscribers who pay a fixed monthly fee.

hegemonic power The dominant nation in the world system.

heterosexual One whose preference is for sexual relations with persons of the opposite sex.

hidden curriculum The concepts that students must learn in order to succeed in school that are not part of the formal curriculum, such as obedience to authority.

high-tech industry An industry, such as computers, that is based on rapidly changing and sophisticated technology.

highway lobby The powerful lobby supporting construction of new roads and highways.

holistic medicine A medical approach that focuses on the overall health of the patient and not on individual symptoms.

home schooling Educating students at home rather than in public or private schools.

homicide The killing of a human being.

homophobia The fear of homosexuality.

homosexual One whose preference is for sexual relations with persons of the same sex.

human immunodeficiency virus (HIV) The virus that causes AIDS.

hydroelectric power Electric power generated by the movements of water.

identity crisis The personal crisis, typical of adolescence, in which people try to define who they are and how they fit into society.

ideology of individualism The belief that each individual is personally responsible for his or her own economic success or failure.

imperialism The creation or expansion of an empire.

incapacitation The prevention of crime by imprisoning criminals so that they cannot commit more crimes against the public.

incest taboo The prohibition of sexual relations between close relatives (e.g., parents and their children).

income The amount of money a person makes in a given year.

individualistic capitalism A capitalist economic system that emphasizes the importance of the individual over the group or community.

individual psychotherapy Psychological therapy with a single patient and therapist.

industrial revolution The change from an agricultural to an industrial society.

inflation An increase in the overall prices consumers must pay for the goods they buy.

infrastructure The basic physical necessities of modern society (e.g., roads, power plants, and sewers).

institutional discrimination Discrimination against minority groups that is practiced by economic, educational, and political organizations rather than by individuals.

integration A national system in which ethnic backgrounds are ignored and all individuals are treated alike.

interactionism A theory that explains behavior in terms of each individual's social relationships.

intermediate technology Machines that are less complicated than expensive, energy-intensive machines but more efficient than human and animal power.

international war Prolonged armed conflict between the governments of two or more nations.

job retraining A program to teach workers new skills.

juvenile delinquency Behavior by minors (usually defined as individuals below the age of 18) that is in violation of the criminal law or the special standards set for juveniles.

labeling theory A theory that sees crime, mental illness, and other types of deviance as labels applied to those who break social norms, and which holds that branding someone as deviant encourages rather than discourages further deviant behavior.

laissez-faire capitalism An economic ideology that argues the government should stay out of economic affairs and allow the free market to regulate itself.

land reform The redistribution of land from wealthy landlords to peasant farmers.

latent function A hidden function performed by a social institution or agency.

lean production An approach to manufacturing that attempts to use the smallest possible amount of labor.

legalization The proposal that the use and sale of a drug be made legal, with government regulation.

legitimacy Consent of the governed based on a belief that those who govern have the right to do so.

lesbian A female homosexual.

less developed countries (LDCs) Nations with a low level of economic development and a low standard of living; also called the Third World.

life cycle The regular progression of persons through the age grades of their society as they grow older.

limited war A war whose goals are restricted to a set of specific objectives and in which a rather small group of military personnel do the fighting.

lobbying The activities of special-interest groups aimed at convincing lawmakers to pass the kind of legislation they desire.

lower class The social class at the bottom of the social hierarchy, composed of people whose incomes are below the poverty line.

macro theory A sociological theory that is concerned with the behavior of large groups and entire societies.

madam Someone who runs a house of prostitution.

magnet schools Schools with special enriched programs designed to attract students from all ethnic groups, thus encouraging integration.

malpractice Incompetent or negligent practice by a physician or other professional.

managed care A system of health care in which the treatments and services available to patients are tightly controlled to hold down costs..

manslaughter The unlawful killing of another person without malice.

Medicaid A U.S. program designed to help the poor, the blind, and the disabled pay for medical care.

Medicare A U.S. program that pays for medical care of people over 65 years old.

megalopolis An area in which several large cities are fused together.

meltdown An accident in which the cooling system of a nuclear power plant fails, allowing the heat of the nuclear reaction to melt the reactor's core, thus releasing huge amounts of radiation.

melting pot theory The belief that U.S. society acts as a sort of crucible in which people from around the world are blended together to form a new and distinctive culture.

mental disorder A mental condition that makes it difficult or impossible for a person to cope with everyday life.

methodology The study of how to do research.

metropolitan statistical area (MSA) The U.S. Bureau of the Census term for a central city and the surrounding suburbs that depend on it.

micro theory A sociological theory that is concerned with the behavior of individuals and small groups.

middle class The social class composed of professionals, managers, and most bureaucrats and white-collar workers.

midlife crisis The crisis faced by middle-aged persons in which they must accept the passing of their youth and the limitations on their earlier aspirations.

migration The movement of people from one geographic area to another.

militarism (1) Glorification of war and combat. (2) Strong belief in "defense" combined with huge military expenditures.

military-industrial complex The powerful interest group formed by the military and the civilian corporations that supply it with the services, materials, and equipment it needs.

misdemeanor A minor offense, usually punishable by confinement in a local jail or by payment of a fine.

modernization The process by which a nation moves from a traditional agricultural society to an industrialized state.

monogamy The practice of being married to only one person at a time.

monopoly The situation existing when a single corporation has gained complete control of a market.

mood disorder A mental disorder involving severe disturbances in behavior and emotion.

mores Customs whose violators are punished or otherwise strongly condemned.

multicultural education Education which reflects the perspectives of many different cultural groups.

multinational corporation A corporation that does business in many different nations.

murder The unlawful killing of a human being with malice.

mutual assured destruction (MAD) A political standoff in which two or more enemy nations realize that each has the power to destroy the other.

National Crime Victimization Survey (NCVS) A yearly survey of Americans that attempts to determine how many have been victimized by crime.

national health care A system of medical care for all the residents of a country.

nationalism A form of ethnocentrism based on a sense of identification with and devotion to one's nation.

neo-Malthusian Someone who believes that we are quickly approaching a crisis because of overpopulation, resource depletion, and environmental destruction.

noncategorical program A welfare program with no restrictions on eligibility.

nonrenewable resource A resource with a fixed supply that cannot be replenished.

norm A social rule telling us what behavior is acceptable in a certain situation and what is not.

nuclear family A married couple and their children.

nuclear proliferation The spread of nuclear weapons to an ever larger number of countries.

nuclear war Any war employing nuclear weapons.

nuclear winter The sharp decline in average temperatures produced by dense clouds that would cover the earth after a major nuclear war.

nurse practitioner A nurse who is trained to take full charge of patients' basic health care.

occupational crime A crime committed in the course of the offender's occupation but without the support or encouragement of his or her employer.

old age The last age grade, usually considered to start around age 65.

oligopoly The situation existing when an industry is dominated by a few large companies.

opiate Any of a group of natural and synthetic drugs with pain-relieving properties, including opium, codeine, morphine, heroin, meperidine, and methadone.

organic waste Waste products with a biological origin.

organizational crime A crime committed by someone acting on behalf of a larger organization, often his or her employer.

overeducation Training more people for occupations than there are jobs available in those occupations.

ozone depletion The reduction in the protective layer of ozone in the upper atmosphere.

parole Release of a criminal from prison after part of his or her sentence has been served.

participant observation A research method in which the researcher participates in the activities of the group under study.

passive smoking Inhalation of secondhand tobacco smoke by nonsmokers.

patriarchy/patriarchal system A society or social system dominated by men and run in their interests.

periphery The poor nations of the world, which are subject to the economic and political domination of the core nations.

personal interview A research method that asks people about their activities and attitudes.

personality The relatively stable characteristics and traits that distinguish one person from another.

personality theory A theory holding that social behavior is determined by differences in personality.

photochemical smog A group of noxious compounds produced by the action of sunlight on oxygen, hydrocarbons, and nitrogen oxides.

photosynthesis The process by which green plants convert solar energy to food.

photovoltaic cells Cells that produce electricity from the sun.

physician's assistant Medical personnel trained to carry out particular medical services traditionally performed by physicians.

pimp A man who solicits customers or performs other services for a prostitute in exchange for a share of the profits.

plea bargaining A process by which a defense attorney and a prosecutor agree to let a defendant plead guilty in return for a reduction in the charge or other considerations.

pluralism A national system in which several ethnic groups maintain a high level of independence and equality.

pluralist One who believes that political decisions are made by changing coalitions of political forces.

police brutality The use of excessive and unnecessary force by police officers in the performance of their duties.

political decentralization Transferring power from centralized government to local communities and agencies.

political economy The economic and political system of a community, nation, or group of nations.

political party An organized group whose goals are to get its members elected to political office and to influence the decisions of those who already hold office.

political socialization The process by which people learn their political values and perspectives.

pollution The release of harmful substances into the environment.

polygamy The practice of having more than one husband or wife at a time.

population explosion The rapid increase in the human population of the world.

pornography A form of entertainment judged to be obscene.

positive school A theoretical school in criminology that rejected the classical theory's assumption that crime was based on free choice.

poverty (1) The state of having an income below some specified level. (2) The state of having significantly less income and wealth than the average person in the society of which one is a member.

power The ability to force other people to do something whether they want to or not.

power elite A group of wealthy and powerful persons who, according to C. Wright Mills, pursue their own interests at the expense of the average citizen.

prejudice Antipathy, either felt or expressed, based on a faulty and inflexible generalization and directed toward a group as a whole or toward an individual because he or she is a member of that group.

preliminary hearing A hearing at which a judge decides whether the evidence against an accused person is sufficient to justify further legal proceedings.

premarital intercourse Sexual intercourse before marriage.

prep school A private school designed to prepare students for college.

preventive medicine The theory or practice of staying healthy by maintaining good health habits.

price-fixing Collusion by several companies to cut competition and set uniformly high prices.

probation Suspension of the sentence of a person who has been convicted but not yet imprisoned, on condition of continued good behavior and regular reporting to a probation officer.

productivity The value of the goods or services an average worker produces in a given period of time.

proletariat The working class in an industrial society.

property crime A crime directed against property.

proportional representation An electoral system in which offices are won on the basis of the proportion of the vote each party receives, and not on a winner-take-all basis.

prostitution The practice of selling the services of oneself or another person for purposes of intercourse or other sexual activities.

psychedelic A drug that produces hallucinations and other significant alterations in the user's consciousness.

psychoanalysis Long-term therapy designed to uncover the repressed memories, motives, and conflicts assumed to be at the root of a patient's psychological problems.

psychosis A mental disorder in which a person has lost contact with reality and may suffer hallucinations, delusions, and the like.

psychotherapy Any program for helping patients with their psychological problems.

pushouts Children who leave their family homes because they are no longer wanted there.

race A group of people who are thought to have a common set of physical characteristics but who may or may not share a sense of unity and identity.

racism Stereotyping, prejudice, and discrimination based on race.

rational choice theory A theory that holds crime to be the result of the rational choice of the offender.

real wages The actual value of wages after a correction for inflation has been made.

rehabilitation The process of changing a person's criminal behavior by nonpunitive methods.

relative approach Dividing the poor from the nonpoor on the basis of the wealth and income of the average person.

relative deprivation The situation in which persons have considerably less income, wealth, or prestige than they believe they deserve.

relative deprivation theory Holding that revolutions are caused by differences between what people have and what they think they should have.

renewable resource A resource that is replenished through natural processes.

replacement rate The average number of children each woman must have to keep the population of a nation from growing or shrinking.

repressive terrorism Terrorism intended to protect the existing political order in a nation.

resegregation A return to racial or ethnic segregation that occurs after official desegregation problems have started.

retirement communities Planned communities for elderly people.

retribution The idea that the goal of the criminal justice process should be to make criminals suffer for their crimes.

reverse discrimination Discrimination against white males.

revolutionary terrorism Terrorism intended to bring about major political changes in a nation.

revolutionary war Armed conflict between an official government and one or more groups of rebels.

rite of passage A ritual that marks the transition from one state of life to another, especially from childhood to adulthood.

robbery The unlawful taking of another person's property by force or threat of force.

role A set of expectations and behaviors associated with a social position.

role conflict The feelings experienced by people when two or more of their social roles place conflicting demands on them.

romantic love The powerful attraction that is expected to form the basis of marriage in most Western societies.

runaways Children who move away from their homes without parental consent.

salad bowl theory The belief that ethnic groups should maintain their distinct identity in a multicultural community.

sample A cross section of subjects selected for study as representative of a larger population.

scapegoat A person or group that is unjustly blamed for the problems of others.

schizophrenia A mental disorder involving extreme disorganization in personality, thought patterns, and speech.

sedative-hypnotic A drug that depresses the central nervous system.

segregated schools Schools in which students are separated according to their racial, ethnic, or class background.

segregation The practice of keeping ethnic or racial groups apart.

self-concept The image one has of who and what one is.

self-report study A survey that asks respondents to report the crimes or other deviant actions they have committed.

semiperiphery The partially industrialized nations that have characteristics of both the core and the periphery.

service occupations Jobs that provide a service to someone else rather than making a product or extracting a natural resource.

sexism Stereotyping, prejudice, and discrimination based on gender.

sexual harassment Unwanted sexual comments, gestures, or physical advances.

sexual orientation A person's identity as heterosexual, homosexual, or bisexual.

sexual stereotyping The portrayal of all females or males as having similar fixed traits.

sexually transmitted disease A disease passed from one person to another during a sex act.

single-parent family A family in which only one parent lives with one or more children.

situationalists Those who believe that the unique social characteristics of poor people are caused by their unique social situation and not a culture of poverty.

social behaviorism A more sophisticated version of behaviorism that emphasizes the social aspects of human behavior.

social class A category of people with similar shares of the things that are valued in a society.

social disorganization The condition that exists when an institution is poorly organized and fails to perform its social functions.

socialization The process by which individuals learn the ways of thinking and behaving of their culture.

social institution A relatively stable pattern of thought and behavior centered on the performance of an important social task.

social movement A group of people who have banded together to promote a particular cause.

social problem (1) A condition that a significant number of people believe to be a problem. (2) A condition in which there is a sizable difference between the ideals of a society and its actual achievements.

social psychology The study of the behavior of individuals and small groups and their relationship with the larger society.

Social Security A government-administered old-age pension program whose formal title is Old Age and Survivors Insurance.

social structure The organized patterns of human behavior in a society.

society A group of people in the same geographic area who share common institutions and traditions.

sociology The scientific study of societies and social groups.

sociopathic personality An antisocial person with a complex of personality characteristics including impulsiveness, immaturity, and a lack of concern for other people.

sodomy A legal term applying to what are called "unnatural" sex acts; usually some form of homosexual behavior.

solar energy The energy supplied by the sun.

special-interest group People who have a stake in a specific area of public policy.

specific deterrence Punishment of criminals in order to change their ways.

spoils system A political system in which government jobs and favors are handed out in exchange for political support.

standard English The English dialect spoken by the middle and upper classes.

status (1) A social position made up of rights and obligations. (2) Prestige inherited from one's family or derived from occupation and life-style.

status offense A juvenile offense that does not violate the criminal law.

statutory rape Sexual intercourse with someone below the legally defined age of consent (usually 16 or 18).

stimulant A drug that arouses the central nervous system, increases the metabolic rate, and reduces drowsiness.

strain theory A theory holding that crime is caused by the strain produced when societies tell people that wealth is available to all but nevertheless restrict access to the means for achieving wealth.

streetwalkers Prostitutes who get their clients on the streets and in other public places.

stress theory A theory that holds that an individual will experience serious psychological problems if exposed to excessive levels of stress.

strip mining A mining technique in which long strips of soil are dug up and processed.

structuralist One who believes that the structure of capitalist society forces the government to support the interests of the privileged few.

structural unemployment Unemployment resulting from long-term changes in the economy, such as technological changes.

subculture A culture that exists within a larger culture and is influenced by it but has its own unique ideas and beliefs.

sub-Saharan Africa Africa south of the Sahara desert.

substance abuse disorder A category of mental disorder applied to people who use excessive amounts of alcohol or other drugs.

suburb A district, usually residential, located on or near the outskirts of a city; often a separately incorporated city or town.

suicide The taking of one's own life.

Supplemental Security Income (SSI) A program that gives financial assistance to those who are blind, disabled, or have other special problems.

surrogate mothering One woman bearing a child for another.

survey A research method that asks people about their attitudes and activities, either in personal interviews or by means of questionnaires.

sustainable society A stable society that does not exceed the carrying capacity of its environment.

syndicated crime Crime committed by a group of individuals working together over a period of time.

temperature inversion A condition in which a layer of warm air moves over a layer of cool air, sealing in pollutants that would otherwise rise into the upper atmosphere.

Temporary Aid to Needy Families (TANF) A welfare program providing temporary financial aid to poor mothers.

term limits Legislation that limits the number of times a person can be reelected to the same office.

terrorism Attacks against civilians to achieve political ends.

theft Unlawful taking of property.

therapeutic community A live-in community for drug treatment.

Third World The poor agricultural nations of the world.

tolerance (1) The immunity to the effects of a drug that builds up after repeated use. (2) The practice of ignoring behavior patterns that are personally objectionable.

total fertility rate The number of children a woman in a particular group is likely to have in her lifetime.

total war A war whose goal is unconditional surrender of an enemy nation and in which both military personnel and ordinary citizens participate.

tragedy of the commons The destruction of common resources in the pursuit of individual benefits.

underclass The lowest social stratum, made up of the long-term poor who are excluded from the mainstream of society.

underemployment The problem suffered by workers who want full-time work but can find only part-time or temporary work.

unemployment The problem suffered by workers who want a job but are unable to find one.

Uniform Crime Reports A national summary of all the crimes reported to the police.

Universal Declaration of Human Rights A United Nations declaration that sets forth a list of basic human rights.

upper class The social class at the top of the social hierarchy, composed of the very wealthy, who often hold top positions of corporate power.

urbanization The movement of people from rural areas to cities.

urban renewal A program, usually financed by the government, intended to upgrade decaying city areas.

urban subsistence economy The way of life of the city dwellers in poor countries who make just enough to get by.

value conflict A clash in the attitudes and beliefs held by different social groups.

victimization survey A survey in which people are asked in personal interviews to report whether they have been the victims of various kinds of criminal offenses.

victimless crime A crime in which the harm, if any, is not suffered by anyone except the offender.

villages Small, traditional communities in rural areas.

violence Behavior intended to cause bodily pain or injury to another; may be legitimate or illegitimate.

violent crime Crime that involves physical harm or the threat of physical harm to an individual.

voucher system An educational system in which the government gives students vouchers that can be used to pay for education at any school they or their parents choose.

war A protracted military conflict between two or more organized groups.

wealth A person's total economic worth (e.g., real estate, stocks, cash).

weapons of mass destruction Military weapons that indiscriminately kill large numbers of people.

white backlash The negative response of whites to affirmative action or other programs designed to assist disadvantaged racial minorities.

white-collar crime Crime committed by people of respectability and high social status in the course of their occupations.

white-collar workers Persons employed in nonmanual labor, such as business managers or office workers.

white ethnics Americans of European descent who maintain a distinct ethnic identity.

withdrawal The sickness that a habitual drug user experiences when the drug is discontinued after a period of steady use.

worker alienation The feeling of estrangement and powerlessness among workers.

working class The social class made up of blue-collar and lower-level service workers.

world economy The international system of economic relationships in which all countries participate.

world system The network of economic and political relationships that links the nations of the world together.

youth culture The distinctive subculture created by adolescents in industrial society.

Credits

Photo Credits

1 © Joe Bensen/Stock Boston; 5 © Bob Daemmrich/Stock Boston; 12 © Chromosohm/Sohm 1992; 21 © B. Daemmrich/The Image Works; 31 © Tom McCarthy/The Picture Cube; 36 © S.Gazin/The Image Works; 43 © M. Bridwell/PhotoEdit; 51 © Jeffrey Myers/Stock Boston; 53 © E. Pedrick/The Image Works; 65 © Tom McCarthy/ PhotoEdit; 75 © Michael Newman/PhotoEdit; 77 Charles Gupton/ Stock Boston; 83 © Mark Richards/PhotoEdit; 90 © Bob Daemmrich/ Stock Boston; 98 © David Young-Wolff/PhotoEdit; 105 © M. Justice/The Image Works; 108 © Bill Aron/PhotoEdit; 113 AP/Wide World; 125 © Jim Daniels/The Picture Cube; 134 © Mark Reinstein/The Image Works; 136 © R. Crandall/The Image Works; 146 AP/Wide World; 148 © David Wells/The Image Works; 162 © Michael Newman/ PhotoEdit; 167 Dorothy Littell/Stock Boston; 174 © P. Davidson/ The Image Works; 181 AP/Wide World; 195 © Tom McCarthy/The Picture Cube; 201 © David Young- Wolff/PhotoEdit; 215 © McGlynn/The Image Works; 217 left: © Bill Bachman/PhotoEdit; 217 right: © Christopher Brown/Stock Boston; 225 DorothyLittell/Stock Boston; 232 © B. Daemmrich/The Image Works; 236 © Richard Sobol/Stock Boston; 248 Gary Conner/ PhotoEdit; 255 Corbis-Bettmann; 259 AP/Wide World; 267 © M. Stravato/Sygma; 269 © William Campbell/Sygma; 273 UPI/Corbis-Bettmann; 285 © B. Daemmrich/The Image Works; 293 © Michael Newman/ PhotoEdit; 296 © Jeff Greenberg/The Picture Cube; 304 © Lawrence Migdale/Stock Boston; 307 © A. Lichtenstein/The Image Works; 312 © Denise Marcotte/Stock Boston; 315 © W. Hill/The Image Works; 317 Irven DeVore/Anthro-Photo; 319 © Lawrence Migdale/Stock Boston; 326 AP/Wide World; 331 © Archive Photos; 345 © Vanessa Vick/Photo Researchers; 350 UPI/Corbis-Bettmann; 354 © Bob Strong/ The Image Works; 359 © Spencer Grant/The Picture Cube; 363 © Tony Clark/The Image Works; 366 © Bob Daemmrich/Stock Boston; 380 © Phil Savoie/The Picture Cube; 384 AP/Wide World; 396 © Granitsas/The Image Works; 399 © T. Clark/The Image Works; 402 © J. Griffin/The Image Works; 413 © Mark Richards/PhotoEdit; 422 AP/Wide World; 427 © Rhoda Sydney/PhotoEdit; 433 © Regis Bossu/Sygma; 439 © Mark Richards/PhotoEdit; 455 © Paul Conklin/PhotoEdit; 458 © Monkmeyer/Wolf; 464 © Mulvehill/The Image Works; 468 © Jonathan Nourok/PhotoEdit; 471 © Jane Schreibman/The Picture Cube; 475 © M.Richards/PhotoEdit; 485 © Carey/The Image Works; 490 © JohnEastcott/VVA Momatiuk/The Image Works; 492 © Schiller/The ImageWorks; 494 © 1991 James Prince/Photo Researchers; 496 AP/WideWorld; 501 © David Austen/Stock Boston; 513 © Topham/The Image Works; 517 top: © Phil McCarten/PhotoEdit; 517 bottom: © Bob Daemmrich/The Image Works; 521 Tom Walker/Stock Boston; 526 NASA; 539 Bruce W. Wellman/Stock Boston; 548 AP/Wide World; 552 © Jim Smalley/The Picture Cube; 555 top: © Bob Daemmrich/Stock Boston; 555 bottom: Robert Caputo/Stock Boston; 566 AP/Wide World; 567 © Richard Lord/The Image Works; 579 AP/ Wide World; 584 © Scott Camazine/Photo Researchers; 587 AP/Wide World; 592 UPI/Corbis-Bettmann; 600 AP/Wide World; 610 AP/ Wide World; 612 © Louise Gubb/The Image Works; 613 Photofest.

Literary Credits

141 Paul N. McCloskey, Jr., "Congressional Politics: Secrecy, Senility and Seniority." In *Truth and Untruth: Political Deceit in America* (New York: Simon & Schuster, 1972). Copyright © 1972 by Paul N. McCloskey, Jr. Reprinted by permission of the author; 173 Christine Gorman, "None But the Brave," *Time*, October 6, 1997, p. 76; 278 Malcolm X, *The Autobiography of Malcolm X,* by Malcolm X with Alex Haley (New York: Ballantine Books, 1964), pp. 35-36; 465 Excerpts from *Do or Die* by Leon Bing. Copyright © 1992 by Leon Bing. Reprinted by permission of HarperCollins Publishers, Inc.; 536 Reprinted from *Beyond the Limits.* Copyright © 1992 by Meadows, Meadows and Randers. With permission from Chelsea Green Publishing Co., White River Junction, Vermont and the Canadian Publishers, McClelland & Stewart, Inc.; 553 Excerpt from *I, Rigoberta Menchu: An Indian Woman in Guatemala,* edited by Elisabeth Burgos-Debray, translated by Ann Wright. Translation copyright © 1984 Verso. Reprinted by permission of Verso.

Name Index

Subject Index